SAP PRESS Books: Always on hand

Print or e-book, Kindle or iPad, workplace or airplane: Choose where and how to read your SAP PRESS books! You can now get all our titles as e-books, too:

- By download and online access
- For all popular devices
- And, of course, DRM-free

Convinced? Then go to www.sap-press.com and get your e-book today.

SuccessFactors™ with SAP® ERP HCM

SAP PRESS is a joint initiative of SAP and Galileo Press. The know-how offered by SAP specialists combined with the expertise of the Galileo Press publishing house offers the reader expert books in the field. SAP PRESS features first-hand information and expert advice, and provides useful skills for professional decision-making.

SAP PRESS offers a variety of books on technical and business-related topics for the SAP user. For further information, please visit our website: *www.sap-press.com*.

Justin Morgalis and Brandon Toombs
SAP ERP HCM Processes and Forms
2013, 344 pp., hardcover
ISBN 978-1-59229-425-1

Joe Lee and Tim Simmons
Talent Management with SAP ERP HCM
2012, 388 pp., hardcover
ISBN 978-1-59229-413-8

Dirk Liepold and Steve Ritter
SAP ERP HCM: Technical Principles and Programming
2013, 732 pp., hardcover
ISBN 978-1-59229-431-2

Jeremy Masters, Christos Kotsakis, and Venki Krishnamoorthy
E-Recruiting with SAP ERP HCM
2010, 358 pp., hardcover
ISBN 978-1-59229-243-1

Amy Grubb, Luke Marson, and Jyoti Sharma

SuccessFactors™ with SAP® ERP HCM

Bonn • Boston

Galileo Press is named after the Italian physicist, mathematician, and philosopher Galileo Galilei (1564–1642). He is known as one of the founders of modern science and an advocate of our contemporary, heliocentric worldview. His words *Eppur si muove* (And yet it moves) have become legendary. The Galileo Press logo depicts Jupiter orbited by the four Galilean moons, which were discovered by Galileo in 1610.

Editor Emily Nicholls
Acquisitions Editor Katy Spencer
Copyeditor Julie McNamee
Cover Design Graham Geary
Photo Credit iStockphoto.com/17439285/© 36clicks
Layout Design Vera Brauner
Production Graham Geary
Typesetting Publishers' Design and Production Services, Inc.
Printed and bound in the United States of America, on paper from sustainable sources

ISBN 978-1-59229-845-7

© 2014 by Galileo Press Inc., Boston (MA)
1st edition 2013, 1st reprint 2014

Library of Congress Cataloging-in-Publication Data
Grubb, Amy.
 SuccessFactors with SAP ERP HCM / Amy Grubb, Luke Marson, and Jyoti Sharma. — 1st edition.
  pages cm
 ISBN 978-1-59229-845-7 — ISBN 1-59229-845-1 — ISBN 978-1-59229-846-4 — ISBN 978-1-59229-847-1
 1. SAP ERP. 2. Personnel management—Data processing. 3. Personnel management—Computer programs. 4. Manpower planning—Computer programs. 5. SuccessFactors (Firm) I. Marson, Luke. II. Sharma, Jyoti. III. Title.
 HF5549.5.D37G78 2013
 658.300285'53—dc23
                                  2013022028

All rights reserved. Neither this publication nor any part of it may be copied or reproduced in any form or by any means or translated into another language, without the prior consent of Galileo Press GmbH, Rheinwerkallee 4, 53227 Bonn, Germany.

Galileo Press makes no warranties or representations with respect to the content hereof and specifically disclaims any implied warranties of merchantability or fitness for any particular purpose. Galileo Press assumes no responsibility for any errors that may appear in this publication.

"Galileo Press" and the Galileo Press logo are registered trademarks of Galileo Press GmbH, Bonn, Germany. SAP PRESS is an imprint of Galileo Press.

All of the screenshots and graphics reproduced in this book are subject to copyright © SAP AG, Dietmar-Hopp-Allee 16, 69190 Walldorf, Germany.

SAP, the SAP logo, ABAP, BAPI, Duet, mySAP.com, mySAP, SAP ArchiveLink, SAP EarlyWatch, SAP NetWeaver, SAP Business ByDesign, SAP BusinessObjects, SAP BusinessObjects Rapid Mart, SAP BusinessObjects Desktop Intelligence, SAP BusinessObjects Explorer, SAP Rapid Marts, SAP BusinessObjects Watchlist Security, SAP BusinessObjects Web Intelligence, SAP Crystal Reports, SAP GoingLive, SAP HANA, SAP MaxAttention, SAP MaxDB, SAP PartnerEdge, SAP R/2, SAP R/3, SAP R/3 Enterprise, SAP Strategic Enterprise Management (SAP SEM), SAP StreamWork, SAP Sybase Adaptive Server Enterprise (SAP Sybase ASE), SAP Sybase IQ, SAP xApps, SAPPHIRE NOW, and Xcelsius are registered or unregistered trademarks of SAP AG, Walldorf, Germany.

All other products mentioned in this book are registered or unregistered trademarks of their respective companies.

Contents at a Glance

1	Introduction	21
2	Implementing SuccessFactors	47
3	Integration with SAP ERP HCM	63
4	Technical Considerations	117
5	Using SuccessFactors	145
6	Employee Central	165
7	Employee Profile	203
8	Performance & Goals	223
9	Compensation	241
10	Recruiting Execution	291
11	SuccessFactors Learning	317
12	Succession & Development	339
13	SAP Jam	371
14	Workforce Analytics	387
15	Workforce Planning	423
16	Onboarding	473
17	BizX Mobile	481
18	Further Resources	491

Dear Reader,

As an editor, it's always a pleasure when one project leads to another as SAP solutions mature and evolve. SAP's 2012 SuccessFactors acquisition announcement came as we were working on our recent Talent Management title. Though it was clear that SAP was taking large strides forward in cloud computing, it wasn't initially evident how the new acquisition would affect users with existing on-premise systems. As the dust settled on the announcement, it was evident that the HCM community had already begun searching for answers. And so *SuccessFactors with SAP ERP HCM* was born.

Over the next year, Luke Marson assembled the incomparable team of SuccessFactors experts who could offer insight and guidance into the innovative functionality offered by the cloud-based HCM solution. His coauthors Amy Grubb and Jyoti Sharma and contributors Regan Klein, Joe Lee, and Atif Siddiqui offer readers invaluable experience implementing, consulting, and networking in the talent management space, together covering all of the SuccessFactors bases. In short, this book offers abundant answers, covering everything from how to implement and integrate SuccessFactors with SAP ERP HCM, to the specific modules and their functionality, to sources of upcoming announcements.

As always, we appreciate your business and welcome your feedback. Your comments and suggestions are the most useful tools to help us improve our books for you, the reader. We encourage you to visit our website at www.sap-press.com and share your feedback about *SuccessFactors with SAP ERP HCM*.

Emily Nicholls
Editor, SAP PRESS

Galileo Press
Boston, MA

emily.nicholls@galileo-press.com
www.sap-press.com

Contents

Foreword 17
Acknowledgments 19

1 Introduction 21

    1.1   Terminology and Concepts 21
           1.1.1   Cloud Computing 22
           1.1.2   Software-as-a-Service 23
           1.1.3   Cloud and SaaS Trends 25
    1.2   About SuccessFactors 27
    1.3   SuccessFactors BizX Suite 29
           1.3.1   Employee Central 31
           1.3.2   Performance & Goals 32
           1.3.3   Compensation 33
           1.3.4   Recruiting Execution 34
           1.3.5   Learning 35
           1.3.6   Succession & Development 37
           1.3.7   Workforce Planning 38
           1.3.8   Workforce Analytics 39
           1.3.9   Onboarding 40
           1.3.10 SAP Jam 41
           1.3.11 BizX Mobile 42
    1.4   SAP Strategy and Roadmap 42
           1.4.1   Product Strategy and Roadmap 43
           1.4.2   Hybrid Model 44
           1.4.3   Full Cloud HCM Model 45
           1.4.4   SAP's Cloud Strategy 45
    1.5   Licensing 46
    1.6   Summary 46

2 Implementing SuccessFactors 47

    2.1   Implementation Considerations 47
           2.1.1   Setting the Strategic Objectives of the Project 48

		2.1.2	Planning for the Implementation	48
		2.1.3	Business Processes	50
		2.1.4	Competencies and Job Roles	50
		2.1.5	Employee Data	51
	2.2	Project Structure		51
		2.2.1	Implementation Consultants	52
		2.2.2	Project Manager	53
		2.2.3	Project Sponsor	53
		2.2.4	Technical Resource	53
		2.2.5	Functional/Business Resource	54
		2.2.6	Stakeholder Group Representatives	54
		2.2.7	Training/Communication Resource	54
	2.3	Project Methodology		55
		2.3.1	Phase 1: Prepare	55
		2.3.2	Phase 2: Realize	57
		2.3.3	Phase 3: Verify	59
		2.3.4	Phase 4: Launch	60
	2.4	Project Delivery		61
	2.5	Summary		62

3 Integration with SAP ERP HCM ... 63

	3.1	Integration Strategy		63
		3.1.1	Integration Pillars	65
		3.1.2	Integration Scenarios	66
		3.1.3	Integration Packages	66
	3.2	Integration Technology		66
		3.2.1	Flat-File Integration	68
		3.2.2	SAP NetWeaver Process Integration	69
		3.2.3	SAP HANA Cloud Integration	71
		3.2.4	Dell Boomi AtomSphere	72
		3.2.5	SAP Data Services	73
		3.2.6	Single Sign-On	73
		3.2.7	Other Integration Technology	73
	3.3	iFlows		74
		3.3.1	Integration Add-On 1.0 for SAP ERP HCM and SuccessFactors BizX	75
		3.3.2	Integration Add-On 2.0 for SAP ERP HCM and SuccessFactors BizX	95

3.4		Other Integration Content	111
	3.4.1	Cookbooks	111
	3.4.2	Employee Central and Employee Central Payroll	112
	3.4.3	Social Media ABAP Integration Library	114
	3.4.4	SAP Data Services Adapter	114
3.5		Summary	115

4 Technical Considerations ... 117

4.1		Technical Architecture	118
	4.1.1	Database Layer	119
	4.1.2	Application Layer	119
	4.1.3	Communication Layer	121
4.2		Metadata Framework	122
	4.2.1	Technical Aspects	123
	4.2.2	Metadata Objects	124
	4.2.3	Rules Engine	126
	4.2.4	PickLists	127
	4.2.5	Configuration Options	127
	4.2.6	Workflows	131
	4.2.7	Hooks	131
	4.2.8	Limitations	132
	4.2.9	Summary	132
4.3		Security	133
	4.3.1	Authentication Security	133
	4.3.2	Layer Security	134
	4.3.3	Role-Based Permissions	135
4.4		OneAdmin	135
4.5		Extending SuccessFactors with Custom Applications	142
4.6		Summary	143

5 Using SuccessFactors ... 145

5.1		User Interface and Navigation	146
	5.1.1	Modular UI Provides Ready-to-Use System	146
	5.1.2	Ease of Use Drives Adoption	146
	5.1.3	Cross-Functional Relevance	150
5.2		Tiles	151

		5.2.1	Welcome Tile	151
		5.2.2	My Info Tile	152
		5.2.3	To-Do Tile	154
		5.2.4	My Team Tile	154
		5.2.5	Quick Links Tile	156
		5.2.6	SAP Jam Tile	156
		5.2.7	My Admin Favorites Tile	157
	5.3	Key Features		157
		5.3.1	General Navigation	158
		5.3.2	Organizational Chart	158
		5.3.3	People Search	160
		5.3.4	Analytics and Reporting	161
	5.4	SAP Jam		162
	5.5	Summary		163

6 Employee Central 165

	6.1	Employee Central Business Drivers		166
		6.1.1	"Glocalization"	166
		6.1.2	Self-Services	167
		6.1.3	Data Quality and Consistency	167
		6.1.4	Integration with Talent Management	167
		6.1.5	Integration with Third-Party Providers	168
		6.1.6	Mobility	169
	6.2	Employee Central Data Objects		169
		6.2.1	Foundation Objects	170
		6.2.2	Generic Objects	174
		6.2.3	HR Data	176
	6.3	Employee Central Processes and Transactions		184
		6.3.1	Add New Employee	185
		6.3.2	Mass Changes	186
		6.3.3	Proxy Management	186
		6.3.4	Create and Manage Workflows	187
		6.3.5	Changes, Transfers, and Workflows	188
		6.3.6	Position Management	190
		6.3.7	Absence Management	190
		6.3.8	Global Assignment	191
		6.3.9	Employee Central Reporting	192
	6.4	Implementing Employee Central		196

6.5		Employee Central Payroll	197
	6.5.1	Access and Data Replication	198
	6.5.2	Myth versus Reality	199
6.6		Summary	200

7 Employee Profile 203

7.1		Public Profile	204
	7.1.1	Badges	206
	7.1.2	Tags	207
7.2		Employee (Talent) Profile	209
	7.2.1	Employee Overview	209
	7.2.2	Background Elements	209
7.3		Scorecard	213
	7.3.1	Employee Overview	214
	7.3.2	Nomination Portlet	215
	7.3.3	Competency and Objective Portlets	216
	7.3.4	Talent Information	216
	7.3.5	Performance and Potential	217
7.4		Other Features	218
	7.4.1	Facebook	218
	7.4.2	LinkedIn	218
7.5		Configure Employee Files	218
7.6		Summary	220

8 Performance & Goals 223

8.1		Goal Management	224
	8.1.1	Maintaining Goals	226
	8.1.2	Aligning and Cascading Goals	229
	8.1.3	Goal Execution	230
8.2		Performance Management	232
	8.2.1	Performance Review Structure	233
	8.2.2	Team Overview	234
	8.2.3	Writing Assistant and Coaching Advisor	237
8.3		360 Multi-Rater Assessment	238
8.4		Calibration	239
8.5		Summary	240

9 Compensation ... 241

- 9.1 Compensation Solution ... 242
  - 9.1.1 Compensation Plan ... 246
  - 9.1.2 Setup Data ... 249
  - 9.1.3 Plan Setup ... 254
  - 9.1.4 Manage Compensation Forms ... 265
  - 9.1.5 Plan and Approve Recommendations ... 269
  - 9.1.6 Reports ... 274
  - 9.1.7 Executive Review ... 276
  - 9.1.8 Reward Statements ... 277
- 9.2 Variable Pay Solution ... 278
  - 9.2.1 Plan Setup ... 279
  - 9.2.2 Manage Variable Pay Forms ... 288
  - 9.2.3 Approve Recommendations ... 289
  - 9.2.4 Executive Review ... 289
  - 9.2.5 Reward Statements ... 290
- 9.3 Summary ... 290

10 Recruiting Execution ... 291

- 10.1 Recruiting Execution Foundation ... 293
  - 10.1.1 Recruiting Roles ... 293
  - 10.1.2 Recruiting Templates ... 294
- 10.2 Requisition Creation and Approval ... 295
  - 10.2.1 Requisition Creation ... 296
  - 10.2.2 Requisition Approval Workflow ... 297
- 10.3 Job Posting and Sourcing ... 297
- 10.4 Candidate Experience ... 301
  - 10.4.1 Career Sites ... 301
  - 10.4.2 Candidate Profile ... 303
- 10.5 Candidate Data Model ... 305
- 10.6 Candidate Selection Management ... 307
  - 10.6.1 Candidate Workbench ... 308
  - 10.6.2 Interview Central ... 309
- 10.7 Offer Management ... 312
- 10.8 Hiring and Onboarding ... 315

	10.9	Employee Referral	315
	10.10	Summary	316

11 SuccessFactors Learning ... 317

	11.1	User Interface	318
		11.1.1 User Interface Home Page	319
		11.1.2 Learning History	324
	11.2	Supervisor Interface	325
		11.2.1 Manage Team Member Learning Plan	326
		11.2.2 Manage Training Approvals	327
		11.2.3 Other Supervisor Actions	328
	11.3	Administrator Interface	328
		11.3.1 Administrative Home Page	329
		11.3.2 Users Menu	331
		11.3.3 Performance Menu	332
		11.3.4 Learning Menu	333
		11.3.5 Content Menu	333
		11.3.6 System Administration Menu	334
	11.4	Security and Access	335
		11.4.1 Domains	335
		11.4.2 Workflows	336
		11.4.3 Roles	336
		11.4.4 Admin Accounts	336
		11.4.5 Organizations	336
	11.5	Summary	338

12 Succession & Development ... 339

	12.1	Succession	340
		12.1.1 Organizational Charts	341
		12.1.2 Matrices	344
		12.1.3 Talent Profile and Scorecard	347
		12.1.4 Talent Search	348
		12.1.5 Talent Pools	352
		12.1.6 Nominating Successors	354
		12.1.7 Position Management	356
		12.1.8 Reporting and Analytics	358

12.2	Development		359
	12.2.1	Development Plan	360
	12.2.2	Career Worksheet	365
	12.2.3	Learning Activities	368
12.3	Summary		369

13 SAP Jam — 371

13.1	Using SAP Jam		372
	13.1.1	Informal and Social Learning	373
	13.1.2	Social Onboarding	374
	13.1.3	Sales	374
	13.1.4	BizX Mobile	374
13.2	Features and Social Networking Capabilities		374
	13.2.1	Profile	376
	13.2.2	Feeds, Comments, and Notifications	378
	13.2.3	Groups	379
	13.2.4	Content Creation and Sharing	382
	13.2.5	Gamification	383
13.3	Administration		383
13.4	Integration		385
13.5	Summary		386

14 Workforce Analytics — 387

14.1	The Foundation of Workforce Analytics		388
	14.1.1	Implementing Core Workforce & Mobility	388
	14.1.2	Metrics Packs	390
	14.1.3	Metric Methodology	393
	14.1.4	Analyzing Your Data	394
14.2	The Benchmarking Program		400
	14.2.1	Benchmarking Methodology	400
	14.2.2	Benchmarking Categories	401
	14.2.3	Applying Benchmarks	402
14.3	Analytical Tools		407
	14.3.1	Query Workspace	407
	14.3.2	Report Designer	412

		14.3.3 Analytics Workspace	416
14.4		Headlines	418
		14.4.1 Using Headlines	419
		14.4.2 Headlines BizX Mobile Integration	420
14.5		Summary	421

15 Workforce Planning — 423

15.1		Defining Strategic Workforce Planning	424
15.2		The Five Steps of SuccessFactors WFP	426
		15.2.1 Forecast List	428
		15.2.2 Creating a Strategic Forecast	429
15.3		Forecasting	443
		15.3.1 Demand Forecasting	444
		15.3.2 Capabilities	448
		15.3.3 Supply Forecasting	451
		15.3.4 Gap	452
15.4		The Act Module	453
		15.4.1 Highlighting Rules	454
		15.4.2 Risk Identification	455
		15.4.3 Strategy Management	457
		15.4.4 Impact Modeling	459
		15.4.5 Action Planning	462
15.5		What-If Financial Modeling	464
15.6		Operational Workforce Planning Forecasts	467
15.7		Summary	471

16 Onboarding — 473

16.1	Pre-hire Verification Steps	474
16.2	Introductory Information	475
16.3	Activities	476
16.4	Paperwork	478
16.5	Integration	479
16.6	Summary	479

17 BizX Mobile ... 481

17.1 Org Chart and Directory ... 482
17.2 SAP Jam on BizX Mobile ... 483
17.3 Mobile Learning ... 485
17.4 Recruiting ... 485
17.5 Employee Central To-Dos ... 486
17.6 Performance Manager To-Dos ... 487
17.7 BizX Mobile Touchbase ... 488
17.8 Data and Security ... 489
17.9 Summary ... 490

18 Further Resources ... 491

18.1 SuccessFactors ... 491
18.2 SAP ... 493
    18.2.1 SAP Help Portal ... 493
    18.2.2 SAP Service Marketplace ... 493
    18.2.3 SAP PartnerEdge ... 496
    18.2.4 SAP Community Network ... 496
    18.2.5 SAP Jam ... 497
18.3 Social Media ... 498
    18.3.1 LinkedIn ... 499
    18.3.2 Google Plus ... 499
    18.3.3 Twitter ... 499
    18.3.4 YouTube ... 500
18.4 Publications ... 500
18.5 Conferences ... 500
18.6 SAP User Groups ... 500

The Authors ... 503
Index ... 507

Foreword

We live in one of the most important and interesting days in the history of enterprise software. Our industry is going through a major transformation, and, without a doubt, cloud software is at the forefront of these changes. The cloud enables software to be created, delivered, updated, and consumed quickly and inexpensively.

But cloud is not the only interesting trend—myriad factors have converged to create this shift. Millennials are replacing Baby Boomers in the workforce. Consumer software, such as Facebook, Twitter, and Google, has changed our lives by creating new expectations around user experience, immediacy, and content accessibility, all wrapped up in the ability to connect with similar users while doing everything on the go. Companies such as Apple have introduced us to beautiful, sleek, and easy-to-use devices. SAP HANA has introduced the world to in-memory platform at scale. And the list goes on.

Here at SuccessFactors, we are incredibly lucky to be at the intersection of these trends. We get to build software that is relevant to today's workforce and that is social, mobile, and engaging employees to deliver business results every day. We are grateful to learn and benefit from thousands of customers with tens of millions of employees, who teach us every day. They share their best practices with us, allow us to incorporate these practices into our software, and share this knowledge with others. We get to observe trends in the consumer software market, learn from them, and then deliver enticing experiences to enterprises. We consider ourselves fortunate to be at the right place, at the right time, moving at the right speed in the right direction, to deliver our innovative solutions to customers. I am convinced that when we look back on this period in our professional lives many years from now, we will appreciate it even more.

SuccessFactors for SAP ERP HCM is the first book to broadly describe the capabilities we have been building for more than a decade. The book highlights different parts of the suite and how they fit together. It goes into detail about key areas of the product—core HR, payroll, talent management, learning, recruiting, compensation, social, and mobile—from both functional and experiential perspectives. Finally, it covers important elements that are required to fully understand the solution, including management, configuration, security, and maintenance of the system. Authors Luke, Jyoti, and Amy, along with contributors Joe, Regan, and Atif, have done a great job learning the software, looking under the covers, and describing it to the readers in an accessible yet detailed way.

I think you will find this well-written and comprehensive book to be useful, and I hope you will use the software to transform your business and help your employees achieve their dreams.

Dmitri Krakovsky
Senior Vice President, Global Product Management
SuccessFactors

Acknowledgments

We would like to dedicate this book to all those who have supported us in this long and exciting journey. We have sacrificed a great deal of time and effort to produce this book, and we greatly appreciate the support our loved ones have provided during the long nights and even longer weekends.

We also appreciate the support that SAP, SuccessFactors, and members of the community have given to ensure that we are able to provide a book of the highest caliber. The SAP ERP HCM industry is currently in a time of transition, and it is disconcerting to read and hear inaccuracies and myths regarded as cutting-edge information. For this reason, we are grateful to all those who have helped ensure that this title provides our readers with confidence in its authenticity, accuracy, and relevance.

We are especially thankful to Dmitri Krakovsky, Senior Vice President of Global Product Management at SAP Cloud, for taking the time, energy, and passion to write an excellent foreword to this book.

In addition to expressing appreciation for each others' hard work and dedication, each author would like to thank specific individuals that have provided support and/or input that has positively affected the final result of this book.

Amy would like to thank Don Grubb, Brandon Toombs, Derek Everett, Kara Pastorek, Mary Poppen, Jeff Pytel, Paige Cherny, Donna Cohen, Steve Bradley, Margaret Black, Ed Steiger, Melissa Scruggs, Matt Jones, Jerry McBrayer, Nicole Mercurio, and Craig Rumbaugh.

Luke would like to thank Kira Swain, Andrea Meyer, Prashanth Padmanabhan, Henner Schliebs, Frans Smolders, Kouros Behzad, Yannick Peterschmitt, Volker Stiehl, Bianka Woelke, Mike Rossi, Heiko Zintgraf, Petra Ligthart, Chiara Bersano, Udo Paltzer, Philip Haine, Paru Sankar, Dmitri Krakovsky, Dagmar Becker, Adrienne Whitten, Oliver Conze, David Ludlow, Yariv Zur, Brandon Toombs, Tim Simmons, Jörg Schreiber, Matthew Partridge, and Jarret Pazahanick.

Acknowledgments

Jyoti would like to thank Willem Spies, Leendert van der Bijl, Jonathan Tager, Tim Simmons, Paul Snyman, Tony Ashton, Chiara Bersano, Abhijit Salvi, Philip Haine, and Heiko Lenk for their support during the writing of this book.

Atif would like to thank Anup Yanamandra and Paul Hopkins.

Regan would like to thank Dana Reinitz, Lyndal Hagar, Tony Ashton, and Kouros Behzad.

Joe would like to thank Liz and Connor Lee.

Last, but not least, we would collectively like to give a big thank you to Emily Nicholls, Katy Spencer, Jon Kent, Kelly Harris, Graham Geary, and the rest of the team at SAP PRESS who put up with missed deadlines, extension requests, spelling mistakes, and grammar faux pas and ensured that we were able to deliver this title to the required standard.

A leader in talent management and social collaboration software in the cloud, SuccessFactors provides a full range of human capital management solutions that are suitable for any organization.

1   Introduction

With the rapid growth of the Software-as-a-Service (SaaS) talent management field, it was inevitable that SAP would move into this market. Having spent some years developing its Career OnDemand solution with little success, SAP made the shocking announcement in December 2011 that it had entered into an agreement to buy SuccessFactors for $3.4 billion.

Although this move came as a total surprise to many, SAP's intentions made sense for several reasons: SAP had not had a lot of success in its early cloud endeavors, SaaS human capital management (HCM) vendors have been making inroads into the market, and analysts such as Bersin by Deloitte and Gartner had not been complimentary about SAP's range of talent management solutions. By acquiring SuccessFactors, SAP immediately became a global cloud player and inherited the "cloud DNA" of SuccessFactors co-founder Lars Dalgaard. However, prior to the acquisition, many did not really know much about SuccessFactors as a vendor—or much about cloud computing to begin with.

1.1   Terminology and Concepts

Before we look at the topic of SuccessFactors, it's worth understanding what the terminology and concepts behind cloud computing really mean. Increased availability of the Internet has forever changed personal computing and the spread of information. More recently, the Internet has provided a platform to revolutionize professional computing.

Enterprise software, particularly from SAP, is rooted in client-server technology and based on older but highly customizable architectures. Despite being flexible, these systems often have user interfaces (UIs) that, by twenty-first century standards, are antiquated and complex.

By contrast, modern applications such as those on computers, in the cloud, or via mobile apps have slick graphics and easy-to-use functionality. As a result, many users find a mismatch between the applications they use in the workplace and the applications they consume on the Internet and on their personal mobile devices. The rise of smartphones and tablets means that attractive and simple applications are available for a cost-effective price—quite often free—and can easily be used for leisure and professional use.

The Internet effectively allows software to be consumed as a service (rather than as a product that is owned and maintained) by organizations and individuals any time and anywhere. *Bring Your Own Device* (BYOD) policies allow employees to use their own smartphones or tablets to perform work-related activities more efficiently and easily wherever they are. Security concerns have led some organizations to opt for a *Choose Your Own Device* (CYOD) policy instead, so that employees can pick the preapproved smartphone or table device that they need to be more productive.

Providing employees with a means of working anywhere lets them perform tasks that were once restricted to the workplace. For example, many employees are likely to check their email outside of work, or submit their timesheet when they are travelling home. This essentially means that time spent in the workplace is more productive because employees are performing smaller, bite-size activities at times where they would otherwise be out of the office and unproductive—during "dead" time. Because of these shifts in application consumption, workers are becoming more productive outside of the workplace, whether this is travelling or during leisure time. It is not unheard of for busy individuals to keep on top of their workload while on vacation!

Of course, whether this is a positive or negative for employees depends on the view of the individual, but businesses benefit because increased efficiency and productivity ensure survival in a competitive marketplace.

1.1.1 Cloud Computing

For many, *cloud computing*—or simply *cloud*—seems a strange and new concept, yet it is something that has been around almost as long as the Internet. In the past, these services, often called "hosted" services, were commonplace within large networks and more so once the Internet became more widespread. In addition, modern cloud services such as Hotmail, Facebook, Twitter, and Flickr are well-known cloud applications that have been in mainstream use for some years. But when it comes to enterprise software, cloud computing is indeed a new concept. Although cloud-based software vendors have existed for a while, they have only become prominent within the past five years or so.

So what is cloud computing? To put it simply, cloud computing is when software or servers are hosted remotely and accessed via a network, such as the Internet. Cloud software exists "in the cloud."

This type of technology is beneficial for both users and organizations for numerous reasons. Essentially, cloud is a platform to provide services. For a subscription fee—or sometimes free of charge!—it provides servers or software that might be used regularly, rather than for a one-off capital expenditure and, in some cases, ongoing maintenance or upgrade fees.

Modern-day hardware and the speed of common Internet connections have made it possible to offer cloud-based services that are truly as effective as those operated on an organization's premises. And because there is now significant uptake in cloud services, costs are becoming easily affordable by individual consumers and companies. With no need to host, install, maintain, or upgrade software, cloud computing is hassle-free for individuals or organizations who simply want software that is easy to consume. In particular, the *SaaS* concept allows organizations to consume enterprise resource planning (ERP) software through the cloud.

1.1.2 Software-as-a-Service

Software-as-a-Service (SaaS) is a concept in cloud computing that can be considered an extension or evolution of *Application Service Providers* (ASP). The SaaS delivery model provides software—most commonly business and enterprise software applications—as a service over the Internet using a subscription-based payment model. If the cloud is the platform to provide services, then SaaS is the application that provides those services.

Because SaaS applications are relatively new and leverage the latest technological advancements coined collectively as Web 2.0, they are often much more visually attractive and easier to use than typical enterprise software applications. Many of the SaaS vendors, particularly in the HCM area, use highly innovative features in their application to provide a superior user experience than what can be achieved with traditional enterprise software.

Since the introduction of SaaS, traditional enterprise software has been termed *on-premise*. In addition to SaaS and on-premise delivery methods, *mobile* is also widely used and is often an integral part of a SaaS vendor's offering. Another integral component of SaaS offerings is the regular delivery of updates to applications, which can be as often as every quarter. These updates often contain new features and bug fixes with a focus on introducing enhancements to the core application in every release. This strategy creates a focus on product development and innovation so that customers can get new features quickly, rather than waiting on the common 12-, 18-, or 24-month cycles that are typical for enterprise software releases.

SaaS offers customers additional benefits. For example, customers do not need to pay for hardware, maintenance and support, or solution upgrades because the vendor handles all of these.

A key architectural difference from on-premise is the use of *multi-tenancy, in which* each customer uses the same instance of the software but has its own unique configuration of the software. This type of architecture has a number of benefits for customers. First, it facilitates improved system maintenance because every customer uses the exact same version of the software. Second, it's the main driver for the regular release cycle because of the shared software version. And finally, it enables benchmark analytics to be produced based on anonymous aggregates of the analytical data in all tenants where the customer has approved of this usage. This is a feature of SuccessFactors Workforce Analytics and will be covered in Chapter 14. This type of scenario is simply not possible in an on-premise scenario.

Of course, SaaS also has its downsides. It requires that customers trust their vendor to adequately maintain the system and protect their sensitive employee data. Multi-tenant systems give only limited control to the customer, who must work within the vendor's guidelines. Having to rely on the vendor for professional services can also be inadequate for some customers. While vendors are very good at producing software, they can be less adept at delivering high-quality professional services.

While SaaS systems are strong on configuration in relation to on-premise systems, they are comparatively weak on customization. Although this can be a disadvantage for many customers, the inability to do heavy customizing means that systems are easy to upgrade and extend while remaining stable and high performing.

There are some misconceptions about SaaS, and, although some of these are valid, they often vary between different vendors rather than being common across vendors. For example, security (both the protection of data stored in the cloud and in day-to-day operations) is a key concern for customers, and each vendor has different standards and systems for protecting data. Limited customization possibilities in a SaaS application reduce the availability of complex authorizations. For some organizations, there is a clear risk that they cannot protect data from being accessed by the wrong employees.

All-in-all, SaaS demonstrates how a cloud-based delivery model can provide a wealth of benefits for customers, not just from a practical perspective but also from the innovation that these young enterprise software companies are investing in. The growth in SaaS clearly shows that this new age of application delivery is the future of enterprise software.

1.1.3 Cloud and SaaS Trends

The information technology research and analyst firm Gartner estimated the value of the overall SaaS market to be approximately $14.5 billion in 2012. They estimate that by 2015, this will exceed $22 billion. In North America, where SaaS is most popular, it accounts for almost two-thirds of global revenue. In Western Europe, it accounts for somewhere between one-fifth and one-quarter of global revenues.

These figures show that SaaS is due to grow rapidly between 2012 and 2015, particularly in Western Europe where growth of nearly 20% was seen in 2012 compared to the previous year. While the North American and Western European markets will continue to grow considerably, growth will be slow outside of these regions with gradual but upward adoption in APAC and Eastern Europe.

The 2012 ERP Report by Panorama Consulting, a consultancy specializing in helping firms evaluate and select ERP software, found that of all ERP implementations, SaaS accounted for 16% of implementations in 2011, up from only 6% in 2010.

Looking specifically at HCM, the leading research and analyst organization Constellation Research believes that spending on SaaS HCM systems will increase from 30% in 2012 to 70% by 2016. The company's research also indicates that by 2016, more than 70% of organizations rely on SaaS HCM systems, which is an increase of 67% from 2012. Constellation Research also predicts that on-premise ERP systems are not experiencing the same level of replacement, and therefore a "hybrid" approach to HCM is becoming more prevalent to bridge the gap between investments in on-premise core HR and SaaS talent management.

Mobility is a strong focus of SaaS vendors, and the growth of smartphone and tablet devices is exceptionally high. Gartner predicted sales of around 820 million devices in 2012 with growth of 50% in 2013. Purchases of tablets by business will increase three-fold to around 50 million devices between 2012 and 2016. By 2016, 40% of the workforce is expected to be mobile, with the focus being on tablet devices.

SaaS vendors are responding to the explosion of mobility within a professional context by attempting to provide complementary mobility that comes at an additional cost with on-premise vendors.

The growth of the Internet and cloud computing has enabled SaaS to become a viable option for enterprise software customers. With a lower total cost of ownership (TCO) and new innovative features delivered on a regular basis, SaaS is proving to be an exciting alternative to traditional on-premise enterprise software. Just as client-server technology was the next step from mainframe computing, SaaS is the next step from client-server technology. Although there are concerns about flexibility in cloud versus on-premise that are providing reasons not to move to the cloud, in the long-term, SaaS will prove a highly attractive option for the majority of organizations. Whether this is an upgrade from an on-premise system or the first move to enterprise software, SaaS will be the clear choice for many customers.

Unprecedented growth in mobile and tablet devices is fuelling new working methods and increased productivity. SaaS vendors are pioneering mobility, and many are providing mobile solutions free-of-charge as part of their offering. Because many on-premise vendors are still charging extra for these applications, SaaS vendors will have the upper hand with regard to mobility until this situation changes.

When mobility is combined with an attractive UI and engaging user experience, SaaS solutions really come to the fore. Because most SaaS applications have been built on modern technology, they possess a graphical framework that is superior to the older on-premise systems of their competition. Because many of the younger workers entering the workforce have become accustomed to simple and appealing applications on their mobile devices, using traditional on-premise enterprise software can often seem like a step back in time and the mark of an outdated organization.

Because the Internet is now a familiar concept and is used by most individuals inside and outside of the workplace on a daily basis, offering software via the cloud begins to seem more and more normal. When many individuals are more used to using Google than a printed encyclopedia, it is easy to see why they would prefer an Internet-based application to an old-fashioned desktop application. The inability of traditional on-premise applications to evolve makes SaaS becoming the mainstream delivery model for enterprise software inevitable.

1.2 About SuccessFactors

SuccessFactors is a SaaS HCM vendor founded in 2001 that focuses on providing "Business Execution" software. SuccessFactors is part of SAP's Cloud Business Unit, which is headed by former Ariba boss Bob Calderoni and was led by SuccessFactors co-founder Lars Dalgaard until his departure in May 2013. Headquartered in San Francisco, USA, SuccessFactors also has offices in more than 35 locations around the world in North and South America, Europe, and Asia-Pacific.

At the time of writing (summer 2013), SuccessFactors boasts more than 3,500 customers in 168 territories using 35 different languages. Among these customers are some highly recognizable companies and brands, including 20th Century Fox, Adobe, American Airlines, Astra Zeneca, Bayer Corporation, Capital One, Comcast, Department of Homeland Security, Drug Enforcement Administration, McAfee, NASA, Siemens, Starbucks, and VMware.

The SuccessFactors products cover the spectrum of HCM processes, including core HR, workforce planning, talent management, analytics, and social collaboration. SuccessFactors has a particular strength in talent management and social collaboration, while its vendor-agnostic analytics solution has 30 years of experience behind it and provides well over a thousand predefined analytics. Its range of talent management solutions covers all of the key process areas: performance management, recruitment, compensation management, learning, succession, and development.

> **Note**
>
> SuccessFactors has a focus on providing business execution and reducing TCO. "Business execution" was described as as "focusing on talent management processes associated with aligning the workforce to deliver business results" in the whitepaper "Driving Business Execution Through Integrated Talent Management" by Steven Hunt, a senior director of Business Execution Practices at SuccessFactors. Business execution influences the design of functionality within the SuccessFactors solutions that support those processes.

SuccessFactors uses its own measurement of project outcomes, return on execution (ROX), instead of the typical metric return on investment (ROI). While ROI is concerned purely with financial cost savings, ROX also focuses on increasing efficiency, executing company strategy, and thus increasing bottom-line results.

In Gartner's 2013 Magic Quadrant for Talent Management suites, SuccessFactors came out a head and shoulders above all other vendors and was ranked as the leader in the Forrest Wave for Talent Management, Q1 2013. In IDC's 2012 Integrated Talent Management MarketScape report, IDC ranked SuccessFactors as a leader in six key areas: Talent Management, Recruiting, Learning, Performance, Compensation, and Social Technology.

SuccessFactors is well known and respected for its company and product marketing and has published a number of videos on YouTube covering all of its product suite, plus topics such as security, architecture, and configuration functionality. SuccessFactors regularly publishes videos about its employees and working at SuccessFactors.

History of SuccessFactors

SuccessFactors was founded in 2001 by Lars Dalgaard and Aaron Au as a vendor of performance management software, and in 2007 floated onto the NASDAQ stock exchange. However, SuccessFactors made a crucial decision in 2009 to extend its product offering from employee performance and goal setting to "business execution software" that fully supports companies by using talent management to execute business strategy. Soon afterwards, the company formally launched the Business Execution (BizX) suite.

The change in strategy and launch of the BizX suite provided a platform for growth of both the company and the products that were offered. Early on, SuccessFactors made a few key acquisitions: a company whose assets were to form the basis of SuccessFactors Workforce Analytics, an enterprise social collaboration and networking software vendor Cubetree (the basis of SAP Jam), and finally a data analysis and calculation software vendor.

In 2011, SuccessFactors' attention was on providing a world-class learning platform. It acquired social learning software vendor Jambok and market-leading learning management system (LMS) software vendor Plateau Systems. In July, SuccessFactors left the NASDAQ stock exchange and became the first company to be listed on three stock exchanges simultaneously: the New York Stock Exchange, Euronext Paris, and the Frankfurt Stock Exchange.

In December, SuccessFactors purchased application tracking and social networking integration software vendor Jobs2Web (the basis for SuccessFactors Recruiting Execution), after the announcement but before the completion of the acquisition by SAP.

In February 2012, SAP's acquisition of SuccessFactors was formally completed, bringing an end to 11 years of growth and success as an independent company and beginning a new era under the ownership of SAP.

Acquisition of SuccessFactors by SAP

On December 3, 2011, SAP made a formal announcement that it had agreed to purchase the entire stock of SuccessFactors for $3.4 billion, which was 52% above the market value of the company. After a period of due diligence and formalities, the purchase was formerly completed, and SuccessFactors became "SuccessFactors, an SAP company."

In recent years, SAP's range of on-premise talent management solutions had received substandard reviews by both Bersin by Deloitte and Gartner. In this period, various SaaS vendors were leading the field in talent management, either as specialist vendors of one discipline or as vendors of end-to-end talent management. In acquiring SuccessFactors, SAP enhanced its range of talent management solutions. The acquisition was significant for SAP in a number of ways; it provided SAP with access to genuine cloud expertise and enabled it to offer a full cloud-based HCM suite. It also gave both SAP and SuccessFactors significant exposure within and outside the SAP ERP HCM ecosystem.

1.3 SuccessFactors BizX Suite

The SuccessFactors BizX suite covers core HCM, talent management, analytics, and social collaboration. Social, mobile, and analytics underpin the suite and are key components of the BizX suite. The suite contains the following modules, which we cover in this book:

- Employee Central
- Performance & Goals

- Compensation
- Recruiting Execution
- Learning
- Succession & Development
- SAP Jam
- Workforce Planning
- Workforce Analytics
- Onboarding
- BizX Mobile

Figure 1.1 is the graphic used by SAP and SuccessFactors to visualize the BizX suite.

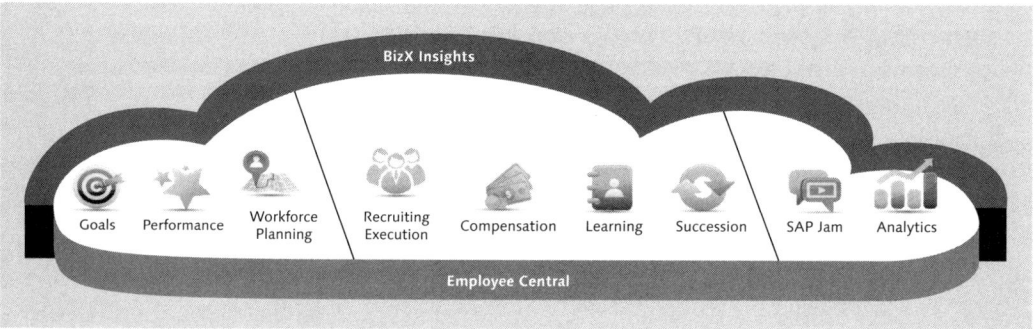

Figure 1.1 The SuccessFactors BizX Suite

The solutions in the BizX suite can be grouped together in three main process areas, as shown in Figure 1.2:

- Attract and retain
- Align and execute
- Develop and learn

Three additional tiers—social collaboration, next-generation core HR, and analytics and workforce planning—can be considered as foundational to supporting these three process areas.

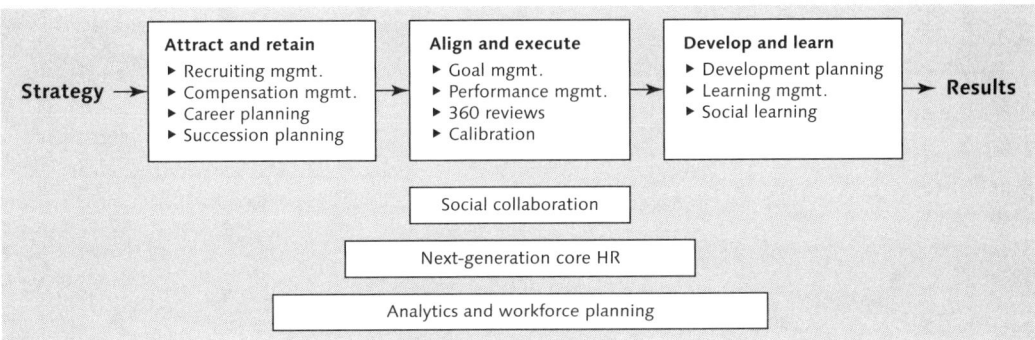

Figure 1.2 Grouping of BizX Solutions into Core Process Areas

> **Note**
>
> At the time of writing (summer 2013), the SuccessFactors Business Execution suite is known as the BizX suite, which is how we refer to it throughout the book. It's possible that the name could change in the future, but this change would not substantially have an impact on the customer.

Let's walk through the 11 key components of the SuccessFactors BizX suite.

1.3.1 Employee Central

SuccessFactors Employee Central is the core HR system of SuccessFactors BizX. It provides enterprise-level HCM functionality in an intuitive UI for HR professionals, managers, and employees. It allows users to view, maintain, audit, and report on employee and organizational data across different countries, cost centers, legal entities, and employee types. It features the built-in ORG CHART shown in Figure 1.3, which gives easy access to employee profiles, employment information, and data from other BizX modules such as Performance & Goals and Succession & Development. Employee Central also integrates with SAP Jam so that HR professionals and managers can engage, track, collaborate, and interact with employees.

Employee Central also offers payroll functionality optionally with SAP's hosted payroll solution, Employee Central Payroll. More information on these can be found in Chapter 6.

1   Introduction

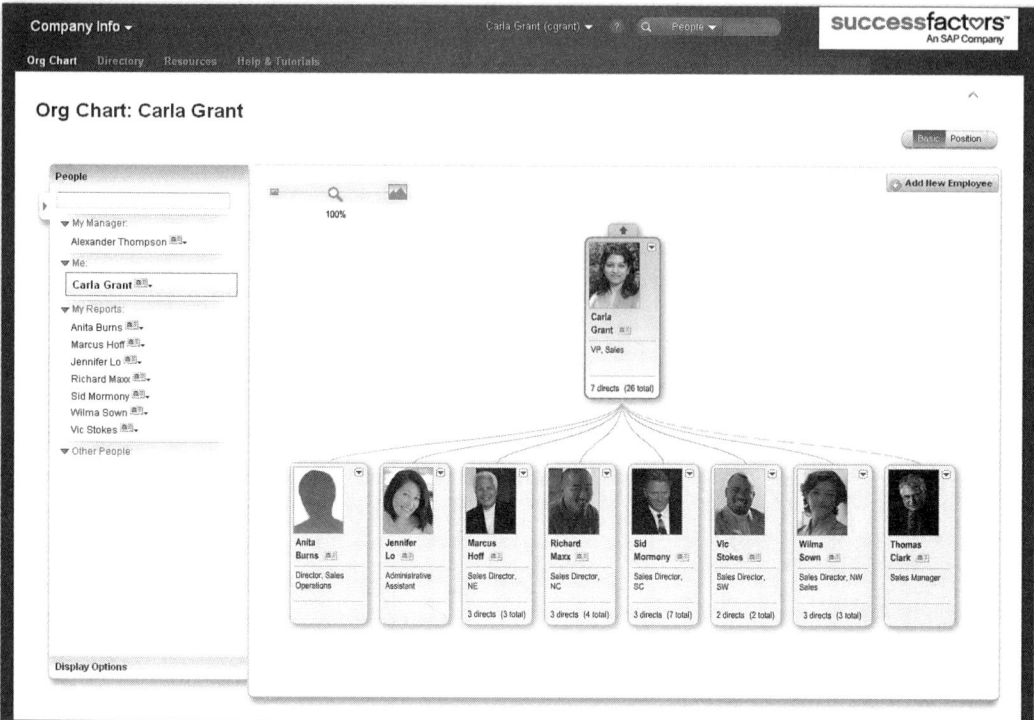

Figure 1.3 The Org Chart in Employee Central

1.3.2   Performance & Goals

SuccessFactors Performance & Goals is the performance management and goal-setting solution. One of the strongest modules of the SuccessFactors BizX suite, it is feature-rich, supports organizations to deliver more meaningful employee reviews, and aligns employee goals with business goals by using Measurement by Objectives principles.

To help users assign appropriate goals to employees and cascade those goals back to the managers and departments that assigned them, the application comes with a SMART wizard and library of more than 500 goals. While completing performance review forms, it is easy for managers to add ratings and comments using the writing assistant, coaching advisor, and legal scan to ensure meaningful, legally robust, and compliant remarks.

Other functions available to managers during the assessment process include team overview, team evaluation (as shown in Figure 1.4), calibration, 360 Multi-Rater assessments, competency gap assessments, and dashboards.

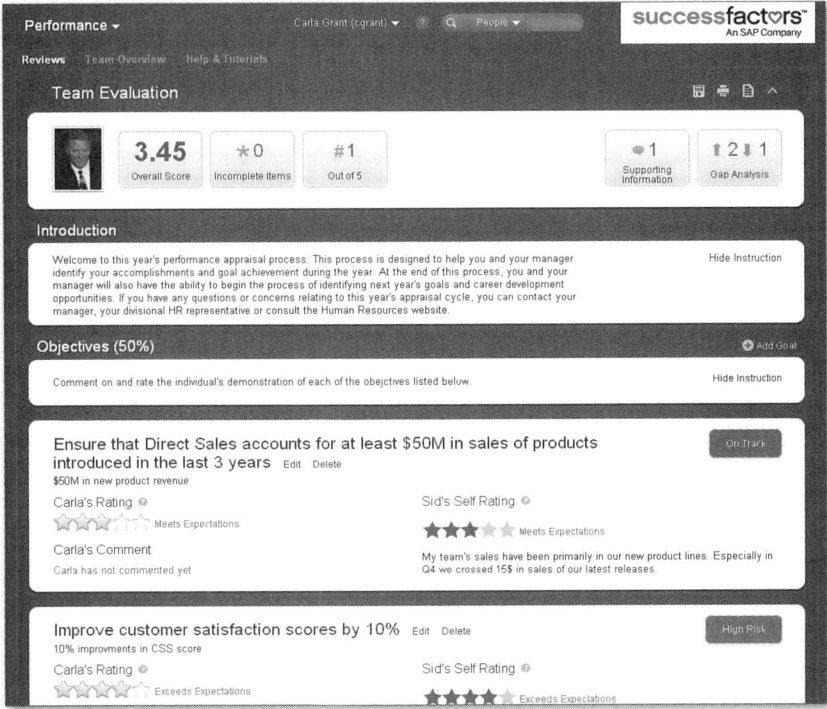

Figure 1.4 Team Evaluation in Performance & Goals

More information on SuccessFactors Performance & Goals can be found in Chapter 8.

1.3.3 Compensation

SuccessFactors Compensation, shown in Figure 1.5, covers the compensation management processes and provides a range of functionality expected in an enterprise-level compensation management solution. For managers, there is a wealth of functionality in compensation planning, including the following:

- Access-controlled compensation plans
- Budgeting
- Calibration

1 | Introduction

- Variable pay options
- Pay-for-performance

SuccessFactors Compensation also features hierarchy-based approvals, departmental budget roll-ups, and total rewards statements. Dashboards and analytics measure the impact of compensation measurements and adjustments on budgets in real time.

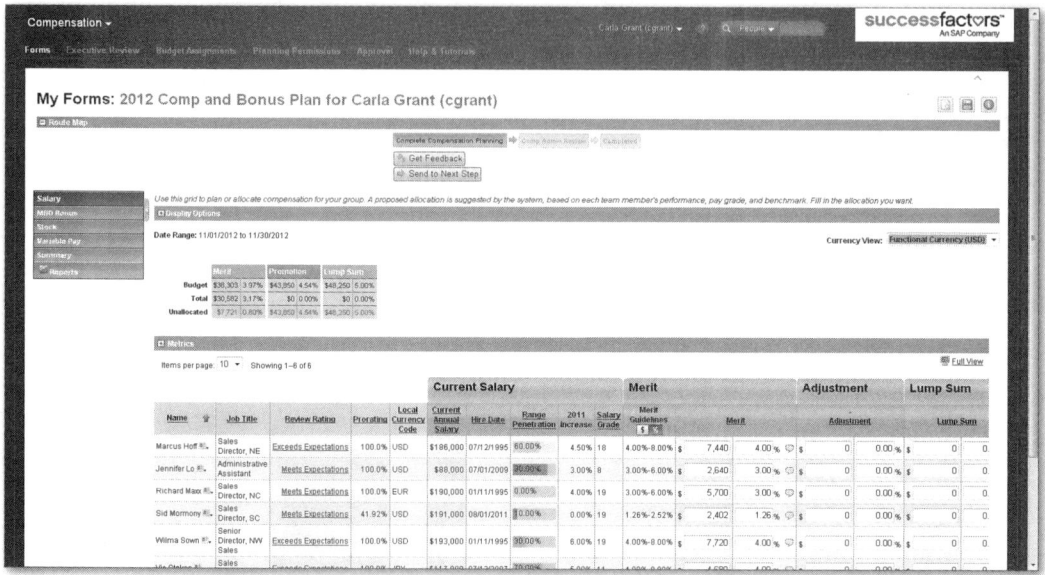

Figure 1.5 Compensation and Bonus Plan in SuccessFactors Compensation

SuccessFactors Variable Pay is a module offered within the SuccessFactors Compensation solution that facilitates the administration of complex bonus programs impacted by business and employee performance measures.

More information on SuccessFactors Compensation can be found in Chapter 9.

1.3.4 Recruiting Execution

SuccessFactors Recruiting Execution supports attracting, engaging, and selecting hires more efficiently. The application compromises two core modules: Recruiting Management (RCM) and Recruiting Marketing (RMK). RCM is a mobile and collaborative recruiting management platform whereas RMK is a social recruiting marketing platform. Together, these aim to make every job opening into a marketing campaign in itself.

By using techniques such as search engine optimization (SEO), customizable job landing pages, and social network integration, SuccessFactors Recruiting Execution can offer a truly attractive twenty-first century recruiting platform to engage applicants. Career site optimization, SocialMatcher, and the use of QR codes help further support the social aspects of recruiting.

Analytics dashboards help recruiters and managers identify the number of visitors, source of visitors, and areas where the recruiting process needs to be adjusted. Integration between candidate sourcing and Employee Central enable accurate evaluation of candidates versus position requirements. Figure 1.6 shows a JOB REQUISITION in SuccessFactors Recruiting.

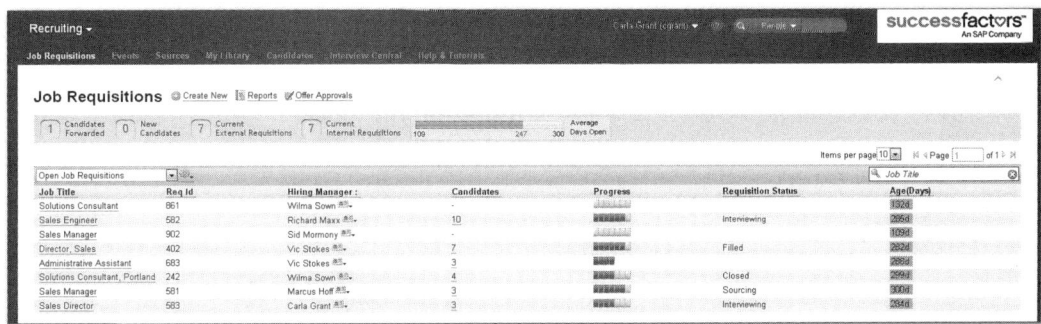

Figure 1.6 Job Requisition in SuccessFactors Recruiting Execution

More information on SuccessFactors Recruiting Execution can be found in Chapter 10.

1.3.5 Learning

SuccessFactors Learning is a learning management system (LMS) that features heavy use of social and mobile features to enhance the learning experience.

With SuccessFactors Learning, courses can be delegated by supervisors and employees can search the course catalog. The To-Do List, Easy Links, and Status pods allow employees to track their learning activities and visit their most frequently performed tasks. Managers can track due and overdue courses (as shown in Figure 1.7) and identify skills gaps for their employees.

Learning administrators have a wealth of options for creating and managing different types of course and course content, in addition to managing overall learning activities across the organization. Analytics dashboards and reports also let them track the benefits of learning activities to the organization in relation to overall goals. E-learning content can be created, managed, and delivered using iContent, which is a *Content-as-a-Service* (CaaS) platform.

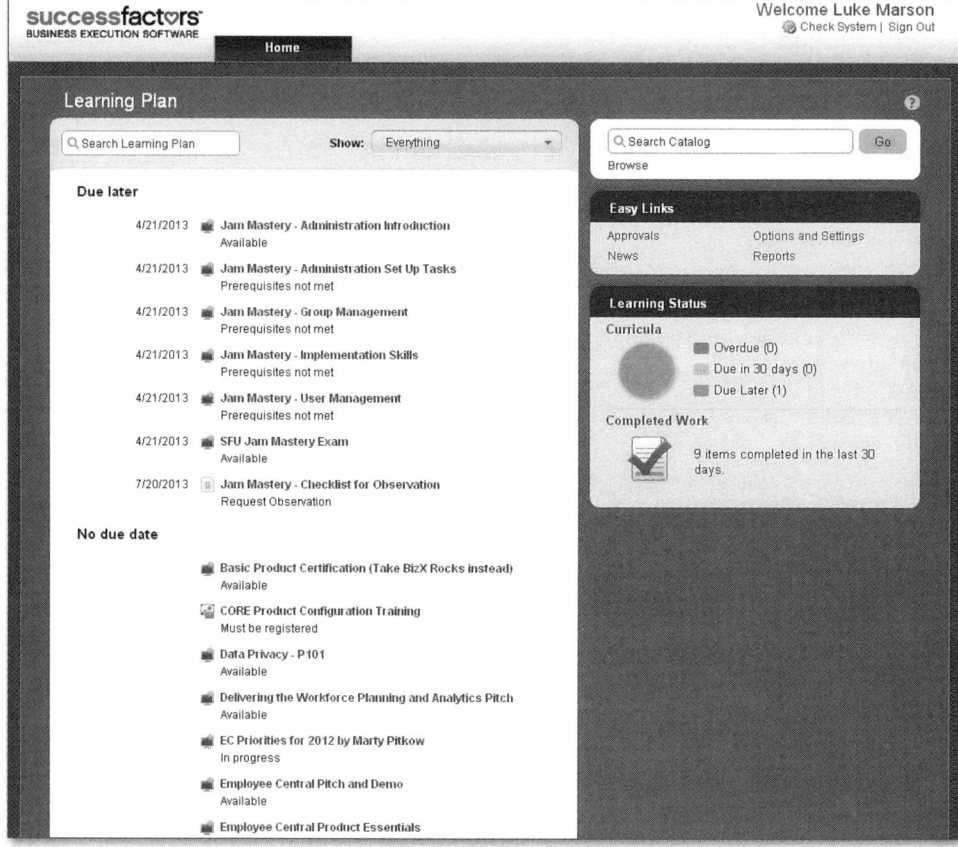

Figure 1.7 Learning Plan in SuccessFactors Learning

More information on SuccessFactors Learning can be found in Chapter 11.

1.3.6 Succession & Development

SuccessFactors Succession & Development is a succession planning and career development solution for helping to objectively identify high-potential individuals, assign successors to key positions, and create development plans for successors.

The Succession Org Chart—built on top of the standard Org Chart functionality—allows an overall view of health of positions, employee risks, and successor readiness. As shown in Figure 1.8, you can highlight key positions, identify the risk and impact of loss of position holders, assess successors' readiness, and make nominations.

The competency-based Talent Search, side-by-side comparison, and Performance-Potential Matrix (nine-box grid) enable talent specialists to find the best employees and successors across the organization. You can use calibration to ensure that performance and potential ratings are adequate for a selection of employees.

You can create development plans to track career development activities for employees and successors. Career Worksheets enable employees to track favored positions and identify the competencies needed to progress toward those roles. Identified competencies can be assigned as Development Goals.

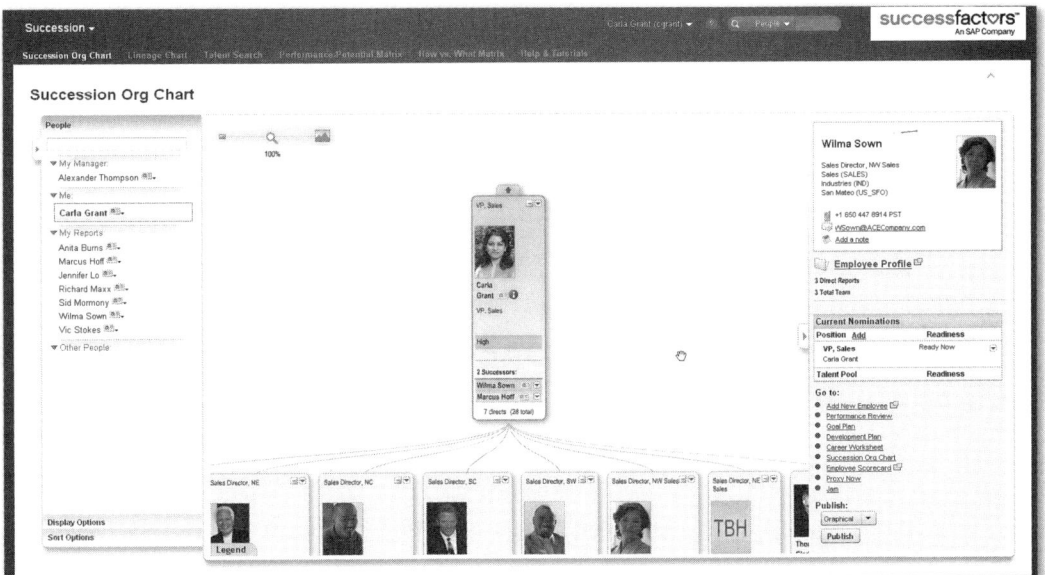

Figure 1.8 The Succession Org Chart and a Successor in SuccessFactors Succession & Development

More information on Succession & Development can be found in Chapter 12.

1.3.7 Workforce Planning

SuccessFactors Workforce Planning, shown in Figure 1.9, enables organizations to match workforce supply to workforce demand in the long-term future. It helps organizations predict long-term workforce needs and forecast the costs and skills associated with meeting those needs.

Strategic workforce plans can be created that forecast demand, supply, and gaps in workforce requirements. You can generate "what-if" scenarios using various data and models made to simulate the cost impact of different scenarios. Predictive capabilities allow SuccessFactors Workforce Planning to forecast how future supply will look if present trends continue, and different variables can be set to produce forecasts and gap analyses of employees and competencies.

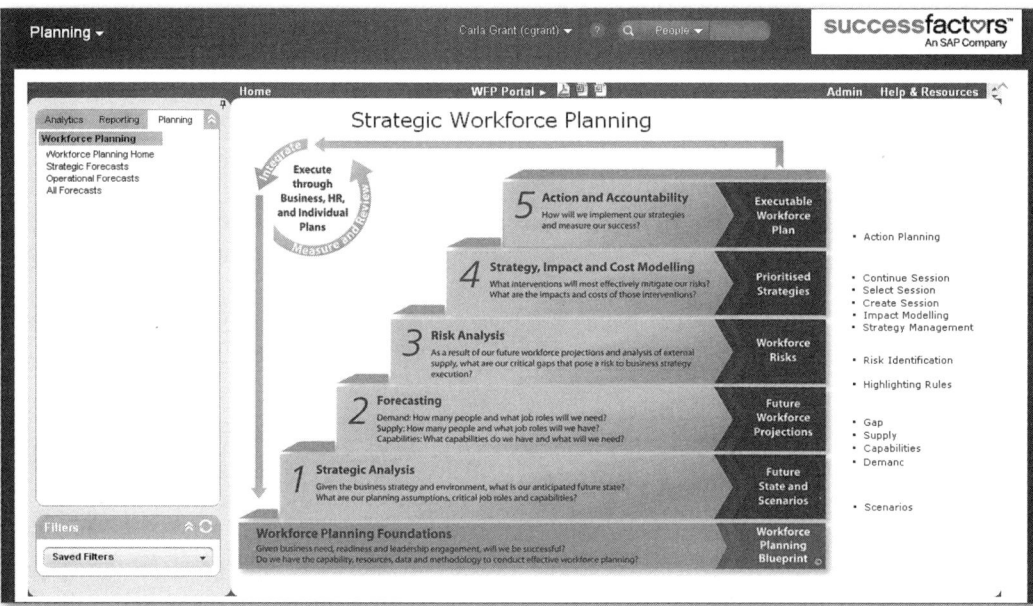

Figure 1.9 The Home Page of SuccessFactors Workforce Planning

More information on SuccessFactors Workforce Planning can be found in Chapter 15.

1.3.8 Workforce Analytics

SuccessFactors Workforce Analytics is a comprehensive vendor-agnostic analytics and reporting solution that comes with more than a thousand predefined analytics and key performance indicators (KPIs). Because it can connect to various systems simultaneously, Workforce Analytics provides a complete and unified view of how various talent-based activities, such as recruiting and learning, impact metrics such as retention, engagement, and performance. Analytics such as headcounts, retention, mobility, diversity, and profit-per-employee can be measured and correlated with business KPIs focused on revenue, profitability, and costs. Figures can also be examined further and deeper with drill-down and slicing capabilities.

The solution also features built-in industry benchmarks so that users can compare various analytics and metrics from their own businesses with like-for-like organizations of similar size, industry, and geographical locations. By using the Questions functionality, organizations can spot trends and then use the interpretation guides to understand data, identify issues, and find resolutions. Ad hoc reports can be built based on on-the-spot requirements, and automated personalized reports can be set up for a set frequency with predefined format and content for each target user, such as managers or executives. Figure 1.10 provides an example of the OBJECTIVE DASHBOARD within SuccessFactors Workforce Analytics.

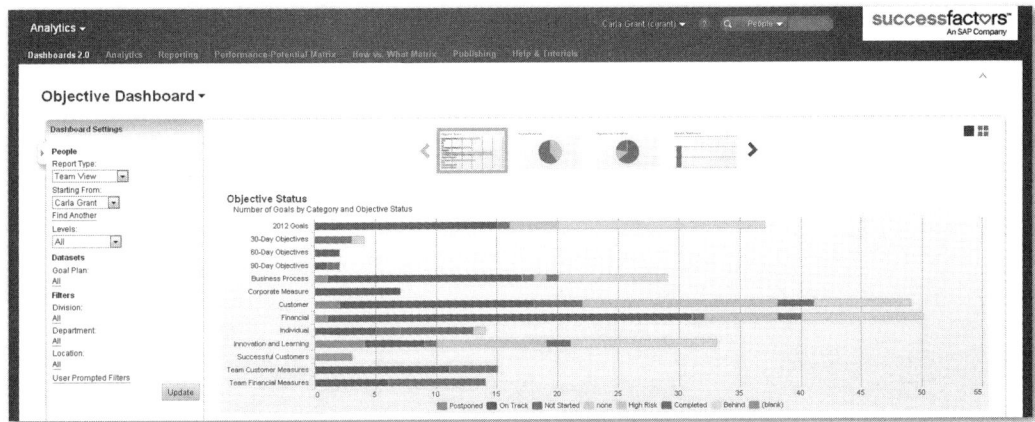

Figure 1.10 Objective Dashboard in SuccessFactors Workforce Analytics

More information on Workforce Analytics can be found in Chapter 13.

1.3.9 Onboarding

SuccessFactors Onboarding is the newest solution in the BizX suite and provides onboarding functionality for new hires. As shown in Figure 1.11, it allows new hires to gain access to the online portal, where they can access and complete required documentation, get an overview of their new team, view their Learning Plan, see and interact in SAP Jam groups, and ask questions of their new colleagues.

In addition, it gives managers and HR professionals an easy way to ensure that new hires get access to the right information, the right documents, and the right people so they can hit the ground running at their new company.

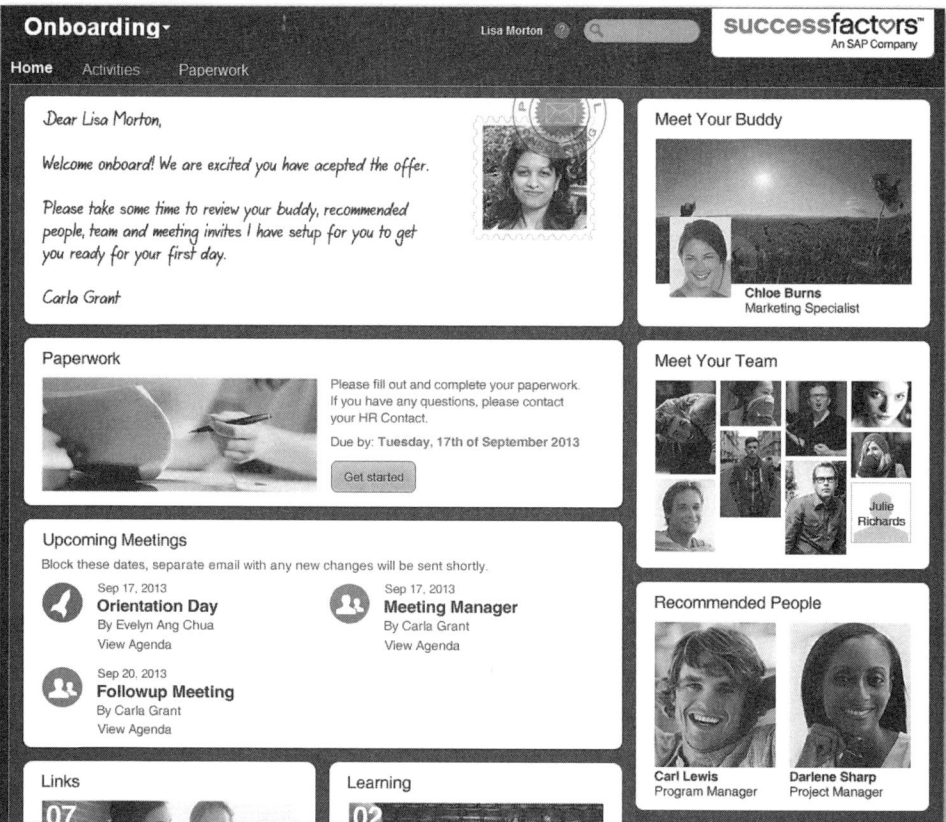

Figure 1.11 Home Page of SuccessFactors Onboarding

More information on Onboarding can be found in Chapter 16.

1.3.10 SAP Jam

SAP Jam—formerly SuccessFactors Jam—is a social collaboration platform that is designed to enhance communication, sharing, content creation, and collaborative working throughout an organization. It is cross-function and designed to be used by employees from different branches across the organization, not just HR. It is modeled after popular social networking sites such as Twitter, YouTube, and Facebook. Figure 1.12 shows the SAP Jam feed.

As a social collaboration platform, it allows users to post documents, articles, and videos, as well as create wikis and groups, either with open membership across the organization or with automated membership for particular target groups or employees. This type of platform can be used to accelerate onboarding, allow informal learning, and encourage knowledge sharing. It also supports managers and HR professionals to view the work and activities that employees are performing, evaluate relationships that they have established, and see who is proactive in helping colleagues achieve their goals and the organization's goals.

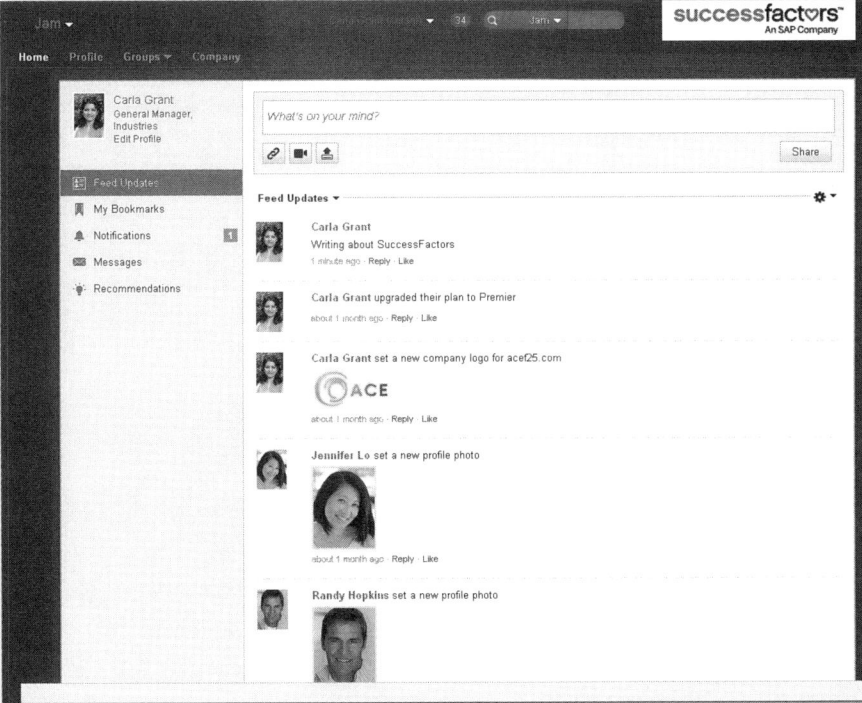

Figure 1.12 The Feed in SAP Jam

More information on SAP Jam can be found in Chapter 13.

1.3.11 BizX Mobile

SuccessFactors BizX Mobile is the mobile solution to view notifications, arrange and review meetings, perform SAP Jam activities, view and manage open To-Do activities, and display the Org Chart while on the go. BizX Mobile is available on Apple, Android, and BlackBerry devices. Figure 1.13 shows BizX mobile on one such smartphone.

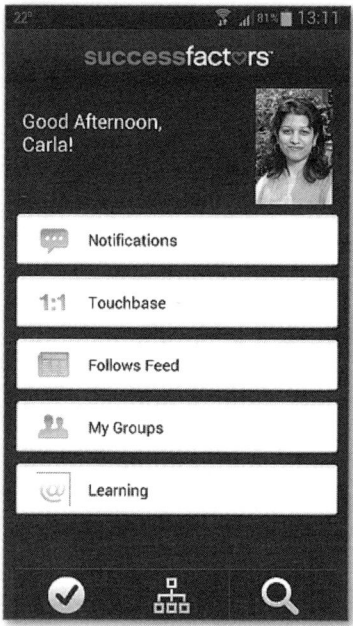

Figure 1.13 The Home Page of SuccessFactors BizX Mobile

More information on BizX Mobile can be found in Chapter 17.

1.4 SAP Strategy and Roadmap

Both SAP and SuccessFactors announced their unified product direction in February 2012, shortly after the acquisition had closed. A keynote speech at the HR 2013 event provided some further details about the product direction announced earlier.

1.4.1 Product Strategy and Roadmap

In SAP and SuccessFactors' unified product direction, the SuccessFactors BizX suite talent management applications (Performance & Goals, Compensation, Recruiting Execution, Learning, and Succession & Development) would be the go-forward solutions for talent management. SAP Jam and SuccessFactors Workforce Planning are the de facto go-forward solutions for social collaboration and workforce planning, respectively, as SAP does not have bona fide on-premise solutions. SAP does have solutions to cover these (SAP StreamWork and SAP BusinessObjects Workforce Planning), but neither have been part of the traditional on-premise portfolio.

> **Go-forward**
>
> SAP defines "go-forward" as the solutions that new customers for a process will be offered. On-premise solutions will still be available and when appropriate, these are the solutions that will be offered to new customers instead of the cloud solutions. Some customers—for example, those in the Defense sector or those with right-to-left language requirements—will be offered on-premise solutions, as these are the best fit for the customer. SAP intends to offer both options for customers, but for talent management, it makes more sense for SAP to offer the SuccessFactors BizX suite because of the continuous and regular innovations that SuccessFactors is working on.

For core HR, workforce analytics, and mobility, both the SAP and SuccessFactors solutions will be the go-forward offerings for new customers. The solutions available in the SAP ERP HCM portfolio are outlined in Table 1.1, with asterisks for the go-forward solutions.

	On-Premise Solution	Cloud Solution
HR Core	SAP ERP HCM*	SuccessFactors Employee Central*
Performance and Goals	SAP ERP HCM	SuccessFactors Performance & Goals*
Compensation	SAP ERP HCM	SuccessFactors Compensation*
Succession and Development	SAP ERP HCM	SuccessFactors Succession & Development*
Recruiting	SAP E-Recruiting	SuccessFactors Recruiting Execution*

Table 1.1 Solution Portfolio for SAP ERP HCM

	On-Premise Solution	Cloud Solution
Learning	SAP Learning Solution	SuccessFactors Learning*
Social Talent Management		SAP Jam*
Workforce Planning		SuccessFactors Workforce Planning*
Workforce Analytics	SAP BusinessObjects for HCM Analytics*	SuccessFactors Workforce Analytics*
Mobile HCM	SAP Mobile apps based on Sybase Unwired Platform*	SuccessFactors BizX Mobile*

Table 1.1 Solution Portfolio for SAP ERP HCM (Cont.)

If you are reading this book, there is a strong likelihood that you are considering or have implemented one or more SuccessFactors BizX solutions. However, if you have any on-premise investments that you want to retain, then be reassured that although SAP intends to focus innovation investments in the go-forward solutions, it will continue to sell, enhance, and support the on-premise portfolio until at least 2020. This was the date to which SAP extended support for the SAP ERP ECC 6.0 suite in 2011. Continuous enhancements will be made to the on-premise Talent Management portfolio, but no further innovations are planned. SAP Talent Visualization by Nakisa (STVN) will remain as the partner solution of choice for on-premise talent visualization for the time being. For core HR and analytics, SAP will continue to make dual investments in innovation in both on-premise and cloud solutions. There will be a period of accelerated investment in SuccessFactors Employee Central, but SAP is also investing in core HR with initiatives such as HR Renewal and SAP Business Suite powered by SAP HANA. SAP Organizational Visualization by Nakisa (SOVN) will remain SAP's on-premise solution suite of choice for organizational visualization and planning. Of course, this information is accurate at the time of writing and may change at any time as SAP sees fit.

SAP has two models for offering SuccessFactors BizX to customers, the *hybrid* model and the *full cloud HCM* model.

1.4.2 Hybrid Model

According to SAP, when customers use SAP ERP HCM on-premise for core HR processes, such as personnel administration and payroll, and SuccessFactors BizX suite for talent management, they are using a hybrid model. SAP Jam, Workforce

Planning, and Workforce Analytics are also considered part of the hybrid model, although from an integration perspective, SAP Jam is treated separately from the rest of the solutions in the hybrid model due to its cross-functional nature. We'll discuss integration in more detail in Chapter 3.

1.4.3 Full Cloud HCM Model

The full cloud HCM model refers to the entire SuccessFactors BizX suite plus Employee Central Payroll. Customers new to SAP can choose either the full cloud HCM model or the hybrid model with SAP ERP HCM as the system of record.

1.4.4 SAP's Cloud Strategy

SAP's cloud strategy is focused on four "pillars," which include SAP's range of on-demand cloud applications and, of course, SuccessFactors:

- People
- Customers
- Money
- Suppliers

Naturally, SuccessFactors falls into the People category. Business ByDesign has recently been added as a fifth pillar but not as a core part of the strategy. Figure 1.14 shows the overall cloud strategy.

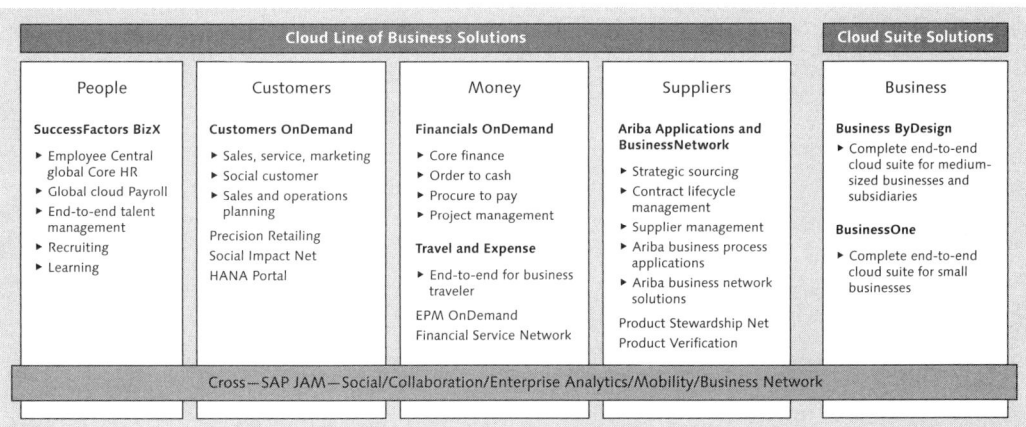

Figure 1.14 The SAP Cloud Strategy

1.5 Licensing

Like most SaaS applications, SuccessFactors is licensed on a subscription basis. Each SuccessFactors BizX solution is licensed for a single fee on a per-user per-year basis, with no additional maintenance costs. In contrast, SAP ERP HCM is licensed for a one-off fee on a per-user basis in perpetuity, plus maintenance at a rate of around 20%. Additional applications, such as Employee Interaction Center or SAP Talent Visualization by Nakisa, are charged additionally on the same basis plus maintenance.

The SaaS licensing module reduces the large capital expenditure for licenses, meaning that customers are only charged for what they use. In the on-premise model, a customer buys a fixed number of licenses at a fixed cost and, if fewer users use the system, the price does not change. In the subscription model, a customer can cancel the contract at the end of the term, which tends to be a year, without incurring any additional costs. In an on-premise scenario, the customer will likely lose that license investment.

1.6 Summary

SAP purchased SaaS HCM vendor SuccessFactors to provide a full HCM suite in the cloud and improve its talent management offering, while simultaneously protecting its position as the world's primary ERP HCM vendor. The acquisition bought genuine cloud DNA and market-leading SaaS HCM functionality into SAP and enabled it to get a foothold in a market where it had previously struggled to establish a presence.

> *SuccessFactors can be designed and configured to support customers' processes and tested and deployed in weeks rather than months. Orienting yourself to the difference between configuration and development is key to understanding the implementation of SuccessFactors.*

2   Implementing SuccessFactors

The SuccessFactors BizX suite is a highly configurable cloud-based system that can be implemented successfully in a compressed timeline and in a remote manner. SuccessFactors has worked for years developing and honing its project methodology to support customers in implementing best-in-class talent management solutions for millions of users in the cloud. By choosing to implement SuccessFactors, you are embarking on a new adventure that will present you with a different way of approaching a systems implementation than you may be accustomed to.

As a cloud technology, SuccessFactors can be implemented from wherever an Internet connection and web browser are available. By focusing on configuration of the system and business process changes rather than developing functionality to close system requirement gaps, you can implement your SuccessFactors suite in a matter of weeks rather than months or years.

This chapter discusses important considerations when embarking upon a SuccessFactors implementation (Section 2.1), provides an overview of a typical project structure (Section 2.2), takes a look at the methodology used to implement SuccessFactors (Section 2.3), and offers insight into how SuccessFactors projects are delivered (Section 2.4).

2.1   Implementation Considerations

There are many things to consider when planning to undertake any systems implementation, and these considerations are no different if you plan to implement

SuccessFactors or an on-premise solution. Take this opportunity to review the applicable business processes, taking care to revisit why you do things the way you do and evaluate how they can be improved. Understand whether the processes exist because they are best practice, because they supported the legacy system, or because that is simply the way business has always been done. This is your chance to adequately prepare the organization for the change that is coming. When implementing SuccessFactors, this change may have the biggest impact on the business process owners in HR rather than on the employee end users.

2.1.1 Setting the Strategic Objectives of the Project

The success of any project, but especially a systems implementation, is dependent upon aligning the project with the strategic objectives of the company. By developing a strong business case for making the move from on-premise to the cloud, you set your success criteria from the beginning.

SuccessFactors has a team that is available to help with business case development and can assist with the heavy-lifting of metrics needed for any business case. Solutions consultants are available to deliver system demonstrations to your key stakeholder groups to help facilitate buy-in and foster enthusiasm for the change. Your implementation partner or an experienced consulting firm will also be able to assist you in preparing sufficiently for a new implementation project.

2.1.2 Planning for the Implementation

Are you looking to implement the full SuccessFactors talent management suite? Not sure where to start? Although there is no set order to implement the modules within SuccessFactors, you should keep some considerations in mind when planning how to approach the implementation. Several modules are very complementary and are usually implemented together as a kind of bundle. Others are more suited to being implemented on their own. Next we walk through some examples of how you might bundle the implementation phases of your full-suite project from a process viewpoint. Keep in mind that implementing the BizX platform is necessary for any modules that you implement and will always be included in the first project phase. The BizX platform includes a minimum level of configuration for business rule settings within the instance, Single Sign-On (SSO), and Role-Based Permissions (RBP).

Performance Review Process

The performance review process most often includes reviewing performance for the previous review period and setting objectives for the coming performance period. In this way, the Performance Management (PM) and Goal Management (GM) modules of SuccessFactors are intricately integrated and are almost always implemented together. Goal plans can be pulled into performance review forms so that employees can be rated on their performance toward the goals from the previous year. Also, it's possible to link the coming year's goal plan in the performance review form so that goal setting can be accomplished at the same time the performance review is completed.

Complementary to PM and GM, the 360 Multi-Rater module is often implemented in conjunction with PM and GM. Results from the 360 Multi-Rater review can be accessed from within the performance review, giving any manager completing an employee review easy access to third-party reviewers.

Performance and Salary Planning Process

Additional complementary modules are PM and GM with Compensation and Variable Pay. Because the merit and bonus planning cycle follows the performance or focal review process, the Compensation and Variable Pay modules are often implemented at the same time as PM and GM. Performance forms can be integrated into the compensation form so managers can view an employee's performance review rating on the salary planning sheet as well as access the details by selecting the hyperlink and opening the performance review in a new window.

Succession Planning Process

The Scorecard is accessed from the Employee Profile of SuccessFactors, and many companies opt to implement these two modules together. If Employee Profile was implemented at an earlier project phase, the Succession Planning implementation is a good time to review the configuration of Employee Profile and make any changes or updates. Succession Planning is also a good candidate for implementation in conjunction with PM and GM.

Career Development and Learning Process

The Career Development Planning (CDP) module is very similar to the GM module and includes defining a development plan where employees and managers can create and maintain development goals. Development goals can be linked with learning activities that are pulled from the learning catalogs assigned to employees in SuccessFactors Learning. Consequently, customers often choose to implement CDP and Learning together.

Recruiting Process

SuccessFactors offers two recruiting modules: Recruiting Marketing (RMK) and Recruiting Management (RCM). These two modules are now offered as Recruiting Execution (RX). While the RMK module is always implemented with or after the RCM module, often customers will choose to implement RCM on its own.

The RCM module contains a lot of functionality, so implementing it in an environment of high-volume sourcing or detailed processes is quite an undertaking. Because these business process owners are often different from those who own the performance and merit processes, implementation of the Recruiting Execution module can also be undertaken in parallel with any other modules, but will have a longer project life due to the complexity of the product and all of the configuration decisions involved.

2.1.3 Business Processes

Before you embark on an implementation, we advise you to spend some time reviewing the business processes involved. Although business process review will be included during the implementation, understanding the weaknesses or limitations of your existing processes will facilitate a more robust kickoff meeting and expedite the system configuration decisions post-kickoff. Because SuccessFactors can be configured but not developed, it's possible that not all system requirements will be met by existing system functionality and configuration possibilities. This is typical of a cloud-based solution, so be prepared to use a combination of system configuration and business process change to address outstanding system requirements. A good understanding of the as-is processes and any legal or corporate requirements becomes key in these situations.

2.1.4 Competencies and Job Roles

Revising or adopting a competency model can be one of the most time-consuming activities you will undertake when implementing any performance management solution; in fact, it's fair to say that you can't begin this preparation soon enough.

If you haven't adopted a competency model for the organization, SuccessFactors offers more than 80 best practice behavioral competencies that can be used in the performance and development processes. If your company already has a behavioral competency model, SuccessFactors lets you create and maintain custom competencies as well.

Another critical activity is to determine how you'll manage job roles within the organization and how these will be represented within SuccessFactors. This should include a thorough review of how your jobs and positions are defined and organized in SAP ERP HCM, so this activity may also require some modification on the SAP ERP HCM side before bringing these over to SuccessFactors. Although your implementation consultant can assist you through these reviews and decisions, this is something that should be undertaken during the initial planning phases of the project to ensure adequate time before go-live.

2.1.5 Employee Data

SuccessFactors will leverage a set of employee data that is brought over from SAP ERP HCM. Numerous standard fields such as Name, Manager, Address, Job Title, and others are supported; up to 15 custom columns may also be defined to house additional data necessary to support the talent management processes completed in SuccessFactors. This is covered in detail in Chapter 3. As with competencies and job roles, the sooner you begin reviewing the employee data requirements, location, and cleanliness, the less impact there will be on the overall project schedule.

2.2 Project Structure

Although the project structure of a SuccessFactors implementation will vary depending on the number of modules undertaken at one time, you can expect to see some baselines. Whether you have a team from SuccessFactors Professional Services or an implementation partner, your consultants should have product expertise in the module(s) implemented, coupled with process and best practice expertise.

The project team can be comprised of the following types of resources:

- Implementation consultant(s)
- Project manager

- Project sponsor
- Technical resource
- Functional/business resource
- Stakeholder group representatives
- Training/communication resource

Let's look at each of these resources.

2.2.1 Implementation Consultants

SuccessFactors prepares all consultants with best practices and starter configuration files. When it rolled out the Consultant Certification Program in early 2013, SuccessFactors took steps to ensure that partner consultants are adequately trained in the functionality of the modules they plan to implement as well as the methodology of implementing the solution.

You may have several consultants implementing on your team, but it's also normal for one consultant to implement multiple modules. For example, you could have one consulting resource implementing GM, PM, 360 Multi-Rater, and Employee Profile.

Implementation consultant responsibilities include the following:

- Conducting the kickoff meeting
- Conducting regular (usually weekly) project meetings by module
- Addressing customer questions on functionality, best practices, and system functionality
- Guiding the customer in completing the configuration workbook
- Configuring the system to customer requirements, as defined in the configuration workbook
- Testing the configuration to ensure completeness and functionality
- Leading the customer through testing each iteration configuration
- Conducting administrator training for customer administrators
- Maintaining project plan, issues log, and risks for their respective module(s)

2.2.2 Project Manager

As on any project, the project manager's role is to manage the work plan, project issues and risks, and keep resources aligned and on track. You may have both a consulting project manager and a client project manager working together to manage the entire project. If there isn't a consulting project manager, the implementation consultant may serve in a project management capacity, keeping the work plan updated and assisting the project manager in understanding the BizXpert phases and deliverables.

If you are implementing the entire BizX suite, you will likely have a project manager dedicated by your implementation partner who will remain consistent across all modules. This resource will work closely with the client project manager throughout the life of the project and through all project waves until all modules have gone live and are in support.

2.2.3 Project Sponsor

Project sponsors champion the project within the client organization and assist with issue resolution, when appropriate. They serve as key stakeholders in the change management and communication plan and are often a delivery channel for key messages. They will also ultimately sign off on the business processes and system configuration. Often, the project sponsor is the one who signs off on the configuration workbooks and other project milestone sign-off gates.

2.2.4 Technical Resource

One or more technical resources will be involved with various aspects of implementation, mainly related to data and integration. Traditionally, the technical resources are engaged to provide an extract of employee data to feed SuccessFactors and set up the automated feed after the project has gone live. They also get involved with setting up Single Sign-On (SSO) and any data migration that might be undertaken. For customers moving from on-premise solutions to SuccessFactors, the technical resources will be involved with setting up the various data connectors and integration packages. As SAP works to build total integration between SAP ERP HCM and SuccessFactors, the role of a technical resource in an on-premise to cloud implementation will grow.

2.2.5 Functional/Business Resource

The functional and business resources are possibly the most critical of the project because they define the end-state business processes and the corresponding system configuration. Numerous resources are usually involved per module implemented. We recommend that you keep project-dedicated resources to a minimum while keeping a larger pool of functional/business resources involved for input, validation, and testing. Your core team of functional resources will prove critical to providing business process knowledge and context when working with the implementation consultant in fleshing out system capabilities to arrive at a satisfactory configuration that meets system and business process requirements.

Functional/business resources should be engaged early in the project planning so they can begin working on the competency and job role work previously mentioned, review the applicable business processes, and assist with communication and training strategies.

2.2.6 Stakeholder Group Representatives

Stakeholder group representatives play a key role in project communication and training strategies and execution. Like project sponsors, they deliver key project messages and drive user adoption after the project is live. Key stakeholders should be involved in various times throughout the project to help validate the to-be business processes, participate in testing, and provide input to training plans. These will be your change champions within the organization.

2.2.7 Training/Communication Resource

The key to any successful systems implementation is consistent and frequent communication to stakeholders and appropriate, just-in-time training for all end-user groups. Even though SuccessFactors is an extremely intuitive solution with "toy-like" qualities, the training plan should not be overlooked. Often, you will be rolling out SuccessFactors in conjunction with significant process updates; ensuring that your employees and managers are informed and prepared for the change is just as important for a SuccessFactors implementation as it is for an SAP ERP HCM implementation. Involve the training and communication resources early in the project and keep them engaged through to post-go-live.

Now let's shift our focus to how SuccessFactors' modules are implemented by discussing project methodology.

2.3 Project Methodology

Prior to March 2013, SuccessFactors had various project methodologies to implement modules within the suite. Core BizX modules utilized the Empower methodology, SuccessFactors Learning utilized Enable, and Employee Central, Workforce Planning and Analytics, and Recruiting Marketing were each implemented with a slightly different methodology. In March 2013, SuccessFactors introduced a new project implementation methodology that unifies implementation across all SuccessFactors modules: *BizXpert*.

The BizXpert methodology draws from the strengths of the existing project methodologies and includes best practices from industry standards (such as PMP, PRINCE2, and Agile) while leveraging best practices from the SAP cloud experience. Readers familiar with SAP implementations will recognize many components in BizXpert.

As shown in Figure 2.1, the BizXpert methodology includes four phases: Prepare, Realize, Verify, and Launch.

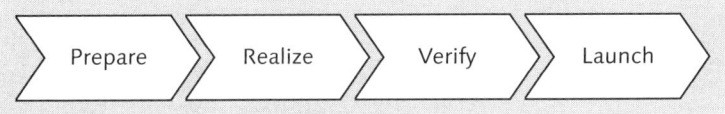

Figure 2.1 BizXpert Project Methodology Phases

We'll take a high-level look at each phase in the succeeding pages.

2.3.1 Phase 1: Prepare

The Prepare phase lays the groundwork for a successful implementation. Tasks are focused on kicking off the project and developing the implementation project plan as well as ensuring that the customer is prepared for the implementation process and the key differences in a cloud-based implementation. Key tasks in the Prepare phase include the following:

- Project team orientation
- Kickoff meeting
- Requirements-gathering workshops
- Project plan development

Project team orientation includes orienting the team to the project framework, guidelines, and schedule. It may also include some project team tool training on the particular module(s) being implemented.

The kickoff meeting will focus on the following:

- Project scope
- Methodology
- Key project business drivers
- Initial timeline/project plan
- Customer resources such as Customer Community
- Project team roles and responsibilities

Table 2.1 lists the estimated duration of kickoff meetings by module.

Module	Kickoff Meeting Duration
Goal Management	2-3 hours
Performance Management	3-4 hours
360 Multi-Rater	1-2 hours
Employee Profile	2-3 hours
Succession Planning	3-5 hours
Recruiting Management	6-8 hours
Recruiting Marketing	6-8 hours
Learning	1-3 days
Compensation Management	6-12 hours
Variable Pay	6-12 hours
Employee Central	1-2 days
Workforce Planning & Analytics	2 days

Table 2.1 Kickoff Meetings by Module

Requirements-gathering workshops are the focus of the Prepare phase. This is when the consulting team identifies the customer's system requirements and details the business processes impacted by the implementation. The entire project team, consultants, and business stakeholders work together to identify the system configuration required to meet the customer's needs.

Requirements gathering is typically conducted as part of the kickoff meeting, and the length of the sessions are determined by the modules being implemented. For modules such as PM and GM, these sessions can likely be covered in a day. But for modules such as Learning, Compensation, and Employee Central, it may take several days or more to talk through the configuration options and document decisions. The end result of these sessions is completion of a detailed configuration workbook, which consultants will then use to complete the system configuration.

Data migration and technical workshops (if applicable) are centered on ancillary implementation work such as migrating legacy data and implementing custom connectors or other third-party integrations. These are conducted on an as-needed basis; the length of the workshops will be determined by the services required and the complexity of the scope of work.

Project plan development is also completed during this phase, outlining key tasks, deliverables, and milestones necessary for project success. As with any implementation, project planning is an ongoing task throughout the project.

2.3.2 Phase 2: Realize

During the Realize phase, the focus is on system configuration and data migration (if applicable). The system design and requirements identified during the Prepare phase are built in the customer's test instance. The implementation consultants are responsible for configuring all modules, with the exception of Learning and SAP Jam. For these modules, the customer is heavily involved in configuration, guided by the implementation consultant. Configuration for these modules is heavy in administrative tasks and can be done directly via the administrative interface in the instance.

Configuration Cycles

The configuration is completed in the test instance, with the exception of SAP Jam, which is completed directly in the production instance. Customers are typically given one SAP Jam instance, which is integrated with their BizX production instance. The following is a simplified process for most modules:

1. Consultant completes configuration per the requirements identified during the Prepare phase.
2. Configuration is made available to the customer to test.
3. Customer tests the configuration to the business processes impacted and provides feedback to the consultant on necessary changes.

Depending on the modules being implemented, you could have up to three cycles of configuration updates and testing. This is dependent upon the complexity of the requirements and the business processes impacted. Each cycle of configuration will consist of smaller requirements-gathering sessions. These are typically conducted virtually and can occur over a series of meetings. Configuration workbooks are updated and given back to the consultant to update system configuration. The customer then retests the updated configuration, and the cycle repeats itself until complete. Traditionally, there are three iterations of configuration and testing.

In the case of the Learning module, the customer provides feedback on the configuration, and the consultants work closely with the customer administrator to refine the system configuration. With Learning, the majority of the configuration is master data that is controlled directly in the instance. By involving the customer administrator from the beginning, training and knowledge transfer occurs throughout the project, resulting in a fully capable customer administrator by go-live.

Data Migration or Other Technical Services

If the customer is migrating data from a legacy system or has included other technical services or custom connectors in the project scope, data migration or other technical activities run parallel to the configuration cycles during the Realize phase. Much of the data migration activities focus on getting the customer up to speed on how data is brought into SuccessFactors. Many self-service tools, videos, documents, and sample files are available to the customer team in the Customer Welcome Kit.

If the customer is migrating data into Learning, then a small sample file is created so that the customer can test the upload via OneAdmin or via the Secure File Transfer Protocol (SFTP). Data cleansing and validation is critical during this testing phase. After the sample file loads cleanly, the larger data file can be prepared. It is advisable to load the full file into the customer's test instance toward the end of the Realize phase and before the Verify phase.

2.3.3 Phase 3: Verify

Once configuration is signed off, the Realize phase concludes and the project transitions to the Verify phase. The tasks conducted during Verify are all focused on testing and organizational readiness for the impending go-live. The customer executes the testing plan developed during the Prepare phase to prove the system is configured as designed and is "fit for purpose." Because the test plan and script development is a key customer deliverable, samples are available in the Customer Welcome Kit, and the implementation consultant can provide input based on project experience as well.

Testing

The types of testing included in the test plan will be familiar as the same testing that occurs in most systems implementations. The customer can determine which testing activities to conduct, but the following are typically included:

- **Unit testing**
  Confirms that each item identified in the configuration workbook has been configured and is working as expected. Unit testing is the responsibility of the implementation consultant.

- **Application testing**
  Confirms that the system configuration meets the customer's functional requirements. It's critical to confirm that the system is ready for end-to-end testing. The customer project team is responsible for application testing.

- **Integration testing**
  Required if other systems will be integrated with SuccessFactors. If integration testing occurs, it is the responsibility of the customer project team, usually focused on IT personnel and key stakeholders representing the systems integrating with SuccessFactors. Because integration deals with existing customer systems, the customer bears responsibility to develop detailed testing scripts. At the conclusion of integration testing, there is often a customer sign-off before moving forward.

- **User acceptance testing (UAT)**
  Confirms that the system is configured to meet the end-to-end business requirements and is the responsibility of the customer UAT team. The most successful user testing includes testers from outside the core project team and has representation from the key business areas impacted by the system.

Preparing the Organization

While testing is underway, the communication and training plans begin execution. Any successful systems implementation hinges on clear communication and preparation of end users. These tasks are owned by the customer, so it's advisable to engage any customer teams that provide change management and training services. Because SuccessFactors modules touch on employee performance, compensation, and career development, it's critical that any change in process or system is deployed with the utmost care and planning. Although SuccessFactors is an intuitive system that can be picked up with minimal training, it is often accompanied by radical process change. These changes, and the business reasons driving the changes, should be "overcommunicated" to employees and management alike.

2.3.4 Phase 4: Launch

The Launch phase is all about preparing for go-live, launching the system, and transitioning to Customer Success for ongoing support. After all testing activities are completed, identified issues are addressed and retested, and final sign-off of testing is achieved, then the implementation consultant will begin cutting over configuration from the test instance to the customer's production instance.

The *cutover checklist* is a critical deliverable of this phase that is used to monitor progress of all cutover activities, responsibilities, and statuses. The implementation consultant will prepare the cutover checklist, and tasks are determined by the modules implemented. Cutting over can take from one day to many days, depending on the complexity of the modules, the configuration, and the business processes impacted. For example, an RMK cutover of moderate complexity with no data migration will take approximately four days, while a PM and GM cutover can be completed in one day. Cutover also includes enabling the production SFTP, the final user connector for employee data, and enabling SSO, if applicable.

At the completion of cutover, including data migration as applicable, the customer begins production validation. After that is complete, the transition to the SuccessFactors' support organization Customer Success begins. The final deliverable of the project is the production readiness sign-off document, which is submitted to Customer Success when submitting the case to have customer accounts created. This process not only provides the customer access to the SuccessFactors support portal but also notifies SuccessFactors that the customer has successfully transitioned into the production instance and is now live.

2.4   Project Delivery

Recall that a big difference between a SuccessFactors implementation and on-premise SAP ERP HCM implementation is that the emphasis is on configuration rather than development. As a SaaS solution, SuccessFactors offers a series of configuration options that can be deployed as needed to support a customer's business processes. There is no custom development involved in a SuccessFactors implementation. If the system cannot be configured to a specific requirement, the applicable business process will need to be changed accordingly. Customers can then submit enhancement requests to SuccessFactors for functionality that they would like to see added to the roadmap and worked into the solution.

Because the project focuses on configuration rather than development, the customer project team can get its hands on the system almost immediately. To support the kickoff meeting, the implementation consultant will often perform some best-practice, baseline configuration in the customer's test instance so the customer project team can log in and "play" in a sandbox environment while discussing and making configuration decisions. This is an excellent way to confirm Iteration 1 configuration decisions before submitting them to the implementation consultant. In this way, the system configuration is being continually tested throughout the entire Realize phase.

A new concept to most on-premise SAP ERP HCM customers is *virtual project delivery*. As a cloud-based solution, SuccessFactors can be configured anywhere an Internet connection and web browser are available. After an onsite kickoff meeting, most of the implementation has traditionally been done in a virtual manner with implementation consultants working from their home offices and supporting the customer project team over regular web conferences.

The main objective of the BizXpert implementation methodology is to empower customers to own their solutions, so activities are designed to give them the tools to do just that. Implementation consultants will work with the project team on a mutually agreed, regular basis (not less than weekly) to review system configuration questions and decisions. The features in the OneAdmin section of SuccessFactors are covered in detail as they apply to the modules implemented.

This virtual project delivery may seem infeasible, but SuccessFactors has more than 10 years of successful implementations using this model with some of the largest companies in the world. Although this model may morph somewhat into more time spent on-site during various project phases, the days of teams of consultants camping in a customer's offices for six months or more are a thing of the past.

2.5 Summary

Implementing your SuccessFactors solution should be an opportunity to review existing business processes and add efficiency while providing enhanced system functionality.

By selecting SuccessFactors, you have taken the first step toward a best-practice core HCM or talent management landscape in your organization. SuccessFactors' BizXpert methodology provides the structure, milestones, and deliverables necessary to ensure a successful project. Staffing your project team appropriately and providing them with the tools to deliver a fully configured system is critical to ensuring that your resulting system meets the needs of the organization and stakeholders. You can ensure successful go-live by teaming up with an experienced implementation partner who has deep business process knowledge and can provide best practices, along with deep knowledge of the SuccessFactors modules you are implementing. Lastly, preparing your organization for the new system and processes that will drive their performance and career planning is crucial to ensuring user adoption. The importance of this element cannot be overstated.

In the next chapter, we'll look at the integration between SuccessFactors and SAP ERP HCM.

SuccessFactors BizX suite has been integrated with SAP ERP HCM hundreds of times with varying approaches and technologies. Since acquiring Success-Factors, SAP has worked on providing standard integration content for a variety of different scenarios.

3 Integration with SAP ERP HCM

For you to use any solutions of the SuccessFactors BizX suite with your SAP ERP HCM system, you need to integrate the two systems. The BizX suite has been integrated with SAP ERP HCM by more than 500 SuccessFactors customers, so there is sufficient evidence of successful integration even if at the time of this writing, a majority of these customers have built their integration autonomously.

Following the acquisition of SuccessFactors, SAP started the process of building and providing standard integration content for the hybrid model that leverages SAP technology. SAP is focusing its efforts on providing data integration, processes integration, and user experience integration that will support a variety of different talent management processes. SAP is also working on providing integration for Employee Central, Employee Central Payroll, and SAP Jam, although these do not fall directly within its hybrid integration strategy.

Because SAP ERP HCM and the BizX suite both store data, it's necessary to create integration so that data can flow between the systems and reside in one central system of record. The process of integration requires technology and mapping of the relevant fields in one system with those in the other and rules for data transformation and validation. Different process steps and triggers can also be part of an integration process, although this will depend on the extent to which integration is required. However integration is designed, a certain level of complexity is required—and SAP intends to reduce this complexity with standard content.

3.1 Integration Strategy

This section covers SAP's main integration strategy, which is focused on integrating SAP ERP HCM with the talent management modules of the BizX suite. This is what SAP calls the hybrid model, as we described in Chapter 1. In this chapter, we'll evaluate the different technologies available to customers who want to integrate SAP ERP HCM and BizX solutions (Section 3.2), plus the standard integration content available from SAP (Section 3.3). We'll also look at some of the additional documentation available from SAP (Section 3.4).

SAP has chosen to center its integration strategy on the hybrid model because a number of customers have invested heavily on creating a robust and effective core SAP ERP HCM system and have no intention of replacing it. However, many SAP ERP HCM customers have reached relative maturity in practicing human capital management and are now looking to invest in talent management solutions, particularly by taking advantage of the new breed of best-in-class, cloud-based talent management solutions that SuccessFactors offers. SAP now intends to provide integration for customers looking to make the move to the cloud for talent management with the BizX suite.

SAP's strategy for providing integration is designed to cater to customers who use the hybrid model. However, it should be noted that SAP is delivering integration content for processes outside of the hybrid model, although these are not considered part of the overall integration strategy.

SAP's aim is to provide "loosely coupled" integration, as opposed to full, real-time integration. This is strategically designed to ensure that changes to data in the BizX suite are only written back to the SAP ERP HCM system at the point in which the data is needed for further processing. For example, the compensation process integration delivered by SAP is strategically designed to only write data to SAP when it needs to be input into the Payroll process.

As a result, the integration that SAP provides is robust, but it is also limited. Additional effort is required to extend the standard integration to add custom logic and to extend the integration beyond the predefined fields.

It's important to note that all data transfers between SAP ERP HCM and the BizX suite are always initiated from the SAP ERP HCM side. No data is "pushed" from the BizX suite; rather, it is always "pulled" from SAP ERP HCM.

SAP's integration strategy has an underlying theme called FAST. FAST is an acronym built from the following characteristics:

- F—Functionally rich
- A—Affordable

- S—Simple to implement, maintain, and support
- T—Trusted, based on SAP's deep domain know-how

Integration content should be delivered prepackaged, yet be feature-rich in content, extensible, and scalable. It should also be affordable, not just in upfront costs but in total cost of ownership (TCO).

3.1.1 Integration Pillars

The integration strategy looks to address three types of integration challenges through three strategic pillars:

- Data integration
- Process integration
- User experience integration

Data integration leverages point-to-point integration to create a basic data foundation within the BizX suite so that talent management processes can be performed. The aim of this integration is to ensure that basic employee and organizational data is not entered into two systems twice. This was delivered in the first integration package.

Process integration is event-driven, bi-directional data integration designed for specific talent management processes. These include the pay-for-performance (compensation management), attract-to-hire (recruiting), and define-to-hire (recruiting) processes. With this type of integration, data may be transferred to SuccessFactors, and data produced in the BizX suite is transferred to SAP, where it can be used in SAP-dependent parts of processes or stored in the system of record. SAP delivers this type of integration on an ongoing basis.

User experience integration is centered on creating a unified, single point of access for end users, irrespective of whether the processes that are being performed are within the SAP NetWeaver Portal or within the BizX suite. This includes Single Sign-On (SSO) and integration of SuccessFactors processes into Employee Self-Services (ESS) and Manager Self-Services (MSS) menus. The intention is that end users can move between Web Dynpro applications and BizX solutions within the SAP NetWeaver Portal or SAP NetWeaver Business Client (NWBC) without being conscious that they have changed applications. SAP delivered the SSO cookbook resource to configure SSO between SAP NetWeaver Portal and BizX suite.

3.1.2 Integration Scenarios

SAP intends to deliver a number of integration scenarios that align with the three pillars of its integration strategy. A number of these scenarios have already been delivered, and SAP intends to continue delivering these scenarios to cover common talent management scenarios for the hybrid model. At the time of writing (summer 2013), the following scenarios had been delivered:

- Basic employee and organizational data
- Data for analytics
- Compensation process
- Recruiting process

The first two scenarios are available for both flat-file and middleware integration methods. The process integration (compensation and recruiting) is only available via middleware platforms.

3.1.3 Integration Packages

To deliver the various integration scenarios, SAP has released a number of integration packages commonly known as iFlows. The idea behind the iFlow is to provide a set of programs, tools, and methodologies to help leverage SAP/SuccessFactors processes seamlessly and with low TCO.

In addition, SAP has also delivered some integration packages for integrating SAP ERP HCM with Employee Central for SuccessFactors Employee Central Payroll. iFlows and other integration content are discussed in detail in Section 3.3 and Section 3.4.

3.2 Integration Technology

Several varied technologies are available to integrate SAP ERP HCM and the BizX suite that offer different costs, features, ease of setup, and flexibility. Previous integrations have used a variety of platforms; many of these are still available for customers, even if they aren't supported by SAP. SAP is focusing integration efforts on its new flagship integration platform, SAP HANA Cloud Integration.

Technologies available for integrating SAP ERP HCM and the BizX suite include the following:

- Flat-file transfer
- SAP NetWeaver Process Integration (SAP NetWeaver PI)
- SAP HANA Cloud Integration
- Dell Boomi AtomSphere®
- Social Media ABAP Integration Library (SAIL)
- Custom-built APIs or other middleware

Although a majority of existing integrations use flat-file integration and custom-built APIs, SAP wants to enable customers to use prebuilt content that leverages either SAP NetWeaver PI or SAP HANA Cloud Integration. For SAP's hybrid model, only the first three technologies are used. The integration options for the hybrid model can be seen in Figure 3.1.

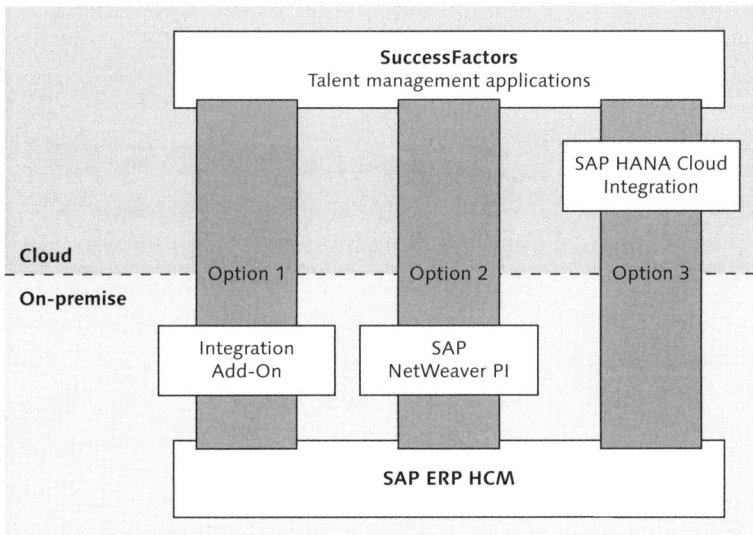

Figure 3.1 Integration Options for the Hybrid Model

We'll now run through these technology options in a bit more detail.

3.2.1 Flat-File Integration

Flat-file integration has been around for a number of years and is still a quick and reliable way to transfer data between two systems, albeit with a lack of standards and much looser security than other mechanisms. Flat-file transfer usually involves extracting a file of data—often a comma-separated values (CSV) or text (TXT) file—from a system and then uploading it to another system. A *File Transfer Protocol* (FTP) or *Secure File Transfer Protocol* (SFTP) server is often used to transfer the file between the systems. Although this method is fairly simple to create and maintain, it does have some disadvantages that might be undesirable by some customers:

- Absence of security or encryption
- No standards or validation for data
- Lack of transformation capabilities
- No field mapping

However, a variety of tools are available that can be used to validate or transform data in flat files, although we won't discuss those in this book. CSV files in this scenario do support *Pretty Good Privacy* (PGP) software to encrypt the file.

In SAP ERP HCM, a report provided in the first iFlow can be used to export a flat file of data that can be uploaded to the BizX suite. No other transactions are available within SAP that allow the export of data within a format accepted by the BizX suite. Within the BizX suite, a flat file of data can be imported from the SuccessFactors FTP using one of the many options in OneAdmin or on a regular basis using a job set up in the MANAGE SCHEDULED JOBS page by your implementation partner within Provisioning. Flat-file transfer can also be used to perform ad hoc or one-time data imports for Metadata Objects, employee data, Employee Central foundation data, translations, and more. These will be covered throughout the specific product chapters.

Figure 3.2 shows the architecture of the flat-file technology. SuccessFactors provides an SFTP site for use in uploading flat files.

Integration Add-On 1.0 for SAP ERP HCM and SuccessFactors (covered later in this chapter) leverage flat-file technology to transfer basic organizational and employee data between SAP ERP HCM and the BizX suite for use in talent management processes. This add-on is also known as Add-On 1.0.

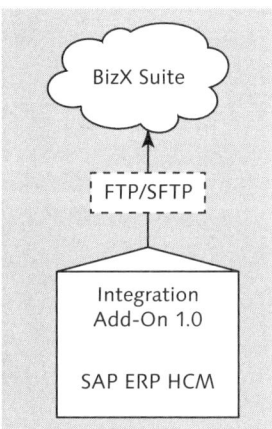

Figure 3.2 Flat-File Integration Using the First iFlow

3.2.2 SAP NetWeaver Process Integration

SAP NetWeaver PI is SAP's reliable/high performance service-oriented architecture (SOA) middleware product for integrating and transferring messages-based data between SAP systems and between other internal or external systems. At the time of writing, approximately 35% of SAP ERP HCM customers currently use SAP NetWeaver PI to integrate SAP systems.

> **Note**
> SAP NetWeaver PI was previously called SAP Exchange Infrastructure (SAP XI) until version 7.0.

SAP NetWeaver PI allows multiple different systems to connect to each other and exchange messages via the central SAP NetWeaver PI Integration Engine component. Various adapters allow connectivity to a variety of systems and handle messages to ensure they are processed correctly by the Integration Engine. Business logic and transformations can be applied to messages to ensure compatibility of data between systems. Figure 3.3 depicts a typical message flow within the SAP NetWeaver PI system.

Although SAP provides a large number of adapters, customers and integration partners can also build their own adapters to fill gaps within the SAP-delivered adapters or to connect to a brand new system such as the BizX suite.

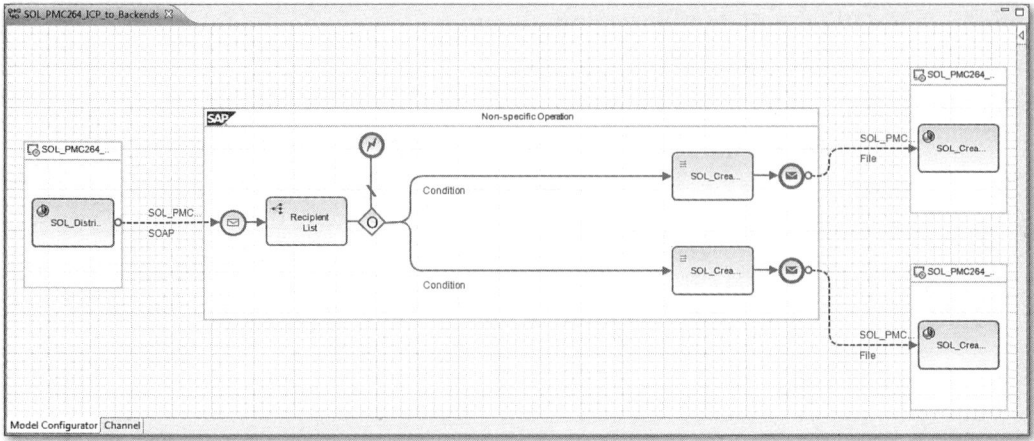

Figure 3.3 Message Flow in SAP NetWeaver PI

For customers who already have an SAP NetWeaver PI instance licensed and implemented, integrating SAP ERP HCM and the BizX suite requires no additional licensing. SAP's integration packages supplied for the hybrid model leverage SAP NetWeaver PI alongside *SAP HANA Cloud Integration*. Figure 3.4 shows the architecture of the middleware technology. Here the integration technology is used as the middleware between SAP ERP HCM and the BizX suite.

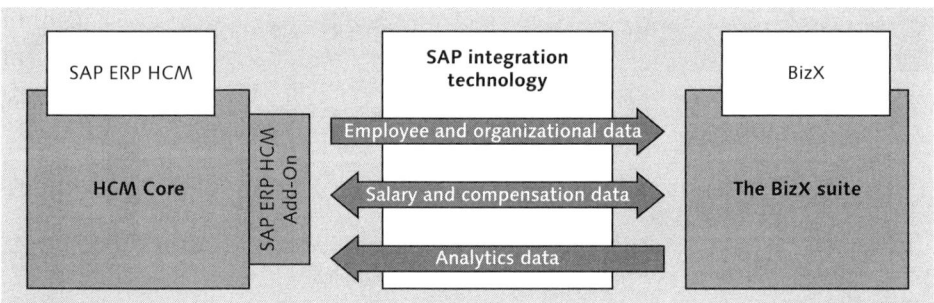

Figure 3.4 Diagram of Middleware Integration Using the First iFlow

> **Additional Resources**
>
> You can read more about SAP NetWeaver PI in the SAP PRESS book *SAP NetWeaver Process Integration (2nd ed.)* by Mandy Krimmel and Joachim Orb (2010).

3.2.3 SAP HANA Cloud Integration

As a cloud-based alternative to SAP NetWeaver PI, SAP HANA Cloud Integration provides the same level of middleware integration between multiple systems as is found in SAP NetWeaver PI. SAP HANA Cloud Integration is an *Integration-as-a-Service* (IaaS) platform.

SAP HANA Cloud Integration is specifically designed to integrate SAP's range of cloud solutions (such as Travel OnDemand and, of course, the BizX suite) with other cloud applications and on-premise systems. However, the platform does support integration of numerous external systems.

For customers who are not using SAP NetWeaver PI, SAP HANA Cloud Integration is a reasonable alternative. Like the BizX suite, it benefits from many of the advantages that a SaaS does, such as leveraging a subscription model, offering multi-tenancy and being hosted and supported remotely. It also offers the same functionality expected from any enterprise-level middleware integration platform. Modeling of integration content is done in web-based UI, as shown in Figure 3.5.

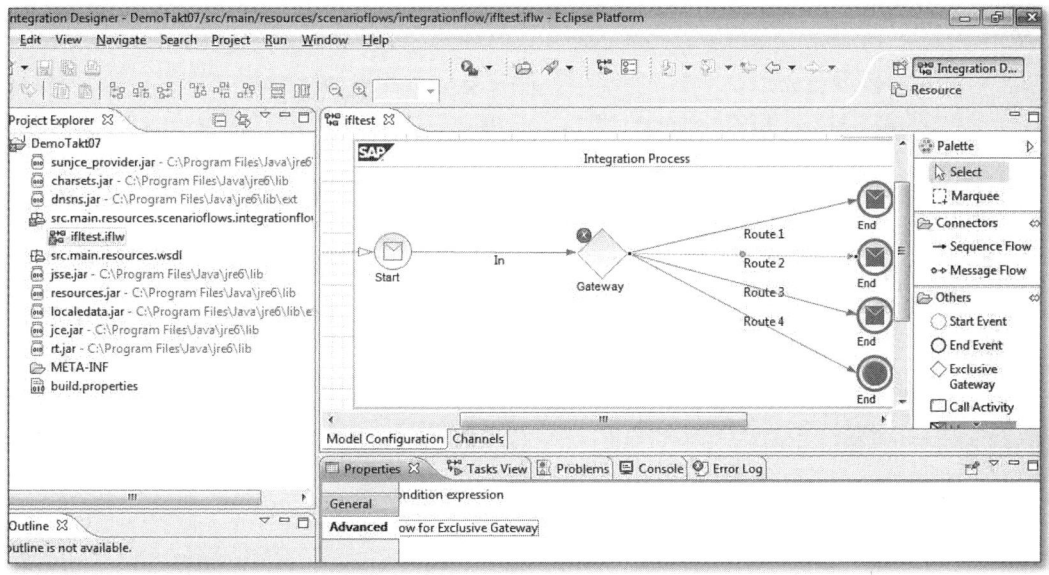

Figure 3.5 Modelling in SAP HANA Cloud Integration

The integration packages that SAP supplies for the hybrid model leverage SAP HANA Cloud Integration alongside SAP NetWeaver PI. Integration content built in SAP HANA Cloud Integration is backward-compatible with SAP NetWeaver PI, meaning that content created by other customers or partners on SAP HANA Cloud Integration can be provided to customers using SAP NetWeaver PI. However, it's worth noting that content created in SAP NetWeaver PI can't be used in SAP HANA Cloud Integration.

3.2.4 Dell Boomi AtomSphere

Dell Boomi AtomSphere is a *Platform-as-a-Service* (PaaS) integration platform designed to integrate on-premise and cloud-based systems with the need for additional coding, software, or technology. Dell Boomi AtomSphere is offered to SuccessFactors customers as part of their base license at no extra cost. This technology is used primarily to integrate SuccessFactors Employee Central, but SuccessFactors offers the platform to support integration of other solutions in the BizX suite. SAP's position is that Dell Boomi AtomSphere should only be used to integrate SAP ERP HCM and SuccessFactors Employee Central (including SuccessFactors Employee Central Payroll).

As a PaaS solution, Dell Boomi AtomSphere benefits from many of the same advantages as SaaS solutions, such as subscription pricing, regular releases, scalability, and lower TCO. In addition, it offers an easy-to-use graphical interface with wizard-based designers that provide the ability to do the following:

- Design workflows using drag and drop
- Create data transformations
- Model complex business logic
- Perform integrity checks and validate data
- Introduce decision handling
- Create event-based messages
- Cleanse data
- Build unique connectors

Dell Boomi AtomSphere also features prebuilt connectors and integration scenarios and leverages newly designed components for all customers.

3.2.5 SAP Data Services

SAP Data Services is a solution that offers data integration, data quality, data profiling, and text data processing. It is primarily used with analytics-based scenarios that require transferring data from SAP ERP to SAP NetWeaver Business Warehouse (SAP NetWeaver BW), SAP HANA, SAP Rapid Marts, SAP Sybase IQ server, and non-SAP data stores.

SAP Data Services is an *extract, transform, load* (ETL) solution, so its primary purpose is to extract data, transform the data, and load the data to and from any application for use in data integration or data warehouse projects. It provides a development workbench, metadata repository, data connectivity layer, runtime environment, and management console.

SAP Data Services can be used to integrate the BizX suite with SAP NetWeaver BW. More details can be found in Section 3.4.4.

3.2.6 Single Sign-On

For user experience integration, SSO technology enables multiple technologies to be integrated from a security and logon perspective so that the user can seamlessly switch between applications. Although visually the switch from one technology to another might not be seamless, from an access perspective, the user is not aware that he has been authenticated against another system using the credentials from his first point of access.

Many systems use a variety of industry standard security mechanisms to provide SSO and protect unauthorized access. The use of HTTPS as a secure protocol is widespread and provides additional security to data that is transmitted over internal or external networks. Technology such as OAuth, Security Assertion Markup Language 2.0 (SAML2) assertion, and Secure Sockets Layer (SSL) are used both between internal systems and with web-based applications.

SAP's Social Media ABAP Integration Library (SAIL) leverages these protocols when integrating SAP ERP HCM with SAP Jam.

3.2.7 Other Integration Technology

Even with all of these technologies, there is still room for a number of other platforms. Customers may be already using another middleware platform, such as Mule ESB or Cast Iron, and they may want to continue leveraging the platform or to build custom *Application Programming Interfaces* (APIs). The SAP NetWeaver platform is open and technology-agnostic, so customers can use various integration technologies to integrate SAP ERP HCM with BizX solutions. This provides a great deal of flexibility and allows customers to retain existing technology and infrastructure that is being used for other solutions.

3.3　iFlows

In May 2012, SAP began delivering on its integration strategy with the first Integration Add-On package (iFlow). This was followed by a number of support packages to extend the functionality delivered in the first release and provide additional stability and bug fixes. A second iFlow was released in 2013; subsequent iFlows are planned for release during 2013 and beyond. At the time of writing, SAP hasn't determined the content of these packages, but it will focus on covering more hybrid model processes. Process integration for the "Qualified for Success" (learning) process will be provided in three packages in 2013 and 2014. Skills and competencies are under consideration.

The iFlows cover the types of data and process integrations shown in Table 3.1.

Integration	iFlow
Employee data	Add-On 1.0
Evaluation data	Add-On 1.0
Compensation data	Add-On 1.0 SP2
Recruitment data	Add-On 2.0

Table 3.1　Integrations Provided with the iFlows

A number of reports and customizing activities introduced in Add-On 2.0 have been designed to be fairly generic so that they can be reused by subsequent integration content that will be released in the future.

The iFlows can be downloaded from SAP Service Marketplace and are available in eight languages: English, German, Spanish, French, Portuguese, Russian, Chinese, and Japanese. The latest versions of the Administrator guides—including all technical prerequisites for the iFlows—can be found on SAP Service Marketplace via the path, RELEASE & UPGRADE INFO • INSTALLATION & UPGRADE GUIDES • SAP BUSINESS SUITE APPLICATIONS • SAP ERP ADD-ONS • INTEGRATION ADD-ON FOR SAP ERP HCM AND SUCCESSFACTORS BIZX. SAP notes can be found on SAP Service Marketplace under component PA-SFI-TM for the hybrid model and PA-SFI-EC for integration with SuccessFactors Employee Central.

Because the iFlows are delivered as an ABAP add-on, customers who are not familiar with this process should consult SAP Note 1708986 (Installation of SFIHCM01 600). Specific details about Add-On 2.0 can be found in SAP Note 1825713 (Release Strategy for ABAP Add-On SFIHCM02 600).

For the middleware integration using SAP NetWeaver PI, version 7.0 of SAP NetWeaver PI and Enterprise Services Repository (ESR) content are required. HTTPS communication between each system and SAP NetWeaver PI is mandatory.

We will now cover the iFlows in detail.

3.3.1 Integration Add-On 1.0 for SAP ERP HCM and SuccessFactors BizX

The first iFlow released by SAP was *Integration Add-On 1.0 for SAP ERP HCM and SuccessFactors BizX*, which was previously known as integration package 1.0 and has the technical name SFIHCM01. This iFlow provided one-way transfer of basic employee and organizational data from SAP ERP HCM to the BizX suite for talent management processes using flat-file technology. It also contains 30 extractors to transfer evaluation data from various infotypes to SuccessFactors Workforce Analytics. Subsequently released support packages introduced additional functionality, including delta handling, middleware integration, Web Dynpro applications for monitoring data transfer, and compensation (pay-for-performance) process integration content.

The iFlow and support packages provide a series of ABAP programs, Web Dynpro applications, authorization roles, and Business Add-ins (BAdIs) to extract a CSV file of data on a periodic basis for import into the BizX suite. The iFlow provides 49 standard fields in total for extraction of employee and organizational data from SAP ERP HCM, of which 34 fields are predefined, and 15 fields are available for customer-specific usage. The extraction of 9 of these fields is mandatory.

The predefined fields are listed in Table 3.2.

Field	Use	Required
STATUS	Employment status from PA0000-STAT2	X
USER ID	Central person ID or person ID from PA0709	X
USER NAME	Employee's user ID or central person	X
FIRST NAME	First name from PA0002	X
LAST NAME	Last name from PA0002	X
MIDDLE NAME	Middle name from PA0002	
GENDER	Gender from PA0002	
EMAIL	Email address	X
MANAGER	Manager using relationship B012 or A002	X
HUMAN RESOURCE	HR administrator from PA0001	X
DEPARTMENT	Organizational unit or cost center from PA0001	
JOB CODE	Job from PA0001	
DIVISION	Company code from PA0001	
LOCATION	Personnel area from PA0001	
TIME ZONE	Time zone of user	X
HIRE DATE	Initial hire date from feature entry	
EMPLOYEE ID	Personnel number	
TITLE	Position or job from PA0001	
BUSINESS PHONE	Business phone number from PA0032 or PA0105 SUBTY 0020	
FAX	Fax number from PA0105 SUBTY CELL	
ADDRESS 1	Description of personnel area from PA0001	
ADDRESS 2	Street of personnel area from PA0001	
CITY	City of personnel area from PA0001	

Table 3.2 Predefined Fields Used in the Extraction and Synchronization Reports

Field	Use	Required
STATE	Region of personnel area from PA0001	
ZIP	ZIP code of personnel area from PA0001	
COUNTRY	Country key or country grouping of personnel subarea from PA0001	
REVIEW FREQUENCY	Performance appraisal frequency	
LAST REVIEW DATE	Date of last performance appraisal	
MATRIX MANAGER	Dotted line manager using relationship A002	
DEFAULT LOCALE *	Default locale of employee	
CUSTOM MANAGER *	Custom manager	
SECOND MANAGER *	Second manager	
PROXY *	Proxy user	
LOGIN METHOD **	Type of login (SSO or PWD)	

Table 3.2 Predefined Fields Used in the Extraction and Synchronization Reports (Cont.)

The fields marked with * are delivered in Service Package 1 (SP1), and the field marked with ** is delivered in Service Pack 2 (SP2). The customer-specific fields are named CUSTOM01, CUSTOM02, and so on, through to CUSTOM15.

For each of the predefined fields, either the predefined source field can be selected or customers can define their own logic via the BAdI implementation HRSFI_B_EMPL_DATA_REPLICATION (Replication of Employee's Data). The custom fields can be customized in the Implementation Guide (IMG) via the menu path, PERSONNEL MANAGEMENT • INTEGRATION ADD-ON FOR SAP ERP HCM AND SUCCESSFACTORS BIZX • INTEGRATION SCENARIO FOR EMPLOYEE DATA • EXTEND EXTRACTION OF EMPLOYEE DATA. The format to be used for the FIRST NAME and LAST NAME fields can be customized in the IMG via the menu path, PERSONNEL MANAGEMENT • INTEGRATION ADD-ON FOR SAP ERP HCM AND SUCCESSFACTORS BIZX • INTEGRATION SCENARIO FOR EMPLOYEE DATA • DEFINE NAME FORMAT FOR FIELDS FIRSTNAME AND LASTNAME.

Figure 3.6 shows the selection screen for the fields in the iFlow extraction report for extracting employee data from SAP.

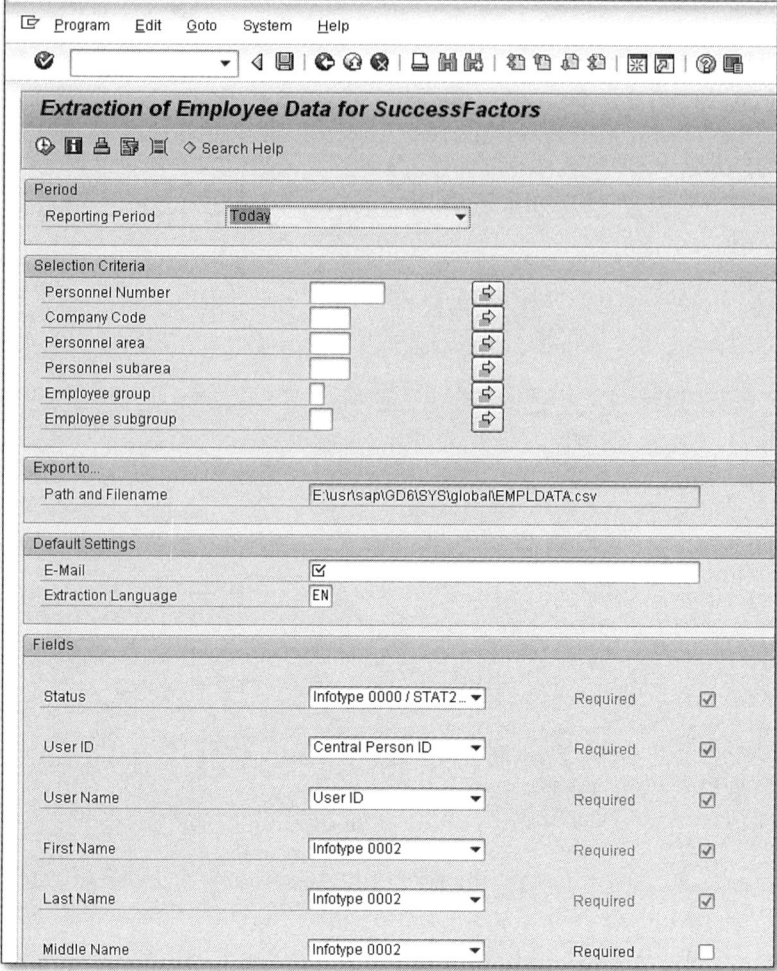

Figure 3.6 Extraction of Employee Data for SuccessFactors Report

The analytic extractors source data from the following infotypes, plus the associated texts tables:

- 0000 (Actions)
- 0001 (Organizational Assignments)
- 0002 (Personnel Data)
- 0007 (Planned Working Time)

- 0008 (Basic Pay)
- 0016 (Contract Elements)
- 0025 (Appraisals)
- 0041 (Date Specifications)
- 0077 (Personnel Actions)
- 0302 (Additional Actions)
- 1000 (Objects)
- 1001 (Relationships)

In SP2.0, an additional report was delivered to handle the synchronization of compensation data for use with a compensation scenario, along with a report to handle cancellation of data transfer for employees and two new Web Dynpro applications for monitoring the transfer of employee/organizational data and compensation data. The report for synchronizing compensation data transfers 39 fields to SuccessFactors for data such as the following:

- Salary
- Payment interval
- Currency
- Capacity utilization level
- Pay grade
- Job level
- Start date
- Bonus eligibility
- Compensation eligibility
- Lump sum eligibility
- Controller

However, the fields that are transferred to the SuccessFactors Compensation module are defined in the IMG via the menu path, PERSONNEL MANAGEMENT • INTEGRATION ADD-ON FOR SAP ERP HCM AND SUCCESSFACTORS BIZX • INTEGRATION SCENARIO FOR COMPENSATION DATA • DATA TRANSFER FROM SAP ERP TO SUCCESSFACTORS BIZX •

DEFINE FIELDS FOR EXTRACTING COMPENSATION DATA. These are also configurable via BAdI `HRSFI_B_COMP_FIELD_EXTRACTOR` (Extraction of Compensation Data).

> **Important Note**
>
> SuccessFactors BizX release 1210 or above is required for the compensation integration.

Figure 3.7 shows the selection screen for the report to transfer compensation data to the BizX suite from SAP ERP HCM. The set of fields to be used for the data export is configured in customizing.

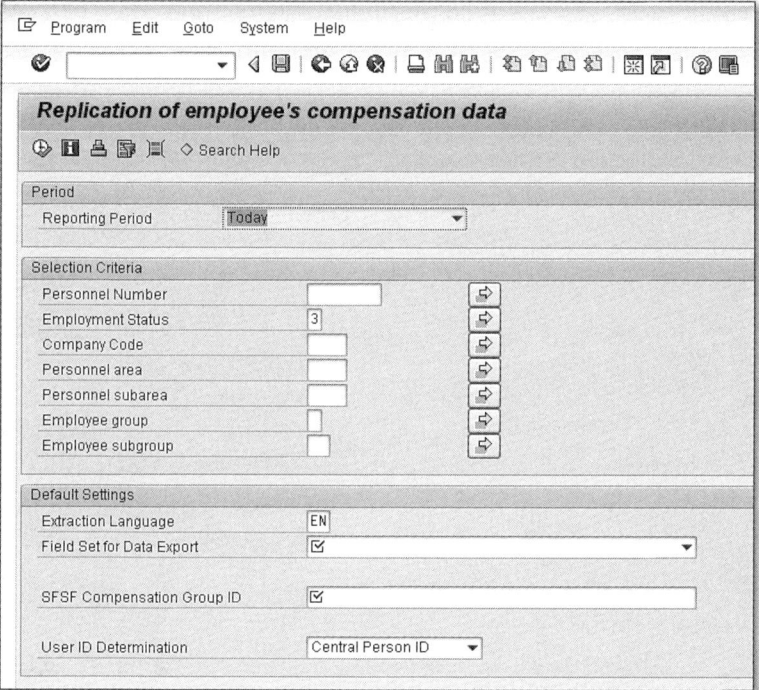

Figure 3.7 Replication of Employee's Compensation Data Report

Figure 3.8 shows the Web Dynpro application used to monitor the import and export of compensation data between SAP ERP HCM and SuccessFactors.

The iFlow considers concurrent employment, but because SuccessFactors currently handles concurrent employment differently than SAP ERP HCM, additional configuration is required before the extraction reports can be run. Each employee with multiple assignments (e.g., multiple personnel numbers [PERNRs]) must have the main assignment defined in infotype 0712 with subtype SFSF. This will then ensure that the main assignment and all related assignments are transferred to the BizX suite. If no main assignment is maintained, then the extraction report will either select one of the assignments for data extraction, or if BAdI HRSFI_B_LEADING_CONTRACT (Determine the Leading Assignment for a Central Person) is defined, then the logic of the active implementation will be used.

Customers should always consider using the iFlow with SP1 or above installed for flat-file integration or SP2 or above for middleware integration. The iFlow currently has an end of mainstream maintenance date of June 30, 2014.

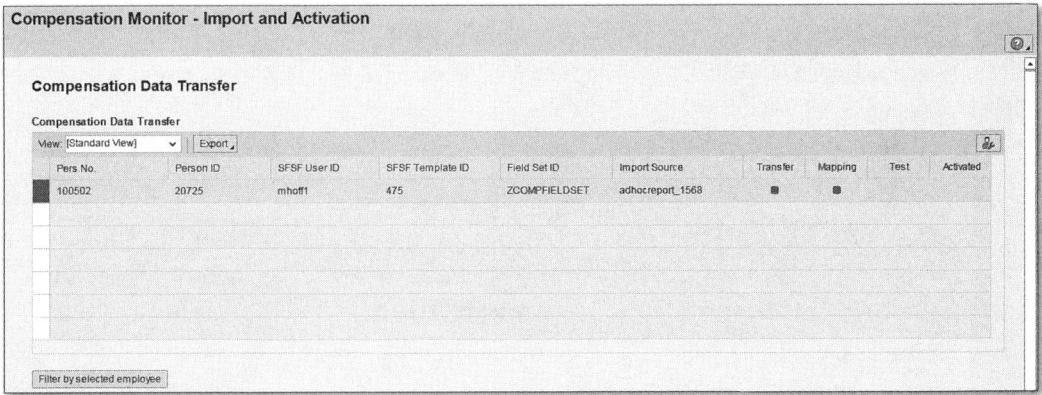

Figure 3.8 Compensation Monitor Web Dynpro Application

Support Packages

Five support packages (SPs) have been released for the first iFlow. The first two support packages introduce new functionality, while subsequent support packages introduce various bug fixes.

Each support package introduced the functionality shown in Table 3.3.

Support Package	Enhancements
SP1	▶ Delta handling for flat-file upload ▶ New field for default locale ▶ New fields for matrix management ▶ New field for proxy determination ▶ Customizing of formatted names ▶ Report to delete inactive employees
SP2	▶ Middleware integration ▶ Web Dynpro for ABAP (WDA) applications for monitoring data transfer ▶ Compensation process integration content
SP3	▶ Report to import data from SuccessFactors for F4 helps ▶ Various bug fixes
SP4 and above	▶ Various bug fixes

Table 3.3 Support Package Releases for the First iFlow

SP2 was the first package to introduce process integration content and support for middleware platforms. All following delivered content is available on middleware platforms only, while previous content can be used with both flat-file and middleware technologies.

Using the iFlow for Employee Data

Data transfer from SAP ERP HCM to the BizX suite is triggered from Report RH_SFI_TRIGGER_EMPL_DATA_REPL for a full data load and from Report RH_SFI_SYNCHRONIZE_EMPL_DATA for a delta load. Both reports require the SAP authorization role SAP_HR_SFI_EMPL_DATA_REPL. Authorization role SAP_HR_SFI_ANALYTICS is required for the analytics extract. If the synchronization report exists, then only this report should be used.

For flat-file transfer, the location of the CSV file and the regular scheduling of the report as a job should be configured in the IMG via the menu path, PERSONNEL MANAGEMENT • INTEGRATION ADD-ON FOR SAP ERP HCM AND SUCCESSFACTORS BIZX • INTEGRATION SCENARIO FOR EMPLOYEE DATA • DEFINE FILE PATH AND NAME FOR STORING THE GENERATED FILES. Both reports can also be scheduled as a job via Transaction SM36. A job must be set up in the BizX suite by an implementation partner to import the flat file. This is set up under Managed Scheduled Jobs in the Provisioning module. Figure 3.9 shows the Create New Job page.

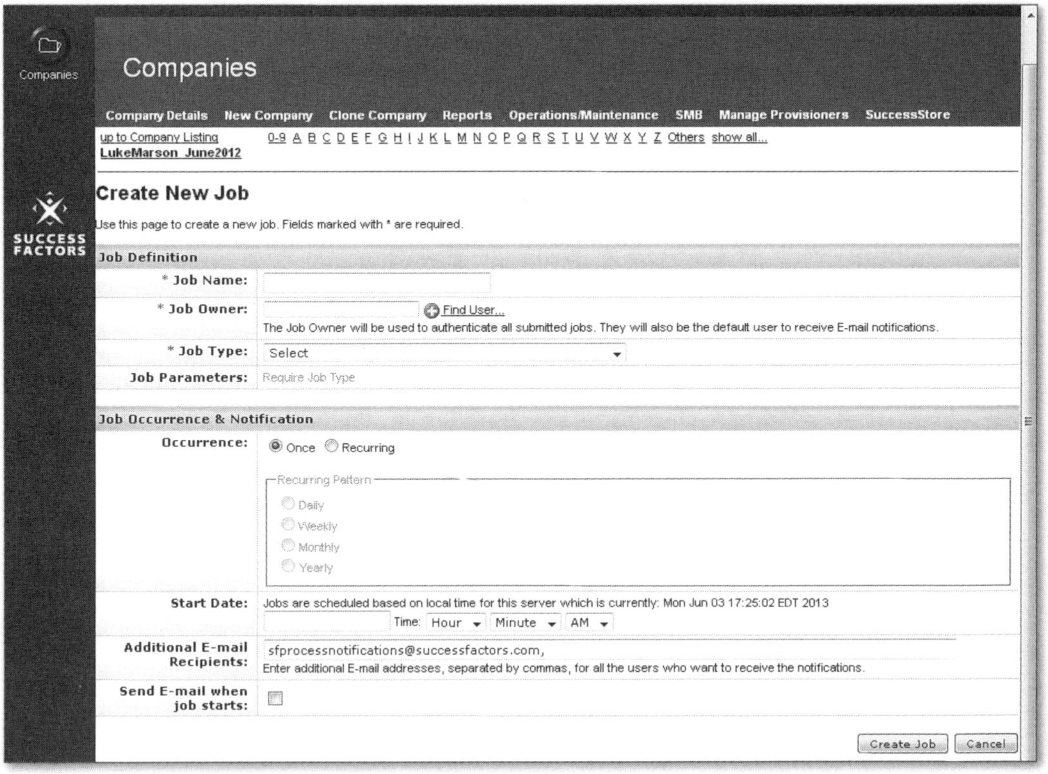

Figure 3.9 Create New Job in the BizX Suite

The flat file can also be imported on an ad hoc basis using the Import Employee Data page under Manager Users in OneAdmin.

For middleware, the middleware integration needs to be configured in the IMG via the menu path, Personnel Management • Integration Add-On for SAP ERP HCM and SuccessFactors BizX • Basic Settings • Settings for Middleware.

Report RH_SFI_TRIGGER_EMPL_DATA_REPL is used to extract a full load of employee and organizational data to import into the BizX suite. If SP1 or above is used, then you shouldn't use this report. When the report is run, the selection screen is displayed, and each of the fields mentioned previously can be configured with the value determination and whether they will be extracted to the flat file.

After the selection is made or verified, the report can be executed. After processing of the flat file is complete, the transfer log will be displayed. After the import job in the BizX suite has run, the data will be available in the BizX suite.

If SP2 or above is used, then you should use Report RH_SFI_SYNCHRONIZE_EMPL_DATA to perform the initial extract and delta updates of employee and organizational data into the BizX suite. This report requires a variant to be used; variants can be created in the IMG via the menu path, PERSONNEL MANAGEMENT • INTEGRATION ADD-ON FOR SAP ERP HCM AND SUCCESSFACTORS BIZX • INTEGRATION SCENARIO FOR EMPLOYEE DATA • SPECIFY ALLOWED VARIANTS FOR DELTA EXTRACTION. If multiple variants are used, they should always be run with the same frequency and in the same sequence.

Various fields are available within the report as selection criteria, including PERSONNEL NUMBER, EMPLOYMENT STATUS, COMPANY CODE, PERSONNEL AREA, PERSONNEL SUBAREA, EMPLOYEE GROUP, and EMPLOYEE SUBGROUP. The type of transfer (middleware of file transfer), default email address, extraction language, and the fields to transfer are configured as part of a variant but can also be changed after a variant has been selected. A default email address must be configured because this is a mandatory field in the BizX suite. The FORCED SYNCHRONIZATION option will force a full data load. After the report is executed, either a flat file is generated, or, if middleware integration is selected, the data is transferred directly to the BizX suite. The log will also be displayed to show any success, warning, or error messages. Figure 3.10 shows an example of the log.

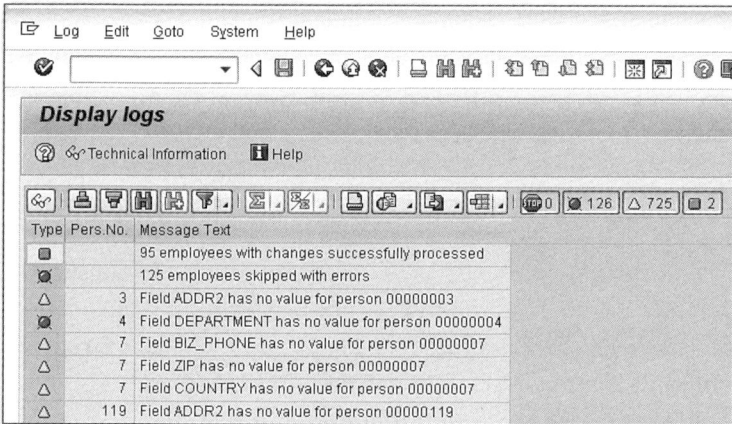

Figure 3.10 Display Log Screen in the Employee Data Synchronization Report

When the report is executed, Table HRSFI_D_EXTR_LOG is updated with all synchronized employees. If an error occurs, the employee is stored in Table HRSFI_D_ERR_LOG, and Table HRSFI_D_EXTR_LOG is not updated for the employee. When the report is executed subsequently, a check is done against Table HRSFI_D_EXTR_LOG to see if any employees have changed, and, if so, they are extracted from SAP ERP HCM. The report also checks for employees marked as inactive in Table HRSFI_D_INACT_EE.

The employee data integration process is now complete.

Using the iFlow for Compensation Data

For compensation data, several reports are used in the integration process. Before the reports can be used, the field sets for the data export and data import need to be configured in the IMG via the menu path, PERSONNEL MANAGEMENT • INTEGRATION ADD-ON FOR SAP ERP HCM AND SUCCESSFACTORS BIZX • INTEGRATION SCENARIO FOR COMPENSATION DATA. As with the fields for the employee data export, predefined fields are available, but customers can also use their own logic via BAdI HRSFI_B_COMP_FIELD_EXTRACTOR (Extraction of Compensation Data). Some fields can also be set to have their values entered at the time of activation, rather than be predefined. These values can then be changed during the activation part of the process. BAdI HRSFI_B_COMP_DATA_ACTIVATION (Activation of Compensation Data Imported from SFSF) is used to determine how compensation data is imported into and activated in SAP ERP HCM. The BAdI HRSFI_B_COMP_ACTIVATION_CUST (Customizing Information Needed for Compensation Activation) can be used to determine additional data from SAP ERP HCM that is required to activate the imported compensation data but that cannot be imported from the SuccessFactors Compensation module.

The Compensation form should already be created in the SuccessFactors Compensation solution and assigned to a Compensation Group ID. This Compensation Group ID is required as part of the synchronization reports in SAP. An ad hoc report must be created in SuccessFactors Compensation for the SuccessFactors API to extract the data for import into SAP ERP HCM; this report must contain the columns for the form template ID and the user ID and must only extract data for complete forms. The column for the user ID must have the property CONSTRAINABLE.

3 | Integration with SAP ERP HCM

> **Important Note**
>
> No configuration is required in the SAP ERP HCM Enterprise Compensation Management module.

Compensation data is transferred to the BizX suite using Report RH_SFI_SYNCH_COMP_DATA. The report selection screen requires the reporting period to be selected, alongside the extraction language, the set of fields to be used, the Compensation Group ID from SuccessFactors Compensation, and the field to determine the employees' user IDs. The field to determine the user ID of employees should be the same that is defined for the employee data extraction. Additionally, the same selection criteria fields that are available in the employee data synchronization report are also available in this report. After the report is executed, the data is transferred directly to the BizX suite, and the log will also be displayed to show any success, warning, or error messages. Figure 3.11 shows the selection screen for the report to export compensation data to SuccessFactors Compensation.

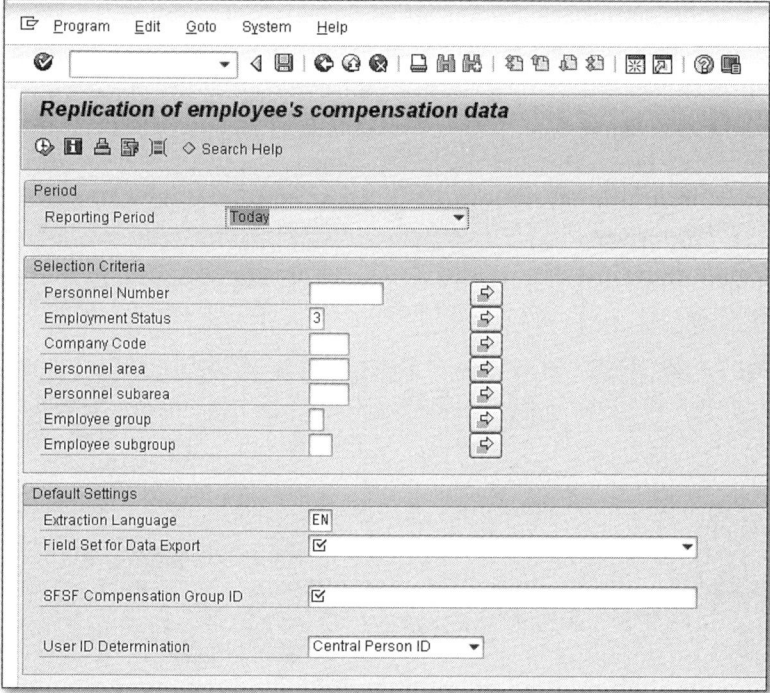

Figure 3.11 Replication of Employee's Compensation Data Report

After the compensation planning process has been performed in SuccessFactors Compensation, the resultant data can be imported into SAP ERP HCM using Report RH_SFI_IMPORT_COMP_DATA. The report selection screen requires the reporting period to be selected, alongside the set of fields to be used, the name of the ad hoc report in SuccessFactors, and the field to determine the employees' user IDs. The field to determine the employees' user IDs should be the same that is defined for the employee data extraction. Additionally, the same selection criteria fields that are available in the compensation data synchronization report are also available in this report. After the report is executed, the data is imported into the staging tables in SAP ERP HCM, and the log is also displayed to show any success, warning, or error messages.

The final stage of the compensation integration process is activating the data in SAP ERP HCM so that it is available within the Payroll infotypes. This is done with Report RH_SFI_ACTIVATE_COMP_DATA. The report selection screen requires the reporting period to be selected, alongside the set of fields to be used and the SuccessFactors Compensation Template ID. Additionally, the same selection criteria fields that are available in the compensation data synchronization report are also available in this report. The report can be run in test mode by selecting the TEST ONLY checkbox. During the configuration of the field set to be used, if some fields were selected to be entered during the activation stage, then these can be changed using the ENTER FIELDS button. After the report is executed, the data is imported from the staging tables into the basic pay and associated infotypes in SAP ERP HCM. The log will also be displayed to show any success, warning, or error messages.

The compensation data integration process is now complete.

Using the iFlow for Evaluation Data

Data is transferred to SuccessFactors Workforce Analytics from SAP ERP HCM using a text (TXT) file. Many predelivered reports must be adapted to customer-specific needs. These reports can be used as standard but can be configured to use customer-specific logic or fields in Transaction SE38. In total, 35 reports can be run to export a text file to be uploaded into SuccessFactors Workforce Analytics:

- RH_SFI_HRP1000
- RH_SFI_HRP1001
- RH_SFI_PA0000
- RH_SFI_PA0001

- RH_SFI_PA0002
- RH_SFI_PA0007
- RH_SFI_PA0008
- RH_SFI_PA0016
- RH_SFI_PA0025
- RH_SFI_PA0041
- RH_SFI_PA0077
- RH_SFI_PA0302
- RH_SFI_T001
- RH_SFI_T001P
- RH_SFI_T500P
- RH_SFI_T501T
- RH_SFI_T503T
- RH_SFI_T505S
- RH_SFI_T510A
- RH_SFI_T510G
- RH_SFI_T512T
- RH_SFI_T513F
- RH_SFI_T527O
- RH_SFI_T529T
- RH_SFI_T529U
- RH_SFI_T530T
- RH_SFI_T542T
- RH_SFI_T545T
- RH_SFI_T548T
- RH_SFI_T549T
- RH_SFI_T554T
- RH_SFI_T5U13
- RH_SFI_T5UEE

- RH_SFI_THOC
- RH_SFI_THOL

These reports should be run as a batch job periodically to create the TXT files for the FTP/SFTP server to retrieve. Each report can be run individually and contains basic selection criteria to run the report for a group of employees or a group of objects.

Monitoring Data Transfers

Two Web Dynpro applications are provided in the iFlow for monitoring the transfer of employee and organizational data (HRSFI_MONITORING_EMPL) and the transfer of compensation data (HRSFI_MONITORING_COMP). These applications are available in the SAP NetWeaver Portal or SAP NetWeaver Business Client (NWBC) to users with the composite role SAP_HR_SFI_C.

The application HRSFI_MONITORING_EMPL (Success Factors – Transfer Monitoring) provides monitoring of the backend and the transfer process when transferring employee data and compensation data to the BizX suite. The application is split up into two lists. Both the EMPLOYEE DATA TRANSFER and the COMPENSATION DATA TRANSFER lists display messages that have been triggered during the data transfer process. The messages are displayed with a status, message type (error, warning, or success), employee number and SuccessFactors user ID, extraction variant, and date and time. For the compensation transfer, the SuccessFactors Compensation template ID and field set name is also displayed. Any fields can be hidden from display using the SETTINGS DIALOG option.

Messages can be viewed by type:

- **Back-end messages**
  Messages that were triggered in SAP ERP HCM.
- **Transfer messages**
  Messages that were triggered during transfer of data.
- **Successfully processed**
  List of employees with successful data transfer.

Some actions can be taken to track and re-extract data for issues. The status can be switched to SOLVED and back to UNSOLVED using the SET TO 'SOLVED' and SET TO 'UNSOLVED' buttons. After issues with the employee data extract have been manually corrected in the backend and marked as SOLVED, they can be re-extracted on

3 | Integration with SAP ERP HCM

an ad hoc basis. This is done by selecting a record and using the RELOAD EMPLOYEE button; it uses the same variant as in the original processing.

In Figure 3.12, the EMPLOYEE DATA TRANSFER area shows several backend messages.

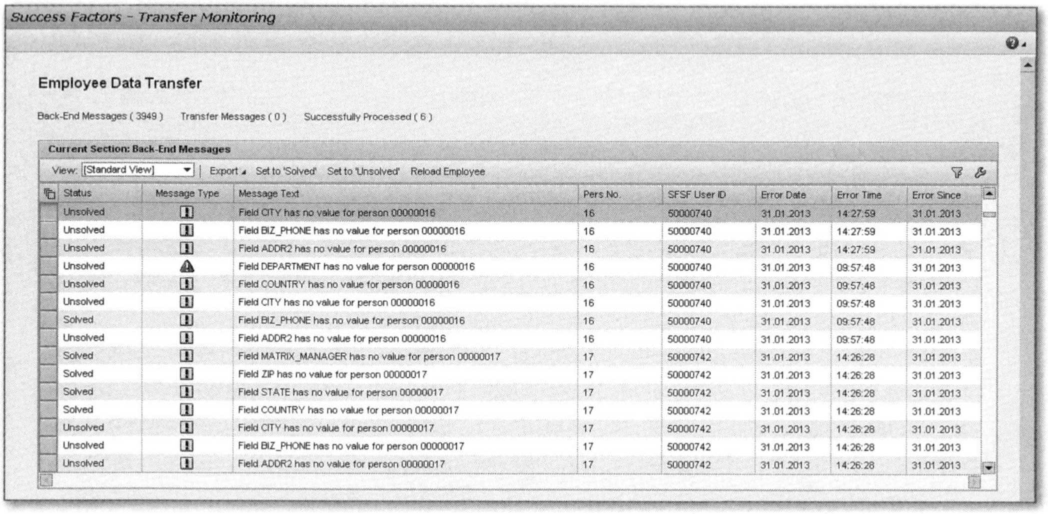

Figure 3.12 Employee Data Transfer Area of the Transfer Monitoring Application

In Figure 3.13, the COMPENSATION DATA TRANSFER area shows several backend messages of error and warning status.

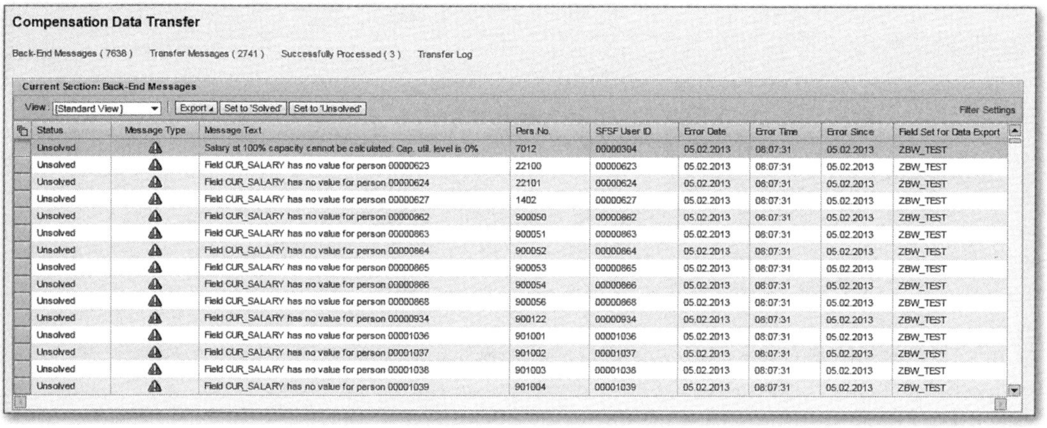

Figure 3.13 Compensation Data Transfer Area of the Transfer Monitoring Application

The HRSFI_MONITORING_COMP (Compensation Monitor – Import and Activation) application is similar to the employee data transfer monitoring application. The application is split up into two lists:

- The COMPENSATION DATA TRANSFER list displays an overview for each of the processes (TRANSFER, MAPPING, TEST, and ACTIVATED) in the importing and activation of data from SuccessFactors Compensation to SAP ERP HCM. It uses a traffic light system of icons to show whether there were errors, warnings, or success messages for employees in each of the four processes. These can be seen in Figure 3.12. The list displays the personnel number, person ID, SuccessFactors user ID, the SuccessFactors Compensation Template ID, the set of fields used, the SuccessFactors ad hoc report, and a column for each of the four processes.

- The ALL EMPLOYEES list displays messages that have been triggered during the data transfer process for each employee. It displays the status, message type, message text, personnel number, SuccessFactors user ID, SuccessFactors Compensation Template ID, the field set, the SuccessFactors ad hoc report, and the date and time. The status of each message can be switched to SOLVED and back to UNSOLVED using the SET TO 'SOLVED' and SET TO 'UNSOLVED' buttons, as with the other monitoring application.

As with the employee monitoring application, any fields in either list can be hidden from display using the SETTINGS DIALOG option.

Messages in both lists can be viewed by type:

- **Transfer messages**
  Messages that were triggered during transfer of data to SAP ERP HCM.
- **Mapping messages**
  Messages that were triggered during transformation of data.
- **Messages on test activation**
  Messages that were triggered during the test run of the activation.
- **Messages on activation**
  Messages that were triggered during the activation.

The main screen of the application was shown previously in Figure 3.8, which shows the status of each step of the compensation integration process.

Data Administration and Cleanup

Several reports are available to administer data used in the transfers. We discuss them in this section.

After employees leave the company and the period of data retention has passed, Report RPUDELPP can be used to delete the personnel IDs of those individuals in the synchronization logs. The BAdI implementation HRPAYXX_DELETE_PERNR (Personnel Number Deletion Reports) is used to define the logic for selecting the employee(s) to be deleted. There is a dual control principle for the authorization object P_DEL_PERN that is used by the report. Both the role used for requesting the deletion and the role used for performing the delete must have this authorization object assigned.

The extraction of employee data can be stopped for one or more employees by using Report RH_SFI_WITHDRAW_VARIANT. This report can be used to halt the extraction for employees using the same selection criteria available in the employee data synchronization report or the compensation extraction report.

Data in the internal log tables used for the transfer of compensation data can be deleted by using Report RH_SFI_CLEANUP_COMP_REPL (for data synchronization with the BizX suite) and Report RH_SFI_CLEANUP_COMP_IMP (for importing data into SAP ERP HCM).

Objects in the iFlow

The reports listed in Table 3.4 are provided with the iFlow for employee, organizational, and compensation data.

Report	Description/Use
RH_SFI_SET_CRDNTLS_EMPLDATA	Store Credentials for Employee Data Scenario
RH_SFI_SET_CRDNTLS_COMPDATA	Store Credentials for Compensation Data Scenario
RH_SFI_SET_CRDNTLS_MAIN	Store Credentials for the Consumer Scenarios
RH_SFI_TRIGGER_EMPL_DATA_REPL	Extraction of Employee Data for SuccessFactors

Table 3.4 Reports Provided with the iFlow

Report	Description/Use
RH_SFI_SYNCHRONIZE_EMPL_DATA	Sync Employee Data with SuccessFactors (with Delta and Inactive Logic)
RH_SFI_WITHDRAW_VARIANT	Discontinue Data Sync with SuccessFactors for Group of Employees
RH_SFI_SYNCH_COMP_DATA	Replication of Employee's Compensation Data
RH_SFI_CLEANUP_COMP_REPL	Cleanup of Internal Tables After Exporting Compensation Data
RH_SFI_IMPORT_COMP_DATA	Import of Employee's Planned Compensation Data
RH_SFI_ACTIVATE_COMP_DATA	Activation of Employee's Planned Compensation Data
RH_SFI_CLEANUP_COMP_IMP	Cleanup of Internal Tables after Importing and Activating Compensation Data
RH_SFI_SYNCH_COMP_F4	Importing Data from SuccessFactors BizX for Use in Input Helps
RPUDELPP	Delete Personnel Numbers Completely

Table 3.4 Reports Provided with the iFlow (Cont.)

Thirty-five reports are provided for transferring analytics data. Further details can be found in the Administrator Guide.

The BAdIs listed in Table 3.5 are provided with the iFlow for recruiting data:

BAdI	Description/Use
HRSFI_B_LEADING_CONTRACT	Determining the Leading Assignment for a Central Person
HRSFI_B_EMPL_DATA_REPLICATION	Replication of Employee's Data
HRSFI_B_EMPL_DATA_REPL_LABEL	Labels for Fields of Data Replication
HRSFI_B_ENHANCE_EMPL_DATA_REP	Enhancement of Employee Data Replication

Table 3.5 BAdIs Provided with the iFlow

3 Integration with SAP ERP HCM

BAdI	Description/Use
HRSFI_B_FILE_NAME	Provide File Name for File Storage
HRSFI_B_COMP_FIELD_EXTRACTOR	Extraction of Compensation Data
HRSFI_B_COMP_DATA_ACTIVATION	Activation of Compensation Data Imported from SFSF
HRSFI_B_COMP_ACTIVATION_CUST	Customizing Information Needed for Compensation Activation

Table 3.5 BAdIs Provided with the iFlow (Cont.)

Two new implementations of the SAP standard BAdI HRPAYXX_DELETE_PERNR (Personnel Number Delete Reports) were introduced in the iFlow:

- HRSFI_DEL_EXTR_LOG (Delete Personnel Numbers from Extraction Log)
- HRSFI_DEL_COMP_LOGS (Delete the PERNR from Compensation Integration Logs)

A new implementation of the SAP standard BAdI SECSTORE_APPLICATION (Administration of Entries in Secure Storage ABAP/DB) was also introduced. This implementation is HRSFI_SECSTORE_APPL (SECStore Application).

The Web Dynpro applications listed in Table 3.6 are provided with the iFlow.

Application	Description/Use
HRSFI_MONITORING_EMPL	Monitoring Employee and Organizational Data Transfer
HRSFI_MONITORING_COMP	Monitoring Compensation Data Transfer

Table 3.6 Web Dynpro Applications Provided with the iFlow

The security roles listed in Table 3.7 are provided with the iFlow.

Security Role	Description/Use
SAP_HR_SFI_EMPL_DATA_REPL	SuccessFactors Integration: Employee Data Replication
SAP_HR_SFI_COMP_DATA_REPL	SuccessFactors Integration: Employee Compensation Data Replication

Table 3.7 Security Roles Provided with the iFlow

Security Role	Description/Use
SAP_HR_SFI_COMP_DATA_IMPORT	SuccessFactors Integration: Compensation Data Import and Activation
SAP_HR_SFI_ANALYTICS	SuccessFactors Integration: Analytics Reports
SAP_HR_SFI_C	SuccessFactors Integration: Composite Role

Table 3.7 Security Roles Provided with the iFlow (Cont.)

The role SAP_HR_SFI_C is a composite role that contains all of the single roles specified in Table 3.7.

Rapid Deployment Solution (RDS)

SAP offers a Rapid Deployment Solution (RDS) package that can be implemented by SAP and its partners. It provides all of the features available in the first iFlow for a fixed-price, fixed-duration implementation. Details can be found on SAP's website.

3.3.2 Integration Add-On 2.0 for SAP ERP HCM and SuccessFactors BizX

The second iFlow released by SAP was *Integration Add-On 2.0 for SAP ERP HCM and SuccessFactors BizX*, which was previously known as integration package 2.0 and has the technical name SFIHCM02. This package provided process integration content for the attract-to-hire recruiting process in SuccessFactors Recruiting Execution. This enables requisition requests to be created in SuccessFactors Recruiting Execution using employee, organizational, and vacancy data from SAP ERP HCM, and allows hiring and transfer actions to be started in SAP ERP HCM after an employee has been hired into a position in SuccessFactors Recruiting Execution. Subsequent support package releases will include functionality for an end-to-end recruiting process using SuccessFactors Recruiting from planning vacancies through to filling vacant positions.

Unlike the previous iFlow, this integration package contains various integration points between SAP ERP HCM and SuccessFactors Recruiting Execution. In the first iFlow, the compensation data was transferred to SuccessFactors before the compensation planning process was performed in SuccessFactors Compensation, and then the resultant data was transferred back to SAP ERP HCM. With this iFlow, data is transferred from one system to another at different stages of the recruiting process. This will be detailed shortly.

The process for this iFlow is as follows:

1. An ad hoc report in SuccessFactors Recruiting Execution is triggered from SAP ERP HCM to retrieve all JobApplication objects with status SentToSAP into a staging table in SAP ERP HCM.
2. For each JobApplication object that was sent to SAP ERP HCM, the status field in SuccessFactors Recruiting Execution is updated to TransferedToSAP if the transfer was successful or to TransferedToSAPError if the transfer was unsuccessful.
3. SuccessFactors Recruiting Execution fields are mapped to SAP ERP HCM fields.
4. Transaction HRSFI_RCT_HIRE is run to check the data from the data import.
5. A personnel action is performed to hire, rehire, or transfer the candidate in the JobApplication object.
6. The status of the JobApplication object in SuccessFactors is set to HiredAtSAP, and the date is saved in the EXPORTED ON field.
7. The new employee's data is transferred to the BizX suite using integration content delivered in Add-On 1.0.

The flow of data between SAP ERP HCM and the BizX suite is illustrated in Figure 3.14.

The objects provided and the process required to use this iFlow differ from the previous iFlow. While reports, authorizations, and BAdIs are included in this iFlow, a program is delivered to monitor the transfer and support post-import processing in SAP ERP HCM. Additional IMG activities are provided for setting up authorizations and middleware integration.

The iFlow provides mappings for 32 SuccessFactors Recruiting Execution fields for four different SuccessFactors Recruiting Execution objects that are used in the data transfer process, although not all fields are mapped to SAP ERP HCM fields. Some fields are used for technical or display purposes and aren't stored within the SAP ERP HCM system. The fields to be imported from SuccessFactors Recruiting Execution can be configured in the IMG via the menu path, PERSONNEL MANAGEMENT •

INTEGRATION ADD-ON FOR SAP ERP HCM AND SUCCESSFACTORS BIZX • INTEGRATION SCENARIO FOR RECRUITING DATA • TRANSFER OF DATA FROM SUCCESSFACTORS BIZX TO SAP ERP • DEFINE FIELDS FOR IMPORTING DATA FROM SUCCESSFACTORS BIZX. All but two of the fields are for JobApplication and JobRequisition objects.

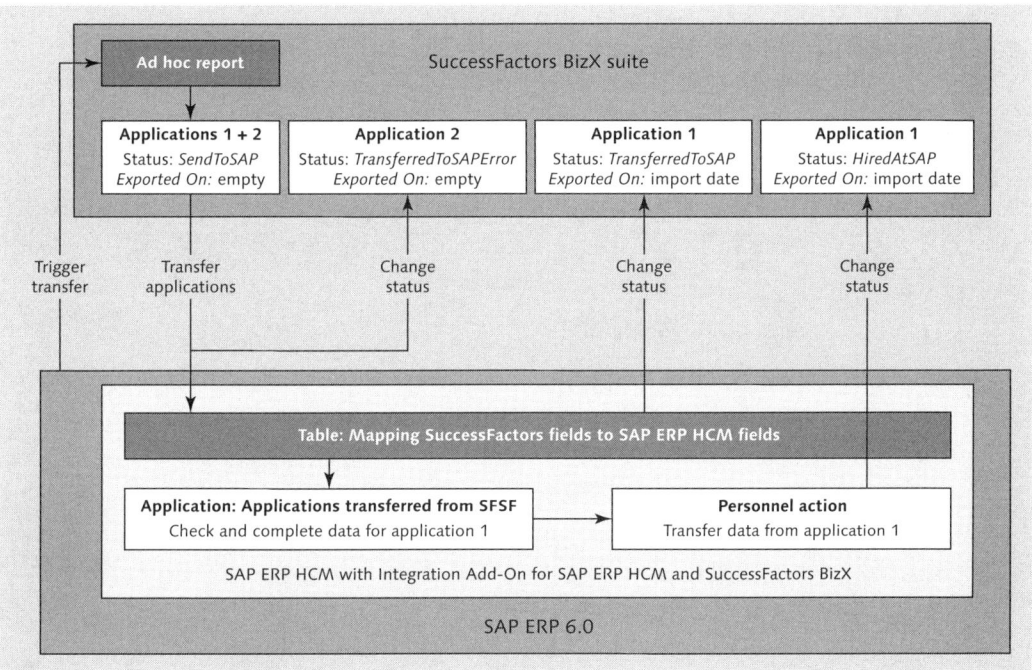

Figure 3.14 Process Flow of Add-On 2.0

The predefined fields for the JobApplication object are listed in Table 3.8. All of the fields except E-MAIL ADDRESS are country-specific.

Field	SuccessFactors Field	SAP ERP HCM Field	Required
APPLICATION ID	RCM_APPLICATION_CAN_JOB_MAP_ID		X
APPLICATION STATUS	RCM_APP_STATUS_STATUS_NAME		X
APPLICANT ID	RCM_APPLICATION_CANDIDATE_ID		

Table 3.8 JobApplication Object Fields Transferred to SAP ERP HCM

Field	SuccessFactors Field	SAP ERP HCM Field	Required
Template ID	APP_TEMPLATE_APP_TEMPLATE_ID		X
Export Date	RCM_APPLICATION_EXPORTED_ON		
First Name	RCM_APPLICATION_FIRSTNAME	PA0002-VORNA	
Last Name	RCM_APPLICATION_LASTNAME	PA0002-NACHN	
Middle Name	RCM_APPLICATION_MIDDLE_NAME	PA0002-MIDNM	
Gender	RCM_APPLICATION_GENDER	PA0002-ANRED	
Date of Birth	RCM_APPLICATION_DOB	PA0002-GBDAT	
Address	RCM_APPLICATION_ADDRESS	PA0006-STRAS SUBTY 1	
City	RCM_APPLICATION_CITY	PA0006-ORT01 SUBTY 1	
Zip Code	RCM_APPLICATION_ZIP	PA0006-PSTLZ SUBTY 1	
State	RCM_APPLICATION_STATE	PA0006-STATE SUBTY 1	
Country	RCM_APPLICATION_COUNTRY_CODE	PA0006-LAND1 SUBTY 1	
Telephone Number	RCM_APPLICATION_EMAIL_HOME_PHONE	PA0006-TELNR SUBTY 1	
E-mail Address	RCM_APPLICATION_EMAIL_ADDRESS	PA0105-USRID_LONG SUBTY 0030	
Former Employee	RCM_APPLICATION_FORMER_EMPLOYEE		
Error in SAP ERP	sapError		

Table 3.8 JobApplication Object Fields Transferred to SAP ERP HCM (Cont.)

The predefined fields for the JobRequisition object are listed in Table 3.9.

Field	SuccessFactors Field	SAP ERP HCM Field	Required
REQUISITION ID	RCM_JOB_REQ_JOB_REQ_ID		
TEMPLATE ID	RCM_JOB_REQ_TEMPLATE_ID		
HIRING MANAGER	HiringManager_USER_SYS_ID		
HIRING MANAGER – FIRST NAME	USERS_SYSINFO_JobReqOperator_ForHiringMgr_USERS_FIRSTNAME		
HIRING MANAGER – LAST NAME	USERS_SYSINFO_JobReqOperator_ForHiringMgr_USERS_LASTNAME		
COUNTRY	RCM_JOB_REQ_COUNTRY		
LOCATION	RCM_JOB_REQ_JOB_LCATION		
DEPARTMENT	RCM_JOB_REQ_JOB_DEPARTMENT		
AREA	RCM_JOB_REQ_JOB_DIVISION		
PERSONNEL AREA IN SAP HCM	RCM_JOB_REQ_EXT_PICKLIST1		
ID OF PERSONNEL AREA	RCM_JOB_REQ_EXT_PICKLIST2	PA0001-WERKS	
PERSONNEL SUBAREA IN SAP HCM	RCM_JOB_REQ_EXT_PICKLIST3		
ID OF PERSONNEL SUBAREA	RCM_JOB_REQ_EXT_PICKLIST4	PA0001-BTRTL	
EMPLOYEE GROUP IN SAP HCM	RCM_JOB_REQ_EXT_PICKLIST5		

Table 3.9 JobRequisition Object Fields Transferred to SAP ERP HCM

Field	SuccessFactors Field	SAP ERP HCM Field	Required
ID of Employee Group	RCM_JOB_REQ_EXT_PICKLIST6	PA0001-PERSG	
Employee Subgroup in SAP HCM	RCM_JOB_REQ_EXT_PICKLIST7		
ID of Employee Subgroup	RCM_JOB_REQ_EXT_PICKLIST8	PA0001-PERSK	
Position in SAP HCM	RCM_JOB_REQ_EXT_TEXT2		
ID of Position in SAP HCM	RCM_JOB_REQ_EXT_TEXT1	PA0001-PLANS	
Organizational Unit in SAP HCM	RCM_JOB_REQ_EXT_TEXT4		
ID of Organizational Unit	RCM_JOB_REQ_EXT_TEXT3	PA0001-ORGEH	

Table 3.9 JobRequisition Object Fields Transferred to SAP ERP HCM (Cont.)

The other two objects are the LastOfferDetail and Candidate objects, which have one field each in the iFlow. The predefined fields for these objects are listed in Table 3.10.

Field	SuccessFactors Field	SAP ERP HCM Field	Required
Hiring date	OFFER_DETAIL_LATEST_JOB_REQ_JOB_START_DATE	PA0000-BEGDA	X
User ID of applicant	RCM_CANDIDATE_USER_SYS_ID		

Table 3.10 LastOfferDetail Object and Candidate Object Fields Transferred to SAP ERP HCM

The package requires Add-On 1.0 with SP3 or SP5 installed. The iFlow currently has an end of mainstream maintenance date of March 31, 2015. At that time, it will probably be replaced by a later version of the iFlow.

Support Packages

SP2 for Add-On 2.0 introduces process integration content for the define-to-hire process, which supports the end-to-end recruitment process. It introduces the triggering of a requisition creation in recruiting based on the information of a vacant position in SAP ERP HCM. Further support packages may be released during the lifecycle of this iFlow.

Preparation of the iFlow for Recruitment Data

Prior to using the iFlow, you need to configure various settings in the IMG in SAP ERP HCM and in SuccessFactors Recruiting Execution.

Settings for credentials and package size for transferring recruiting data need to be configured in the IMG via the menu path, PERSONNEL MANAGEMENT • INTEGRATION ADD-ON FOR SAP ERP HCM AND SUCCESSFACTORS BIZX • BASIC SETTINGS • SETTINGS FOR MIDDLEWARE. Customer-specific logic for authorizations and super users can be defined in the IMG via the menu path, PERSONNEL MANAGEMENT • INTEGRATION ADD-ON FOR SAP ERP HCM AND SUCCESSFACTORS BIZX • BASIC SETTINGS • BADI: AUTHORIZATION CHECK FOR SFSF INTEGRATION. This can also be done with BAdI `HRSFI_B_AUTHORITY_CHECK` (Authorization Check for SFSF Integration), which is called whenever the list of imported data is viewed in SAP ERP HCM and displays the data records that the user has authorization to view.

Additionally, settings for defining how the personnel numbers and SuccessFactors user IDs are determined (e.g., if there are duplicates) are performed in the IMG via the menu path, PERSONNEL MANAGEMENT • INTEGRATION ADD-ON FOR SAP ERP HCM AND SUCCESSFACTORS BIZX • BASIC SETTINGS • BADI: DETERMINATION OF SAP ERP PERSONNEL NUMBERS AND SFSF USER IDS. These are also configurable via BAdI implementation `HRSFI_RCT_PERNR_USERID` of BAdI `HRSFI_B_PERNR_USERID` (Determination of SAP ERP Personnel Numbers and SFSF User IDs).

Settings for defining how the country grouping and personnel actions are determined are performed in the IMG via the menu path, PERSONNEL MANAGEMENT • INTEGRATION ADD-ON FOR SAP ERP HCM AND SUCCESSFACTORS BIZX • INTEGRATION SCENARIO FOR RECRUITING DATA • TRANSFER OF DATA FROM SUCCESSFACTORS BIZX TO SAP ERP • BADI: DETERMINATION OF FURTHER DATA FOR RECRUITING SCENARIO FROM SFSF. These are also configurable via BAdI `HRSFI_B_RECRUIT_MAPPING`

(Determination of Further Data for Recruiting Scenario from SFSF), although no standard implementation exists within the system.

For the application HRSFI_RCT_HIRE, there are three customizing activities available in the IMG via the menu path, PERSONNEL MANAGEMENT • INTEGRATION ADD-ON FOR SAP ERP HCM AND SUCCESSFACTORS BIZX • INTEGRATION SCENARIO FOR RECRUITING DATA • FURTHER PROCESSING OF IMPORTED DATA. With these, you can do the following:

- Define more columns for the TRANSFERRED JOB APPLICATIONS list.
- Specify the headers and field labels.
- Change the PDF overview for job requisition overview.

Within SuccessFactors Recruiting Execution, you'll need to make several settings. It is a prerequisite that the JobApplication object has the field SAPERROR available and that the HIRE status category can be filtered. Four statuses must be made available in the CandidateStatus selection list that is used by the APPLICATION STATUS (RCM_APP_STATUS_STATUS_NAME) field:

- SFSF_APPL_STATUS_HIRED: HiredAtSAP
- SFSF_APPL_STATUS_SEND_SAP: SendToSAP
- SFSF_APPL_STATUS_TRANSFERRED: TransferredToSAP
- SFSF_APPL_STATUS_TRANSF_ERR: TransferredToSAPError

The statuses can be changed in SuccessFactors Recruiting Execution and, if so, must also be changed in the IMG via the menu path, PERSONNEL MANAGEMENT • INTEGRATION ADD-ON FOR SAP ERP HCM AND SUCCESSFACTORS BIZX • INTEGRATION SCENARIO FOR RECRUITING DATA • TRANSFER OF DATA FROM SUCCESSFACTORS BIZX TO SAP ERP • CHANGE APPLICATION STATUS VALUES USED IN SUCCESSFACTORS BIZX.

An ad hoc report needs to be created to transfer all JobApplication objects to SAP with the status SEND TO SAP, including the fields to be transferred. Those marked as required in Section 3.3.2 must be included in the ad hoc report. Importantly, the XML templates for the SuccessFactors Recruiting Execution objects must contain all of the required fields.

After the customizing in SAP ERP HCM has been performed, and the ad hoc report has been created in SuccessFactors Recruiting Execution, then Report

RH_SFI_SYNCH_METADATA needs to be run. This report imports the SuccessFactors ad hoc reports and fields that are used in the data transfer process. When any of these objects change in SuccessFactors, the report must be run to re-import the objects. When running the report, there is only one option that can be run for recruiting data: SFSF Ad Hoc Reports. This report can also be used to import compensation metadata from SuccessFactors Compensation.

After the report has been run, the imported ad hoc report needs to be mapped to field sets. This is performed with Transaction S_NWC_37000012 or in the IMG via the menu path, Personnel Management • Integration Add-On for SAP ERP HCM and SuccessFactors BizX • Integration Scenario for Recruiting Data • Transfer of Data from SuccessFactors BizX to SAP ERP • Assign SuccessFactors BizX Objects to Field Sets.

> **Important Note**
>
> The customizing performed in Assign SuccessFactors BizX Objects to Fields Sets is not transportable and must be completed in each of the target SAP ERP HCM systems.

After assigning the SuccessFactors ad hoc report to a field set, the fields to be used in the field set must be defined in the IMG via the menu path, Personnel Management • Integration Add-On for SAP ERP HCM and SuccessFactors BizX • Integration Scenario for Recruiting Data • Transfer of Data from SuccessFactors BizX to SAP ERP • Define Fields for Importing Data from SuccessFactors BizX. Here each SuccessFactors Recruiting Execution field can have its mapping mode defined (Mapped via Table, Mapped via BAdI, or Not Individually Mapped, e.g., display-only), whether the field is country group-dependent, and whether the field should be a required field.

The mapping for each field in the field set from SuccessFactors Recruiting Execution to a field in SAP ERP HCM can then be defined in the IMG via the menu path, Personnel Management • Integration Add-On for SAP ERP HCM and SuccessFactors BizX • Integration Scenario for Recruiting Data • Transfer of Data from SuccessFactors BizX to SAP ERP • BAdI: Mapping of SFSF Fields to SAP ERP Infotype Fields. These are also configurable via BAdI `HRSFI_B_FIELD_MAPPING` (Mapping of SFSF Fields to SAP ERP Infotype Fields). It is important to note that not every field needs to be mapped via a BAdI.

Multiple fields can be mapped to one or more fields in the IMG via the menu path, PERSONNEL MANAGEMENT • INTEGRATION ADD-ON FOR SAP ERP HCM AND SUCCESSFACTORS BIZX • INTEGRATION SCENARIO FOR RECRUITING DATA • TRANSFER OF DATA FROM SUCCESSFACTORS BIZX TO SAP ERP • BADI: MAPPING OF SFSF FIELDS TO ERP IT FIELDS: CHANGE OF MAPPING RESULT. These are also configurable via BAdI HRSFI_B_CHANGE_MAPPING_RESULT (Mapping of SFSF Fields to ERP Infotype Fields: Change of Mapping Result).

Using the iFlow for Recruitment Data

After the configuration has been completed in SAP ERP HCM and SuccessFactors Recruiting Execution, then the integration process can begin. There are two steps to the data integration process: data import and further processing.

After a job offer has been accepted by a candidate and the requisition has been marked as such in SuccessFactors Recruiting Execution, the status of the requisition can be changed to SENTTOSAP so that the JobApplication object and related data can be imported into SAP ERP HCM. The first step—data import—is performed using Report RH_SFI_IMPORT_RECRUITING_DATA. In the report selection screen, select the ad hoc report to be run in SuccessFactors Recruiting Execution. This will also select the field set defined for the ad hoc report during customizing. After the report is executed, the data is transferred from the BizX suite into the staging table, and the log is also displayed to show any success, warning, or error messages. Figure 3.15 shows the selection screen for the report to import recruiting data to SAP ERP HCM.

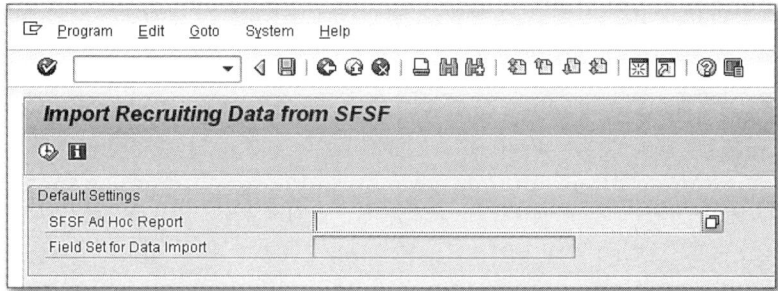

Figure 3.15 Selection Screen of Report RH_SFI_IMPORT_RECRUITING_DATA

Report RH_SFI_IMPORT_RECRUITING_DATA can be scheduled to regularly transfer data from SuccessFactors to SAP ERP HCM.

The second step is the further processing of the imported Recruiting Execution data. This is performed in Transaction HRSFI_RCT_HIRE. The transaction displays a list of all job application data that has been transferred to the SAP ERP HCM staging area. The first three columns of the list display icons: the check status (green if a personnel action can be started, or red if one cannot), notes (either the CREATE NOTE or CHANGE NOTE icons), and an icon if any messages were generated during the transfer. Selecting the MESSAGE icon will show the messages that were generated.

The following nine columns display the applicant first name and last name, start date, personnel number, action type, application ID from SuccessFactors Recruiting Execution, country grouping, status, and company code. Selecting any record provides information in the bottom panel of messages, notes, or details for the selected employee. The DETAILS tab displays data about the applicant, the application, the data from SuccessFactors, and the last processor of the data/record.

Figure 3.16 shows the main screen for Transaction HRSFI_RCT_HIRE.

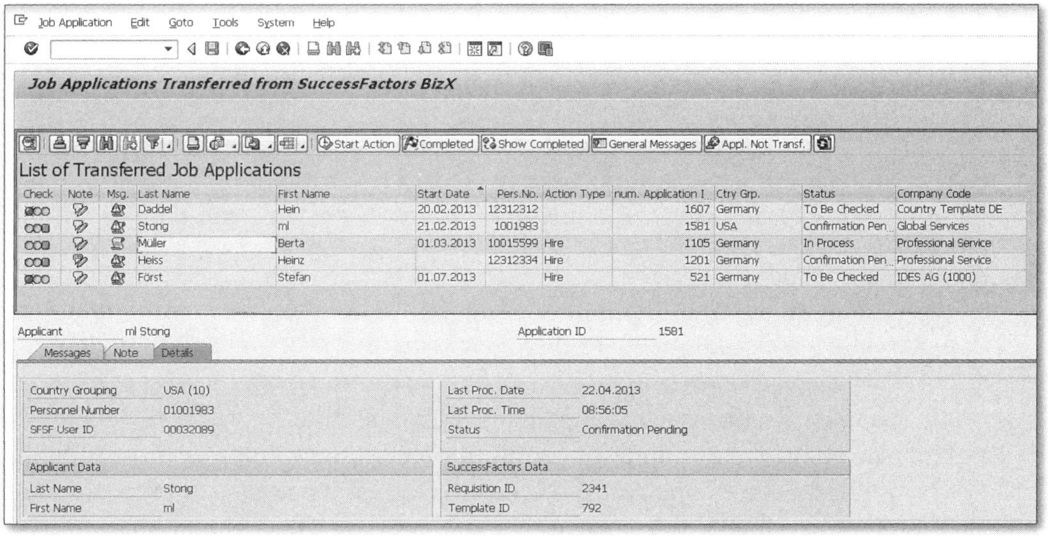

Figure 3.16 Selection Screen of Transaction HRSFI_RCT_HIRE

Above the list are several options. In addition to the standard options for an SAP List Viewer (ALV) list, such as sorting and exporting, there are several application-specific actions:

- DATA OVERVIEW (PDF)
  Display a PDF of the job application information.
- START ACTION
  Trigger a personnel action for the job application.
- COMPLETED
  Manually mark the job application as COMPLETED.
- SHOW COMPLETED
  Display records that are marked as COMPLETED.
- GENERAL MESSAGES
  Display records that have general messages (e.g., middleware connection issues).
- APPL. NOT TRANSF.
  Display job applications that were not transferred correctly to SAP ERP HCM.

The PDF produced when selecting the DATA OVERVIEW (PDF) button displays basic information about the application, the fields and data transferred from SuccessFactors Recruiting Execution to SAP ERP HCM, the SAP ERP HCM fields that data has been transferred to, and what data has been transferred to the SAP ERP HCM fields. Figure 3.17 shows an example of the first page of the PDF document.

The STATUS column indicates whether the record requires action, can be processed, or is being processed. When a record is set to TO BE CHECKED, then the record requires action before it can be set to START ACTION and processed further.

To set the status to START ACTION, the record must be completed. Selecting the red light in the CHECK column opens the CHECK AND CHANGE DATA window. Here any potential duplicates are displayed, and the COUNTRY GROUPING and PERSONNEL ACTION fields are displayed in the PROCESS DATA section. SAP ERP HCM uses the first name, last name, and date of birth to check for any employees may already exist in the system. If a potential duplicate is found, then the correct record must be selected. If either value is missing in the PROCESS DATA section, then the correct value must be selected from the available dropdown values. In the PERSONNEL ACTION dropdown, the type of action that should be started is selected. The COUNTRY GROUPING field must be selected because this selects the country-specific infotypes used during the selected Personnel Action. Figure 3.18 displays the Check and Change Data window.

Job Application Data

Name	Mark RECR4	Transfer Date	01/29/2013
Start Date	02/01/2013	Transfer Time	13:51:19
Requisition	1602	Status	New
Country Grp.	Germany (01)	Last Changed	GUNDELFINGER
Action	Hire (01)	Ad Hoc Rep. ID	AdhocReport_3482
Application	682	Ad Hoc Report	Hire Data SFI Final 2

SFSF Field	Content
Template ID	792
HiringManager_USERS_SYS_ID	RECR3
OFFER_DETAIL_LATEST_JOB_REQ_JO	2013-02-01
RCM_APPLICATION_ADDRESS	Colima Avenue NW
RCM_APPLICATION_CANDIDATE_ID	1041
	682
RCM_APPLICATION_CITY	San Diego
RCM_APPLICATION_COUNTRY_CODE	US
RCM_APPLICATION_DOB	
RCM_APPLICATION_EMAIL_ADDRESS	reiner_do@yahoo.de
RCM_APPLICATION_EXPORTED_ON	
RCM_APPLICATION_FIRSTNAME	Mark
RCM_APPLICATION_FORMER_EMPLOYE	N
RCM_APPLICATION_GENDER	
RCM_APPLICATION_HOME_PHONE	858-123456
RCM_APPLICATION_LASTNAME	RECR4
RCM_APPLICATION_MIDDLE_NAME	
RCM_APPLICATION_STATE	California
RCM_APPLICATION_ZIP	85413
RCM_APP_STATUS_STATUS_NAME	SendToSAP

Figure 3.17 PDF of Job Application Data in HRSFI_RCT_HIRE

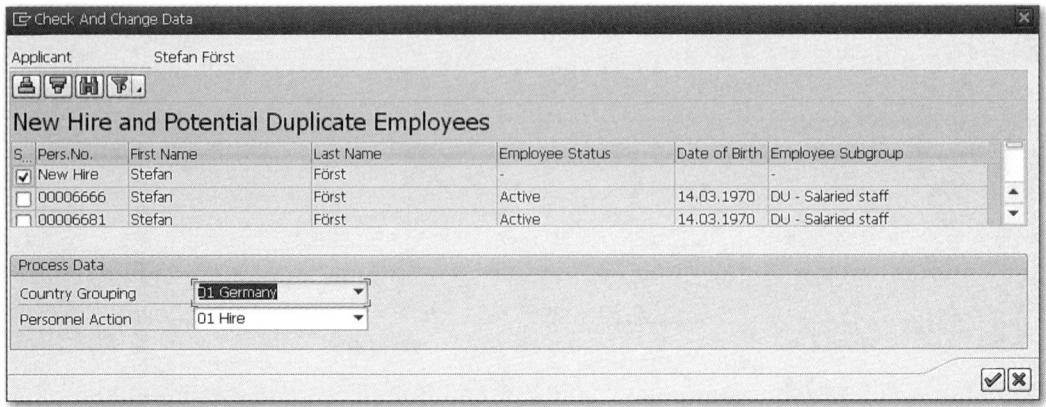

Figure 3.18 Check and Change Data Window in Transaction HRSFI_RCT_HIRE

After the record is corrected and the window closed, then the record will be set to START ACTION in the STATUS column.

A personnel action can be started by selecting a record with the status START ACTION and selecting the START ACTION button. Transaction PA40 (Personnel Actions) will open for the appropriate action and will prefill the relevant data that has been sent over from SuccessFactors Recruiting Execution. By default, this is the start date, position ID, personnel area, employee group, and employee subgroup in the CREATE ACTIONS screen (infotype 0001), first name and last name in the PERSONNEL DATA screen (infotype 0002), and address details in the CREATE ADDRESSES screen (infotype 0006).

After the action is completed, the candidate is now hired into the SAP ERP HCM system and Personnel Actions (Transaction PA40) is closed. The list of job applications in HRSFI_RCT_HIRE is once again displayed, and the record that has been processed in Personnel Actions is no longer displayed in the list. By using the SHOW COMPLETED button, the record can be displayed along with all other completed job applications. In SuccessFactors Recruiting Execution, the STATUS column of the job application changes to HIRED AT SAP.

A job application can be closed manually by selecting the record and selecting the COMPLETED button. This may be used if a personnel action needs to be manually performed (for example, if insufficient data is sent from SuccessFactors Recruiting Execution or if a personnel action has been performed already).

It's possible to retransfer one, multiple, or all job applications from SuccessFactors Recruiting Execution in the TOOLS menu using either the REMAP DATA FOR JOB APPLICATION or the REMAP DATA FOR ALL JOB APPLICATIONS menu options. It's also possible to retransfer the status update for a job application marked as COMPLETED to SuccessFactors Recruiting Execution if the original message was not sent (e.g., if the middleware was unavailable). This is done in the TOOLS menu using menu option RESEND FAILED CONFIRMATIONS TO SFSF.

A job application that is no longer required for processing can be removed from the list. This doesn't remove the job application in SuccessFactors Recruiting Execution, however. To perform the deletion, the user must have super user authorization. This also means that the user will see *all* job applications in the list. The deletion can be performed in the JOB APPLICATION menu using the DELETE menu option.

Objects in the iFlow

The reports listed in Table 3.11 are provided with the iFlow for recruiting data.

Report	Description/Use
RH_SFI_SET_CRDNTLS_RECRUITING	Store Credentials for Recruiting Data Scenario
RH_SFI_SYNCH_METADATA	Importing Metadata from SuccessFactors BizX
RH_SFI_IMPORT_RECRUITING_DATA	Importing Recruiting Data from SFSF
RH_SFI_RECRUIT_PROCESS_APPL	Further Processing of Imported Recruiting Data

Table 3.11 Reports Provided with the Second iFlow

The application listed in Table 3.12 is provided with the iFlow for recruiting data.

Application	Description/Use
HRSFI_RCT_HIRE	Further Processing of Imported Recruiting Data

Table 3.12 Application Provided with the Second iFlow

The BAdIs listed in Table 3.13 are provided with the iFlow for recruiting data.

BAdI	Description/Use
HRSFI_B_AUTHORITY_CHECK	Authorization Check for SFSF Integration
HRSFI_B_FIELD_MAPPING	Mapping of SFSF Fields to SAP ERP Infotype Fields
HRSFI_B_CHANGE_MAPPING_RESULT	Mapping of SFSF Fields to ERP Infotype Fields: Change of Mapping Result
HRSFI_B_RECRUIT_MAPPING	Determination of Further Data for Recruiting Scenario from SFSF
HRSFI_B_PERNR_USERID	Determination of SAP ERP Personnel Numbers and SFSF User IDs
HRSFI_B_REQUIRED_FIELDS	Object-Type Dependent Required Fields

Table 3.13 BAdIs Provided with the Second iFlow

The security roles listed in Table 3.14 are provided with the iFlow.

Security Role	Description/Use
SAP_HR_SFI_RECRUITING	SuccessFactors Integration: Recruiting
SAP_HR_SFI_C2	SuccessFactors Integration: Composite Role

Table 3.14 Security Roles Provided with the Second iFlow

The role SAP_HR_SFI_C2 is a composite role that contains all of the single roles specified in Table 3.7 and Table 3.14.

Rapid Deployment Solution (RDS)

SAP also offers a Rapid Deployment Solution (RDS) package for the second iFlow that can be implemented by SAP and its partners. Like the first RDS, it provides all of the features available in the second iFlow for a fixed-price, fixed-duration implementation. Details can be found on SAP's website.

3.4 Other Integration Content

In addition to the standard iFlows that have been and will be released, SAP has also released various other types of content for integrating SAP ERP HCM with the BizX suite (or vice versa). This content takes different forms, from "cookbooks" to add-ons to standard delivered integration.

3.4.1 Cookbooks

To provide customers and partners with the ability to create user experience integration and connect multiple systems to the BizX suite, SAP released two "cookbooks." These cookbooks are essentially how-to documents on enabling this connectivity. These types of documents are released when human intervention is required more than a standard software solution. SAP has released two cookbooks to date:

- *Integration of SuccessFactors Business Execution into SAP NetWeaver Portal via Single Sign-On*
- *Integration of Multiple SAP ERP Human Capital Management Systems with SuccessFactors Business Execution*

The *Integration of SuccessFactors Business Execution into SAP NetWeaver Portal via Single Sign-On* cookbook provides information on the prerequisites for setting up SSO integration between the SAP NetWeaver Portal and the BizX suite solutions, as well as the steps to do the following:

- Configure SAML2.0 in the SAP NetWeaver Portal.
- Collect required information from SuccessFactors.
- Configure SSO in SuccessFactors.
- Create links within the SAP NetWeaver Portal.

The *Integration of Multiple SAP ERP Human Capital Management Systems with SuccessFactors Business Execution* cookbook discusses various scenarios and the impact of those scenarios when integrating multiple instances of SAP ERP HCM with one instance of SuccessFactors. It covers SAP ERP HCM as both the source system and as the target system.

Both of the cookbooks can be downloaded from the SAP Help website at *http://help.sap.com/erp_sfi_addon20*.

3.4.2 Employee Central and Employee Central Payroll

For integration of SAP ERP HCM with SuccessFactors Employee Central and SuccessFactors Employee Central Payroll, SAP delivered the *Employee Mini-Master Integration Package* in early 2013. This iFlow is also known as *Employee Central On-Demand*.

This iFlow integrates employee, job, work contract, and payroll data between SAP ERP HCM and SuccessFactors Employee Central. It's also used for integration between SuccessFactors Employee Central and SuccessFactors Employee Central Payroll, and for SuccessFactors Employee Central to SAP ERP HCM. The iFlow covers integration for common types of systems, such as payroll, time and labor, benefits, master data, and identity management services. Integration is also available between Employee Central Payroll and SAP Finance OnDemand and SAP Travel OnDemand.

The Dell Boomi AtomSphere platform is a requirement for the iFlow because it contains predefined mappings content. Both components PA_SE_IN 100 (Message-Based Employee Replication from Employee Central to SAP ERP) and ODTFINCC 600 (File-Based Cost Center Replication from SAP ERP to Employee Central) are required for the integration scenarios.

The iFlow is configured in the IMG via the menu path, PERSONNEL MANAGEMENT • PERSONNEL ADMINISTRATION • INTERFACES AND INTEGRATION • INTEGRATION OF SAP ERP MASTER DATA AND SUCCESSFACTORS EMPLOYEE CENTRAL. Two handbooks have been available since early 2013 that support the configuration of these scenarios:

- The *Employee Central–SAP ERP: Implementation and Integration Handbook* was released for integrating SuccessFactors Employee Central data into SAP ERP HCM using Dell Boomi AtomSphere. It provides information and configuration steps for setting up Employee Central, SAP ERP HCM, and middleware.

- The *SuccessFactors Employee Central Payroll: Implementation and Integration Handbook* that is provided for the integration package contains extensive information on setting up the following:
    - Integration between SAP ERP HCM and Employee Central
    - Integration between Employee Central and Employee Central Payroll
    - Users and roles
    - Employee Central Payroll

- Integration between Employee Central and Benefitfocus
- Integration between Employee Central Payroll and Workforce Software

The guide also contains troubleshooting and localization information.

The iFlow itself has predefined standard mappings for various SAP infotypes related to basic employee data and payroll information, including the following:

- 0000 (Actions)
- 0001 (Organizational Assignments)
- 0002 (Personnel Data)
- 0003 (Payroll Status)
- 0006 (Addresses)
- 0007 (Planned Working Time)
- 0008 (Basic Pay)
- 0009 (Bank Details)
- 0014 (Rec. Payments/Deductions)
- 0015 (Additional Payments)
- 0105 (Communications)

From a technical perspective, the process works on the following basis:

1. Data in Employee Central is passed to Dell Boomi AtomSphere by the SuccessFactors API.
2. Dell Boomi AtomSphere maps the data to the SAP ERP Web Services.
3. SAP ERP Web Services pushes the data into SAP ERP HCM.
4. The HR infotype framework is leveraged to execute the appropriate actions and update employee data in the applicable infotypes.
5. If other SAP systems are dependent on this data, then an Application Linking and Enabling (ALE) message will be triggered per the standard on-premise functionality.

Further integrations are planned to integrate Employee Central with various other on-premise and cloud solutions by SAP, such as on-premise Payroll, Customer Relationship Management (SAP CRM), and Supplier Relationship Management (SAP SRM).

3.4.3 Social Media ABAP Integration Library

To integrate SAP Jam with SAP modules—including SAP ERP HCM—the Social Media ABAP Integration Library (SAIL) was delivered by SAP in late 2012. SAIL is part of SAP NetWeaver and is available as of SAP_BASIS versions 7.02 SP11, 7.30 SP07, and 7.31 SP03. To use SAIL, the business function `BC_SRV_STW_01` must be activated.

SAIL allows for SAP Jam objects, such as groups and feeds, to be available in multiple applications, such as SAP ERP HCM, SAP CRM, or custom applications. Integration is focused on two parts:

- Establishing an HTTP connection between SAP and SAP Jam
- Setting up authentication between SAP and SAP Jam

Unlike other integration activities between SAP and the BizX suite solutions, SAP Jam doesn't require any mapping of fields. Rather, because the application is focused on social media activities, collaboration, and sharing non-SAP data, there is no requirement for SAP data to be stored outside of the SAP system.

SAIL is configured in the IMG via the menu path, APPLICATION SERVER • BASIS SERVICES • COLLABORATION. In the first release of SAIL, the SAP STREAMWORK subnode is used, but as of SAP_BASIS 7.31 SP06, the SAP JAM subnode is used.

Authentication is via OAuth, Security Assertion Markup Language 2.0 (SAML2) assertion, and Secure Sockets Layer (SSL) for HTTPS communication.

Full details of configuring integration of SAP Jam using SAIL can be found in the SAP guide *SAP Jam ABAP Integration – Configuration Guide*, which is available as a document on the SAP Community Network in the Social Software space at *http://scn.sap.com/community/socialsoftware*. There are two versions of the configuration guide: one version for SAP_BASIS version 7.31 SP06, and one version for SAP_BASIS versions 7.31 SP05, 7.30 SP08, and 7.02 SP12.

3.4.4 SAP Data Services Adapter

A standard SuccessFactors adapter is provided in SAP Data Services 4.1 SP1 to integrate talent data from the BizX suite into SAP NetWeaver BW or SAP HANA. Potentially, data can also be transferred bi-directionally into the BizX suite.

The adapter connects to the SuccessFactors API and extracts database tables that can be processed and sent to SAP NetWeaver BW or SAP HANA. The data can also be subject to transformations and quality checks during processing. It is worth noting that the standard talent management InfoCubes in SAP NetWeaver BW don't map entirely with data from the BizX suite, so new InfoCubes may need to be created.

For more information, see the *SAP BusinessObjects Data Services 4.1 Support Package 1 (14.1.1.0) Integrator's Guide*, available on SAP Help at *http://help.sap.com/boall*.

3.5 Summary

SAP is at the beginning of a long journey to build robust standard integration content. It has already laid out a detailed foundation of how to reach its goal, which is to ensure that customers have relevant, specific, and maintainable integration content. SAP has set its strategy and chosen to leverage SAP and Dell Boomi AtomSphere technology to provide bi-directional middleware integration between SAP ERP HCM and the BizX suite.

Shortly after completing the acquisition of SuccessFactors, SAP delivered the first of its packages of predefined integration content (iFlows) and followed these up with cookbooks to facilitate additional integration scenarios such as SSO for the SAP NetWeaver Portal. SAP continued to deliver additional integration content to cover talent management (hybrid model) process integration for compensation and recruitment processes.

Having read this chapter, you should now be familiar with SAP's strategy, the integration technology and content that SAP offers, and how to configure and use this content for employee, compensation, and recruitment process scenarios. Next, we'll look at the technical aspects and considerations of the BizX suite.

SuccessFactors is very different from on-premise SAP ERP HCM. Because of multi-tiered data structure and multi-tenant architecture, SuccessFactors can house many customers on a single database and streamline security, custom objects, and administration within the system.

4 Technical Considerations

Although the technical architecture and system design of SuccessFactors is very different from that of SAP ERP HCM, SuccessFactors is able to maintain highly scalable and effective procedures not only to store and run data but also to maintain secure data while keeping applications fast and stable.

The approach for examining the technical architecture of SuccessFactors varies greatly from on-premise SAP ERP HCM solutions in several ways. The days of creating custom tables from scratch and implementing completely custom functionality in-house using specialized skillsets are no more. And because SuccessFactors is a cloud solution, everything from security to moving configuration from one system to another system is different.

But that's not to say that SuccessFactors is not flexible. SuccessFactors delivers significant functionality by default and also uses the Metadata Framework and the Rules Engine to customize your own objects and screen elements. The flexibility of the architecture allows for endless customization.

In this chapter, we'll take a look at the technical architecture of SuccessFactors, the technical aspects of the solution, and how it differs from SAP (Section 4.1). We'll also walk through the Metadata Framework (MDF) that is used to manage custom objects in SuccessFactors (Section 4.2) and have a look at security from a technical level as well as how security is applied on a user level (Section 4.3). Finally, we'll take a quick look at the administration part of SuccessFactors (Section 4.4).

Now, let's take a look at the basics of how this technology works.

4   Technical Considerations

4.1   Technical Architecture

As with all applications, data must live somewhere. In the case of the SuccessFactors BizX suite, which is a cloud solution, the SuccessFactors organization hosts the data and the application on its own servers. However, the SuccessFactors architecture allows for very fast, stable, and customizable solutions that remain performant from the hosted location. Let's take a look at the high-level architecture for all SuccessFactors solutions.

In Figure 4.1, you can see that the overall architecture of the SuccessFactors application landscape runs similar to many other web-enabled applications. There is the core application and database in the SuccessFactors Data Center, and then there is the client-side web browser that consumes the application from the Data Center.

Architecturally, SuccessFactors is split into three layers; two are within the Data Center and one connects the Data Center to the client:

- Within the Data Center, the Database layer contains the underlying application metadata configuration and also the customer data.
- The Application layer, also within the Data Center, contains the application and logic of the BizX suite.
- The Communication layer lies between the Application layer and the client web browser.

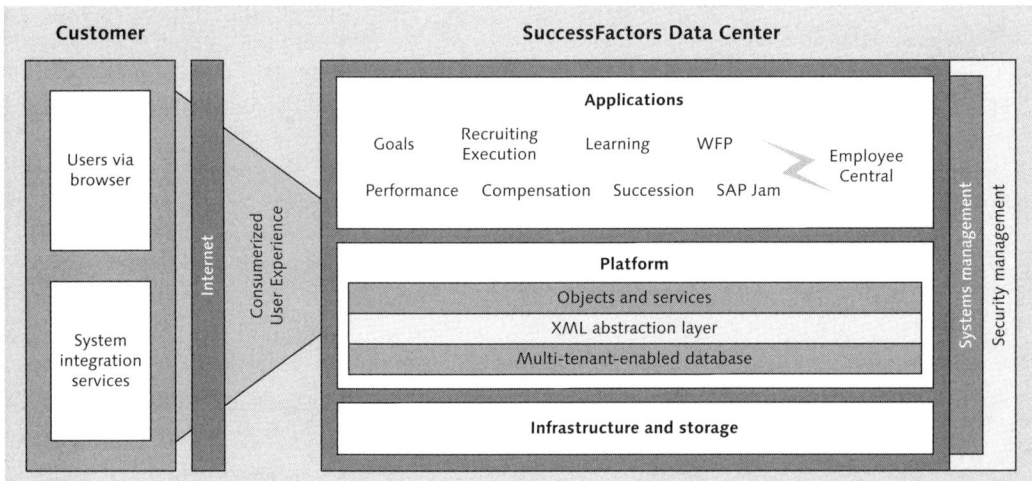

Figure 4.1 SuccessFactors Structure Stack

As with all cloud applications, security is generally a main concern. We'll cover security in depth later in this chapter. First, we'll briefly look at each of the layers.

4.1.1 Database Layer

SuccessFactors houses all of the customer's data in an Oracle database but plans to switch this to an SAP HANA database in late 2013. Because it uses what is known as a multi-tenant architecture, multiple customers' data lives in the same database, with each customer using the same instance of the software but each having its own set of configuration (the tenant). This greatly reduces the required hardware needed to host clients and increases speed and reliability.

Of course, sharing database space with another customer's sensitive HR data raises some obvious security concerns to those not familiar with the technical architecture of the database landscape. We'll address how SuccessFactors rigorously tests each level of the stack to ensure data security in Section 4.3 of this chapter.

Because the SuccessFactors BizX suite is a multi-tenant Software-as-a-Service (SaaS) suite, customers share infrastructure, web servers, database instances, and the application itself. However, each customer has its own partition in the database, along with the customer-specific database schema. This allows for high flexibility and the export of any customer data from the database at any time with no effect on any other customer. Because the database partition is separated from other customer data and is linked specifically to the customer's tenant, this means that data cannot be accessed from any place except the customer's instance of SuccessFactors. It also means that configuration in one customer tenant does not affect any other customer tenant running on the same instance of the software.

4.1.2 Application Layer

One of the most important aspects of a SaaS solution is that it is multi-tenant. Because of the multi-tenant architecture, all of the users share the same core code base of the application, but they each have their own tenant of configuration. This differs from on-premise solutions, where each instance of the system requires different hardware, versions, and operating systems. Having all users on the same code base has many advantages:

- **Scheduled releases**
  The SuccessFactors development team is constantly updating the software to

perform better and increase functionality. Users get regular scheduled updates automatically, instead of paying to upgrade their own on-premise software. New features are delivered in a way in which they must be activated to be used, so there are no "nasty surprises" for customers.

- **Latest version across all customers**
  With the scheduled releases, all customers will be up to date on the latest version all the time. This means that there are no more costly upgrades, creating different versions for different customers.

- **No hardware, operating systems, or database licenses**
  One single subscription licensing fee is paid to use SuccessFactors and includes all necessary costs for hardware, database, and support.

- **Optimal hardware and software combination**
  SuccessFactors resides on hardware that is optimized for its own software.

- **Consistent performance and stability**
  Because all customers use the same software and hardware, the fast, stable, and secure experience is shared by all customers.

- **More manageable and efficient support and maintenance**
  SuccessFactors can easily support and maintain its software because it is standardized.

- **Data mining and aggregation for analytical benchmarking**
  Analytics can easily be pulled with maximum efficiency due to the standardization of software and hardware.

Now, let's take a closer look at the application architecture itself. Figure 4.2 shows a more in-depth overview of the SuccessFactors components within the application engine.

The application and modules themselves are written in the Java programming language using Java Platform Enterprise Edition (J2EE) specifications, meaning it conforms to a standard set of programming logic.

The Java application then uses JavaScript Object Notation (JSON) to send the data to the client or end user. With JSON, the web page that the user sees is dynamically created and rendered using JavaScript. This makes it a very lightweight application on the client side and allows for a dynamic display of data. This also lets the application perform many of the user-friendly animations that appear and gives great flexibility within the design of the user interface (UI). We'll cover the UI itself in Chapter 5.

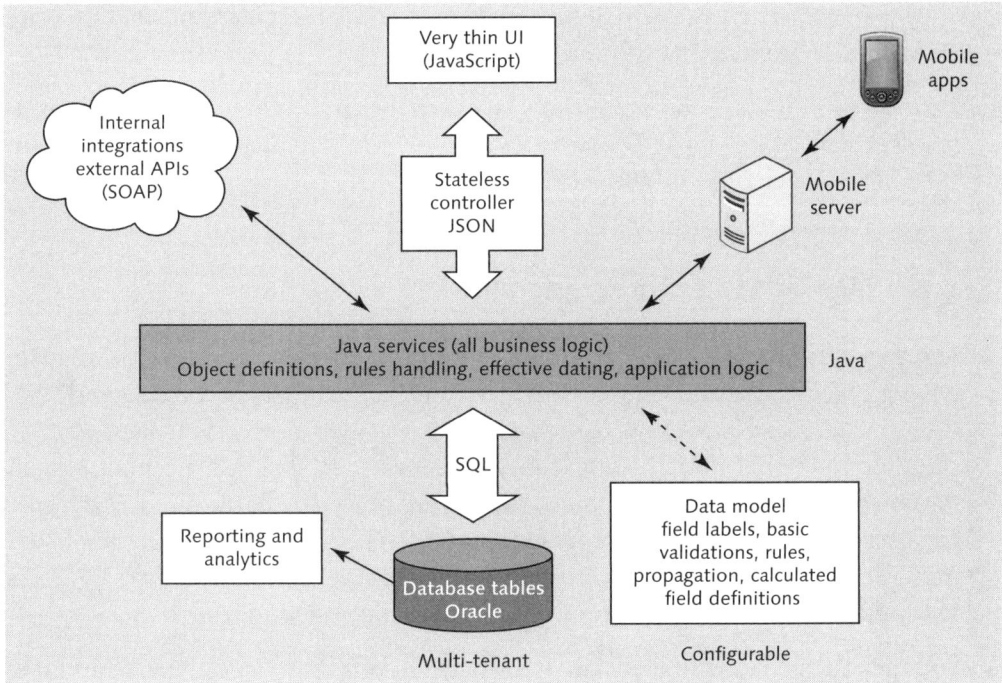

Figure 4.2 Technologies Used with SuccessFactors

Because the JSON interchange allows for efficient and powerful exchange of the data from the Java application to the end user, it makes SuccessFactors applications *stateless*. Stateless application design means that there are no static HTML pages being called from the server. Each page is dynamically created and sent securely to the end user. This allows for complete flexibility and lightweight application design.

Also within this layer are the connectors to other Web Services (e.g., Recruiting Management can connect to Job Boards), mobile application services, and all the logic that drives the entire application.

4.1.3 Communication Layer

The Communication layer transports the data for the application to the web browser for rendering and communications data calls to and from the Data Center. This is important from an architectural perspective because this layer is sending sensitive application and personal HR information across the Internet. As a result, SuccessFactors has implemented well-known standards for data transfer, including Secure

Shell (SSH), VeriSign-certified Secure Sockets Layer (SSL)/Transport Layer Security (TLS), and Secure File Transfer Protocol (SFTP).

Now that you understand the various layers of the application, let's take a look at the Metadata Framework, which is a very powerful architecture that allows for customized logic, objects, and dataflow.

4.2 Metadata Framework

The Metadata Framework (MDF) is a mechanism for creating, modifying, and maintaining objects within the SuccessFactors system. It consists of a framework that uses metadata to allow easy creation and maintenance of objects using a generic set of components that are re-used by all objects. As a result, nothing related to new objects or the enhancement of existing objects is hard-coded within the SuccessFactors system and no programming or coding is required — even for objects introduced by SuccessFactors. In fact, it means that it is easier for SuccessFactors to introduce new objects and functionality into the system.

The specialized nature and design of the MDF means that you can create multiple objects while retaining a high level of performance within the system. For individuals from a solely SAP-based background, the concept of the MDF may seem new and unfamiliar.

The objects created in the MDF are called *Metadata Objects*; they can be new objects, new screens for existing objects, new rules, or new fields — for example, a job classification or a work center. A screen and a set of rules could also be configured through the MDF — for example, to support administration of the company car plan. Metadata Objects are easily configurable through the OneAdmin interface without programming or editing application XML files. However, some applications within the BizX suite do not yet leverage the MDF, although SuccessFactors aims to complete rolling this out fully across the entire BizX suite in the near future.

For customers or consultants who are used to creating new objects and infotypes in SAP, the MDF may seem simplistic or alien. However, simplicity offers some advantages:

- Reliance on technical or external assistance to add new objects or fields is no longer required.
- Stability and upgradability are maintained because standard objects or components are not changed.

- There is a consistency across objects, such as the look and feel of the UI, searching, and auditing.
- A minimal level of training is required to use the MDF because it has an easy-to-use GUI and it isn't necessary to understand the technical aspects.
- The performance of Metadata Objects is superior to the performance of standard SuccessFactors objects.
- The standard UIs delivered by SuccessFactors are fully compatible with the MDF and can leverage Metadata Objects.

We'll now take a look at the technical aspects so that you can understand how the MDF and Metadata Objects work.

4.2.1 Technical Aspects

Each object within the SuccessFactors data model is made up of a number of components, including the following:

- API
- Controller
- User Interface (UI)
- Workflow implementation
- Data Access Object (DAO)
- Database Table
- Implementation of Role-Based Permissions (RBP) security
- Logic Services
- Set of Java Services
- Reporting integration

Many of the standard objects within the SuccessFactors system have their own instances of these components. Within the MDF, only one instance of each of the components exists; this instance is used for all Metadata Objects. Through the definition and structure of the metadata, these generic components can operate without error no matter how the objects are created and no matter what metadata is used.

Because the components required for Metadata Objects already exist, only their behavior needs to be configured. For example, the name of the fields, the field data type, and the rules used for validation must be configured. However, you don't even need to take the UI, object controller, and database tables into consideration when configuring the object. This means that the overall complexity of creating new or extending existing objects in SuccessFactors is reduced significantly through this framework. SuccessFactors will also leverage the MDF to create new objects in the future rather than use the traditional XML method also used by implementation consultants.

The objects created in the MDF are also automatically exposed via the OData Rest APIs, which means that they can be integrated with other systems, such as SAP ERP HCM. As a result, data can be transferred to or from custom objects created in the MDF with these systems. Import templates for new objects are automatically generated.

The UI supports translations as well as the history UI to show effective-dated records. Approvals can be configured and rule-based validations added for fields, which we will cover in Section 4.2.3.

The MDF has a transaction flow that sees a number of hooks at different stages of actions in the system. A *hook* is a point when a rule can be triggered. For example, rules can be triggered during initialization, field change, pre-save and post-save of data, and so on. In total, there are around nine points within the transaction lifecycle where hooks exist. Hooks can be configured on the object level or the field level and are explained in Section 4.2.7.

4.2.2 Metadata Objects

The structure of a Metadata Object—called a *Generic Object* within the SuccessFactors system—is defined by the SuccessFactors data model.

Metadata Objects have a number of fixed attributes that must be defined during creation; some are compulsory, and others are optional. In addition to these attributes, up to 200 fields can be configured for each Metadata Object. Attributes are stored as fields, and the attributes that are required for each Metadata Object include the object type, use of effective dating, and the object label. Labels can be maintained in multiple languages for systems that have more than one language enabled. Optional fields include workflow configuration, the "to-do" category, and additional fields.

Other fields are also stored for a Metadata Object, including the internal ID, external code, creator, creation date, last modifier, and last modified date. These are assigned automatically by the system.

Like standard objects, Metadata Objects can have associations assigned to them. Associations designate a relationship with another object and define attributes of these relationships. Associations have the following attributes:

- Name: Name of association
- Type: Composite (the associated object can only exist as a child of the object) or Valid When (valid with or without the existence of the associated object)
- Multiplicity: One-to-One (one object can only be related to one object) or One-to-Many (one object can be related to many objects)
- Destination object ID: ID of the destination object type
- Required: Yes (at least one child record is required) or No
- Visibility: Editable (users can view, add, edit, or delete child records), Not Visible (users cannot see the child records), or Read Only (users can only view the child records)
- Label: Label for the association on the UI

For example, a position object has an association called parentPosition that is between the position object and another position object. The following attributes state how these two types of objects are associated to each other:

- Type: Valid When
- Multiplicity: One-to-One
- Destination object ID: Position
- Required: No
- Visibility: Editable

Each Metadata Object can have searchable fields assigned, just as standard objects do. As the term suggests, these are fields of the object that can be searched upon.

You can also assign Role-Based Permissions (RBP) to a Metadata Object. After you select a permission category from a PickList, the object is then subject to the permissions of that permission category.

The attributes, data model, and metadata for the new Metadata Object are saved in the database used for the SuccessFactors instance. Two new database tables are created for the object to store all of the necessary information about it. The structure of these tables is controlled by the overall SuccessFactors data model, but the data model allows for a possible 200 additional fields.

4.2.3 Rules Engine

Rules allow you to apply business logic to certain actions or to configure input field entry selection or validation. Rules result in the sort of flexibility that is found in the SAP system with functionality such as user exits, Business Add-ins (BAdIs), F4 Helps, and data elements. Rules are modeled with statements (using conditions such as "and" and "or") and flow logic to define the business logic used; once created, they can be assigned to fields or objects. Through this functionality, you can easily modify standard system behavior or add your own business rules or logic to a host of actions or data fields throughout the SuccessFactors system using the various GUIs of the MDF. Rules are supported by the Rules Engine, which processes the rules as necessary.

A system administrator retains the flexibility to modify, add, or remove rules at any time through OneAdmin. Rules are configured in the same area of OneAdmin as objects in the MDF; we'll discuss this configuration in Section 4.2.5.

Rules have a standard logic flow. They are configured with four sections:

- Rule information (rule name and base object type)
- If logic
- Then logic

For *If* logic, "and" and "or" conditions are used to model statements that can reference any object field or object field attribute. These statements determine the action to take, which is defined in the Then logic. With *Then* logic, an object field, object field attribute, or system variable can be set to a specific value. The If logic can be set to be Always True, which means that the Then logic is always actioned when the rule is triggered.

Now let's look at an example of a rule. Imagine that we want to create a rule to validate that an employee's pay grade level does not exceed their position's pay grade level during a transfer. Using the MDF, we can configure a rule that checks that both the employee's pay grade and the position pay grade have the same value, for each value available in the pay grade scale. We can then set the event reason (to TRANSFER) and the action (CONTINUE PROCESSING or CANCEL PROCESSING WITH ERROR). After we have defined this rule, we can now go to the transfer object and add this rule to the pay grade field.

4.2.4 PickLists

A *PickList* is a list of input values that a user must choose from when entering data, usually accessed as a dropdown list of values. These are very similar to the F4 Help selection menus found in the SAP system. Once created, PickLists like the one shown in Figure 4.3 can be assigned to fields in Metadata Objects for input selection. This reduces data errors in fields that are using standard entries.

You can modify PickLists assigned to standard SuccessFactors objects to add new values or change existing values.

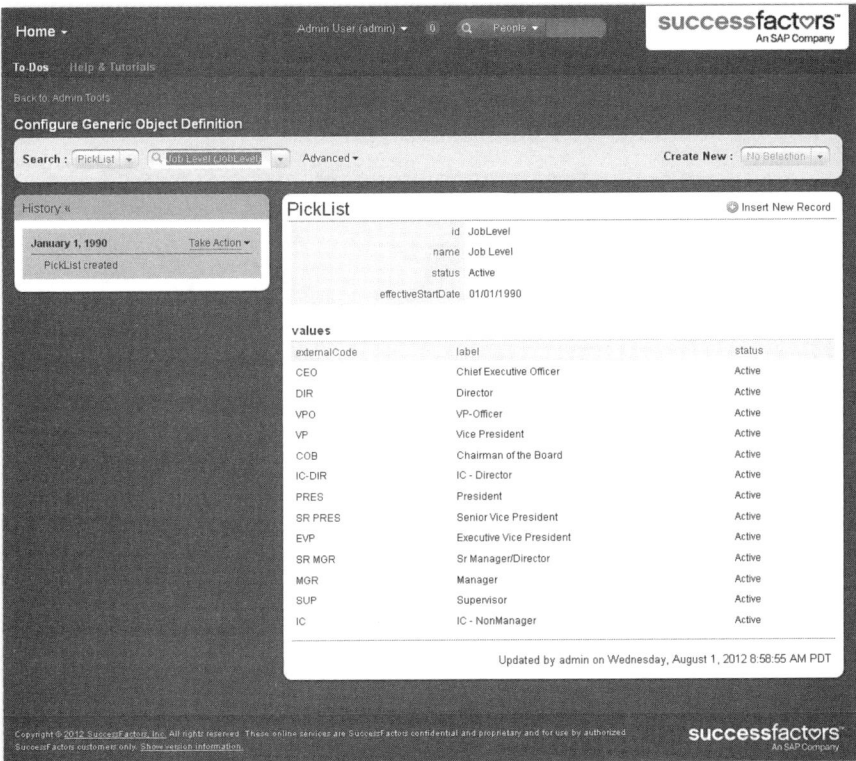

Figure 4.3 The Job Level PickList in the Metadata Framework

4.2.5 Configuration Options

The options for configuring the MDF are found in OneAdmin under COMPANY SETTINGS and EMPLOYEE FILES. In the old Admin Tools they can be found under the GENERIC OBJECTS heading. Eight options are available:

4 | Technical Considerations

- CONFIGURE GENERIC OBJECT DEFINITION
- MANAGE GENERIC OBJECTS
- MANAGE RULE OBJECTS
- MANAGE POSITION OBJECTS
- MANAGE TIME OFF STRUCTURES
- MANAGE TIME OFF CALENDARS
- MANAGE CONFIG UI
- GENERIC OBJECTS IMPORT/EXPORT

New Metadata Objects are created or modified in the CONFIGURE GENERIC OBJECT DEFINITION screen, which is shown in Figure 4.4. In this screen, a user can create and amend existing Metadata Objects and PickLists.

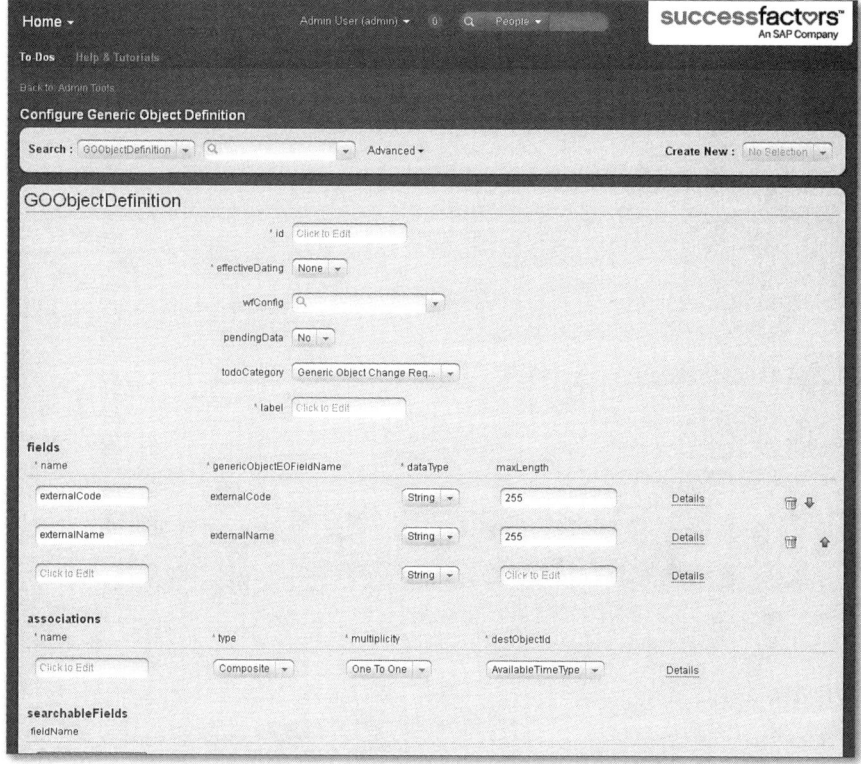

Figure 4.4 Creating a New Metadata Object in the Metadata Framework

In the MANAGE GENERIC OBJECTS option, a user can view and modify specific instances of Metadata Objects. For example, the user can search, view, and modify any position or work schedule objects in the SuccessFactors system. The MANAGE POSITION OBJECTS option leverages the exact same UI, except it is specifically for position objects. Figure 4.5 shows the VP, OPERATIONS position record in MANAGE GENERIC OBJECTS screen.

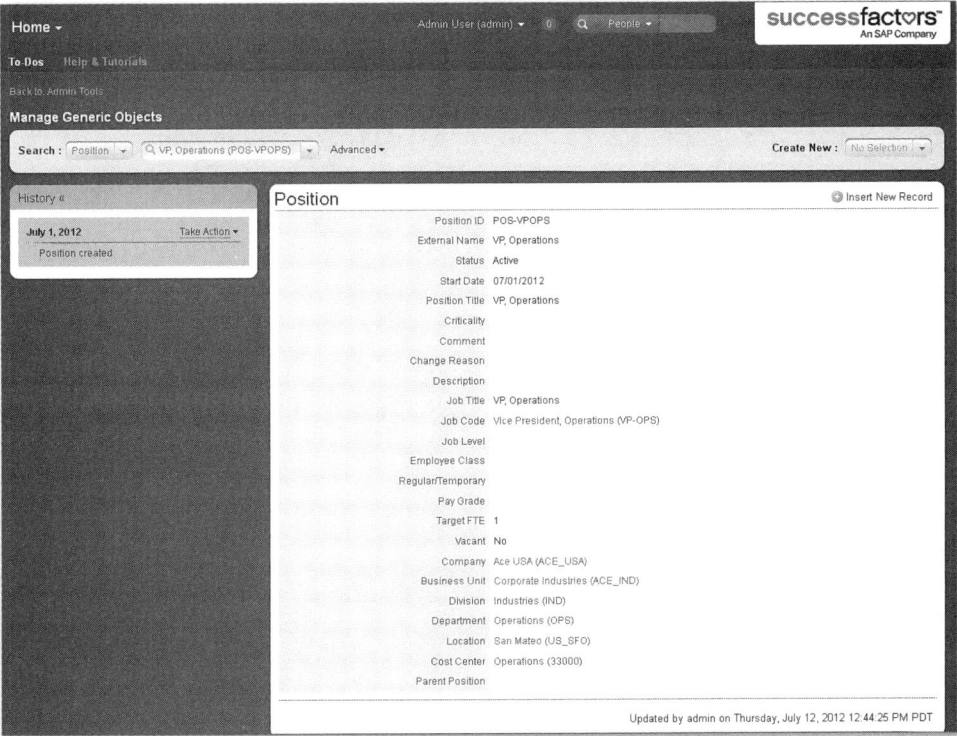

Figure 4.5 The VP of Operations Position in Manage Generic Objects

Through GENERIC OBJECTS IMPORT/EXPORT, it's possible to import a Microsoft Excel spreadsheet of objects for any of the Metadata Objects that exist within the system. You can also download a template file, either empty or with all data of existing objects for the selected Metadata Object.

The MANAGE RULE OBJECTS option provides an easy and intuitive UI for creating rules, as described in Section 4.2.3. The rule UI provided makes it simple to create rules using point-and-click actions to add statements and logic within these statements. Figure 4.6 shows the rule designer in action.

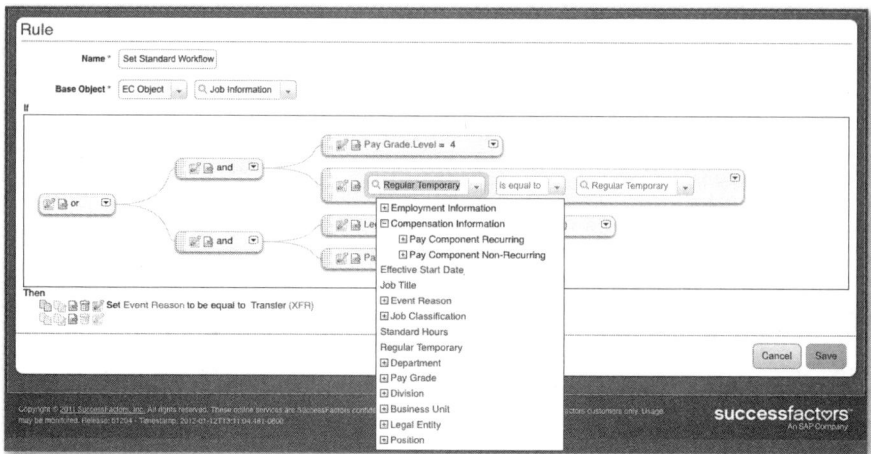

Figure 4.6 Creating a New Rule in the Metadata Framework

The MANAGE CONFIG UI designer is a what-you-see-is-what-you-get (WYSIWYG), drag-and-drop UI editor that lets users style the UI for a Metadata Object exactly as they require. New fields and groups of fields (called *field groups*) can be added, and different attributes and styles can be assigned to the field groups. Field groups can be assigned titles, have borders, and be collapsible. The default theme is still applicable and is not changed in the MANAGE CONFIG UI designer. Figure 4.7 shows a new UI being created in the MANAGE CONFIG UI designer.

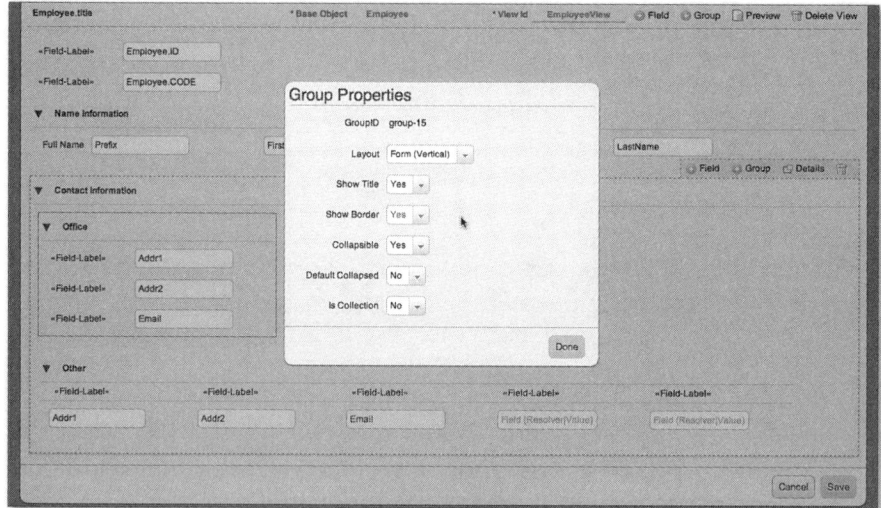

Figure 4.7 Creating a New Metadata Object UI

4.2.6 Workflows

Workflows are configured on the object level and require a rule in order to be operational. Three fields must be configured for a workflow:

- WORKFLOW ROUTING: The foundation objects workflow configuration that defines the steps in the workflow
- PENDING DATA: The value that defines whether the data is only available in the system if approved (Yes) or if the data is displayed immediately (No)
- TODO CATEGORY: The name of the To-Do category where the workflow notification should be shown for the receiver

In addition, the field wfConfig should be made visible, if hidden.

It is worth noting that only approver steps are supported in workflows added in the MDF; contributor steps are not supported. In addition, dynamic roles are not supported in workflow steps and the only actions supported are approve, decline, withdraw request, and comment.

4.2.7 Hooks

Hooks are points or situations in which a rule can be triggered. They are configured at object level or field level.

At the object level, rules can be added by selecting DETAILS under the RULES heading. A pop-up will display four sections with dropdowns from which to select one or more rule. Please note that multiple rules can be added for each type of hook, such as the following:

- initializeRules: These rules are triggered in the initialization phase after the object is created and can be used to provide default values for fields.
- validateRules: These rules are used for validation.
- saveRules: These rules are triggered when the object is being saved and can be used for activities such as ensuring that related fields are populated, etc.
- deleteRules: These rules will be triggered on deletion of the object and can be used to delete the entire object hierarchy (e.g., children of the related parent object).

Field Level

You can add rules at the field level by selecting DETAILS next to the field. A pop-up will display the details of the object. Under the RULE REFERENCES heading, a rule can be selected from the dropdown box or the ADD RULE icon can be selected to create a new rule. Multiple rules can be selected for each field. The rules are triggered for "On Change" events and can be used for validation or propagating values to other fields.

4.2.8 Limitations

Despite all of the benefits of the MDF, there are naturally a few limitations. Although the MDF functionality exists across the BizX suite, some applications (such as SuccessFactors Performance & Goals, Learning, and Recruiting Execution) do not yet make full use of it. Some other modules (such as SuccessFactors Compensation) are not built on the MDF, although the integration module that integrates SuccessFactors' solutions will call the MDF. Future releases will increasingly leverage the MDF as SuccessFactors builds out this functionality across the BizX suite.

Another limitation is that customers cannot change what has already been delivered, although sometimes objects created in the MDF can override things such as rules. Predelivered functionality in SuccessFactors can be disabled through OneAdmin, but because this core functionality may be updated in a future release, it can't be removed or changed. This ensures that the SuccessFactors system remains stable during operation, upgrades, and introduction of new functionality.

4.2.9 Summary

The MDF is a powerful, flexible, and safe mechanism for customers and consultants to extend the SuccessFactors system and introduce custom objects and data. It provides an easy-to-use interface for customers to create and maintain Metadata Objects that are stable and unaffected by upgrades or introduction of the quarterly releases. Rules are an effective way to ensure that customer-specific business logic and validations can be used throughout the SuccessFactors system and can be modeled simply and easily.

The MDF reduces a large proportion of the technical aspects required to create new objects in an HR system and puts control in the hands of business users and system administrators. The possibility to extend the SuccessFactors system is no longer reliant on technical consultants or deep knowledge of complex structures or procedures; now customers can benefit from a system that is flexible and can be changed at will to meet the ever-changing demands of the business.

4.3 Security

SuccessFactors takes security very seriously. Because its systems store sensitive HR data from multiple customers, every aspect of technology used is thoroughly tested and includes many security standards to ensure proper security.

4.3.1 Authentication Security

SuccessFactors has many different levels of security on all layers. It supports the Secure Socket Layer (SSL) or Transport Security Layer (TLS) encryption languages that are leveraged by standard web providers, in addition to the following authentication methods:

- **Internal authentication**
  Using an internal repository of user profiles, this authentication occurs on the SuccessFactors side when customers choose not to integrate their own identity management system.

- **Federated authentication (SSO)**
  SSO implementation requires users to first be authenticated through their own authorization systems (LDAP) using tokens (MD5, SHA-1, HMAC encryption, DES, 3DES) or Security Assertion Markup Languages (SAML 1.1, 2.0). The user will then be redirected to the SuccessFactors instance using HTTPS.

- **SSO without federation**
  This method uses a public encryption key that is sent to the customer's authentication server from SuccessFactors. By using this key, users can connect to SuccessFactors by using a preestablished authentication method.

- **Separate security modules**
  Because authorization is usually deeply integrated in source code in standard solutions, SuccessFactors uses a separate authorization and authentication module than that of the data and functions. This allows for future growth of security throughout the application as needed. This security module logs every action of the user and validates each request to prevent cross-site scripting (XSS) attacks.

▶ **Password protection**
Strong passwords with regular password changes are required by SuccessFactors. Administrators can also set custom rules for passwords that users must abide by.

4.3.2 Layer Security

The SuccessFactors environment is made up of multiple layers of security. The security layers and the accompanying encryption and technology are shown in Figure 4.8.

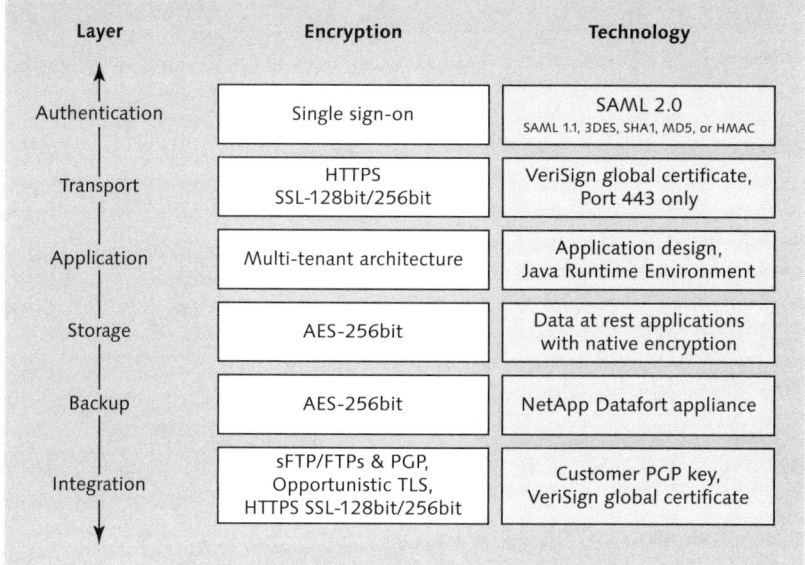

Figure 4.8 The Security Layers of SuccessFactors Applications

The data center itself also conforms to many security standards:

- EU 95/46 EC
- PCI-DSS
- ISO 27002
- BS7799
- ASIO-4

- FIPS Moderate
- BS10012
- SSAE-16/SOC2

Because of these safeguards, customers' information is encrypted and protected, so even if the data is stolen, it will be inaccessible and unusable.

Now that you understand how the data and layers are secured, let's explore security from another point of view. As mentioned before, security is not based on individual users but rather on their role within the organization. The next section explores how fields on the screen are regulated by the use of roles.

4.3.3 Role-Based Permissions

The SuccessFactors BizX suite empowers the user with Role-Based Permissions (RBP) management. Also known as the RBP framework, it allows the user to have as many roles in the system as the company requires while granting each role a different level of permission granularity. RBPs allow all of the security to be managed at all levels, including function, transaction, field, and data levels. Unlike in other human capital management systems, RBPs rely on placing security around the context of a user's responsibility rather than around the user. This is considered a best practice by most large enterprise systems.

4.4 OneAdmin

Administrators within SuccessFactors have many powerful tools at their fingertips, including those that enable administration of features such as employee and organizational data, forms used in various BizX suite solutions, and notification emails. In this section, we'll explore the OneAdmin tool (previously known as Admin Tools) and see how it supports easy configuration of the SuccessFactors instance.

When you log in to your SuccessFactors instance as an administrator, click your user name and then select ADMIN TOOLS from the menu to access OneAdmin. (If configured, it can also be accessed from a tile on the home page.) Here, many useful administration tools are available to enable an administrator to set up various features, functions, objects, and data imports. Figure 4.9 shows the new OneAdmin home page.

> **Note**
>
> You can also switch back to the old Admin Tools, which is a text-based list of the options available in OneAdmin.

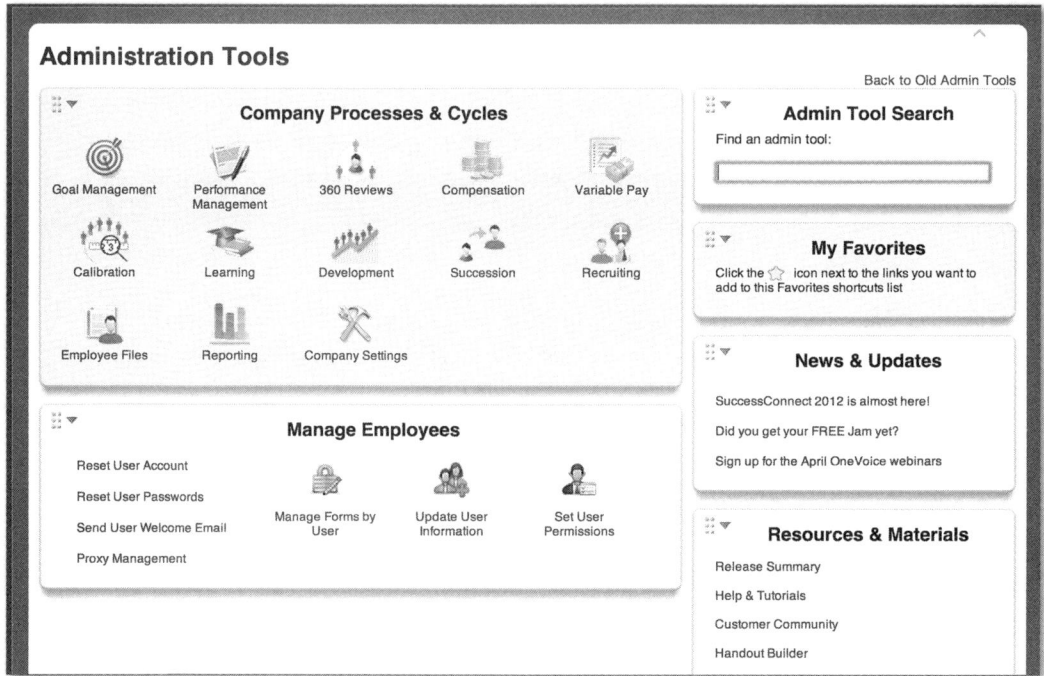

Figure 4.9 OneAdmin Home Page

The icons on the screen in Figure 4.9 display some of the standard functions that are available for those particular modules (e.g., GOAL MANAGEMENT, PERFORMANCE MANAGEMENT, and 360 REVIEWS). When you choose an icon, a dynamic menu appears on the screen to show its functions. Figure 4.10 shows an example of the SuccessFactors Recruiting Execution module dynamic menu.

Here, you can see many useful functions of the Recruiting Management module of the SuccessFactors Recruiting Execution solution. The administrator can easily navigate to these key functions all within the same page. Notice that many functions are available, which can be overwhelming for new users who are not familiar with the system.

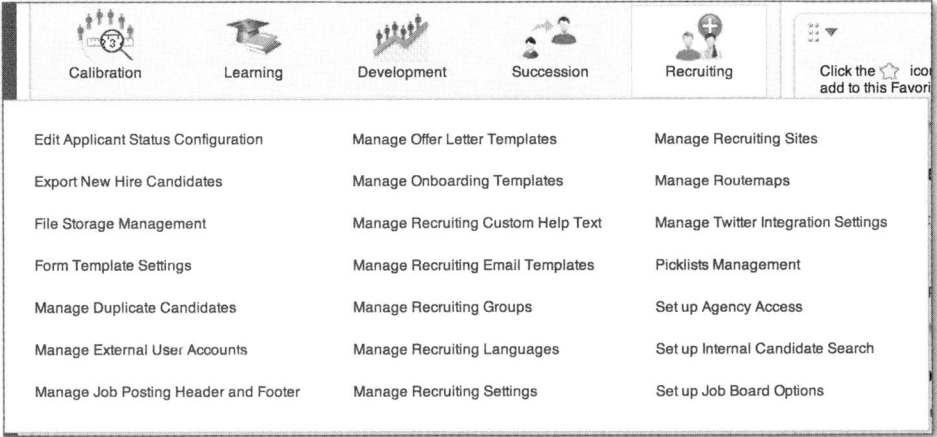

Figure 4.10 Choosing the Recruiting Icon in OneAdmin

Thankfully, SuccessFactors comes with a live search function right on the OneAdmin home page (see Figure 4.11). This useful function displays the search results as you type, making navigation within the OneAdmin home page very easy.

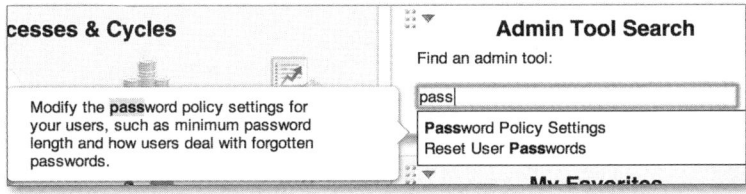

Figure 4.11 Live Search Function in OneAdmin

Now that you're familiar with the home page and how to navigate, let's explore a few of the user administration tools. Let's first discuss how to update user information.

If you choose the UPDATE USER INFORMATION icon shown in the bottom left of Figure 4.12, the system presents you with some of the tools that can be used to maintain user data.

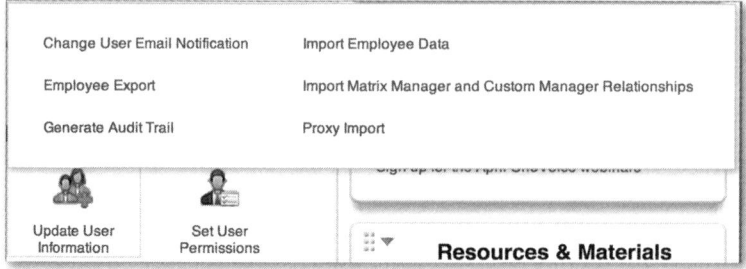

Figure 4.12 Update User Information Icon Tools

In this menu, an administrator is able to upload users using the IMPORT EMPLOYEE DATA function. This important function allows an administrator to upload a spreadsheet containing all of the users, user names, roles, and hierarchy. Figure 4.13 shows the IMPORT EMPLOYEE DATA screen and some of the useful options that administrators can use to populate users in the system.

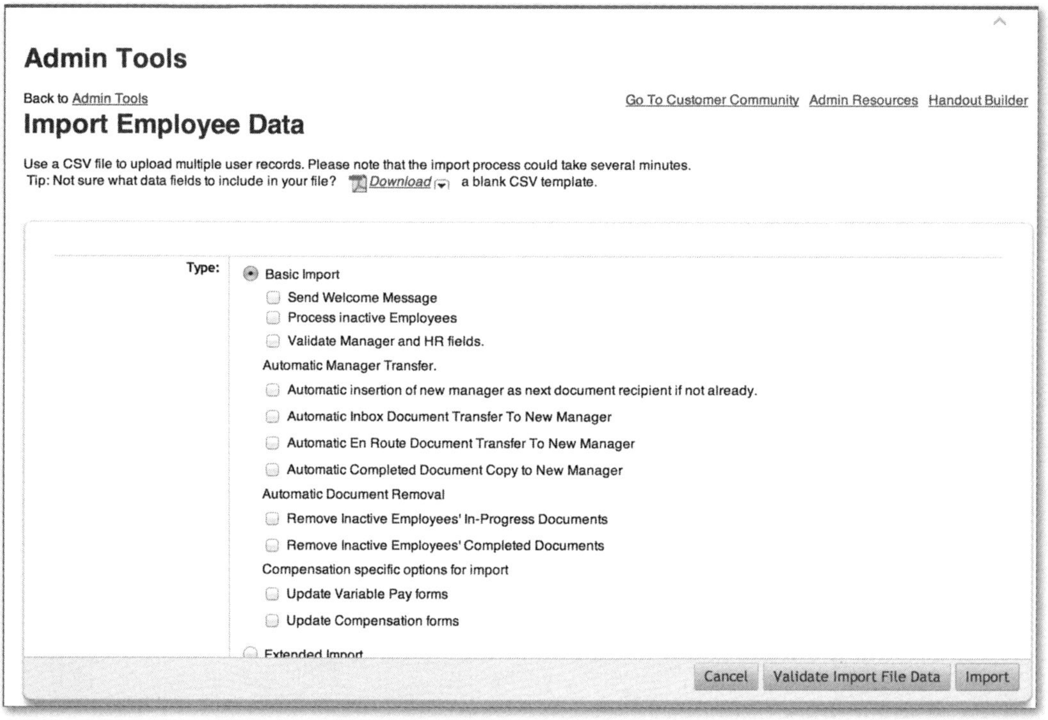

Figure 4.13 Import Employee Data

Here, administrators can easily import users into the system by downloading a CSV template directly from this page. Also within the user administration tools is the ability to manage proxy users. *Proxy users* enable users to act as delegates for other users—for example, to access another user's data and functions. This, of course, needs to be carefully maintained because you are viewing sensitive data that belongs to others.

Proxy users can be maintained via the PROXY MANAGEMENT option in the MANAGE EMPLOYEES section of the OneAdmin home page. The PROXY MANAGEMENT screen, which is shown in Figure 4.14, has many different options that allow careful control over all modules within SuccessFactors.

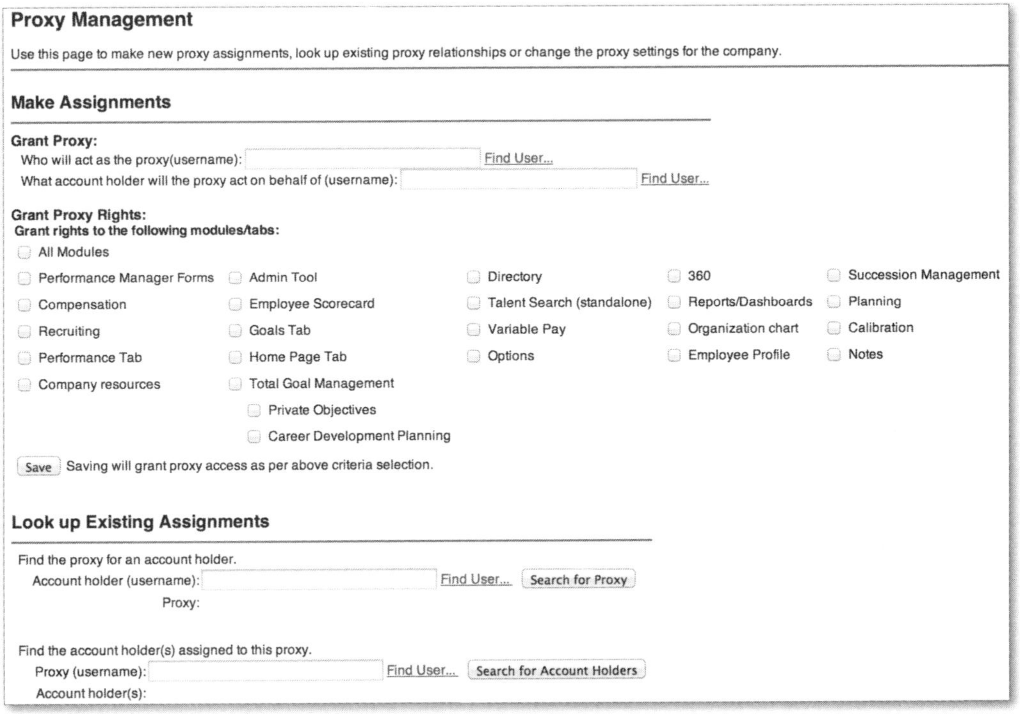

Figure 4.14 Proxy Management Screen

Another useful user administration tool is the ability to manage users' access and passwords. If a user has attempted too many failed password attempts, for example, there is an easy way to unlock the user so the user can enter the system again. Figure 4.15 shows the RESETTING USER ACCOUNTS tool, which allows an administrator to easily reset a user's account and information.

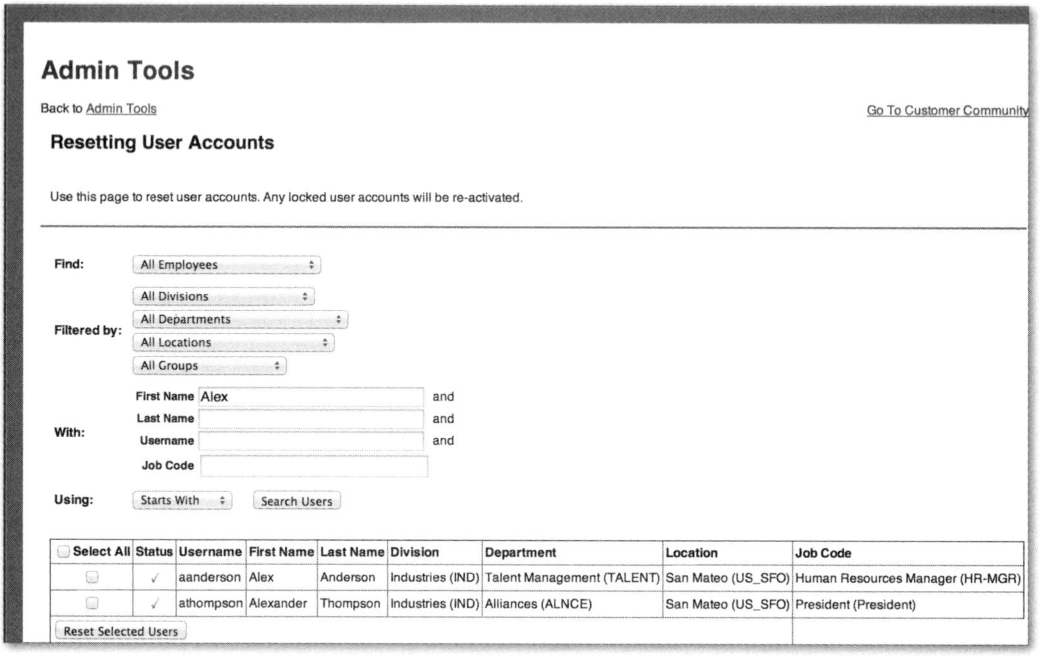

4 | Technical Considerations

Figure 4.15 Resetting User Accounts Administrator Tool

Along the same lines with user administration, administrators need to be able to set new passwords, reset passwords, and set password rules for users. Setting and resetting passwords can be done by all users, not just administrators. Figure 4.16 shows the PASSWORD RESET option for all users.

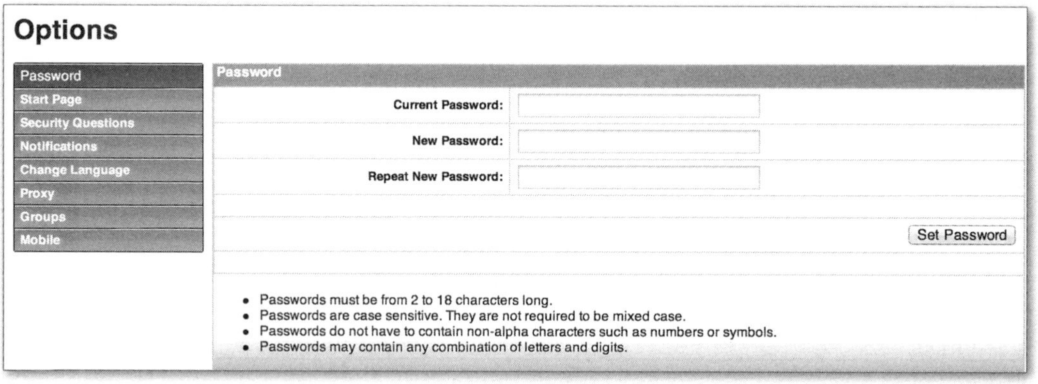

Figure 4.16 Password Reset

Beyond user administration, another important function that is used by all modules within SuccessFactors is the *email notification*. Notifications are a powerful way to communicate system information to users. By using these administrator tools, an administrator can easily and efficiently change a notification to fit into an organization. Email notifications can easily be customized by administrators within OneAdmin. Figure 4.17 shows a sample list of the EMAIL NOTIFICATIONS TEMPLATES that can be activated and customized.

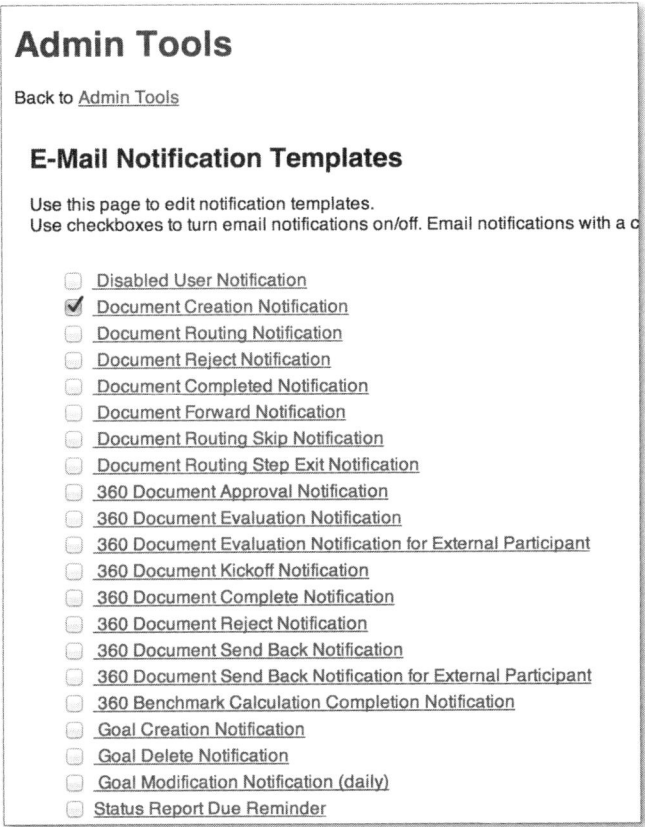

Figure 4.17 Sample List of Notification Activation

After activating email notifications, the actual notification can be customized to change the text on the screen or add a logo. Each module has its own notifications that can be customized. Figure 4.18 shows the notification customization.

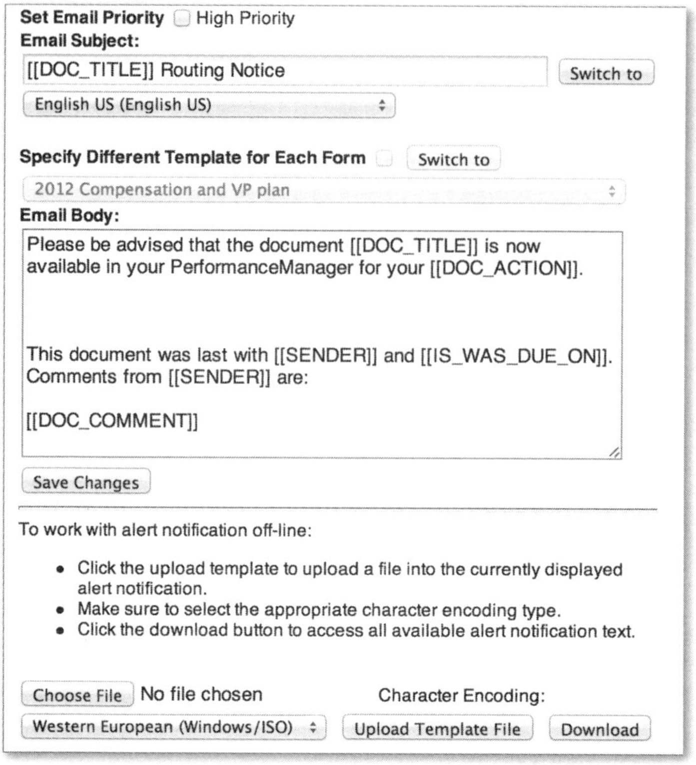

Figure 4.18 Notification Customization

4.5 Extending SuccessFactors with Custom Applications

With SAP HANA Cloud Platform and the SAP HANA Cloud Portal, a Platform-as-a-Service (PaaS), it is possible to create custom applications to embed within Success-Factors BizX suite solutions. At the time of writing, this is focused on adding new capabilities to SuccessFactors Employee Central.

SAP HANA Cloud Platform is a cloud-based platform for developers to create scalable applications that can leverage the speed, power, and scale of SAP HANA and can integrate into cloud-based applications such as SuccessFactors or applications within SAP's other cloud pillars (Money, Customers, and Suppliers). It also leverages the MDF and integrates with mobile and SAP Jam. One of the key platform services is the SAP HANA Cloud Portal, which enables the quick creation of mobile-ready, highly brandable sites without coding. Looking at the combination of sites and applications, the SAP HANA Cloud Portal "Extensions" to Employee Central combine a SaaS solution with a PaaS development platform.

Applications built for SuccessFactors Employee Central integrate with it using SSO and leverage the SuccessFactors API to fetch employee details. These applications also integrate with home screen (so they can be shown as tiles) and with the theme and navigation of SuccessFactors BizX. Figure 4.19 shows the HR Support application that has been created on the SAP HANA Cloud Platform and is integrated into the SuccessFactors BizX suite.

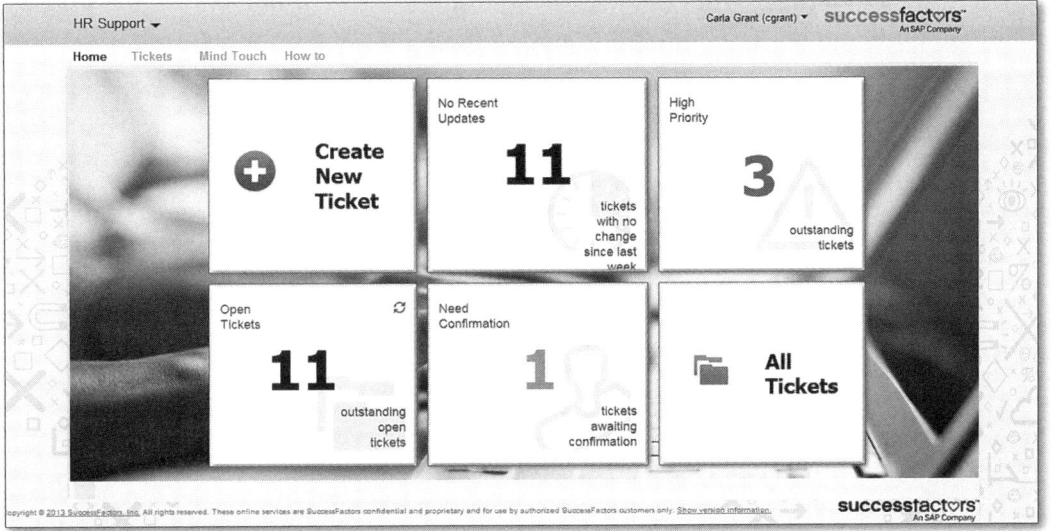

Figure 4.19 HR Support Application in SuccessFactors

4.6 Summary

We started this chapter with the technical architecture of SuccessFactors and the various layers of the architecture. Because this is a cloud solution, the architecture must be light, scalable, and powerful. SuccessFactors delivers this by using a dynamic backend technology, coupled with a JavaScript frontend that creates a very powerful architecture.

We also discussed the MDF — a growing configuration platform in SuccessFactors for creating data objects and customizing flow logic. The Rules Engine is a future-proof way to create your own business and flow logic, as well as data validations, without worrying about future releases affecting the changes.

Security is of the utmost importance to SuccessFactors. Therefore, every layer of technology within SuccessFactors contains its own strong security and is independently penetration-tested to ensure that the data, code, and connections are secured every step of the way.

Within SuccessFactors, permissions are based on the role of the user logged in. This unique approach allows for an intuitive and efficient way to manage what is displayed on the screen. The template configurations contain the ability to maintain permissions for buttons, sections, actions, and fields in the system.

Administrators within the SuccessFactors system have a home page containing many useful functions that can be searched upon, categorized, and easily displayed right within the home page. These functions include user administration, password, and notification functions.

Now that you understand some of the technology and functions that make SuccessFactors run, let's explore what will be displayed to most of the users that access the system. SuccessFactors has a fantastic UI that is aesthetically pleasing and consistent throughout its modules. Chapter 5 will explore some of these UI features.

SuccessFactors is a highly intuitive, easy-to-use solution that provides an attractive user interface and engaging user experience. You should be able to use any of the solutions within the SuccessFactors suite with minimal training or experience using other enterprise software applications.

5 Using SuccessFactors

The SuccessFactors user interface (UI) has been designed to provide an engaging and enriching user experience (UX) for the end user. The simple design provides powerful benefits to employees and managers who have minimal training or exposure to SAP or SuccessFactors.

When designing UIs for SuccessFactors BizX solutions, SuccessFactors considered a number of design principles:

- **The SMART (Social, Mobile, Analytical, Rich, and Toy-like) principles**
  These tenets are behind everything that SuccessFactors does, providing a foundation for achieving the company's design goals.

- **Extensibility**
  This design principle takes into account the future configuration of the system through adding, extending, or enhancing functionality.

- **Business execution strategy**
  When new functionality is created, SuccessFactors designers deeply consider how the software will help the business execute better and how it can help individual employees succeed better at their jobs.

In this chapter, we'll look at the key aspects of the UI and navigation in SuccessFactors. We'll show you the various features that enable seamless access to functionality across the products in the BizX suite and empower you to perform people processes and organizational functions with improved efficiency and accuracy, resulting in an engaged and productive workforce.

5.1 User Interface and Navigation

This section covers the benefits that you can derive from the intuitive and easy-to-use UI and the seamless navigation abilities provided in the BizX suite. Although the UI is largely unified, some modules have their own specific navigation options based on the unique functionality. The user-friendly UI empowers employees, managers, and system administrators to execute their job functions smoothly and enhance productivity by incorporating the key areas of their job function into an intelligent system design.

Let's start by examining the factors that make the UI and navigation intuitive and easy to use.

5.1.1 Modular UI Provides Ready-to-Use System

The BizX suite's agility addresses the key productivity areas for your job functions whether you are an individual contributor, a manager, or a system administrator. For example, the Admin Alerts tile provides ready-to-use information to system administrators for areas that need their attention. This design gives organizations a platform to provide a unified experience to their users. The products have been intelligently assembled so that the functionality can be leveraged to access common data and processes (e.g., Employee Profile data, Performance & Goals information, and Workforce Analytics).

The organic structure of the modular BizX suite enables organizations to utilize and license according to their needs, provide a user-specific experience to their employees at all levels, lower their annual maintenance and support budgets, and enhance employee productivity with a UI that is high on both aesthetics and functionality.

5.1.2 Ease of Use Drives Adoption

Navigation across screens in SuccessFactors is designed to be intuitive and require minimal training for end users. For example, the HOME page consists of a highly adaptable set of tiles, as shown in Figure 5.1; each tile reflects an area of interest to the user. For example, a manager would see team member photographs in a MY TEAM tile, whereas an HR administrator would see a tile highlighting exceptions that require attention.

User Interface and Navigation | **5.1**

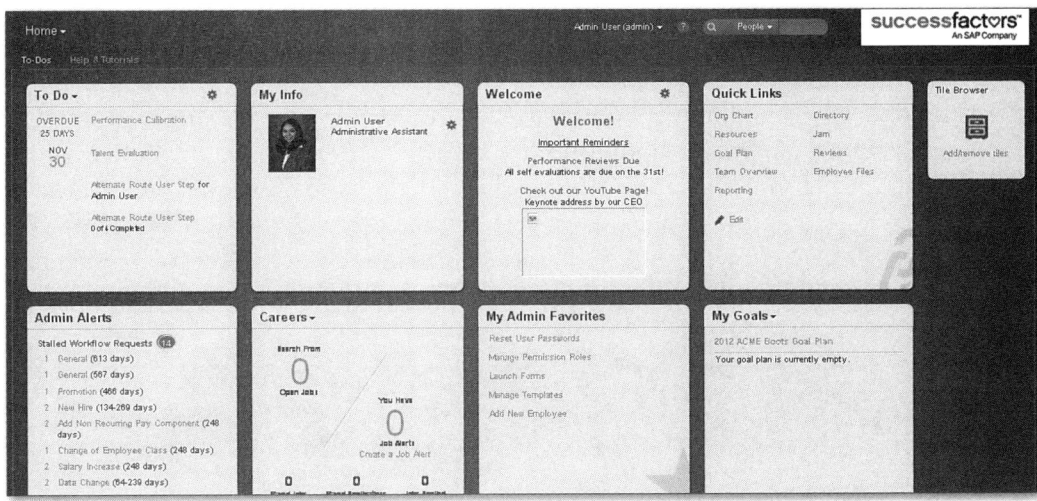

Figure 5.1 SuccessFactors Home Page Showing Tiles

Let's zoom into a few of the tiles present on the HOME page. Figure 5.2 shows the CAREERS tile, which allows any employees to see what other open jobs in the company are currently available to them. They can access the INTERNAL CAREERS tab, search for jobs, track past applications, and create job alerts.

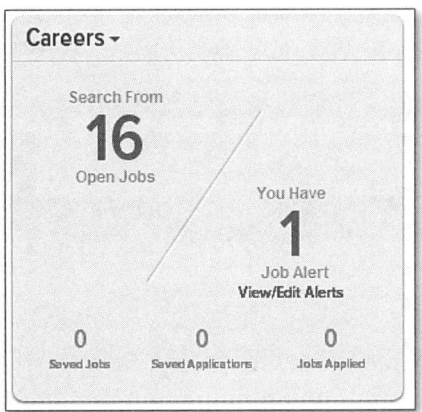

Figure 5.2 Careers Tile on the Home Page

MY ADMIN FAVORITES, typically seen by business partners or administrative users, allows users to access shortcuts to the frequently used administration operations.

Having these links on the HOME page gives instant one-click access, instead of requiring that the user drill through the application to access the operation.

For example, an administrator would use the ADD NEW EMPLOYEE operation to hire employees. This operation resides in the OneAdmin (the old Admin Tools) section of the application and requires a few clicks before you can access it. Figure 5.3 displays the ADD NEW EMPLOYEE link on the user's MY ADMIN FAVORITES tile. The user can click on this link and go directly to the ADD NEW EMPLOYEE operation in the application. This saves time and enhances user experience and productivity.

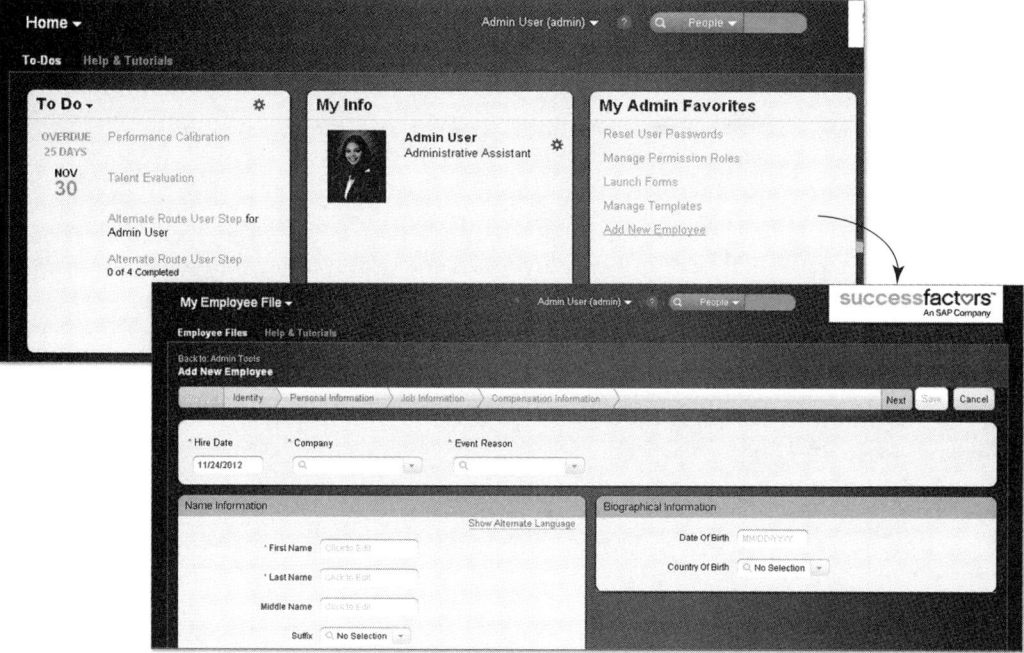

Figure 5.3 Access Add New Employee via My Admin Favorites on the Home Page

When administrators need to perform administration activities, they can navigate to OneAdmin—the home base of administrative functions. Here, large icons divide the extensive administrative functions by area. To add a new employee, the administrator needs to follow the path, ADMIN TOOLS • UPDATE USER INFORMATION • ADD NEW EMPLOYEE to access the ADD NEW EMPLOYEE feature. Figure 5.4 and Figure 5.5 show how to access ADD NEW EMPLOYEE via ADMIN TOOLS.

User Interface and Navigation | **5.1**

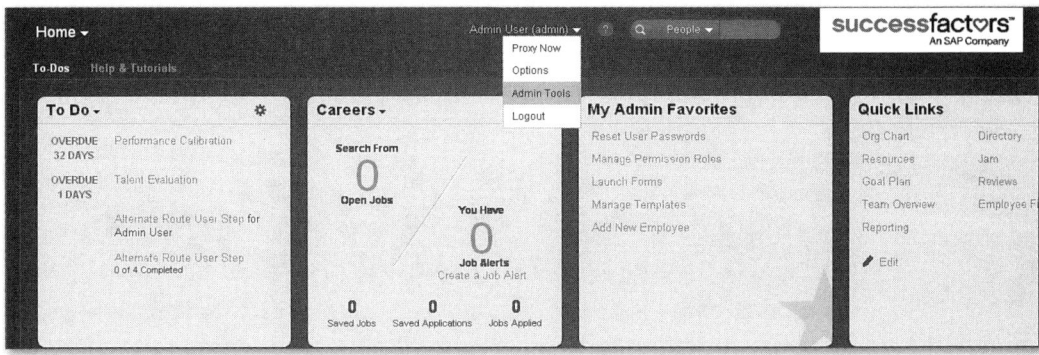

Figure 5.4 Go to Admin Tools from the Home Page

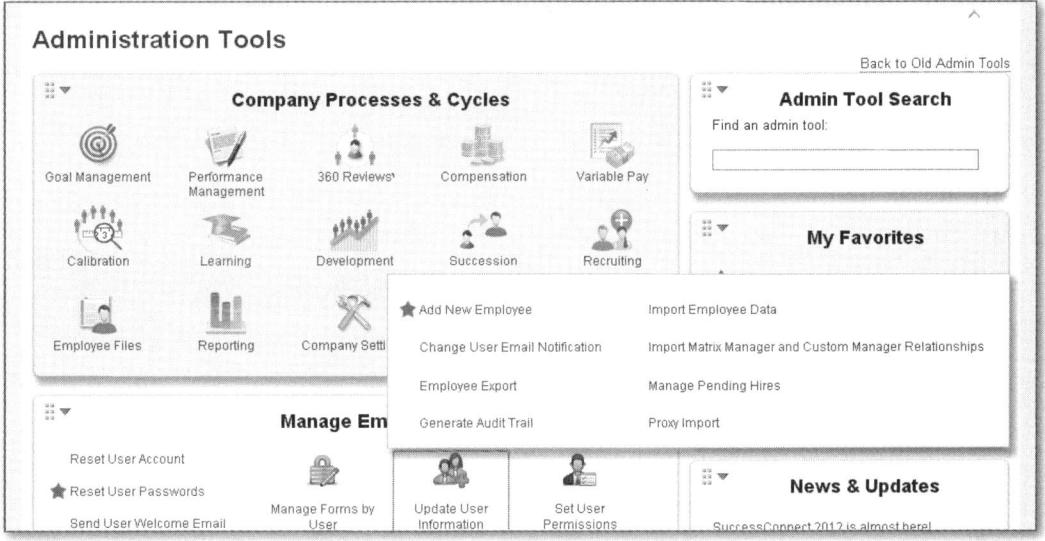

Figure 5.5 Access Add New Employee via Admin Tools

An important navigation feature of the SuccessFactors UI is the module navigation menu in the top-left corner. This module navigation menu lets the user navigate to any section in the BizX suite from anywhere else. Based on the set of SuccessFactors solutions that have been implemented by the customer, users can choose any of the applications from the menu. For example, you can go to the Succession module by simply clicking on the module navigation menu and selecting that module name.

149

In Figure 5.6, the user is in the ADD NEW EMPLOYEE section of the application; using the module picker, the user can navigate from the ADD NEW EMPLOYEE section to the HOME page or to any other part of the application.

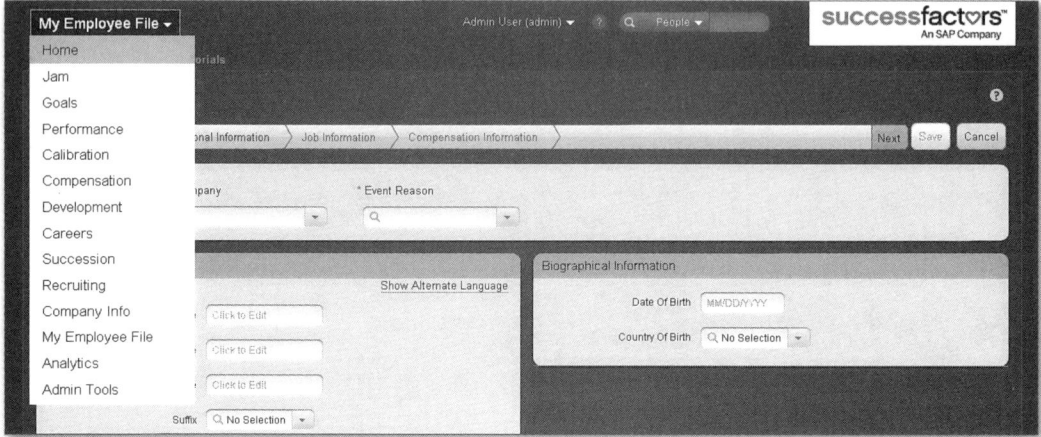

Figure 5.6 Module Navigation Menu

As the name suggests, the ADD OR REMOVE TILES link allows users to add or remove tiles on their HOME page. Every tile has to be individually selected to either add it to or remove it from the HOME page.

Users can also move the tiles around on the HOME page based on their personal preferences.

5.1.3 Cross-Functional Relevance

The BizX suite is built to conform to the needs of organizations of various sizes that operate in a wide array of industries and territories. Unlike traditional software applications that target one level of user in an organization, this solution is designed to adapt to the different needs of various types of users, from C-level executives, to HR business partners, to line managers, and to entry-level employees.

Now that we've covered the basic UI and navigation principles offered in the BizX suite, let's discuss the general features and functionality of the BizX suite.

5.2   Tiles

In this section, we'll look at some of the key tiles on the HOME page. These tiles offer quick access to the most frequently used areas of the application and significantly enhance the user experience. They allow users and administrators to design their own HOME page based on job functions and form the core of bringing critical functions and information to users at the entry point of the BizX suite.

> **Note**
>
> Functionality specific to respective modules such as Employee Central, Learning, and Recruiting Execution will be covered in detail in later chapters. At the end of this section, you should feel comfortable with tiles and be equipped to explore more advanced functionality covered in upcoming chapters.

Now let's examine the HOME page tiles discussed earlier in this chapter in more detail. The HOME page tiles link to the most frequently visited places. Recall that they also provide a unique experience to every user as the user can add or remove tiles from the HOME page and also change their placement on the HOME page. Customers can create custom tiles on the HOME page and also manage RBP groups and permission roles for these tiles. For example, a customer wants only the C-suite of executives to have access to information from a shareholder annual review meeting. Now organizations have more opportunities to brand the HOME page and communicate business processes and information exclusively to different groups of the organization—in this case C-level executives. Let's look at examples of tiles on the HOME page.

5.2.1   Welcome Tile

The WELCOME tile, which is shown in Figure 5.7, is the place for the company—usually the HR department—to promote key information to the workforce. It can be used to communicate an important initiative being undertaken by the company, important reminders, or an advertisement for a company event. The WELCOME tile is created as a custom tile and can be formatted according to the customer's needs.

The WELCOME tile is a custom tile created by customers according to their needs. Like most tiles, it can be expanded or shrunk depending on how much space the user would like the tile to occupy on the HOME page.

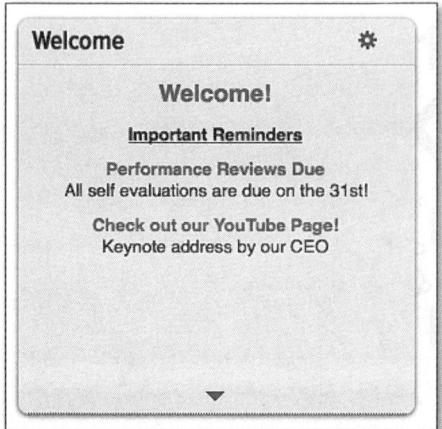

Figure 5.7 Welcome Tile

5.2.2 My Info Tile

This tile is the main access point for everything directly pertaining to the *logged in* user. It shows the badges granted to the employee by colleagues and available time off balances. Figure 5.8 shows an example of the MY INFO tile for the employee Carla Grant, whose position and badges are also shown. Additional MY INFO LINKS can be accessed by clicking on the gear icon to get further information about the *logged in* user.

Figure 5.8 My Info Tile

Figure 5.9 shows an example of the links available when the user clicks the MY INFO LINKS. The user can click any of these links to access his information.

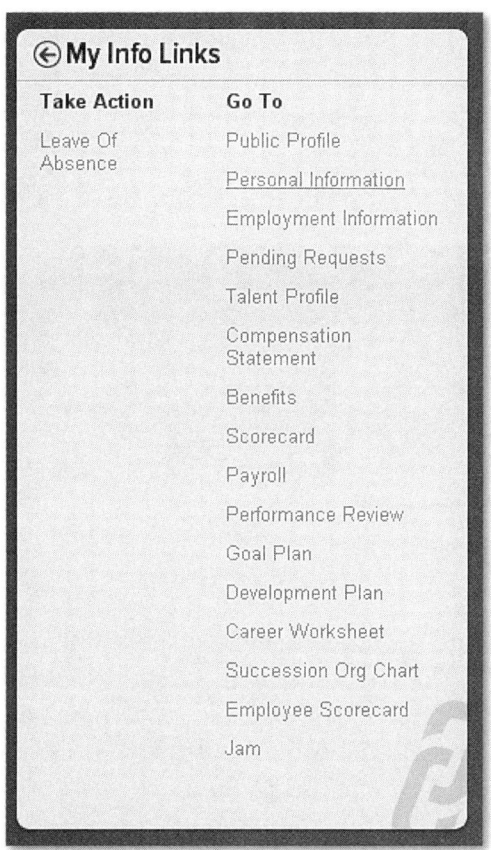

Figure 5.9 My Info Links

If you click on the PERSONAL INFORMATION link from MY INFO LINKS in Figure 5.9, you are taken to the PERSONAL INFORMATION page shown in Figure 5.10. From here, the logged in user can change information such as address or emergency contacts.

5 | Using SuccessFactors

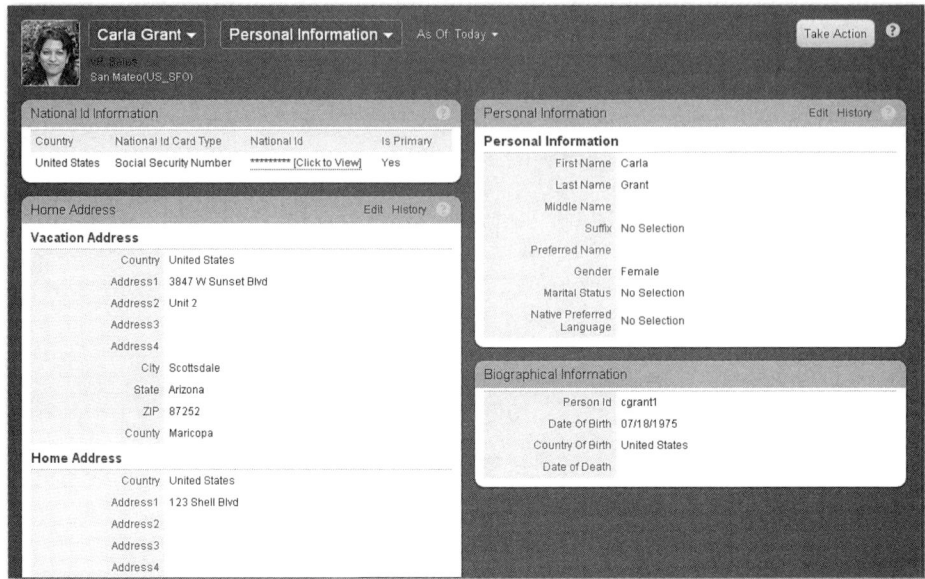

Figure 5.10 Go to the Personal Information Page from My Info Links

5.2.3 To-Do Tile

The To-Do tile hosts a list of all action items, upcoming activities, and completed items across the entire suite, in one place. The To-Do tile is an excellent tool for system administrators and managers to receive reminders from the application. You can sort tasks by date (tasks in descending order of days overdue) or type (tasks of one type or category; e.g., all employee change requests together).

It also allows the user to filter activities by the following criteria:

- Active
- Active and Upcoming

5.2.4 My Team Tile

The My Team tile is visible only to managers. It lets them instantly access their direct reports and see the status of their tasks.

Figure 5.11 shows an example of the My Team tile for the logged in user, Ashley N. Brooks.

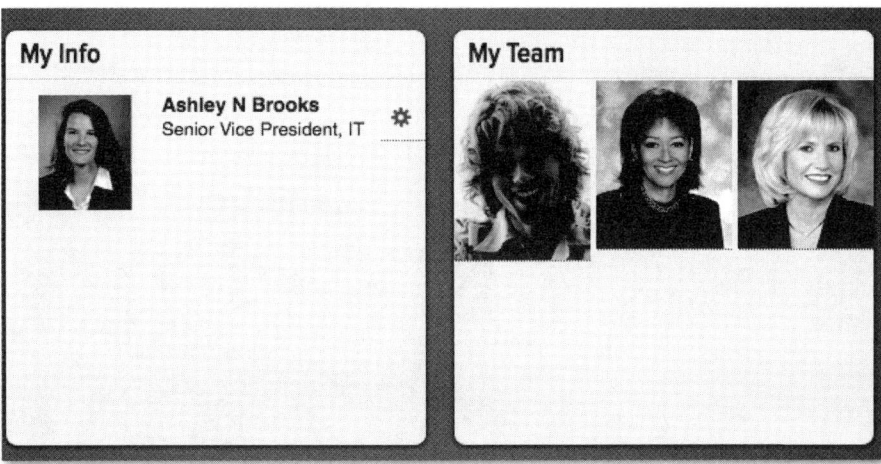

Figure 5.11 My Team Tile with Team Members in the BizX Suite

When the user clicks on any of the team members, the user can view issues or action items for that team member. Figure 5.12 shows the four overdue tasks associated with team member Richard Maxx.

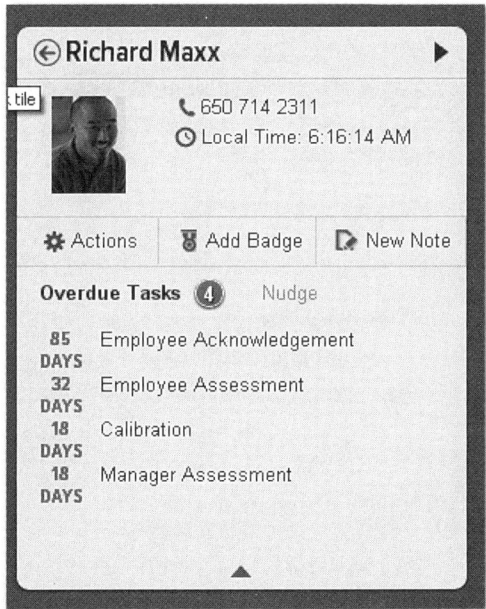

Figure 5.12 Team Member's Action Items

5.2.5 Quick Links Tile

The QUICK LINKS TILE shown in Figure 5.13 allows you to add shortcuts to frequently used pages and forms. You can edit the QUICK LINKS tile and add or remove links by selecting the checkbox for tiles in the AVAILABLE column to move them to the SELECTED column.

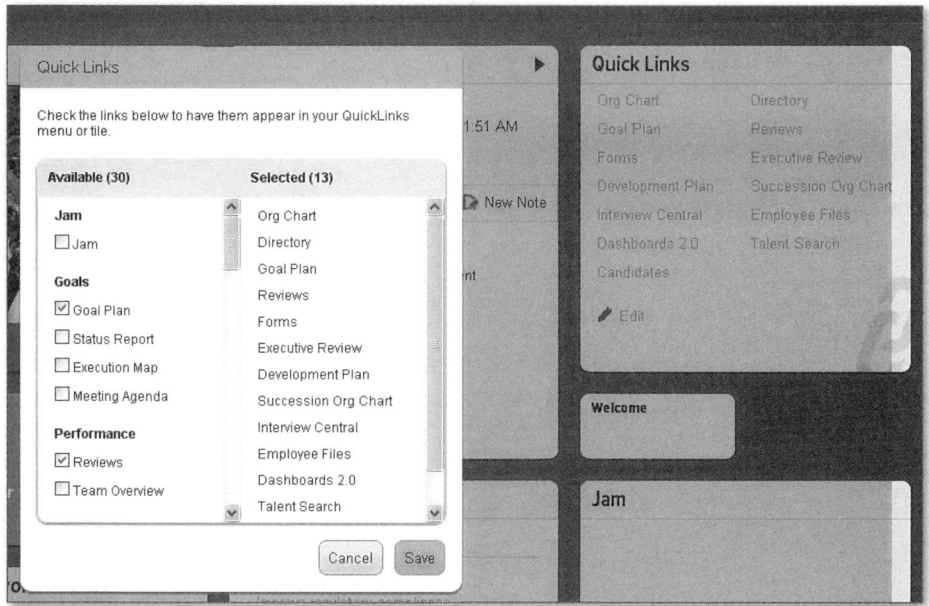

Figure 5.13 Edit Quick Links Tile

5.2.6 SAP Jam Tile

The tile devoted to the social collaboration solution SAP Jam gives the user a view of their SAP Jam feed. This allows the user to see what their colleagues are doing in SAP Jam. The tile lets the user see recent activity at a glance on the most recently visited groups. By simply hovering over the face of a group member, the user can see the activity of that person. It is even possible to instantly reply to a message, download a posted document, or navigate into an SAP Jam group.

5.2.7 My Admin Favorites Tile

The MY ADMIN FAVORITES tile gives administrators and HR business partners shortcuts to their most frequently used administrative tasks. To add a link to the ADMIN FAVORITES tile, the user can go to OneAdmin and click on the star next to a link.

Figure 5.14 shows that RESET USER PASSWORDS, MANAGE TEMPLATES, and MANAGE PERMISSION GROUPS have been added to the MY FAVORITES section within OneAdmin.

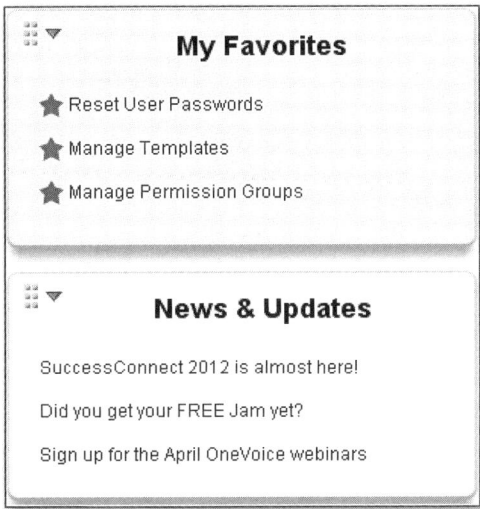

Figure 5.14 My Favorites in OneAdmin

You should now be comfortable with navigating the HOME page and general user navigation available in the application. We also touched on some activities that the user can perform from these tiles, such as viewing issues and action items related to a team member through the MY TEAM tile. Before we dive into the core modules in later chapters, let's examine some of the key features of the BizX suite that are not found in other HCM solutions.

5.3 Key Features

To derive maximum advantage from the later chapters that detail core functionality, we'll now cover the key features that empower users to interact across modules.

The integration of these key features is a classic example of how the BizX suite interlaces the key components of the solution to bring a well-rounded experience to the user.

5.3.1 General Navigation

The user menu located beside the username on the HOME page is a powerful section of the application. It provides access to those areas of the application that allow for a personalized experience of the application for the user. The following options are available:

- OPTIONS
  The user is sent to a page where he can do a number of activities such as change the language settings, change the password, set the start page at login, choose accessibility settings, and activate a mobile device. Users can also choose whether to receive email notifications from the system.
- PROXY
  The user menu also allows you to log in on behalf of another user if the administrator has assigned proxy rights to you on behalf of another user (e.g., administrative assistants can proxy on behalf of their managers).
- ADMIN TOOLS
  The user menu provides another gateway to OneAdmin.

The HELP AND TUTORIALS link sends the user to a page where standard content such as "show me" videos can be found to help users get familiar with the system.

5.3.2 Organizational Chart

The Org Chart is a central component of the Employee Central and Succession & Development modules. In Employee Central, the ORG CHART can be accessed by clicking on COMPANY INFO in the module navigation menu, and by selecting SUCCESSION in the navigation menu in Succession & Development module.

Figure 5.15 shows an example of the fictitious Carla Grant's direct reports in her ORG CHART.

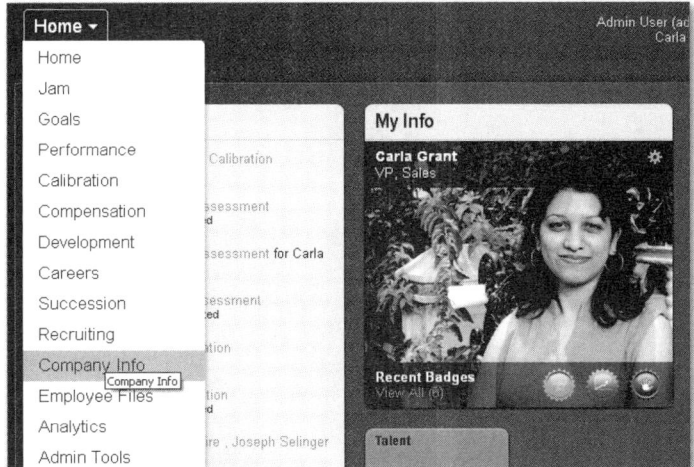
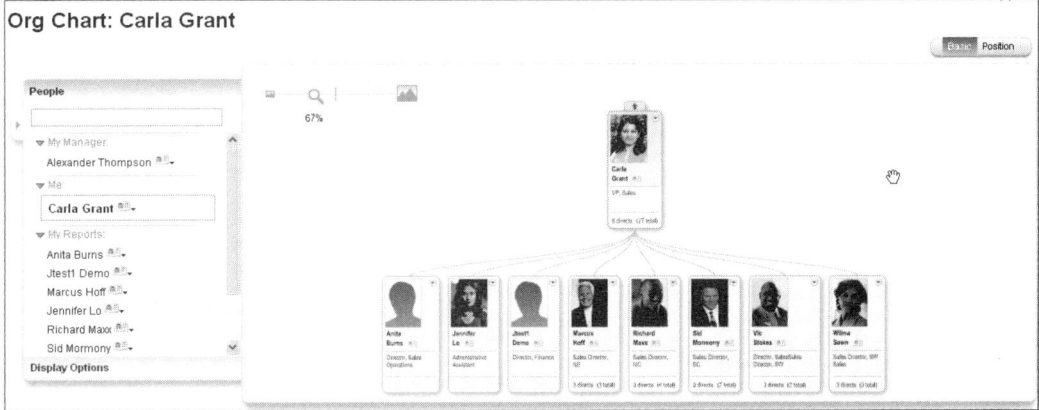

Figure 5.15 Company Info Shows the Logged In User's Org Chart

If one of Carla Grant's direct reports logs in to the system and goes to the COMPANY INFO page, the user will see the ORG CHART starting from his own position in the company. For example, Figure 5.16 shows Richard Maxx's ORG CHART; you can see on the left PEOPLE panel that he is one of Carla Grant's subordinates.

Clicking on another individual changes the perspective. That is, the logged-in user can always click on his manager's name and see the entire Org Chart from the team's perspective. The user can see the entire team that reports to the manager. You can control access to the Org Chart using RBP, which we cover in detail in Chapter 6.

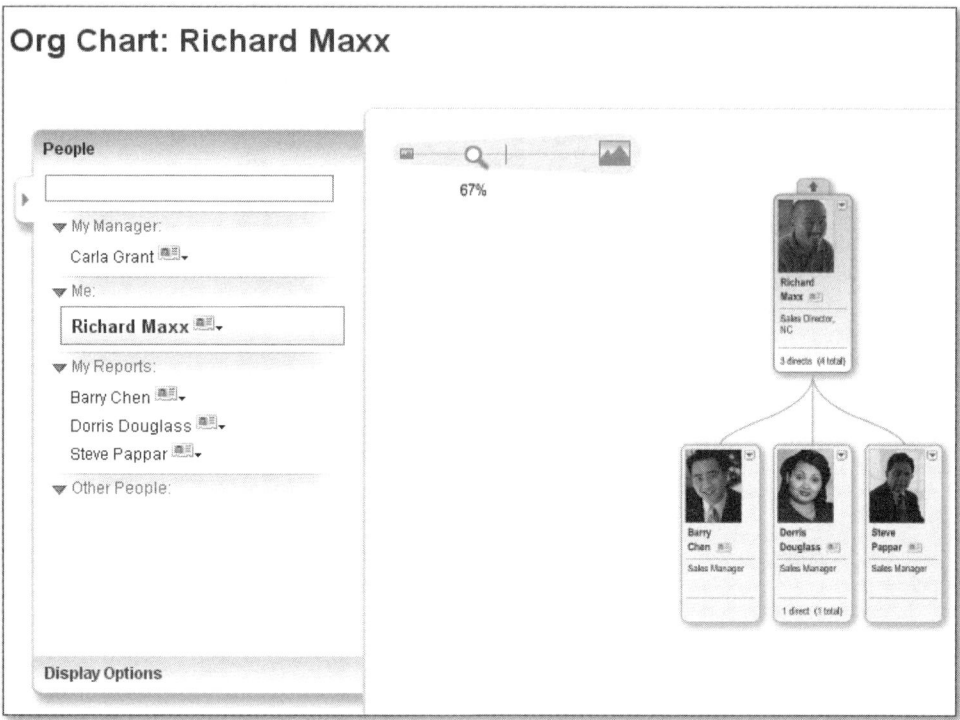

Figure 5.16 Org Chart for Richard Maxx

5.3.3 People Search

The quickest way to look up any other employee and access their profile is to use the PEOPLE search feature available from the HOME page and other pages in the application. The logged-in user searches for Richard Maxx in Figure 5.17.

The most important information is shown on this contact card, such as the user's contact information, manager and the size of the team.

To take action on the employee, click TAKE ACTION to reveal choices. These choices are permissioned to the user, meaning that a manager or HR manager, for example, can access information and take actions that regular employees cannot, such as initiating a change on the employee or viewing the employee's salary information.

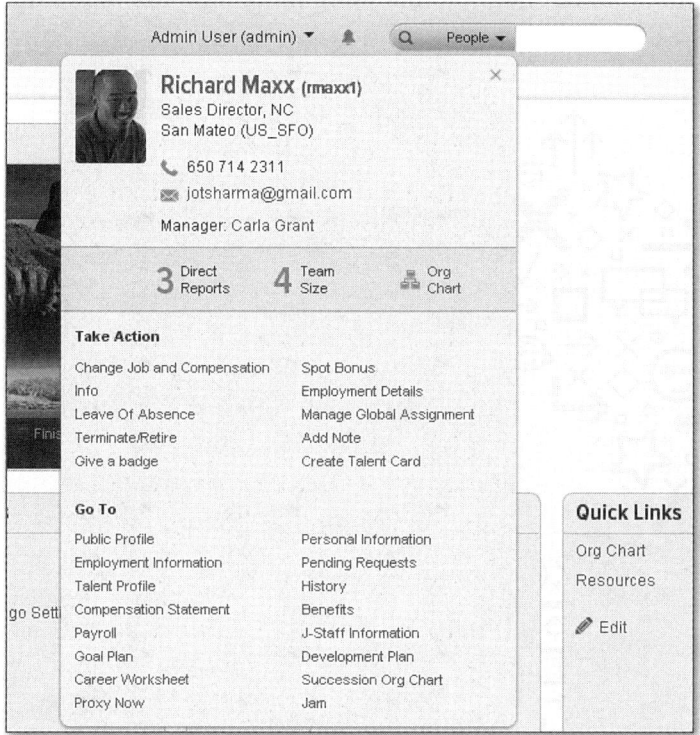

Figure 5.17 An Example of People Search

Through the EMPLOYEE PROFILES pages, users, especially managers and HR, access *all* of the information the suite has about the selected employee. For example, you can access the employee's personal and employment information by going to the PERSONAL INFORMATION and EMPLOYMENT INFORMATION pages, respectively.

5.3.4 Analytics and Reporting

Every module comes with its standard reporting and dashboard feature, which we'll cover in respective chapters. Analytics and reporting will be covered in detail in Chapter 14 of the book. The reporting feature can be accessed from the HOME page by clicking on the ANALYTICS button in the HOME menu. You can run reports online and offline and generate them in CSV, PDF, Excel, and PowerPoint formats.

5.4 SAP Jam

As previously mentioned, SAP Jam is a social collaboration solution integrated into a user's HOME page. We'll cover SAP Jam in more detail in Chapter 13, but for now, let's consider its UI.

Figure 5.18 shows the SAP Jam SIGN IN TO JAM screen and the FEED UPDATES. The main navigation sits on the left-hand pane of the screen. Here, you can move directly to your FEED UPDATES, MY BOOKMARKS, NOTIFICATIONS, MESSAGES, RECOMMENDATIONS, and RECENTLY VIEWED ITEMS.

Figure 5.18 Feed Updates Page on SAP Jam

Additional navigation sits above the main window through the GROUPS link that allows you to view your news feed, profile, any groups you belong to, and your company page. In Chapter 13, we'll explore these navigation features in detail.

5.5 Summary

This chapter introduced the intuitive UI and navigation capabilities of the SuccessFactors BizX solution, enabling you to navigate on the HOME page and personalize it by adding and removing tiles. You should also have an understanding of how each of the tiles enables employees and managers to perform their functions effectively. We have examined some key concepts such as accessing the ORG CHART and using PEOPLE search that make for an engaging and productive user experience.

The next chapter will talk in detail about the Employee Central product of SuccessFactors, which lays the foundation of a Human Resource Information System (HRIS) for customers. In the Employee Central coverage and subsequent chapters, we'll employ what we learned here regarding customizing the HOME page according to a user's needs, adding Admin Favorites, viewing the team, and viewing the To-Do items.

SAP's core HR system in the cloud is SuccessFactors Employee Central. Employee Central is a robust, innovative, and evolving solution for managing the enterprise. Coupled with its attractive user interface, Employee Central is an excellent foundation for the entire SuccessFactors BizX suite.

6   Employee Central

Organizations large and small are undergoing people and process transformations now more than ever before. They require a true Human Resource Information System (HRIS) that streamlines processes and data flows to achieve efficiencies while allowing them to build strategic HR programs and manage the enterprise efficiently and cost-effectively.

SuccessFactors Employee Central achieves all of this and more through its organic and robust design and superior user interface (UI). Employee Central is continuously evolving based on the dynamically changing needs of global organizations and SAP's global co-innovation partners. Employee Central Payroll provides one of the many options that Employee Central customers have to run in-house payroll within the convenience of the cloud.

In this chapter, we'll examine the Employee Central and Employee Central Payroll offerings, their key features, and the pivotal role they play in transforming organizations with the value of an efficient people- and process-centric core HRIS. We'll look at the various business drivers that are making Employee Central a popular choice for cloud HRIS solutions (Section 6.1), objects that lay the foundation of organizational and personnel data in Employee Central (Section 6.2), HR processes and transactions supported by the system (Section 6.3), and some of the key functionalities that can be implemented to further enhance the standard delivered product offering (Section 6.4). Section 6.5 will walk you through the payroll offering in the cloud and how Employee Central Payroll complements Employee Central to provide customers with a true HRIS in the cloud.

6　Employee Central

6.1　Employee Central Business Drivers

Employee Central is a genuine SaaS twenty-first century core HCM system that offers flexibility, usability, and the principal functionality needed to manage the enterprise in a constantly challenging and changing world. HR professionals, managers, and executives can leverage these characteristics to more effectively manage personnel and organizational processes. Although it is lacking in the same depth of functionality as SAP ERP HCM, Employee Central does offer a broad range of features and functionalities that are user friendly and flexible to change however and whenever the business requires. There are some key drivers behind the use of Employee Central in addition to SAP ERP HCM, which we'll take a look at now.

6.1.1　"Glocalization"

A large number of customers that are evaluating a strategy to transition to the cloud are organizations that have disparate HR systems; with increased unification of business processes and revenue pools, they are looking to construct an HRIS that can serve as a global system of record with localized business processes.

For example, Job Info is an HRIS element that stores job-related information for an individual. So how are these standard elements delivered for localized data? If you choose USA as the country to maintain the national identification ID, Employee Central gives you an option of Social Security Number; if you select UK instead, Employee Central provides the option of National Insurance Number. All the validations are built into the system without requiring any additional coding; Canada's Social Identification Number, for example, uses the Luhn Algorithm for its validation, which is delivered as a standard functionality in Employee Central.

Employee Central offers you a global core HR system with a modern, easy-to-use interface and out-of-the-box integration to Talent Management. It provides you with a template solution that offers frequently used data elements as a standard offering. This provides you with a powerful launch pad when setting up your system. Employee Central meets the burning necessity of organizations to be "glocal" by enabling them to implement local country requirements but on a platform that can be extended to the global compliance needs.

6.1.2 Self-Services

It is evident that self-service capabilities of a core HRIS are increasingly viewed in a more progressive dimension than in the past. The advent of Employee Self-Service (ESS) and Manager Self-Service (MSS) found its source in the need to decentralize administrative and service functions via HR solutions that enable employees and managers to handle most of their own processes and data maintenance activities. But complex business needs require employees to understand myriad complex processes; having a modern core HRIS that leverages self-service capabilities with an intuitive UI simplifies the complex job functions performed by employees and managers and increases the employee productivity and profitability of an organization.

6.1.3 Data Quality and Consistency

Sophisticated analytics are only as good as the data they are based on. How can you ensure that you don't suffer from poor data quality or data inconsistencies that affect critical data-reliant processes such as payroll, talent management, or analytics? Bad data can be caused by user error, nonintegrated data, and poor system validations. You can prevent these by investing in a core HRIS that inherently provides robust data validations to enable accurate and consistent data.

Employee Central comes with built-in data validations and standard-delivered HRIS elements for localized data. *HRIS elements* are the building blocks of the Extensible Markup Language (XML) that forms the core of the Employee Central data model. Being built on the XML platform considerably minimizes the time required to design a system from scratch and drives organizations to a more standard and globally acceptable system. Customizations can be made where required, but they are not necessary in order for Employee Central to serve your core HRIS needs.

The functionality of *associations* in Employee Central is a powerful feature to ensure consistent data. For example, if a department is associated with one or more cost centers, only the associated cost centers are proposed by the system when the department is selected.

6.1.4 Integration with Talent Management

Employee Central is built with seamless integration to the Talent Management solutions in the BizX suite. This allows for powerful workforce decision making using the data that already exists within the system, in that having your employees' complete profile and their core and talent information will help you make better informed "people decisions." When performing goal management or recruitment activities, it makes sense to be able to leverage the data, security, and foundation that is already used within the core HR system seamlessly and intelligently.

6.1.5 Integration with Third-Party Providers

SAP delivers several pre-packaged integrations and generic connectors to integrate Employee Central with the SAP ERP HCM, SAP cloud applications, and third-party applications and services. To ensure a full cloud offering for Time, Benefits, and Payroll, customers have the option of leveraging the open integration platform provided by Dell Boomi AtomSphere. Dell Boomi AtomSphere is the middleware included with the Employee Central subscription and is covered in Chapter 3.

Benefitfocus and Workforce Software are some of the preferred partners that have integration available with Employee Central for Benefits and Time and Attendance applications, respectively. EPI-USE America offers an SAP-certified Rapid Deployment Solution (RDS) for cloud payroll that can be leveraged for Employee Central Payroll, while Workforce Software has entered into a partnership to help provide workforce management services. Co-innovation is taking place at a significant pace within the partner ecosystem to provide customers with the flexibility of choice with their integration technology. SAP has already announced over 30 co-innovations with partners for third-party integrations and it has many more on its roadmap in 2014 and beyond. Partnership with Kronos is an important step in that direction.

At the time of writing SAP offers several predelivered integrations from Employee Central to SAP:

- Employee Master Data in Employee Central to SAP Payroll and Employee Central Payroll, and Employee Mini Master to SAP Finance
- Organizational Data in Employee Central to SAP Payroll, SAP Finance, SAP Cloud Finance and SAP Cloud Travel
- Over 145 integrations with third-party solutions

Chapter 3 delves deeper into the various integration platforms, scenarios, and architecture.

6.1.6 Mobility

Mobility is an increasingly important part of an HR technology strategy and the use of mobile devices for workplace activities is on the rise. Employee Central helps to facilitate mobility through functionality provide in the SuccessFactors BizX Mobile application. Although SAP's mobility platform—which comprises Sybase Unwired Platform and Gateway technology—scores high on scalability with the number of deployed applications and the heterogeneity of deployed application types, cost and required ROI can be prohibitive obstacles to rolling out mobility within the enterprise. SuccessFactors BizX Mobile is not only free but also requires no additional infrastructure setup and is simple to download and activate.

We have seen the key business drivers that reiterate the need for a core HRIS that is not just a repository of employee and organizational data but truly enables business execution. Employee Central is built for business execution; let's examine how in more detail in the upcoming sections.

6.2 Employee Central Data Objects

Employee Central has an agile and easy-to-adapt design for customers' changing HR business requirements. It moves away from the structured design of SAP ERP HCM and the concept of infotypes and toward a free-flowing platform of flexible XML-based data models that allows you to store and manage data through simple and easy-to-configure attributes. XML data models provide the basic structure that can be used to store your data within the predefined parameters of the structure.

Employee Central is based on a template-based UI with XML forming the spinal column of the architecture. As with all solutions in the BizX suite, the framework for maintaining Employee Central is through the OneAdmin UI, formerly known as Admin Tools.

We'll now spend some time understanding the four data objects that comprise the architecture of the Employee Central data framework: foundation objects, generic objects, person objects, and employment objects. Upon examining these objects, we'll see how they fit into the transactional aspect of Employee Central. So let's get started.

6.2.1 Foundation Objects

Foundation objects define the company data for an organization. They are database objects that hold information about enterprise-level objects such as a business unit or cost center. The foundation object tables capture detailed information about a company's organization, pay, and job structures. Each object has a set of standard fields, custom fields, and country-specific fields to house country-specific data. Of course, you are not expected to remember any table names or transactions to access the information housed in these objects! Let's look at each of these structures and understand their importance in building your core HR system through a few examples.

- **Organizational structures**
  Organizational structures are the building blocks that organizations can use to structure their organization to custom fit their needs. Eight standard organizational structures are delivered (legal entity, business unit, location group, geo zone, location, division, department, and cost center), but the system can create custom organizational structures to suit your needs. For example, a division may have an additional level of subdivision in the organizational hierarchy.

  You can create subdivision as a custom organizational structure and link it to (associate it with) the division. We'll explain associations in more detail in Section 6.4.

- **Job structures**
  Job structures functionality can be used to create job codes and job functions in your organization. Similarly to the organizational structures, job structures empower you to maintain the job-related information that is not employee-specific, such as pay grade, job title, and so on. The two job structures are job classification and job function.

- **Pay structures**
  Pay structures are used to store the remuneration components of any employee. They include pay group, pay component, pay component group, pay grade, pay range, pay calendar, and frequency.

> **Note**
> Let's draw some similarities here to SAP ERP HCM. Pay group is the equivalent of a payroll area, pay components are analogous to wage types, and pay component groups are comprised of pay components just like wage type groups are made up of wage types.

These pay components and pay component groups can be easily configured in OneAdmin UI, where you can perform actions such as identifying them as an earning or deduction, specifying the tax treatment (e.g., whether it is a regular earning or a gross-up), and specifying whether the particular pay component will be used for compensation planning or not.

Now that we've covered the foundation objects, let's talk about what they do. Within Employee Central, there is a feature to populate information to gain efficiencies and reduce user entry error. For example, an HR manager entering a new hire into the system must enter information such as the following:

- Job Code: ENG00253
- Job Title: Java Engineer
- Local Job Title: Java Engineer
- Standard Hours: 40
- FLSA Status: Exempt

This information can be stored on the job code foundation object and be populated on the screen when a new hire is assigned the job code. In SAP ERP HCM, this is similar to creating a job object and maintaining this data against that specific object. Figure 6.1 illustrates how data maintained at the job code level, such as standard hours and pay grade, can be populated on the employee record when that job code is assigned.

You are also empowered to store country-specific details on foundation objects. For example, perhaps you need to store country-specific fields such as FEDERAL EMPLOYER IDENTIFICATION NUMBER (FEIN) for a US-based legal entity or company code, but you need to keep the remaining fields applicable to all countries.

> **Note**
>
> Foundation objects are configured in the corporate data model. The country-specific requirements are configured in the country-specific (CSF) corporate data model.

The foundation objects make the application agile. We'll discuss a few examples of foundation objects to illustrate the adaptability and flexibility of Employee Central.

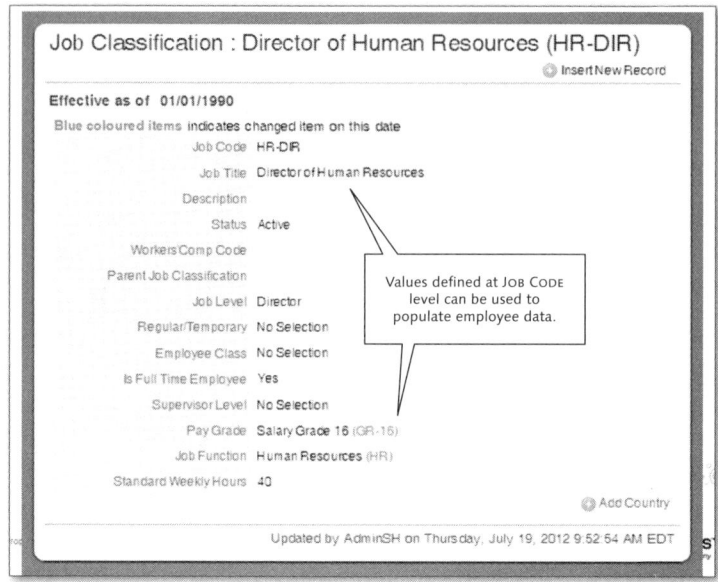

Figure 6.1 Job Code Foundation Object

Country-Specific Fields

Figure 6.2 shows an example of the country-specific fields configured for the USA on the legal entity foundation object ACE USA.

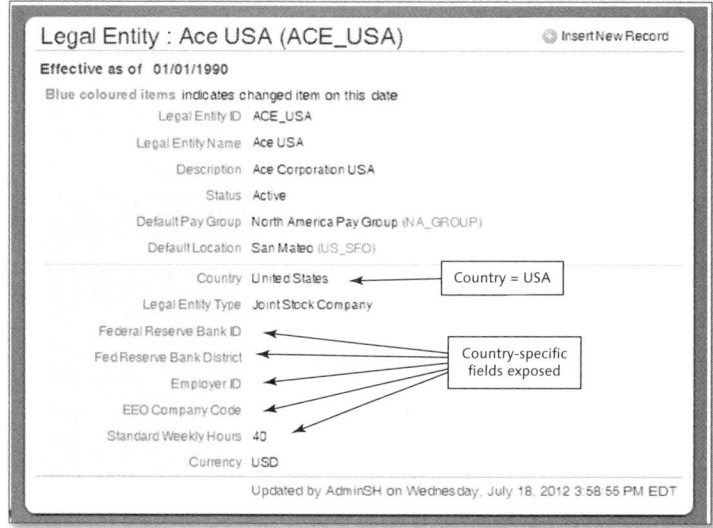

Figure 6.2 Country-Specific Fields on Legal Entity

Location Group

Customers can group multiple locations into a location group (see Figure 6.3). Location groups are generally used for Equal Employment Opportunity (EEO) reporting in the United States.

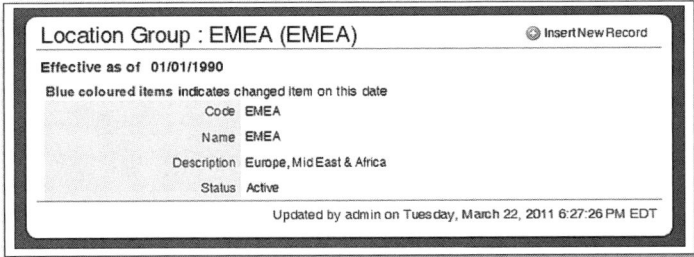

Figure 6.3 Example of Location Group

Geo Zone

Customers can group multiple location groups into one Geo Zone, like the ASIA PACIFIC zone shown in Figure 6.4. The ADJUSTMENT PERCENTAGE field determines the adjustment factor for the pay range based on specific factors for a location in a Geo Zone, such as cost of living.

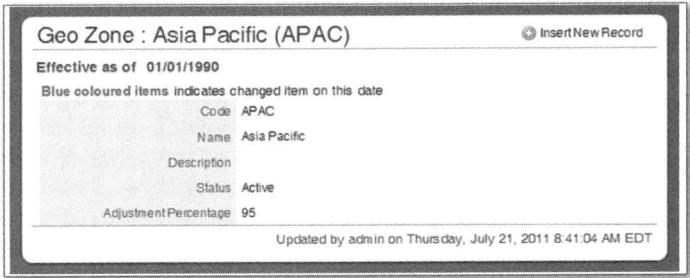

Figure 6.4 Example of APAC Geo Zone to Group APAC Locations

Pay Component Group

Multiple pay components can be grouped into a pay component group. The amount of a pay component group is equivalent to the pay components it includes. The system automatically performs annualization and currency conversion during the calculation of the annual salary, as shown in Figure 6.5. For example, if the frequency maintained on the pay component is bi-weekly, the annualization will be done on that basis.

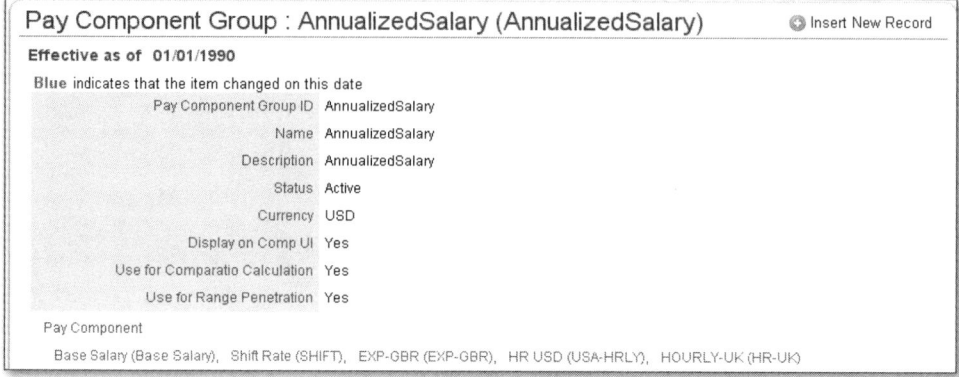

Figure 6.5 Annualized Salary Pay Component Group Showing Pay Components

6.2.2 Generic Objects

Generic objects are the building blocks of the Metadata Framework (MDF). Recall from Chapter 4 that the MDF is a generic platform that provides a rich configurable UI and provides customers with out-of-the-box functionality to define objects, configure object relationships, and create rules and workflows.

For example, a position is a generic object that enables you to implement Position Management in Employee Central. It is integrated with the employment object—job information—and appears on the UI as part of the job information for an employee, as shown in Figure 6.6.

Customers can define custom fields on generic objects and also determine the data type. In Figure 6.7, you see the position object with the DIVISION field that uses the division foundation objects as a source. When the position is created, the system will present the list of divisions stored in the system.

Employee Central Data Objects | **6.2**

Figure 6.6 Position Object on Job Information

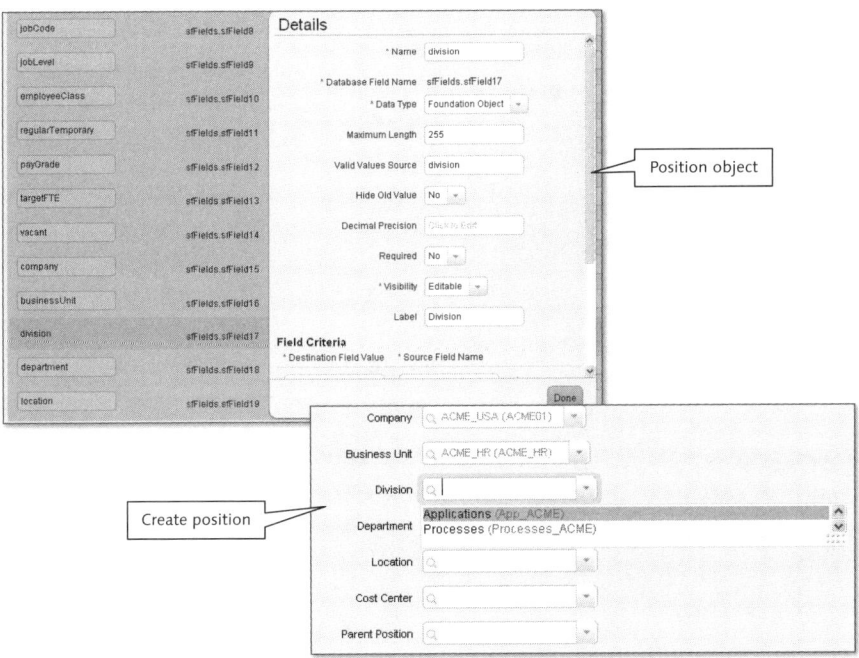

Figure 6.7 Example of Position Object and Creating a Position

You can also define rules and link to generic objects both at the object level and field level. Figure 6.8 is an example of a rule to synchronize information on the position to the job information of the employee. When the information on the Position object is changed and an employee is assigned to that position, the system will automatically sync the position information to the Job Info element on the employee's record.

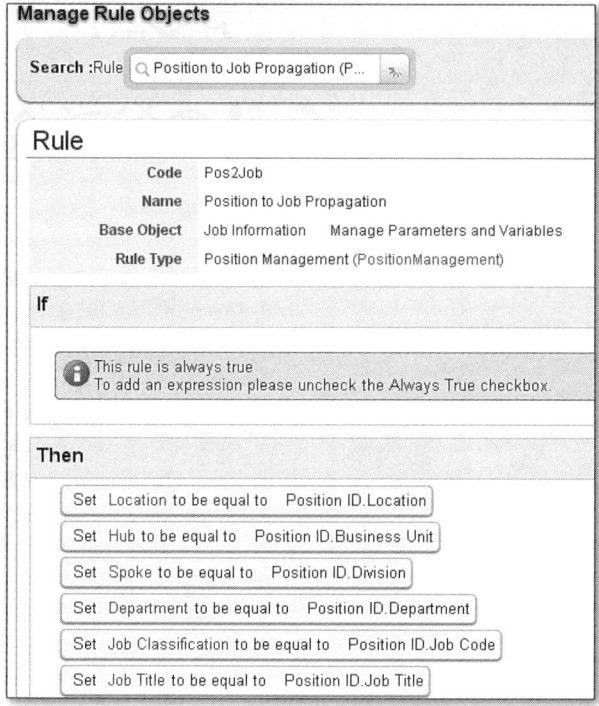

Figure 6.8 Position to Job Sync Rule

6.2.3 HR Data

HR data objects are separated into person objects and employment objects. These objects appear as sections on the UI called *portlets*. In Figure 6.9, you see various portlets for NATIONAL ID INFORMATION, PERSONAL INFORMATION, HOME ADDRESS, and BIOGRAPHICAL INFORMATION. Customers can rename these portlets if desired.

6.2 Employee Central Data Objects

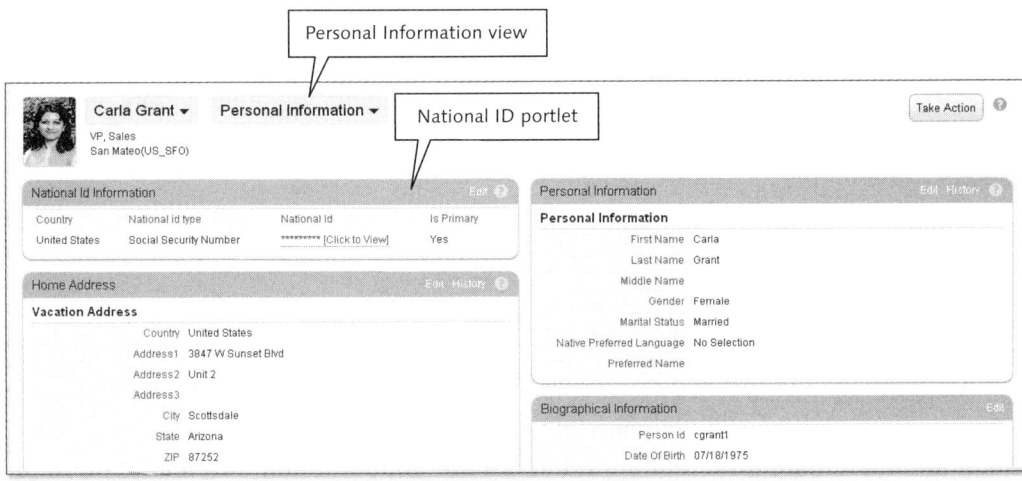

Figure 6.9 Example of Portlets and Views

HR data is stored in a menu called EMPLOYEE VIEWS. Figure 6.9 illustrates the various views that contain employee information; in this screenshot, the PERSONAL INFORMATION view is in use. We'll take a look at these views and incorporated objects in the upcoming sections.

> **Note**
>
> Standard HRIS elements defined in the Succession and Country-Specific (CSF) Succession data models appear on the UI as portlets, as shown in Figure 6.9.

Before we examine these objects in more detail, let's review some of the common characteristics of HR data objects.

Effective Dating

The majority of the information captured in HR data objects is effective dated. This means that data about an object (e.g., an employee's address) is time-dependent and that multiple instances of data can exist over time. An exception to this rule is the National ID (e.g., Social Security number); this information is not provided with an effective date because typically it doesn't change. In this case, you won't see a HISTORY link on the screen.

6 | Employee Central

Figure 6.10 shows the difference between an effective-dated and non-effective-dated data object on the UI.

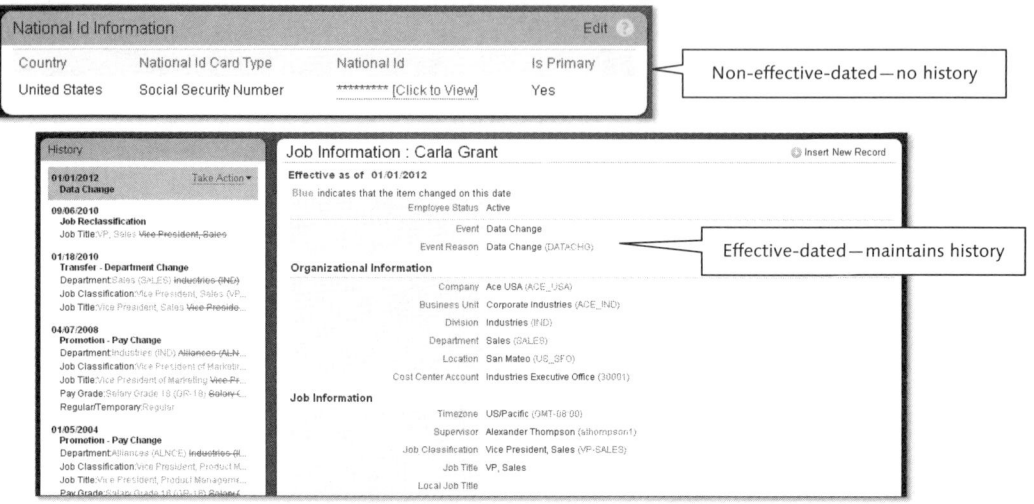

Figure 6.10 Example of Effective- and Non-Effective-Dated Data

Integration

All HR data information is fully integrated with the rest of the SuccessFactors BizX suite, such as SuccessFactors Performance & Goals, Compensation, and Succession & Development. Customer who have implemented SuccessFactors Employee Central and Performance & Goals can access all information within the same UI. They can view the GOAL PLANS and the EMPLOYEE INFORMATION by selecting options from the quick card or from the main dropdown menu.

Figure 6.11 shows the user accessing the GOAL PLAN from the contact card in Employee Central.

Role-Based Permissions

All HR data is controlled by a powerful tool called Role-Based Permissions, also known as the RBP framework. We've explored it in previous chapters; it supersedes the traditional methods of granting security and permissions by adding more granularity. Customers not only control the access by a certain population but also control the target population that a role can access. You are able to further define the level of access as Edit and/or View.

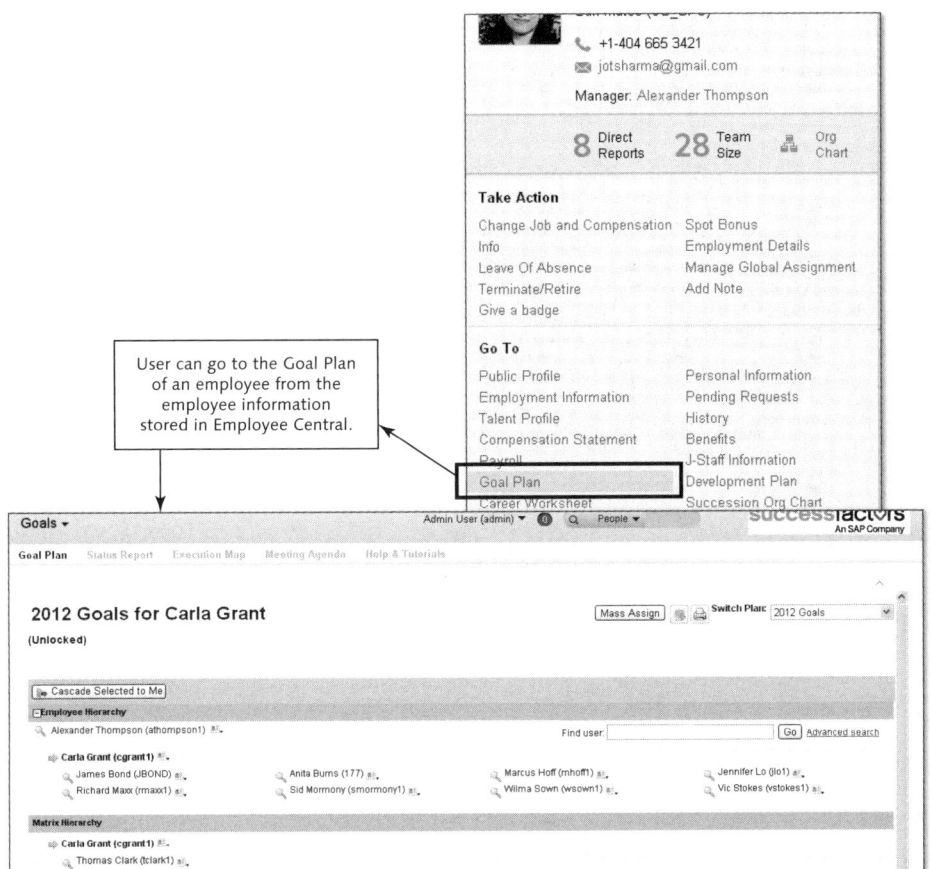

Figure 6.11 Example of Integration between Employee Central and Goal Management

Let's walk through an example to cement our understanding using Figure 6.12. A company needs to give select individuals with the power user role the permission rights to access data for employees from their own country. The same role needs to be assigned to all managers, but they must be able to access only their direct reports. The RBP framework enables you to address this requirement with the help of permission groups and permission roles. Permission groups are created, and the required roles are assigned to these groups. You'll see the RBP framework in more detail in a later section.

In Figure 6.12, the PowerUser R/W role is assigned to different groups of users with unique access to target populations. Here, PowerUser USA can access only USA employees.

6 | Employee Central

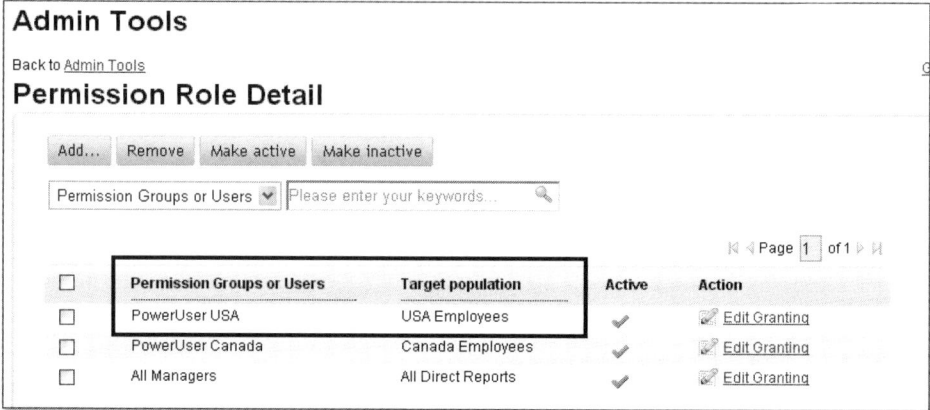

Figure 6.12 Example of a Permission Role Assigned to Permission Groups

Person Objects

The intelligence of Employee Central is obvious when you handle HR data objects. We saw that foundation objects pertain to information controlled at the enterprise level, such as the job code. Person objects, on the other hand, apply to information independent of the organization that is determined at the "person" or "employee" level. Such distinction between these objects ensures ease in managing HR information.

The person objects are stored under the PERSONAL INFORMATION view shown in Figure 6.13, which contains the following portlets of information on the employee:

- PERSONAL INFORMATION
- PERSONAL GLOBAL INFORMATION
- BIOGRAPHICAL INFORMATION
- ADDRESS INFORMATION

Employee Central Data Objects | **6.2**

- EMAIL INFORMATION
- PHONE INFORMATION
- SOCIAL ACCOUNTS INFORMATION
- DIRECT DEPOSIT INFORMATION
- NATIONAL ID INFORMATION
- EMERGENCY CONTACT INFORMATION

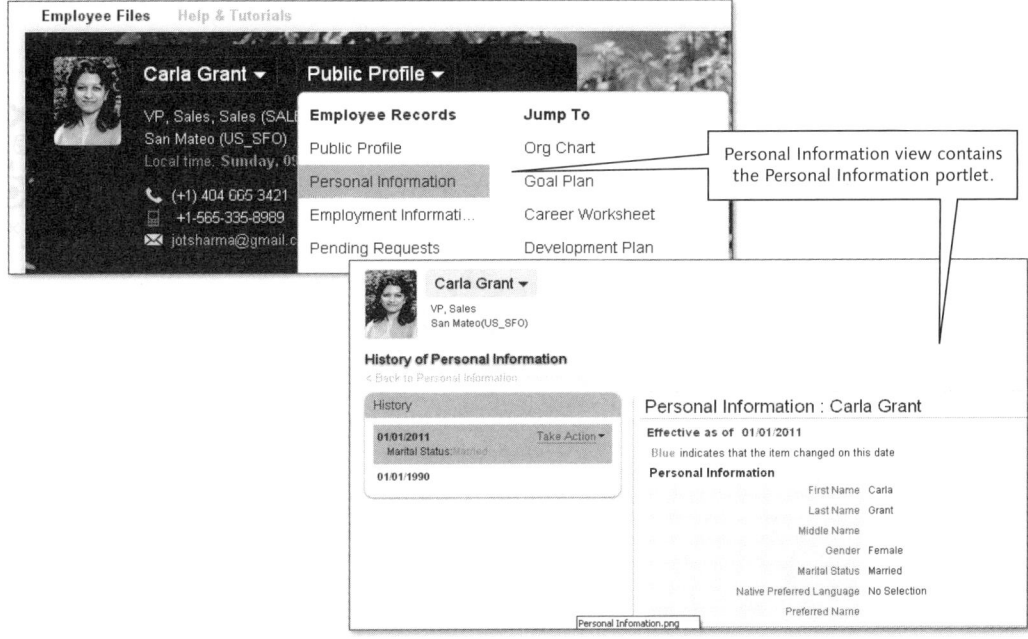

Figure 6.13 Personal Information Portlet Showing Employee Information under the Personal Information View

Similar to foundation objects, the person objects consist of a set of standard fields, custom fields, and country-specific fields.

Personal Information
The PERSONAL INFORMATION portlet contains information such as first name, last name, marital status, and so on. Name and marital status information can change often, requiring in storage of effective dated information in the system. The customer

can also store name information in an alternative language based on the language packs that have been activated.

> **Note**
>
> Personal Information is the name of a view as well as a portlet on the UI. Customers can rename the views as well as the portlet titles.

Address Information

The ADDRESS INFORMATION portlet contains the address for an employee. You can specify country-specific address formats. Figure 6.14 shows the different address formats for the UNITED STATES and CHINA.

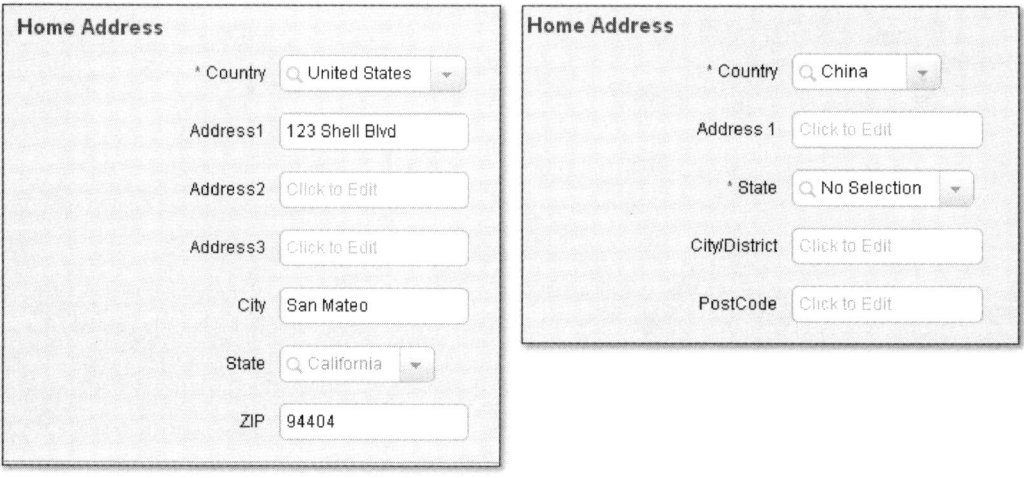

Figure 6.14 Country-Specific Address Formats

> **Note**
>
> Address information is defined in Succession data model, while the country-specific format is defined in the CSF Succession data model.

Contact Information

In the CONTACT INFORMATION portlet, you can store information such as email, phone, and social accounts such as Facebook and Twitter. You are able to define the type of email and phone information to store, such as cell, work, and home. The system requires that you define primary email and phone information. The purpose of this is that in the event of multiple email and phone details, the primary contact details will be used by the system, requiring no additional user input.

Employment Objects

Employment objects include job-related information about a person such as compensation information and hire date. The employment objects are stored under the EMPLOYMENT INFORMATION view, as shown in Figure 6.15. These objects are person-related and independent of the enterprise.

- Employment details
- Job information
  - Position information
  - Job information
  - Organization information
  - EEO information
  - Time off

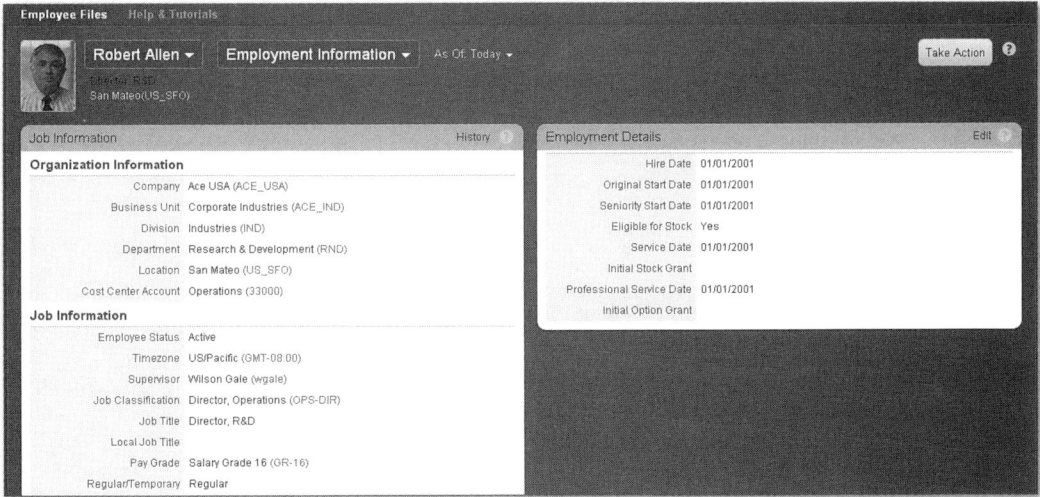

Figure 6.15 Example of Employment Information

- Job relationships
- Compensation information
- Spot bonus
- Direct deposit

> **Note**
> Employee Central supports country-specific localization for 51 countries in 37 languages.

In this section, we examined the foundation objects, generic objects, and person and employment objects that form the building blocks of Employee Central and are integral to satisfying customers' HR needs. These data objects provide an engaging UI and powerful tools for performing HR transactions and processes. We'll scrutinize these transactions and processes next.

6.3 Employee Central Processes and Transactions

Employee Central supports a wide range of HR processes and transactions, making it a complete HR system of record in the cloud. The following processes are supported in Employee Central:

- HR transactions
- New hires and onboarding
- Changes and transfers
- Position management
- Absence management
- Reporting compliance and auditing
- Global payroll for 22 countries

Let's look at a few examples of these processes to understand the value that Employee Central can add.

Employee Central Processes and Transactions | **6.3**

6.3.1 Add New Employee

New hires can be added through a slick ADD NEW EMPLOYEE transaction. You can use event reasons to determine the appropriate reason for the hire. Because the system comes with a standard list of event reasons that are sufficient in most cases, additional configuration is not required from the customer. Figure 6.16 shows an ADD NEW EMPLOYEE TRANSACTION. You can see in the boxed bar in the figure how the system walks you through each step starting with setting up the identity, followed by entering personal information and employment information, and finally by entering the compensation information for the new hire.

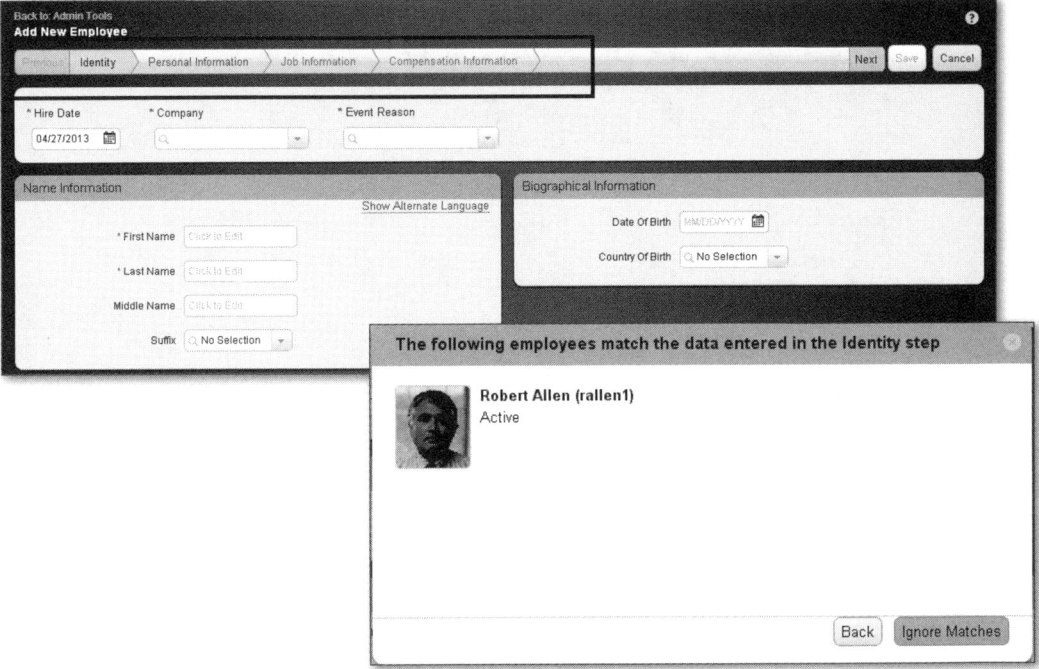

Figure 6.16 Hiring an Employee with Add New Employee Transaction

PERSON ID can be generated automatically by the system or entered manually. If a PERSON ID entered on the new hire screen already exists, the system validates it and informs the user of the duplicate entry, as shown in Figure 6.16. You can choose to go back and enter new credentials. If you click on IGNORE MATCHES,

185

6 | Employee Central

the system will give you an error and prompt you to enter a unique value for the PERSON ID.

6.3.2 Mass Changes

Administrators can create mass changes such as organizational changes, job relationship changes, and so on. After a mass change action has been created, the system gives you the two SAVE buttons shown in Figure 6.17: SAVE and SAVE AND INITIATE. Saving will create the mass change action but not execute it, while saving and initiating will execute the change as well.

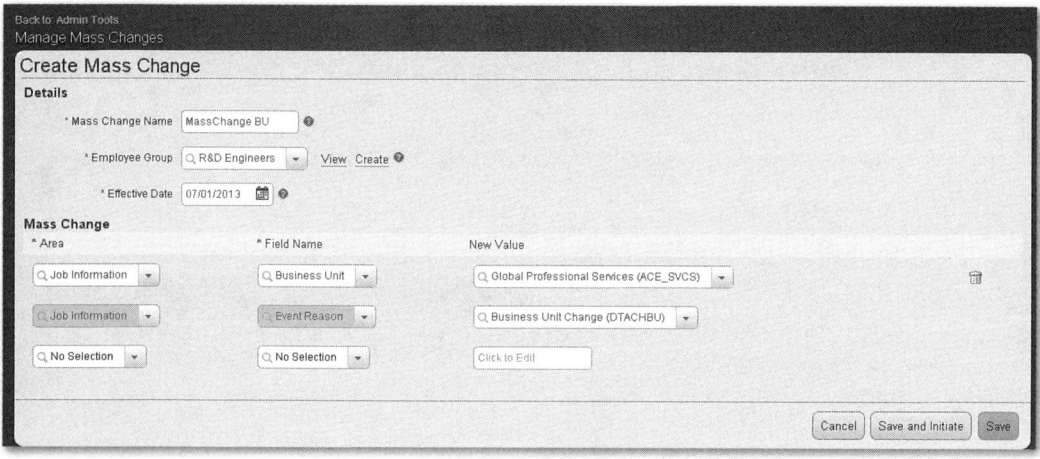

Figure 6.17 Create a Mass Change

6.3.3 Proxy Management

Administrators in Employee Central can easily assign proxies for selected users. By definition, a proxy has the power or authority to act for someone else. For example, if an executives want their personal administrator to carry out transactions on their behalf, the personal administrators can be assigned as a proxy user for these executives either by the executives or by system administrators. Figure 6.18 shows the PROXY MANAGEMENT page, where you select the proxy user, the proxy target, and the modules for which the proxy rights are granted.

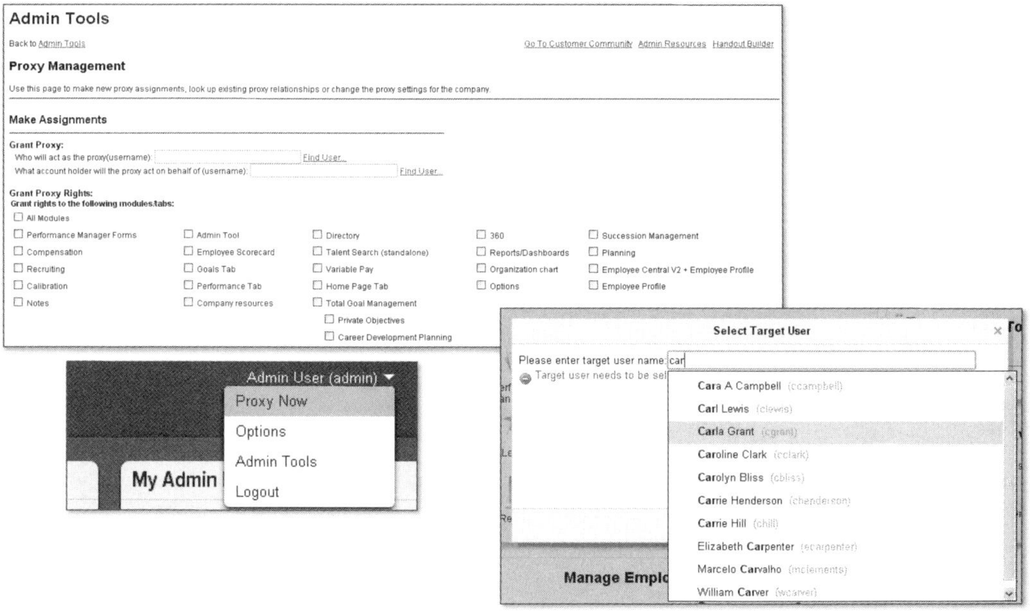

Figure 6.18 Proxy Management

6.3.4 Create and Manage Workflows

System administrators can easily create workflows and assign approver types in OneAdmin. There are three approver types:

- **Role**
  The approver is the employee, the employee's manager, the manager's manager, or the employee's HR responsible person. The administrator can also select whether the old or new manager must approve a step when the employee's manager changes.

- **Dynamic role**
  Dynamic role means that you let the system find the right approver. For example, let's assume that the head of the business unit is defined as the approver. Depending on the business unit of the person for whom data has been changed, the system will select the head of the business unit as the approver.

- **Dynamic group role**
  Dynamic group is group of several approvers that the administrator can set up before creating workflows. If a dynamic group role is assigned as an approver

type, any member of the dynamic group can approve the transaction. For example, you can create a dynamic group consisting of Talent Management administrators who can approve a particular change to employee data.

Figure 6.19 shows an example of the WORKFLOW: HIRE (NEW OR REHIRE) screen.

Workflow : Hire (New or Rehire)				Take Action
	Workflow ID	HIRE		
	Name	Hire (New or Rehire)		
	Description			
Step 1				
Approver Type	Approver Role		Context	Edit Transaction
Role	Employee Manager		Target	No Edit
Step 2				
Approver Type	Approver Role		Context	Edit Transaction
Role	Employee Manager Manager		Target	No Edit
Step 3				
Approver Type	Approver Role		Context	Edit Transaction
Dynamic Role	Finance Controller (FIN-CONT)		Target	No Edit
Step 4				
Approver Type	Approver Role		Context	Edit Transaction
Role	Employee HR		Target	No Edit
Workflow Contributer				
CC Role				
CC Role Type	CC Role			Context
Role	Employee Manager			Target
Role	Employee Manager Manager			Target

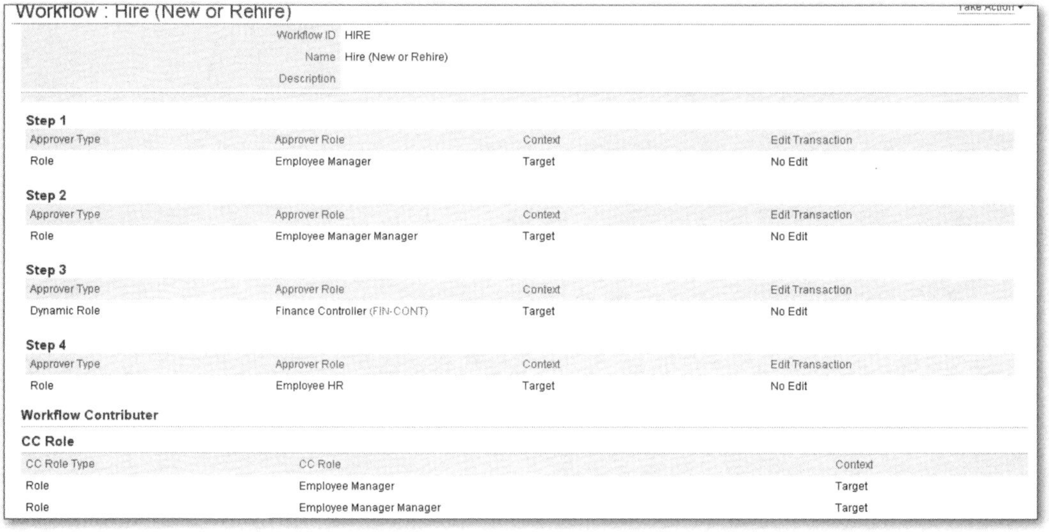

Figure 6.19 Workflow: Hire (New or Rehire) Screen

The approver can make in-flight changes (changes made while the approval is still being processed) based on which the system recalculates the approval route. Notification-only workflows are also available. For example, a home address change may require a benefits eligibility or payroll tax information change. The system is equipped to handle such workflow requests.

6.3.5 Changes, Transfers, and Workflows

Managers can initiate changes and transfers for their direct reports. These changes can be associated with workflows.

Consider the scenario begun in Figure 6.20. Manager Wilson Gale initiates a business unit change for his team member Penny Welsh that is effective from April 27, 2013. This change is associated with a workflow that involves the president (Alexander Thompson) and VP of operations (Julie Olsen).

After the change is submitted, the workflow is triggered and needs to be approved before the changes can take place. Figure 6.21 shows that the workflow was triggered, and the president approved the workflow.

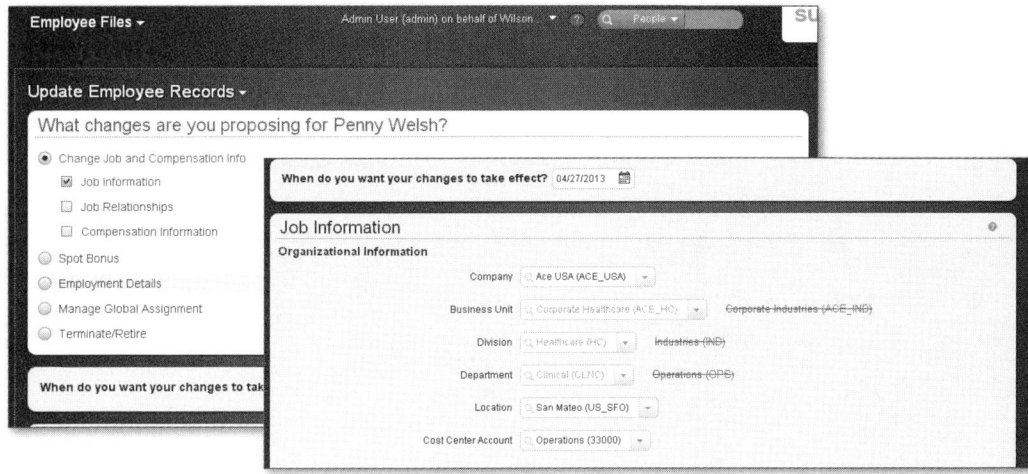

Figure 6.20 Initiate a Change

Figure 6.21 Trigger and Approve a Workflow

The change takes place after all the approvers have approved the request and it appears on the employee's record (in this case, Penny Welsh's EMPLOYMENT INFORMATION, which is shown in Figure 6.22).

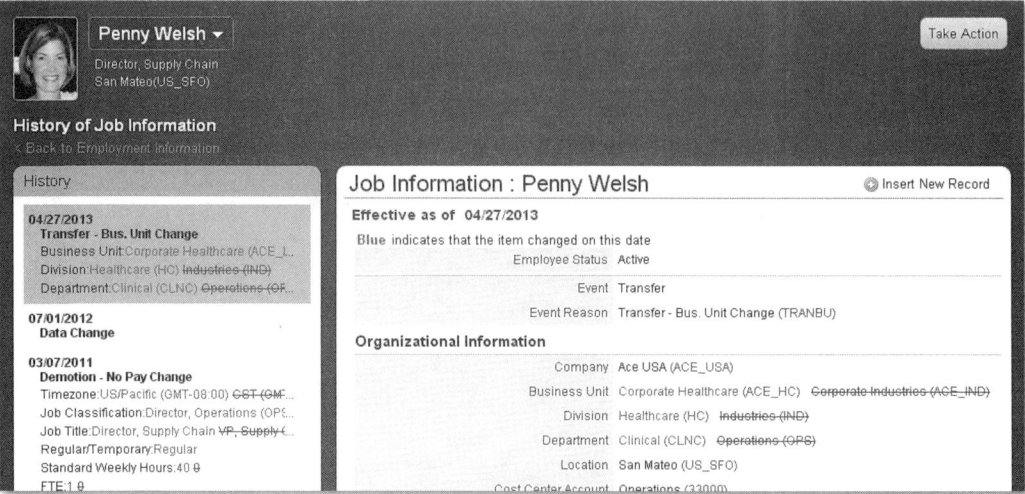

Figure 6.22 Change in Employment Information after Approval of Workflow

6.3.6 Position Management

Through the Position Management feature you can create, fill, and activate positions for displaying a position hierarchy, which can be different from the reporting line structure. Position information can be changed and synchronized with the job information of an employee. You can also define default values—for example, that full-time employee (FTE) should always be equal to 1 when creating new positions. This is done by creating rules in the MDF and linking them to the position object. You can track vacancies and reporting relationships.

Figure 6.23 shows a basic organizational chart being compared with a position organizational chart.

6.3.7 Absence Management

The Employee Central Absence Management feature allows companies to manage their employees' time off. Employees can request time off via web or mobile or tablet devices, and managers can approve time-off requests in the same way. Generic objects such as holiday calendar, time types, work schedules, time profiles, and time account types can be configured in the system; employees are provided access through the RBP framework. Holiday calendars, which can vary country to country, can be maintained by country. The system allows you to create employee work schedules and approval workflows. Positive time recording is provisioned by SuccessFactors partners Workforce Software and Kronos, which offer standard integrations with Employee Central.

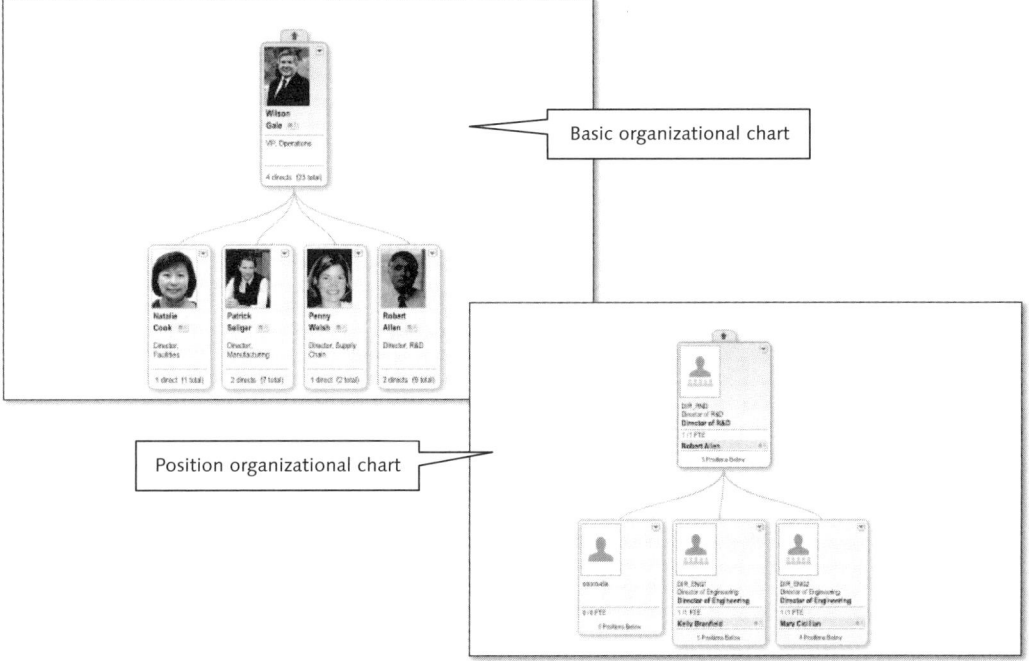

Figure 6.23 Basic Organizational Chart Compared with a Position Organizational Chart

6.3.8 Global Assignment

With the Global Assignment feature shown in Figure 6.24, you can add or end global assignments for expatriate employees. When the global assignment is active, there is one home and one host for the expatriate employee. When the administrator or manager ends the host employment, the home assignment will become active again. Global Assignment can be set as obsolete for use cases when the assignment is no longer active, but the assignment should be retained.

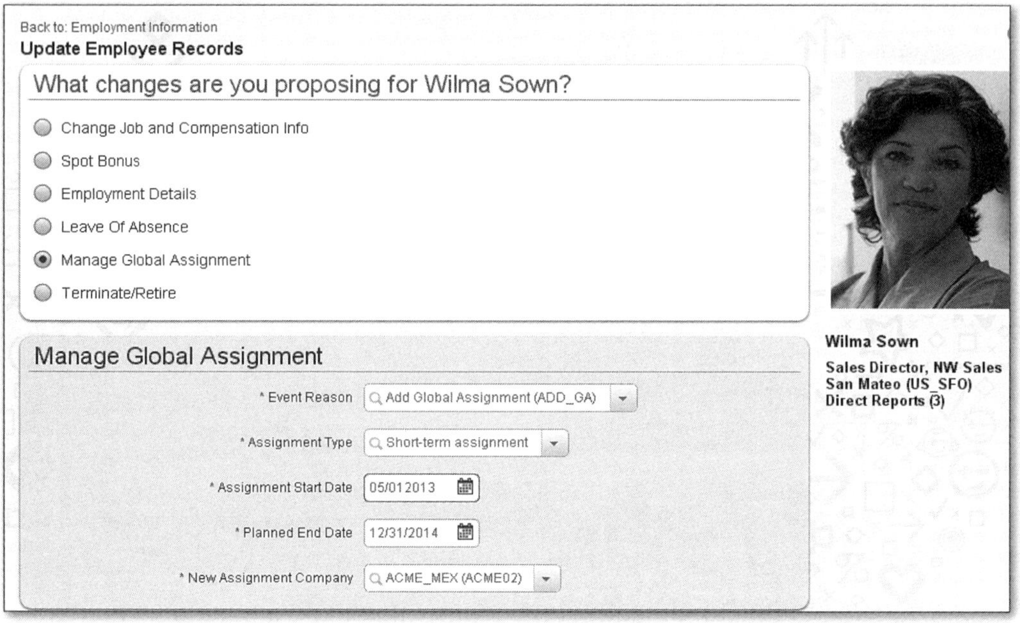

Figure 6.24 Example of Global Assignment

> **Note**
>
> The configuration for Position Management, Absence Management, and Global Assignment is done in the Succession data model.

6.3.9 Employee Central Reporting

Reporting in Employee Central is done through various tools that source data from Employee Central objects. Reports can be *single domain* or *cross domain*. Single-domain reports comprise information from a single product (e.g., Employee Central), while cross-domain reports can extract information from multiple products (e.g., Employee Central and Performance & Goals). You can schedule reports with the help of your implementation partner. System administrators can use the MONITOR JOBS FEATURE in OneAdmin to administer the status of scheduled reports.

The reporting feature in Employee Central equips you to answer the critical questions outlined in Table 6.1 when creating a report. Your aim is to get the desired output of shareable reports, which enable "As of date reporting" as well as "date range reporting."

Employee Central Processes and Transactions | **6.3**

People	Views	Filters
Who will be running the report?	What information do I need to see displayed in my report?	Is there a specific characteristic to the data I need?
What permissions exist for this user?	Is there specific information I need for future analysis?	Do I need to refine further based on business need?
Who is the audience for the report?	Is there a preferred order of the information?	How will the information be presented?

Table 6.1 Employee Central Reporting Parameters

Let's examine the various reporting tools that help answer these questions: Ad Hoc Report Builder 2.0, Online Report Designer, and YouCalc dashboards.

Ad Hoc Report Builder 2.0

Ad Hoc Report Builder gives users a flexible, intuitive platform to easily create custom reports and share them across the organization, as shown in Figure 6.25. It is permissioned by the user, with the option for users to act either as a report creator or just a viewer. Ad Hoc Report Builder 2.0 consists of standard-delivered subdomain schemas that are used to create reports.

The system also delivers standard reports that can be modified per the customer's requirements. These reports can be exported in Excel, CSV, or PowerPoint formats.

Figure 6.25 List of Ad Hoc Reports Created for Some Foundation Objects in Employee Central

193

Advanced Employee Central Reporting with Online Report Designer

The Online Report Designer tool is now equipped to provide advanced Employee Central reporting. You have the option to create near real-time transactional reporting on Employee Central data. You can query the transactional data to create list style reports or aggregate the list data to create charts and pivoted tables, as shown in Figure 6.26.

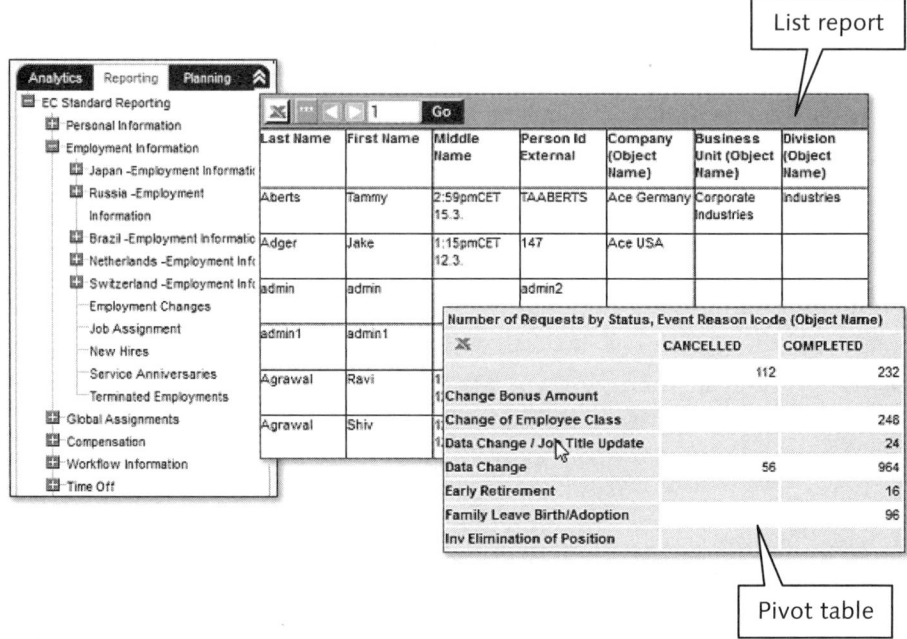

Figure 6.26 Advanced Employee Central Reporting with Online Report Designer

Comparing Ad Hoc Report Builder and Online Report Designer

To get a comprehensive view of the reporting capabilities in Employee Central, let's compare the Ad Hoc Report Builder and the Online Report Designer using Table 6.2. In general, the Ad Hoc Report Builder 2.0 presents you with a user-friendly interface to create reports, but the Online Report Designer presents you with superior features.

Report Feature	Ad Hoc Report Builder 2.0	Online Report Designer
Build report	Use standard-delivered subdomain schemas that extract data from Employee Central objects. Customers are confined to the delivered schemas	Use Online Report Designer to extract every object in Employee Central.
Customize report	Does not allow much customization or data manipulation.	Allows relabeling of fields and creation of custom calculations and concatenations. If/then/else statements are possible.
Design report	Minimal flexibility for report design.	Allows custom page layouts that can be formatted with images, text, and so on.
Export report	Exportable in most available formats.	Exportable as PPT, PDF, Word, and Excel.
Present report	Reports need to be formatted for presentation.	Reports already formatted and presentation-ready in tabular list formats, pivot tables, and a variety of chart styles.
Schedule report	Need consulting support to schedule reports.	Use Report Distributor (also customer facing) to schedule and distribute reports.

Table 6.2 Ad Hoc Report Builder versus Online Report Designer

YouCalc Dashboards

You can use YouCalc dashboards to convert any ad hoc reports into a dashboard that can be uploaded as a tile on the HOME page or as a standalone dashboard. We covered details on the HOME page and associated tiles in Chapter 5. Customers have controlled access to change the configuration on the YouCalc dashboards and can provide a unique name for the dashboard in many different languages. Changes can also be made to the data and interface of the dashboards via ADMIN TOOLS • MANAGE YOUCALC DASHBOARDS • ADD LANGUAGE.

6.4 Implementing Employee Central

You've now seen that Employee Central is a core HRIS where customers can maintain HR data and company processes and transactions. It also serves as a global system of record that caters to localized country requirements.

When you are implementing Employee Central there are some key technical attributes of the BizX platform that are implemented to provide you with the desired level of system configuration and capabilities. A detailed implementation walkthrough is outside the purview of this book, but we'll look at some of these key system attributes:

- **Metadata Framework (MDF)**
  Recall that MDF is a generic platform that allows you to define objects, configure object relationships, create rules and workflows, and use a rich, configurable UI. Employee Central is suited to meet diverse customer needs through MDF. For example, objects such as position and time off account types are created through MDF in OneAdmin by customers and don't require engagement of technical consultants. Chapter 4 covers MDF in more detail.

- **PickLists**
  PickLists enable you to maintain custom lists for data elements. You can configure any data field as a PickList. The customer can then maintain custom lists of values that appear on the UI. These PickLists can be modified at any time based on the customer's changing requirements.

- **Associations**
  Associations allow customers to maintain context-specific dropdown filters. For example, a particular business unit may contain one or more divisions, but a division can't belong to more than one business unit. In this case, when an association is built between a business unit and a division, only the relevant divisions are available to be selected by the user based on the business unit selected.

- **Translations**
  One of the biggest advantages of Employee Central is its ability to function as a global system of record. Currently it supports 37 languages in 51 countries. Customers can switch on relevant language packs and enable translations for the required fields. The system provides standard translations that can be replaced with customer-required translations.

▶ **Propagation**
Employee Central is enabled with a feature called *propagation*. Propagation allows for information to be defaulted, effectively reducing manual input and user entry errors. The information stored in the foundation objects can be propagated to job information. For example, standard hours stored on the job code (foundation object) can be propagated to JOB INFORMATION when an employee is assigned to a job code. This is accomplished through the Propagation data model.

Now that you've implemented Employee Central, and all your employee data resides in an intelligent and intuitive platform in the cloud, it's time to use that data to pay your employees as well. This brings us to our next topic: Employee Central Payroll.

6.5 Employee Central Payroll

A core HRIS is not complete if you don't have an option to process payroll utilizing the core HR data. Employee Central customers have a number of options for running payroll: you can leverage your existing investment in SAP ERP HCM payroll on-premise, outsource payroll processing to a *Business Process Outsourcing* (BPO) provider, use a third-party in-house payroll provider, or manage payroll in-house with the convenience of the cloud with Employee Central Payroll.

Employee Central Payroll is a cloud-hosted payroll system available for Employee Central customers *only*. It gives you the advantage of controlling your payroll within the convenience of the cloud. The Employee Central Payroll engine is hosted in the cloud by SAP at a data center in Germany. Upgrades, patches, legal changes, and tax updates are applied to the payroll engine without the customer ever having to experience the inconvenience of applying these upgrades, as is the case in the on-premise payroll engine.

The customer has full control of the payroll implementation and processing. With Employee Central Payroll, customers have the world's most proven payroll solution that currently supports 7,000 organizations in 90 countries. As of fall 2013, Employee Central Payroll is available for 23 countries with a roadmap to build for up to 51 countries depending on market demand.

6.5.1 Access and Data Replication

Access to Employee Central and Employee Central Payroll can be best understood by viewing the roles of users who need to access the application. These roles can be divided into employees and managers, HR administrators, and payroll managers. The core HRIS data is maintained in Employee Central while the payroll-related master data is maintained in the cloud-hosted payroll engine. Employees and managers maintain data and execute transactions in Employee Central. This data is replicated in the payroll engine through delivered integration for purposes of payroll processing. HR administrators and payroll managers can access the payroll engine to maintain payroll master data and payroll execution. Figure 6.27 shows how access to Employee Central and Employee Central Payroll changes based on the role of the individual.

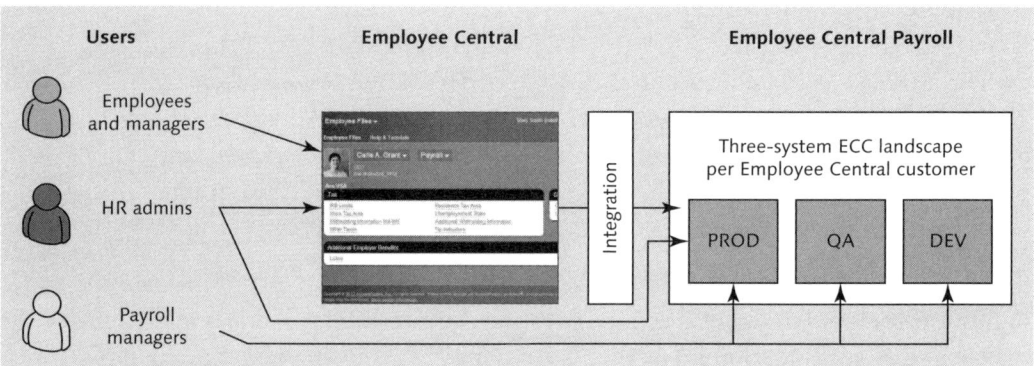

Figure 6.27 Employee Central Payroll Access Based on Role of the User

> **Note**
>
> Employee Central Payroll is available for 23 countries: Australia, Austria, Brazil, Canada, China, Finland, France, Germany, Hong Kong, India, Ireland, Italy, Japan, Malaysia, Mexico, Netherlands, Russia, Singapore, Spain, Sweden, Switzerland, the United Kingdom, and the United States.

The HR data objects (person and employment objects) that we covered in Section 6.2.4 and Section 6.2.5 are replicated to Employee Central Payroll:

- Personal data
- Addresses

- Nationality
- Compensation
- First day worked
- Cost center
- Payment method
- Bank details
- IBAN
- Earnings
- Contact information
- Job information

Any historical data items (including changes and deletions) are also replicated in the payroll engine. Currently, replication of employee data is available for 11 countries. One of the key features is the availability of the online pay statement on the UI in Employee Central.

Currently, integration between Employee Central and Employee Central Payroll is delivered using Dell Boomi AtomSphere. Employee data stored in Employee Central is mapped to the corresponding fields in the SAP ERP backend required by the payroll engine hosted in the cloud. Standard delivered integrations are also available between the hosted payroll and SAP Financials on-premise. More details on integration can be found in Chapter 3.

6.5.2 Myth versus Reality

Note that Employee Central Payroll is not a standalone offering. It's available for Employee Central customers only. Employee Central Payroll is not a new code but is instead SAP's proven payroll engine that has been used for a number of years and supports a large customer base. SAP's largest payroll customer pays 1.3 million people. Employee Central Payroll is also not a BPO or service bureau type offering. You are in complete control of your implementation and configuration of the system.

Payroll master data is maintained in a hosted payroll UI; all processes are executed via hosted payroll.

> **Myth**
>
> "Employee Central Payroll can be used if a customer maintains employee master data on the SAP ERP HCM on-premise platform."
>
> Because Employee Central Payroll utilizes SAP's payroll engine available for on-premise SAP ERP HCM applications, it's frequently interpreted that Employee Central Payroll is another option for executing payroll transactions for customers maintaining master data on the on-premise platform. However, this is not the case. Employee Central Payroll is available for use *only* if master data is maintained using Employee Central on the BizX platform.

You can execute the following processes in Employee Central Payroll:

- Master data maintained in Employee Central and replicated to Employee Central Payroll
- Gross pay calculation based on time entered
- Gross-to-net calculation of paychecks
- Retroactive pay calculation
- Garnishment calculation
- Paychecks and deposit advices
- Direct deposit of paychecks
- Payroll tax forms to be filed
- Quarterly and year end reports and forms
- End-to-end payroll process interfacing with the General Ledger

Employee Central Payroll is an optimal choice for Employee Central customers who want a complete cloud offering for their core HRIS and payroll system.

6.6 Summary

SuccessFactors Employee Central is the foundation of the entire SuccessFactors BizX suite. Additionally, it's an excellent core HR system that can be used with or without SAP ERP HCM as the system of record.

In this chapter, we introduced the unique features and functionalities of Employee Central that offer a competitive advantage to customers looking for a global core HRIS integrated with the Talent Management solutions of the BizX suite. We explored the XML data models that form the spinal column of the Employee Central framework and the OneAdmin interface that empowers customers with a configurable UI. Coupled with a robust global core HRIS in Employee Central, Employee Central Payroll enables customers to control payroll processes as well, thereby providing a complete HRIS in the cloud.

In Chapter 7, we'll discuss Employee Profile, which is the foundation of the Talent Management offerings such as SuccessFactors Performance & Goals and Succession & Development of the BizX suite. Employee Central provides a sound core HRIS, but for customers who are only interested in implementing the Talent suite and want to retain their existing HR systems, the BizX suite offers Employee Profile, which allows you to store the key data elements that are prerequisites for the talent planning tools.

Employee Profile drives workforce performance by connecting employees, enabling widespread knowledge sharing and collaboration, and providing ready access to the most comprehensive employee information needed to make informed talent decisions.

7   Employee Profile

Employee Profile is the foundation for much of the talent planning tools within SuccessFactors. With widespread user adoption, it becomes the housing area for employee history, accomplishments, and employment performance details. Employee Profile helps encourage employee engagement by providing employees with a place to connect with their colleagues and actively participate in their personal career and development planning.

Employee Profile enables customers to create a continuously updated, easily searchable directory of employee skills, interests, and expertise. Employees can maintain their own data, find colleagues with relevant or similar skills and interests, and publicly recognize their peers. Managers can view workforce information to identify skill gaps in their organization and ensure that they are working with the right people and on the right things, aligning them with team and company objectives.

In this chapter, we take a look at the features within Employee Profile and discuss how they can be utilized to develop a culture of collaboration and teaming within an organization.

Employee Profile is comprised of numerous elements that work together to provide a complete picture of an employee's Talent Profile. These elements are used by many people in an organization to view data about an employee. Managers use the data stored on Employee Profile and Scorecard as data points into the Talent and Succession Planning process. Other employees can view the Public Profile to quickly get contact information for their colleagues. Tags help employees identify interests with which they want to associate themselves, as well as help find other employees with the same interests or skills.

In this chapter, we'll review the Public Profile, looking at both Standard and Expressive options, as well as functionality such as Tags and Badges (Section 7.1). In Section 7.2, we'll review the Employee Profile in detail with a look at all of the background elements that can be defined to capture information about an employee. We discuss the Scorecard as a data collection point for Succession Planning and other Talent Planning in Section 7.3. We'll conclude with a discussion of how customers can build their own Employee Profile through OneAdmin with relative ease (Section 7.4 and Section 7.5).

7.1 Public Profile

The Public Profile was introduced as part of the SuccessFactors v12 release of Employee Profile. The Public Profile provides an attractive, usable view for employees to access data on colleagues. It provides all employees with a snapshot of anyone in the organization, along with that person's contact information such as job title, department, phone, and email information, as shown for Carla Grant in Figure 7.1. Colleagues can view details such as a brief description about the employee and what the employee's interests, contact information, organization chart, local time, badges, and tags.

An employee's Public Profile can be Standard or Expressive. Through the Expressive Public Profile, SuccessFactors provides employees the opportunity to visually express themselves to their colleagues by choosing a background photo. They can choose from images already provided by SuccessFactors or can upload their own personal photo, depending on company guidelines. This provides a personalized feel that allows employees to stand out to their colleagues.

The Standard Profile, which is shown in Figure 7.2, contains the same elements as the Expressive Profile but is displayed like the rest of Employee Profile. Many customers choose to maintain a uniform appearance to their Employee Profile and elect to have only the Standard Profile deployed.

Figure 7.1 Expressive Public Profile

Figure 7.2 Standard Profile

An editable profile allows employees the opportunity to provide a snapshot of themselves to colleagues. Features such as recording audio and video files to share personal and professional profile information make Public Profile an interactive experience, as shown in Figure 7.3.

7 | Employee Profile

Figure 7.3 Editing Expressive Public Profile

7.1.1 Badges

SuccessFactors incorporates Web 2.0 functionality with badges, which are used to recognize colleagues' achievements and efforts. Badges allow employees and managers to recognize each other outside of the normal performance and compensation management processes, which are often private. Badges are meant to be awarded by others; employees cannot award badges to themselves.

Badges are selected from a static BADGES menu and displayed on the employee's PROFILE. At this time, there is no configuration supported for adding new badge types or hiding existing badge types; you can choose to either deploy the BADGE background element shown in Figure 7.4 or not deploy it. Administrative configuration of custom badge types is planned for a later phase of badges development. Permissions for viewing badges have the same configuration and behavior as other data elements and are governed by the RBP model created in the instance and the permissions defined in the Succession data model.

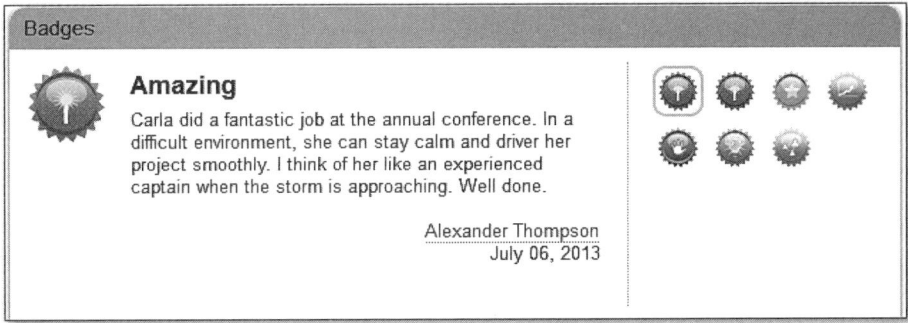

Figure 7.4 Badges Background Element

Permissions for adding or deleting badges have the same configuration and behavior as the edit permissions for any other data elements, except that you must be the creator or recipient of a badge to delete it—that is, employees cannot delete other employee's badges at will. Editing of existing badges isn't supported.

Badges are also displayed in the MY INFO tile on the v12 HOME page (see Figure 7.5).

Figure 7.5 Badges Displayed in My Info Tile

7.1.2 Tags

Further expanding Web 2.0 functionality into the system, tags provide a way for users to self-identify group affiliation such as professional associations/organizations and community activity groups, both internally and externally; several examples are shown in Figure 7.6. You are able to see all employees who have selected certain tags and leverage the system to stay connected to those in the tag group. Unlike badges, users can add tags to their own profile to identify with groups or interests within the organization with which they want to be affiliated. Tags can also be assigned by other users.

Figure 7.6 Tags

Because tags are displayed on the COMPANY INFO page when searching the Employee Directory, shown in Figure 7.7, and on the PUBLIC PROFILE, you can more easily find other employees who share the same tags, thereby increasing company cohesiveness and fostering a greater sense of community and collaboration.

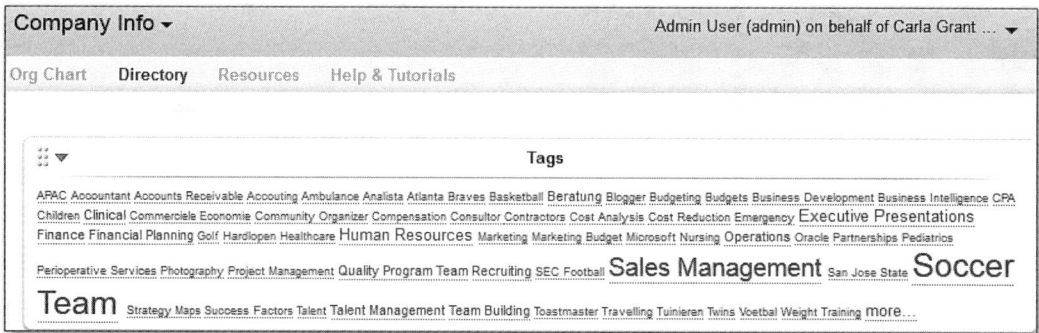

Figure 7.7 Tags in the Company Directory

7.2 Employee (Talent) Profile

The Employee or Talent Profile serves as an employee's online résumé by providing an area to add details about the employee's background, work history, job experience, and skills. SuccessFactors provides numerous standard background elements in the Succession data model that can be configured on the Employee Profile to capture the information pertinent to each company. These portlets display system-generated information together with employee-generated data on the Talent Profile to provide a holistic view of an employee.

7.2.1 Employee Overview

The Talent Profile generally begins with an overview of the employee displayed in the OVERVIEW and EMPLOYEE INFORMATION background elements, as shown on the left in Figure 7.8. Here, information from the employee's data record in the BizX suite can be displayed because it's pertinent to the talent process. These fields can be permissioned for viewing and editing based on role and in the Succession data model.

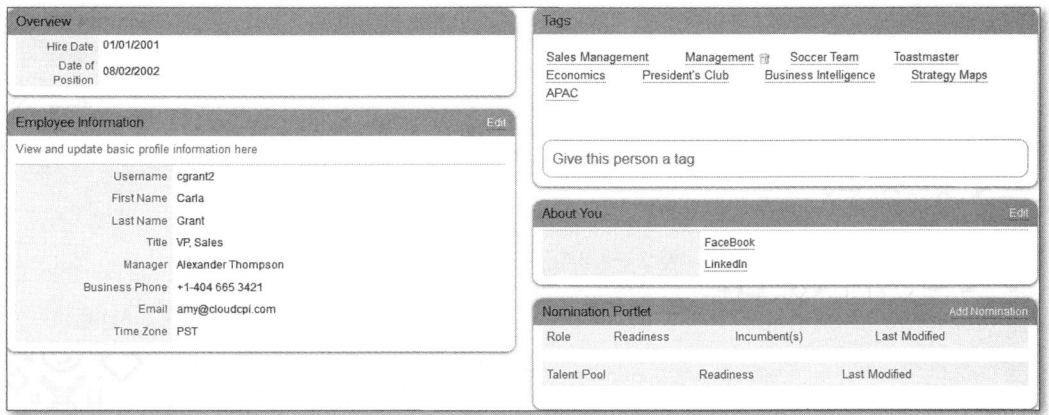

Figure 7.8 Employee Overview in the Talent Profile

7.2.2 Background Elements

The SuccessFactors data model comes with standard background elements that can be configured on the Profile via the OneAdmin feature in the instance. These background elements can be used as they come or can be modified to add or remove fields and make fields required or optional. We'll look at these background elements in the following sections.

Experience

An employee's experience is captured in numerous background elements that are designed to reflect the roles employees have held within the company, the type of functional experience they've had in those roles, any leadership experience they have had, and previous employment. This information can be captured in the following standard background elements, which are shown in Figure 7.9:

- DOCUMENTS
- WORK EXPERIENCE WITHIN COMPANY
- FUNCTIONAL EXPERIENCE
- LEADERSHIP EXPERIENCE
- PREVIOUS EMPLOYMENT

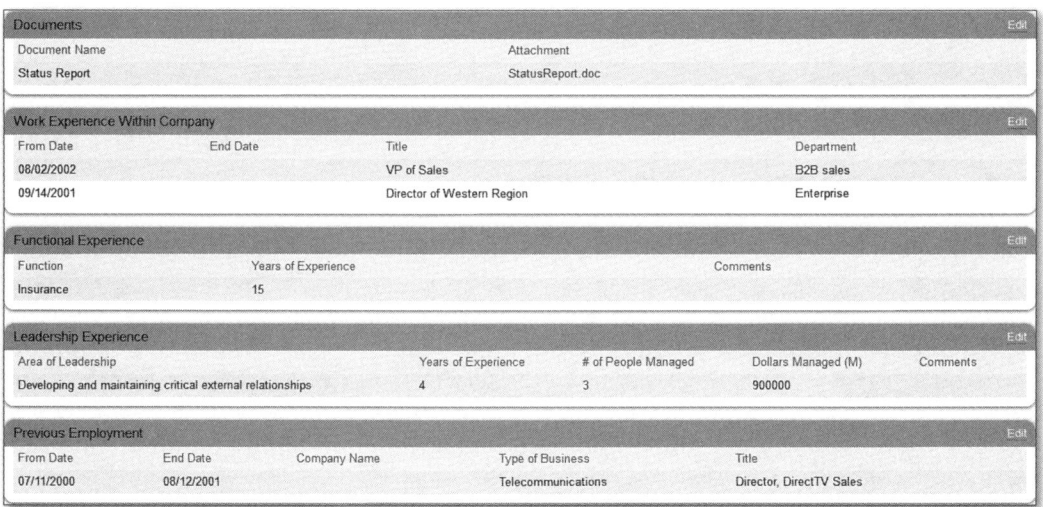

Figure 7.9 Work/Experience Background Elements

Education and Interests

An employee's educational background and specialty interests can be captured in standard background elements as well. Along with gathering information on whether an employee is open to relocating, these background elements capture their career goals and interests to assist managers and HR in career planning for the employee.

Finally, this section also documents any special assignments, roles, or projects the employee has participated in that aren't directly tied to their role but are relevant to their experience and development. This information can be captured in the following standard background elements, which are shown in Figure 7.10:

- Formal Education
- Career Goals/Interests
- Geographic Mobility
- Special Assignments/Projects

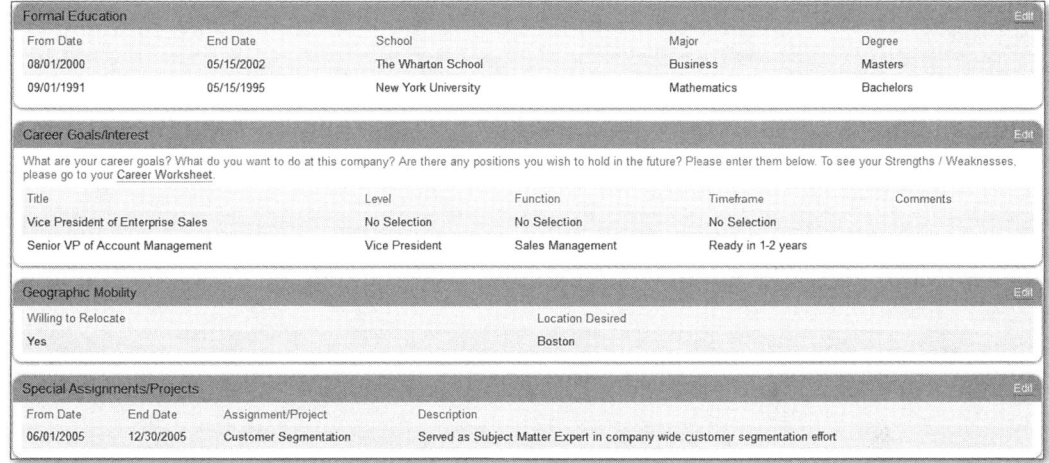

Figure 7.10 Education and Interests Background Elements

Other Employee Skills

Finally, companies are able to gather data around outside training and certifications that employees have obtained, as well as languages spoken. An employee's professional memberships, honors, and community involvement can also be documented in various background elements. This information can also be critical to the talent and development processes because it underscores the qualifications employees have for future positions and other roles within the company. This information can be documented in the following background elements, which are shown in Figure 7.11:

- COURSES/WORKSHOPS/SEMINARS
- CERTIFICATIONS/LICENSES
- LANGUAGE SKILLS
- PROFESSIONAL MEMBERSHIPS
- HONORS/AWARDS
- COMMUNITY/VOLUNTEER INVOLVEMENT

Figure 7.11 Other Employee Skills

Other Considerations

While all of these background elements are provided for use, it's important to keep in mind that you don't need to use all of them. You can decide which background elements to deploy while implementing Employee Profile. Every customer's data model contains all of the standard background elements. These can be used as-is, modified at the field level per requirements, or custom configured by your implementation consultant. Also, the Employee Profile can be edited in OneAdmin so companies have the option to add or remove background elements at any time. Often, new customers may find the thought of deploying all background elements to be overwhelming, especially if the company hasn't previously attempted to capture this data. SuccessFactors offers total flexibility to utilize this powerful tool in the time and manner that best meets customers' needs.

7.3 Scorecard

The Scorecard is the section of the Employee Profile that is used as key data input to the Succession Planning process. The Scorecard is not visible to employees—only managers and other roles designated with permission to view the Scorecard. A series of standard portlets and background elements are intended to provide data specifically geared for evaluating employees for placement on the nine-box report and finding successors for key positions. We'll discuss Succession Planning in more detail in Chapter 12; this section is intended to cover those touch points between Succession Planning and Employee Profile.

The portlets and background elements that capture Succession-related data can reside anywhere. Many companies prefer to keep all data on one tab and combine the elements of the Employee Profile and Scorecard together, using permissions to govern who can see and do what. Other organizations prefer to keep these two separated, as they come out of the box. This is a configuration decision that will be made during implementation.

Regardless of where the data resides, the important point to note here is that this type of information is typically considered highly confidential and isn't made available for viewing to a wide population. Again, this is a configuration decision that will be made according to the company's process and data requirements, but the system allows a great amount of flexibility and a granular level of security through RBP and adding permissions to data and background elements in the Succession data model. Your implementation consultant will help guide you through considerations for making these critical configuration decisions.

7.3.1 Employee Overview

From a Scorecard perspective, several portlets can be configured to give a snapshot of the employee and provide an overview of the employee's Succession data, such as performance and potential rating and placement on the nine-box report. The OVERVIEW portlet shown in Figure 7.12 is generally only visible to the manager, upline managers, HR representatives, and the custom manager (if that role is utilized in Succession Planning).

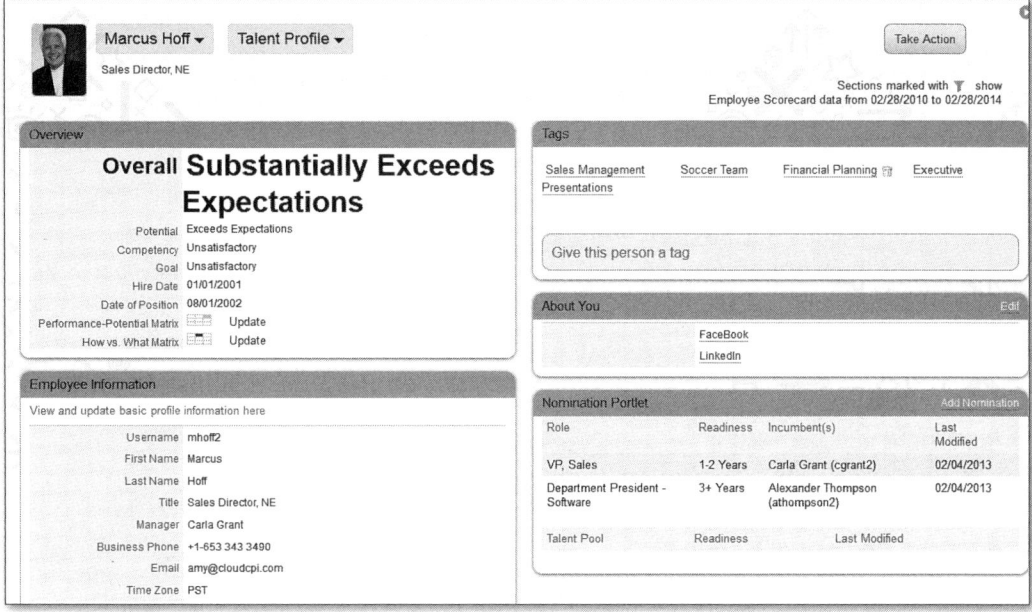

Figure 7.12 Overview Information on the Scorecard

Given the correct permissions, managers and HR personnel may be able to update an employee's placement on both the PERFORMANCE-POTENTIAL matrix (see Figure 7.13) and the How vs. What matrix reports directly from the OVERVIEW portlet. By selecting the UPDATE link, users can update the placement by selecting the correct box and entering effective date information. These matrices are discussed in detail in Chapter 12.

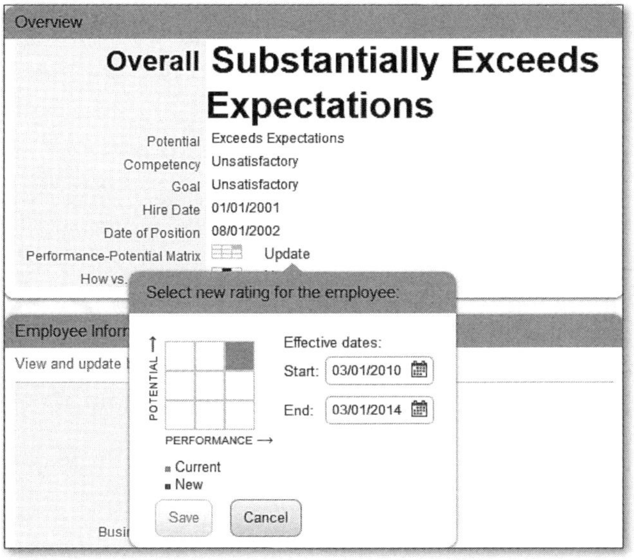

Figure 7.13 Update Performance-Potential Matrix Placement

7.3.2 Nomination Portlet

The standard background element NOMINATION PORTLET displays an employee's existing Succession nominations and enables managers to add new nominations directly in the portlet, as shown in Figure 7.14. Nominations can also be made on the Succession Org Chart (as discussed in Chapter 12).

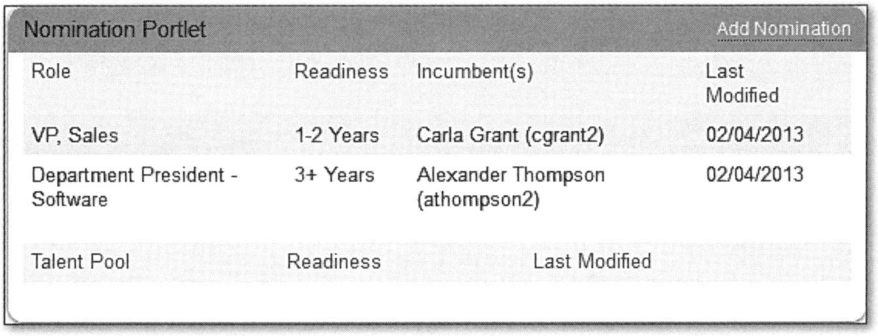

Figure 7.14 Nomination Portlet

7.3.3 Competency and Objective Portlets

Companies can choose to display standard background elements that display an employee's competencies, objectives, and related ratings. This information may be relevant and helpful during the talent review and Succession Planning process by providing ready access to how employees are developing and performing against their core and job-specific competencies. Easy access to the COMPETENCY and OBJECTIVE portlets prevents managers and talent planners from navigating away from the Talent Profile to the REPORTS tab or pulling up the employee's past performance reviews to get this data; these are shown in Figure 7.15.

Competency Portlet — Edit

Start Date	End Date	label	Source	Module
09/01/2011	12/31/2013	2.0-Meets Expectations	Calibration	Calibration
11/25/2013	11/25/2013	0.0-	Performance Review	Performance Manager
09/01/2013	10/31/2013	1.0-Exceeds Expectations	Calibration	Calibration
09/01/2013	10/31/2013	1.0-Exceeds Expectations	Calibration	Calibration
09/01/2013	10/31/2013	1.0-Exceeds Expectations	Calibration	Calibration
09/01/2011	10/31/2013	1.0-Does Not Meet	Calibration	Calibration
03/01/2013	03/01/2013	1-Does Not Meet	Scorecard	Scorecard
03/01/2013	03/01/2013	1-Does Not Meet	Scorecard	Scorecard

Objective Portlet — Edit

Start Date	End Date	label	Source	Module
09/01/2011	12/31/2013	1.0-Does Not Meet	Calibration	Calibration
11/25/2013	11/25/2013	0.0-	Performance Review	Performance Manager
09/01/2013	10/31/2013	1.0-Exceeds Expectations	Calibration	Calibration
09/01/2013	10/31/2013	1.0-Exceeds Expectations	Calibration	Calibration
09/01/2013	10/31/2013	1.0-Exceeds Expectations	Calibration	Calibration
09/01/2011	10/31/2013	1.0-Does Not Meet	Calibration	Calibration
03/01/2013	03/01/2013	1-Does Not Meet	Scorecard	Scorecard
03/01/2013	03/01/2013	2-Meets Expectations	Scorecard	Scorecard

Figure 7.15 Competency and Objective Portlets

7.3.4 Talent Information

The TALENT INFORMATION portlet shown in Figure 7.16 captures data that can be used as flags and icons on the Succession Org Chart. Talent flags like the following are determined by each customer during implementation:

- Risk of loss
- Impact of loss
- Reason for leaving
- Bench strength

- Future leader
- Key position

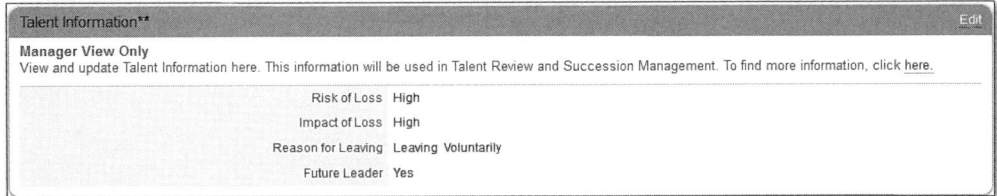

Figure 7.16 Talent Information Portlet

7.3.5 Performance and Potential

Two background elements are available to display historical information around performance and potential ratings (see Figure 7.17). The PERFORMANCE **MANAGER VIEW ONLY and POTENTIAL **MANAGER VIEW ONLY portlets are not available to employees. These are intended to store historical performance/potential ratings relevant to Succession Planning and are an input into the OVERALL rating in the OVERVIEW portlet (discussed in Section 7.3.1) on the Scorecard. These two portlets can be permissioned so managers or custom managers can add both performance and potential scores directly in the background elements during the Succession Planning process.

Performance **Manager view only			Edit
Start Date	End Date	Rating Label	
09/01/2011	12/31/2013	HIGH	
10/23/2013	11/22/2013	HIGH	
09/01/2013	10/31/2013	HIGH	
09/01/2013	10/31/2013	HIGH	
09/01/2011	10/31/2013	HIGH	
08/01/2013	10/30/2013	HIGH	
08/17/2013	08/17/2013		
08/17/2013	08/17/2013	HIGH	
07/14/2013	08/13/2013		
03/01/2013	03/01/2013	SOLID	
01/01/2012	12/31/2012	Unsatisfactory	

Potential **Manager view only			Edit
Start Date	End Date	Rating Label	
09/01/2011	12/31/2013	3.0-HIGH	
10/23/2013	11/22/2013	3.0-HIGH	
08/07/2013	11/05/2013	3-HIGH	
09/01/2013	10/31/2013	2.0-SOLID	
09/01/2013	10/31/2013	2.0-SOLID	
09/01/2011	10/31/2013	2.0-SOLID	
03/01/2013	03/01/2013	2-SOLID	

Figure 7.17 Performance and Potential **Manager View Only

7.4 Other Features

SuccessFactors has other features available on the Employee Profile to keep employees linked to social media and professional networking applications. The ABOUT YOU background element can link to an employee's Facebook and/or LinkedIn profiles (see Figure 7.18).

Figure 7.18 About You

7.4.1 Facebook

Facebook integration allows you to easily look up an employee in the *Facebook.com* application. You can click on the FACEBOOK link to search for all users in Facebook.com with the same first and last name as the employee that you are looking for. If you sign up as a Facebook user and accept the *Facebook.com* cookie, you'll experience seamless integration between SuccessFactors and Facebook.

7.4.2 LinkedIn

LinkedIn integration allows you to easily look up an employee in the *LinkedIn.com* application. You can click on the LINKEDIN link to search for all users at *LinkedIn.com* with the same first and last name as the employee that you are looking for.

7.5 Configure Employee Files

The beauty of Employee Profile and all of its components is that it's highly configurable directly from the OneAdmin interface, putting the control in the hands of the customer. After the requisite data and background elements are configured in the Succession data model, the customer may add, remove, and reorder the elements on the Employee Profile and Scorecard, as well as copy and create new views as required.

Any system administrator with the appropriate permission may choose to configure employee files directly from the OneAdmin page by clicking the CONFIGURE EMPLOYEE FILES option shown in Figure 7.19. Any changes made to the employee files are effective immediately upon saving the dashboard, so it's critical that this administrative privilege not be widely dispersed and that care is taken to make changes that won't impact users during business hours.

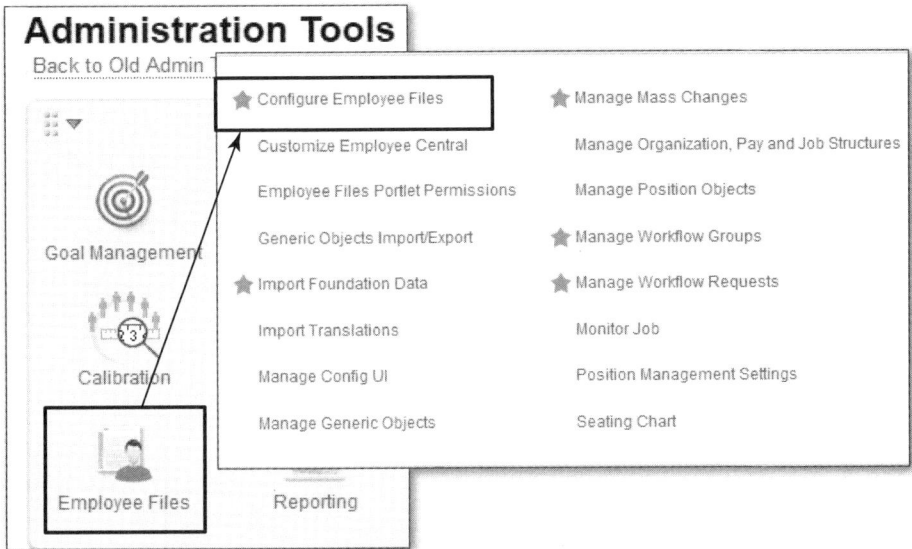

Figure 7.19 Configure Employee Files from OneAdmin

You can add, copy, or delete employee file layouts. Not all layouts may be deleted — there are some standard layouts that cannot be deleted — but they do not have to be displayed. This is controlled from the SHOW/HIDE column shown in Figure 7.20.

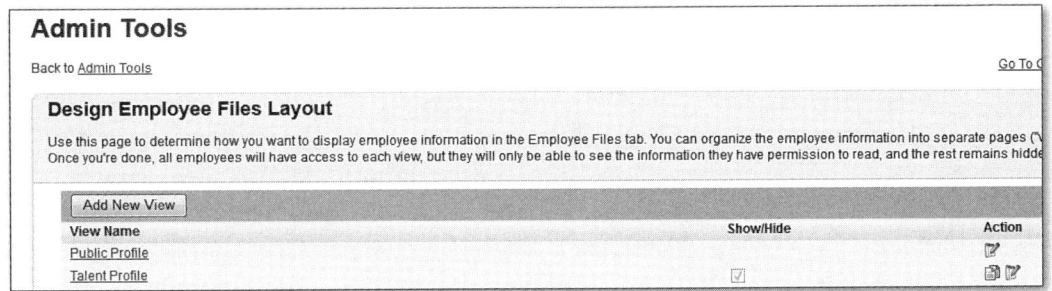

Figure 7.20 Design Employee Files Layout

Within each layout, or dashboard, you can move layout elements around in a matter of mouse clicks. Use the up, down, left, and right arrows to place the elements where they should live. Use the red DELETE icon shown in Figure 7.21 to remove the element from the layout. To edit each background element, select the edit icon under the ACTION column. Here you can rename the portlet and make other changes, depending on the portlet with which you are working.

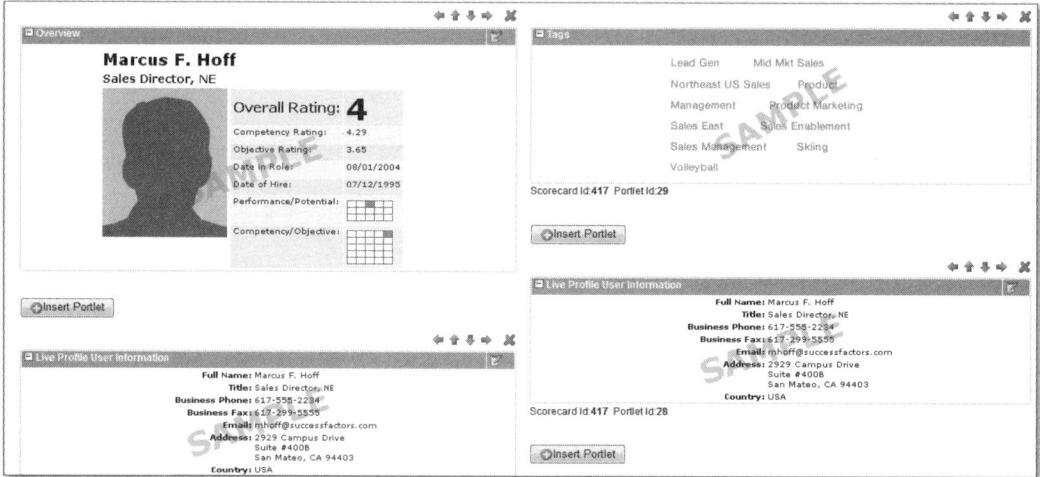

Figure 7.21 Editing an Employee Files Layout

7.6 Summary

Employee Profile brings together many BizX modules into one place and encourages employees and managers to collaborate with each other. As companies implement the other BizX modules, Employee Profile makes gains in richness and application, and, in turn, other modules benefit from a robust Employee Profile because it makes a complete employee picture available.

Employee Profile allows employees to express their personal identity outside the work environment through the Expressive public profile. Background elements provide a place for employees to document information on their professional qualifications and experience, and allow them to be a resource to each other and the company. Badges assist employees in recognizing each other for accomplishments and skillsets, and tags assist employees in searching for others with like interests. Managers gain a richer understanding of their team through both the Employee Profile and the Scorecard, and can utilize each team member in a more efficient capacity to achieve company, department, and personal objectives. Finally, the company benefits generally by having an accurate, well-rounded view of its people resources to better utilize them throughout the organization to meet corporate objectives.

In the next chapter, we will look at how SuccessFactors' Performance Management and Goal Management modules provide visibility and alignment to an organization's objectives, and efficiency and best practices for reviewing performance.

One characteristic of high-performing businesses is that they conduct multiple performance reviews each year. The Performance Management and Goal Management modules provide businesses with the tools to align their employees to corporate objectives and optimize workforce performance to achieve business execution results.

8   Performance & Goals

In today's competitive business environment, business execution is a key buzzword that corporations globally are striving to achieve. But many companies struggle to execute on their business strategy and never achieve the results they seek because they are unfocused or have either outdated or nonexistent technology to help them execute.

SuccessFactors provides tools to align an organization to corporate objectives. Through the Performance Management (PM) and Goal Management (GM) modules in the BizX suite, a company can drive alignment across the organization through a series of goals that are cascaded to every employee. Progress toward these goals can be tracked from the top; executives can be sure that their entire team of employees is aware of the corporate strategy and the role each individual plays in executing on that strategy. This helps drive focus toward the right things, provides visibility of progress of the entire organization, and heightens accountability.

BizX provides a series of robust tools to take performance and goal processes to the next level. One such tool is Stack Ranker, which lets managers rate their team at once against each other; with 360 Multi-Rater, they gain a well-rounded view of their employee's performance that serves as input to the overall performance assessment. New features of Team Rater take Stack Ranker to the next level, providing managers a one-stop shop for completing their team's reviews. Calibration enables managers to level set ratings across their team for input to other performance processes such as Compensation and Succession Planning.

While PM and GM are two separate modules within the BizX solution, they work hand in hand to support talent development processes. In this chapter, we'll take a look at PM and GM. Performance reviews are incomplete without input from goal progress, and goals are only so meaningful in the absence of a formal performance review process. We'll discuss the tools available in the scope of the performance process. Specifically, we'll review the following PM and GM components:

- Goal Development and Execution
- Performance Reviews
- Team Rater
- 360 Multi-Rater
- Calibration

Let's begin by examining the performance process with Goal Management.

8.1 Goal Management

SuccessFactors is known for helping align an organization against company-wide goals. This is an area that remains critical to the development of the BizX suite because of its foundational importance to business execution.

The performance process begins with goal setting and continues as employees progress toward goals throughout the performance year. The BizX suite facilitates the creation, alignment, monitoring, and measurement of both organizational and personal goals as represented in Figure 8.1. The *goal plan* is the basis for GM in BizX. The goals that appear in the goal plan are easy to create and edit throughout the year, by both the employee and manager.

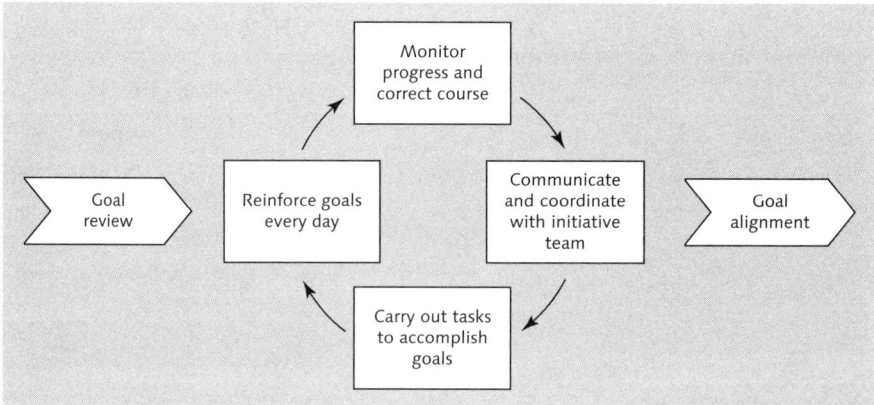

Figure 8.1 Goal Alignment through Execution

The goal plan is comprised of the following elements:

- **Goal categories**
  Categories are used to organize goals on the goal plan. Standard goal categories are based on the Balanced Scorecard methodology, but customers may configure additional or different goal categories to meet their tracking and reporting requirements.

- **Align and Link**
  This functionality encourages organizational goal adoption throughout business units, departments, and other organizational groups. Cascading goals from the top of the organization down through the organizational structure ensures company alignment to individual and group objectives. Linking goals allows alignment and tracking across the organization.

- **SMART Goal Wizard**
  This powerful tool provides employees a step-by-step wizard to walk through creating goals that are Specific, Measurable, Attainable, Relevant, and Time Bound—the tenets of SuccessFactors development.

- **Best-Practice Goal Library**
  This best-practice collection of goals provides more than 500 ready-to-use, role-specific goals that customers can leverage as corporate or individual goals.

- **Goal Alignment Spotlight**
  What use is goal alignment if you have no visibility? This feature provides full line-of-sight visibility to goals across and down through the organization.

- **Dashboards and spotlights**
  This feature provides managers and other organizational leaders dashboard visibility into progression of the organization against corporate goals. From dashboards, managers can track how their team is performing against corporate strategy.

Goal plans like the one shown in Figure 8.2 are structured for ease of use by employees and managers. Each category is clearly labeled with corresponding categorized goals that are numerically ordered under each category. Display options are user defined, so each user can display the information that is most pertinent and helpful to achieving the goals of that particular user. Managers may easily navigate to their team's goal plans with a single mouse click. Aligned (cascaded) goals may be tracked directly from the user's goal plan by selecting the ALIGNED UP or ALIGNED DOWN display options to the left. Outlook calendar integration is

8 | Performance & Goals

available so goal-related due dates can be added to a user's calendar. STATUS of the goal is clearly labeled with a colored bar to indicate goal progress.

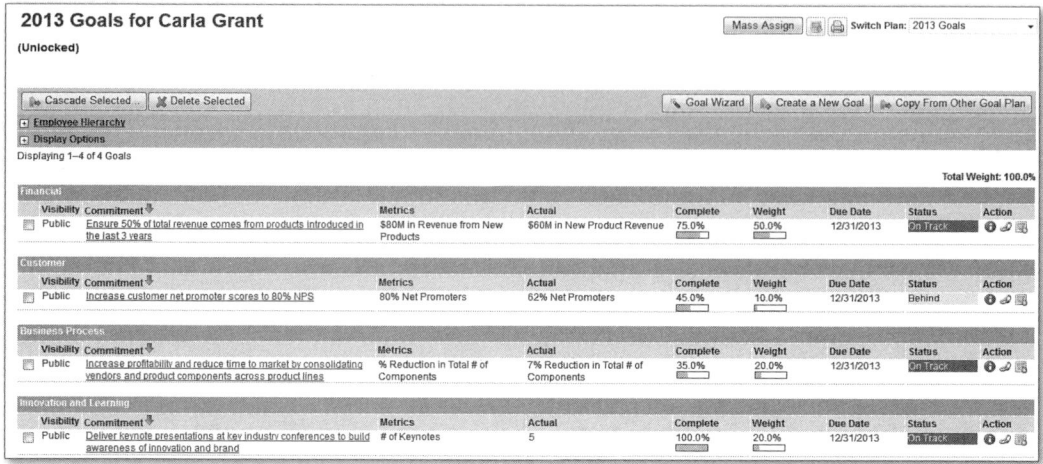

Figure 8.2 Goal Plan

8.1.1 Maintaining Goals

You can create or edit goals at any time. New or custom goals can be created in several ways:

- Create a custom goal.
- Use the Goal Library.
- Use the Goal Wizard.
- Create the goal from another goal plan.

A user can create his own goal by selecting the ADD GOAL button (see Figure 8.3), which allows the user to populate all fields in the goal plan, or the user can also choose CREATE A LIBRARY GOAL.

Regardless of which option a user chooses, the user ends up at the same screen. The ADD GOAL dialog layout will depend on the configuration decisions made during the design phase of implementation. The example in Figure 8.4 contains many fields, but customers can design a much more streamlined goal structure if desired. Two critical features to note are the VISIBILITY and CATEGORY fields, which are boxed.

Goal Management | **8.1**

Figure 8.3 Create a New Goal Dialog

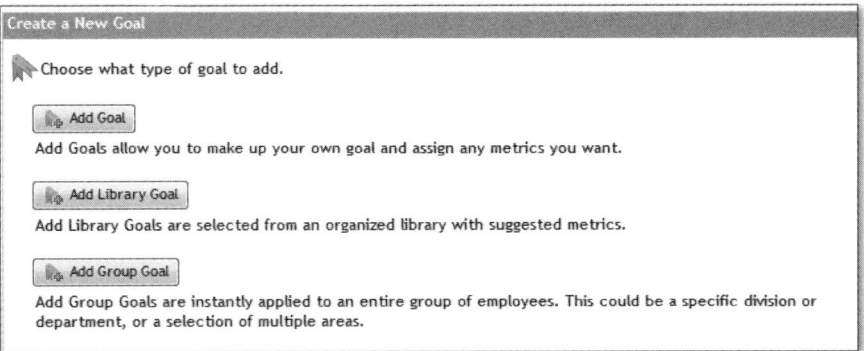

Figure 8.4 Adding a Goal

VISIBILITY determines whether a goal is public, meaning anyone who can view the goal plan may also view the goal, or private, meaning only the employee, the employee's manager (and possibly second-level manager), and HR personnel may view the goal. This permission is determined in the configuration of the goal plan template to meet customer requirements. Default visibility will be configured in the goal plan, but employees may choose to change this after the goal is created.

A category for each goal must be selected to correctly order the goals on the plan. The category can always be updated after the goal is created, but having goals incorrectly categorized could impact downstream reporting and alignment spotlights.

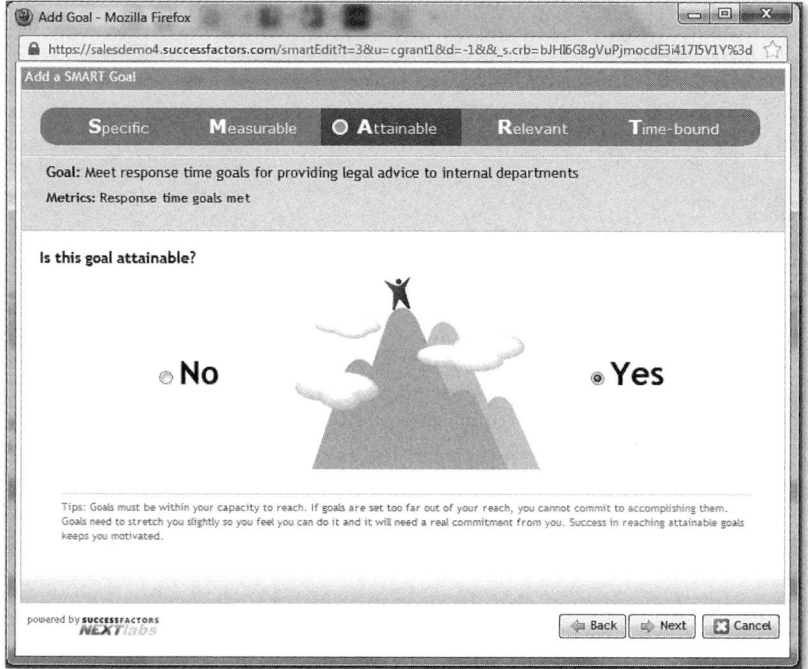

Figure 8.5 SMART Goal Wizard

Users unfamiliar with SMART goals may opt to utilize the SMART Goal Wizard and have the system guide them through creating a SMART goal, as demonstrated in Figure 8.5. The Goal Library is also leveraged in the SMART Goal Wizard so users can select a library goal as a starting point by typing their goal in the GOAL NAME box. They are offered possible matches based on what they are typing. Users are taken through each step of a SMART goal until they have met all elements and are then presented the ADD GOAL dialog box, as displayed earlier in Figure 8.4. Here they can add any additional details that may be required and then save the goal.

8.1.2 Aligning and Cascading Goals

After goals are created, they can be cascaded up or down the reporting chain. Through this alignment of goals, a company has visibility to the goals that employees are working toward, as well as whether they are corporate or personal goals. Anyone with direct reports may cascade a goal down to their team or matrix reports. If goal plan permissions allow, goals may also be cascaded up. It's possible for mangers to cascade a goal up to themselves from their direct report's goal plan, or for employees to cascade a goal up to their managers.

Goals may be cascaded individually or in a group to one or more team members. The Cascade Goal wizard walks through the steps necessary to cascade the goal(s) to the appropriate people, as shown in Figure 8.6. After they are cascaded, display options will keep the user up to date on progress of aligned goals, as demonstrated in Figure 8.7.

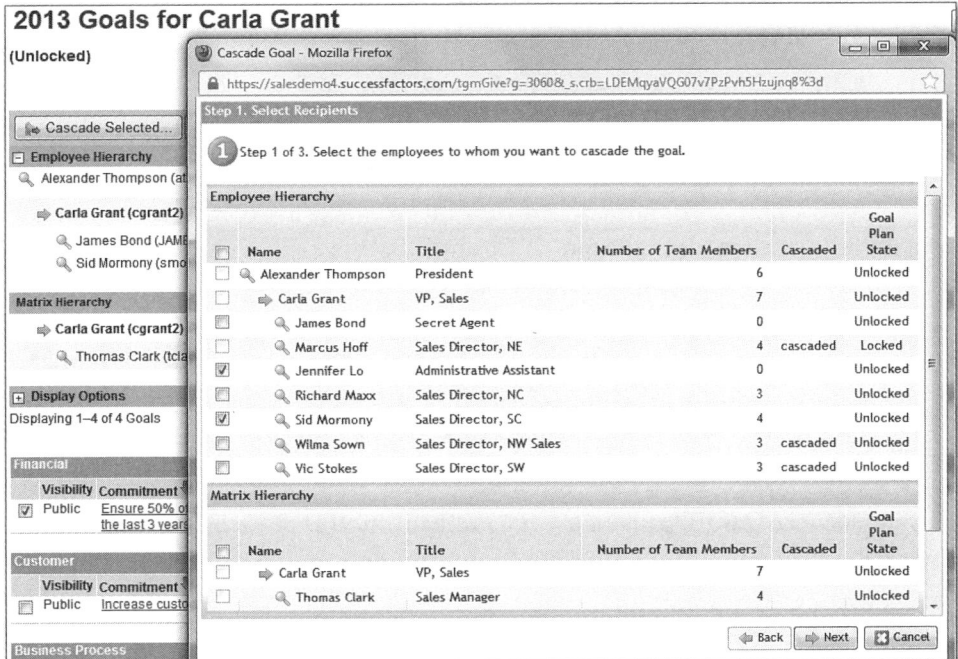

Figure 8.6 Cascade Goal Wizard

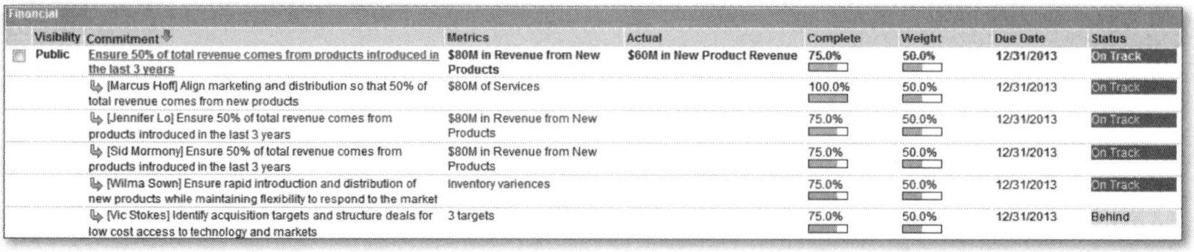

8 | Performance & Goals

Visibility	Commitment	Metrics	Actual	Complete	Weight	Due Date	Status
Public	Ensure 50% of total revenue comes from products introduced in the last 3 years	$80M in Revenue from New Products	$60M in New Product Revenue	75.0%	50.0%	12/31/2013	On Track
	[Marcus Hoff] Align marketing and distribution so that 50% of total revenue comes from new products	$80M of Services		100.0%	50.0%	12/31/2013	On Track
	[Jennifer Lo] Ensure 50% of total revenue comes from products introduced in the last 3 years	$80M in Revenue from New Products		75.0%	50.0%	12/31/2013	On Track
	[Sid Mormony] Ensure 50% of total revenue comes from products introduced in the last 3 years	$80M in Revenue from New Products		75.0%	50.0%	12/31/2013	On Track
	[Wilma Sown] Ensure rapid introduction and distribution of new products while maintaining flexibility to respond to the market	Inventory variences		75.0%	50.0%	12/31/2013	On Track
	[Vic Stokes] Identify acquisition targets and structure deals for low cost access to technology and markets	3 targets		75.0%	50.0%	12/31/2013	Behind

Figure 8.7 Aligned Goals Display

8.1.3 Goal Execution

Goal Execution is a part of GM that assists employees and managers to reinforce goal progress and achievement. Through Goal Execution, managers have tools to help them ensure their team is focused on the right goals and working toward achieving them on a daily basis.

> **Note**
>
> Goal Execution is meant for companies that update and monitor goals on a regular basis. It's also intended for organizations that align goals by cascading them down through the reporting hierarchy. There are configuration considerations to be aware of when implementing Goal Execution; your implementation consultant will review those with you if you choose to roll out this powerful set of tools.

Goal Execution facilitates goal achievement by providing an interface to visualize goals and monitor progress every time a user logs in. Employees and managers, or executives at the highest level, can view individual goals and corporate goals to which they are aligned. Managers can track progress of goals and drill into each goal for more information on issues that may impede progress. The Execution Map illustrated in Figure 8.8 gives managers a visual representation of their team's goal progress. On-track goals are shown in green, while goals that are lagging are shown in red. From the Execution Map, the manager can drill into each goal to view details and determine what issues may be impeding progress.

Workflows are available to allow employees to regularly update progress toward goals and level of effort, gauge the probability of success of each goal, and provide comments. This is visible via the status report shown in Figure 8.9.

Goal Management | 8.1

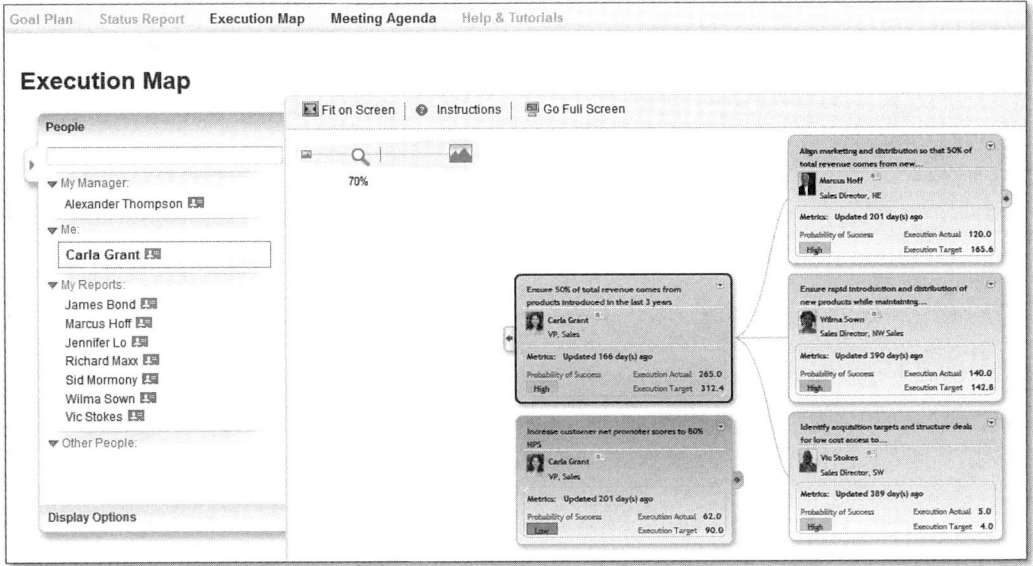

Figure 8.8 Execution Map

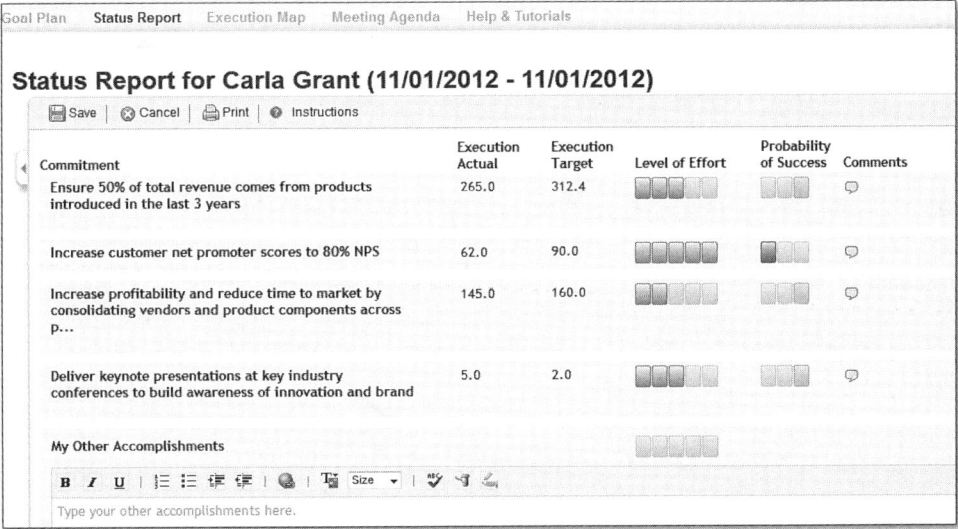

Figure 8.9 Goal Status Report

Additional tools available with Goal Execution assist managers in communicating with their team on goal progress. The MEETING AGENDA subtab shown in Figure 8.10 provides an easy interface from which to build items for discussion with each employee about goal progress; it even provides Outlook integration so that managers can set up meetings with employees all from one place.

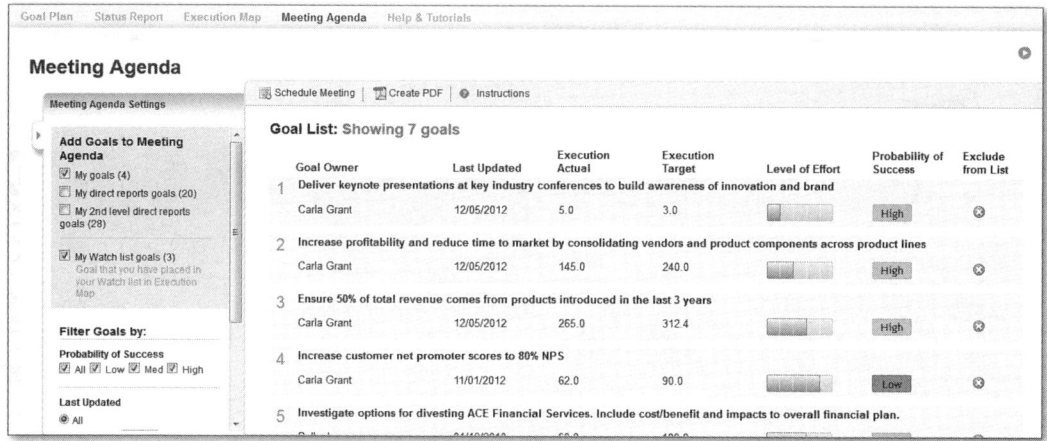

Figure 8.10 Meeting Agenda

8.2 Performance Management

As goals are established and tracked, they become part of the performance review process. Performance reviews in PM and GM assists companies in measuring individual performance against company objectives and competencies, as well as personal objectives and competencies. This information feeds into any number of other talent processes such as SuccessFactors Compensation Management, Succession Planning, Learning, and Career Development. Performance reviews are designed on best practices and provide numerous tools to assist all participants in the process to produce the best possible performance feedback. Highlights of PM tools and functionality include the following:

- **Writing Assistant and Coaching Advisor**
  This powerful tool provides best-practice content for commenting on competency feedback. It's available to both employees and managers and will greatly increase the effectiveness of meaningful feedback in the performance process.

- **Flexible workflows**
  Each form has a route map that determines who touches the performance review, what they can do with it, and when each step is due. Tools such as iterative steps to allow the form to go between two users before moving forward, and collaborative steps where the form resides in two user's inboxes simultaneously, help increase completeness of performance reviews.

- **Legal Scan**
  This tool works much like a spell check and reviews and flags potentially inappropriate language in a performance review.

- **Team overview**
  A feature of Performance Management v12, this interface allows managers a dashboard-like view of their team's review status. Review feedback and workflow steps can be managed from this view.

- **Ask for Feedback**
  Soliciting feedback from others as input to a performance review is effortless with the enhanced Ask for Feedback functionality. Requests are sent and respondents can reply via email, and the responses are visible from within the performance review form.

8.2.1 Performance Review Structure

Though performance reviews can be configured to include items specific to customer's needs, the best-practice performance review includes three main content sections:

- The goal plan
- Core competencies
- Role-specific competencies

Each section is given a weight of the overall performance score, or selected to be excluded from the overall score. In the newest interface, ratings are as easy as hovering over the star icon and clicking the mouse to save the entry as displayed in Figure 8.11; the form auto-saves as the reviewer moves through each item. Comments can be collected at the goal or competency item level, for the entire section, or both. The Writing Assistant is available for competencies. Each comment box can have spell check and Legal Scan available for use.

8 | Performance & Goals

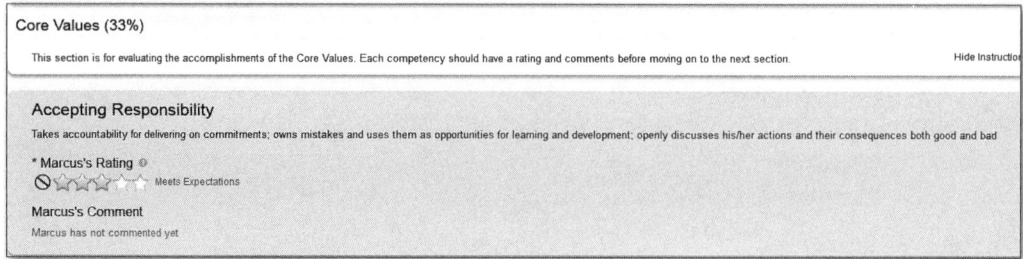

Figure 8.11 Sample Performance Review Section

Customers may choose to also include an INDIVIDUAL DEVELOPMENT PLAN section in the form; this is common for customers who are not implementing the Development module. Note that any development goals created in this section will only be available in the form if linked to the *development plan* in the Development module. The Development module is covered in detail in Chapter 12.

Finally, the form has an OVERALL PERFORMANCE SUMMARY section. This is visible to the manager and displays a summary of the rated items in the form. The OVERALL SCORE is also displayed at the top of the form in the SCORE POD, AS SHOWN IN Figure 8.12. Other pods that are available track the number of incomplete items in the review and where the current employee ranks in the overall team.

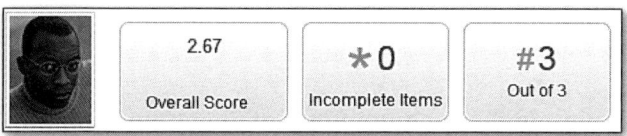

Figure 8.12 Manager View of Performance Form

8.2.2 Team Overview

Managers now have access to the TEAM OVERVIEW subtab where they can manage all performance reviews in one view, which can be seen in Figure 8.13. In the TEAM OVERVIEW subtab, they can see who has completed a self-review or which team members still need to be rated, use the ASK FOR FEEDBACK function, and track the form along the workflow until it's completed.

Ask for Feedback

As managers prepare to complete a performance review, they may find it helpful to have feedback from others who have worked with the employee throughout the year. Outside of a formal *360 Multi-Rater assessment*, managers can use the ASK FOR FEEDBACK mechanism to solicit immediate feedback from others for input into the performance review. Feedback can be requested from internal employees or sent to those external to the organization. The manager can customize the email that accompanies the request or use the standard language. Responses are tracked from the TEAM OVERVIEW tab, or from within the performance form itself in the SUPPORTING INFORMATION pod. An example of the ASK FOR FEEDBACK form can be seen in Figure 8.14.

Figure 8.13 Team Overview

Team Rater

When self-reviews have been completed and all requested feedback has been received, managers can commence with rating their team's performance. The Team Rater feature builds on the Stack Ranker concept in BizX to allow managers to rate all employees against the same competencies at the same time. This tool allows the managers to see how their team members stack up against each other, as demonstrated in Figure 8.15.

8 | Performance & Goals

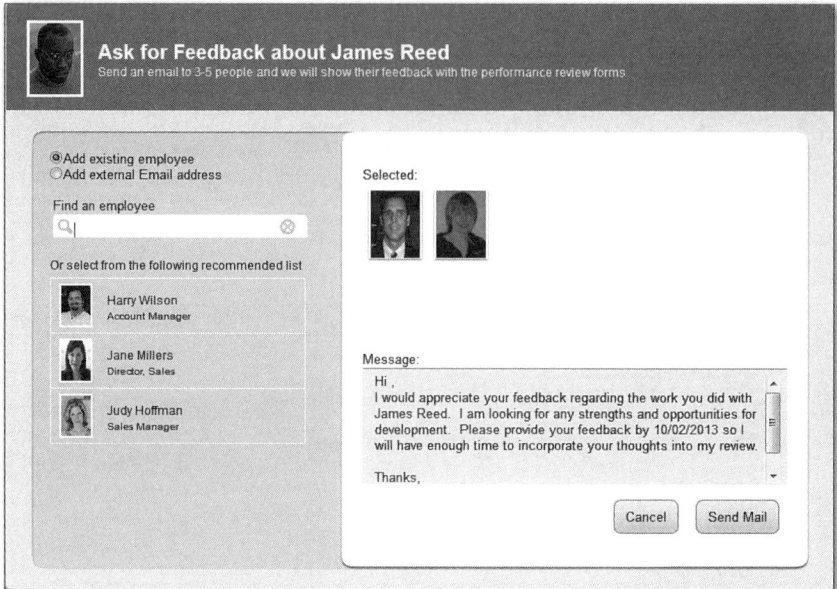

Figure 8.14 Ask for Feedback Form

Figure 8.15 Team Rater

Managers can easily rate against each competency and add comments to each competency as they go along. Scores are summarized along the bottom, and managers have instant feedback as to the employee's ratings. This information is also displayed along the right side of the screen, and each employee is given a ranking based on the employee's competency scores. The employees in Figure 8.16 have been ranked 1-3 according to their competency scores.

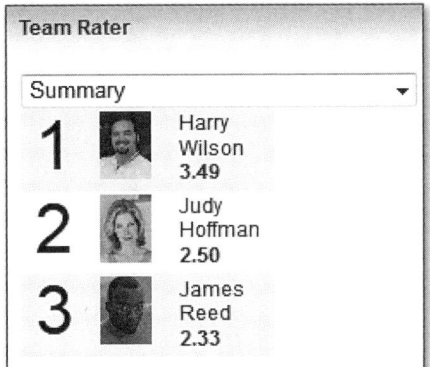

Figure 8.16 Stack-Ranked Employees

8.2.3 Writing Assistant and Coaching Advisor

The Writing Assistant and Coaching Advisor tool helps managers provide accurate and meaningful feedback to their employees regarding their competency performance and coaching where needed. By offering suggested feedback that is tempered by the competency rating, this tool eliminates the age-old issue of "writer's block" when it comes time to provide feedback. The system begins with the competency description and rating and also provides suggested statements to include as comments, as shown in Figure 8.17. The suggested statement can be used as a template, made more positive or less positive at the user's discretion, and then placed in the comment box. Comments can then be edited to be more personal, depending on the individual and situation. In this way, managers are giving competency-based feedback in such a way that employees can take action in developing in the future.

Figure 8.17 Writing Assistant

8.3 360 Multi-Rater Assessment

The 360 Multi-Rater assessment facilitates gathering performance feedback on goals and competencies from everyone (i.e., both internal employees and personnel external to the organization). The 360 Multi-Rater assessment is different from the Ask for Feedback feature in that it's an actual form that allows raters to provide feedback and even rate an employee against the competencies assigned to that employee. This mechanism can collect quantitative and qualitative data from a wide range of respondents: the employee, the manager, peers, direct reports, and others.

The 360 Multi-Rater assessment supports adding internal and external raters and has a configurable workflow just like the performance review. Writing Assistant is available to help respondents provide meaningful feedback to the form subject. Detailed reporting that accompanies this feedback can be made available to the employee, the manager, or both.

If necessary, the 360 Multi-Rater evaluations can be made anonymously. Most customers solicit anonymous evaluations to encourage the most frank feedback from colleagues.

The detailed report, displayed in Figure 8.18, breaks down the ratings by rater and provides all rater's comments in one view as well. This report can be permissioned, and it's the customer's decision to make this report available to the employee. This report can be accessed by managers from within the performance review form and can provide additional input into competency ratings and comments for performance review.

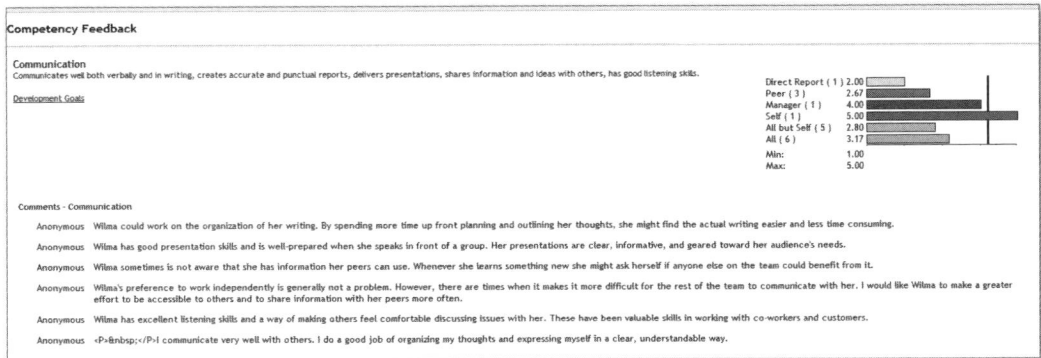

Figure 8.18 Detailed 360 Multi-Rater Report View

8.4 Calibration

Many customers perform calibration of performance ratings across an ogranization to rationalize the rating distribution. Performance ratings are changed during the calibration exercise. The Calibration tool helps make employee calibration a simpler and more efficient exercise, bringing objectivity to a process that can often be too subjective. This is critical when the outcome influences an individual's career growth, compensation, and Succession Planning decisions.

To assess performance accurately, the Calibration feature shown in Figure 8.19 provides a visual comparison of employees, much like the Stack Ranker view when rating competencies. It allows managers in calibration sessions to see their team against each other and make the most informed decisions, eliminating variability across managers. They can see performance ratings, compensation, and potential distributions in both bin and grid views.

The easy-to-use UI allows you to drag and drop employees from one bin to another to calibrate the ratings. This tool identifies a company's true high performers because

239

all employees are viewed together. Managers are trained to assess performance more objectively and accurately when they see the results their ratings have on downstream processes such as compensation and succession.

Figure 8.19 Calibration Session

8.5 Summary

SuccessFactors Performance Management (PM) and Goals Management (GM) modules and the accompanying functionality in 360 Multi-Rater and Calibration provide a manager with a robust set of tools to accurately develop and track corporate, team, and individual goals and ensure progress is on track and aligned with the overall corporate strategy. Goal Execution makes GM an easy daily task rather than a chore. Performance reviews can become real avenues to development as tools such as the Writing Assistant help managers provide meaningful feedback that can be turned into action by employees.

Gathering informal feedback from others as input to the performance review is facilitated right from the TEAM OVERVIEW page. And tools such as 360 Multi-Rater provide another source of ratings against goals and competencies that managers can take into account when performing the year-end process. Finally, the Calibration sessions give visibility across the organization to ratings among managers and help restore objectivity to identifying and rewarding a company's true top performers.

In Chapter 9 we will look at SuccessFactors' Compensation module and how it facilitates managing merit, bonuses, and stock plans.

Designing an effective compensation system is crucial to an organization's talent management and total rewards strategy because compensation management plays a big factor in attracting and retaining talented employees. The SuccessFactors Compensation module provides the toolsets to design, automate, and launch a solid compensation program.

9 Compensation

Economic trends are forcing organizations to adopt pay-for-performance strategies because tying worker's pay to actual business results provides more visibility and control into the compensation payout, improves budget accuracy, and reduces risk. This helps enforce a culture where everyone in the organization is awarded fairly according to individual contribution and organizational performance in areas such as teams, projects, and business units. It provides incentives for the workforce to align and deliver on the goals of an organization in a tangible way. This enables organizations to drive toward profitability and thus provide a bigger pool to reward employees that helped create that additional profitability.

SuccessFactors Compensation is a comprehensive solution that enables an organization to streamline the following planning components:

- **Base pay**
  Merit, salary, promotion, and lump sum.
- **Long-term incentive pay**
  Restricted stock, stock options, performance units, and cash.
- **Short-term incentive pay**
  Bonus.
- **Variable pay**
  Bonus.

Some common methods of calculating employee compensation are to leverage spreadsheet tools or deploy custom software. This complex and nonintegrated approach is inflexible to the changing dynamics of an organization and introduces data inconsistencies between Human Resource Information Systems (HRISs) and Compensation systems.

SuccessFactors Compensation as a solution of the BizX suite provides a single source of all employee data to be utilized for calculation of compensation components. Data from SuccessFactors Employee Central or SAP ERP HCM is integrated, thus providing a single source of truth for the compensation process.

The SuccessFactors Compensation solution has the following two suite offerings:

- **Compensation (Section 9.1)**
  This is an engine for calculating merit, stock, and bonus data in relation to employee performance and guidelines.

- **Variable Pay (Section 9.2)**
  This complex and robust bonus calculation engine allows you to tie business goals and individual results to the payout amount.

Let's begin by taking a look at SuccessFactors Compensation.

9.1 Compensation Solution

SuccessFactors Compensation leverages standard BizX functionality that is essential in delivering a complete end-to-end compensation process:

- **Calibration**
  "Nine-box" sessions review compensation data across teams, departments, and the entire organization to ensure fairness in the compensation process. Performance data from BizX solutions can be leveraged to align performance and goals with compensation. Compensation data can be leveraged during the Succession Calibration session; Figure 9.1 shows an output of a Calibration session.

- **Live Metrics**
  As shown in Figure 9.2, these offer graphical visibility into employee and compensation data, such as performance distribution by employees or pay versus performance matrix.

- **Rewards Statement**
  You can generate compensation and variable pay statements for employees using standard fields and custom text.

Compensation Solution | 9.1

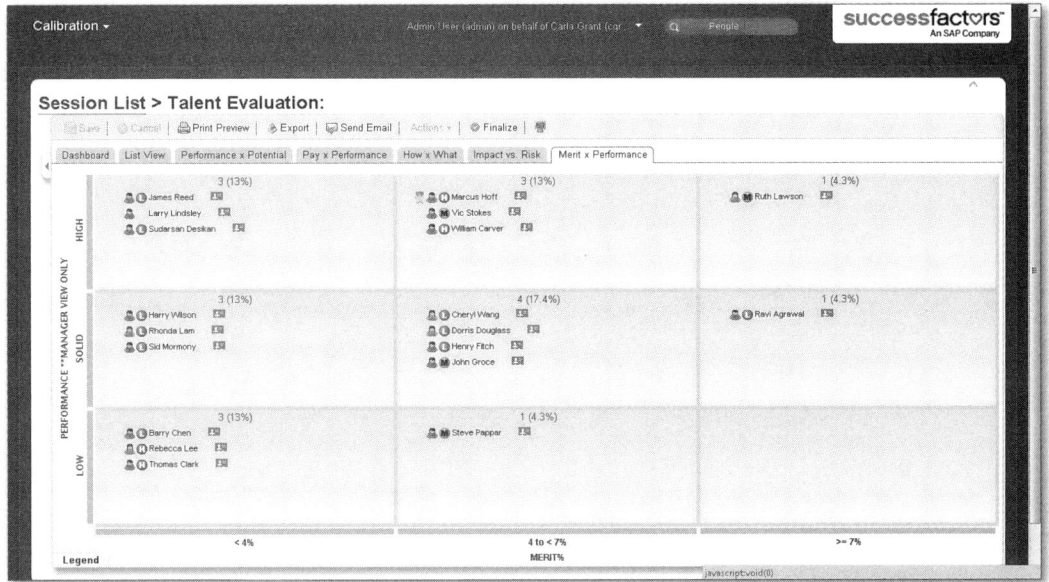

Figure 9.1 Calibration Session with Compensation, Performance, Succession, and Gender Data

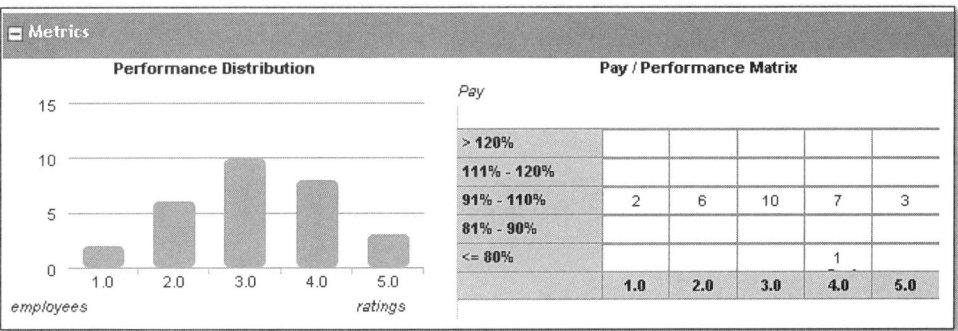

Figure 9.2 Live Metrics in Compensation Worksheet

- **Executive Review**
  This provides visibility into all compensation and variable pay data. Employees can be viewed according to security permissions, reporting structure, organization levels, and views.

- **Compensation Profile**
  This lets compensation planners make recommendations while viewing employee history and graphical view of position. Figure 9.3 shows a planner's view of an employee compensation profile.

243

9 | Compensation

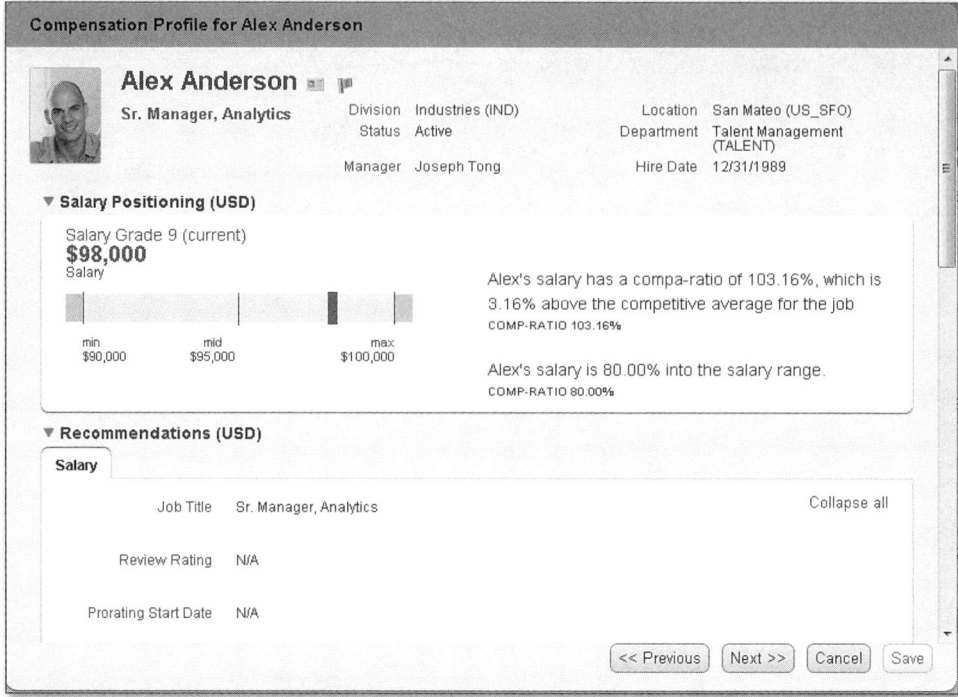

Figure 9.3 A sample Employee Compensation Profile

SuccessFactors Compensation enables compensation planners and HR professionals to access information quickly, make required changes, and complete the compensation cycle in an efficient and simple manner.

Out-of-the-box and configurable workflow provides flexibility to launch the compensation cycle, whether using standard approval hierarchy or a custom compensation hierarchy. The OneAdmin tool provides configuration flexibility for each step of the compensation cycle. Approval of the compensation cycle is also a seamless process for both planners and HR professionals in the organization. As the compensation cycle progresses through the workflow steps, Compensation notifies the appropriate planner or administrator through emails and dashboard alerts if an action is required on their part.

To successfully launch a compensation cycle, you must set up a compensation plan template and perform the configuration and setup activities that meet the design needs of your organization. These activities are performed under the COMPENSATION HOME menu found under OneAdmin in Figure 9.4.

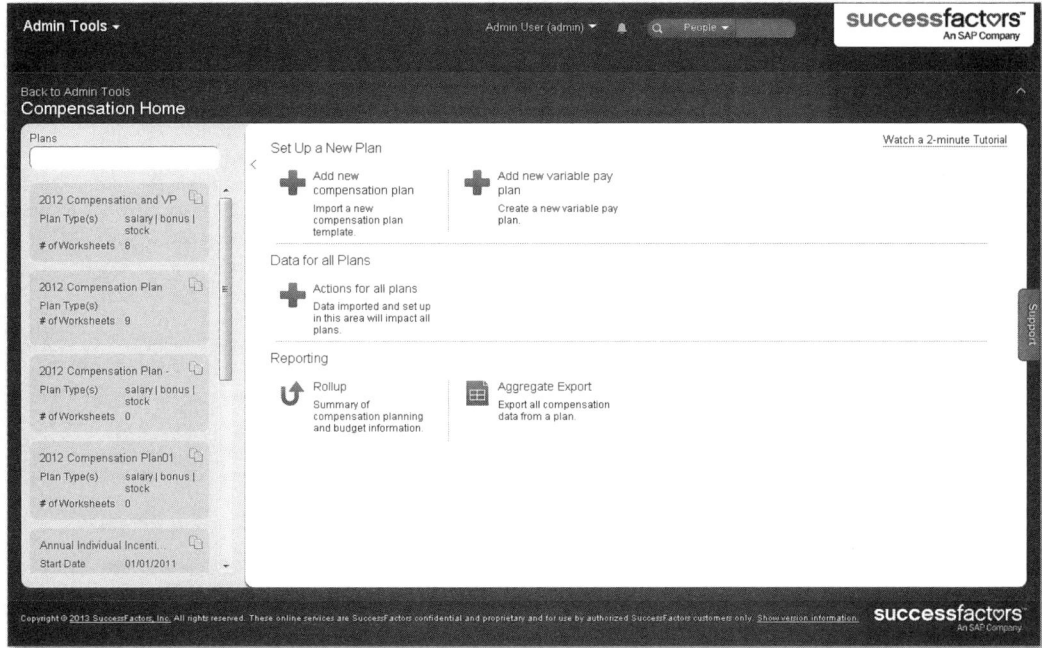

Figure 9.4 Compensation Home

The next step is to generate compensation worksheets (forms), which are created based on current data in the system. As the compensation cycle progresses toward completion, compensation forms will require updates based on certain data elements that may have been updated during the compensation cycle.

The final step is to review and approve all of the compensation worksheets by the respective planners. Once completed, data is ready to be consumed by your HRIS for further action. Rewards statements and reports are generated after approval of the compensation forms.

With SuccessFactors Compensation, you can configure the following three compensation components:

- **Salary**
  You can configure any combination of merit increase, promotion, adjustment, lump sum, or bonus calculations. Performance ratings can be leveraged from the SuccessFactors Performance Management (PM) solution or alternatively uploaded into the solution as required for the compensation guidelines. You can prorate bonus calculations based on the employee hire date and end date

9 | Compensation

for the year. Standard and custom fields set up for this component leverage the Lookup Tables, Salary Pay Matrix, and Job Code & Pay Grade Mapping tables to perform functions and calculations that are reflected on the compensation form.

▶ **Bonus**
Management by Objective (MBO) can enforce a pay-for-performance bonus configuration, as opposed to a formula-based bonus. Goal attainment data is integrated from PM, and the bonus amount is calculated as a percentage of bonus targets.

▶ **Stock**
You can configure stock options, restricted share units, performance units, and cash. Standard and custom fields set up for this component leverage the Lookup Tables, Stock Value, and Stock Factor tables to perform the calculations.

9.1.1 Compensation Plan

Most organizations have an annual compensation cycle; each compensation cycle should have a corresponding plan in the system. Figure 9.5 illustrates the summary of a sample compensation plan for all eligible employees. Plans are generally not personalized and represent an entire population of the organization under a specific hierarchy.

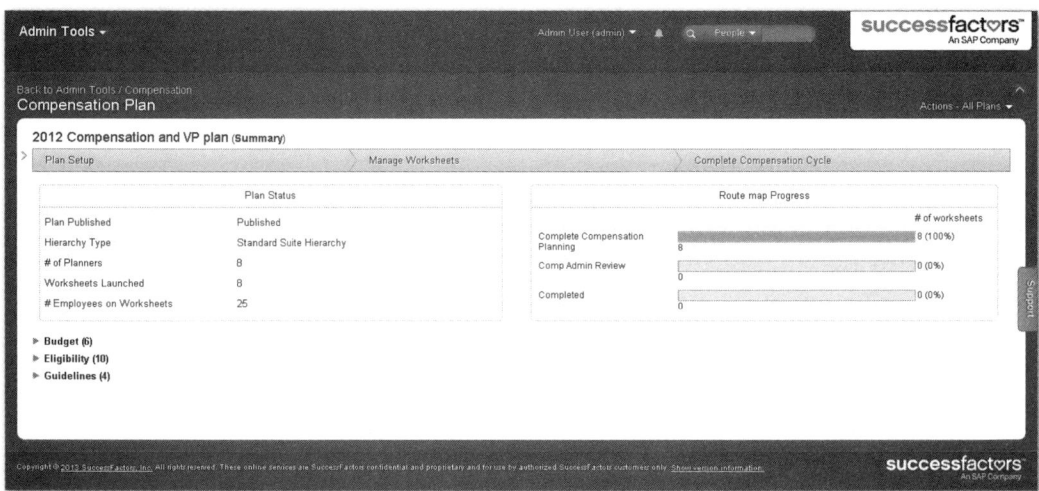

Figure 9.5 Summary View of the Compensation Plan

The Plan Status section on the left provides a high-level summary about the plan; the Route map Progress section on the right illustrates the progress of the compensation cycle.

Figure 9.6 illustrates the Budget status for each compensation component within the plan, such as merit, promotion, lump sum, and so on.

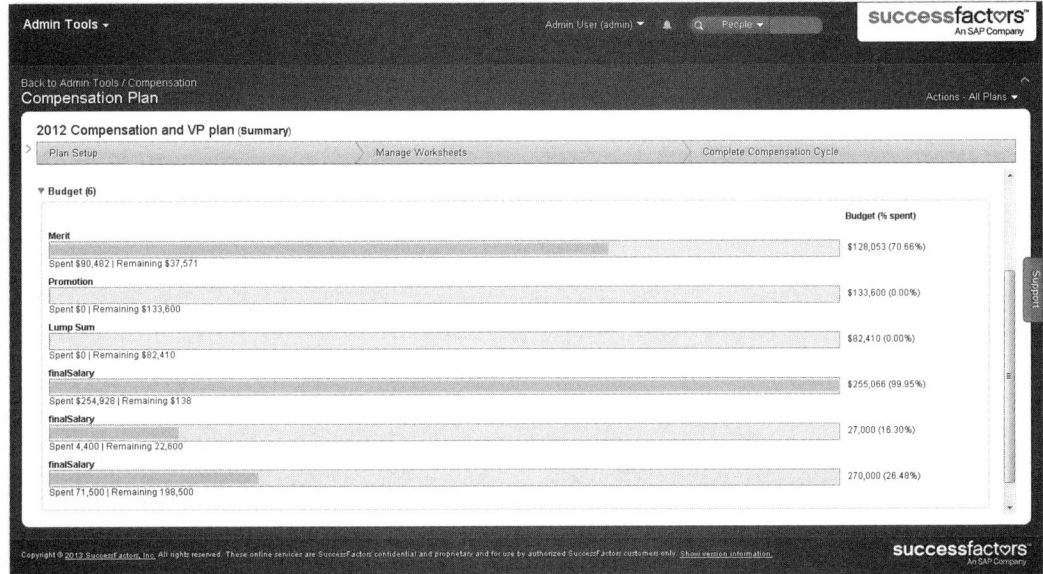

Figure 9.6 Budget Overview of the Compensation Plan

Figure 9.7 illustrates the employee Eligibility statistics—comparing the number eligible and ineligible—for the plan components.

Figure 9.8 illustrates the Guidelines assignment statistics for employees. This provides a quick analysis of how many employees meet the guidelines configured for the compensation plan template.

9 | Compensation

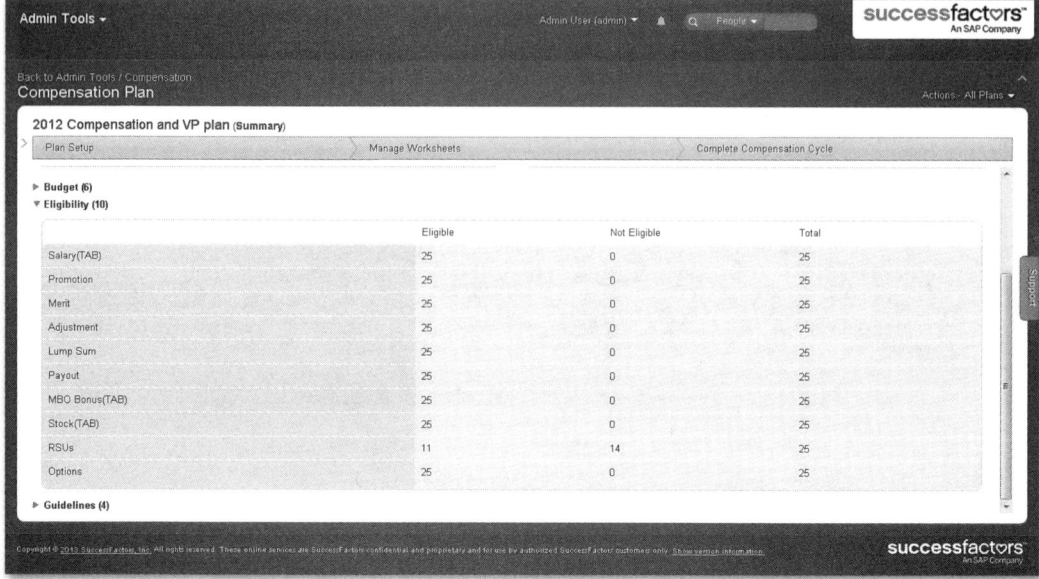

Figure 9.7 Eligibility Overview of the Compensation Plan

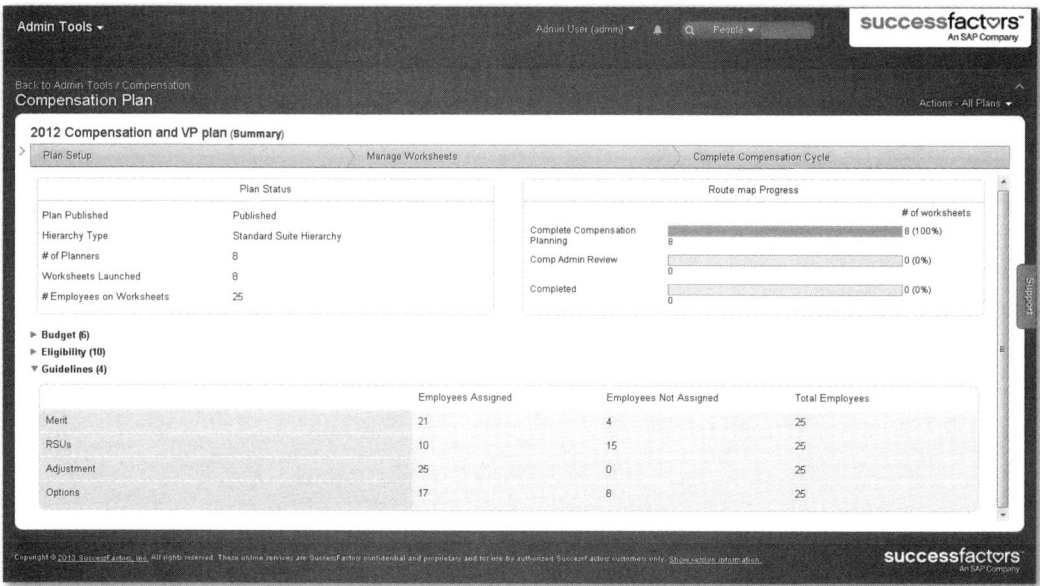

Figure 9.8 Guidelines Analysis of the Compensation Plan

9.1.2 Setup Data

Before you initiate the setup of the compensation plan, you must populate the required base setup tables with data. These data elements are in the IMPORT/EXPORT DATA section under the COMPENSATION HOME page, as shown in Figure 9.9.

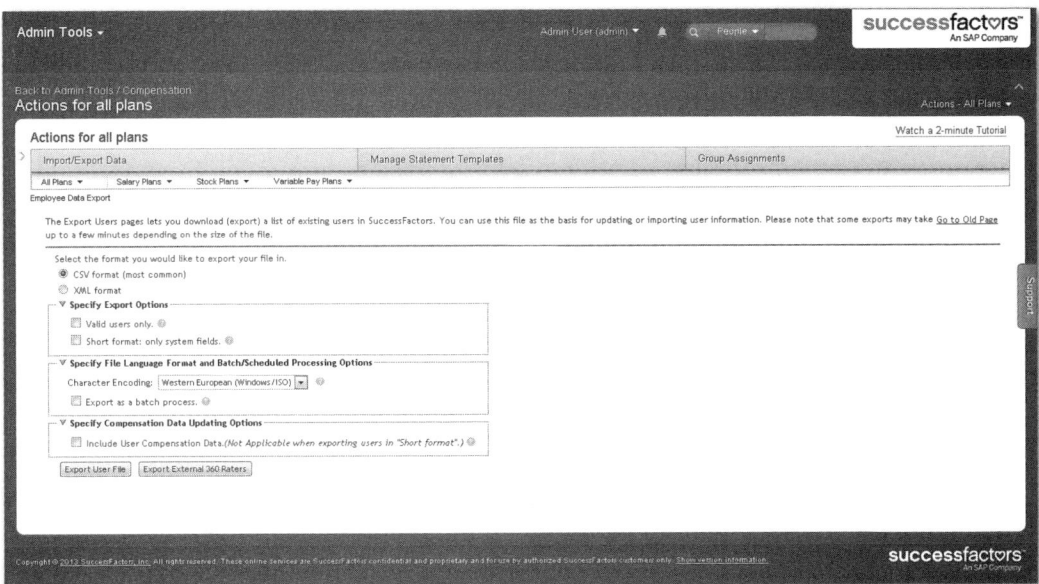

Figure 9.9 Data Import, Export and Setup Options for a Compensation Plan Template

All Plans

The ALL PLANS subsection of the IMPORT/EXPORT DATA section has the following options:

- EMPLOYEE DATA EXPORT
  This option is very useful for troubleshooting employee data issues. You can use the export file as a basis for importing or updating employee data.

- CURRENCY CONVERSION TABLE
  You can import currency conversion tables through this option. Figure 9.10 shows a sample table that charts the rates of conversion between U.S. dollars and other currencies.

9 | Compensation

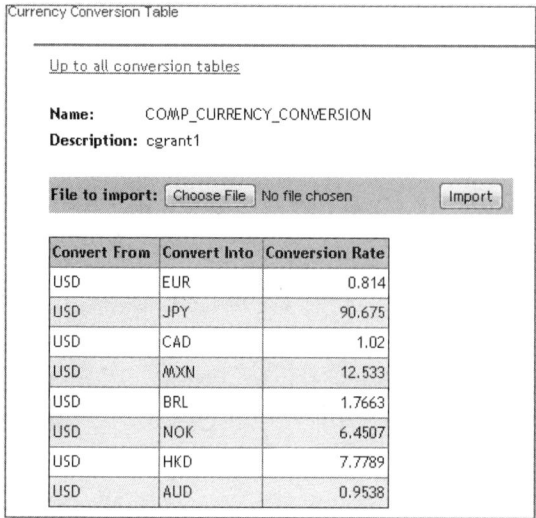

Figure 9.10 Currency Conversion Table

▶ LOOKUP TABLES

You can set up as many Lookup Tables (Figure 9.11) as required under this option. Your compensation plan design will include gathering any requirements for setting these tables. Input and output columns form the structure of the lookup table, which is then referenced in the formula box of the compensation plan template.

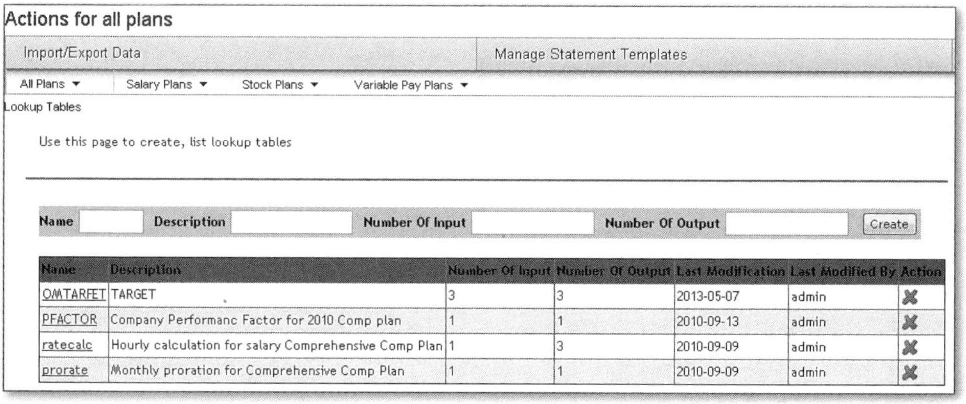

Name	Description	Number Of Input	Number Of Output	Last Modification	Last Modified By	Action
OMTARFET	TARGET	3	3	2013-05-07	admin	✗
PFACTOR	Company Performanc Factor for 2010 Comp plan	1	1	2010-09-13	admin	✗
ratecalc	Hourly calculation for salary Comprehensive Comp Plan	1	3	2010-09-09	admin	✗
prorate	Monthly proration for Comprehensive Comp Plan	1	1	2010-09-09	admin	✗

Figure 9.11 List of Lookup Tables

Salary Plans

The SALARY PLANS subsection of the IMPORT/EXPORT DATA section has the following options:

▶ SALARY RANGES

You can upload or export salary pay matrices like the one shown in Figure 9.12 using this option. Salary pay matrices contain the salary ranges for each distinct value of pay grade. Values in the salary pay matrix are set up in functional currency and also drive the Compa-Ratio and Range Penetration calculation on the compensation form for each employee.

The PROMOTABLE flag is used to define whether the pay grade is eligible for promotion. The ATTRIBUTE 1, ATTRIBUTE 2, and ATTRIBUTE 3 columns can be utilized to have different salary ranges for the same pay grade. At the bottom of this section, you have the option to upload a related MANAGER PROMOTION MAP as shown in Figure 9.13.

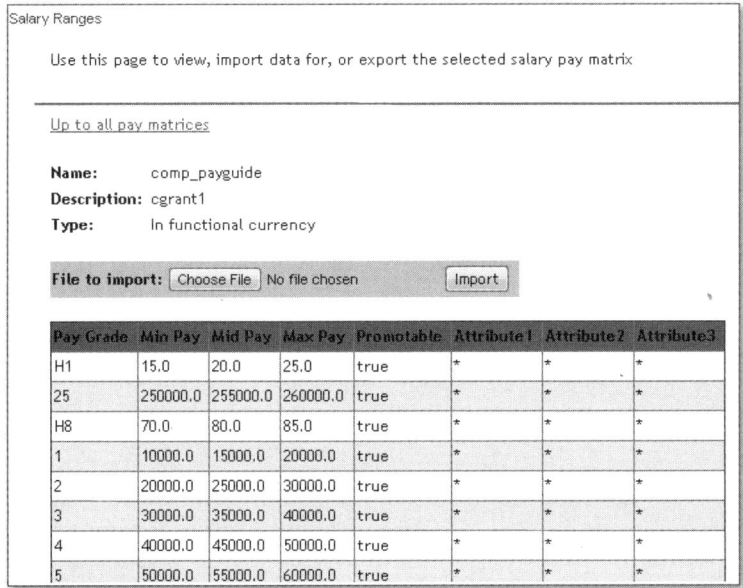

Figure 9.12 Salary Pay Matrix

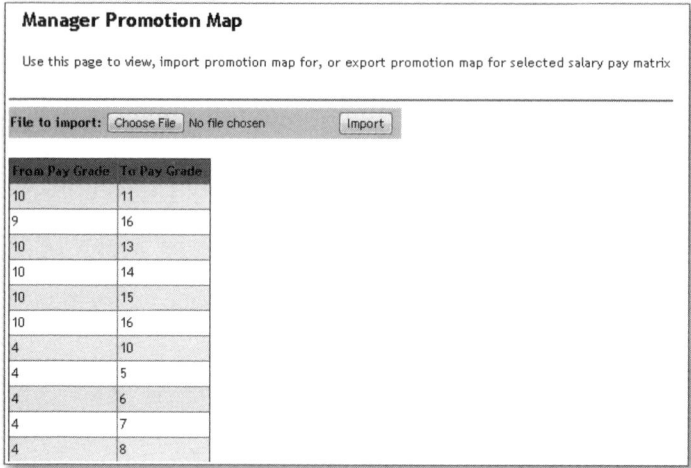

Figure 9.13 Promotion Map Table

- Job Code & Pay Grade Mapping

    This area maintains the Job Code & Pay Grade Mapping table, which is shown in Figure 9.14.

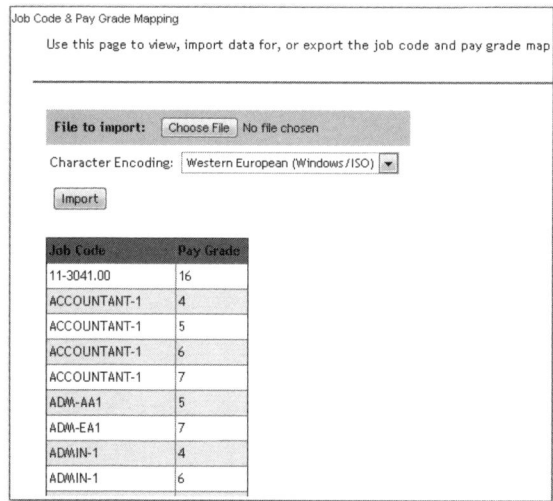

Figure 9.14 Job Code & Pay Grade Mapping Table

Stock Plans

The Stock Plans subsection of the Import/Export Data section has the following options:

▶ STOCK VALUE TABLES

You can maintain this table (Figure 9.15) with numerical values for each different type of stock. This numerical value can represent the purchase price of the stock or price per unit of a stock, depending on your design requirements.

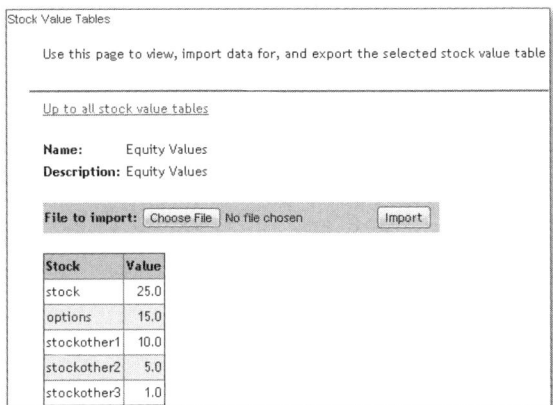

Figure 9.15   Stock Value Table

▶ STOCK FACTOR TABLES

You can maintain this table (Figure 9.16) to automatically calculate the appropriate mix of stock types for your employees. The KEY column represents the job level.

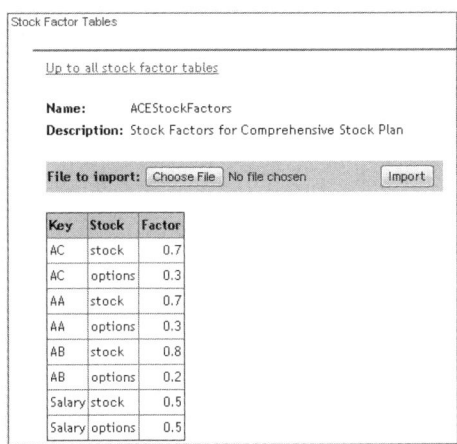

Figure 9.16   Stock Factor Table

9.1.3 Plan Setup

The PLAN SETUP section of the COMPENSATION PLAN shown in Figure 9.17 contains the compensation plan template configuration and is where setup activities are performed.

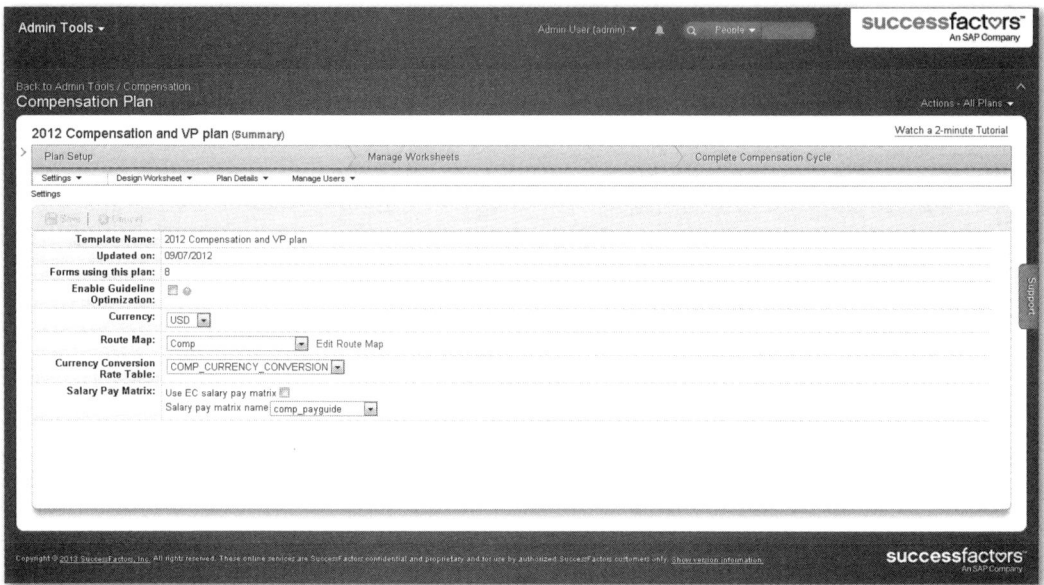

Figure 9.17 Plan Setup Section of the Compensation Plan Template

Settings

The SETTINGS subsection is where the following details are visible and configurable:

- TEMPLATE NAME
  As a best practice, choose a template name that reflects the year of the compensation cycle and the compensation components being planned against.

- UPDATED ON
  This is the compensation plan template update date.

- FORMS USING THIS PLAN
  This is the number of forms generated based on this compensation plan template.

▶ ENABLE GUIDELINE OPTIMIZATION
By default, this option isn't checked. If your organization has many compensation guidelines that are slowing down the performance of your system, check this option to improve performance.

▶ CURRENCY
This is the default functional currency of the form. If your organization has planners that plan in multiple currencies, the CURRENCY CONVERSION RATE TABLE will convert the functional currency to the default currency of the form.

▶ ROUTE MAP
The route map is the sequence of workflow steps associated to all forms that have been generated based on this compensation plan template. Routing maps are configured to generate compensation forms with employees and their respective planners or HR administrators. Each route map has several steps; each step type can be assigned to a single role, be iterative between two people to exchange feedback, or be collaborative to allow for group review. Figure 9.18 shows a sample configuration screen for ROUTE MAP.

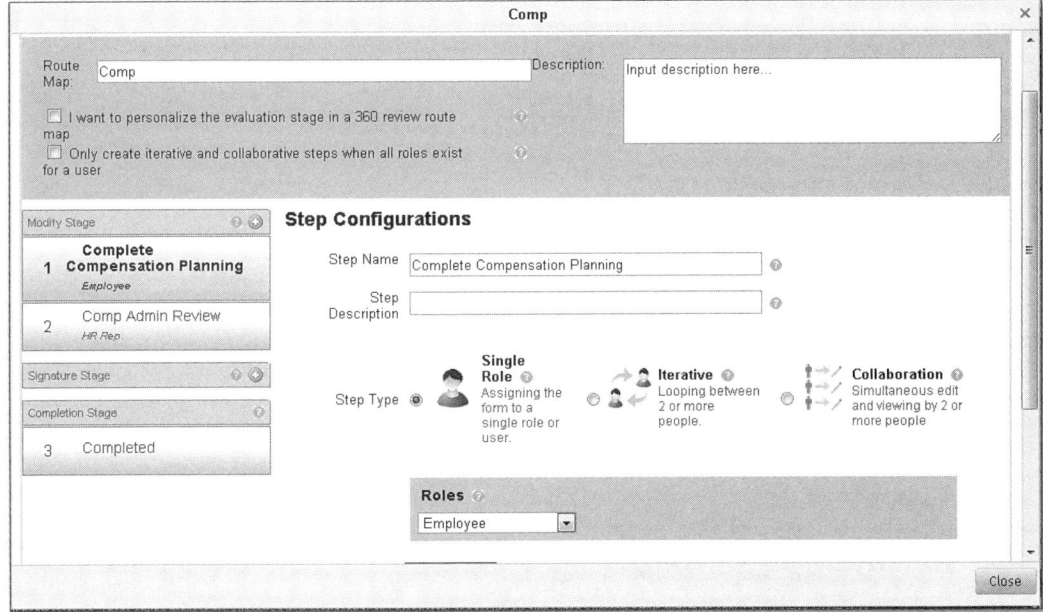

Figure 9.18 Route Map Configuration

▶ CURRENCY CONVERSION TABLE
This is a mandatory currency conversion table per your organization's needs and setup.

▶ SALARY PAY MATRIX
If you are a SuccessFactors Employee Central customer, you can choose to use the salary pay matrix as defined in the Employee Central solution. For non-Employee Central customers, you must select a salary pay matrix.

The ADVANCED SETTINGS subsection is the central location for managing the compensation plan template settings, such as form behavior, workflow, security, and functions. Figure 9.19 illustrates the ADVANCED SETTINGS area for the compensation template.

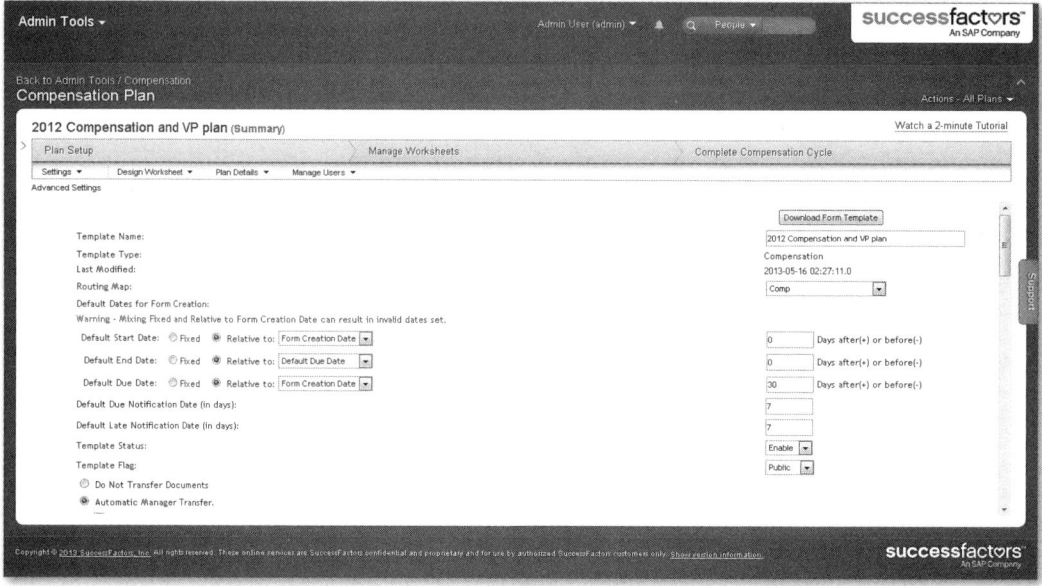

Figure 9.19 Advanced Settings for a Compensation Plan Template

> **Note**
> After the compensation forms are generated, settings changed on the compensation plan template won't take effect unless the compensation forms are deleted and generated again.

Compensation Solution | 9.1

Design Worksheet

The DESIGN WORKSHEET subsection (Figure 9.20) is where you design the layout of your compensation form and configure the fields for the compensation components that are required as part of the compensation plan template.

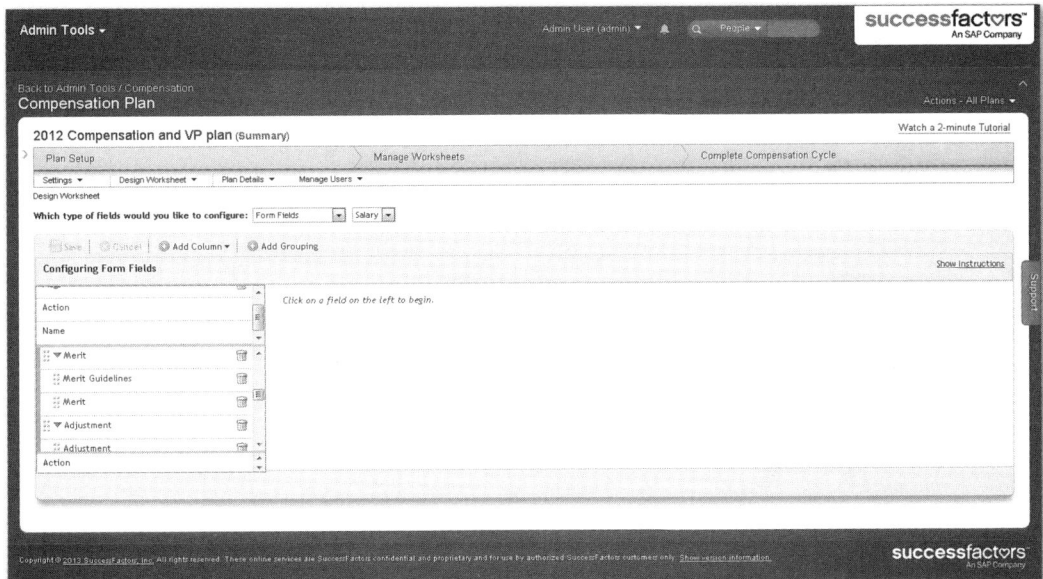

Figure 9.20 Compensation Plan Template Designer

Figure 9.21 illustrates the list of standard fields available when selecting the ADD COLUMN option in the compensation plan template. These options are based on the BizX instance configuration for your organization.

Figure 9.22 shows how a custom column is added to the compensation plan template. The column properties such as title, read-only, visibility, type, format, and formula, among many others, can be adjusted. The FORMULA box is where you can enter mathematical calculations, If logic, conversions, and reference lookup statements pointing to the lookup tables. Each custom field can also be hidden if not required to be visible for the planner, be reloadable if data in this field will change frequently based on data import, be reportable to make available in reports and extracts, and have a unique import key associated with it, as shown in Figure 9.23.

9 | Compensation

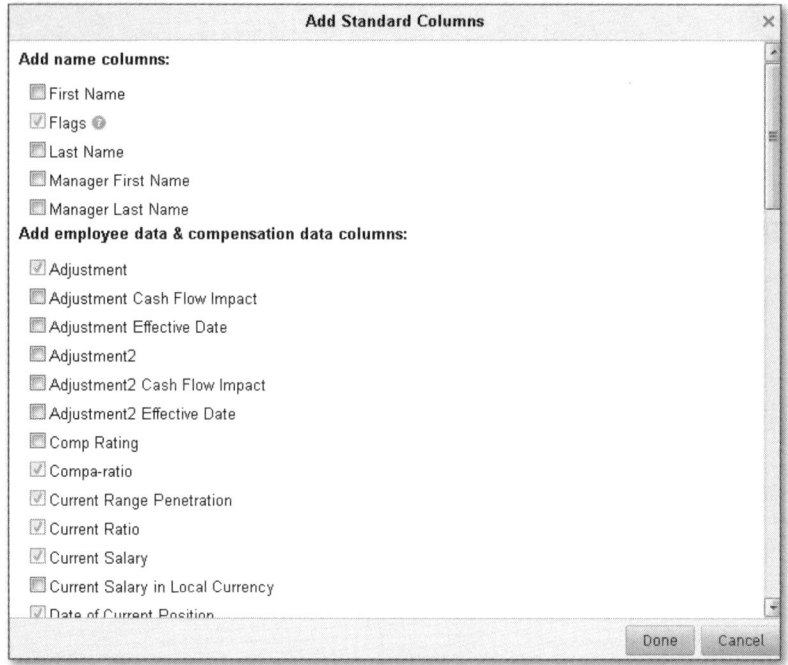

Figure 9.21 List of Standard Columns Available

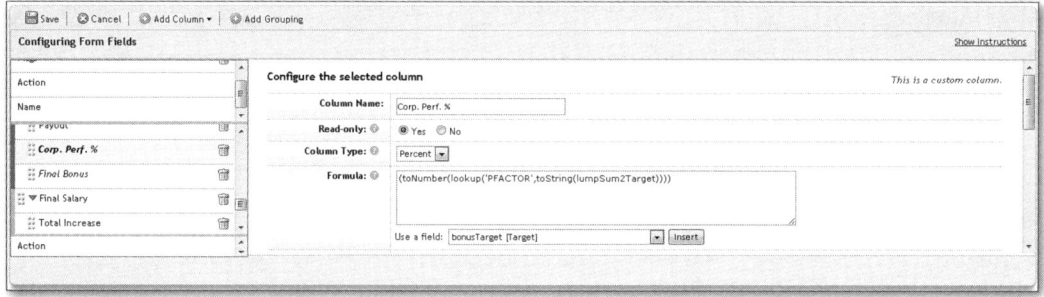

Figure 9.22 Custom Column Configuration

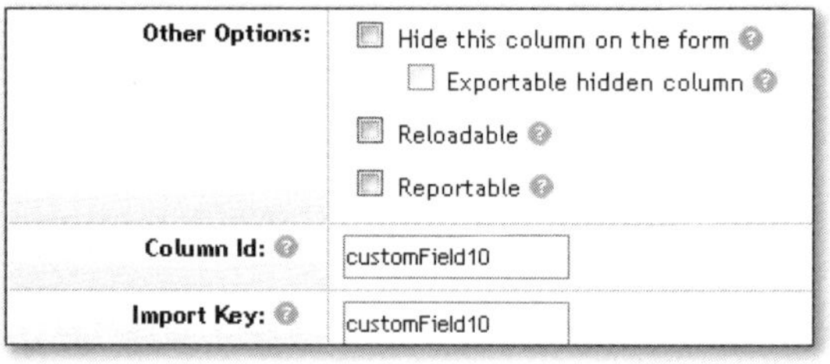

Figure 9.23 Custom Column Configuration Options

After the STANDARD and CUSTOM columns have been configured, another logical step in the configuration process is to group relevant columns by selecting the ADD GROUPING option. Each grouping can be visibly shown separately on the compensation form by configuring it with its own HEX COLOR CODE, as shown at the bottom of Figure 9.24. This helps the planner identify employee and planning information easily on the compensation form.

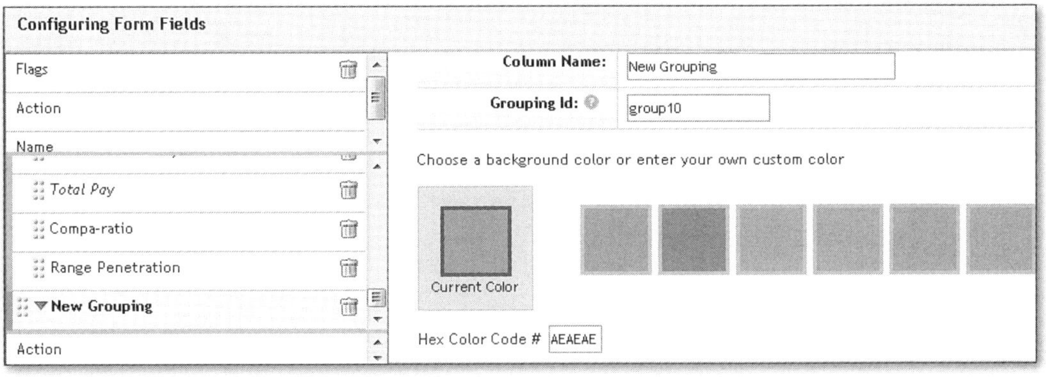

Figure 9.24 Grouping Configuration

To add custom messages to be visible on the compensation form, the PLAN INSTRUCTION option under the DESIGN WORKSHEET subsection facilitates this process. Figure 9.25 illustrates the custom messages area available for SALARY, BONUS, STOCK, and SUMMARY sections of the compensation form. These messages appear on top of the compensation form.

Plan Details

The PLAN DETAILS subsection allows for configuration of the following options:

▶ ADD BUDGET CALCULATION
This enables the planner to view budget calculation status on the compensation form. Figure 9.26 shows the configuration options available for this section, such as the budget calculation mode shown on the form, the planning components the budget is used for, the default budget value, and who to base the budget calculation on. Multiple budget calculation options can be configured within the compensation plan template shown in Figure 9.27.

9 | Compensation

Figure 9.25 Default Custom Messages for a Compensation Plan Template

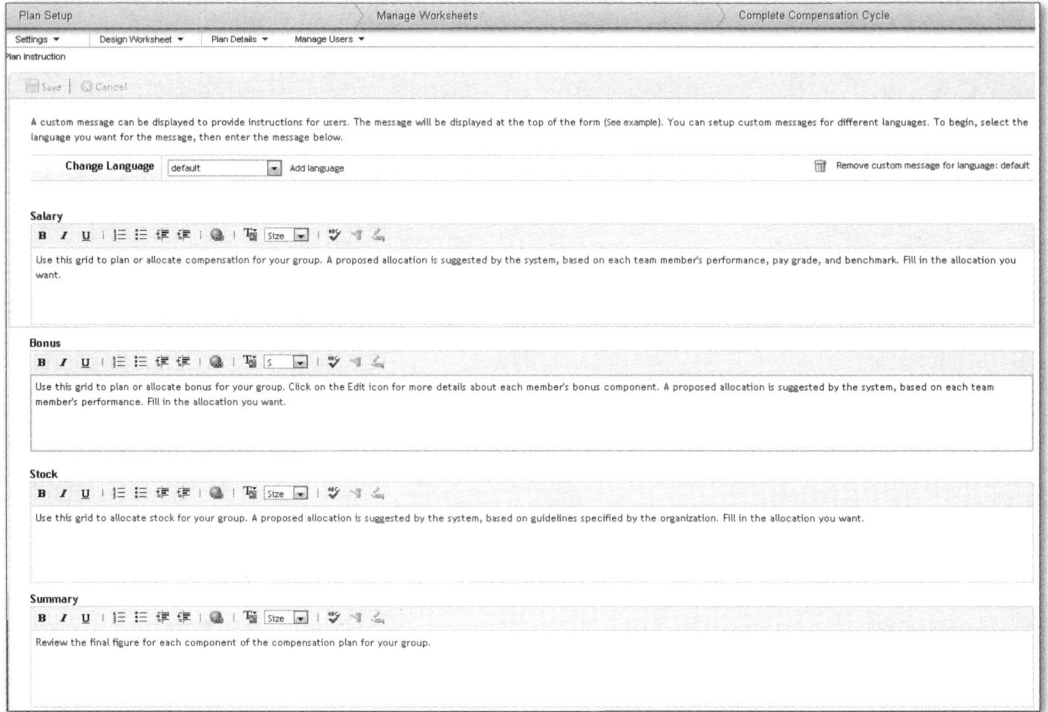

Figure 9.26 Budget Calculation Options

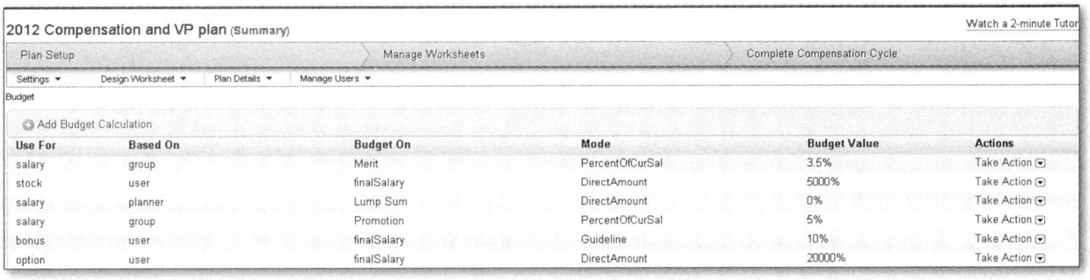

2012 Compensation and VP plan (Summary)
Watch a 2-minute Tutor
Plan Setup
Manage Worksheets
Complete Compensation Cycle
Settings
Design Worksheet
Plan Details
Manage Users
Budget
Add Budget Calculation
Use For | Based On | Budget On | Mode | Budget Value | Actions
salary | group | Merit | PercentOfCurSal | 3.5% | Take Action
stock | user | finalSalary | DirectAmount | 5000% | Take Action
salary | planner | Lump Sum | DirectAmount | 0% | Take Action
salary | group | Promotion | PercentOfCurSal | 5% | Take Action
bonus | user | finalSalary | Guideline | 10% | Take Action
option | user | finalSalary | DirectAmount | 20000% | Take Action

Figure 9.27 Budget Calculations Setup for a Compensation Plan Temple

- ADD BUDGET RULE
  This option, shown in Figure 9.28, allows for the rule setup for budget calculations. You can choose to allow, warn, or disallow planners to exceed budget calculations and whether to save the compensation form if the budget has been exceeded. Options for entering warning messages are available in this area as well. You can set up multiple rules for each compensation plan template.

Add Budget Rule
Use For
all
Allow Exceed
allow
Allow Save On Exceed
Yes
No
Language Add
Budget Exceed Warn Message
Default
Allocation total exceeds budget, do you want to save?
Save
Cancel

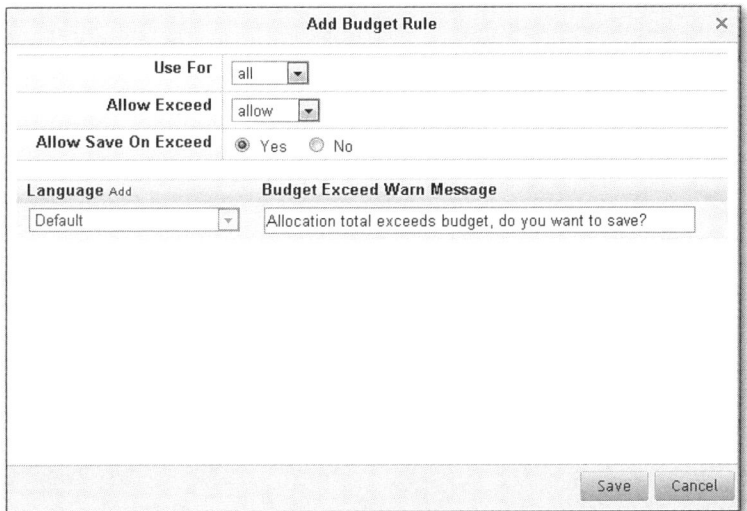

Figure 9.28 Budget Enforcement Rule Configuration

- ELIGIBILITY
  Multiple eligibility rules can be configured for the compensation plan template as shown in Figure 9.29. Undertake designing each eligibility rule carefully because it affects the planner's ability to enter planning details against each employee on the compensation form. Rules can be anchored on standard fields

available on the compensation plan template such as pay grade or performance ratings.

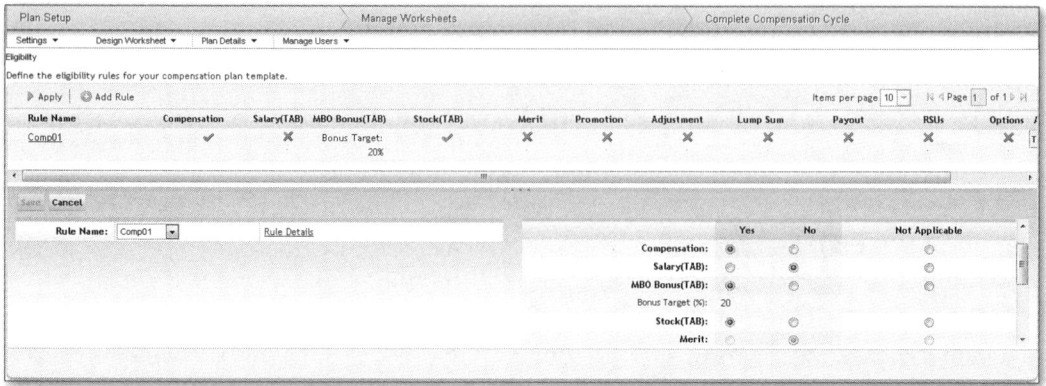

Figure 9.29 Eligibility Rules Setup

▶ GUIDELINES

Compensation guidelines, which are shown in Figure 9.30, are the rules a planner follows to effectively plan employee compensation for each component on the compensation form. Multiple rules can be set up per compensation plan template. As shown in Figure 9.31, each rule setup has much input: standard field criteria (RULE NAME, TYPE, FORMULA CRITERIA), MODE (AMOUNT or PERCENTAGE) for that rule, BENCHMARK field against this rule, HARD LIMIT toggle, and WARNING option if the planner exceeds or falls below the rule limit. Each rule contains formulas that calculate the default planning component on the compensation form and also contain the MIN (minimum), LOW, DEFAULT, HIGH, and MAX (maximum) value for the component calculation. Figure 9.32 illustrates formulas set up for the rule; these can be imported, exported, or entered manually.

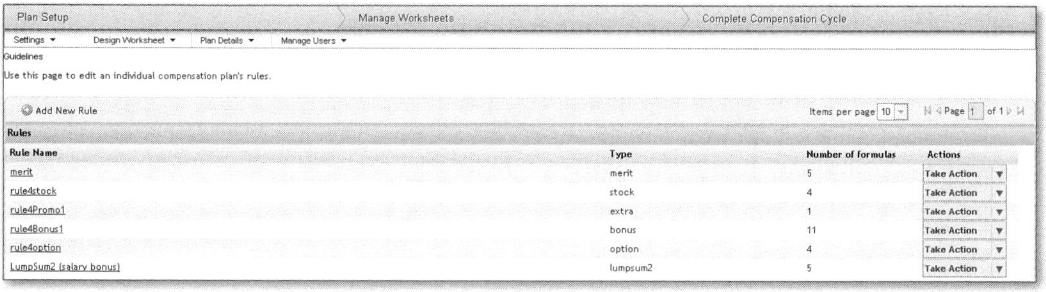

Figure 9.30 Guidelines for a Compensation Plan Template

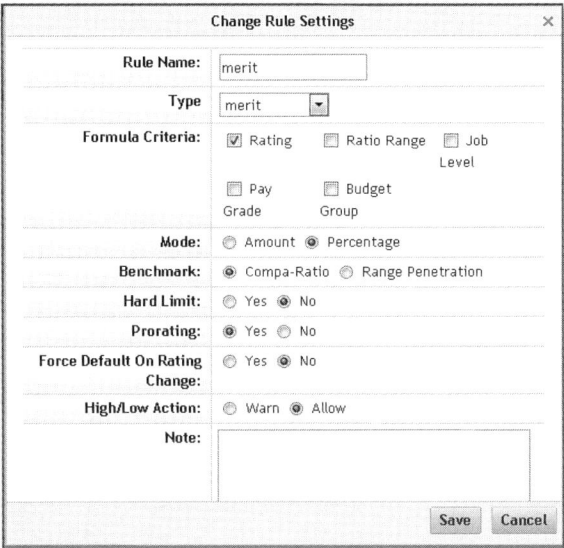

Figure 9.31 Rule Setup

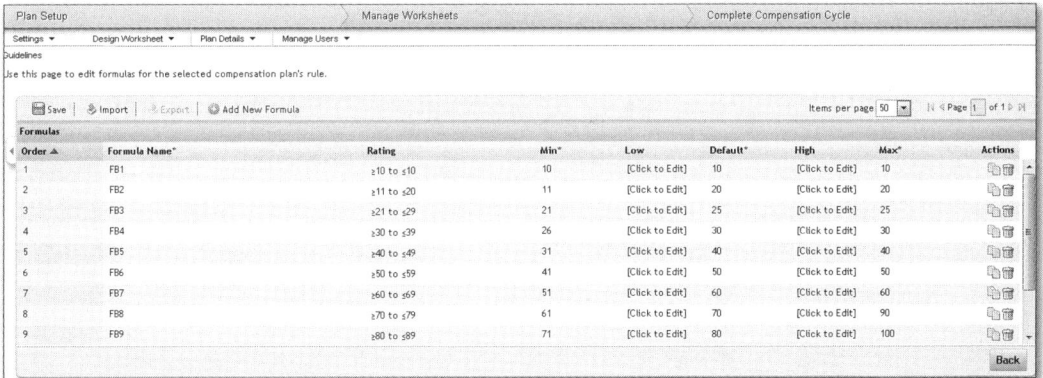

Figure 9.32 Formulas Grid

▶ RATING SOURCES

This option as shown in Figure 9.33 allows for configuration of the employee performance rating source. You can import these ratings or leverage them from other BizX solutions.

9 | Compensation

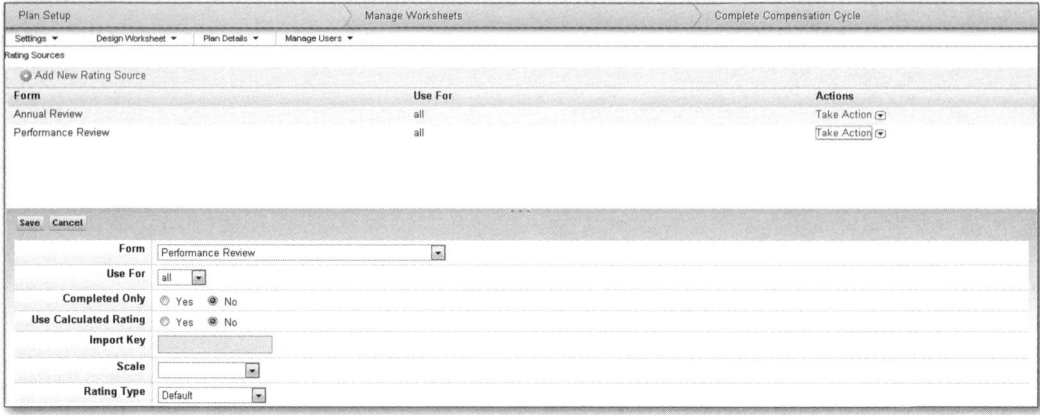

Figure 9.33 Rating Sources Setup

Manage Users

In the DEFINE PLANNERS subsection shown in Figure 9.34, you define the hierarchy structure compensation forms that will be generated for planners to plan employee compensation. The default option is to use the STANDARD SUITE HIERARCHY, which is based on the employee and the employee's manager set up in the BizX suite. Another option, the ROLLUP HIERARCHY, allows for planning responsibilities to be assigned to managers higher up in the organization. A custom hierarchy can also be configured as required to meet your organization's needs. This subsection is also leveraged for troubleshooting employee and planner hierarchy setup.

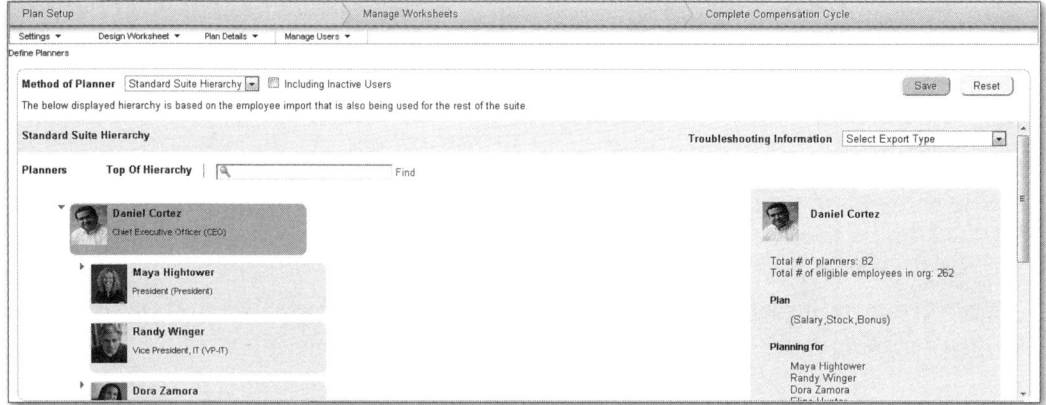

Figure 9.34 Standard Suite Hierarchy

9.1.4 Manage Compensation Forms

After all setup and configuration activities have been completed for the compensation plan template, the next step in the process is to generate compensation worksheets. Worksheets are forms that reside with the planners to enter compensation planning details and submit for further action. The MANAGE WORKSHEETS section shown in Figure 9.35 is the central location to launch compensation forms and manage the lifecycle of the forms generated for the related compensation plan template.

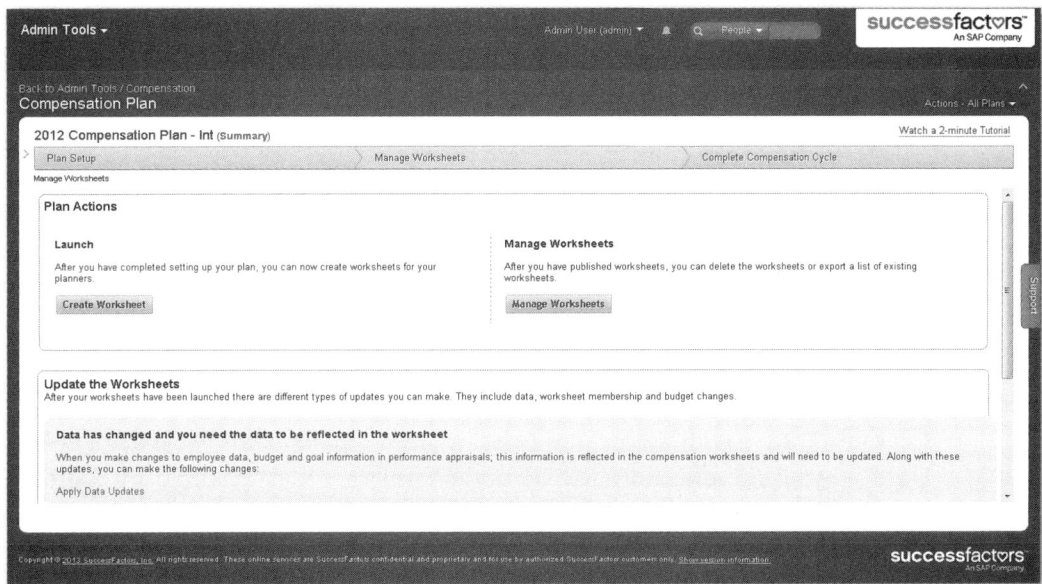

Figure 9.35 Manage Worksheets Section

Launch Forms

The CREATE WORKSHEET option under the PLAN ACTIONS subsection opens the panel as shown in Figure 9.36 to provide step-by-step details for form generation.

The following steps are involved:

1. COMPENSATION PLAN
   Enter the form name visible to the planner. The planner's name is appended to this name automatically.

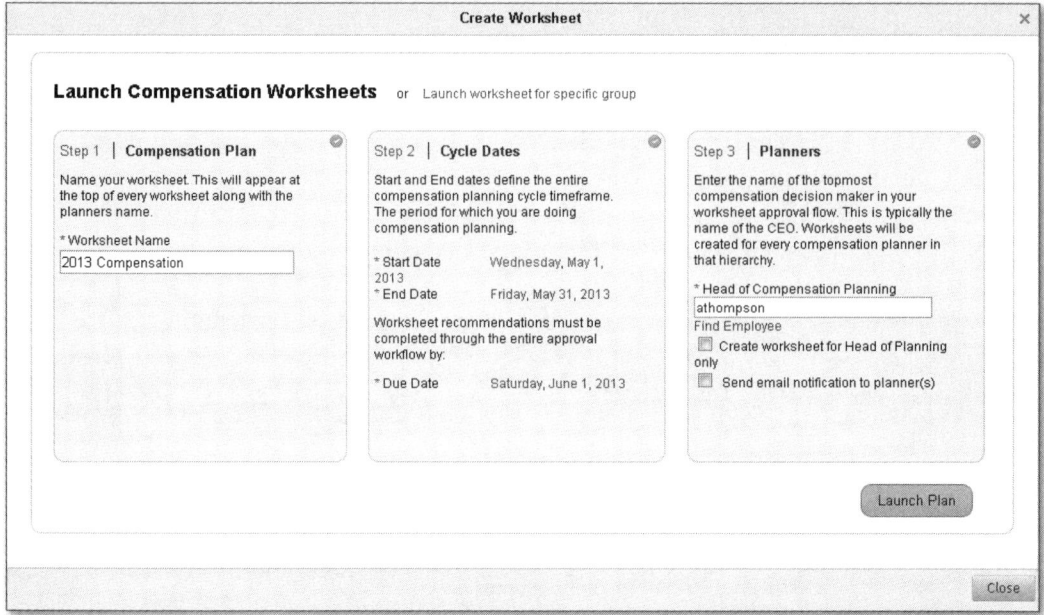

Figure 9.36 Launch Compensation Worksheets

2. CYCLE DATES

   Choose the start and end date of your organization's planning cycle. The DUE DATE controls the workflow activity of the form such as when to notify planners based on date criteria.

3. PLANNERS

   Select the topmost planner in your organization hierarchy. This will launch forms for all planners in the organization per the hierarchy configuration setting of the compensation template. If the requirement is to only generate forms for the specific planner, check the CREATE WORKSHEET FOR HEAD OF PLANNING ONLY option. You can choose to notify planners of compensation form availability by email. Planners will be able to view the compensation form under the COMPENSATION section of SuccessFactors solution, as shown in Figure 9.37.

After all of the details are entered, click on the LAUNCH PLAN option to start the request for the form-generation process. Upon completion of the process, an email notification will be sent with details on how many compensation forms were generated. At this stage, the compensation forms are considered in-progress.

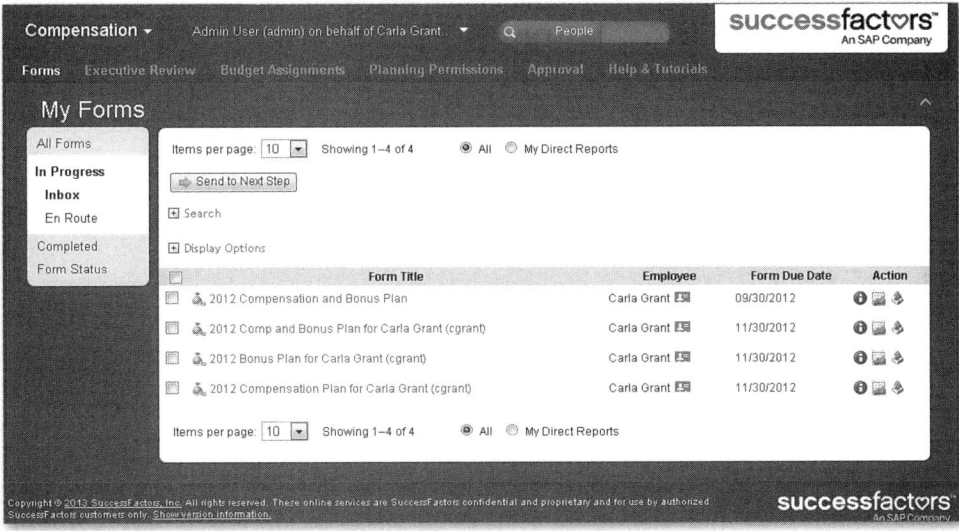

Figure 9.37 Manager's View of the Compensation Home Screen

Manage Worksheets

The MANAGE WORKSHEETS option under the PLAN ACTIONS subsection, as shown in Figure 9.38, gives you visibility into the individual forms generated as part of the compensation plan template.

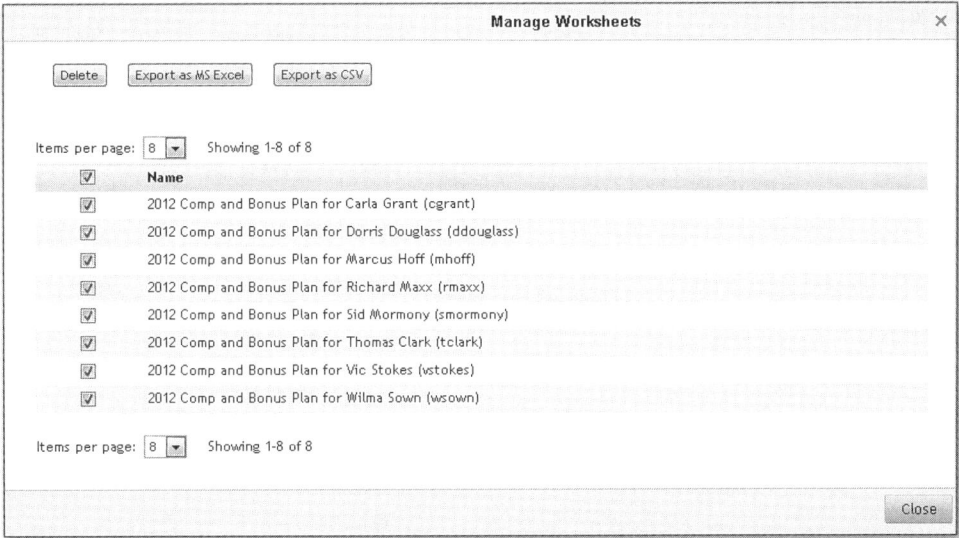

Figure 9.38 Manage Worksheets Options

9 | Compensation

In this example, there are forms for Carla Grant, Dorris Douglas, Marcus Hoff, and their colleagues. From this option, you can choose to DELETE the form, EXPORT AS MS EXCEL, or EXPORT AS CSV.

Update the Worksheets

After the compensation forms have been generated, you may need to periodically update data, update compensation form membership, or account for budget changes until the compensation planning cycle reaches completion. These activities are performed under the UPDATE THE WORKSHEETS subsection under the MANAGE WORKSHEETS section, as shown in Figure 9.39.

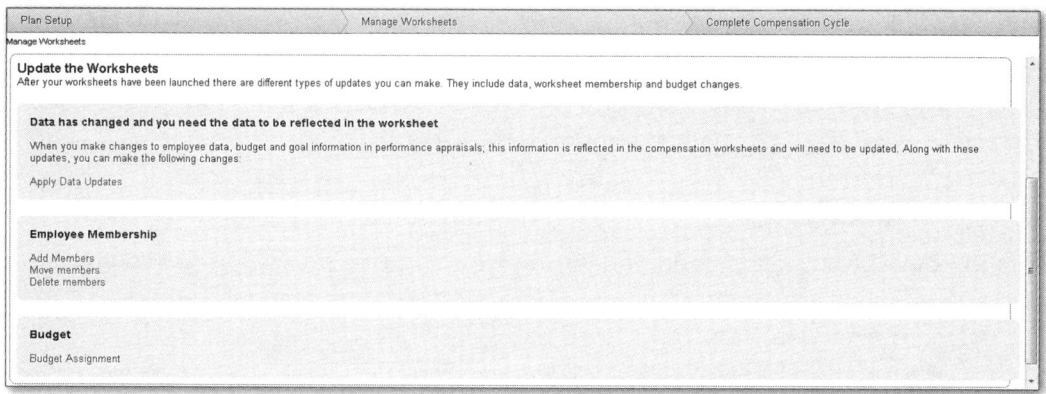

Figure 9.39 Update Worksheets Options

The following options are available in this subsection:

▶ APPLY DATA UPDATES
Clicking on this option opens the panel shown in Figure 9.40. You can choose the settings that reflect the data change being applied, such as hire of a new employee, termination of an employee, budget changes, or change in organization hierarchy structure. Any changes in compensation eligibility criteria can be updated through this option. This option also allows for updates to completed compensation forms as well.

▶ ADD MEMBERS
Add members (employees) to existing compensation forms.

- MOVE MEMBERS

  Move members (employees) from one compensation form to another existing compensation form.

- DELETE MEMBERS

  Delete members (employees) from existing compensation forms.

- BUDGET ASSIGNMENT

  Update the budget pool available for the compensation cycle. Additional budgets can be propagated and distributed to planners in the organization. Cascading budgets can't be propagated if the amount spent exceeds the new budget amount.

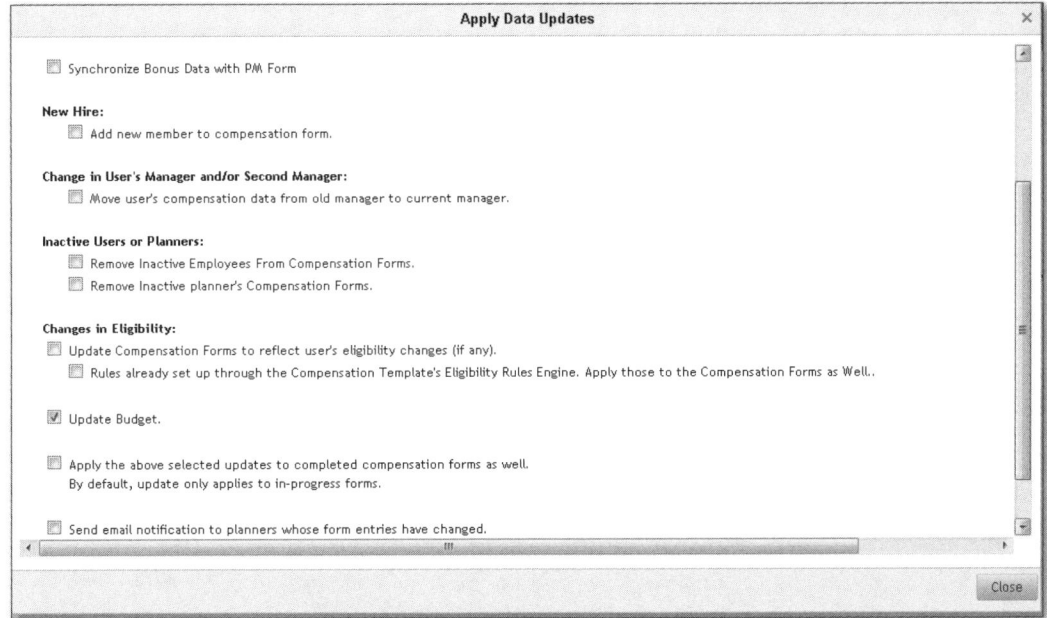

Figure 9.40 Apply Data Updates options

9.1.5 Plan and Approve Recommendations

Each planner in the organization is responsible for timely recommendations for employees as part of the compensation planning cycle process. These activities are performed on the compensation forms generated for each planner. Figure 9.41 shows a sample compensation form with the salary compensation component configuration.

9 | Compensation

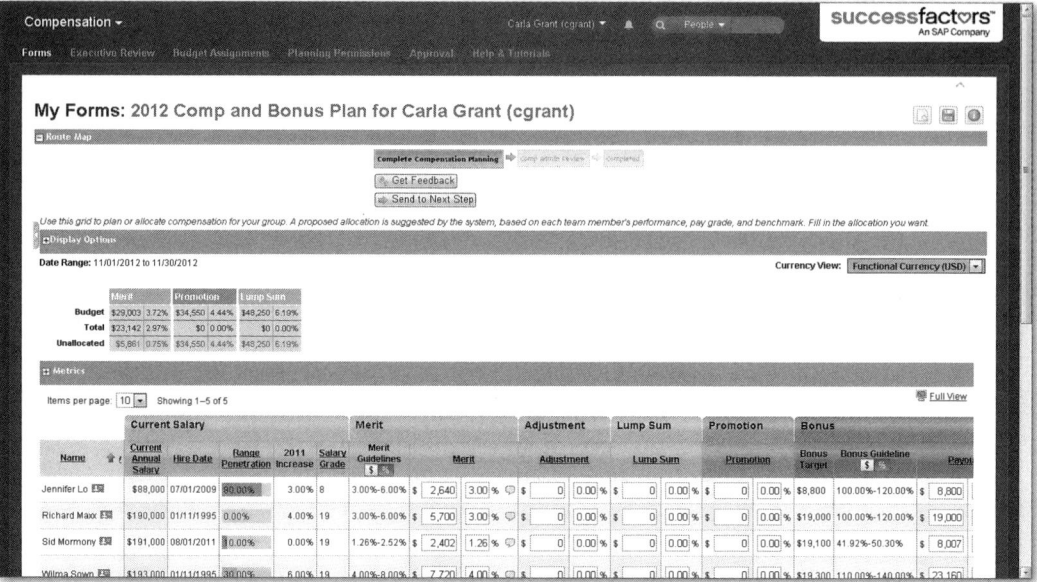

Figure 9.41 Planner's View of the Compensation Form

Planners can adjust the display options on the form to get the information desired about the employee by expanding the DISPLAY OPTIONS option, as shown in Figure 9.42.

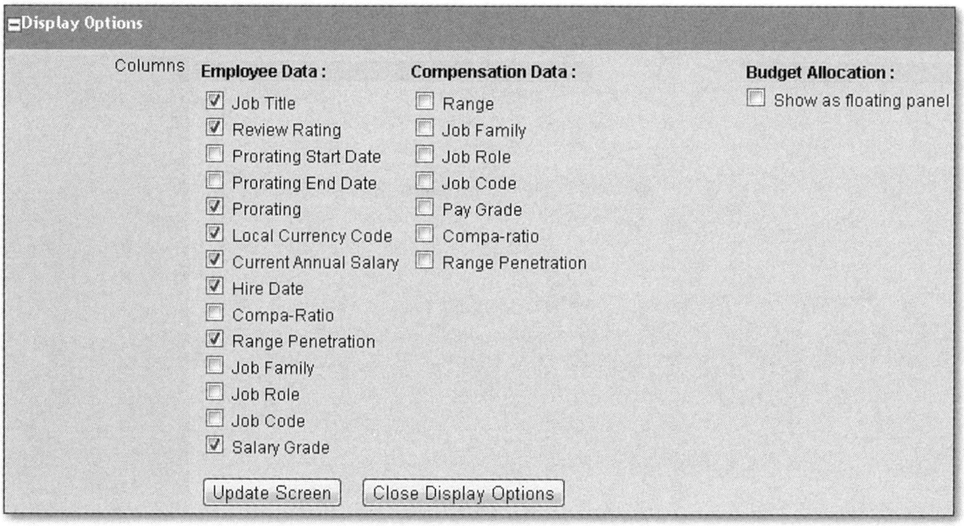

Figure 9.42 Display Options on the Compensation Form

Input Recommendation

Planners can choose to accept the calculated recommendations for the employees based on the compensation plan template setup or to override the system-calculated recommendations. Planners also have the flexibility to view the compensation guidelines as a percentage value or numerical value by adjusting the toggle available in the appropriate column. Figure 9.43 illustrates a planner (Richard Maxx) changing the initial recommendation exceeding the threshold of the component being planned against and being prompted for further action.

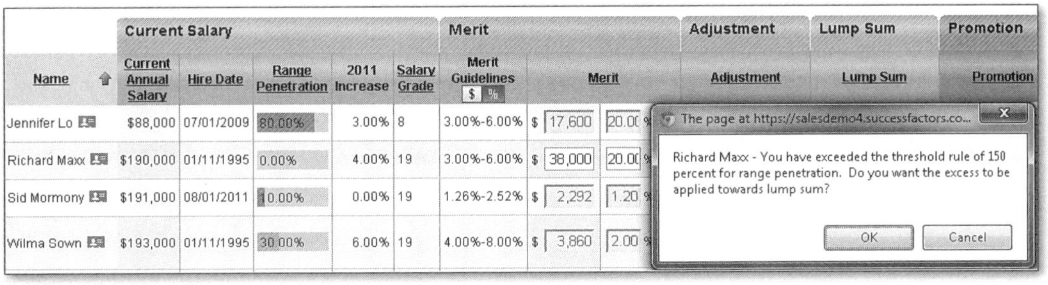

Figure 9.43 System Prompt for Exceeding Thresholds Established in the Guidelines

The planner must also provide mandatory comments in response to the adjustment of the initial recommendation value if the user exceeds the maximum limits established as part of the compensation guidelines (see Figure 9.44).

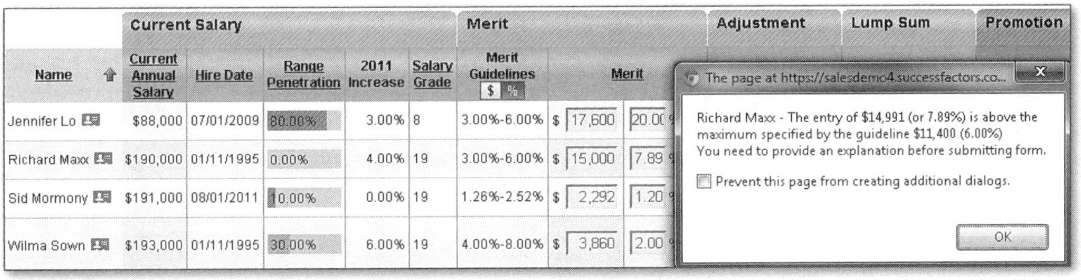

Figure 9.44 A System Prompt for the Planner to Provide an Explanation

Depending on how the compensation plan template is configured, a planner can also view multiple compensation planning components as separate tabs, as shown in Figure 9.45. The SUMMARY tab is shown in Figure 9.46.

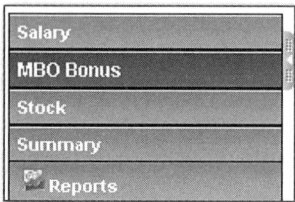

Figure 9.45 Multiple Compensation Components View on Compensation Form

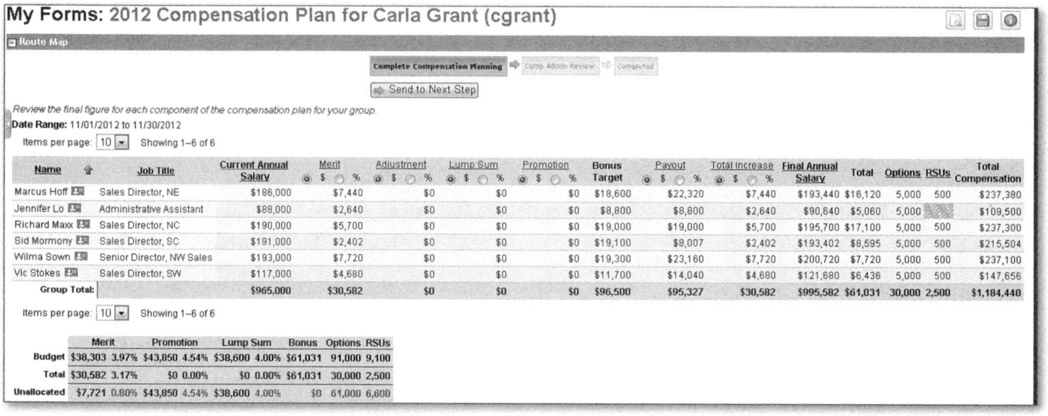

My Forms: 2012 Compensation Plan for Carla Grant (cgrant)

Route Map

Complete Compensation Planning → Comp Admin Review → Completed

Send to Next Step

Review the final figure for each component of the compensation plan for your group.

Date Range: 11/01/2012 to 11/30/2012

Items per page: 10 Showing 1–6 of 6

Name	Job Title	Current Annual Salary	Merit ($ / %)	Adjustment ($ / %)	Lump Sum ($ / %)	Promotion ($ / %)	Bonus Target	Payout ($ / %)	Total Increase ($ / %)	Final Annual Salary	Total	Options	RSUs	Total Compensation
Marcus Hoff	Sales Director, NE	$186,000	$7,440	$0	$0	$0	$18,600	$22,320	$7,440	$193,440	$16,120	5,000	500	$237,380
Jennifer Lo	Administrative Assistant	$88,000	$2,640	$0	$0	$0	$8,800	$8,800	$2,640	$90,640	$5,060	5,000		$109,500
Richard Maxx	Sales Director, NC	$190,000	$5,700	$0	$0	$0	$19,000	$19,000	$5,700	$195,700	$17,100	5,000	500	$237,300
Sid Mormony	Sales Director, SC	$191,000	$2,402	$0	$0	$0	$19,100	$8,007	$2,402	$193,402	$8,595	5,000	500	$215,504
Wilma Sown	Senior Director, NW Sales	$193,000	$7,720	$0	$0	$0	$19,300	$23,160	$7,720	$200,720	$7,720	5,000	500	$237,100
Vic Stokes	Sales Director, SW	$117,000	$4,680	$0	$0	$0	$11,700	$14,040	$4,680	$121,680	$6,436	5,000	500	$147,656
Group Total:		**$965,000**	**$30,582**	**$0**	**$0**	**$0**	**$96,500**	**$95,327**	**$30,582**	**$995,582**	**$61,031**	**30,000**	**2,500**	**$1,184,440**

Items per page: 10 Showing 1–6 of 6

	Merit		Promotion		Lump Sum		Bonus	Options	RSUs
Budget	$38,303	3.97%	$43,850	4.54%	$38,600	4.00%	$61,031	91,000	9,100
Total	$30,582	3.17%	$0	0.00%	$0	0.00%	$61,031	30,000	2,500
Unallocated	$7,721	0.80%	$43,850	4.54%	$38,600	4.00%	$0	61,000	6,600

Figure 9.46 Summary of All Compensation Components

Figure 9.47 shows a sample compensation form with the bonus compensation component configuration.

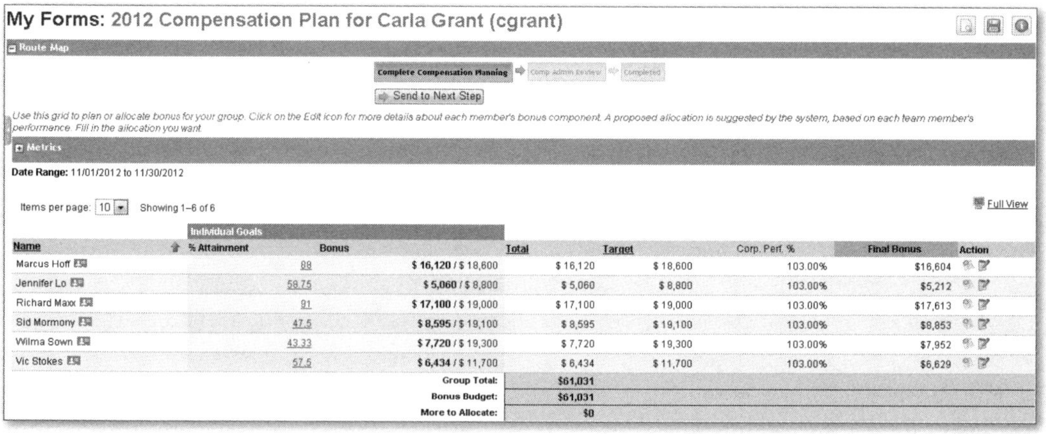

My Forms: 2012 Compensation Plan for Carla Grant (cgrant)

Route Map

Complete Compensation Planning → Comp Admin Review → Completed

Send to Next Step

Use this grid to plan or allocate bonus for your group. Click on the Edit icon for more details about each member's bonus component. A proposed allocation is suggested by the system, based on each team member's performance. Fill in the allocation you want.

Metrics

Date Range: 11/01/2012 to 11/30/2012

Items per page: 10 Showing 1–6 of 6 Full View

	Individual Goals						
Name	% Attainment	Bonus	Total	Target	Corp. Perf. %	Final Bonus	Action
Marcus Hoff	88	**$ 16,120** / $ 18,600	$ 16,120	$ 18,600	103.00%	$16,604	
Jennifer Lo	58.75	**$ 5,060** / $ 8,800	$ 5,060	$ 8,800	103.00%	$5,212	
Richard Maxx	91	**$ 17,100** / $ 19,000	$ 17,100	$ 19,000	103.00%	$17,613	
Sid Mormony	47.5	**$ 8,595** / $ 19,100	$ 8,595	$ 19,100	103.00%	$8,853	
Wilma Sown	43.33	**$ 7,720** / $ 19,300	$ 7,720	$ 19,300	103.00%	$7,952	
Vic Stokes	57.5	**$ 6,434** / $ 11,700	$ 6,434	$ 11,700	103.00%	$6,629	
		Group Total:	**$61,031**				
		Bonus Budget:	**$61,031**				
		More to Allocate:	**$0**				

Figure 9.47 A Planner's View of the Bonus Component on the Compensation Form

Figure 9.48 shows a sample compensation form with stock compensation configuration.

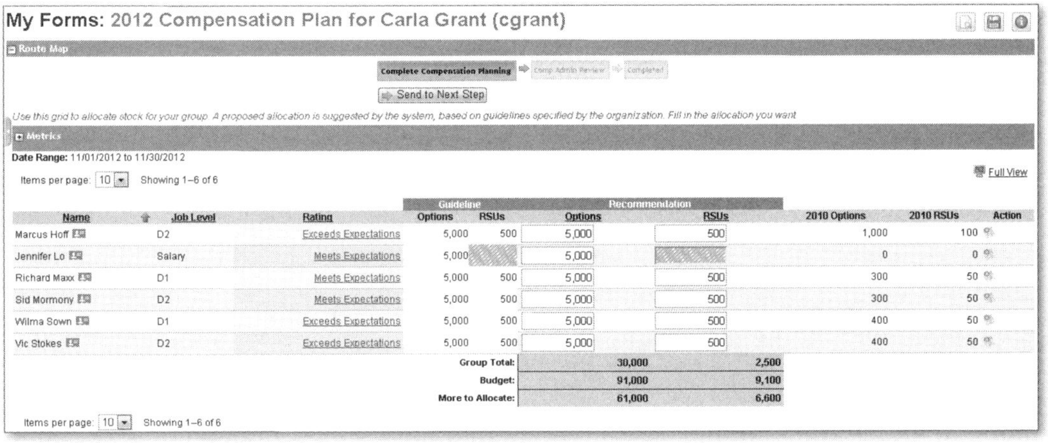

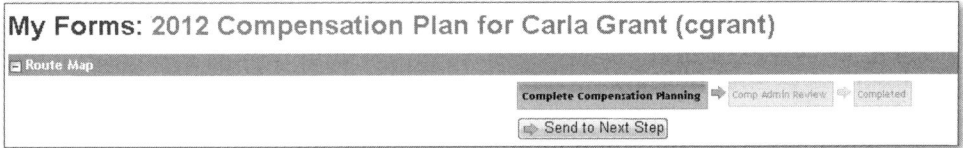

Figure 9.48 A Planner's View of the Stock Component on the Compensation Form

Approval Workflow

After a planner has completed making their recommendations on the compensation form, the next step is move the form to the next logical part in the workflow process. To perform this, a planner must click on the SEND TO NEXT STEP button at the top of the compensation form, as shown in Figure 9.49.

Figure 9.49 Compensation Form Workflow Steps

Hierarchy-Based Approval

Another option for approval of the planner recommendations is to enable *hierarchy-based approval* as part of your solution design. It provides a simple approval model based on tree structure navigation that is built on the organization hierarchy. This configuration option eliminates the need to generate forms or send forms to the next step in the approval process. Figure 9.50 shows the planner view of the compensation components using hierarchy-based approval configuration.

9 | Compensation

Figure 9.50 Hierarchy-Based Approval Configuration

9.1.6 Reports

The two standard options for compensation reporting are ROLLUP and AGGREGATE EXPORT; these are available as part of the COMPENSATION HOME menu.

Compensation Aggregate Export

This is an export of all employee and planning data available within a specific compensation plan template. The extract includes all standard and custom fields (if marked as reportable) defined on the compensation plan template. A sample compensation aggregate export is shown in Figure 9.51.

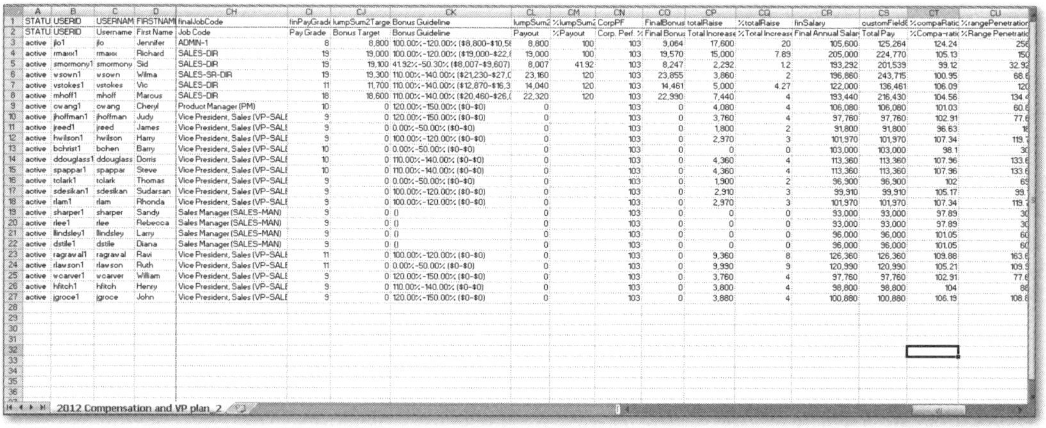

Figure 9.51 Compensation Aggregate Export

Compensation Rollup

This option allows for the generation of the compensation planning and budget information report based on a planner's hierarchy for the selected compensation plan template. Figure 9.52 illustrates the menu for generation of this report. The reports are generated as a ZIP file with the rollup summary report and a detailed report as Excel files, as shown in Figure 9.53 and Figure 9.54, respectively.

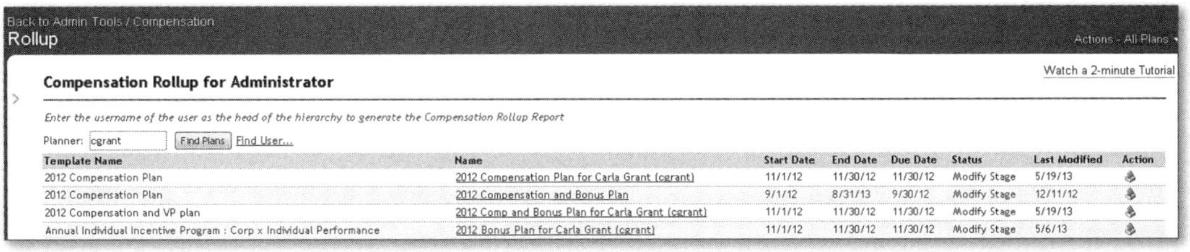

Figure 9.52 Compensation Rollup Generation Menu

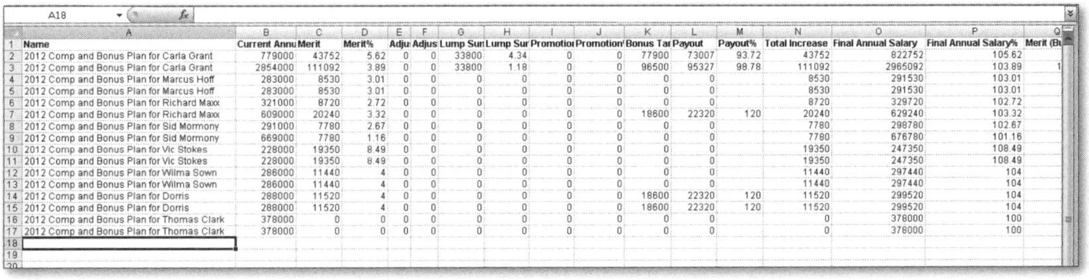

Figure 9.53 Compensation Rollup Summary Report

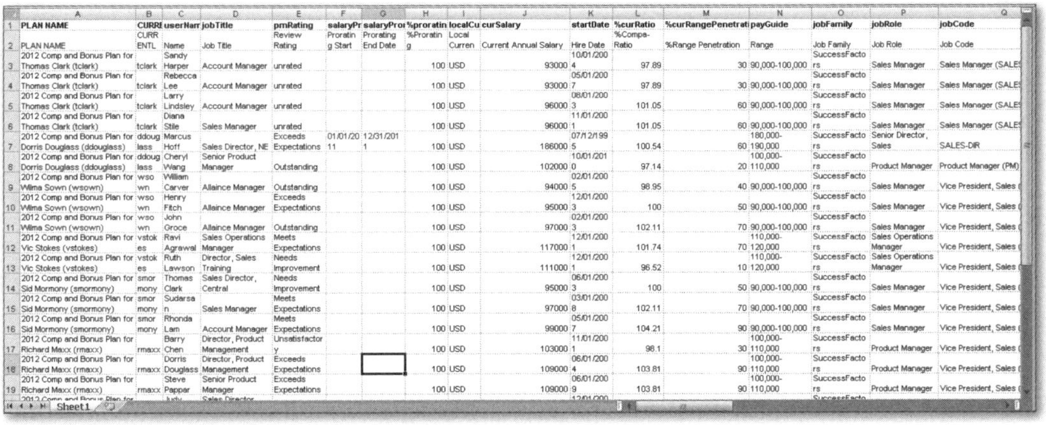

Figure 9.54 Compensation Rollup Detail View

9.1.7 Executive Review

The Executive Review functionality in the Compensation solution enables any active BizX user to review (read) or adjust (write) compensation recommendations made for all employees in the organization. The user must be granted this functionality as part of the RBP framework and be assigned proper data access to the employee population. At any given time, data generated within a single compensation plan template can be accessed with EXECUTIVE REVIEW, as shown in Figure 9.55.

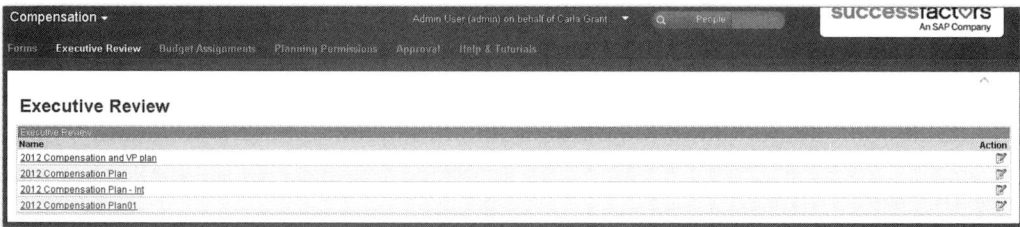

Figure 9.55 User Access to Executive Review

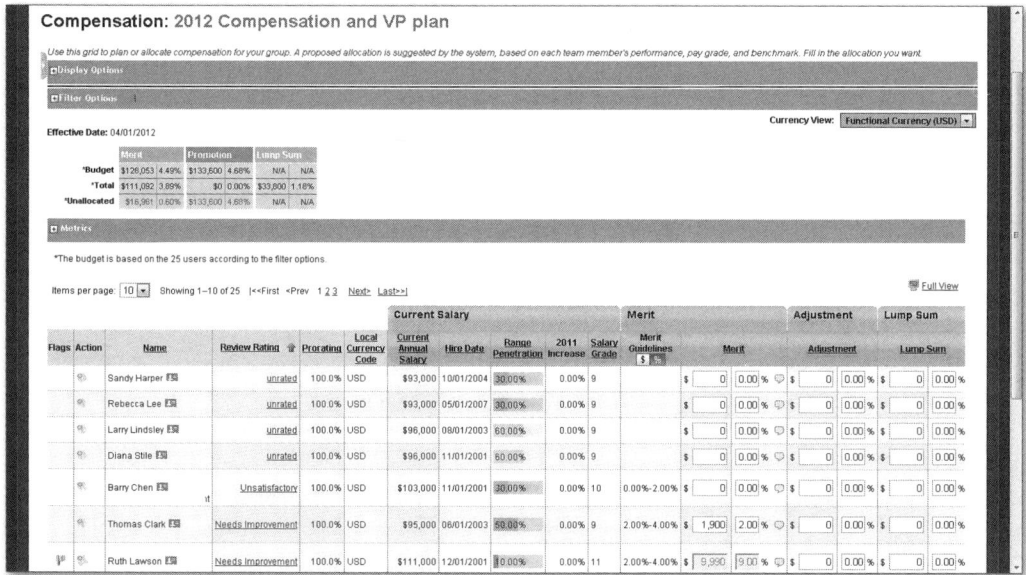

Figure 9.56 Executive Review for a Compensation Plan Template with Write Access Enabled

After the compensation plan template is chosen, the user is presented with a page that exactly matches the design and layout of the compensation plan template, as shown in Figure 9.56. This page isn't to be mistaken with the compensation form for a planner. Executive Review neither relies on a compensation form's workflow state nor behaves like a form. If compensation data is modified in Executive Review, you can send an email notification to the planners or reviewers of the affected underlying compensation form.

The real advantage of using Executive Review is the ability to filter data by expanding the FILTER OPTIONS, as shown in Figure 9.57. This can provide for a detailed analysis and update of compensation data by the administrators, HR professionals, and managers in your organization. Data visible on the EXECUTIVE REVIEW screen can also be exported in CSV format.

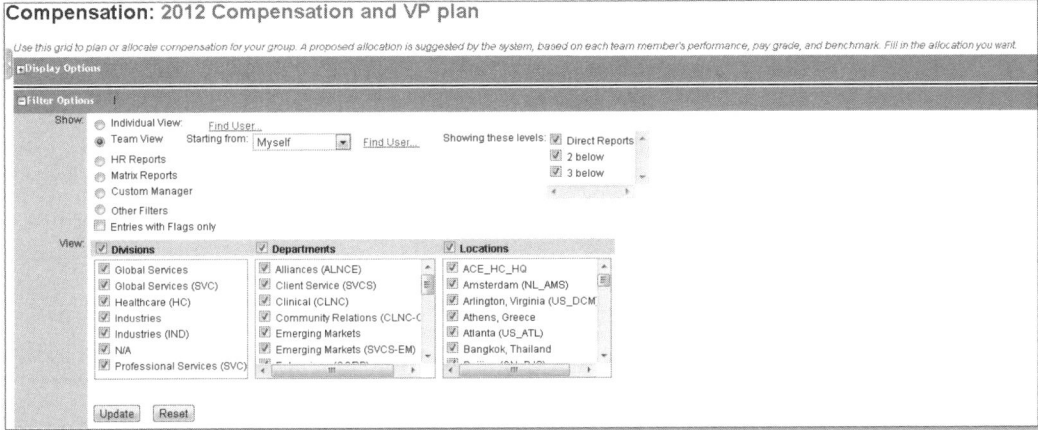

Figure 9.57 Filter Options for Executive Review

9.1.8 Reward Statements

Leading industry practices call for providing each employee with a Personal Compensation Statement highlighting the employee's compensation results at the end of the compensation planning cycle. The Compensation solution facilitates this process by providing the capability to create a PERSONAL COMPENSATION STATEMENT template, as shown in Figure 9.58. You can modify the template with your organization's text, logo, multiple sections, and standard fields on the compensation plan template.

9 | Compensation

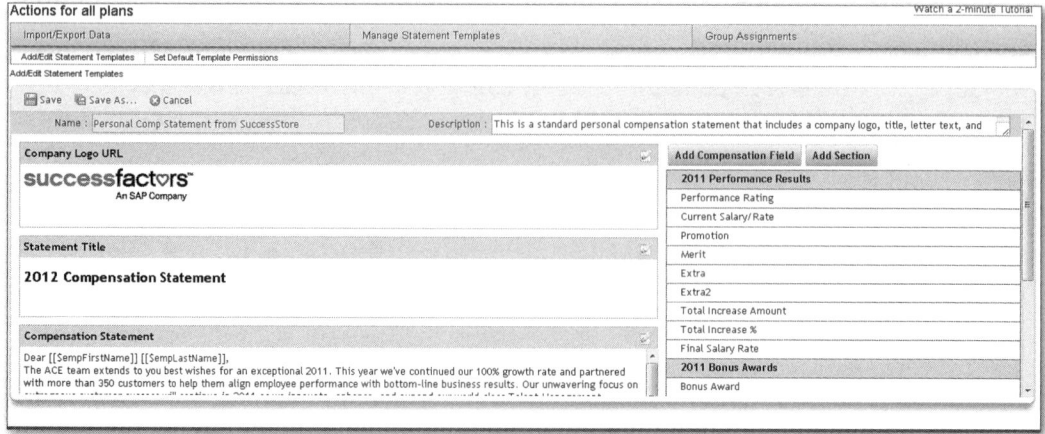

Figure 9.58 Personal Compensation Statement Template

After all compensation forms have been reviewed and marked completed, only then can a Personal Compensation Statement be generated for each employee. The Personal Compensation Statement for an employee is available on the Employee Profile.

9.2 Variable Pay Solution

SuccessFactors Variable Pay is a robust solution that calculates employee bonus based on quantitative business performance and individual performance measures. An organization can decide whether to use either the bonus calculation feature of the SuccessFactors Compensation solution or the Variable Pay solution as part of the compensation planning cycle design.

The following are keys features of the Variable Pay solution:

▶ Proration of bonus calculation for an employee who has held two or more positions in the organization, has had two or more pay grades, has had a salary change, or is associated with multiple scorecards

▶ Manage several bonus plans with weighted business goals

▶ Modeling of "what-if" scenarios to forecast bonus payout

▶ Integration of employee performance in bonus calculation

- Support for additive or multiplicative formulas
- Multiple time-based payout cycles such as monthly, quarterly, and annually

Let's walk through the configuration steps required to create a Variable Pay program.

9.2.1 Plan Setup

The first step is to configure a variable pay plan within the PLAN SETUP section shown in Figure 9.59.

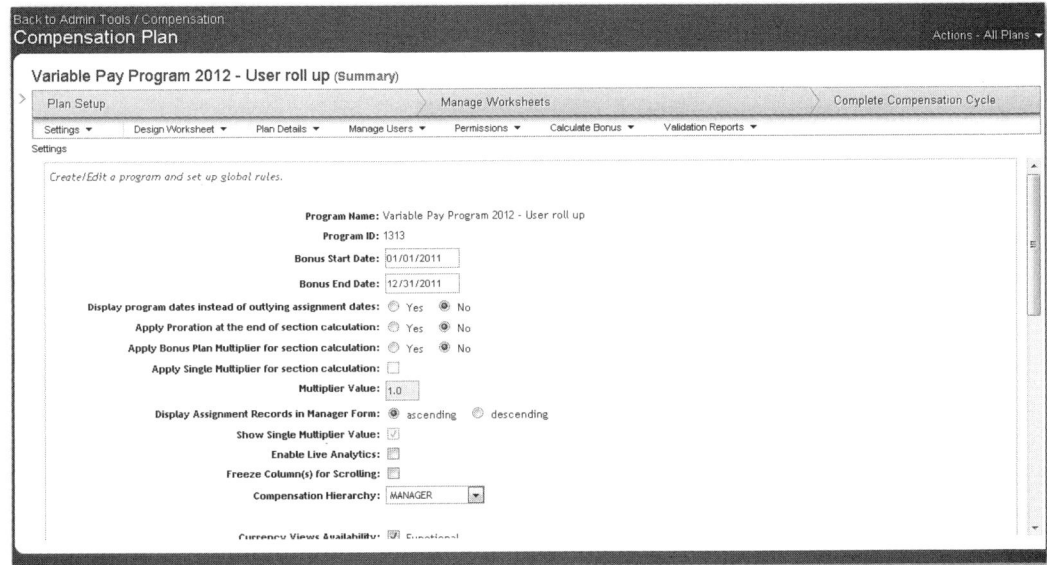

Figure 9.59 Variable Pay Plan Setup

Settings

The SETTINGS subsection is where the following details are visible and configurable:

- PROGRAM NAME
  Enter a unique program name to identify the variable pay program type.
- PROGRAM ID
  This is a system-generated unique ID for the variable pay program.
- BONUS START DATE/BONUS END DATE
  These are start and end dates for the variable pay program. This should match the time frame for which the bonus is being calculated.

- ▶ DISPLAY PROGRAM DATES INSTEAD OF OUTLYING ASSIGNMENT DATES
  Choose the best option based on your organization's design requirements.
- ▶ APPLY PRORATION AT THE END OF SECTION CALCULATION
  Select the best option based on your organization's design requirements.
- ▶ APPLY BONUS PLAN MULTIPLIER FOR SECTION CALCULATION
  Select the best option based on your organization's design requirements.
- ▶ APPLY SINGLE MULTIPLIER FOR SECTION CALCULATION
  Select the best option based on your organization's design requirements.
- ▶ MULTIPLIER VALUE
  Enter the value to be used in bonus calculation.
- ▶ DISPLAY ASSIGNMENT RECORDS IN MANAGER FORM
  Select the best option based on your organization's design requirements.
- ▶ SHOW SINGLE MULTIPLIER VALUE
  Select the best option based on your organization's design requirements.
- ▶ ENABLE LIVE ANALYTICS
  Select this option to enable onscreen calculation capability.
- ▶ FREEZE COLUMN(S) FOR SCROLLING
  Select this option to prevent screen scrolling if large numbers of columns are present.
- ▶ COMPENSATION HIERARCHY
  Select the hierarchy for the variable pay program.
- ▶ CURRENCY VIEWS AVAILABILITY
  This option enables the variable pay form to be viewed using multiple views if selected.
- ▶ CONVERSION RATE TABLE
  Currency conversion table to be used by the variable pay program.
- ▶ IF USING CURRENCY CONVERSION, IMPORT BASIS AND CUSTOM FIELDS USING
  Select the LOCAL CURRENCY or FUNCTIONAL CURRENCY option based on your organization's design requirements.
- ▶ APPLY GATES FOR BUSINESS GOALS
  Select the best option based on your organization's design requirements.
- ▶ APPLY ACCELERATORS FOR BONUS GOALS
  Select the best option based on your organization's design requirements.

- APPLY PRORATING ROUNDING
  Select the option and date parameters based on your organization's design requirements for proration rounding, if date-sensitive.
- MANAGER INSTRUCTION
  Text entered in this box is visible at the top of the variable pay form.
- LEGAL NOTICE
  Enter any legal text required.

The SET BONUS CALCULATION subsection has the following configuration options:

- IS THIS BONUS BASED ON ASSIGNMENTS?
  Select this option if the bonus calculation is based on employees having different assignments in the year.
- BONUS CALCULATION EQUATION
  Select the appropriate bonus calculation for your organization's design of the variable pay program. The calculation options are shown in Figure 9.60.

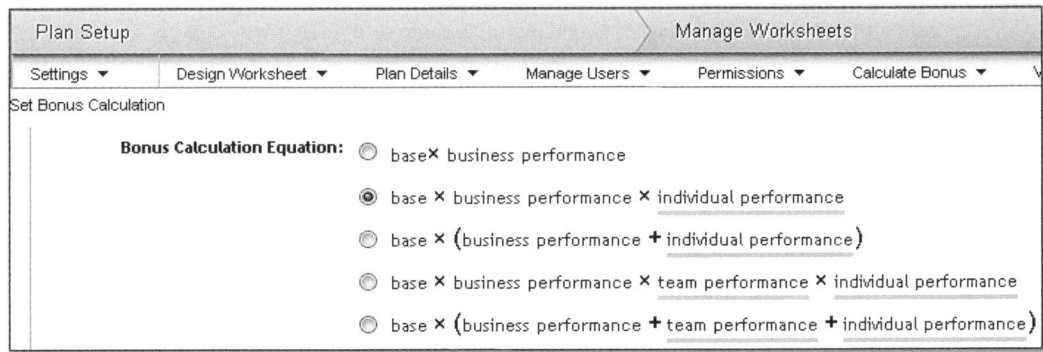

Figure 9.60 Bonus Calculation Equation for Variable Pay

- BUSINESS GOAL NAME
  Select the required business goal for variable pay program.
- PERFORMANCE RATING SOURCE
  Select the option to import performance rating by employee or assignment history. If integration with PM is required, select the TEMPLATE NAME and RATING option, as shown in Figure 9.61.
- DEFINE BONUS CAPS
  Select the option to apply bonus caps.

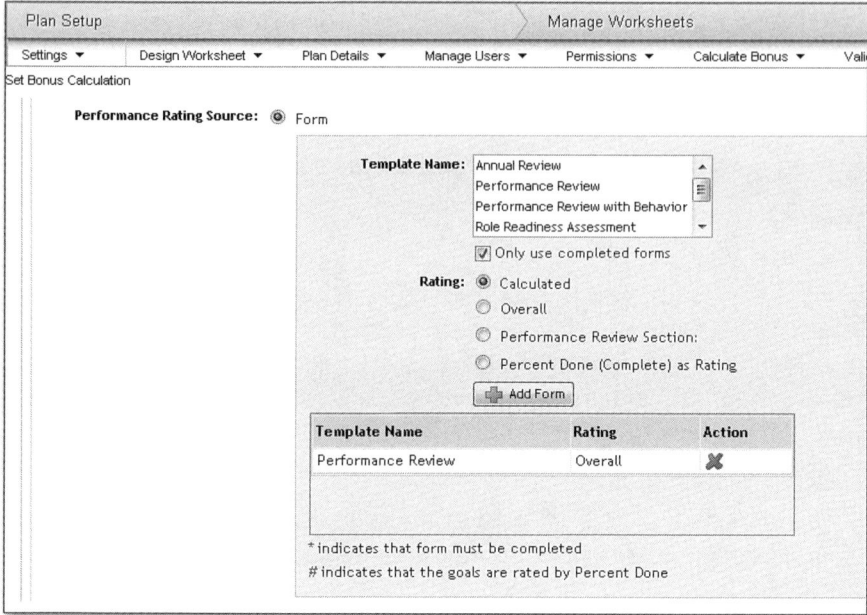

Figure 9.61 Performance Rating Source Configuration

The SET NUMBER FORMAT RULES subsection, as shown in Figure 9.62, enables the creation of number formatting rules. These rules are referenced for each value in the variable pay calculation.

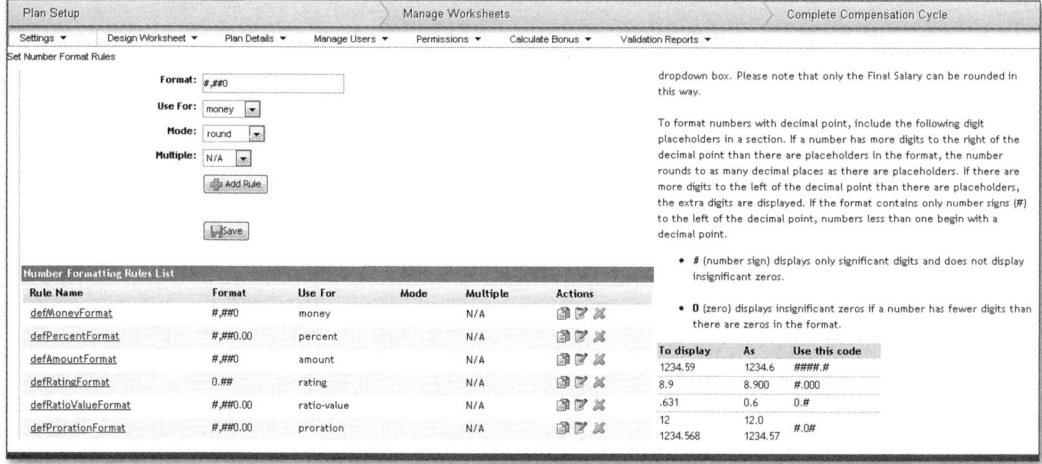

Figure 9.62 Set Number Format Rules Configuration

Design Worksheet

The CONFIGURE LABEL NAMES AND VISIBILITY subsection, as shown in Figure 9.63, controls the visibility of variable pay sections, fields, and label names.

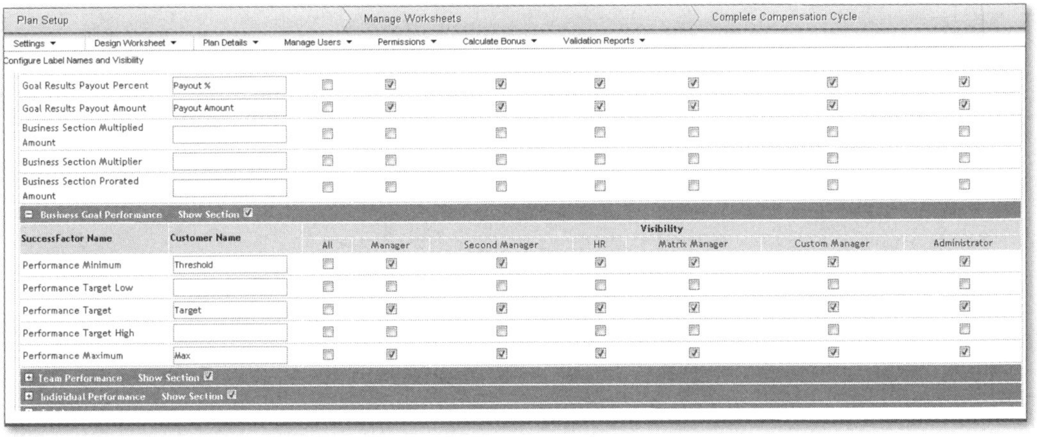

Figure 9.63 Configure Label Names and Visibility

The COLUMN DESIGNER subsection is very similar to the DESIGN WORKSHEET option in the SuccessFactors Compensation solution. You can add standard or custom fields, as well as custom groups to create the variable pay form layout.

The SET NUMBER FORMATS subsection shown in Figure 9.64 is where you set the number format for each value in the variable pay calculation.

Plan Details

The PLAN DETAILS subsection allows for configuration of the following options:

- BONUS PLANS 1. IMPORT BUSINESS GOALS
  Import a CSV file that contains the business goal definitions, goal forecasts, and goal results. This file is produced as part of the variable pay program design and is required for the configuration of the variable pay program.

- BONUS PLANS 2. IMPORT BONUS PLANS
  Import a CSV file that contains the bonus plan definition. This file is produced as part of the variable pay program design and is required for the configuration of the variable pay program.

- BONUS PLANS 3. CONFIGURE BONUS PLANS
  Adjust the imported bonus plans parameters as shown in Figure 9.65.

9 | Compensation

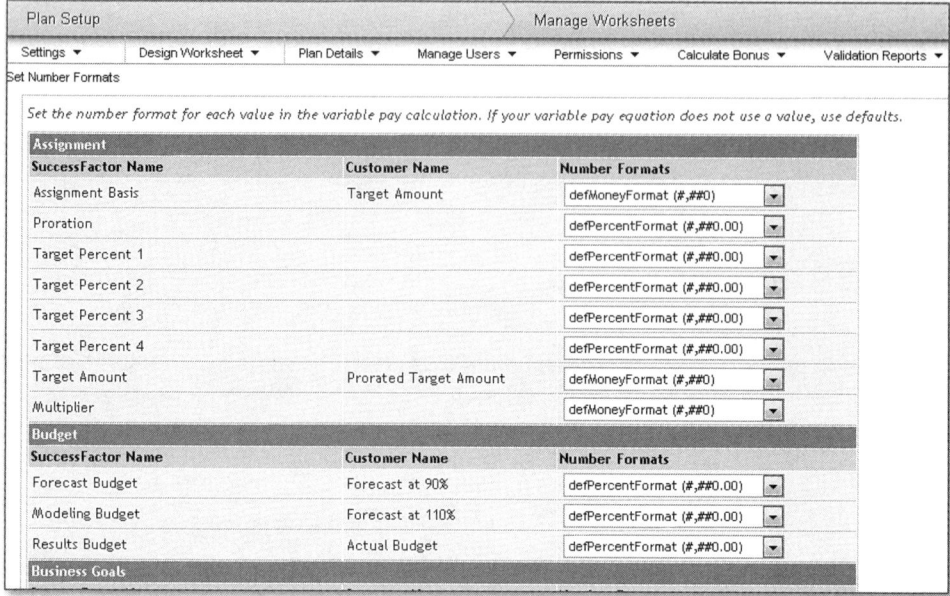

Figure 9.64 Set Number Formats for Variable Pay

Figure 9.65 Configure Bonus Plans for Variable Pay

▶ IMPORT BUSINESS GOAL WEIGHTS
Import a CSV file that links the business goals to the bonus plans and assigns unique weighting. This file is produced as part of the variable pay program design and is required for the configuration of the variable pay program.

▶ ELIGIBILITY
Import a CSV file that contains the eligibility rule for the bonus plans. This file is produced as part of the variable pay program design and is required for the configuration of variable pay program.

▶ BUDGET
Configure budget visibility and percentages, as shown in Figure 9.66.

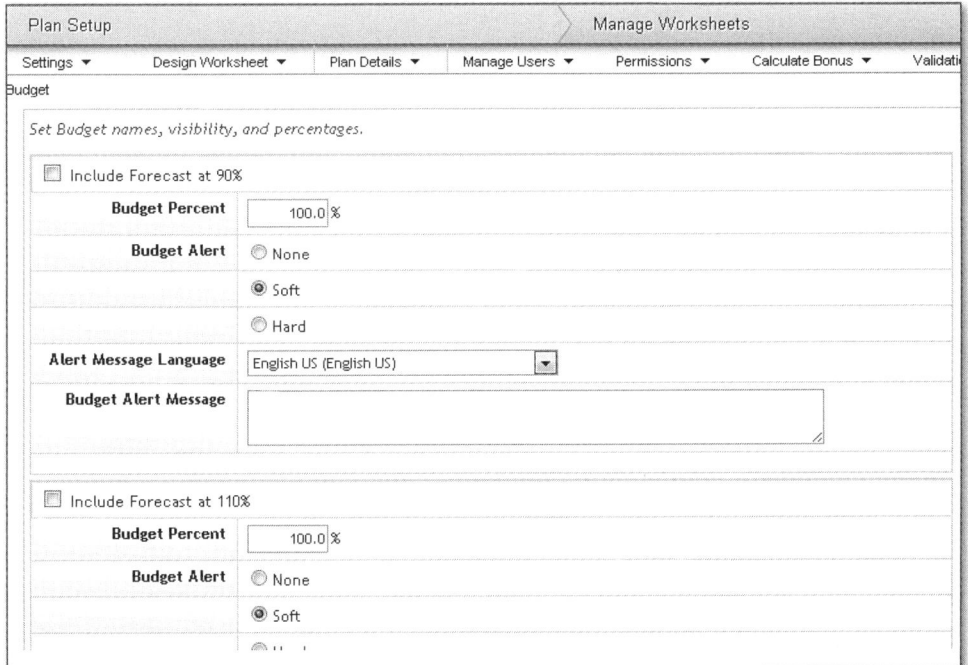

Figure 9.66 Budget in Variable Pay

▶ INDIVIDUAL GUIDELINE
Configure the mapping of employee performance rating sources to input guidelines, as shown in Figure 9.67.

9 | Compensation

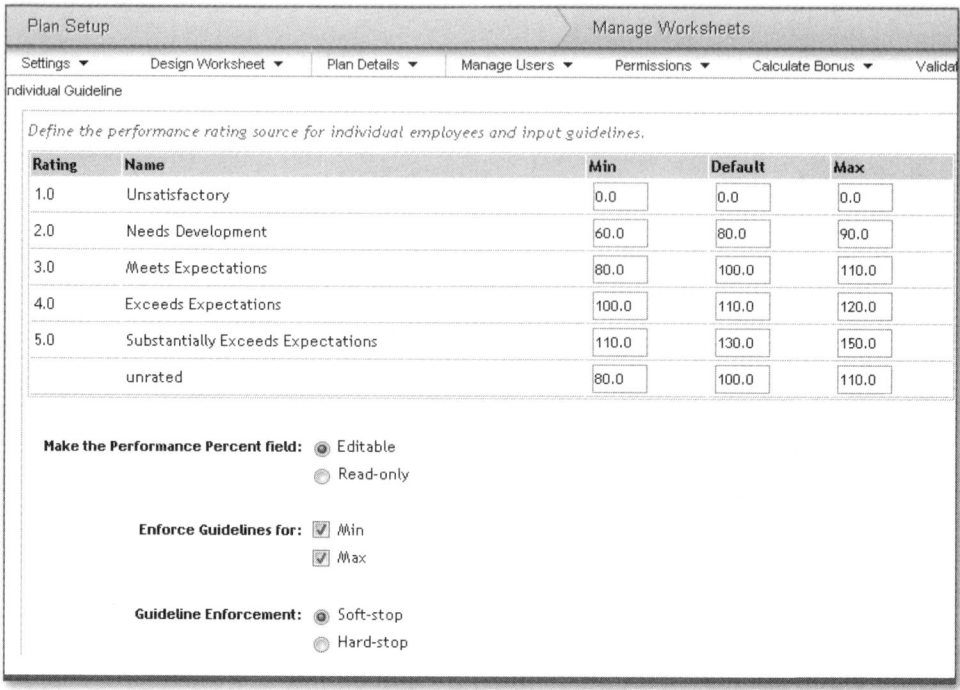

Figure 9.67 Individual Guideline for Variable Pay

- TEAM GUIDELINE
  Configure the mapping of team performance rating sources to input guidelines.
- ADVANCED GUIDELINES
  Configure the formulas for individual guidelines.

Manage Users

The MANAGER USERS subsection is where you import the employee's date-effective history file in a CSV format. This is a required file for variable pay plan setup and calculation. This subsection is also used for performing an online edit of the employee history rows. Figure 9.68 shows the EDIT EMPLOYEE HISTORY screen with rows uploaded in the system.

The employee history can also be processed from the PM solution if required.

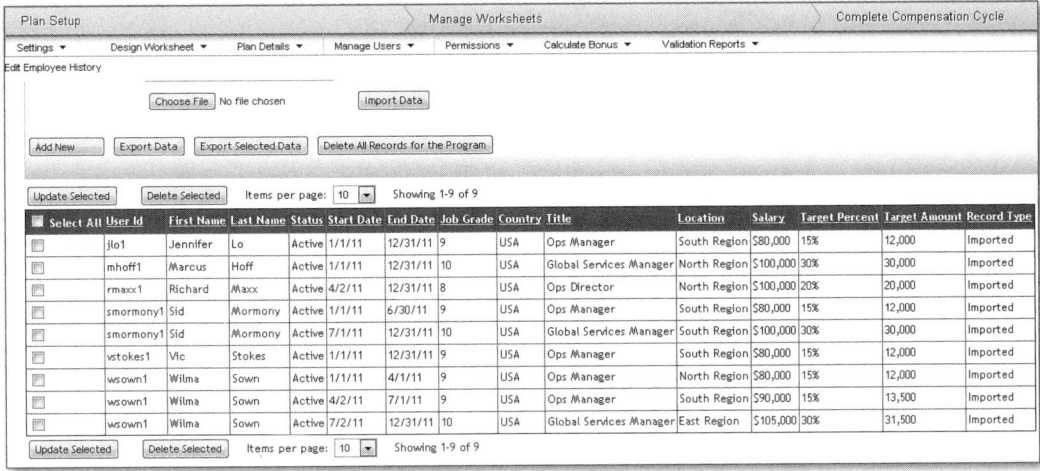

Figure 9.68 Employee History File for Variable Pay

Calculate Bonus

After all setup activities have been performed and employee history data is uploaded into the system, the next step is to trigger the BONUS PAYOUT calculation process as shown in Figure 9.69. The calculation can be made for one of the bonus plans, a manager, and an employee.

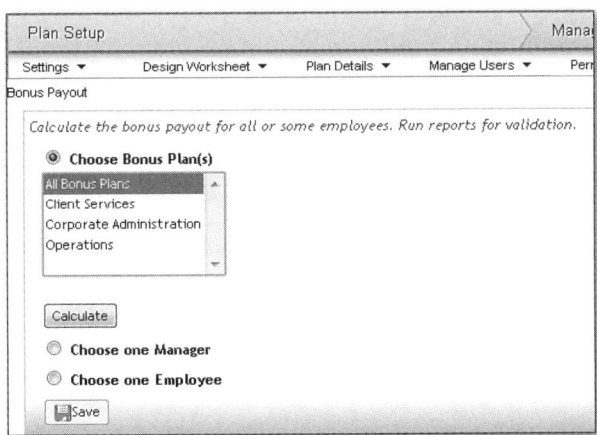

Figure 9.69 Bonus Payout Calculation

The user who initiated the process will be notified by email of the successful completion of the bonus payout calculation.

Validation Reports

The Variable Pay solution is delivered with the reports shown in Figure 9.70, which help validate the variable pay program setup.

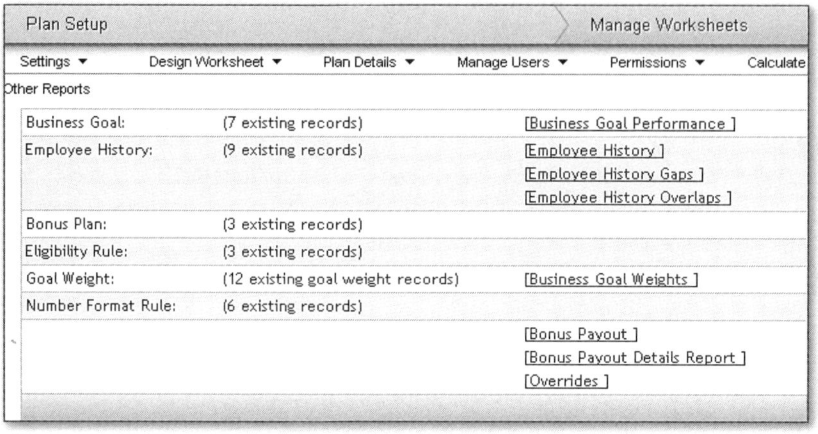

Figure 9.70 Validation Reports in Variable Pay

9.2.2 Manage Variable Pay Forms

After the Variable Pay setup is complete, the process to generate variable pay forms is exactly the same as for generation of compensation forms discussed in Section 9.1.4. After the forms are generated, the planner can review the forms as shown in Figure 9.71.

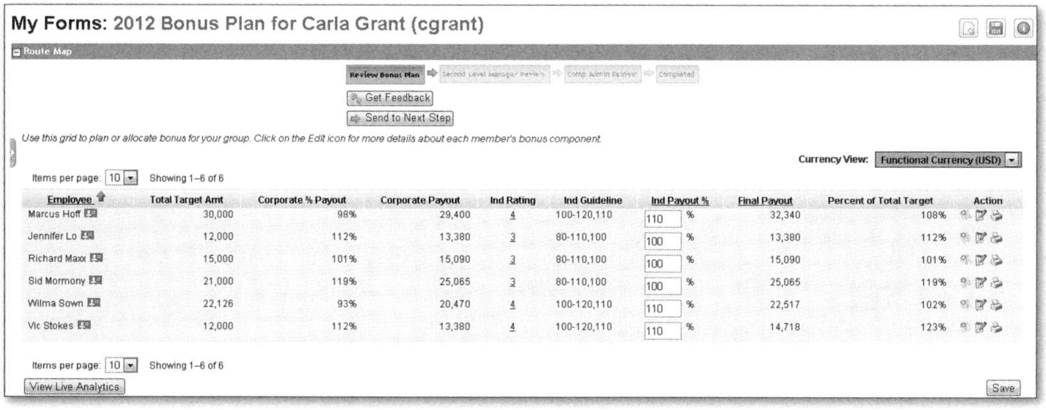

Figure 9.71 Variable Pay Form

If the planner wants to view detailed calculations instead of this overview, the planner can click the PLAN DETAILS icon in the ACTION column. The plan details include details such as target amounts, proration, goals, weighting, and payout amounts, as shown in Figure 9.72.

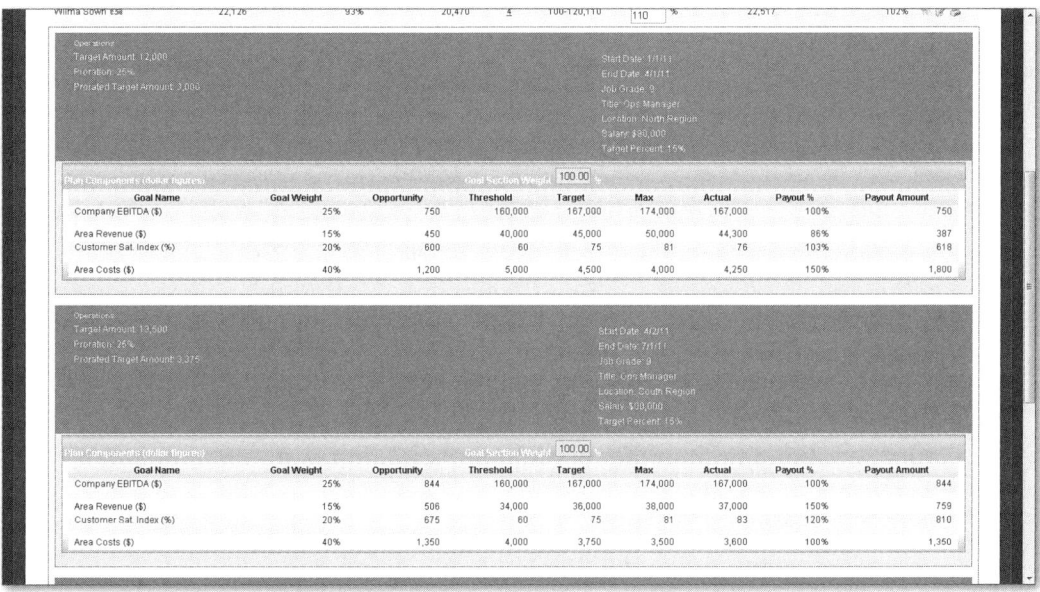

Figure 9.72 Employee Plan Details on Variable Pay Form

9.2.3 Approve Recommendations

After the planner is satisfied with the calculations on the variable pay form, clicking the SEND TO NEXT STEP button at the top of the variable pay form moves it into the next step in the workflow.

> **Note**
>
> The hierarchy-based approval configuration for approving compensation forms isn't available for the Variable Pay solution.

9.2.4 Executive Review

The Executive Review functionality in the Variable Pay solution behaves exactly the same way as the SuccessFactors Compensation solution discussed in Section 9.1.7.

9.2.5 Reward Statements

The Variable Pay solution provides the capability to create a Personal Variable Pay Statement template. You can modify the template with your organization's text, logo, multiple sections, and standard fields available on the variable pay program.

9.3 Summary

The SuccessFactors Compensation and Variable Pay solutions provide a robust platform to meet the complex needs of an organization's compensation design and truly enforce a pay-for-performance culture. The solution offerings in SuccessFactors Compensation provide the organization the agility needed to effectively manage a successful compensation cycle by streamlining the planning process. Integration capabilities with SAP ERP HCM and Employee Central provide the benefit of not having to manage multiple data points.

In this chapter, you learned what is required for the setup of the yearly compensation forms and how to design your compensation worksheets. You also learned how to execute a compensation review and complete the compensation process. We covered the SuccessFactors Variable Pay module and how this can offer you the ability to perform compensation reviews for individuals whose pay varies based on different business factors.

In the next chapter, we'll look at the SuccessFactors Recruiting Execution solution and how this can support both recruiting management, applicant tracking, and recruiting marketing activities.

Recruiting in today's competitive environment encompasses three phases that are all critically important to ensuring that you hire the right candidates to drive business results. SuccessFactors Recruiting Execution provides all of the tools to attract, engage, and select the best talent for your organization.

10 Recruiting Execution

Legacy Applicant Tracking Systems (ATS) have focused almost exclusively on selecting candidates. While many tools are now available on the market to help companies find and engage candidates, most aren't connected to the application and selection processes and tools. But in today's competitive hiring environment, finding the best candidates isn't enough. You need to get them engaged and moving through your hiring process quickly so you don't risk losing them to a different opportunity.

The SuccessFactors Recruiting Execution module (hereafter RX) brings together Recruiting Marketing (RMK) and Recruiting Management (RCM) to combine the best features of an ATS, application processing and candidate management features, and high-powered tools to attract and engage candidates in one solution. This complete recruiting solution sits inside the BizX suite, enabling customers to connect it to their other BizX solutions such as SuccessFactors Workforce Analytics, Workforce Planning, Succession Planning, Learning, Performance Management, Goal Management, Compensation, and other collaboration solutions. As shown in Figure 10.1, RX is an integral piece of a complete HCM solution that drives business execution results and is the first step for customers to optimize their workforces—finding the right people for the right jobs.

RX not only manages the transactional components of a traditional ATS from a requisition and application perspective but also goes beyond that, providing tools that ensure customers can attract and engage the best candidates in their recruiting process.

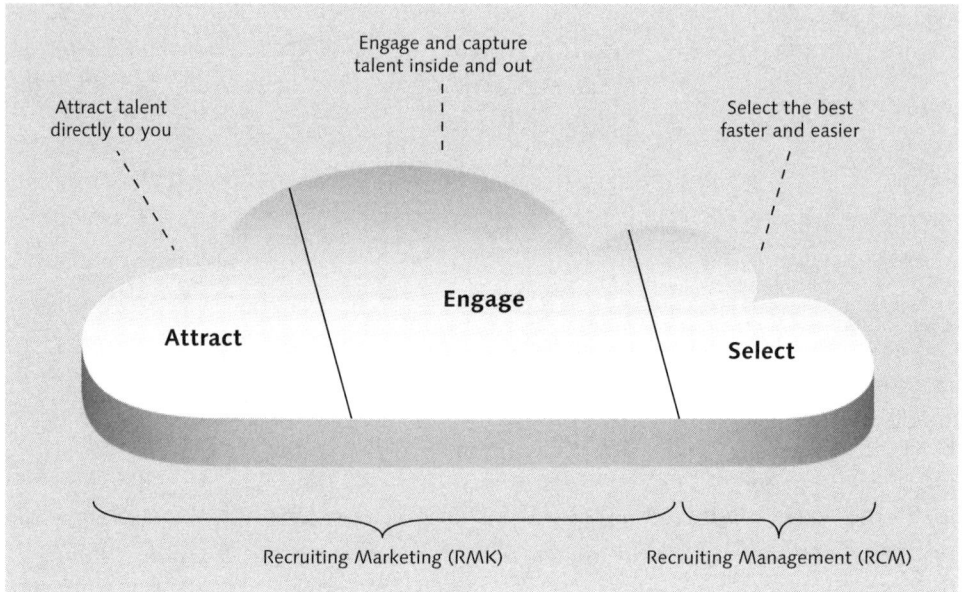

Figure 10.1 Recruiting Execution Landscape

The recruiting process with RX is driven by collaboration. It allows different players in the process from recruiters, hiring managers, coordinators, and others to actively participate in managing an open position, reviewing and assessing candidates, and eventually selecting the right candidate for hire.

The system is intuitive and easy to use; any player in the process can log in and understand what to do and where to do it with very little training. For recruiters that spend all day in the system, RX saves time and frustration by reducing the number of mouse clicks to complete an action from maintaining a requisition to moving candidates through the Talent Pipeline to eventually processing the successful candidate for hire.

RMK features introduce the concepts of Search Engine Optimization (SEO) and social media integration to attract top talent and help them find the jobs customers are sourcing. Advanced RMK analytics provide never-before-available insight into how marketing strategies and dollars are being utilized and facilitate real-time adjustment.

Other tools such as the Requisition dashboard give recruiters an overview of the critical pieces of data on their open positions. The Candidate Workbench provides many tools for recruiters to evaluate and communicate with candidates and share qualified candidates with other colleagues.

Interview Central facilitates competency-based assessment of candidates. It leverages the BizX Stack Ranker functionality to allow interviewers to evaluate candidates against each other and give an overall rating and comments. Recruiters can build interviewer teams for requisitions and assign the same team to each candidate being interviewed, saving time and increasing recruiter efficiency.

RX provides one of the most comprehensive metrics engine in the industry. Providing metrics such as cost per hire, time to hire, and candidate quality by source, location, and other criteria, RX provides the raw data customers need to evaluate the effectiveness of their recruiting process and tools.

As with the rest of the BizX suite, RX is highly configurable. It offers more than 30 standard fields available for use on the requisition and application and supports unlimited custom fields. The customer's branding and messaging is supported by SuccessFactors' best practices and platform.

10.1 Recruiting Execution Foundation

Before we look at the features of RX, let's outline some foundational concepts that are helpful to understand.

10.1.1 Recruiting Roles

Roles associated with the recruiting process are identified by each customer based on who needs to approve requisitions and view candidates. These process roles are then associated with the standard RX roles, which define the following:

▸ Field, button, and feature permissions on the requisition

▸ Field, button, and feature permissions on the candidate application

▸ Which role will create the approval workflow for the requisition and review the requisition

Within the RX module, seven roles can be permissioned. These roles are separate from roles created in Role-Based Permissions (RBP) and are defined and permissioned directly in the requisition template configuration. Roles correspond to operator fields on the requisition (for example, the RECRUITER in the example provided in Figure 10.2). The following recruiting roles are available:

- Originator
- Recruiter
- Hiring Manager
- Sourcer
- Coordinator
- Second Recruiter
- VP of Staffing
- Approver

Figure 10.2 Requisition Operator Roles

Unless an operator field is tied to a dynamic group, thereby limiting the users who can be selected as an operator in that field, then any user in the system can be selected as an operator on the requisition. This provides a great amount of flexibility in who can participate in the recruiting process.

10.1.2 Recruiting Templates

There are three main components of configurable templates within RX: the Job Requisition Data Model, the Candidate Data Model template, and the Candidate Profile Template.

Job Requisition Data Model

A requisition defines the requirements of the position being filled. Requisitions are created from a template that is configured during implementation. The template is called the Job Requisition Data Model (JRDM) and specifies the fields on the requisition and who has permissions to read and write to each field. Requisitions are created manually by operators in the recruiting process, such as a hiring manager or recruiter. In future releases, it will be possible for requisitions to be created via integration with SAP ERP HCM position management. Requisitions are tied to a route map (or workflow) for approval before they are open and can be posted to the Career site. The JRDM is completely configurable to meet customer requirements using either the standard fields for requisitions or any number of custom fields that may be required.

Candidate Data Model

The Candidate Data Model (CDM) is RX's application. It defines information about a candidate who is applying for a position, and contains identifying information such as name and contact data, job-specific requirements the candidate possesses, and other demographic data the customer needs to capture, such as Equal Employment Opportunity (EEO) status. The application template is also completely configurable and can utilize the standard application fields or any custom fields required to support the customer's needs.

Candidate Profile Template

The Candidate Profile Template (CPT) is the candidate's online résumé. It leverages BizX Employee Profile functionality and can be designed to capture static information about a candidate such as education, work experience, and references. The CPT can by synched to the Employee Profile for internal candidates so that this information is entered only once.

Now that we've laid a foundation to discuss RX, let's take a look at the recruiting process.

10.2 Requisition Creation and Approval

The recruiting process in RX begins with creating a requisition and sending it through the approval workflow, or route map. This gives each operator in the approval workflow an opportunity to review the position requirements, make additions or correct data, and send it back if there is an issue that needs to be addressed. After the requisition is approved, it can be posted to the internal and external career portals, job boards, or the agency portal.

10.2.1 Requisition Creation

As mentioned earlier, requisitions are created manually. Future releases of RX will include integration with SAP ERP HCM position management so that open positions in SAP ERP HCM will generate a requisition created in RX. For manually created requisitions, any user that has been granted permissions to create the requisition form can start the requisition process. The user who creates a requisition, like the one shown in Figure 10.3, is known as the originator and has permissions on the requisition that have been granted in the requisition configuration for the originator role. The originator role completes the operators that will need to approve the requisition and any other fields for which they have permissions.

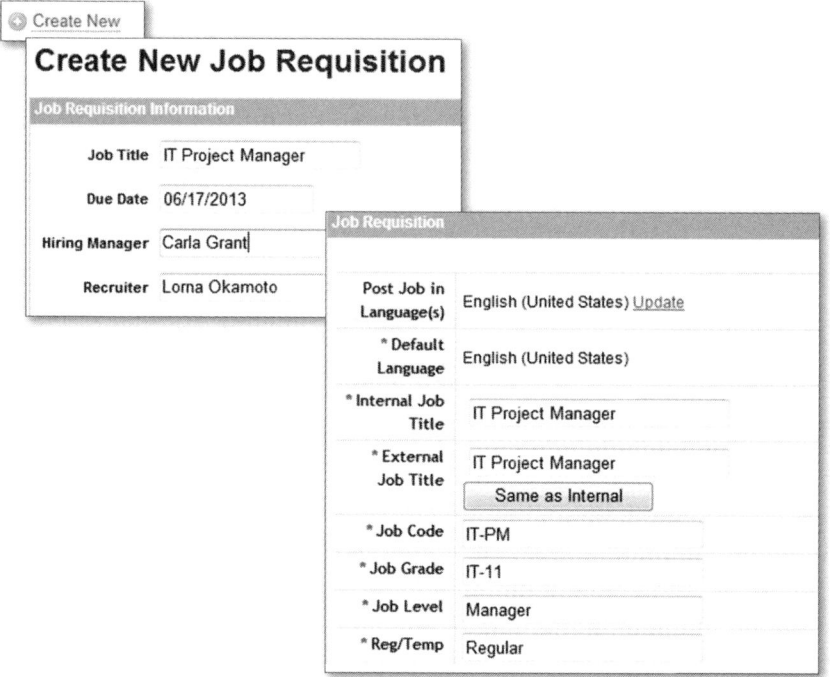

Figure 10.3 Creating a New Requisition

For requisitions created through integration, the functionality required for requisitions generated from open positions created within SAP core HR is on the RX Product Roadmap, but no release date is available. It is likely this functionality will be made available later in 2013.

10.2.2 Requisition Approval Workflow

Each job requisition template can be associated with one approval workflow, called a route map. A *route map* electronically moves a requisition from one user to the next until all appropriate approvals have been received (see Figure 10.4).

Figure 10.4 Requisition Route Map

While the route map defines which users will touch the requisition, the permissions assigned to each role in the route map define what the users can see and do to the data in the requisition. Steps in the route map can be linear, or iterative. Iterative steps involve two parties and allow the requisition to be sent back and forth between the two parties until it's ready to move forward. After the requisition has been approved, it can be posted, and candidates can view it on the career portal. We'll cover this step next.

10.3 Job Posting and Sourcing

Open requisitions can be posted so candidates can search for them and apply. Job posting is where the power of RX's marketing capabilities come into play and illustrate SuccessFactors' dedication to candidate engagement. SuccessFactors is committed to delivering data-driven and user-centric best practices that optimize site conversion rates and maximize the user's experience.

The power of SuccessFactors Recruiting Marketing (RMK) is making job postings available to the brightest and best talent possible. A common problem facing talent acquisition professionals is that their jobs aren't easy to find. RMK leverages proven marketing techniques such as SEO, social media integration, and customized landing pages while applying them to talent sourcing in new ways to drive applicant flow. Talent communities capture passive candidates that may have been previously lost to recruiters. SuccessFactors implemented RMK internally in early 2012, and within 10 months of implementation, visitors to its career site increased from 10,000 to more than 80,000, resulting in more than 150 hires. Now the company can track more than 50% of its hires directly back to the source.

Easily accessible sourcing analytics provide new visibility to marketing strategies and their effectiveness at any given time. Dashboards on recruiting marketing sources provide real-time data on where candidates are coming from, enabling customers to evaluate and adjust recruiting marketing strategies and dollars in an agile manner. These advanced analytics support tracking candidates from sourcing to hire to retire.

SuccessFactors treats every job as a campaign to attract candidates to your sites based on their interests and skill sets. Customized landing pages attract candidates based on their particular interests and drive them to the main Career site within RCM. Talent communities are candidate-centric, automated recruiting pools that grow over time. They connect talent with the company's brand, store contacts in a centralized place, and track visitors to a customer's site who begin the application process but don't complete it. Talent communities open communication channels with candidates that would not otherwise exist.

Jobs are posted through the JOB POSTINGS page and, from there, are picked up and distributed to the predetermined channels based on the criteria established during implementation.

As shown in Figure 10.5, approved requisitions are available for posting in various places within RCM:

- Internal posting (internal career site)
- External posting (external career sites)
- Job board postings (via eQuest integration)
- Agency listings (SuccessFactors' Agency Portal)

Jobs posted to the intranet will appear on the CAREERS tab within BizX and be available to all employees. Corporate postings are those made to the microsite created for external candidates. Customers have one default microsite but can create additional sites as requirements dictate. This flexibility enables sites to focus on certain populations or target candidates. However, the decision to create additional microsites should be made in the context of the RCM strategy employed by each customer.

Jobs can be posted for a specific period of time by providing a POSTING START DATE and a POSTING END DATE. If a job should be posted indefinitely, no POSTING END DATE is provided, and it will stay posted until the posting is removed by the recruiter.

Figure 10.5 Job Postings in RX

Job board postings are an add-on service provided by SuccessFactors' partner eQuest. The job boards available depend on a customer's separate contract and subscription with eQuest. This aggregator allows recruiters to post jobs to multiple places via one interface. Specific fields must be configured on the requisition template to support the fields eQuest requires to post.

SuccessFactors supports working with agencies using its Agency Portal. There is one Agency Portal that is shared by all customers, and each customer sets up individual agency accounts for those agencies they want to post jobs for, as shown in Figure 10.6.

After agencies have been set up in OneAdmin and granted access to the Agency Portal (see Figure 10.7), recruiters can post jobs to the portal, and agency users may submit candidates for open positions. Agency candidates are easily identifiable from the Candidate Workbench as well as within the Candidate Snapshot.

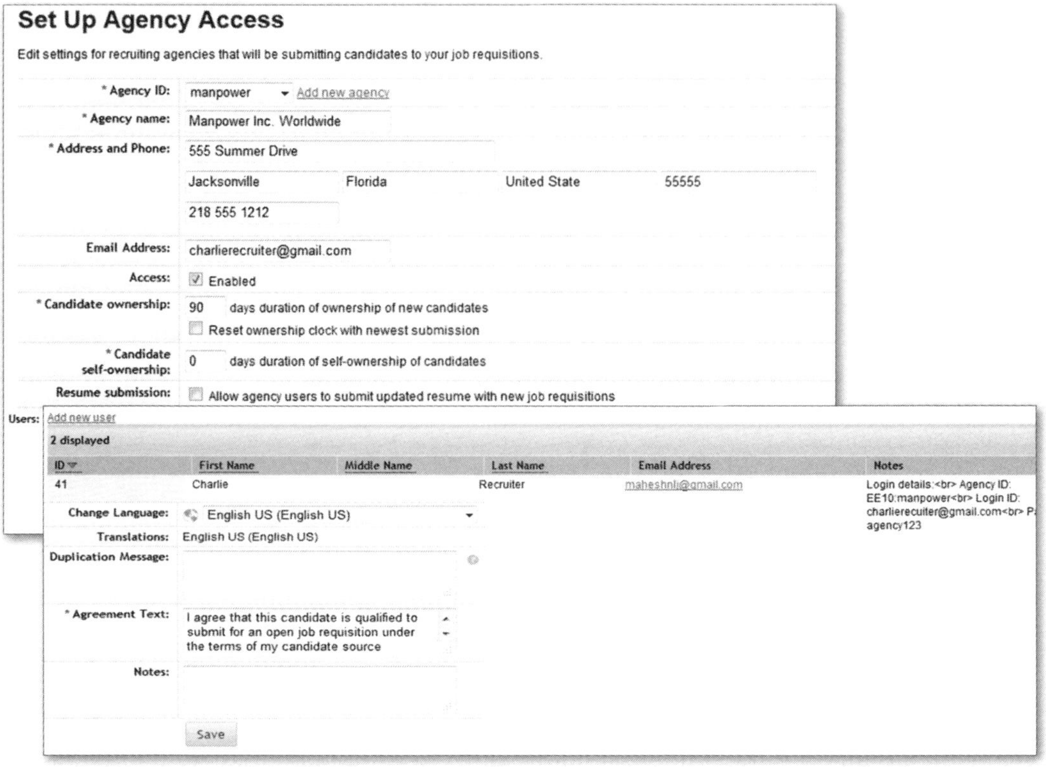

10 | Recruiting Execution

Figure 10.6 Setting Up Agency Access in OneAdmin

Figure 10.7 The SuccessFactors Agency Portal

10.4 Candidate Experience

Candidates interact with the system in several ways. They can search for open positions and set up a Candidate Profile, apply for jobs, manage job applications already submitted, and set up job alerts to be notified of future positions that become available.

The Candidate Profile and Candidate Data Model are two big elements of the candidate's job search experience as they work together to provide recruiters and hiring managers a complete picture of the candidate. This picture is used to evaluate the candidate against the job requirements, leading to the selection of a qualified candidate. This section will look at how the two elements of the candidate experience—the Candidate Profile and Candidate Data Model—work together to provide recruiters and hiring managers with a complete picture of a candidate's background and qualifications for a position.

10.4.1 Career Sites

As we saw in Section 10.3, jobs are posted in two places within RX: an internal careers page (where internal employees go to find open positions for which to apply through BizX) and microsites (where external candidates can view jobs and set up an account via one or more external Career sites). External sites like the one in Figure 10.8 are generated in OneAdmin, and a customer can have multiple microsites within its RX system. Each site has its own URL and can be used for marketing jobs to specific audiences. This is irrespective of other channels that funnel jobs in RMK.

Search Criteria

From the CAREER page, candidates can use search criteria to find positions that interest them. By selecting the VIEW JOBS button, they can display more detail on each position before drilling into job descriptions to view the requirements of each position, as shown in Figure 10.9. Customers can define welcome messages in the right two-thirds of the CAREER page. This is also done in OneAdmin, and it supports graphics, hyperlinks, and deep links to other URLs.

10 | Recruiting Execution

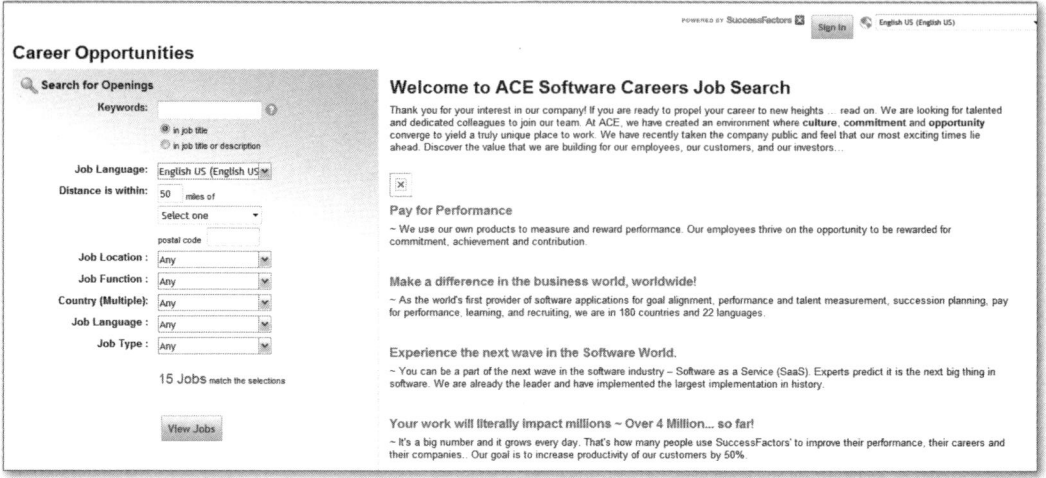

Figure 10.8 External Career Site

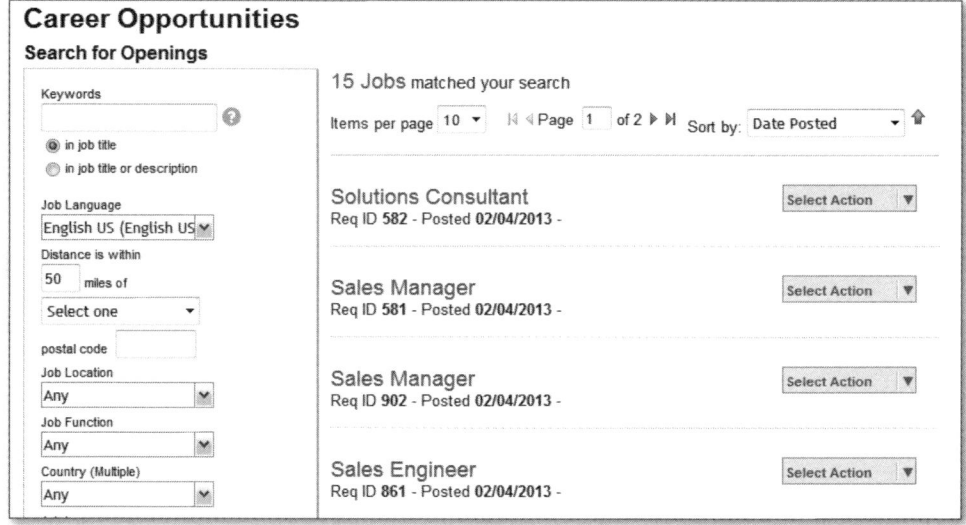

Figure 10.9 View Job Search Results

Search criteria are defined by the customer during implementation. There are standard search criteria that can be activated, such as keyword search and radial search. And customers may define unique search criteria that use data from the requisition to help candidates find positions of interest.

Candidates can create an account to set up a Candidate Profile and apply for jobs. External candidates are identified by their email address, which is also their user ID.

Candidate Home Page

After candidates log into the Career site, they are taken to a HOME page like the one in Figure 10.10. This provides additional space for the company to communicate with candidates and gives candidates an easy way to jump to actions they want to perform, such as searching for a job or maintaining their profile. Whether to use a HOME page is a configuration decision, and it can be turned on and off depending on the customer's requirements.

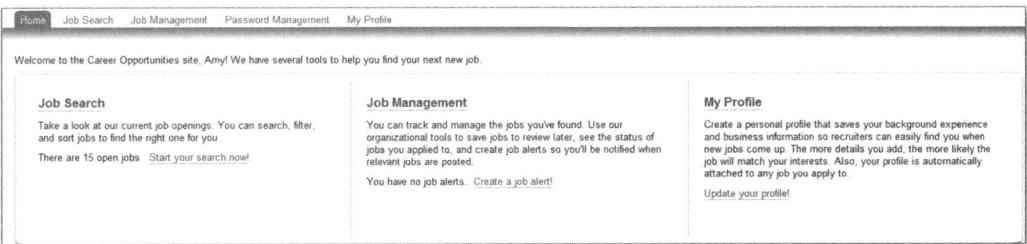

Figure 10.10 Career Page Home Page

10.4.2 Candidate Profile

The Candidate Profile serves as a candidate's online résumé. It leverages Employee Profile functionality to capture static candidate information such as name and contact information, work history, education, languages spoken, geographic mobility, among others, as shown in Figure 10.11. It serves to capture all of the information about a candidate that isn't job specific and applies to any position to which the candidate applies. Candidates enter this data just once in a central location that is visible to and searchable by recruiters. The Candidate Profile exists for all potential candidates, including all existing employees with access to BizX and external candidates who create an account.

Data collected on the Candidate Profile is searchable by recruiters who may be sourcing positions and others who have been permissioned to conduct candidate searches. To ensure consistency for internal employees between Employee Profile and Candidate Profile, the system supports mapping of the data elements configured on each Profile template. Fields that reside on both the Employee Profile and Candidate Profile can be synched so that internal employees only need to maintain information in one place. The trend is moving toward capturing more information on the Candidate Profile, rather than the application (or CDM) so candidates have one place to update information that remains fairly constant from one position to another.

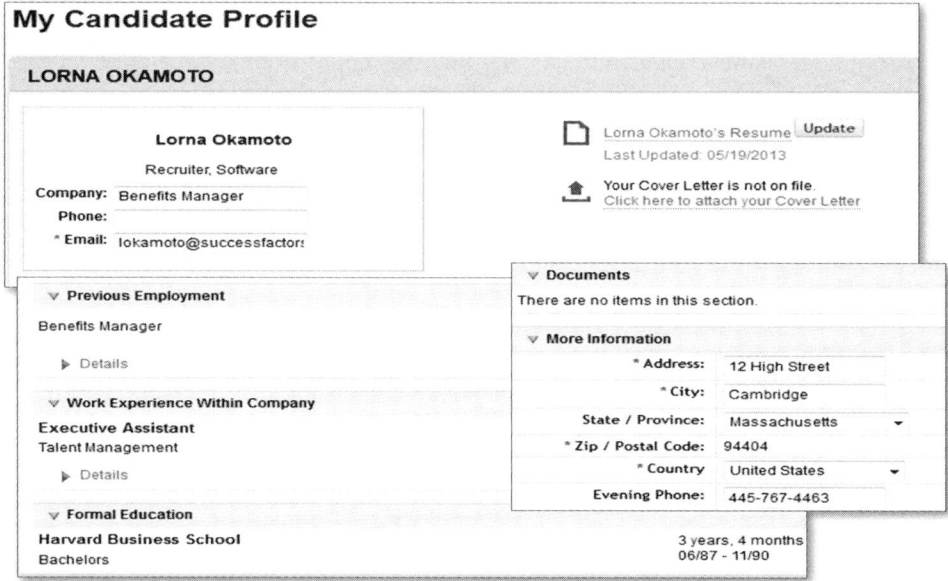

Figure 10.11 Candidate Profile

There is only one CPT that is used for both internal and external candidates. This is critical to keep in mind during design because both types of candidates need to use the same template but often have varying data needs. RX supports configuration for internal and external audiences to assist with this situation.

It's possible to have fields configured on the CPT that are only visible to internal candidates; likewise, fields that apply and are visible to external candidates only can also be configured. For internal candidates, background elements on the Candidate Profile that are duplicates of Employee Profile background elements can be mapped so that data is synced between the two. This alleviates the internal candidate from having to maintain the same data in two places in the system.

10.5 Candidate Data Model

The CDM that is shown in Figure 10.12 defines the data that is to be submitted by the applicant to apply for a job. The CDM captures job-specific information such as special qualifications and skills that are applicable to the position for which the candidate is applying.

The CDM and Candidate Profile can be configured so that data entered into one is mapped to the other. So, for example, if the candidate opens the application and completes the Candidate Profile first, information such as name, address, email, and phone number are populated on the application. Any documents such as résumé and cover letter uploaded to the Candidate Profile will also be available on the CDM. Updates to documents made on the CDM will be updated on the Candidate Profile also.

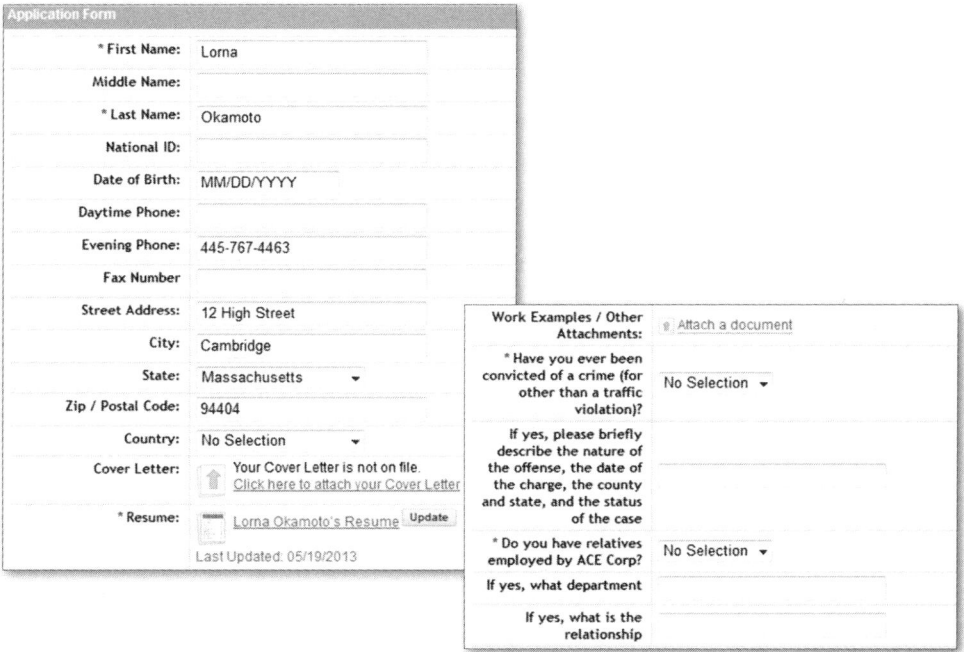

Figure 10.12 The Candidate Data Model

The CDM also controls what individuals in the recruiting process see when viewing candidates who have applied to positions. For example, the hiring manager may be permissioned to see all fields on the CDM except self-identification fields such as gender and veteran status, while the recruiter can see all fields.

Country-specific field configuration is also supported if a customer has a need to display certain fields to only candidates in a certain country. For example, a customer that sources jobs in the United States will often collect EEO data from candidates. Of course, they would not want these fields to be displayed to a candidate applying for a job in Canada or the United Kingdom because they aren't applicable. Country-specific configuration can be applied to these fields so that they appear only for positions based in the United States.

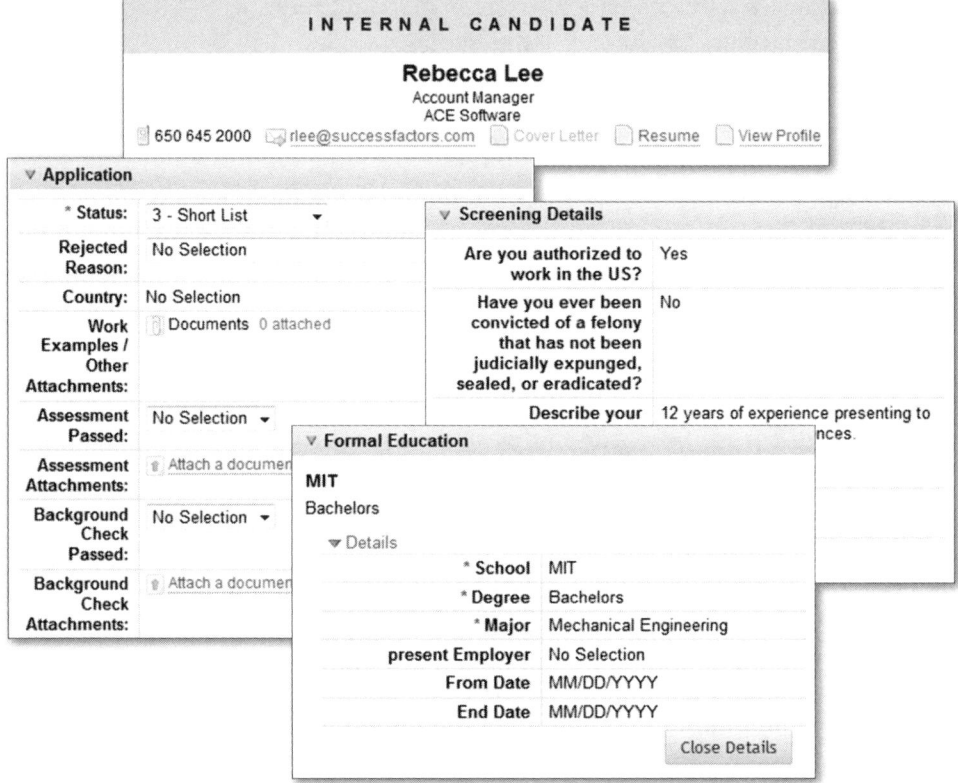

Figure 10.13 The Candidate Snapshot

Together, the Candidate Profile and CDM present the complete picture of the candidate to the recruiter and others evaluating them for a position. This complete picture is presented in the Candidate Snapshot (see Figure 10.13) and gives the recruiter the full view of a candidate's experience, qualifications, and interests. From the Candidate Snapshot, recruiters can view the résumé, cover letter, Candidate Profile, and the Candidate Profile elements and any screening details from questions that were added to the requisition. Every type of candidate is identified by the banner across the top as internal candidate, external candidate, or agency candidate.

By default, the system is configured so that a candidate may choose to complete the Candidate Profile before or after submitting an application. However, there is a setting that will mandate that the Candidate Profile must be completed prior to submitting the application. This recommended setting requires candidates to provide as much background information as possible for recruiters and hiring managers to use to evaluate the candidate for the position. With the trend being toward a more robust Candidate Profile and streamlined CDM, the required fields to be completed on the application may be very few, so without completing the Candidate Profile before applying for a job, candidates wouldn't otherwise be providing a well-rounded representation of their skills and experience. The CPT view provided to recruiters in the CANDIDATE DETAIL view is a "snapshot" of the CPT at the time the candidate submits an application. If the candidate has not yet completed the Candidate Profile, much data about the candidate's education, experience, and other qualifications won't be available in this view.

The advantage of setting up this configuration is that customers can ensure that candidates have completed all required fields on the Candidate Profile before submitting an application. Any subsequent applications submitted will follow the same process of taking the candidate to the Candidate Profile to update any necessary information or provide an updated résumé before continuing with the application submission.

10.6 Candidate Selection Management

After jobs are posted and candidates begin applying, the recruiter has numerous tools available to evaluate candidates and make sure the best quality candidates are identified and ushered through the hiring process quickly. The two main tools are the Candidate Workbench and Interview Central.

10.6.1 Candidate Workbench

The Candidate Workbench is the place recruiters spend most of their time. It gives them access to the applications and profiles of candidates who have applied to each position and shows how candidates rate against the requirements established in the requisition (see Figure 10.14). From here, recruiters begin dispositioning candidates—or moving them through the Talent Pipeline—in multiple ways:

- Select one or more candidates and use the ACTION column to perform any number of actions against a candidate such as changing their status or emailing them.
- Update the STATUS field within the Candidate Snapshot.
- Use the MOVE CANDIDATE button to update the candidate status in the Candidate Snapshot.
- Drag and drop a candidate into the appropriate status.

Name		Status	Rating	Source	Phone Number	Source:
Caroline Clark		3 - Short List	100.0	Internal Referred		
Aaron Allen	New	1 - New Application	50.0	Corporate Site	(713) 382-7188	Corporate Website
Tiffany Peters	New	1 - New Application	50.0	Corporate Site	303-888-8888	Hot Jobs
Gina Walker		Hireable	50.0	Internal Referred	408-555-1214	
Jonathan Burns		Hireable	50.0	Corporate Site	303-333-3030	Corporate Website
Brad Jones		Auto Disqualified	0.0	Corporate Site		Corporate Website

Figure 10.14 The Candidate Workbench

The TALENT PIPELINE contains all of the statuses in the hiring process as well as some system default statuses (see Figure 10.15). It organizes the candidates as they are evaluated against job requirements and moved through the process. It is divided into three sections:

- **Default statuses**
  The FORWARDED and INVITED TO APPLY statuses are tied to specific functionality in the system whereby a user can forward a candidate to a job through Candidate Search and then invite the candidate to apply via an email link to the job posting, if their qualifications match up to the those of the position. These statuses can't be edited or disabled.

- **In-progress statuses**
  This section of the pipeline contains all new applications and is configured to represent all of the stages of a customer's hiring process such as résumé review,

interview, background check, offer, and hire. In-progress statuses should encompass all stages of a customer's hiring process for candidates that remain under consideration until they are disqualified for any reason.

▶ **Disqualified statuses**
These statuses capture the reasons that candidates aren't selected to move through the process, including the system status of AUTO-DISQUALIFIED, which is tied to a candidate answering required questions on the requisition incorrectly.

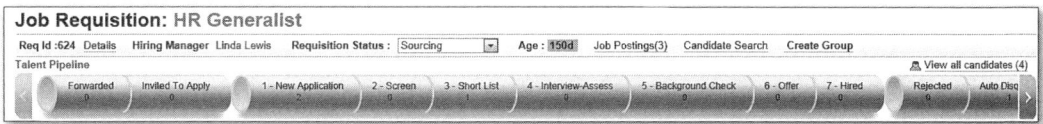

Figure 10.15 The Talent Pipeline

Statuses in the TALENT PIPELINE are completely configurable by the customer, with the exception of the system statuses of FORWARDED, INVITE TO APPLY, and AUTO-DISQUALIFIED. The customer can create any number of statuses required for assessing candidates for hire, or dispositioning them to a disqualified status that is reportable. While the number of statuses will dictate the length of the pipeline visually, the system scrolls through the pipeline by using the left- and right arrows on each end of the pipeline, making navigation quick and easy.

Several of the actions recruiters can make against candidates, such as scheduling interviews or generating offer approvals and letters, are controlled by a Features Permissions functionality that is configured within the requisition template. This means that customers can decide when they want recruiters to have access to the SET UP INTERVIEWERS portlet or the Offer functionality, as an example. These decisions will be made during implementation and configured directly into the requisition. Customers can also decide what roles can perform certain actions. So if they want recruiting coordinators to set up interviews but not generate offers, then that is possible using the Feature Permissions functionality.

10.6.2 Interview Central

Interview Central is where candidates may be evaluated by the interview team. RX is based on competency evaluation and leverages the competency library within BizX. Customers may define a competency library that contains interview-related

10 | Recruiting Execution

competencies that are added to the requisition and then are available to rate candidates against in Interview Central.

Setting Up Interviews

Setting up interviews is a Feature Permission functionality that can be configured against one or more in-progress statuses in the Talent Pipeline. When a candidate is moved into one of these statuses, such as INTERVIEWING, the SET UP INTERVIEWERS portlet shown in Figure 10.16 is available within the Candidate Snapshot. Recruiters can define the interview team and set dates and times for each interviewer to evaluate the candidate. The recruiter also has the option of emailing this information to the interview team and including the candidate's résumé and cover letter.

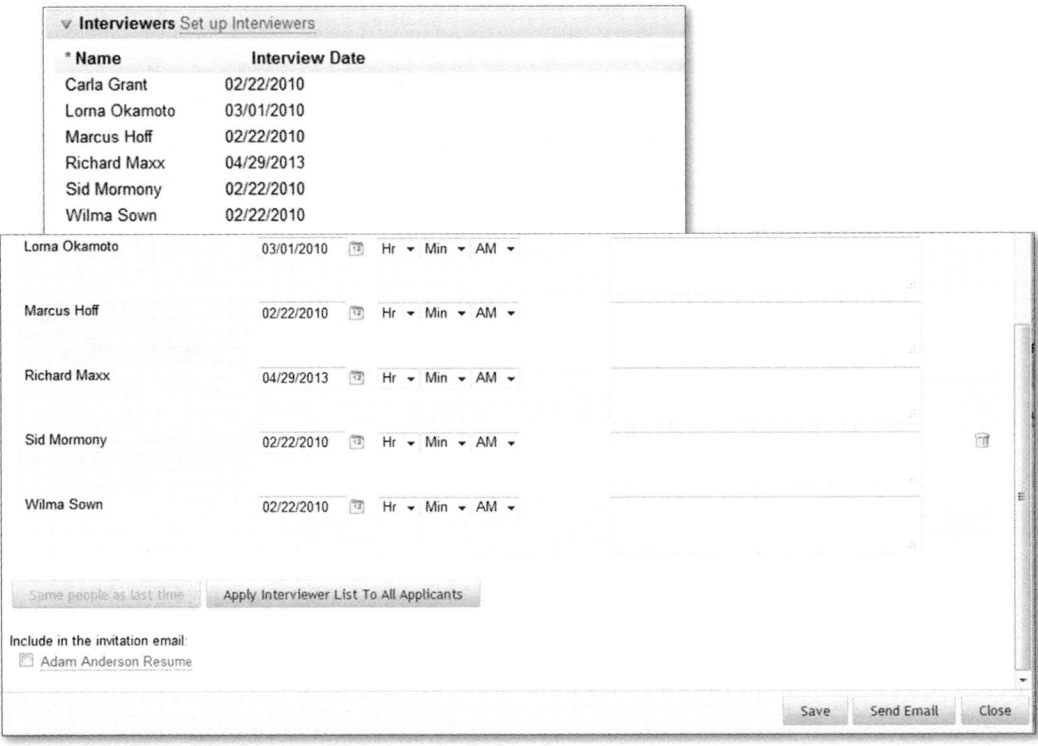

Figure 10.16 Set Up Interviewers

Note that this option does not put a calendar entry on the interviewers' calendar. To do this, the recruiter needs to use the CREATE MEETING button to use email to send a meeting invitation via that avenue.

Evaluating Candidates

Interview Central is where competencies added to the requisition come into play. It provides tools for interviewers to provide feedback and rate candidates against those requisition competencies. They can access all candidates they are scheduled to interview by job. From the main screen shown in Figure 10.17, they can see who has been evaluated, who has yet to be evaluated, and how all candidates stack against each other. Notes from the hiring manager about the particular job, if provided on the requisition, are displayed to all interviewers, and they can choose to use the PRINT AND GO feature to print a hard copy of the candidate's résumé, cover letter, and the job description with competencies to be rated.

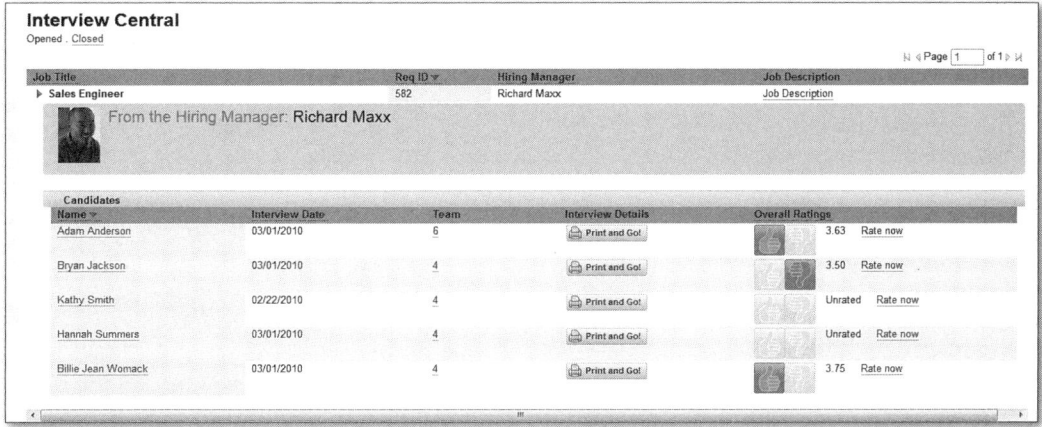

Figure 10.17 Interview Central Main Screen

Evaluating candidates is as easy as selecting the RATE NOW link to see all candidates evaluated for that job. Interview Central utilizes the BizX Stack Ranker functionality to give a visual of all candidates against each other. This also makes rating quick and easy and can be done for all competencies and for all candidates at the same time. As ratings are given, an overall score is generated based on the rating scale defined for the requisition.

Interviewers can provide comments on each competency and overall comments on their rating. They can also upload a document in case they took notes electronically. These notes are available to recruiters managing the position. Finally, interviewers provide an overall rating of THUMBS UP or THUMBS DOWN on each candidate for a dashboard-like view of how the candidates rate against each other (see Figure 10.18).

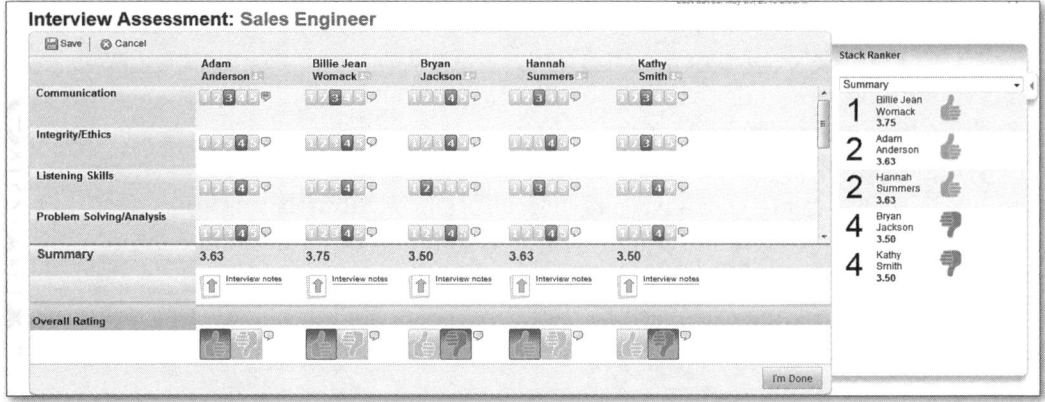

Figure 10.18 Interview Assessment Stack Ranker

10.7 Offer Management

Offer Management in RX offers two alternatives for customers. Offer letters can be generated from the system and sent to candidates, or the offer can be formally approved in the system before creating the offer letter.

RX enables customers to create and maintain multiple offer letter templates to meet a variety of requirements. Recruiting administrators can create or edit offer letter templates at any time in OneAdmin (see Figure 10.19). Tokens are available to embed in each template so that information can be dynamically populated into each offer letter.

Offer letter functionality is tied to statuses in the Talent Pipeline. Offer letters can be made available in one status or several statuses, depending on the customer requirements. Recruiters have the option of generating PDF versions of the offer letter or sending them as text embedded in an email. The offer letter process also supports documenting a verbal offer that may occur. This is illustrated in Figure 10.20. The offer letter and verbal offer will be captured in the audit trail for each candidate.

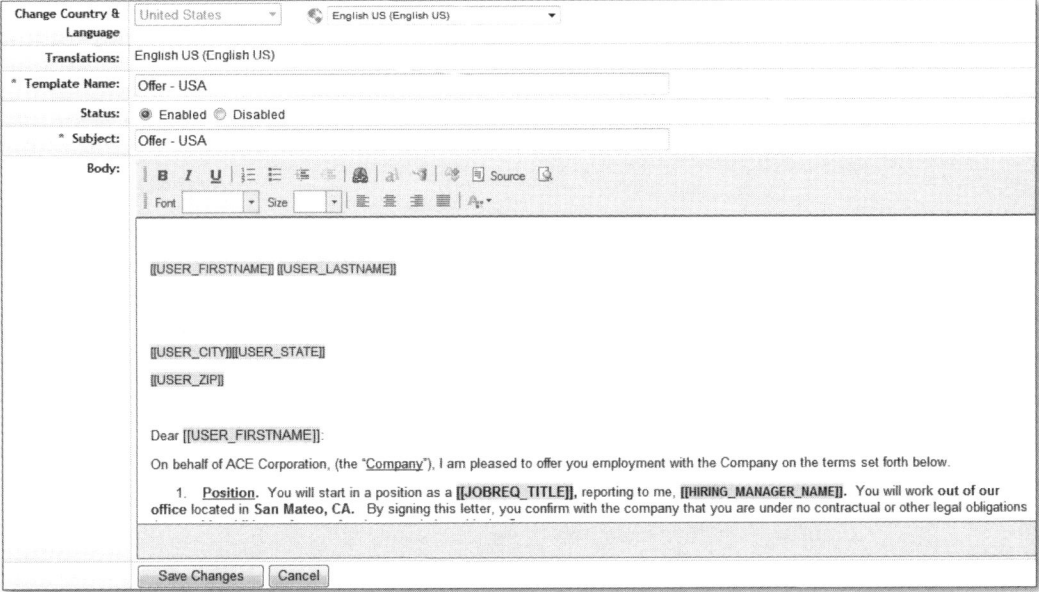

Figure 10.19 Offer Letter Template in OneAdmin

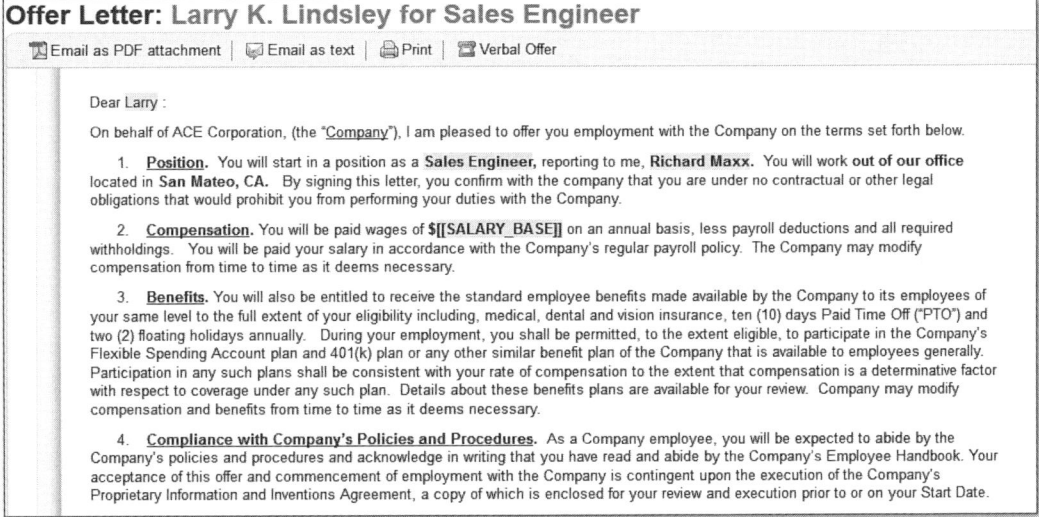

Figure 10.20 Send Offer Letter as PDF, Text, or Make Verbal Offer

For customers that have a more formal approval process for offers, the system supports defining an OFFER DETAILS template like the one shown in Figure 10.21.

This template captures the particulars of each specific offer such as job title, salary offered, vacation, and bonus details, among others. Information can be mapped from the requisition, application, and Candidate Profile so this is already on the offer details at creation. Recruiters can then enter any additional data related to the offer for each candidate.

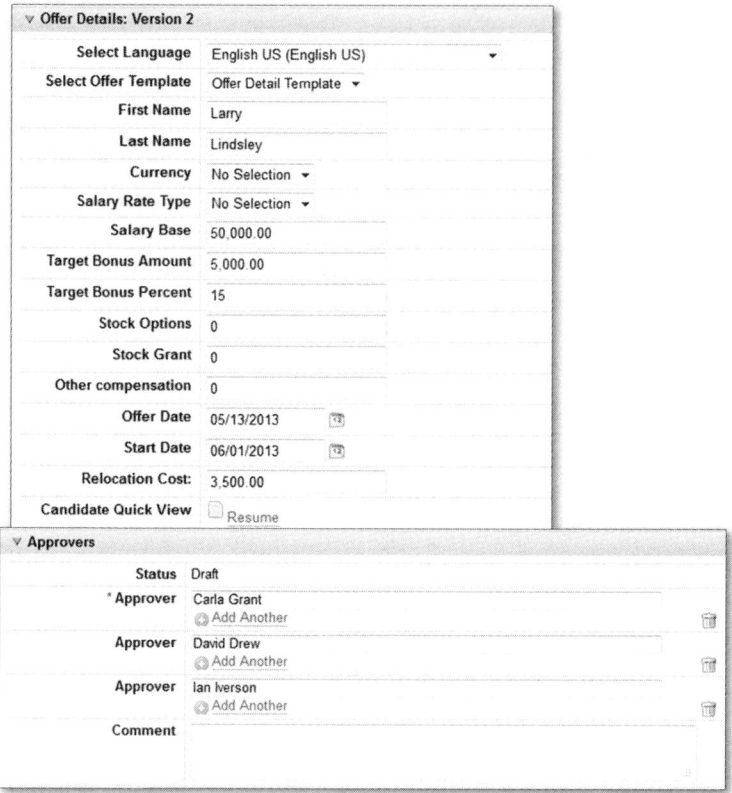

Figure 10.21 Offer Approval Detail Template

The approval chain for an offer detail is completely ad hoc. The recruiter can add anyone from the user database as an approver for an offer approval and can have as many approvers as required. The approval process is defined by the users in the order they are added as approvers. After one user approves the offer, it will be available for the next approver until all approvers have approved the offer. Each approver has the option to decline the offer and add comments for the recruiter about what needs attention in order to approve the offer.

After the offer detail is approved, the offer letter may be generated and sent to the candidate as discussed.

10.8 Hiring and Onboarding

After a candidate has been identified and an offer has been made, RX offers several options for transferring the candidate to Employee Central or core HR and getting them onboarded as employees.

If a customer is running Employee Central as their HRIS, RX has standard functionality to transfer candidates to Employee Central after they are moved into a status with the type of HIRABLE. This status is unique to Employee Central and tells the system to send them over to the Employee Central module as a pending hire.

A configured template defines the data from the recruiting process that should be transferred over to Employee Central in order to complete the hiring process. Data such as job title, job grade, level, salary, and others can be sent directly from RX to prepopulate the foundation objects in Employee Central to ease the hiring process.

SAP provides new hire integration for clients using both SAP ERP HCM and SuccessFactors RX via an integration pack that allows you to transfer applicant data from RX into SAP ERP HCM using SAP NetWeaver Process Integration (SAP NetWeaver PI).

To facilitate this integration, SAP ERP HCM and RX must include certain prescribed configurations. Configuration for both RX and SAP ERP HCM, plus additional details on the add-on, can be found in Chapter 3.

RX offers *onboarding services* through third-party vendors. It's the customer's responsibility to engage the services of these onboarding vendors, and projects are completed in tandem with the RX implementation. While there is minimal configuration required by RX to get the integration working, there is quite a bit of process work that needs to be completed during implementation to ensure the process defined is efficient.

10.9 Employee Referral

A new Employee Referral functionality became available with the b1305 release of RX. This enables customers to increase employee engagement in the recruiting process by providing them with an avenue to participate in building the potential talent pool within the company. While there is existing Employee Referral functionality in RMK, this new release is housed within RCM and leverages LinkedIn and Facebook profiles to allow employees to match their friends and professional contacts to jobs. Existing employees can do the following:

- Match jobs to contacts.
- Refer a contact to a recruiter.
- Track the progress of their referrals.
- Determine what referral bonuses they have earned.

At the time of this writing, this functionality was scheduled to be enhanced in the b1308 release and will continue to be developed over the next several months.

10.10 Summary

With RX, customers have all of the transactional components of traditional Applicant Tracking Systems combined with powerful tools to market their jobs to attract and engage the best candidates possible. The players in the recruiting process are actively involved in creating open positions and reviewing candidates, including approving critical recruiting documents and providing candidate feedback on their mobile devices. RX's intuitive features allow users to log in, understand what to do with very little training, and get up to speed and using the system immediately. This enables companies to accelerate their recruiting process while ensuring that only the most qualified candidates are selected for hire.

In this chapter, we've looked at the foundation for and components of SuccessFactors Recruiting Execution. We've explored creating and approving requisitions, as well as job postings and sourcing. In addition, we've looked at the candidate experience, the selection process of these candidates, and managing offers to candidates. We've also discussed the hiring and onboarding processes that are offering in the solution.

Now you should understand how the SuccessFactors Recruiting Execution solution can provide value for your recruiting, candidate, and application tracking processes. In the next chapter, we will examine SuccessFactors Learning functionality from the employee, manager, and administrator perspective.

SuccessFactors Learning is a robust, state-of-the-art learning management system that can accommodate any organization's learning process and requirements. Its intuitive interface is easy to navigate and is highly configurable to provide employees, managers, and administrators with the best learning experience possible.

11   SuccessFactors Learning

SuccessFactors Learning manages the entire learning lifecycle. As users progress through their development cycle, they search for learning to add it to their Learning Plans, complete online training, and manage their other development requirements. If a user is also an administrator, the user has access to the administrator interface to complete tasks such as maintaining catalogs, assignment profiles, master data, and running reports.

SuccessFactors Learning is highly configurable — and the majority of the configuration occurs in the interface itself. In this way, customer administrators are heavily involved in the implementation; they learn how to "configure" the solution as the project progresses and take ownership of the system configuration almost from the beginning of the project. The functionality delivered by SuccessFactors Learning is enough to fill a book on its own, so this chapter will provide a high-level overview of the features of SuccessFactors Learning and how users of all types can interact with the system.

SuccessFactors Learning can be approached from two directions: the user interface and the administrator interface. SuccessFactors Learning is a user-based system that allows employees and managers to take an active role in assigning and completing learning items. As a user, employees can browse the catalog and add items to their Learning Plan. If items require approval, these will be in a pending status until approved by their manager. Users can also complete online learning and register for classroom-based or virtual learning.

Users who are managers can manage both their own learning and the Learning Plans of their team. Managers can assign learning directly to their employee's

Learning Plans, record learning events (if permissioned), and run reports on the progress of their team.

Then there is the administrator interface, which we'll cover in Section 11.3. Administrators have access to all of the tools and data items that comprise the system "configuration." Administrators are often also users, in which case, they will have two interfaces within which to work.

However, before we begin, we want to introduce a few foundational concepts that should be understood before diving into the solution:

- An *administrator* has privileges to create master data, set up catalogs, manage assignment profiles, set user permissions, launch forms, and run reports. Administrators access SuccessFactors Learning via the administrator's interface.
- A *user* is the end user of SuccessFactors Learning and includes managers and employees. Users log in to the user interface to perform activities such as adding courses to their Learning Plans, participate in courses, and manage their team members' Learning Plans.
- *Domains* control administrative access to records; *catalogs* control what training items are available to employees for self-assignment and enrollment. Users are assigned one or more catalogs from which to choose learning, and can't see any items that don't appear in one of the catalogs to which they have been assigned.
- *Organizations* are other groups of users that are managed by organization owners; they have corresponding dashboards that display pertinent information about the organization's learning activities. Organizations can have slots in scheduled offerings reserved for them and can purchase training.

Let's begin looking at the user interface that supports employees and managers in their learning needs.

11.1 User Interface

Users access the system from their BizX HOME page, as with other BizX solutions. The LEARNING tile on the HOME page will display the five items on a user's Learning Plan that are due the soonest. It will also display a link that will take the user to their MY LEARNING ASSIGNMENTS page in SuccessFactors Learning.

What a user can access in the Learning module is dictated by which catalogs have been assigned to them. User roles can be defined to grant varying levels of access to different kinds of users. For example, a company may have contractors that require access to complete some learning, but they should not have the same level of system access as employees. User roles can be defined for employees and contractors to differentiate the levels of access and then be assigned to users accordingly.

11.1.1 User Interface Home Page

When users land on their Learning HOME page (see Figure 11.1), they are presented with their LEARNING PLAN, as described in this section. The MY LEARNING ASSIGNMENTS area displays items assigned to the user, either by the user's manager, by an automatic assignment, or by self-assignment from the catalog. Catalog searches can be accessed from the FIND LEARNING tile. THE LINKS tile provides quick access to other parts of the system. The MY CURRICULA tile provides a snapshot view for assigned curricula and completed learning items can be accessed from the HISTORY tile. As with the HOME page in the BizX suite, the tiles on the Learning HOME page can be rearranged by users according to their needs.

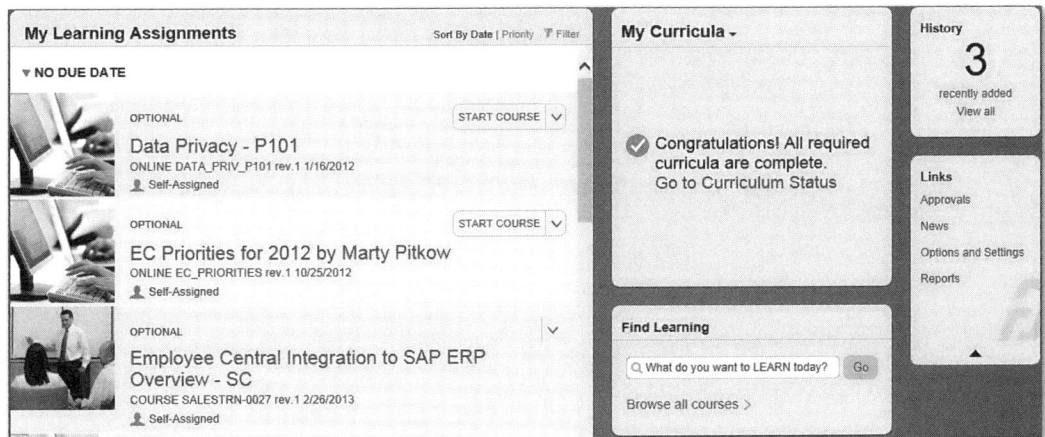

Figure 11.1 User Home Page

Learning Plan

The Learning Plan to-do list items listed on the MY LEARNING ASSIGNMENTS tile can be broken down into buckets of due dates. An administrator can configure these, but the following default values are available:

- OVERDUE
- DUE WITHIN A WEEK

- Due within a month
- Due later
- No due date

Users can view details of items on the Learning Plan by clicking on the link in the item name or clicking MORE to display a quick view of the course description, delivery method, and duration. The MY LEARNING ASSIGNMENTS tile can be seen in Figure 11.2. It displays items that have been assigned to the user by the user's manager, assigned by an administrator, or assigned by the user. Some items may have due dates and others may not. As items are completed, they drop off the to-do list and are moved to the LEARNING HISTORY pod.

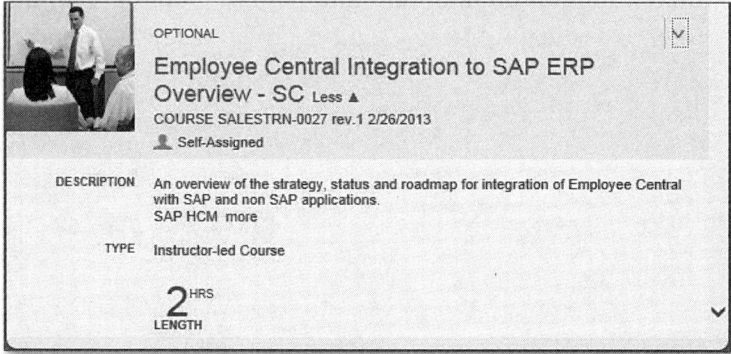

Figure 11.2 Item Details from To-Do List

From the Learning Plan, users can perform a variety of tasks:

- Launch online content.
- Launch an online exam.
- Register for a learning offering.
- Request approval to register for an offering.
- Request a schedule for an offering when it's not available.
- Launch an evaluation survey.

You can filter the Learning Plan to show only certain types of items or all learning, as shown in Figure 11.3. This is a helpful feature for users who have many items on their MY LEARNING ASSIGNMENTS page. As tasks are completed, they will drop off the LEARNING PLAN and will be instead available on the LEARNING HISTORY pod.

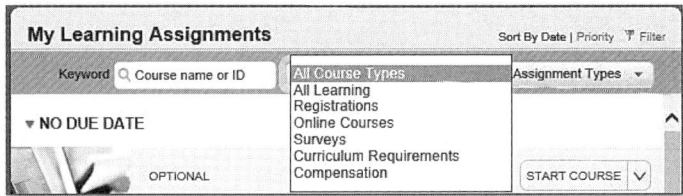

Figure 11.3 Filter My Learning Assignments

Catalog Search

Users can perform a quick catalog search from the search dialog on the HOME page. Entering a key word will return items that match in the item title or description, as can be seen in Figure 11.4.

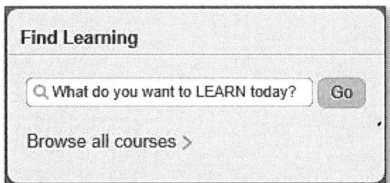

Figure 11.4 Catalog Search

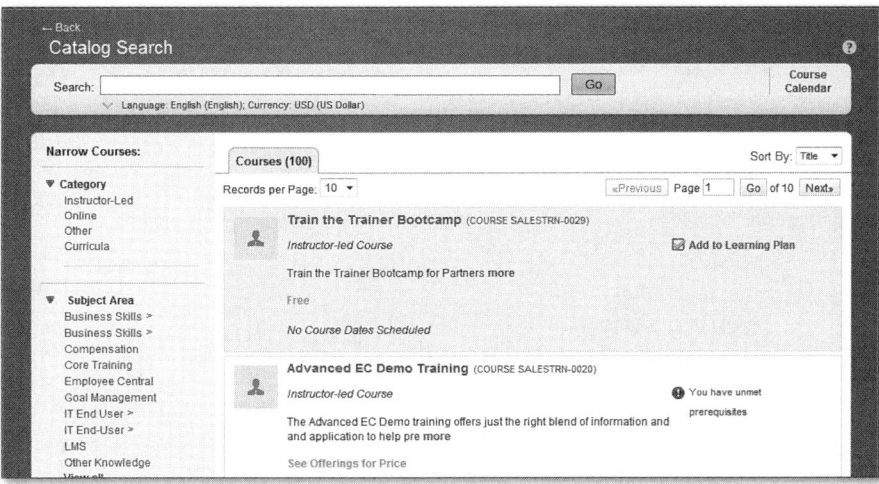

Figure 11.5 Browse Catalog

As shown in Figure 11.5, users can also browse the catalog if they choose. Browsing the catalog takes users to a screen where they can select categories of training such as INSTRUCTOR-LED and ONLINE courses, as well as filter training offerings by the SUBJECT AREAS that have been configured in the administrator interface.

One of the nicest features of the catalog search is the CALENDAR view shown in Figure 11.6, by which users can browse course offerings by dates on a calendar. Days that have offerings scheduled will display links. Selecting the links will take the user to the offering details, where they can register or add to their Learning Plan.

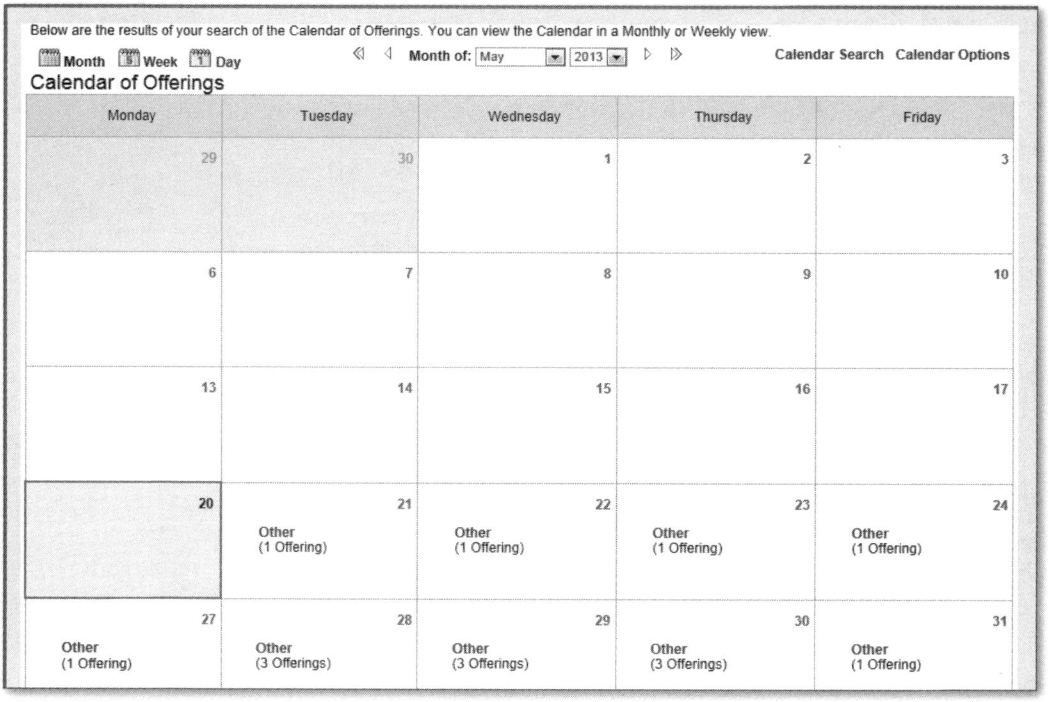

Figure 11.6 Calendar View of Learning Offerings

Easy Links and Learning Status

Also available from the HOME page, users have access to helpful LINKS that will jump them to other parts of the system. There are LINKS provided by default, but administrators can also define up to 10 additional internal or external URLs. The default LINKS include the following:

- APPROVALS

    Managers can jump to the APPROVALS page to manage their team's approvals.

▶ NEWS PAGE
This area can be used to promote learning-related news in the company or provide tips on how to better utilize the system (see Figure 11.7).

▶ OPTIONS AND SETTINGS
Users can change their password, set delegates, set notification preferences, and set locale and time zone settings.

▶ REPORTS
Reports can be run that provide managers with information on their team's enrollments, learning progress, and completions.

LINKS can be limited to groups of users based on user roles that are defined by the administrator.

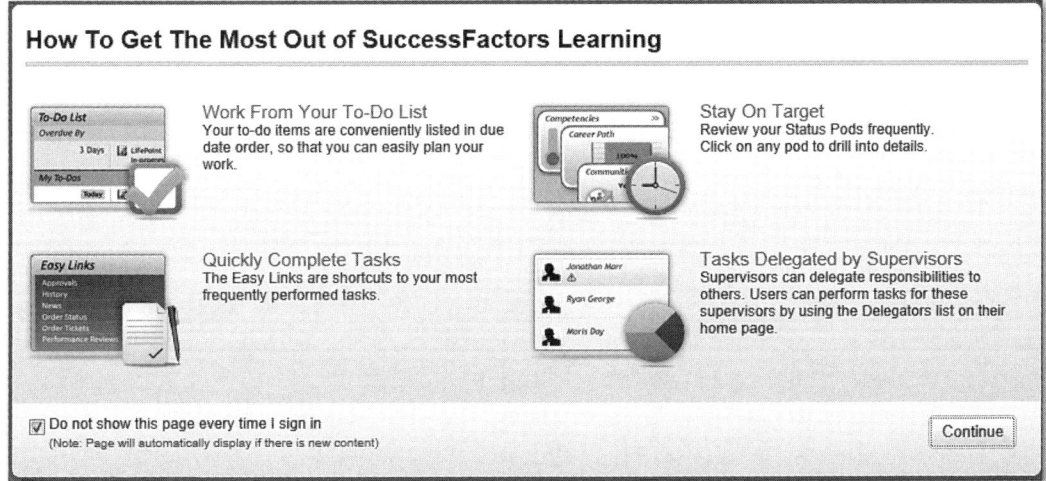

Figure 11.7 News Page

The MY CURRICULA pod shown in Figure 11.8 displays where a user is against curricula and displays completed items. This dashboard view gives users an overview of critical items related to their progress against their assigned learning activities. The CURRICULA status displays a color-coded picture of the status for all assigned curricula. Clicking on the pod will drill down to the details of the related items. It also displays a green checkmark if a user is up to date with all curricula on their Learning Plan.

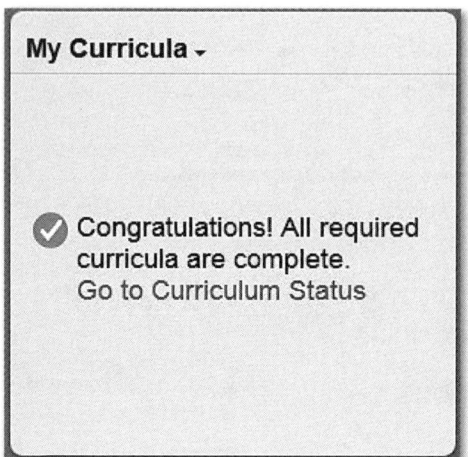

Figure 11.8 My Curricula Pod

11.1.2 Learning History

After users have completed learning items on their learning plan, they are moved to Learning History. Online items such as courses and documents can be accessed again and again from the LEARNING HISTORY pod to enable continuous, just-in-time learning.

Learning History fed from SuccessFactors is also available to display in a background element in Employee Profile. Some companies prefer to make this information available in Employee Profile in addition to the Learning History in SuccessFactors Learning because it can be critical data input to other talent development processes, such as Career Development Planning and Succession Planning. An example of the Learning History background element is provided in Figure 11.9. Data in this portlet is fed directly from the LMS and is not editable by any user in Employee Profile.

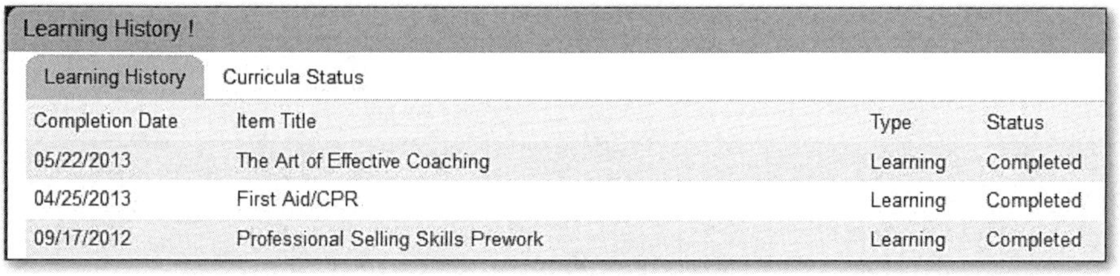

Learning History	Curricula Status		
Completion Date	Item Title	Type	Status
05/22/2013	The Art of Effective Coaching	Learning	Completed
04/25/2013	First Aid/CPR	Learning	Completed
09/17/2012	Professional Selling Skills Prework	Learning	Completed

Figure 11.9 LMS Portlet

Users can always access online content for repeated viewing from their Learning History (see the REVIEW CONTENT button in Figure 11.10). This provides continuous, just-in-time learning to support a user's training and development needs as they arise.

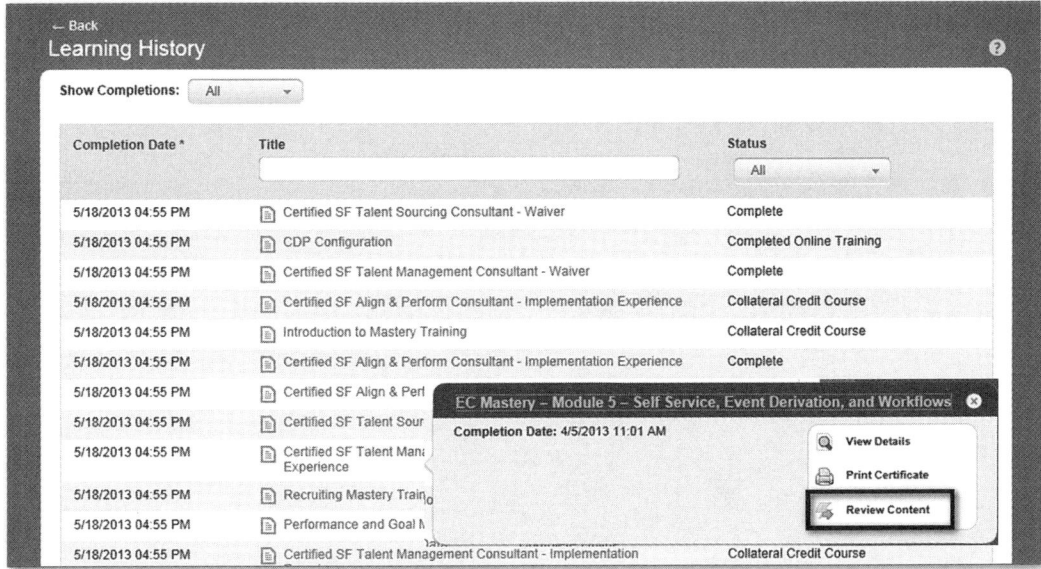

Figure 11.10 Launch Online Content from Learning History

11.2 Supervisor Interface

Anyone who has direct reports in BizX will be recognized as a supervisor in Success-Factors Learning and will automatically have access to their employee's records. Supervisors have access to view all information related to their team members' learning information. The scope of supervisor actions is determined during implementation, at which time customers can determine which actions they would like supervisors to complete, such as the following:

▶ View assigned learning, the curriculum status, and overdue learning for all team members.

▶ Assign learning items and curricula to their team.

- Register team members into scheduled offerings.
- Record learning events/completions for their team.
- Run reports for direct and indirect team members (second level of reporting).
- Delegate responsibilities to other users.
- Assign alternate supervisors for their team.

Managers can also get a bird's-eye view of their team's learning status under MY EMPLOYEES. This is a jump-to link to a view of their team's Learning Plans where they can assign and remove learning, grant approvals for registrations, get a dashboard view of their employees, and run reports. These functions are available in the SUPERVISOR LINKS pod, as displayed in Figure 11.11.

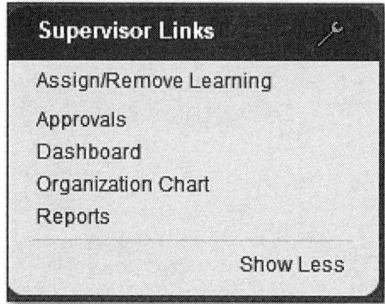

Figure 11.11 Supervisor Links

11.2.1 Manage Team Member Learning Plan

Supervisors are able to add and remove items to their team member's Learning Plan. The system walks them through the process using a wizard. It's possible to select one or more users to assign or remove learning in five easy steps, as numbered in Figure 11.12:

❶ Choose ADD ITEMS AND CURRICULA or REMOVE ITEMS.

❷ Select the team member(s) for whom to perform the action.

❸ Search the catalog for the appropriate items to add.

❹ Select the items to add from the search results.

❺ Set required dates, if applicable.

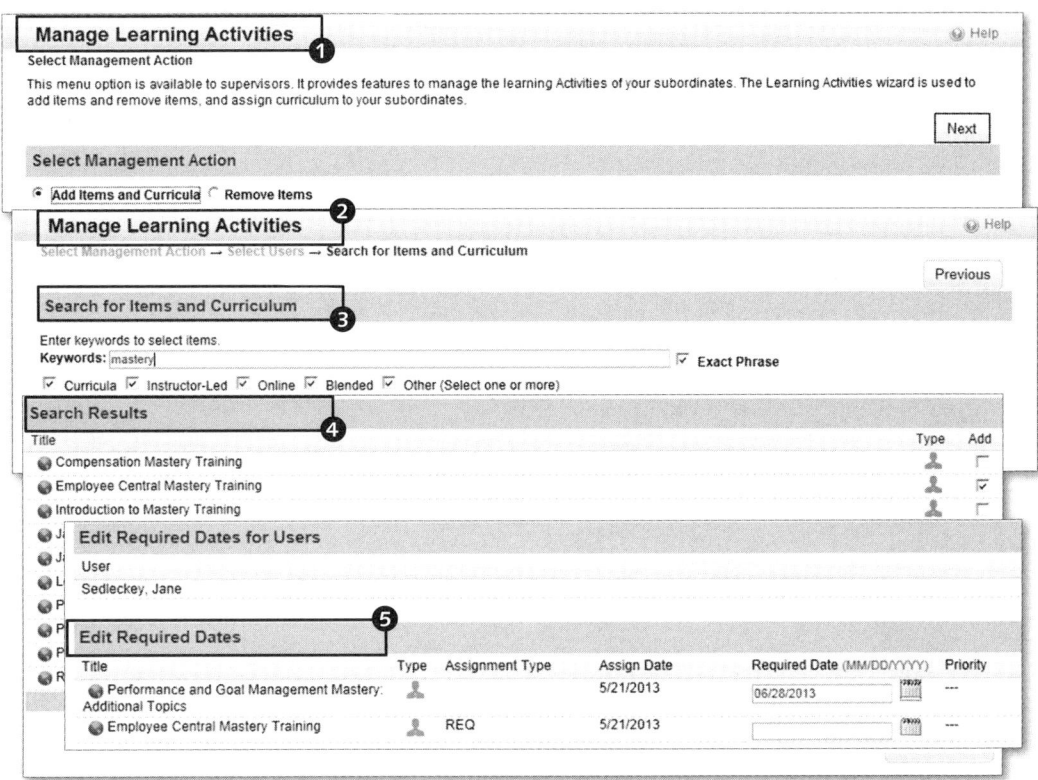

Figure 11.12 A Manager Adding Items to Learning Plan

11.2.2 Manage Training Approvals

Supervisors can approve or deny requests from their team to attend or complete training, including scheduled offerings and online content. Administrators can establish approval workflows to include others besides the direct supervisor. This is a configuration decision and can be set up at any time in the administrator interface.

When a user registers for an offering that requires approval, they will see a status of PENDING APPROVAL. This status will remain until action is taken on the request. The supervisor and other approvers can view the request, approve or deny it, or skip the request for later action. When a request is approved or denied, the user will receive email confirmation that action has been taken on the request and any comments on the action. For example, if the request was denied, the email will include any reason the approver chose for denial.

If an approval workflow contains more than one approval, it must go through all levels of approval before the user can register for a seat in the offering or launch the online content.

11.2.3 Other Supervisor Actions

Supervisors can complete numerous other actions for their team, as shown in Figure 11.13. These are accessible from the callout that appears when you hover over the team member's name. From here, links are available to manage an alternate supervisor and generate reports on this user. Supervisors can also view profile information. Note that this isn't a link to the Employee Profile and only displays minimal information that is maintained within SuccessFactors Learning.

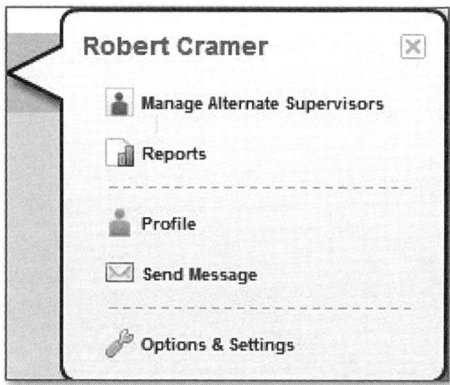

Figure 11.13 Other Supervisor Actions

11.3 Administrator Interface

Recall from earlier in the chapter that administrators access administrative functions via the administrator interface. While the user and administrator interfaces are integrated, a user who is also an administrator will have different access and be able to perform predefined and permissioned tasks within the administrative interface. This section will review a sample of the administrator capabilities in the system. Please note that the administrator capabilities of the system are vast, so this is a very high-level view.

11.3.1 Administrative Home Page

The ADMIN. page is organized with menus across the top navigation bar and QUICK LINKS in the middle of the screen (see Figure 11.14). Six different layouts are available to organize the HOME page: USERS, PERFORMANCE, LEARNING, CONTENT, COMMERCE, and SYSTEM ADMIN. The slide bar between the two sections can also be moved to adjust the size of each area.

Figure 11.14 Administrative Home Page

As shown in Figure 11.15, administrators can set up their own Quick Links or use the default links and choose the layout of their HOME page. Administrators utilize Quick Links often for their common tasks, and it's quite helpful to modify these based on an administrator's role and the tasks that they routinely perform in the system.

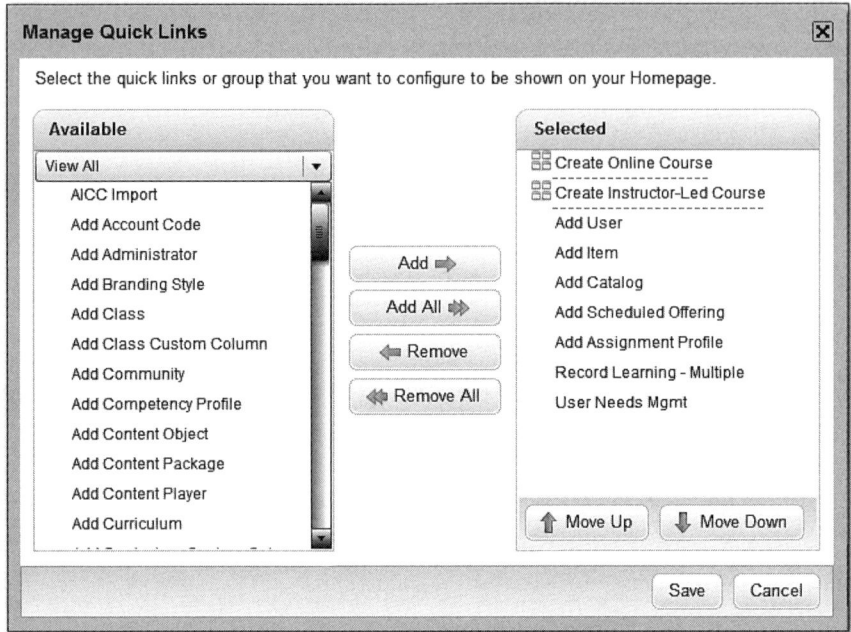

Figure 11.15 Manage Quick Links

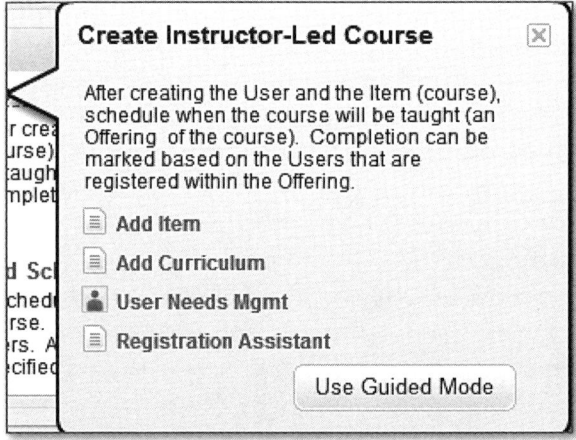

Figure 11.16 Actions Available from Quick Links

Quick Links are an easy way for administrators to get working on the things they need to complete. Hovering over a Quick Link will display the options available within that particular link. The callout box also gives some perspective to where in the process that action should occur. For example, in Figure 11.16, the description for CREATE INSTRUCTOR-LED COURSE tells the administrator that this action is undertaken after user and item have been created. It then explains what can occur after completing this action: learning completions can be recorded.

Also available in the QUICK LINK dialog box is the option USE GUIDED MODE. This is a wizard that will walk the administrator through each step in the process CREATING AN INSTRUCTOR-LED COURSE.

11.3.2 Users Menu

The USERS menu contains all of the actions an administrator can perform related to user records and related information. From the USERS menu, administrators can create and modify the following records, as shown in Figure 11.17:

- USERS
- ASSIGNMENT PROFILES (used to assign learning automatically)
- JOB CODES
- JOB FAMILIES
- POSITIONS

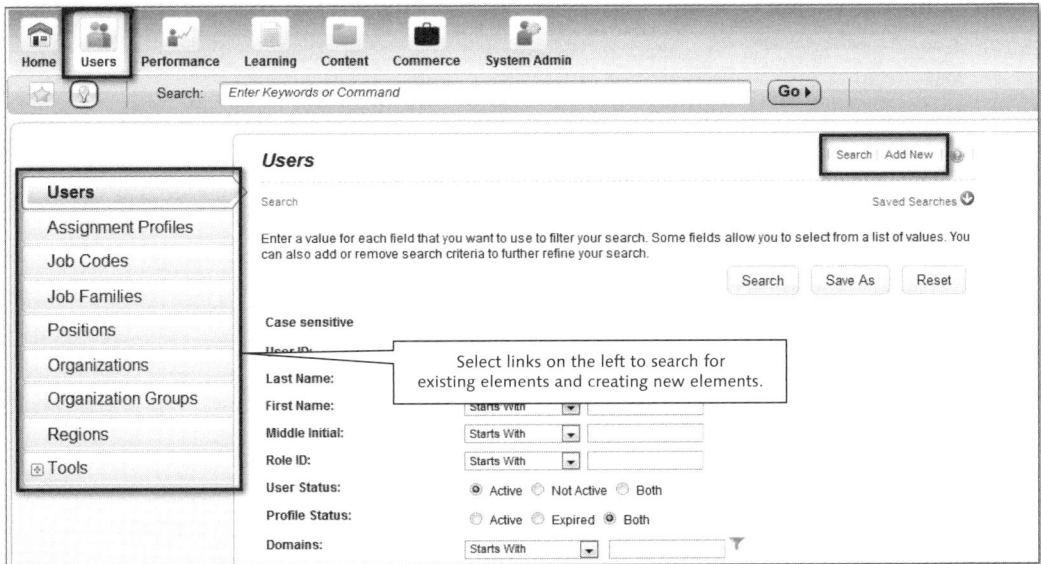

Figure 11.17 Users Menu

- Organizations
- Organization Groups
- Regions

Select a link from the left column of Figure 11.17 to search for or create a new element on it.

Note that several of these elements will be defined in Employee Central, such as users and job codes, and may possibly have been transferred into BizX via the user integration from core HR, so it's likely that only a super administrator would have access to all of these functions.

11.3.3 Performance Menu

This menu is a legacy system functionality related to performance. This is superseded by SuccessFactors Performance & Goals.

Figure 11.18 Learning Menu

11.3.4 Learning Menu

The LEARNING menu actions control the creation and modification of learning items that reside in the catalog(s) and all of their derivations (see Figure 11.18). Here, administrators maintain items, group them into curricula, create new catalogs, and add scheduled offerings to the calendar, among other things. You can create or modify instructors and maintain tasks.

The TOOLS option under the LEARNING menu controls actions related to scheduled offerings such as closing and cancelling, editing required dates, and using the Registration Assistant, which allows an administrator to register, withdraw, or hold seats for users.

11.3.5 Content Menu

As the name implies, the CONTENT menu organizes all of the functions related to online content (see Figure 11.19). An important note about SuccessFactors Learning and online content is that the system points to content that is stored elsewhere. No online content is housed within SuccessFactors Learning. Online content can be a web-based training course or online exam that is attached to an item in the catalog. These are the various content-related elements that can be maintained in the system:

- **Content objects**
  Content objects are records that provide the system instructions to find and launch a unit of online content. Each content object references one launchable file. Content objects in the system can be reused multiple times. Content objects are assigned to items; they aren't in themselves assigned to learning plans, nor are they recorded as completed in the Learning History.

- **Content packages**
  This is a grouping of multiple content objects. Packages are a way to organize all relevant content for an item. Content packages can be created manually or imported via an AICC (Aviation Industry Computer-Based Training Committee) or SCORM (Sharable Content Object Reference Model) import tool.

- **AICC wrapper**
  A feature of SuccessFactors Learning is the AICC wrapper. This allows an administrator to create a content object in the system to "wrap" a document and requires users to read and acknowledge that they either accept or reject it. Users can simply click a button to complete the item rather than launching and

completing an entire online course. This is an excellent way to put "read and understand" training in the system and automate the completion and tracking of this type of training.

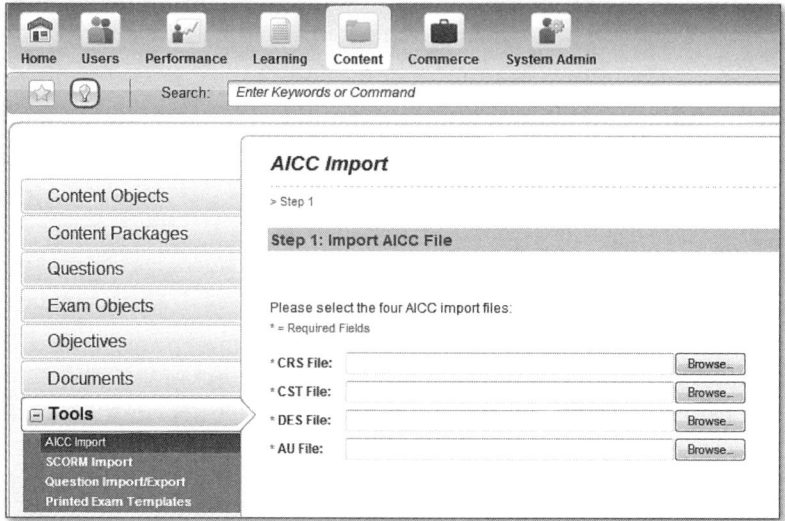

Figure 11.19 Content Menu

- **Content import tools**

   The system provides utilities to facilitate import content that is either AICC or SCORM compliant. The AICC IMPORT button is for a single content object. After the import, the administrator needs to search for the object, add the domain and assignment type ID, and add it to the applicable catalog(s).

   The SCORM IMPORT button imports a single SCORM file, either as a ZIP file or via a URL (for files larger than 1MB). Finally, the SCORM IMPORT utility can be used to import one or more content packages and deploy them to a content server. They can then be configured to an item through the wizard in the system.

11.3.6 System Administration Menu

The last menu, SYSTEM ADMIN, is where all system administration functions occur (see Figure 11.20). This menu should be granted only to "true" system administrators who understand the power of these features. This is where configuration occurs in the system in setting up connectors, creating automatic processes, configuring custom columns, and configuring background jobs.

Security is also a main feature of this menu. This is where domains and domain restrictions are managed. Roles are also created here. Administrators will create multiple roles and then assign these roles to users or groups of users.

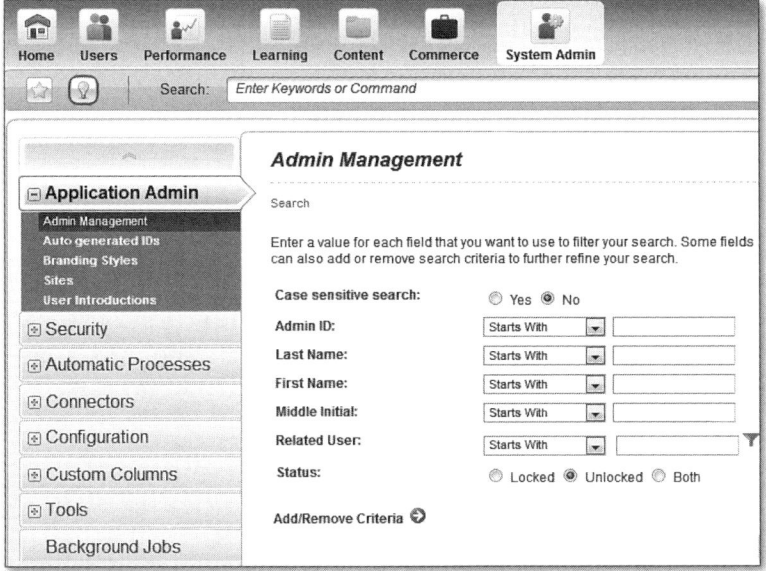

Figure 11.20 System Admin Menu

11.4 Security and Access

SuccessFactors Learning has a multilevel security model that allows administrators access to various functions in the system related to specific data sets. Security in the system can be set up to restrict what information administrators can access and what they can do with this data. This is accomplished through domains.

11.4.1 Domains

Recall that domains restrict what administrators have access to; they also act as filters for data. Domains can be built in a hierarchical, or parent-child, structure. A domain can have many children but only one parent. This structure permits access to data within organizational structures with minimal administrative setup. The domain structure required for a customer's system will be discussed and determined during implementation. However, domains can be maintained by a system administrator, and it's important that these users understand the domains' function and purpose in the system as well as how to maintain them.

A *domain restriction* is a group of domains defined to fit a specific need. Domain restrictions provide a more granular level of security than at an administrator account level. Rather, they are applied to individual data types within a domain to which administrators have access. They can even be applied to operations such as view, add, delete, and so on.

11.4.2 Workflows

Workflows define what administrators can do within SuccessFactors Learning. A *workflow* is comprised of a function that is related to an entity, which can be a user, an item, or a scheduled offering. A *function* is an action such as view, edit, and delete. Example workflows include viewing user data and recording learning events. Administrators can have any number of workflows assigned to them to allow them to perform their required tasks in the system.

11.4.3 Roles

A role is created by a combination of workflows and domain restrictions. The system supports any number of roles required, and they can be broad, finite, or both to suit customer requirements. Roles are assigned to users, and each user can have multiple role assignments.

11.4.4 Admin Accounts

Any user who will log into the administrator interface will need an admin account. This account will have one or more administrative roles assigned to it, depending on the functions that the administrator needs to complete in the system. If an administrator is also a user, it's possible to link the user ID and admin account together so that the user can toggle back and forth between the user interface and the administrator interface.

11.4.5 Organizations

An *organization* is an entity that is used to group users. Organizations can be designed and maintained to completely meet the customer's requirements. They can be designed along functional lines, represent business units, or have any other basis that makes sense in the customer's environment. Organizations can be used as follows:

- Users within an organization can use the account code to pay for learning items that have a cost.
- Organizations can reserve space in scheduled offerings.
- Organizations can have their own branding of the interface.
- Organizations can control multilevel approval workflows (rather than using domains).
- Organizations can be used as search criteria to locate users and as an attribute to assign learning.
- Organizations can have owners identified who can have access to the organization dashboards mentioned earlier in this chapter.

When designing organizations, it's important to keep reporting in mind. These elements can increase the value of assigning learning and generating reports as well as make searching easier.

Organizations are elements that can be used to group and identify users in the system. They provide another level of structure in the system.

Organization dashboards provide a graphical representation of learning-related information that assists organization owners to analyze metrics within the organization(s) that they own. You can filter data based on core attributes, and drill-down capability is available to gain a deeper view of the data behind the attributes. Dashboards are available for the following, as shown in Figure 11.21:

- **Learning item completions**
  Shows the number of items and learning hours completed by each organization within a given time period.
- **Learning projections**
  Displays the number of items and learning hours predicted for delivery within a given time frame.
- **Curriculum status**
  Provides the status of the organization's employee's assigned curricula.
- **Registration status**
  Displays the registration status of all users in the organization.

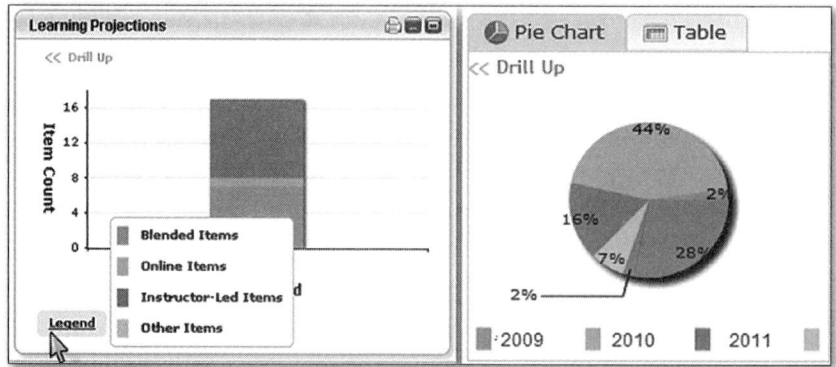

Figure 11.21 Sample Organization Dashboards

11.5 Summary

SuccessFactors Learning's two interfaces, the user interface and administrative interface, and robust functionality provide employees, managers, and administrators with a plethora of tools to manage learning needs for organizational, team, and individual development. It's a best-in-class system that is capable of meeting nearly any business requirement. The user interface puts learning needs and requirements at the fingertips of the individual learners and gives their supervisors tools necessary to monitor and participate in their team's learning activities. It's a critical piece of the BizX talent management picture.

Administrators have a completely flexible system that can be mostly configured directly from the administrator interface. As an active part of implementation, system administrators learn by doing from the beginning how to maintain the system configuration to meet growing and changing requirements within the company.

In this chapter, we've touched on what SuccessFactors Learning can offer an organization from a very high level. We've discussed the types of users of the system, the different interfaces they have, and what actions they have. We've looked at how content can be created and imported into the system, as well as the security and access functionality that is available. You should now have a comprehensive understanding of how SuccessFactors Learning can work for you and your organization.

We now turn our attention to Succession & Development in the next chapter.

Managing succession plans and employee career development is critical to maintaining organizational sustainability and protecting against unmitigated losses. Personal development provides engagement across the workforce and increases competency, productivity, and leadership in critical positions.

12   Succession & Development

Managing succession plans is a crucial exercise, and being able to develop high-performing and high-potential employees into future leaders and holders of your most critical positions is of utmost importance. Hiring and onboarding are costly exercises, and key talent can be difficult if not impossible to replace, particularly at a senior and board-room level. Studies have shown that employees value nontangible benefits such as development and career advancement more than financial benefits, which means employee retention can be directly impacted by ensuring that you offer employees the possibility to develop their career within your organization.

SuccessFactors Succession & Development is a comprehensive and easy-to-use solution that offers all of the core features and functionality of a best practice succession management and career development planning solution. It allows the management of key positions, successors, career plans, and development plans and enables a talent manager or HR professional to view bench strengths, nominated and assigned successors, and key talent data such as performance, potential, and risks. In addition, it also features classic features such as the nine-box grid, organizational chart, talent search, and reports.

The Development Planning functionality provides management of development activities that integrate with the SuccessFactors Learning module and leads to development of competencies. It also gives employees a platform to manage their careers and make choices about where they want to go in your organization.

In short, SuccessFactors Succession & Development features the type of functionality that you would expect in a comprehensive succession planning and career development planning solution. The solution is split into two core modules that are accessed from the module navigation menu: the Succession module and the Development module.

The Succession module focuses on the succession planning process. We'll run through how the Succession module supports it in Section 12.1.

The Development module, which is also known as *Career Development Planning* (CDP), provides development planning, career planning, and learning activities management. In Section 12.2, we'll explore how these support the growth of an employee's competencies and career within your organization and how they can be used to develop successors into the leaders of tomorrow.

12.1 Succession

The succession management process typically kicks off after the annual performance appraisal process has been completed, either in SuccessFactors Performance & Goals or an external performance management system such as Employee Performance Management in SAP ERP HCM. If the succession management process begins before the annual performance process has completed, then Succession & Development offers the opportunity to maintain performance ratings ad hoc. Quite often, employees are reviewed and calibrated before the process so that they can be assigned to talent pools. These talent pools are used to supply talent to the succession plans of key positions. During the process of assigning successors, you can evaluate and rate the potential and possible risks of employees.

After successors have been assigned to succession plans, their Development Plan can be updated to reflect the competency gaps identified during assignment. Learning activities can be assigned to the Development Plan to obtain the required competency. Employees should maintain their career plan on a periodic basis to help inform managers and talent professionals of how they want to move within the organization because this will have an impact on the decision to make them a successor.

Management of key positions is an ongoing activity and isn't generally confined to just the core of the succession planning process. Generally, most key positions will be identified during implementation and set as such, although on occasion new requirements or organizational changes may necessitate the assignment of new key positions or removal of key status of existing positions.

Now let's look at some key functionality that supports this process, and how it supports the management of succession plans.

12.1.1 Organizational Charts

Succession is focused on leveraging one or more Org Charts to support visualization of succession plans across areas of the organization. These charts provide greater breadth of visibility of succession plans, risks, and coverage over teams.

Succession Org Chart

The main focus of the Succession module is the *Succession Org Chart*. This Succession Org Chart, which is shown in Figure 12.1, provides the foundation of organizational-based succession planning and allows an overview of succession plans across different departments within the enterprise.

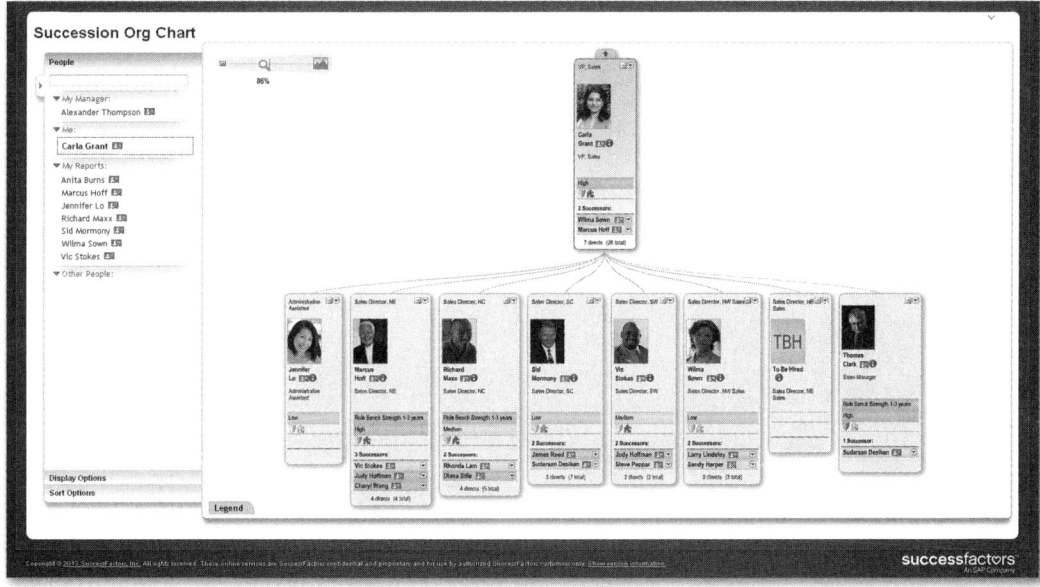

Figure 12.1 Succession Org Chart

The Succession Org Chart displays the logged-in user and all of the user's direct reports. Each of the direct reports of each direct report can also be viewed, and so forth. In addition, there are several options to search within, display, and sort the Org Chart, display the Org Chart and the contents of each box.

Most of the data within the position boxes can be switched on or off, such as photo, risk of loss, impact of loss, newness to company, bench strength, successors, nine-box placement, and successor details. You can also highlight key positions. There are also three modes that can be selected to change the layout of the Org Chart:

- HIERARCHY VIEW
  Displays the "classic" Org Chart as shown in Figure 12.1.

- TEAM VIEW
  Displays all of the reports and their direct reports.

- KEY POSITION VIEW
  Displays only the key positions.

Each box represents a position and has numerous information and options. As with the standard Org Chart, there is a business card available to get an overview of the employee and go to different pages within the SuccessFactors BizX suite. However, the key difference between the two business cards is the Current Nominations for succession plans, and talent pools instead of the employment information and personal information links. Figure 12.2 shows the CURRENT NOMINATIONS box from the business card.

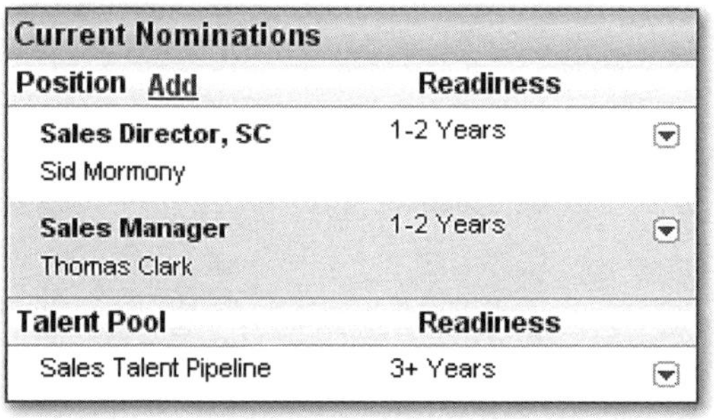

Current Nominations	
Position Add	Readiness
Sales Director, SC Sid Mormony	1-2 Years
Sales Manager Thomas Clark	1-2 Years
Talent Pool	Readiness
Sales Talent Pipeline	3+ Years

Figure 12.2 Current Nominations

Using the ADD link in the CURRENT NOMINATIONS box, you can assign an individual as a successor for a position. We'll cover this in more detail in Section 12.1.6.

The position box action dropdown menu (located in the top-right corner of a position box) provides a number of options that include editing, deleting, and hiding the position; adding a peer or direct report; finding successors; viewing the position in the Lineage Chart; viewing the nomination history; and creating a Job Requisition in SuccessFactors Recruiting Execution. The EDITING A POSITION option refers to setting a position as a *key position*. However, the most interesting feature of the Succession Org Chart is the information available within the position boxes.

The wealth of information that can be either shown in or hidden from the boxes as required provides the opportunity to get an overview of the status of succession across your team and, if required, their reports below. For example, it can be very easy to see the overall risk of loss for each of your team members or get the total coverage of successors and bench strength.

> **Bench Strength**
>
> Bench strength is a subject evaluation of the succession plan and the cascaded succession plans (chain of succession). It provides a way of measuring the readiness of the succession plan of the position so that managers and HR professionals can understand whether the position is adequately covered and how "deep" the bench is.

As with the holder of the position, each nominated successor has a business card icon; you can view details about the person and select options to view the person's nomination details, delete their nomination, and evaluate their readiness from SuccessFactors Performance & Goals from the action dropdown menu.

Lineage Chart

Succession also offers the Lineage Chart, which shows the chain of successors. That is, it shows the user's successors and that user's successors in turn. Use the EXPAND button to expand your view to the next level of successors, and so forth, as shown in Figure 12.3. This provides a quick overview of how well covered a position is and the positions of the nominated successors—something measured with bench strength.

12 | Succession & Development

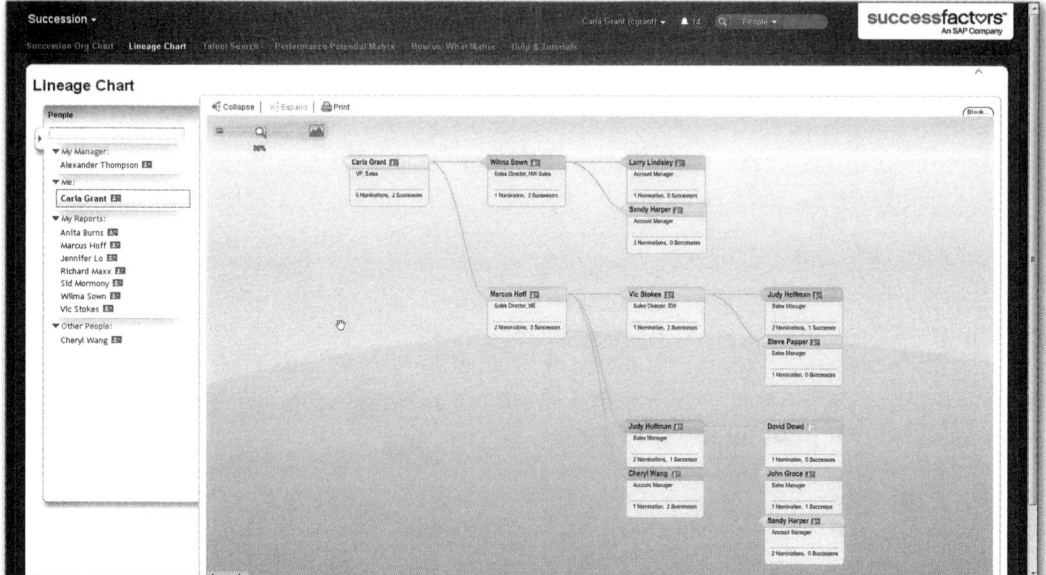

Figure 12.3 Lineage Chart

Now that we've covered the Org Charts that are used in Succession, let's look at the different matrices that can be used for reviewing and identifying the talent that will be used to nominate successors.

12.1.2 Matrices

The performance versus potential nine-box grid is commonly used within a best practice succession planning process. Succession & Development not only features the *Performance-Potential Matrix*, but it also features the *How vs. What Matrix* grid. Both matrices can be used to source talent for succession plans and feature a host of filter options for the search that can encompass large areas of the organization. They are also both separately configurable in OneAdmin, including components such as labels, ratings, and icons. They are both accessed from the options at the top of the page of the Succession module.

For filter options, both matrices allow you to report by your team or the team of a direct report for up to three levels below, the Succession Management and Matrix Report Permissions, or by a group. Groups are custom-made based on specific characteristics, such as job code, department, division, location, and so on. For example, a group may be made for job code Managers in country United States in the Department Sales division. The matrices allow you to view data based on any department, division, or location for any date range.

Performance-Potential Matrix

The Performance-Potential Matrix is used to help identify the high-performing, high-potential individuals that are the most likely to progress through the ranks of your organization. It plots individuals into a grid based on their performance and potential ratings so that it's easy and quick to identify not only which individuals are the top talent within your organization but also which individuals are in need of support to improve their performance. Essentially, this helps provide an overview of how development activities can be focused to ensure that individuals are performing to the level required by your organization.

Figure 12.4 shows the PERFORMANCE-POTENTIAL MATRIX with a number of employees plotted within each square, called a quadrant. Each quadrant on the matrix has a name (e.g., STAR EMPLOYEES or EMERGING STARS), and lists the number of employees, the percentage of the total employees in that quadrant, and the employees themselves with an icon for their business card and historical trend of performance and potential ratings. The HISTORICAL TREND icon opens up a popup window with a graph showing the history of both the performance and potential rating, as shown in Figure 12.5.

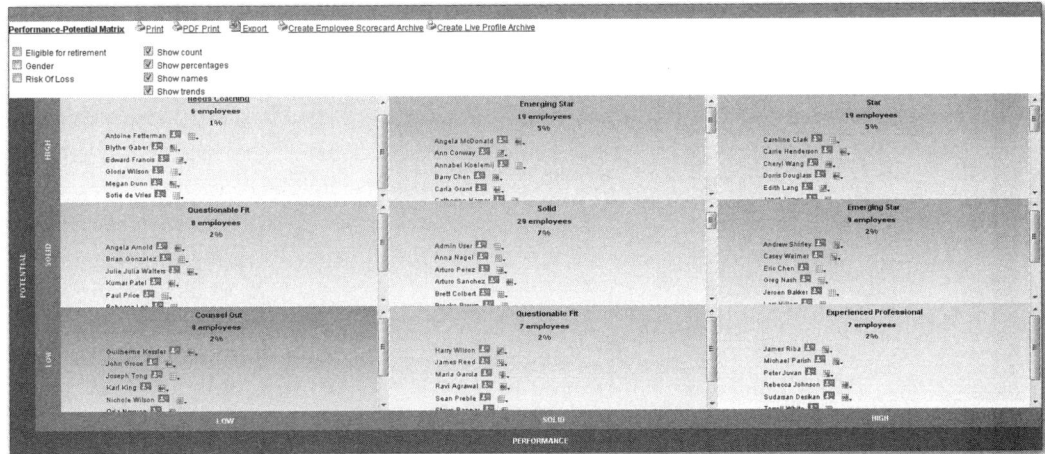

Figure 12.4 Performance-Potential Matrix

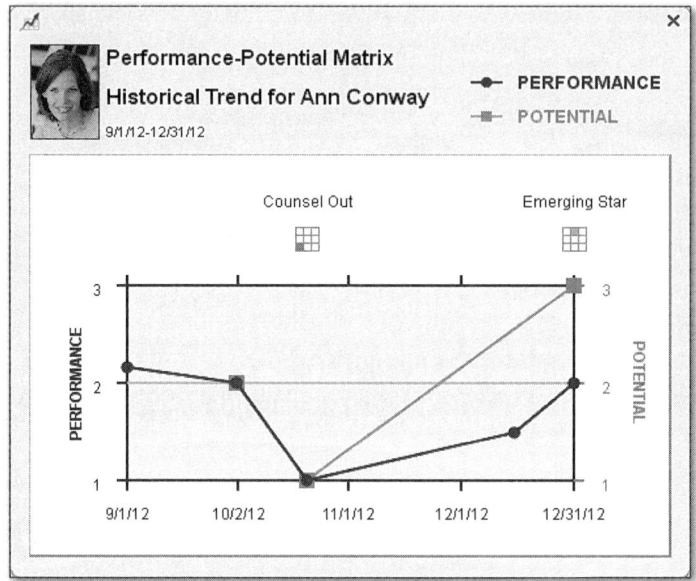

Figure 12.5 Historical Trend Popup Window

The matrix can also have icons displayed for those eligible for retirement, for gender, and for risk of loss to enable balanced and informed decision making to be made. You can also print or export the matrix to a PDF file or Microsoft Excel file to be used in talent review meetings or calibration sessions. Below the matrix, you can display the employees that are too new to rate or that are unrated.

After employees have been reviewed, you can nominate an employee for a succession plan or for a talent pool by selecting the employee's BUSINESS CARD icon, selecting SCORECARD, and taking the necessary action. These are covered in Section 12.1.5 and Section 12.1.6.

How versus What Matrix

A unique feature in the Succession & Development solution is the HOW VS. WHAT MATRIX, shown in Figure 12.6. This grid plots employees based on their competencies ("How") and their objective ratings ("What") so that individuals who are higher achievers and regularly meet their objectives with distinction can be easily identified. Although the outcome of using this matrix is the same as the Performance-Potential Matrix, it provides a different method of achieving it through objectives rather than solely job performance and future potential.

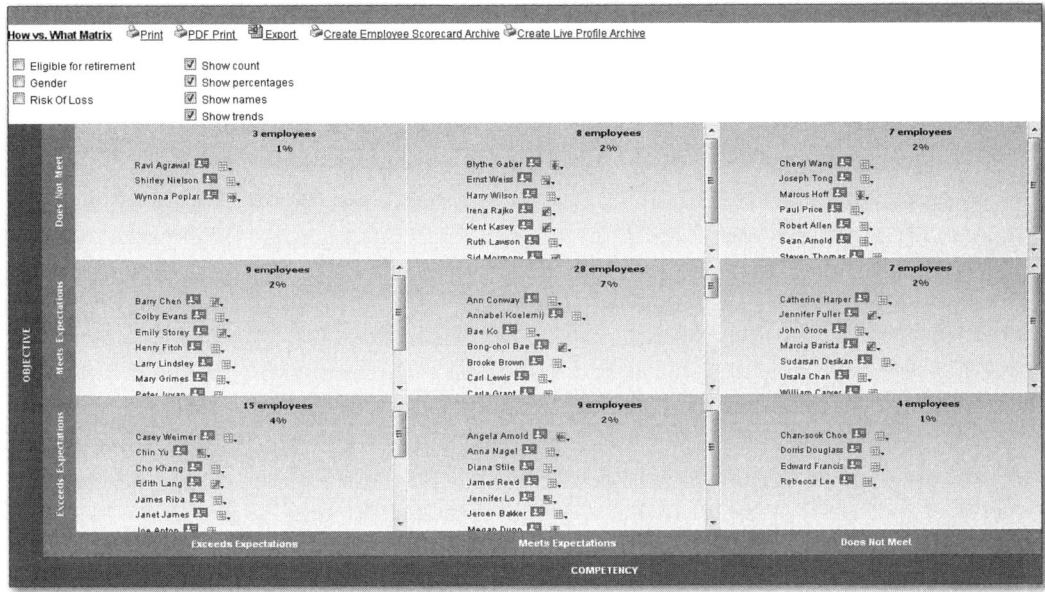

Figure 12.6 How vs. What Matrix

12.1.3 Talent Profile and Scorecard

Although the Talent (or Employee) Profile and Scorecard are covered in Chapter 7, there is some succession planning-specific information on both of these that is worth highlighting. It's also important to note that the Talent Profile and Scorecard are where talent-related information can be maintained.

Talent Profile

The Talent Profile features a host of information that can be used in the succession planning process. More precisely, the NOMINATION PORTLET and TALENT INFORMATION portlet can display and maintain specific succession planning information.

The NOMINATION PORTLET displays nominations for succession plans for talent pools, as shown in Figure 12.7. By selecting the ADD NOMINATION link in the top-right corner, the user can make additional nominations for succession plans, although it's important to note that the user can't nominate the individual for talent pools here.

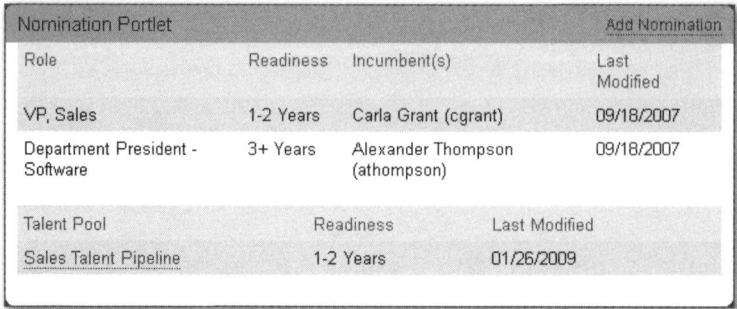

Figure 12.7 Nomination Portlet

The TALENT INFORMATION portlet contains the RISK OF LOSS, IMPACT OF LOSS, REASON FOR LEAVING, NEW TO POSITION, and FUTURE LEADER attributes. This portlet is only visible to the manager or HR specialists, and not to the employee. You can maintain each of these attributes here by clicking the EDIT link.

Scorecard

The Scorecard is more high level than the Talent Profile and therefore contains less information. With regards to succession planning, the Scorecard contains the NOMINATION PORTLET that is featured on the Talent Profile and also the TALENT MANAGEMENT SNAPSHOT portlet. This portlet displays FUTURE LEADER, RISK OF LOSS, and IMPACT OF LOSS fields for the individual, as shown in Figure 12.8. This data can be maintained by clicking the EDIT link.

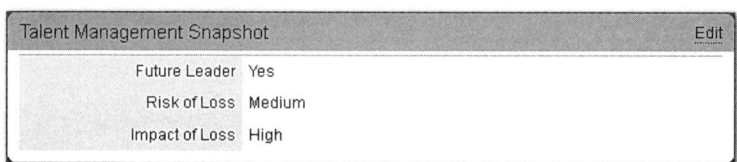

Figure 12.8 Talent Management Snapshot

12.1.4 Talent Search

Talent Search provides a powerful interface for finding, filtering, and matching employees for key positions and talent pools. It provides managers and HR with the ability to search for individuals by numerous criteria, such as job role, background criteria, and competencies. Search criteria can be saved so that it can be reused again, or even created specifically to be used by certain teams or departments within your organization.

> **Note**
> When searching for talent, it may require a number of different searches with different criteria to find the right candidates. Make sure to use all of the search criteria to ensure the best possible results.

Searching

Talent Search is accessed from the options at the top of the page of the Succession module. By default, it opens to the KEYWORD SEARCH, which allows you to enter any search term and execute the search. Below this, you can open the ADVANCED OPTIONS section by clicking the expand button.

The ADVANCED OPTIONS include a host of criteria that can be used to find the right talent, whether you're searching to populate a talent pool or to find a successor. The first part of the ADVANCED OPTIONS section includes criteria fields such as TITLE, JOB CODE, DIVISION, DEPARTMENT, LOCATION, DIVERSITY CANDIDATE, HIRE DATE, RISK OF LOSS, IMPACT OF LOSS, and REASON FOR LEAVING. Below these options, the BACKGROUND CRITERIA can be selected. The dropdown list of background criteria provides 15 options, 3 of which are available within the MANAGER view only. These fields include WORK EXPERIENCE WITHIN COMPANY, PREVIOUS EMPLOYMENT, FORMAL EDUCATION, LANGUAGE SKILLS, LEADERSHIP EXPERIENCE, CAREER GOALS, GEOGRAPHIC MOBILITY, PERFORMANCE, and POTENTIAL, among others.

When one of these criteria has been selected from the dropdown, additional criteria become available that differ for each criterion selected. For example, selecting LEADERSHIP EXPERIENCE provides a dropdown to select the AREA OF LEADERSHIP and then text boxes for YEARS OF EXPERIENCE, NUMBER OF PEOPLE MANAGED, and DOLLARS MANAGED. Clicking the ADD CRITERIA button or green arrow adds this to the criteria list, and then additional background criteria can be added. Within the overall search, you can assign each background criterion a weight so that, for example, years of experience weigh more than number of employees managed.

The third part of the ADVANCED OPTIONS section provides the ability to search by competencies from the competency libraries available in the system. After a competency has been selected from one of the available libraries, click on the green arrow to add it to the list of criteria, just as you did for BACKGROUND CRITERIA. However, for competencies, it's possible to enter a range for the score, select whether the competency is required, and weight these criteria relative to the overall search.

Figure 12.9 shows an example of the possible search criteria that can be selected in TALENT SEARCH.

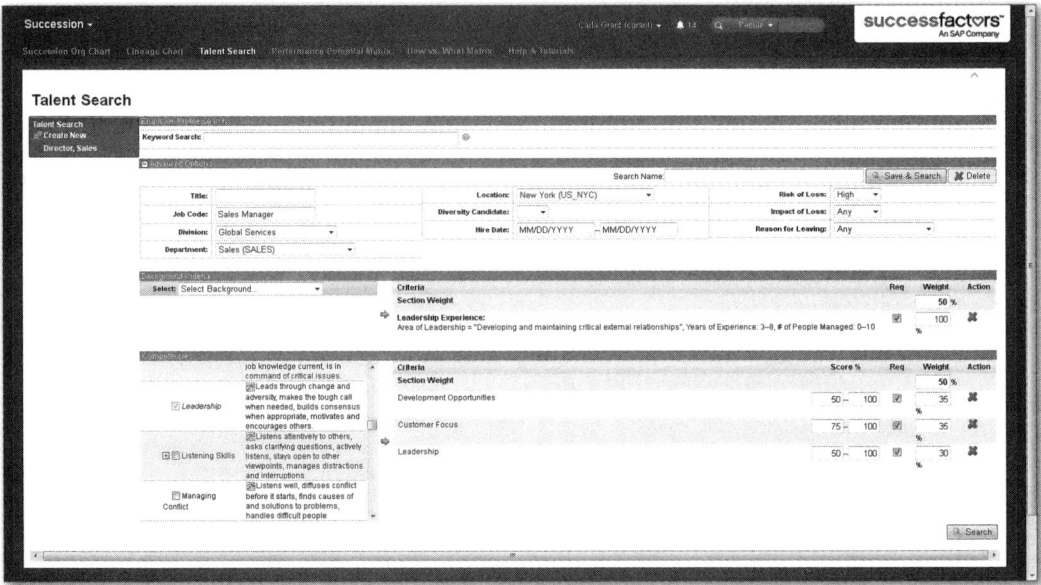

Figure 12.9 Talent Search with Advanced Options

After you've entered search criteria, you can either search using the SEARCH button or enter a name for the search and select SAVE & SEARCH to save this criteria for future use before you execute the search.

> **Note**
>
> The maximum number of search results that Succession can return is 400, although the default maximum is set to 50. It's possible for the system to return 50, 100, 200, or 400 maximum records.

Results

After the search has executed, the results are displayed on a new screen. Each record in the results displays the name, photo, business card icon, background criteria match, competency match, total match, and performance and potential grid icon, as shown in Figure 12.10. The results list can be exported to Excel.

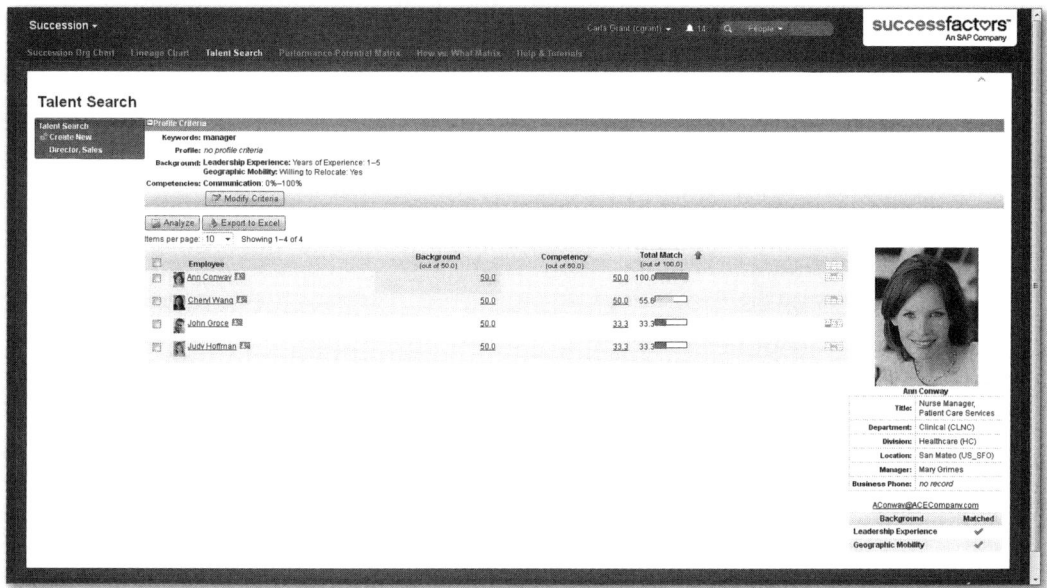

Figure 12.10 Talent Search Results

The most interesting feature of the search results is the Compare Successors analysis report. This option allows individuals selected in the search results to be compared for a variety of different attributes. By comparing multiple individuals, you ensure that the best possible candidates can be chosen.

To open the COMPARE SUCCESSORS window, check the checkbox next to each employee to include, and click the ANALYZE button. Figure 12.11 compares three employees' competencies.

After candidates have been identified, they can be nominated to talent pools or succession plans, as we'll discuss in the next two sections.

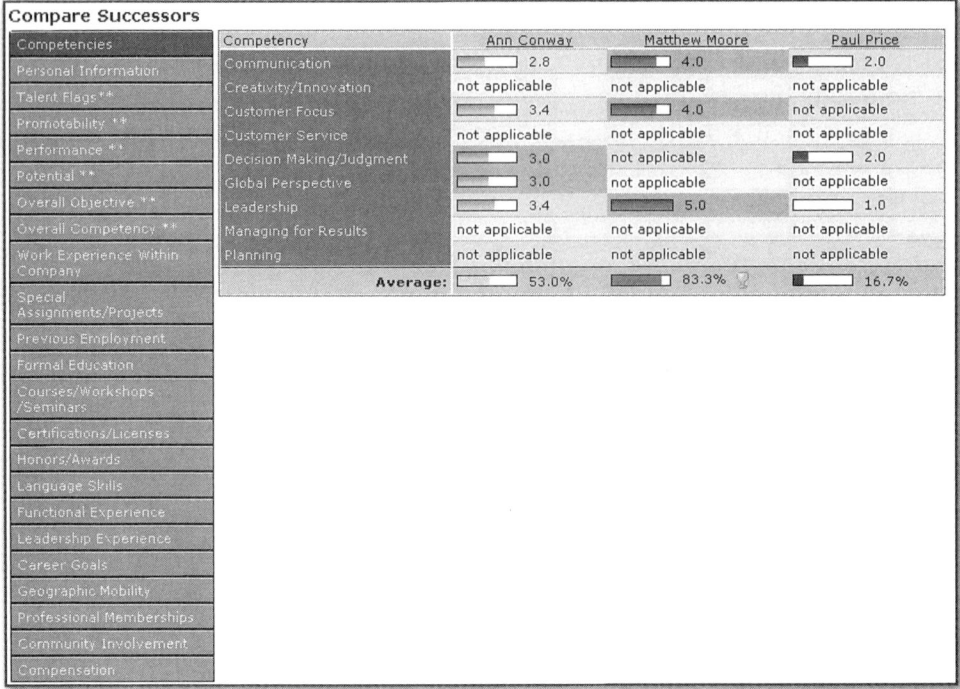

Figure 12.11 Compare Successors Feature

12.1.5 Talent Pools

Talent pools provide a way of classifying and aggregating individuals to similar job roles so that they can be sourced for succession plans. This enables organizations to scale their succession planning effort and begin identifying, tracking, and preparing candidates for future roles even though they may not be nominated as a successor to a position yet.

Talent pools are assigned to job roles; and any employee nominated to a talent pool has the potential to be a successor to the job codes and related positions of the job roles that the talent pool is linked to. Any employee in your organization can be nominated to a talent pool.

> **Note**
>
> Talent pools can be assigned to multiple job roles, although a job role can only have one talent pool. Talent pools are associated to job roles in OneAdmin using the FAMILIES AND ROLES listed under MANAGING COMPETENCIES AND SKILLS in the old ADMIN TOOLS screen.

Any position box within the Succession Org Chart whose job role has a talent pool associated to it will show the TALENT POOL link at the bottom of the box, as shown in Figure 12.12.

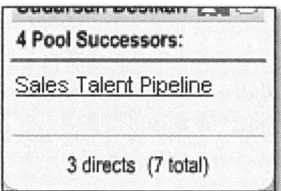

Figure 12.12 Sales Talent Pipeline Talent Pool Link in a Position Box

When the user selects the talent pool link (e.g., SALES TALENT PIPELINE), the talent pool will open in a new window where it will list all of the members of that talent pool, as shown in Figure 12.13. Here you can add, edit, or delete members of the talent pool.

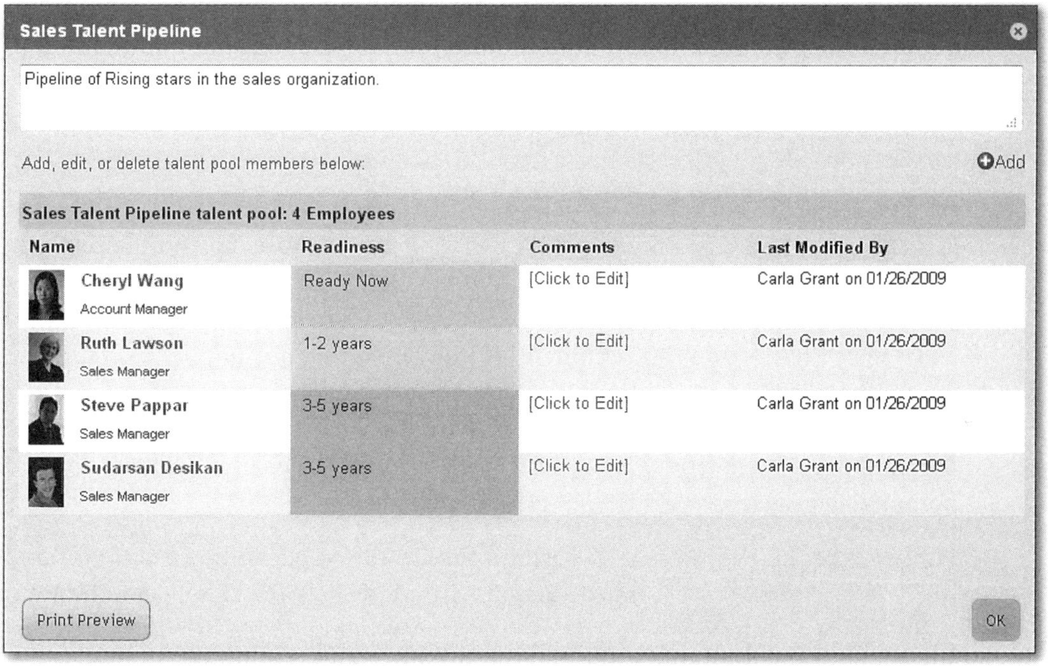

Figure 12.13 Sales Talent Pipeline Talent Pool

You can also open a talent pool from the NOMINATION PORTLET in the Talent Profile or Scorecard and from the business card of any employee that is a member of that talent pool.

12.1.6 Nominating Successors

After you've identified the supply of talent, you can begin the process of nominating successors. In Succession & Development, nominating successors is form-based; you must configure and assign a template in OneAdmin before nominating can begin.

In the Succession module, functionality is provided to seek and nominate individuals *for* a specific position (i.e., from the position perspective) or nominate a specific individual *to* a position (i.e., from the employee perspective). Managers are responsible for nominating successors for positions within their teams, and they can also nominate their direct reports as successors for other positions.

Successors can be nominated to positions in a number of different ways:

- Succession Org Chart
- Lineage Chart
- Scorecard
- Talent Profile

In the Succession Org Chart and Lineage Chart, an individual can be nominated as a successor to the position via the CURRENT NOMINATIONS box on the business card by selecting the ADD link. From the position box action dropdown menu, you can nominate a successor using the FIND SUCCESSORS option. In the Scorecard and Talent Profile, you can nominate an individual to a position by selecting the ADD NOMINATION link in the NOMINATION PORTLET. The process of nominating a successor doesn't differ greatly whether from the position perspective or from the employee perspective. Now, let's walk through an example where you are nominating a successor for the VP of Sales position.

First, you locate the VP, SALES position box in the SUCCESSION ORG CHART and select FIND SUCCESSORS from the actions dropdown menu. This opens the FIND A SUCCESSOR window, where you can search for an employee or add an external candidate. You can either enter a name into the text box or click the ADVANCED TALENT SEARCH link to open the TALENT SEARCH in an external window. In this example, enter "Richard Maxx" into the text box and click GO.

On the next screen, which is shown in Figure 12.14, you can see your nominee RICHARD MAXX and also the existing nominated successors. You also have the option to compare the nominee and existing nominated successors using the Compare Successors feature in the Talent Search by selecting the COMPARE THE NOMINEES link.

After reviewing the successors, select NEXT to go to the screen to select the READINESS and RANKING for your nominee and add any NOTES. You see that Richard Maxx is a competent successor but still needs some time to develop. Therefore, you select the readiness as READY IN 1-2 YEARS from the dropdown and enter a ranking of "3". In the NOTES text box, you add some notes about Richard Maxx needing some competency development before being ready to take the role. After this is done, you select the NOMINATE button to close the window and confirm the nomination. If you now take a look at the VP, SALES position box in the SUCCESSION ORG CHART, you'll see RICHARD MAXX is now listed as a successor.

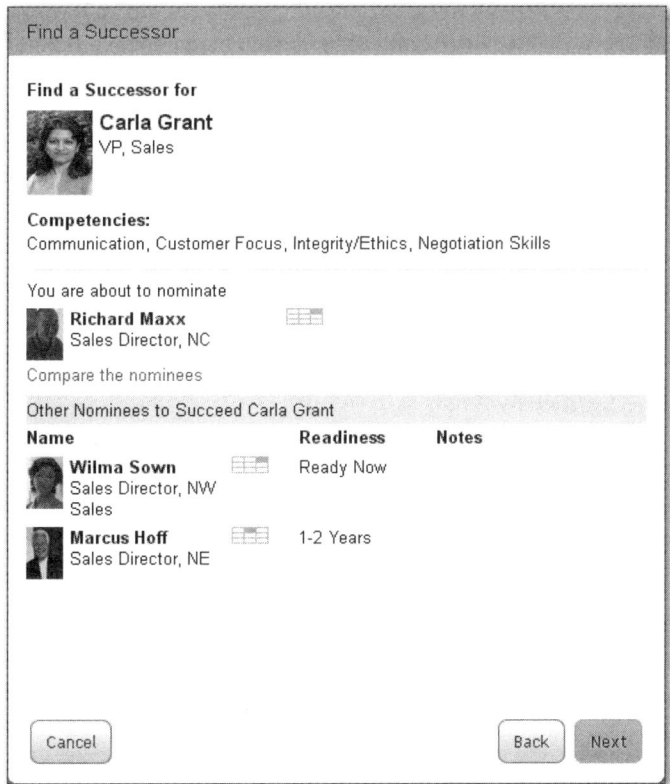

Figure 12.14 Find a Successor Window with the Nominees for VP, Sales

A useful feature of Succession & Development is being able to nominate an external candidate as a successor. This can be a job candidate from SuccessFactors Recruiting Execution or a defined individual such as a candidate that has been head-hunted outside of the standard recruitment process. External candidates are nominated by selecting either FIND EXTERNAL CANDIDATE or ADD A NEW EXTERNAL CANDIDATE in the FIND A SUCCESSOR window (which is the same place where an employee is searched for).

Nomination history can be viewed for a position by selecting NOMINATION HISTORY in the action dropdown menu of a position box in the SUCCESSION ORG CHART. Figure 12.15 shows the nomination history to the VP, SALES position held by CARLA GRANT.

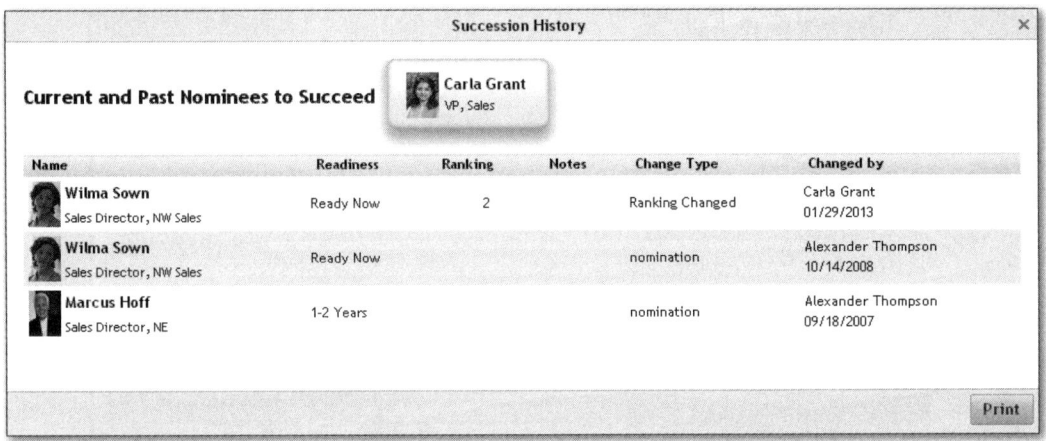

Figure 12.15 Nomination History

12.1.7 Position Management

Succession & Development offers Position Management, which considers positions as a separate entity from a job code and an employee. Because succession planning is focused on positions, and you may not use these objects in your SuccessFactors system, it's necessary to have these objects within the Succession module.

Creating Positions

SuccessFactors offers various ways of creating position objects if they don't exist, including the following:

- **Deriving positions from employee data**
  In OneAdmin, you can use the SYNC POSITION MODEL WITH EMPLOYEE DATA option under POSITION MANAGEMENT to create both the positions and the reporting relationships between the positions.

- **Importing position data**
  In OneAdmin, you can import position data by using the IMPORT POSITIONS option under POSITION MANAGEMENT. The import file must include the position code, the employee's ID, the reporting position, and the job code for vacant positions. Positions can also be marked as a key position within the import file.

- **Using the Succession Org Chart**
  Within the Succession Org Chart, you can create new positions by selecting the ADD DIRECT REPORT option in the ACTIONS dropdown menu on the position box of the parent position.

- **Using the Metadata Framework (MDF)**
  Since the 1305 release, in OneAdmin, you can use the option MANAGE POSITION OBJECTS under GENERIC OBJECTS to both create and manage position objects.

Maintaining Positions

Positions can also be maintained through the Succession Org Chart and the MDF. Within the Succession Org Chart, the EDIT POSITION option in the actions dropdown of a position box allows the user to maintain information about that position (shown in Figure 12.16), while the DELETE POSITION option from the same menu will delete that position. The MDF can also be used to edit position objects, as described in Chapter 4.

12 | Succession & Development

Figure 12.16 Edit Position Window in the Succession Org Chart

12.1.8 Reporting and Analytics

We've already covered a number of tools within Succession that can be used for reporting, such as Talent Search, Scorecard, and Nomination History. In addition to these tools, Succession also offers powerful ad hoc reporting. It's important to note that Succession doesn't offer any predefined analytics.

The Ad Hoc Reports in SuccessFactors allow you to combine specific succession data with demographic or other organizational data to produce your own meaningful reports. They are accessed in the Analytics module by selecting AD HOC REPORTS in the REPORTING tab. From here, users can create their own Ad Hoc Report based on criteria chosen from a list of more than 250 different fields for each of the succession planning domains:

- Succession (incumbent-based nominations)
- Inclusive succession (position-based nominations)
- Succession history (incumbent-based nominations)
- Succession history (position-based nominations)

Figure 12.17 shows an example of an Ad Hoc Report for *inclusive succession* (position-based nominations).

We've examined how Succession empowers organizations to identify key talent and nominate that talent to critical positions with the help of the Succession Org

358

Chart. The next step is to develop the identified talent to ensure readiness for the succession plans to which they have been assigned. We'll now examine the Development module and how it supports these activities.

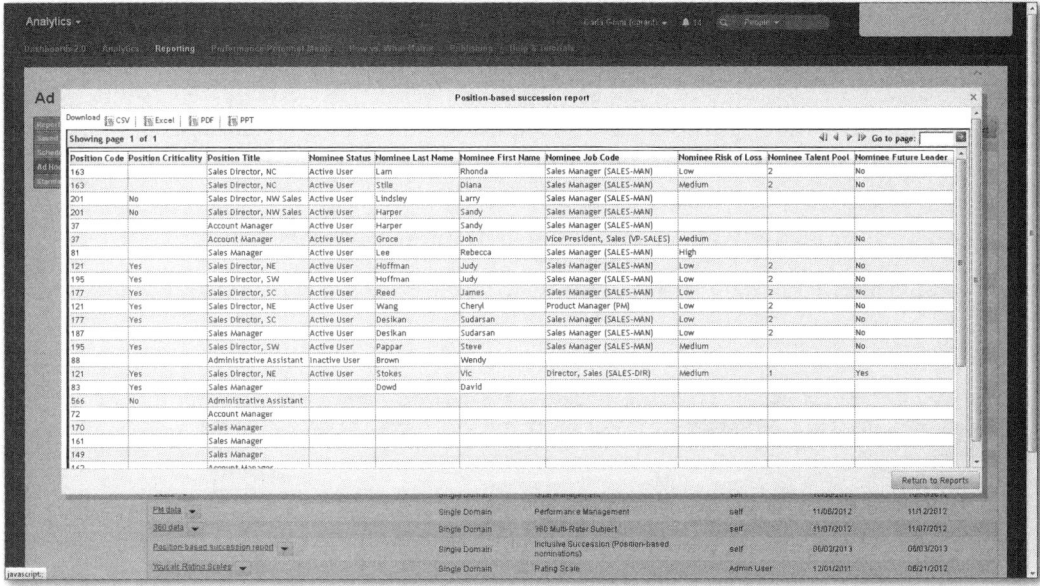

Figure 12.17 Example of an Ad Hoc report on Inclusive Succession

12.2 Development

The Career Development Planning (CDP) or just Development module provides the ability to create Development Plans, link them to career plans, and plan learning activities to support them. This makes the CDP an actionable and powerful tool for companies to close the talent gap and utilize and retain talent with high merit for succession planning and overall personnel development activities.

There are three core components to the CDP module:

▸ Development Plan
▸ Career Worksheet
▸ Learning Activities

Now let's take a look at how each component supports these activities.

12.2.1 Development Plan

After successors have been assigned to succession plans, a suitable Development Plan is required to ensure development and readiness of the successors. The Development Plans are accessible by the individuals, as well as their managers.

Development Plans comprise *development goals*, which are oriented toward developing skills and competencies in the chosen direction for career progression. Unlike goal plans in SuccessFactors Performance & Goals, these plans can span multiple years. The CDP module of the BizX suite comes with a comprehensive and integrated design that enables organizations to accomplish this very important aspect of ensuring that they have the right talent in the right position.

Figure 12.18 illustrates the Development Plan and its various elements for employee CARLA GRANT.

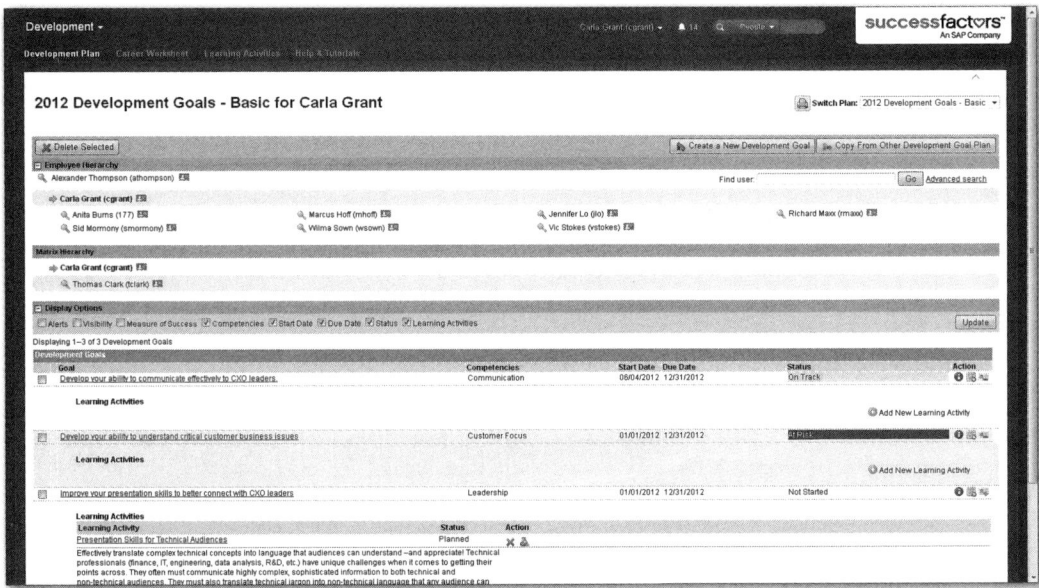

Figure 12.18 Example of a Development Plan

However, similar to the goal plan in the SuccessFactors Performance & Goals (covered in detail in Chapter 8), the Development Plan can be created from a template and configured according to the needs of the organization. Various information of a development goal can be displayed or hidden by selecting it in the DISPLAY options section. This includes ALERTS, VISIBILITY, MEASURE OF SUCCESS, COMPETENCIES, START DATE, DUE DATE, STATUS, and LEARNING ACTIVITIES.

> **Note**
> Although largely an integrated solution, the Development Plan within the CDP module does not integrate with the goal plan in Performance & Goals.

Within each Development Plan, it's also possible for a manager to select their own Development Plan or to select the Development Plan for any of the manager's direct or matrix reports within the EMPLOYEE HIERARCHY section.

Creating Development Goals

Development goals are added to a Development Plan by clicking the CREATE A NEW DEVELOPMENT GOAL button. This opens the ADD DEVELOPMENT GOAL window (see Figure 12.19) where details of the new development goal can be defined. Several different attributes can be chosen for a development goal, although only the GOAL description and COMPETENCIES fields are compulsory:

- VISIBILITY
  Defines whether the development goal will be publicly visible or only visible to the individual and the corresponding manager.

- GOAL
  Freeform text box to describe the development goal.

- MEASURE OF SUCCESS
  Freeform text box to describe the measure of success for the development goal.

- START DATE
  The start date of the development goal.

- DUE DATE
  The date by which the development goal should be completed.

- STATUS
  The status of the development goal, which can be set and changed throughout its lifecycle to one of the different predefined statuses.

- COMPETENCIES
  The one or more competencies from the competency library that will be gained after the development goal is completed.

▶ PURPOSE
Whether the development goal is for a current role, future role, or general skillset.

The GOAL and MEASURE OF SUCCESS fields feature both a spell checker and the Legal Scan feature. The values for STATUS are defined in the Development Plan template.

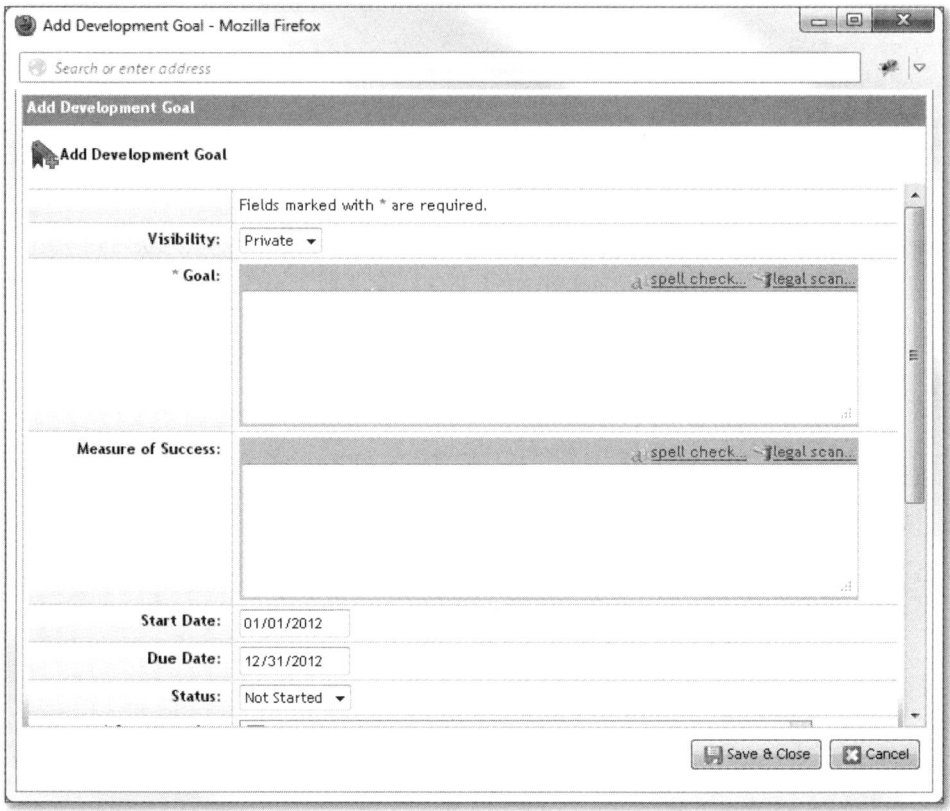

Figure 12.19 Add Development Goal Window

You can also copy development goals from another Development Goal template using the COPY FROM OTHER DEVELOPMENT GOAL PLAN button that is located beside the CREATE A NEW DEVELOPMENT GOAL button.

Assigning Learning Activities

After you've created a development goal, you can assign one or more learning activities to it via the ADD NEW LEARNING ACTIVITY button located directly underneath the development goal. Learning activities can be selected from the learning catalog, or custom activities can be created. This provides organizations with the possibility to assign learning to aid the development of the required competencies of a position for which they are a successor or just to increase their productivity within their existing role. Figure 12.20 shows the addition of a LEARNING ACTIVITY to the development goal.

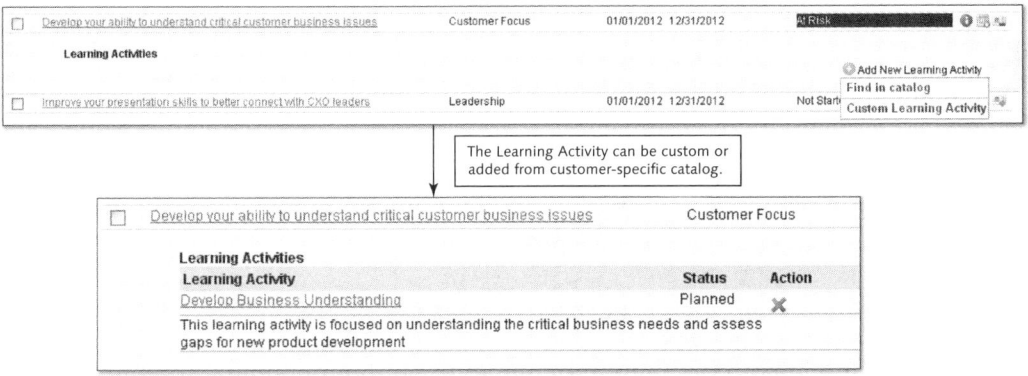

Figure 12.20 Adding a Learning Activity to a Development Goal

After a LEARNING ACTIVITY has been added, the ACTION column provides three icons to edit, delete, or add the LEARNING ACTIVITY to Outlook.

Maintaining and Tracking Goals

Development goals can be edited, removed, or added to Outlook as required. Editing a development goal—including changing its status—can be done freely at any time. This enables development goals to be altered as an employee develops or changes roles and supports tracking of current status.

By selecting the INFORMATION icon in the ACTION column of the development goal, you can see the DETAIL VIEW of that development goal (see Figure 12.21). Although the information is largely the same from that provided when a development goal is created or edited, the DETAIL VIEW screen does show the AUDIT HISTORY of the development goal.

12   Succession & Development

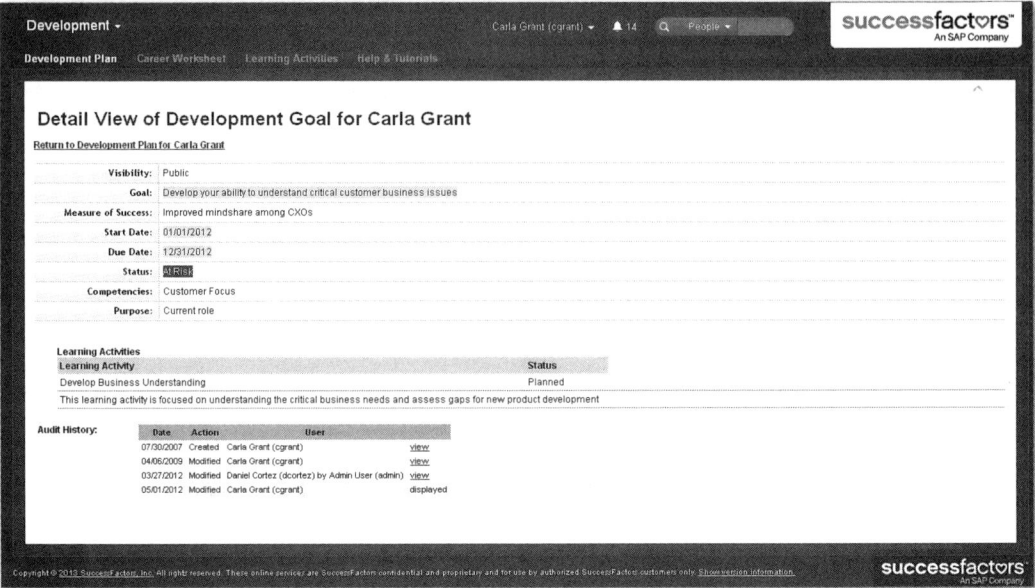

Figure 12.21 Detail View of a Development Goal

You can remove development goals from the Development Plan by selecting them and clicking on the DELETE SELECTED button at the top of the Development Plan.

Publishing to the Scorecard

Managers and employees can view the development goals on the Scorecard, which increases visibility and actionable analytics to the career development processes. This is done by selecting the ADD DEVELOPMENT GOAL IN SCORECARD icon in the ACTIONS menu. After the goal is added, this icon switches to the REMOVE DEVELOPMENT GOAL FROM SCORECARD icon, which can be used to remove the development goal from the Succession Scorecard.

> **Note**
>
> Private development goals can't be published on the Scorecard. They are only visible within the Development Plan by the manager and the employee.

Development Objectives Portlet

The DEVELOPMENT OBJECTIVES PORTLET can be added to the Employee Profile to show all of an employee's development goals, as shown in Figure 12.22.

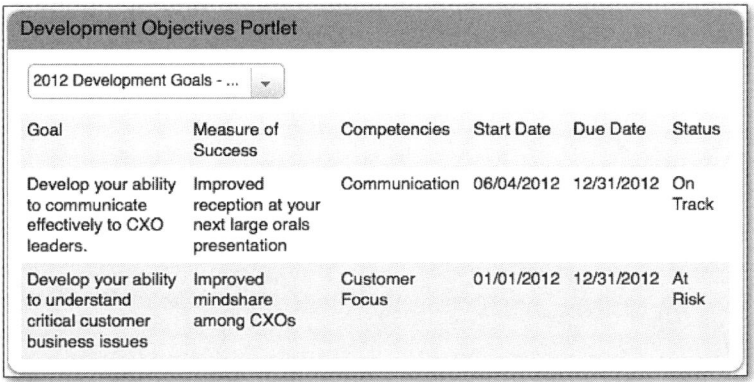

Figure 12.22 Development Objectives Portlet

To maximize returns from a Development Plan, it's imperative that you also align it with the individual's career plan. We'll explore the Career Worksheet and how it enables organizations to integrate the Development Plan with the career path of its talent next.

12.2.2 Career Worksheet

The *Career Worksheet* is the main focus of the CDP module and serves as an actionable view of an employee's career path, current and future roles, and existing and required competencies. Because it's linked to the Development Plan, it's a powerful tool to align your talent's development goals with the planned career progression for current and/or future goals. You can assess the readiness of your talent for a particular role that they have been nominated for using the Career Worksheet (see Figure 12.23).

The Career Worksheet allows an individual or the individual's manager to map out the individual's career by adding potential jobs, viewing competency gaps, and adding development goals aligned with the competencies required to ensure the readiness of the future role. This is based on the assumption that a prior activity has been performed to add competencies for various job roles for your organization. New competencies added to a job role are immediately available for consumption in the CDP module.

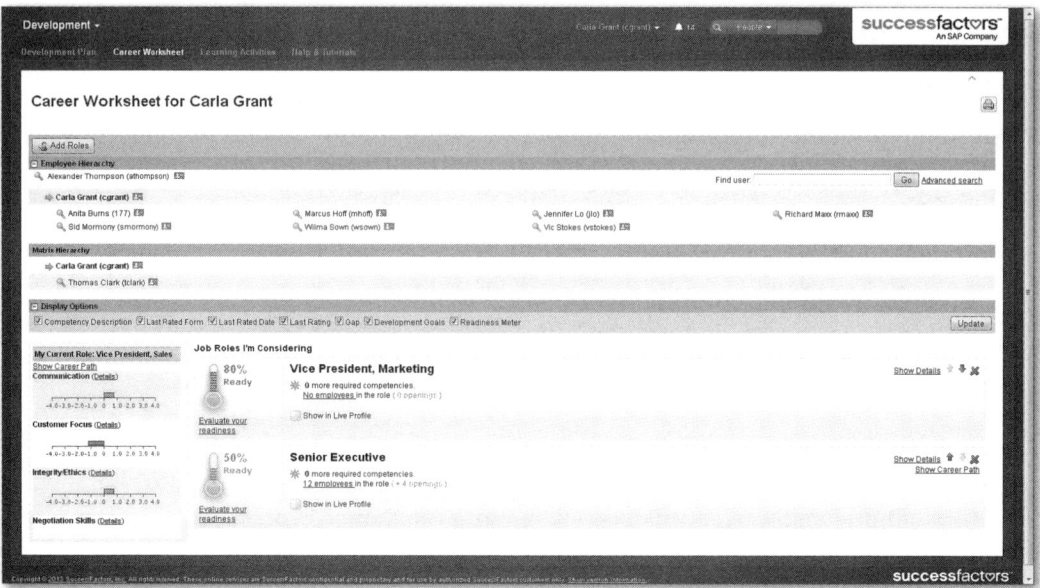

Figure 12.23 Career Worksheet

The bottom-left corner of the CAREER WORKSHEET displays the current job role of the individual along with the competencies of the job role. For each competency, the gap between the previous performance rating and the expected rating is displayed. By clicking on the DETAILS link, you get a popup that features details of the competency and a link to view the development goals that are linked to that competency, as shown in Figure 12.24.

The main part of the Career Worksheet displays the job roles that the individual is interested in pursuing. For each job role, a number of details are displayed, including readiness, the required competencies, and the number of employees in the role with the number of openings alongside. Readiness is based on the employee's skills assessment that was completed in the SuccessFactors Performance & Goals module.

By selecting the SHOW DETAILS link, it's possible to see the competencies of the JOB ROLE along with a gap analysis between the individual's current competencies and those of the job role. Figure 12.25 shows the competencies linked to the job role, VICE PRESIDENT, MARKETING that is being considered by Carla Grant as a future job role. For every competency, you have the ability to add a development goal using the ADD DEVELOPMENT GOAL button. The development goals added here also get reflected in the Development Plan.

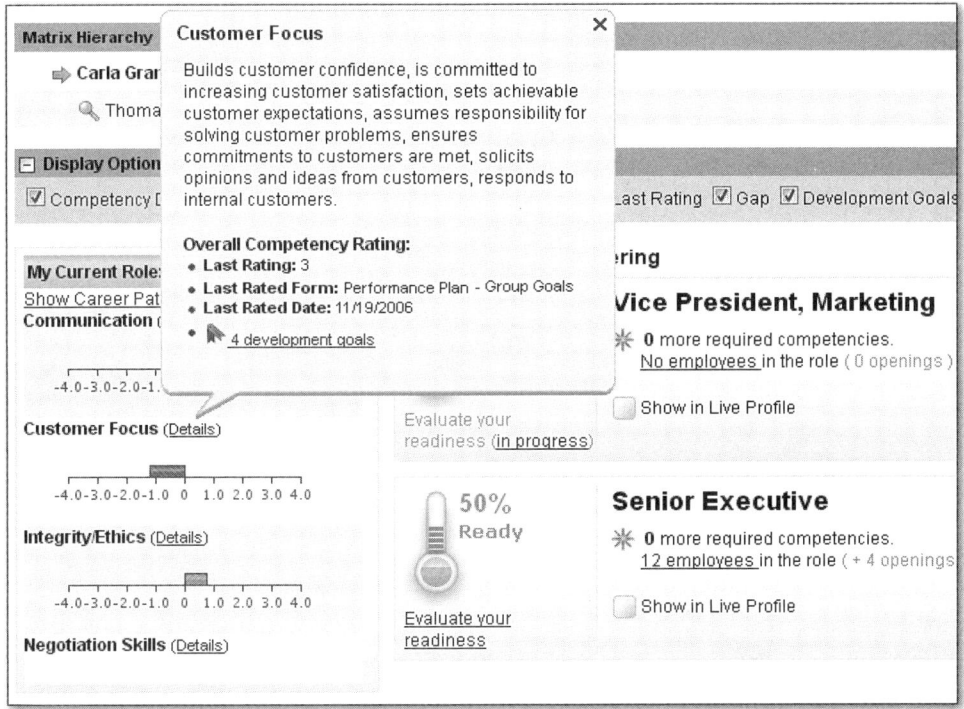

Figure 12.24 Competency Detail Popup

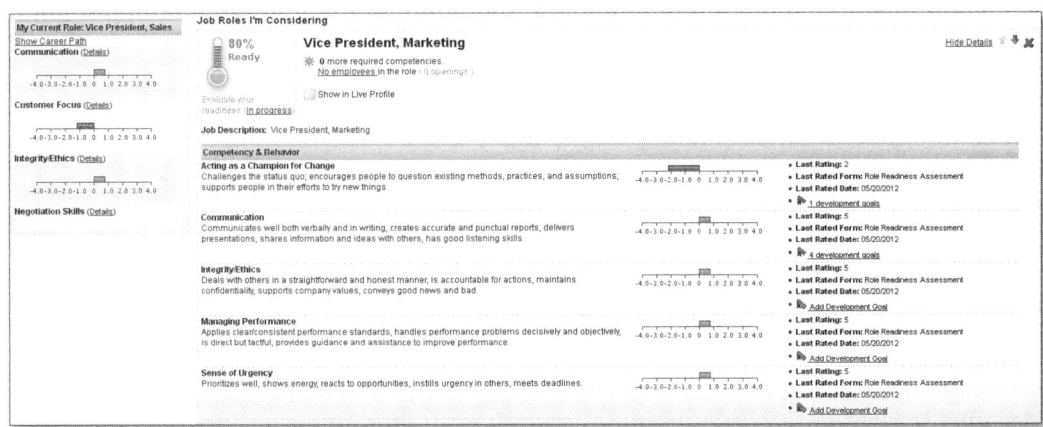

Figure 12.25 Job Roles Being Considered by Carla Grant

We've looked at the required competencies for a particular role and added the relevant development goals to the Development Plan. One of the useful features of the Career Worksheet is the ability to view the CAREER PATH DIAGRAM of a job role, as shown in Figure 12.26.

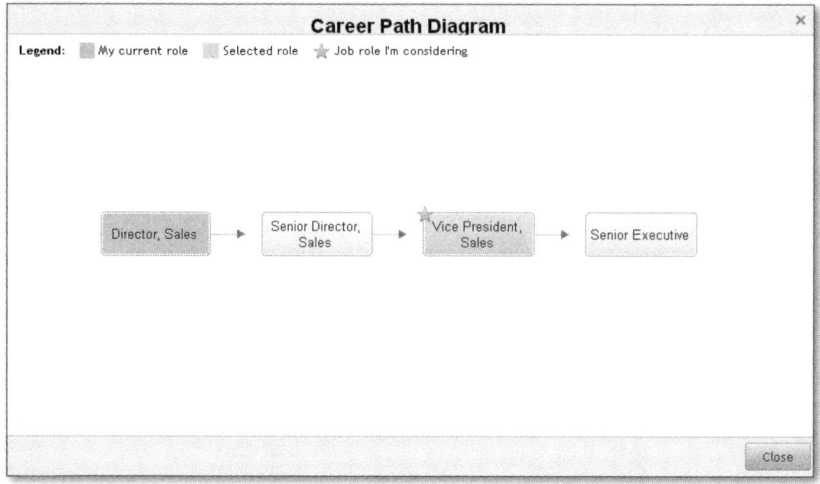

Figure 12.26 Career Path Diagram

You saw in the preceding sections how the Development Plan and Career Worksheet work in tandem to help organizations assess competency gaps for their talent to craft a suitable Development Plan. For your talent to fill the competency gaps, they need to be registered to a learning plan. This brings us to the next feature of the CDP module, Learning Activities.

12.2.3 Learning Activities

Let's look at the LEARNING ACTIVITIES section of the CDP module. The LEARNING ACTIVITIES section allows you to add a training course, certification, and so on to the Development Plan so that employees can achieve their development goals.

Although learning activities can be added directly in the Development Plan itself as discussed in Section 12.2.1, the LEARNING ACTIVITIES page also allows employees or their manager to view all of the learning activities that are assigned to them from a development and career perspective and take actions for each of them. For example, a learning activity can have development goals added or edited, be associated with a development goal, or be launched. You can create a printable version of the learning activities list using the PRINT PREVIEW button.

Figure 12.27 shows how you can link a learning activity to one or more development goals. The system recognizes that a particular learning activity can help you accomplish some of the development goals in your Development Plan that don't require a one-to-one relationship between a learning activity and a development goal.

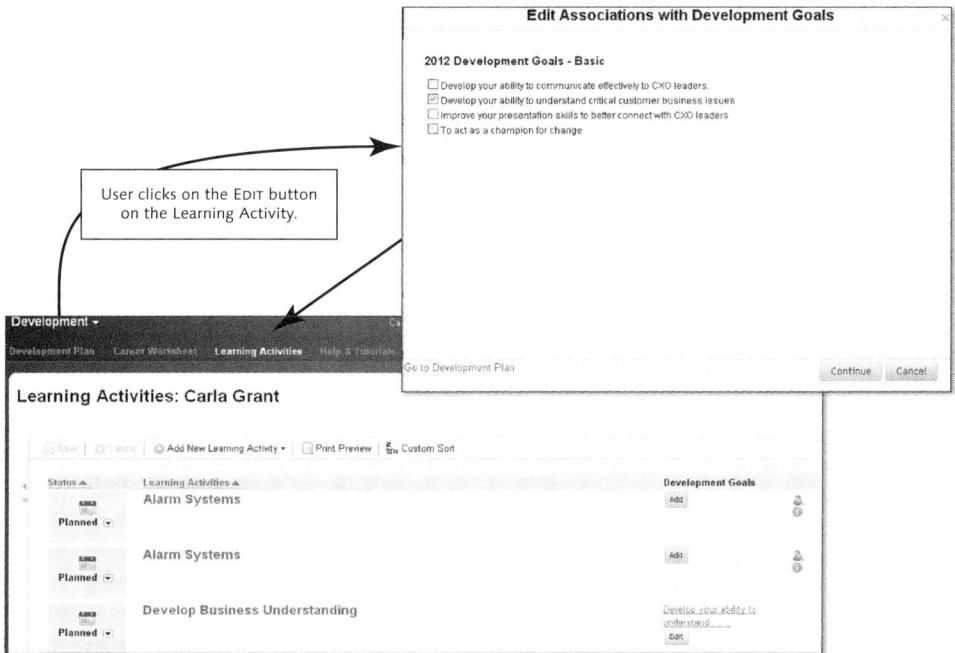

Figure 12.27 Associating Development Goals with a Learning Activity

12.3 Summary

SuccessFactors Succession & Development is a two-fold solution for managing organizational sustainability through succession planning and career development planning. Its core functionality enables full management of the succession planning process and of employee career paths. It also enables employees to make choices about their own careers and actively develop their own skills and competencies.

In this chapter, we've learned how the Succession module supports the full succession planning process through the Succession Org Chart, Scorecard, matrices,

Talent Search, and talent pools, as well as by leveraging Position Management. We also covered the reporting possibilities that exist in the solution.

We explored the Career Development Planning module and how this supports competency growth and career planning for all employees, as well as those planned for critical or leadership positions. We looked at how all of this integrates with other solutions within the BizX suite.

In the next chapter, we'll look at SAP Jam, the social collaboration and knowledge-sharing solution designed to improve cross-functional cooperation and support achieving team, project, and strategic goals and initiatives.

SAP Jam is an innovative and professional social collaboration and networking platform solution that supports cross-functional collaboration, ensuring that organizations leverage their skills, knowledge, and experience to enhance productivity. It brings together people, data, content, and processes to deliver business results in a secure, social foundation.

13 SAP Jam

Social networking is a relatively recent phenomenon that has created new methods for individuals to connect and interact. These networks have become powerful ways of sharing information, opinions, and different types of content. With the increased ability to gain attention and traction, there has been uplift in the level of content creation and sharing. Now, SuccessFactors and SAP have created a solution to leverage this type of social networking, content creation, and sharing in a professional collaboration environment.

SAP Jam—previously SuccessFactors Jam—is a cross-functional social collaboration and networking solution designed to increase productivity and knowledge sharing in a professional environment. SAP Jam brings together the strengths of SuccessFactors Jam and SAP StreamWork to provide a new social experience for SAP customers.

Social collaboration enables sharing knowledge to create empowerment, to engage employees, and to enhance expertise. It increases overall organizational competency levels, facilitates faster decision making, and onboards individuals into an organization more quickly. It also provides a platform for teams to discuss common topics, find answers to problems within their everyday work, and work toward achieving shared goals. SAP Jam also offers the possibility to collaborate with individuals who are based outside of the company, such as partners or customers.

To enable social collaboration, SAP Jam supports business processes in all four of SAP's cloud business pillars: people, customers, money, and suppliers. It uses common social networking features that can be seen in popular social networking platforms such as Twitter, Facebook, and Google Plus. In this chapter, we'll focus on SAP Jam for the people pillar, although we'll briefly cover the benefits it offers across different business areas.

> **Note**
>
> There are four editions available of SAP Jam: *Basic*, *Advanced*, *Advanced Plus*, and *Enterprise Edition*. This chapter covers the Enterprise Edition.

13.1 Using SAP Jam

SAP Jam supports a number of different business scenarios inside and outside of the HCM domain. It covers four main capabilities:

- **Enterprise social networking**
  Groups, feeds, discussions, content creation and sharing, bookmarks, and so on.
- **External collaboration**
  Collaboration with customers, partners, suppliers, and so on.
- **Structured collaboration**
  Brainstorming, problem solving, and decision making with business tools (ranking, pro/con tables, etc.).
- **Business processes**
  People, customer, money, and supplier processes.

The following list gives a set of examples of the business processes and scenarios that SAP Jam supports:

- Employee
  - Informal learning
  - Onboarding
  - Recruiting
  - Collaborative goals and performance management
  - Expert finding
  - Career growth through mentoring

- Customers and sales
  - Opportunity management
  - Campaign management
  - Partner and vendor management
- Suppliers and partners
  - Supplier collaboration
  - Sales and operations planning

Note these are not exhaustive lists of use cases—SAP Jam supports many more possibilities. The flexibility of the solution means that creative organizations may find numerous ways to leverage the functionality for specific internal and external activities. The core to SAP Jam is the groups functionality; using groups to target specific audiences enables targeted sharing and collaboration.

Now we'll look at some of these use cases to understand how SAP Jam can support social collaboration.

13.1.1 Informal and Social Learning

SAP Jam can be used for informal learning or to support learning activities in the SuccessFactors Learning module. By leveraging the groups functionality, groups can be created to share learning materials in the following ways:

- Members can share additional documents to help other members increase their learning.
- Wikis and blogs enable users to add new learning information and post their thoughts on what they have learned.
- The agenda and task functionality allows members a way to complete a structured learning program.
- Videos enable learners to create inline annotations to support the video content from a learning perspective.
- The questions functionality enables members to ask questions, either for the course instructor or for their fellow group members.

13.1.2 Social Onboarding

The process of onboarding new employees can be significantly streamlined in SAP Jam. The availability of a private external group provides new employees with access to an onboarding group before even commencing their employment.

Using the first-time welcome announcement can introduce employees to the purpose of the group, what information and resources they can find in the group, which people to follow, what related groups to join, and what activities they need to perform. Recommendations can help new employees understand what content is important and which contributors are worth following. By familiarizing themselves with new colleagues, the new employees can begin to orient and integrate themselves into their new company.

13.1.3 Sales

Sales organizations can leverage the collaboration aspect of SAP Jam to share critical information to help close team deals, build pro/con tables for sales tactics, ask questions, and request documentation. For teams working with similar products/services or customers, it can be beneficial to collaborate over the handling of accounts or share new information that colleagues can use to position or sell additional products or services. At-risk accounts can be discussed and remedy tasks can be set up to track actions. Marketing colleagues can be invited to groups so that sales and marketing can collaborate on campaign strategy and execution. External vendors can be invited to collaborate on the sales cycle of their products.

13.1.4 BizX Mobile

SAP Jam is also available via SuccessFactors BizX Mobile, but we'll focus more attention on this in Chapter 17.

Now that we've evaluated the ways in which SAP Jam can be used, let's look at the features within the application.

13.2 Features and Social Networking Capabilities

SAP Jam streamlines business processes by making them social. It offers a number of social networking features that Twitter and Facebook users are familiar with.

The Enterprise Social Networking functionality forms the backbone of the process-driven business scenarios that bring business value through social collaboration. For example, when entering the SAP Jam solution, users are taken to the HOME page with their feed, which shows content from all of the groups of which they are a member (see Figure 13.1).

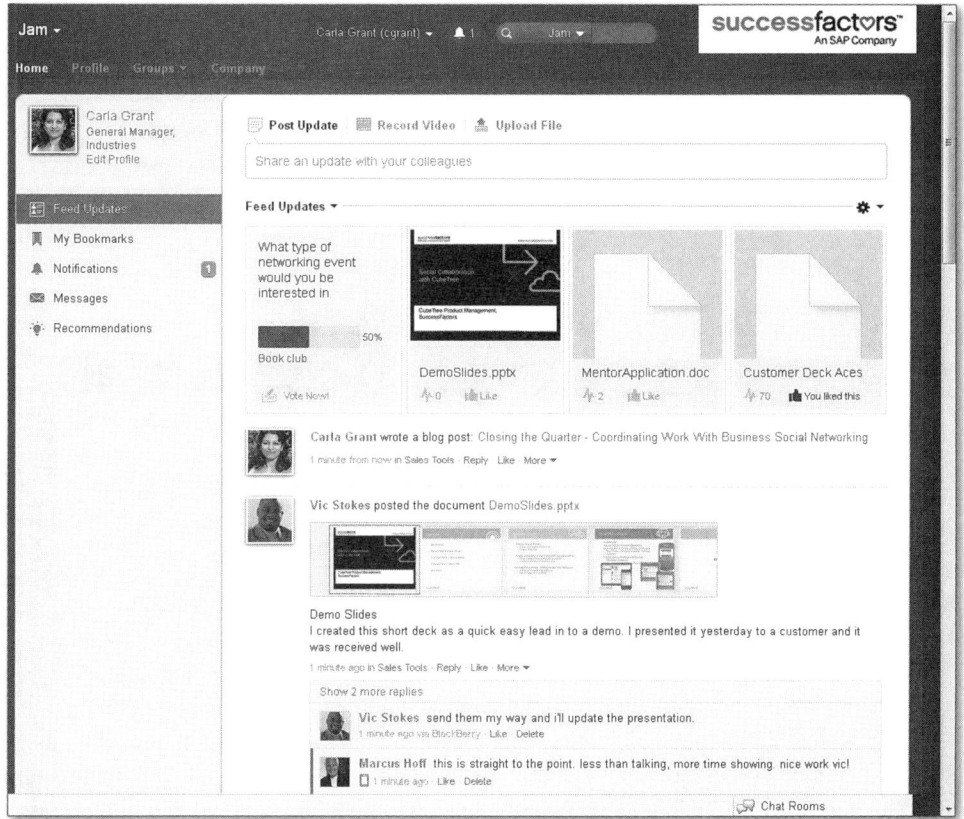

Figure 13.1 The Home Page of SAP Jam

The core functionality and features available in SAP Jam include the following:

- Profile
- Feeds and comments
- Bookmarks and notifications
- Groups

- Content authorship and distribution
- Now let's run through these features.

13.2.1 Profile

SAP Jam gives users the opportunity to create a *profile* about themselves, with some data already populated from SAP ERP HCM. This is accessed by selecting PROFILE at the top of the page. When entering their profile, users are presented with their overview, which displays their basic profile data, such as name and position, and their updates. They can also post updates, record videos, and upload files here, as well as add a variety of other types of content. Additionally, they can check the individuals they follow and the individuals that follow them. Figure 13.2 shows the PROFILE overview of CARLA GRANT.

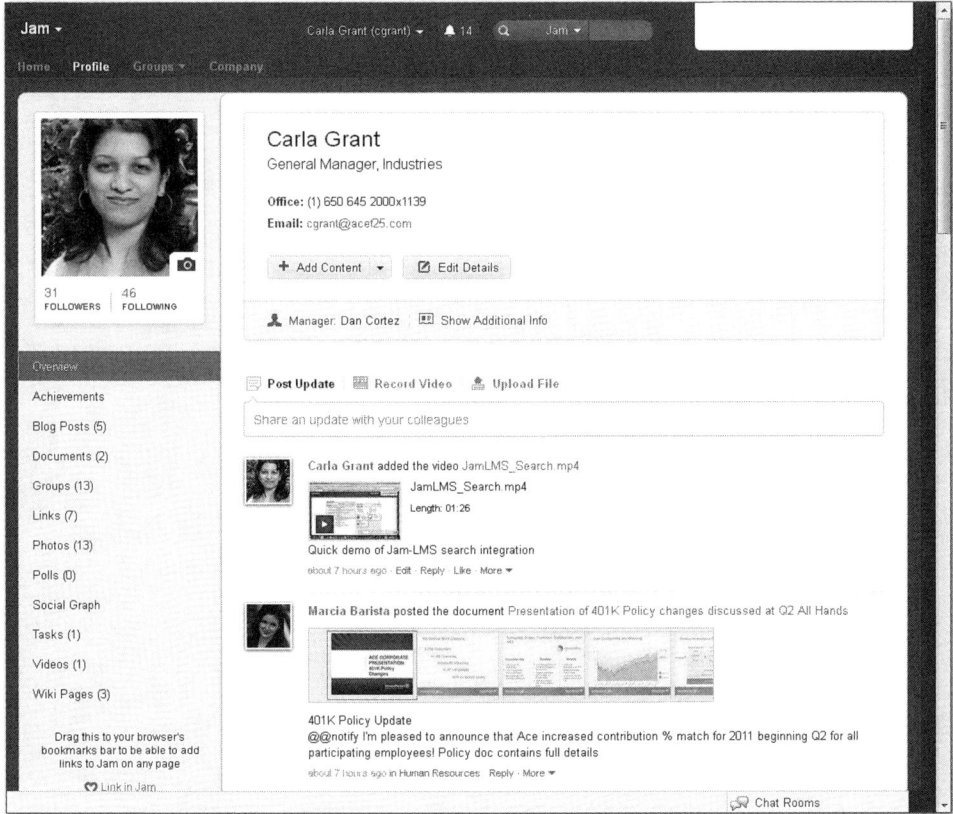

Figure 13.2 Profile Page

The left menu bar gives users access to the following content and details:

- OVERVIEW
- ACHIEVEMENTS
- BLOG POSTS
- DOCUMENTS
- GROUPS
- LINKS
- PHOTOS
- POLLS
- SOCIAL GRAPH
- TASKS
- VIDEOS
- WIKI PAGES

By selecting COMPANY at the top of the page users can access the COMPANY profile page, which contains all of the public feeds from the company, as well as options to see the same content for the entire company in the user's PROFILE page. In addition, the following content and features can be accessed for the company:

- ALUMNI
  Displays all company alumni.
- CHAT ROOMS
  Provides a platform for employees to discuss topics.
- COMPANY WIKI PAGE
  Acts as a company intranet.
- DASHBOARD
  Shows the most followed and most active individuals in the company, as well as how much of the preset (50GB) storage has been used.
- DIRECTORY
  Provides search functionality for company employees.
- EMPLOYEE OF THE MONTH
  Allows employees to vote for the employee of the month.
- LOCATIONS
  Displays the company locations.

▶ TAGS
Allows tagged content to be searched by tags.

▶ TOP CONVERSATIONS
Shows the conversations with the most comments.

13.2.2 Feeds, Comments, and Notifications

Every user, group, and company page has a *feed*. The feed shows actions such as updates (with comments and likes), upload of documents, and replies to questions. Each action in the feed can be commented on, liked, or bookmarked. Administrators also have the ability to delete actions.

At the top of the screen, the number of notifications of new actions or content or actions is displayed. Selecting this will display the most recent notifications.

Figure 13.3 shows the COMPANY NEWS FEED. Here you can also see the notifications icon at the top of the screen.

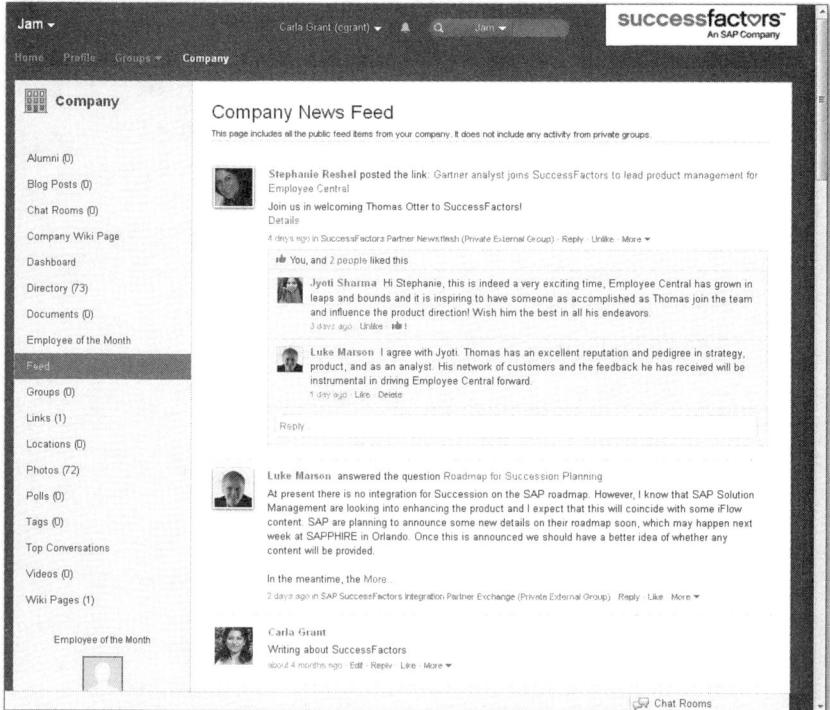

Figure 13.3 Company News Feed Page

13.2.3 Groups

With SAP Jam, users can create, manage, and join internal and external groups. Groups can be created for a variety of topics and purposes and allow individuals to participate in discussions and share and consume content. This forms the backbone of collective collaboration and creates a permanent history of conversations and documents that can be reused in future business scenarios, such as employee onboarding or sales cycles.

Users can access the groups they are members of by selecting GROUPS at the top of the page and selecting either the group from the list or selecting the menu option VIEW ALL GROUPS. All groups will be displayed, and users can view or leave any groups. By selecting a group, users are taken directly to that group. Depending on the group settings, they will either be taken to the ABOUT page or the FEED page. Figure 13.4 shows the SALES LEADS group, as an example.

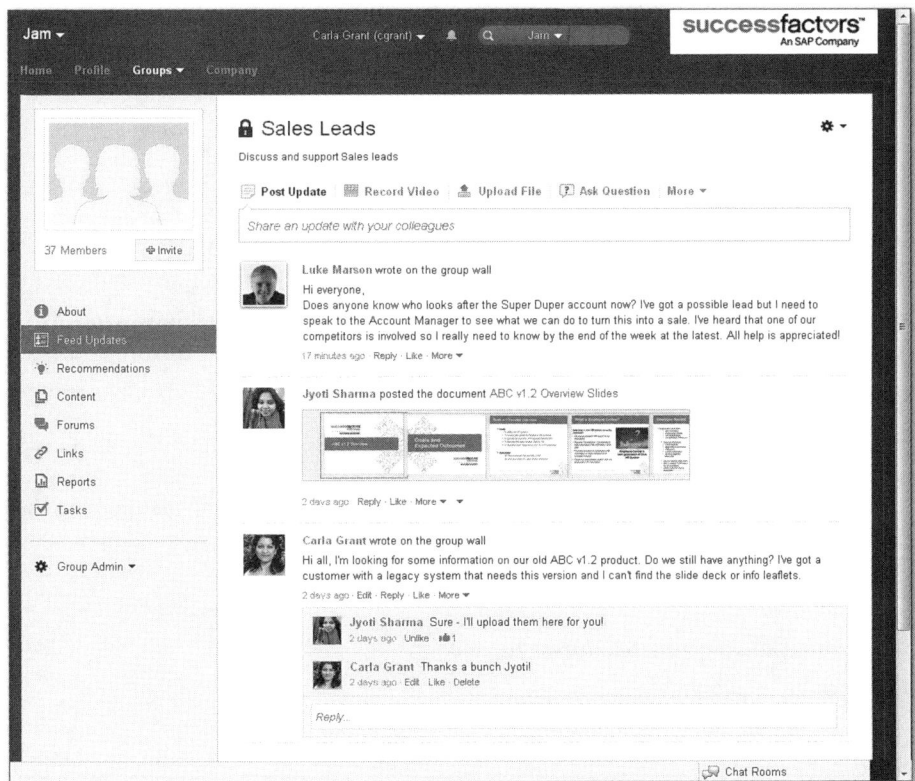

Figure 13.4 The Sales Leads Group

Within groups, there is a lot of the same functionality available in other feeds and profiles, such as posting updates and uploading documents. For example, in groups, users can share links, ask a question, add an idea, start a discussion in the forum, record a video, and add tasks. Members can also get recommendations of the most popular content in the group, as well as stop following a group, change the regularity of their email notifications, invite members (depending on group settings), and leave the group. Within the CONTENT page of a group, members can also create blogs, wiki pages, polls, pro/con tables, and rankings. Administrators can also edit the ABOUT page and download CSV reports of various metrics about activity, consumption, and contributions.

Users can create groups by selecting GROUPS at the top of the page and selecting the menu option CREATE A GROUP. As shown in Figure 13.5, the group creator can define the NAME, DESCRIPTION, GROUP TYPE (PUBLIC INTERNAL, PRIVATE INTERNAL, or PRIVATE EXTERNAL), STATUS (whether to activate the group now or later), and INVITE POLICY (whether all group members or just administrators can invite other individuals to join the group). Additionally, the group creator can configure optional features in the SETUP and PARTICIPATION tabs. In the SETUP tab, the creator can defined features such as providing a welcome announcement on the first visit to the group, using a group photo, setting the ABOUT page as the first page instead of the FEED page, and setting users to be automatically subscribed to notifications.

In the PARTICIPATION tab, the creator can set the allowed participation level for members, the upload policy (all members or just administrators) and whether a moderation policy should apply (the moderation policy applies to documents, photos, videos, wikis, and blogs). The allowed participation has three different levels:

- INFO (READ ONLY)
  Members can only view and download content and discussions; polls, and tasks are disabled.
- EXPERT (LIMITED PARTICIPATION)
  Members edit, post updates, comment, like, and view content.
- FULL PARTICIPATION
  All members have full read and write access.

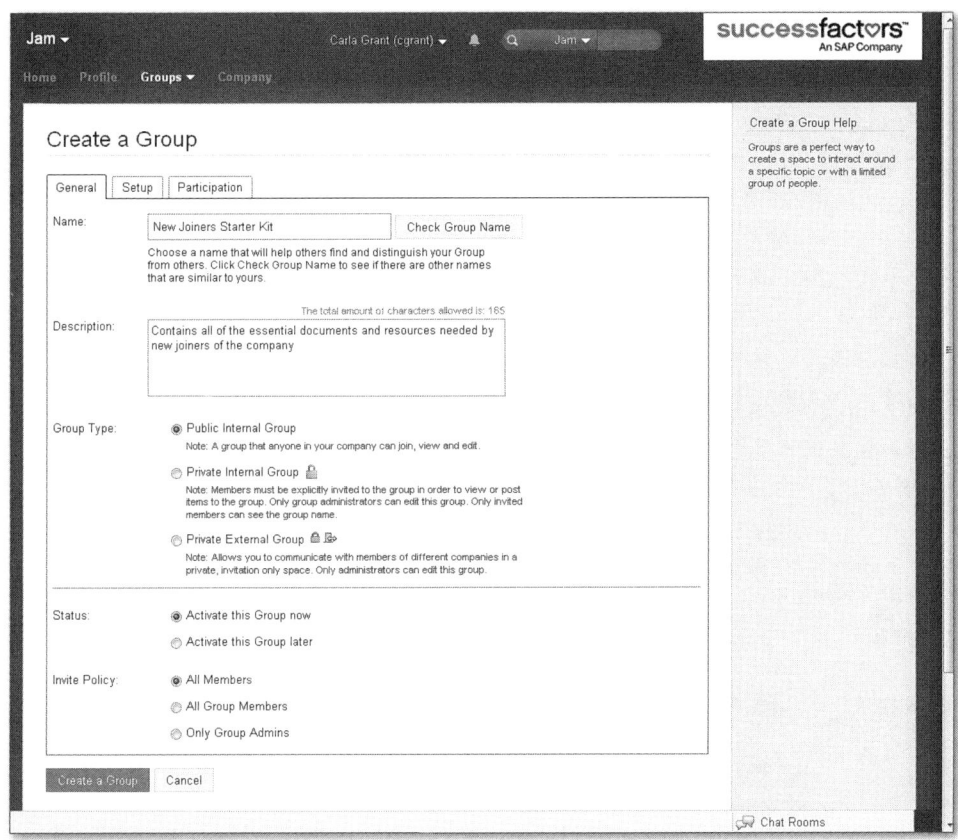

Figure 13.5 Create a Group Page

Groups with auto-membership—called *auto groups*—can be created by administrators in *Jam Admin* (see Section 13.3 for more details on Jam Admin). Auto groups are created using almost the same process as standard groups, except that membership can be set to be automatic. There is a fourth tab called MEMBERSHIP that is grayed out unless automatic membership is enabled. Within this tab, you can configure automatic membership for all employees or for employees with one or more attributes from the following list:

▶ COUNTRY
▶ DEPARTMENT
▶ DIVISION
▶ HAS DIRECT REPORT
▶ HIRE DATE

- Job Code
- Location

After you've selected the attributes, then a value can be selected for each attribute. For example, auto membership could be assigned for employees within the country of United States that have the Job Code of Sales Manager. The Hire Date attribute is defined either as within a specified number of days from today or within a date period. It is also possible to allow automatic membership for employees by specifying their email address.

13.2.4 Content Creation and Sharing

SAP Jam allows various types of content to be created, uploaded, edited, and shared, including photos, videos, documents (such as Word or PowerPoint documents), and blogs. Creating content is simple and intuitive, and uploading content is as easy as opening a file in any application. For example, creating blog posts features a rich text editor (see Figure 13.6), while videos can be recorded using a screen capture of a webcam.

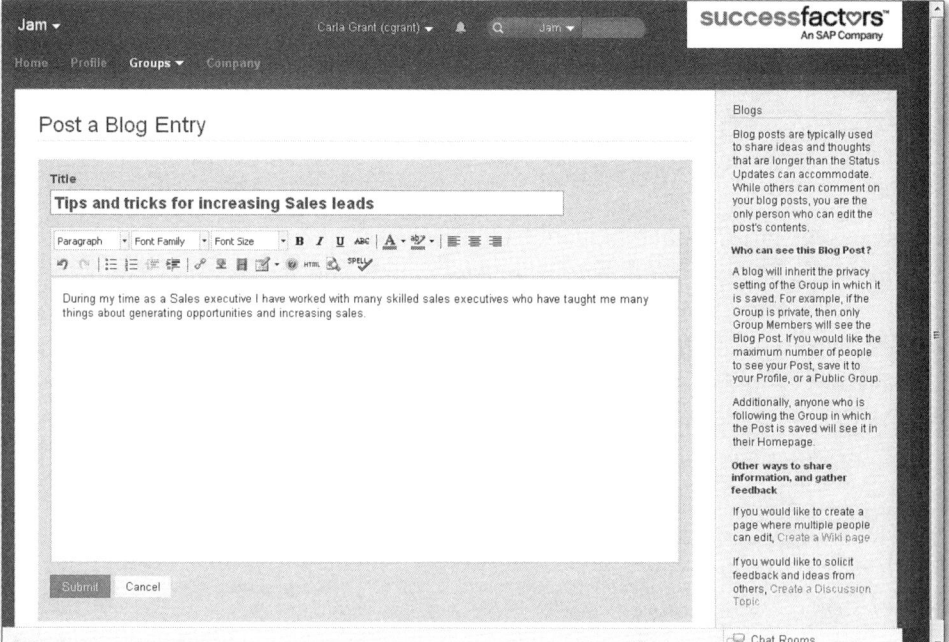

Figure 13.6 Creating a Blog

13.2.5 Gamification

SAP Jam can leverage external gamification platforms to provide a full range of gamification features, such as badges, challenges, missions, and leader boards. These can then be viewed on an individual's PROFILE page, as shown in Figure 13.7.

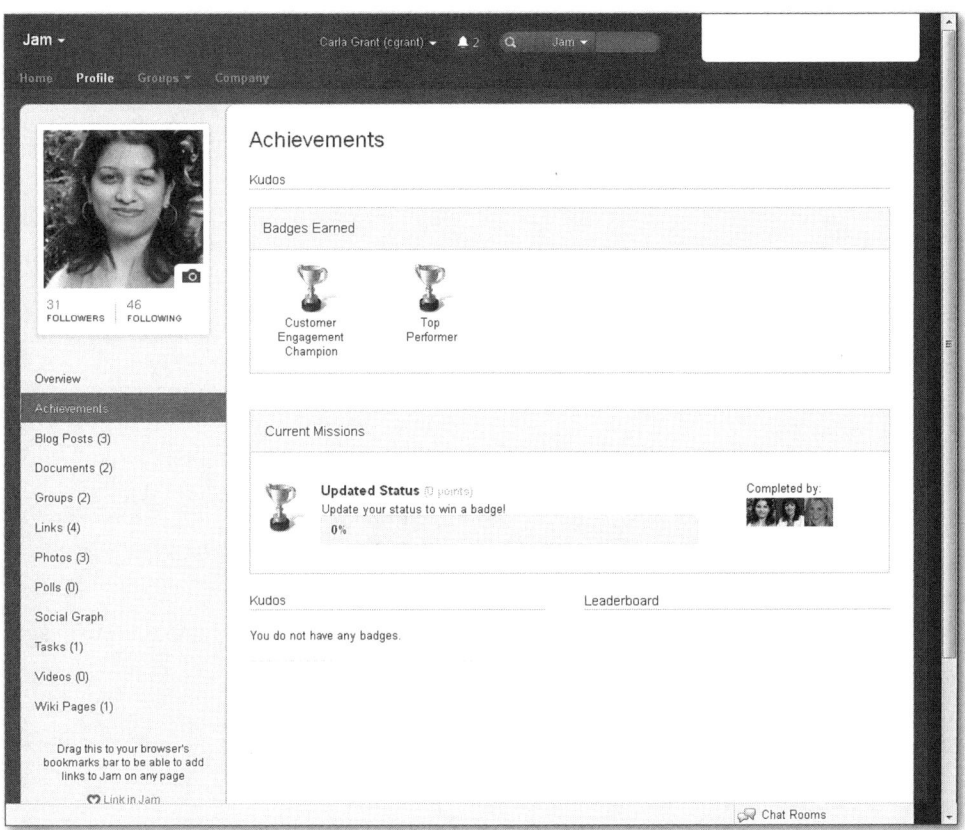

Figure 13.7 Gamification Features in SAP Jam

13.3 Administration

SAP Jam has an excellent set of administration features in the Jam Admin function. Jam Admin is accessed in the user menu by selecting JAM ADMIN. Here an administrator can configure a number of options, including the following (see Figure 13.8):

▶ AUTO GROUPS
Create groups with automatic membership (see Section 13.2.3).

▶ BRANDING
Configure branding features for SAP Jam such as the name, logo, and colors of the instance.

▶ COMPLIANCE
Monitor flagged content, define keywords, and view history.

▶ CONTENT ADMINISTRATION
Enable or disable administration of all content across the SAP Jam instance, set abuse flagging level, and audit users.

▶ FEATURES
Enable or disable many of the features in SAP Jam, such as file sharing, wikis, videos, gamification, and so on.

▶ REPORTS
Download CSV reports of various metrics about activity, consumption, and contributions.

▶ SECURITY
Enable or disable RSS, shared session service, or content creation via email, and set session length, IP restrictions, and valid domains for users.

▶ USERS
Manage users—including assignment of administrator rights—and review usage.

▶ OAUTH CLIENTS
Configure OAuth clients.

▶ SAML TRUSTED IDPS
View and register SAML trusted identity providers.

▶ EXTRANET MANAGEMENT
Manage external access and users for external groups.

A number of the pages include a right HELP sidebar that provides help, tips, and definitions for the administration options.

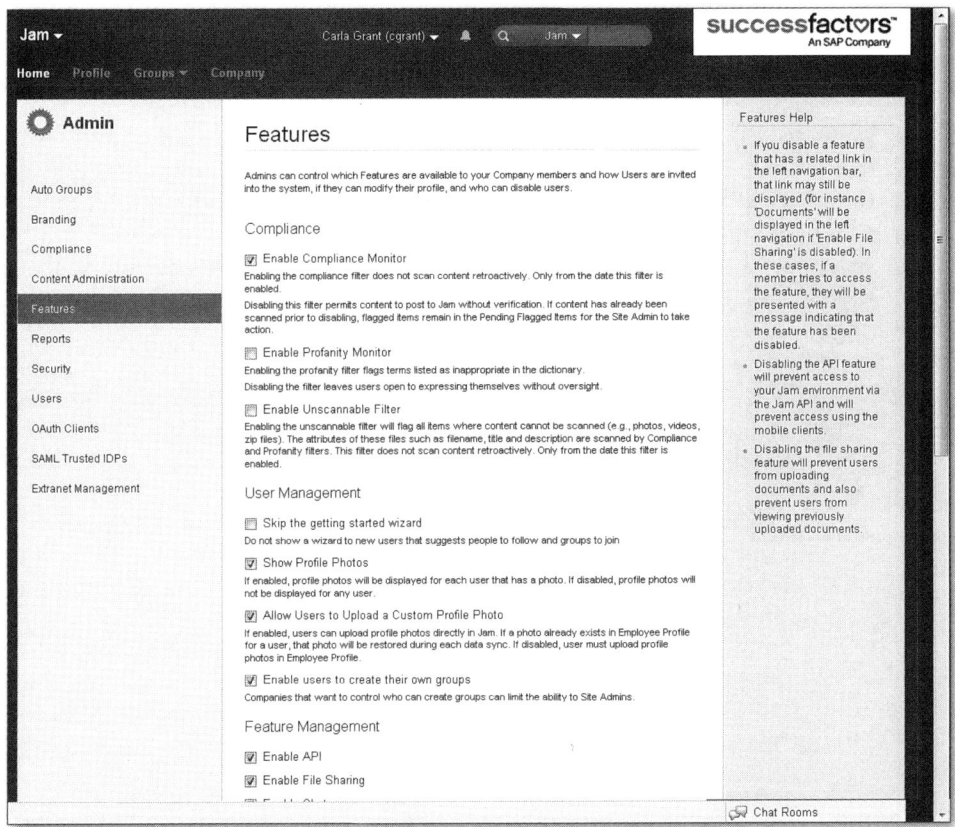

Figure 13.8 Features Page of Jam Admin

13.4 Integration

SAP Jam is integrated within the SuccessFactors BizX suite and can be accessed from the dropdown menu in the same way that other solutions such as SuccessFactors Recruiting Execution and Succession & Development can be accessed, as well as being integrated into SuccessFactors BizX Mobile. It is also integrated with solutions such as Learning so that social learning discussions and activities can take place. SAP Jam leverages employee data such as name, email address, and organizational data (e.g., job code, department, location, etc.).

SAP Jam integrates with SAP ERP HCM for this employee and organizational data, and authentication with Single Sign-On (SSO) is also possible. It also natively integrates with the rest of the SAP Business Suite, SAP Customer Relationship Management (SAP CRM) on-premise, SAP Cloud apps and third-party applications. For more information on integration, refer to Chapter 3.

13.5 Summary

SAP Jam is a powerful tool for increasing collaboration and knowledge sharing within organizations. In this chapter, you've seen the business processes that SAP Jam supports and functionality that the solution provides.

By using SAP Jam, organizations can reduce onboarding time and costs, increase sales, enhance learning opportunities, and produce a more knowledgeable and efficient workforce. Leveraging groups and discussions can be a foundation for targeting focused productivity and giving individuals easy access to tools that can make their everyday work easier and more enjoyable.

In the next chapter, we'll take a deep dive into SuccessFactors Workforce Analytics and how this provides real-time analytical insight and the foundation for SuccessFactors Workforce Planning.

There is a growing trend for organizations to understand the constantly changing dynamics of their human capital and its impact on business outcomes. SuccessFactors Workforce Analytics provides insight into workforce issues, risks and opportunities, and links HR initiatives to organizational strategy through standardized HR metrics, key performance indicators, and analytic investigations.

14 Workforce Analytics

Compared to its predecessors and contemporaries, SuccessFactors Workforce Analytics (hereafter WFA) is on the cutting edge of the HR transformation, making it a key differentiator in the SuccessFactors product suite. By empowering companies to analyze the myriad of data they are already collecting about their people and processes, organizations can obtain a more holistic picture of their workforce, as well as identify areas of opportunity to drive actions resulting in either cost-savings or increased revenue.

The SuccessFactors WFA solution clears the hurdles commonly experienced in launching and sustaining a WFA program by guiding you in what to measure and how to verify the accuracy and validity of your data, and providing methods for utilizing the analysis, visualizing results, and recommending actions. The process of telling stories with data enables HR to transform the decision-making process from being based on gut feelings to data-driven insights. Additionally, companies that utilize WFA can leverage a standardized metrics catalog to compare individual results against various categories of benchmarks, such as industry, geographic region, organization size, or revenue.

In this chapter, we'll provide you with an understanding of the multitude of analytic capabilities delivered by SuccessFactors WFA, including standardized metrics (Section 14.1), the benchmarking program (Section 14.2), and reporting functionality and advanced analytical tools (Section 14.3). The modular design is followed by a detailed description of the metrics methodology, associated metrics packs, and common WFA data sources. The chapter concludes with the Headlines functionality (Section 14.4), which is fully integrated into the BizX suite and with SuccessFactors BizX Mobile.

14.1 The Foundation of Workforce Analytics

In this section, we'll examine the foundation of the WFA application. The modular approach that was discussed in Chapter 5 extends into the WFA solution and facilitates the sourcing of data and calculation of measure values by significantly reducing both the time to implement and the cost of providing a comprehensive reporting and analytics solution. All WFA implementations begin with the base Metrics Pack, known as Core Workforce & Mobility, which is used as a foundation to extend into more specific functional areas (e.g., Learning, Performance, Recruiting Execution, etc.) through additional *Metrics Packs*.

The standards for each Metrics Pack have been defined by the legacy Infohrm group, which was acquired by SuccessFactors in 2010. Based on more than 30 years of consulting experience in the field of Workforce Analytics, Infohrm (and now SuccessFactors) is an influential global presence in the space. By working with hundreds of organizations across industries around the globe, Infohrm standardized an implementation and ongoing consultative process designed to ensure successful client experiences. This proven methodology was quickly adopted by SuccessFactors to maintain global leadership in the WFA field.

14.1.1 Implementing Core Workforce & Mobility

The first phase of any WFA implementation begins with the Core Workforce & Mobility Metrics Pack, which takes between three and four months to complete. The base Metrics Pack is sourced from your Human Resource Information System (HRIS) and consists of more than 150 metrics for headcount, staffing rates, terminations, movements, and hires. In addition, the core implementation typically includes at least 20 analysis options (also referred to as dimensions, analysis options, or dimension hierarchies), which are used to slice and dice your core workforce and mobility metrics. Examples include gender, diversity, job level, pay band, and so on. The final component of the core implementation includes an organizational structure, which typically represents the roll-up of business units (by cost center, supervisor, location, etc.). We will delve deeper into both analysis options and organizational structures at the end of this section.

Let's begin by deconstructing the base Metrics Pack, which forms the foundation of WFA. The Core Workforce & Mobility Metrics Pack supports the necessary data items required to generate measures and reporting structures for a comprehensive HR reporting solution.

The standard metrics included in the Core Workforce & Mobility Metrics Pack are bucketed into operational measure categories and associated subcategories.

> **Note**
>
> The Core Workforce & Mobility Metrics Pack primarily consists of measures in the Workforce Profile and Workforce Mobility categories, and includes a limited number of measures in the Workforce Productivity, Workforce Compensation & Benefits, and Staffing Function categories. If clients choose to purchase additional Metrics Packs, such as the Payroll & Benefits Metrics Pack or Financial Metrics Pack, these categories will become more comprehensive.

- **Workforce Profile**
  Describe and compare an organization's workforce using a range of organizational and personal characteristics, such as organizational structure, age, employment status, occupational group, tenure, gender, and diversity groupings. These measures provide insight into workforce demographics and their implications on workforce skill and experience levels.

- **Workforce Productivity**
  Provide macro indicators that are helpful in the first step of the diagnostic process. This section combines a range of input and output/outcome measures that can be considered together in an examination of organizational effectiveness. The Termination Value per Termination metric is included in the subcategory called Workforce Costs.

- **Workforce Mobility**
  Monitor and compare the flow of the workforce into, and out of the organization. These include measures of staff recruitment, transfer/promotion, and separations. Subcategories include Recruitment, Movement, and Termination.

- **Workforce Compensation and Benefits**
  Monitor and compare the remuneration to reward to motivate employees. For example, the Average Annual Salary metric is included in the subcategory called Compensation.

- **Staffing Function**
  Provide an overview of the effectiveness of the staffing function from a turnover standpoint. For example, the Quick Quits metric Turnover Rate <30/90 Days is included in the subcategory called Staffing Effectiveness.

> **Note**
>
> The full-time equivalent (FTE), external hires, termination, and retirement measures included within the Core Workforce & Mobility Metrics Pack are all requirements for the SuccessFactors Workforce Planning (WFP) solution. The WFP solution allows organizations to create forecasts using either headcount or FTE metrics, and leverages the underlying analytics engine to include projected retirements, terminations, and hires into the forecast. We will study WFP in more detail in Chapter 15.

14.1.2 Metrics Packs

Despite the availability of systems that are continuously collecting workforce data, deriving insights that can be used to make informed business decisions remains a challenge. The following are some of the common reasons hindering the decision-making process; if any of these resonate with you, consider evaluating the WFA product for your organization:

- **Data accessibility**
  IT alone has access to the required data, and HR is still waiting for key data that will be used to facilitate discussions with the business.

- **Incomplete view**
  Business intelligence (BI) tools often lack a holistic view of the workforce, meaning that total workforce issues are not addressed. BI tools are built for finance and IT departments, and they are typically not targeted at analyzing employee issues.

- **Analytical capability**
  HR lacks analytical skills and is not well equipped to interpret data and generate compelling stories.

- **Data quality**
  The business questions the validity and credibility of data provided by HR, due in part to the lack of standardization around HR metrics.

SuccessFactors WFA has been designed to address each of these challenges, and Metrics Packs play a key role in minimizing the effects of these issues. Metrics Packs can be defined as standardized sets of metrics sourced from your HR or business systems, such as SAP ERP HCM, Employee Central, Recruiting Execution, Performance Management, Finance, Sales, and so on. In effect, each functional area has an associated Metrics Pack, and includes standards for sourcing the data, formulas used to calculate metrics, and benchmarks.

The following Metrics Packs are available for you to analyze in conjunction with your core workforce data:

- Core Workforce & Mobility/Workforce Planning
- Absence Management
- Compensation Planning
- Payroll and Benefits
- Employee Relations
- Finance Management
- Health and Safety
- HR Delivery
- Leave Accrual
- Performance Management
- Recruitment
- Succession Management
- Survey
- Talent Flow Analytics
- Learning and Development
- Custom Data Source (e.g., custom Metrics Pack sourced from a system not listed here)

After the Core Workforce & Mobility Metrics Pack is implemented, you can begin to map in additional Metrics Packs from other data sources (e.g., Recruiting Execution, Learning, Finance, etc.). Note that you can use virtually any data source, including homegrown systems and Excel worksheets, as the source of data for any Metrics Pack. The preferred, and most common, method is to extract raw data from a source system because this mitigates the risk of importing incorrect data often held in Excel or other similar data files. Depending on the complexity of the Metrics Pack, the typical length of time to implement ranges between three and twelve weeks. By integrating data from your core HRIS with other systems, you can yield more powerful insights and analyses than a singular view would allow.

For example, the integration of learning data with sales data can allow you to analyze the effect of specific training courses on sales output. Essentially acting as a data warehouse, WFA provides you with a tool to move beyond operational reporting and counting of things (e.g., how many employees took a specific training course) to become a more strategic partner to the business (e.g., sales went up 30% for employees who took the training course).

To provide another example, the Absence Management Metrics Pack helps derive absence measures that can be used to gain insights into an organization's productivity and the profitability per employee. For example, the Absence Management Metrics Pack includes the following metrics:

- Unscheduled Absence Rate
- Total Cost of Sick Leave per FTE
- Absence Duration Days per FTE

When you cross these metrics with your core workforce data, you can begin to answer questions like the following:

- What percentage of our absence days is unscheduled versus scheduled?
- How do our sick leave occurrences differ according to employee generations (Baby Boomers, Gen X, etc.)?
- What is the remuneration value of unscheduled absence per employee? How does it vary across lines of business or geographies?

In summary, each Metrics Pack is based on a highly structured framework that does the following:

- Defines the SuccessFactors standard set of core metrics for each respective functional area (e.g., Core HRIS, Learning & Development, Recruiting Execution, Sales, etc.)
- Defines a standard set of dimensions/hierarchies to support further analysis of results
- Maps requirements to a source set of base data items
- Includes template extract programs and scripts for common and large enterprise HRISs/HRMSs
- Includes common business logic that can be customized for customer-specific requirements

- Includes benchmarks
- Includes logical groupings within categories and subcategories to minimize effort searching for specific metrics

We have examined what constitutes a Metrics Pack and how metrics enable organizations to analyze their workforce issues and organization-wide trends. While the Metrics Packs are based on standardized formulas that represent the most frequently analyzed metrics by function, it is important to note that clients have the ability to add custom metrics or calculations at any time. In the next section, we will cover how the Metrics Packs are used as building blocks to implement the *Metric Methodology*.

14.1.3 Metric Methodology

Now that we've built the case for WFA and defined Metrics Packs, let's take a deeper look at the metric methodology. If we were to ask you what the starting point is for workforce analytics, of course, the answer would be data. However, the tricky part is advancing from mere data points to full-fledged analytics.

The metric methodology is the same for all Metrics Packs, so we'll use the Core Workforce & Mobility Metrics Pack to illustrate the process. The first step is to define the metrics sourcing logic, which are the data fields sourced from the HRIS (e.g., SAP ERP HCM or Employee Central). Data from the core HRIS is mapped to standardized formulas by the SuccessFactors data transformation engine to generate what are called *base input measures* (e.g., FTE) and *dimension hierarchies* (e.g., gender). These base input measures are filtered through the dimension hierarchies to generate a rich set of *derived input measures* (e.g., # of FTE – Female).

Lastly, the derived input measures are combined in formulas to generate *result measures* (e.g., male to female staffing ratio) commonly used in analysis and reporting, and are displayed in the form of rates, ratios, percentages, averages, and so on. In other words, the derived input measures and the base input measures are the numerators and denominators making up each rate or ratio, respectively. Figure 14.1 shows the metric methodology.

All measures (base input, derived input, or result) and dimension hierarchies represented by the dotted box are available to support a customer's reporting and analytics agenda.

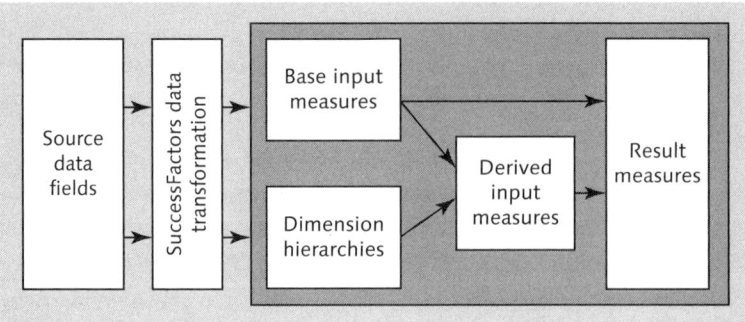

Figure 14.1 Metric Methodology

Now that we've examined how the metric methodology is structured and defined, we'll review the analysis options, organizational structures, and other tools for analyzing the data.

14.1.4 Analyzing Your Data

As data analysts, we often use the phrases "slicing and dicing" or "drilling through the data" to describe the process of dissecting the total organizational result to identify patterns, trends, and insights. Often, this can be a challenging task that requires a high level of manual effort due to the fact that data is usually only available in an aggregate form. WFA includes numerous analysis options for easy slicing and dicing of data results, all located within the ANALYZE BY tab in the FILTERS pane as shown in Figure 14.2. This list is often referred to as the Dimensions list, and it's organized by alphabetical order.

In effect, analysis by dimensions allows for greater insight into the characteristics or performance of a metric by looking at results across different subgroups, which is often referred to as "segmenting the workforce." By segmenting the workforce, we can break down the organizational result and start to see which employee populations or areas of the organization are driving the total result for the organization.

Let's take a look at the example in Figure 14.3, which shows Voluntary Termination Rates by Tenure. In this example, we can see that, at nearly 40%, the 1-<2 YEAR tenure band has considerably higher voluntary turnover than other tenure groups. This may indicate a low tenure turnover problem, which could warrant further investigation, and ultimately, targeted interventions.

The Foundation of Workforce Analytics | **14.1**

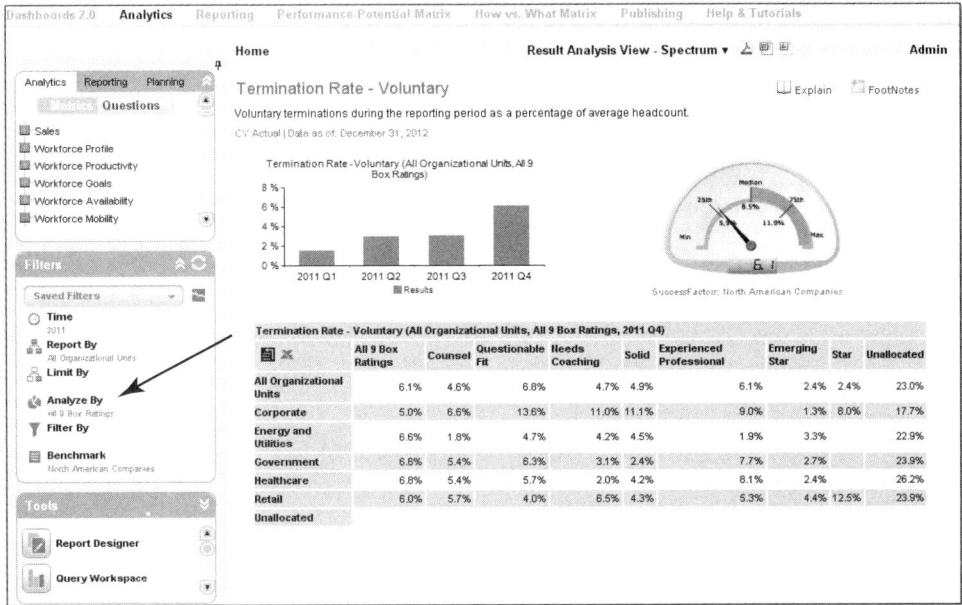

Figure 14.2 Analyze By

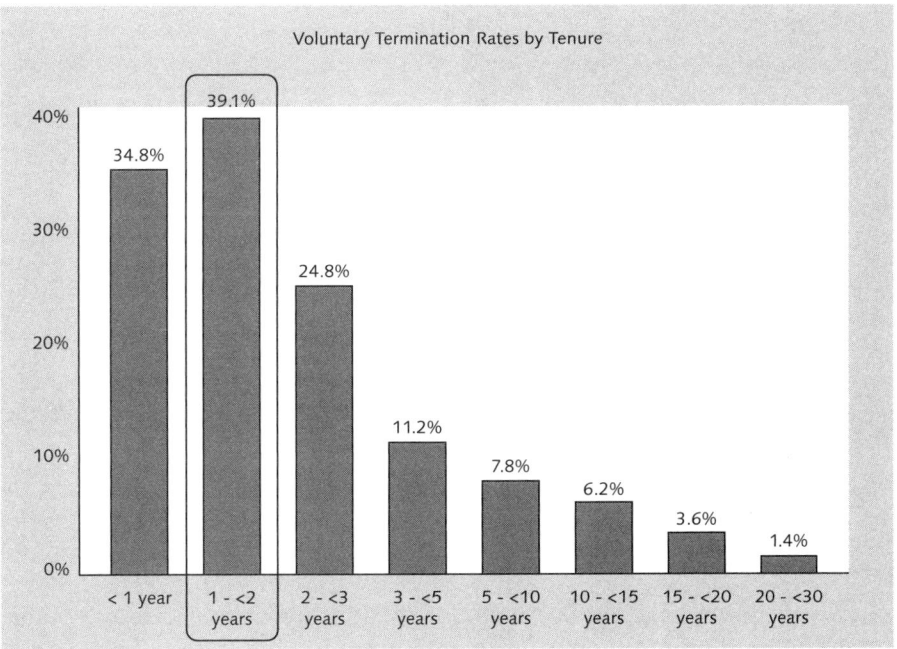

Figure 14.3 Voluntary Termination Rates by Tenure

395

Organizational Structures

The next logical step in the analytics process is to determine where in the organization the low tenure turnover problem is occurring. To do this, we need to drill through the organizational structure to identify locations where voluntary turnover rates are highest for the 1-<2 Year tenure band. Organizational structures represent the hierarchical relationship of business units, cost centers, reporting relationships, or geographic locations. The most common organizational structure is the cost center structure, or business unit roll-up.

In Figure 14.4, we can clearly see that the HEALTHCARE business unit has significantly higher low tenure voluntary turnover rates (78%) than the rest of the organization.

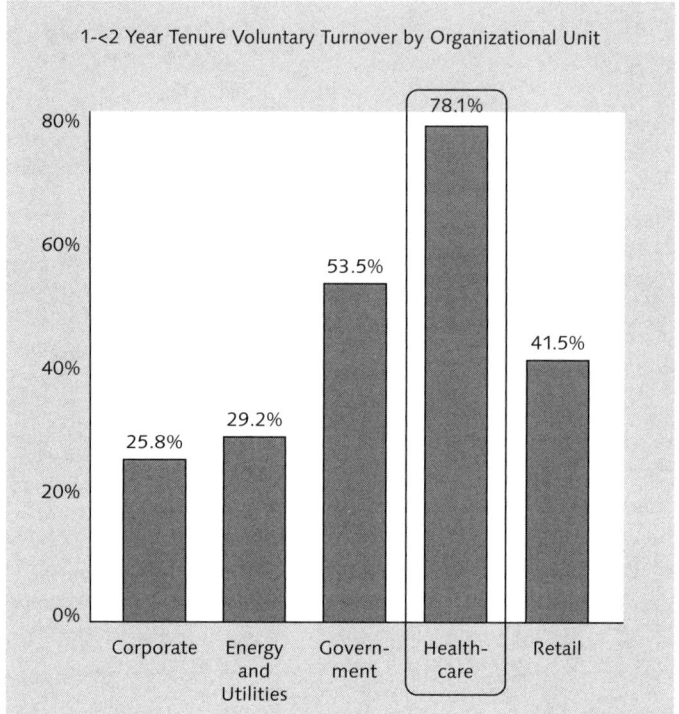

Figure 14.4   1-<2 Year Tenure Voluntary Turnover by Organizational Unit

Analysis Options

Now that we've identified the business unit with a low tenure turnover issue, we can continue to slice and dice our results to understand which populations within the Healthcare business unit are of particular concern. This can be done by applying additional analysis options, such as job family, gender, ethnic group, age group, and so on.

In Figure 14.5, we've analyzed low tenure voluntary turnover within the Healthcare business unit by gender, and you can see that almost all females (almost 84%) have left within the first two years of employment.

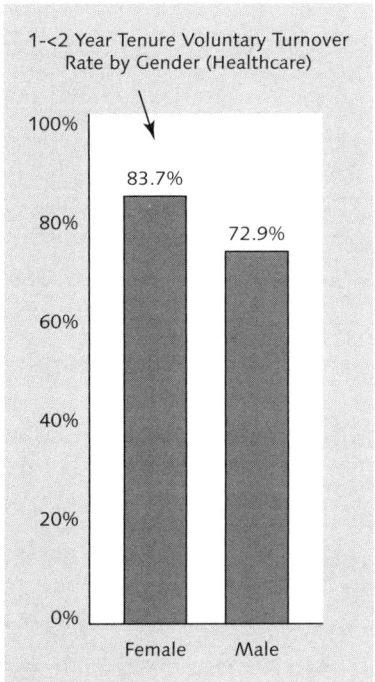

Figure 14.5 Low Tenure Voluntary Turnover by Gender (Healthcare)

Filtering

Sometimes it can be useful to apply a second level of analysis when trying to pinpoint the hot spot in your data, and this is done by using the FILTER BY option (also located in the Analysis pane and shown in Figure 14.2). This feature effectively allows you to go one level deeper into your analysis by limiting the data to one specific node of an ANALYSIS OPTION. For example, we've already sliced the 1-<2 year tenure voluntary turnover in the Healthcare business unit by gender. However, perhaps we want to look at only employees who left that were 20-29 years old. By filtering by the 20-29 year old age group, we can see in Figure 14.6

that 70.2% of employees who left the HEALTHCARE business unit were 20-29 year old females with 1-<2 years tenure.

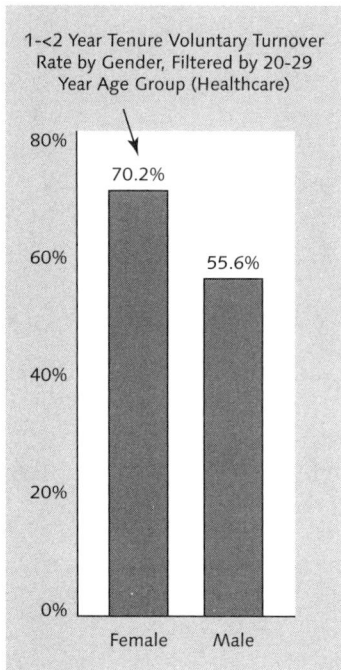

Figure 14.6 Low Tenure Voluntary Turnover by Gender Filtered by 20-29 Age Group (Healthcare)

Now that we've identified a low tenure turnover issue in the Healthcare business unit for females in the 20-29 year old age group, we may want to view the employee level details that make up this population.

Drill to Detail

The Drill to Detail functionality is embedded within the WFA application and allows users to click on any hyperlinked result (e.g., percentage or raw count). By doing so, the tool generates the details of the individual records represented in the result in a transactional list-based view. Customers can limit what is returned in the Drill to Detail view, but in theory, can choose to show any of the fields that are included in the data file that is sent as part of the monthly data refresh cycle. Figure 14.7 shows the hyperlinked result (70.2%) that we can click on to activate the Drill to Detail functionality.

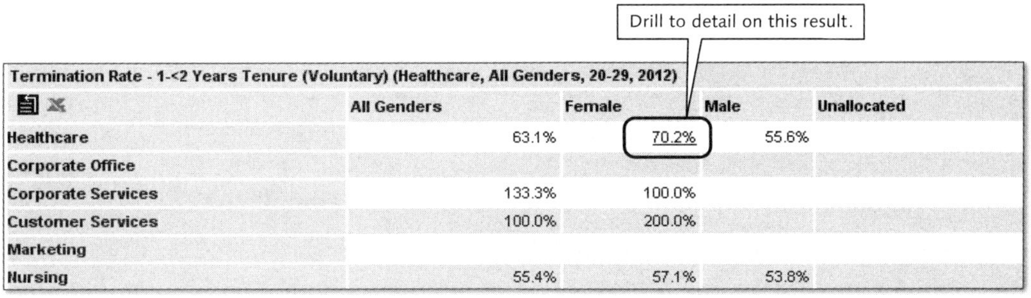

Figure 14.7 Hyperlinked Result for Drill to Detail

If you click on the hyperlink, the system will generate a transactional list of the specific employees that make up the result, as shown in Figure 14.8. Also, note that clicking on the EXCEL icon in the upper-left corner of the table allows a user to export the table for further analysis or distribution. One tip is that if you're accessing WFA through Single Sign-On (SSO), and your organization also utilizes SuccessFactors Employee Profile, you can click on the boxed person icon next to any drill-to-detail record to see that individual's profile.

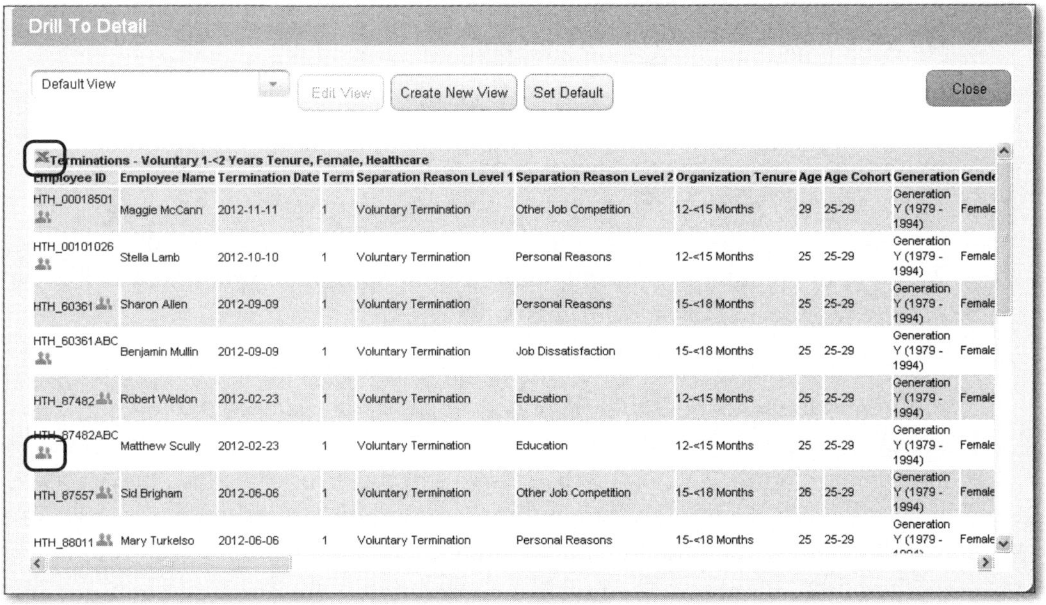

Figure 14.8 Drill to Detail Result

In summary, Drill to Detail enables users to verify which employees are included within a particular result. This customer-driven enhancement is a tool for validating the quality of the data to gain credibility with the business.

In the next section, we'll discuss the Benchmarking program in depth.

14.2 The Benchmarking Program

External benchmarks are extremely useful for organizations to utilize as a reference point to gauge performance against competitors. Additionally, you can leverage benchmarks as an input in the target-setting process or to understand whether your organization is following or deviating from macroeconomic trends over time. Many clients find the Benchmarking program to be a key value-add from their SuccessFactors WFA investment.

In this section, we'll examine the Benchmarking program methodology, the categories and subcategories for viewing benchmarks, and how to access benchmarks in WFA.

14.2.1 Benchmarking Methodology

Every customer using SuccessFactors WFA contractually agrees to share their data for benchmarking purposes. Unlike other popular benchmarking programs (e.g., Saratoga or Watson Wyatt), SuccessFactors does not use a survey methodology to collect data for benchmarking purposes. Instead, SuccessFactors accesses clients' raw data to calculate the benchmarks using standard formulas and definitions. This ensures that all data is being viewed in an apples-to-apples comparison and increases the quality of the benchmark figures.

Another quality assurance check embedded in the Benchmarking program is the minimum sample size criteria. For a benchmark to be calculated, there must be a minimum of eight organizations providing the data elements necessary to generate a benchmark result. This rule also acts as a safeguard for organizational anonymity. Because benchmarks are always reported in aggregates, the minimum sample size also provides confidence that no single organization's individual results will be identifiable. The benchmarks are published once a year, usually during the first quarter after year-end data has become available.

Now we'll look at the various categories of benchmarks available for analysis purposes.

14.2.2 Benchmarking Categories

As the number of SuccessFactors WFA clients grows, so does the Benchmarking program's capability to provide benchmarks for more metrics in the metrics catalog. The total benchmark database is called the SuccessFactors North American Companies; for organizations based in North America, this would be your best bet for finding an acceptable sample size for the metrics you're interested in benchmarking.

However, sometimes it's helpful to look at specific slices of the database, such as by industry, organization size, or revenue. The Benchmarking program provides clients with seven main categories of benchmarks to choose from in addition to the total North American Companies results. Figure 14.9 shows the main categories available to clients for benchmarking purposes.

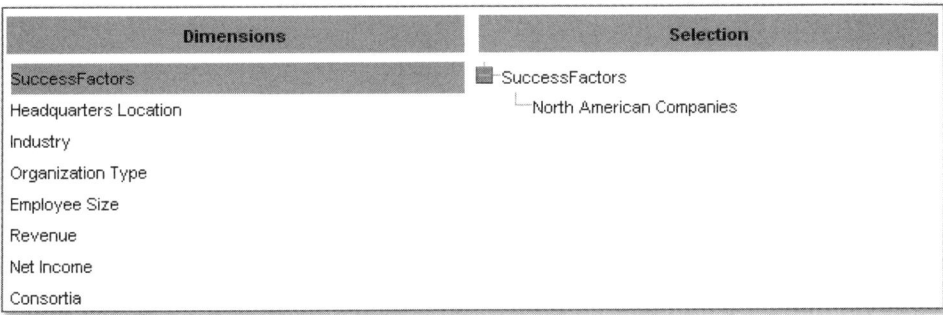

Figure 14.9 Benchmarking Categories

When you select one of the benchmark categories, a list of subcategories appears for you to choose from to further refine your selection. Note that as you restrict your selection, the sample size criteria may not be met, and therefore no benchmark result will be displayed.

Now, we'll look at how to navigate through the WFA application to apply benchmarks to specific metrics.

14.2.3 Applying Benchmarks

Benchmarks are embedded within the WFA technology and therefore cannot be turned "off" on your specific instance. There are a few different methods for accessing the benchmarks, the easiest of which is to navigate to a specific measure page where the benchmark result for that measure is displayed as a component of the standard page layout. For example, if you were interested in seeing the benchmark for voluntary termination rate, then you would see the standard page layout as depicted in Figure 14.10.

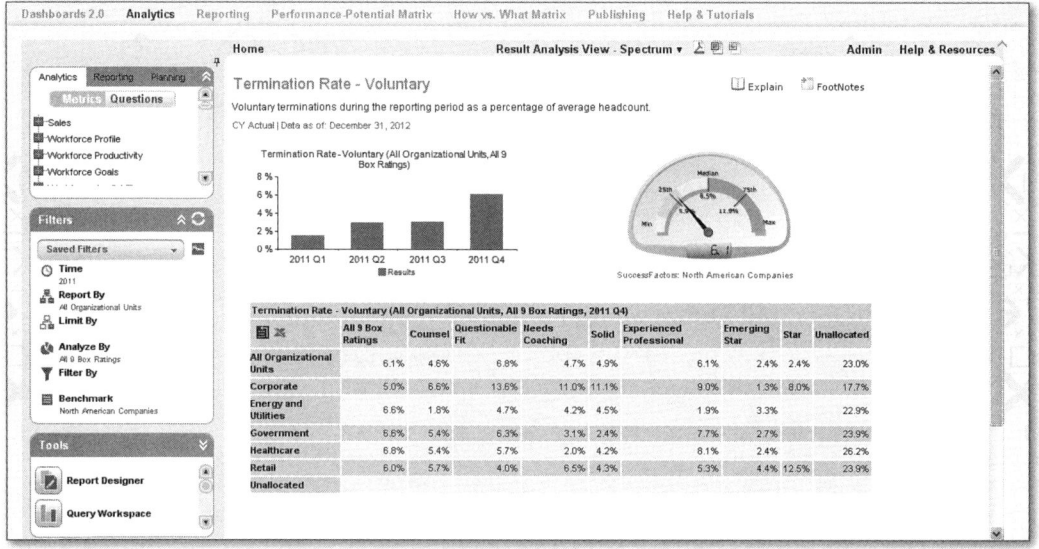

Figure 14.10 Benchmarks on a Measure Page

As you can see, each measure page shows a gauge image for the benchmark result, including breakdowns for the 25TH, 50TH, and 75TH percentiles. The title below the spectrum denotes the benchmark group you're viewing—in this case, the default SUCCESSFACTORS: NORTH AMERICAN COMPANIES. Please note that clients can choose to set their default benchmark group to any of the categories or subcategories available.

The benchmark spectrum also utilizes the stop-light methodology (e.g., red/yellow/green color-coding) to indicate where desirable and undesirable results fall within the ranges provided. Clients can view their organizations' results by either reading the digital result in the bottom of the gauge or by hovering on the needle.

If you wanted to see how your organization's result compares to a different benchmark group, you can easily make this selection in the FILTERS pane. Figure 14.11 illustrates how to make your benchmark selection by clicking on BENCHMARK.

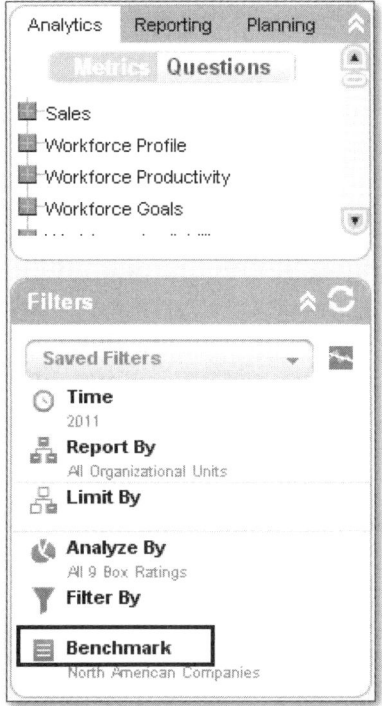

Figure 14.11 Changing the Benchmark Group in the Filters Pane

You can see that the current selection is NORTH AMERICAN COMPANIES, but let's say you want to view benchmarks for the Healthcare industry instead. After clicking on BENCHMARK, a new window will pop up that allows you to select the INDUSTRY category in the DIMENSION window, and then a list of subcategories appears in the SELECTION window. Figure 14.12 shows how to change the benchmark selection.

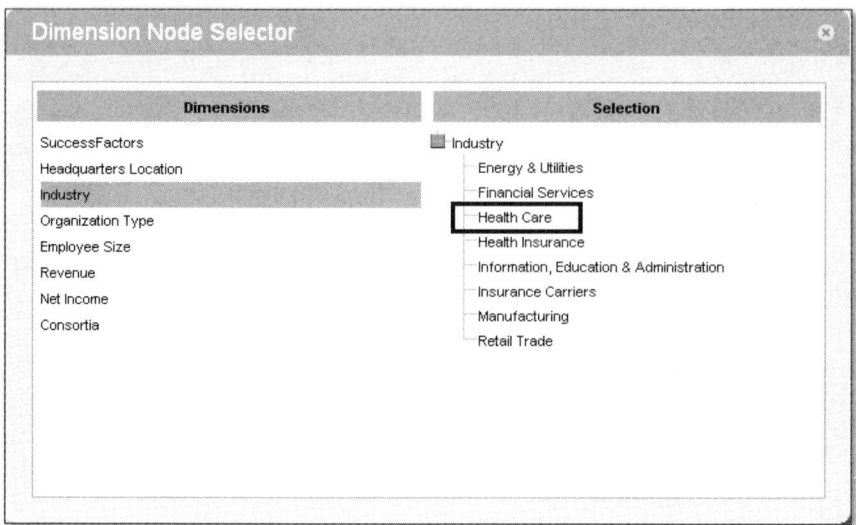

Figure 14.12 Applying Your Benchmark Group Selection

After you click on HEALTH CARE, the window closes, and the benchmark image, title, and percentile ranges change to reflect this selection, as displayed in Figure 14.13.

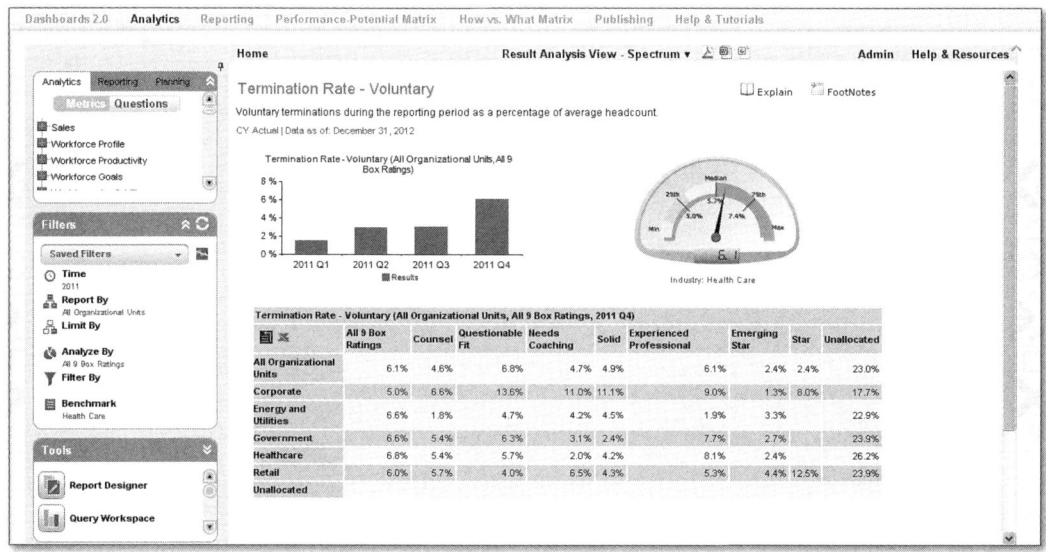

Figure 14.13 Health Care Benchmark Selection on a Measure Page

There are a few additional methods for viewing benchmarks in the WFA application, including the Benchmark View, Benchmark Scorecard, and Benchmark Chart. We'll review each of these in detail, beginning with the Benchmark View.

Benchmark View

Several *views* are available that allow users to change the measure page layout for any measure on the site. The VIEW dropdown is located at the top of any measure page and will include various options such as RESULT ANALYSIS VIEW (default), RESULT TREND VIEW, RESULT INPUT VIEW, and RESULT BENCHMARK VIEW. The view you're currently in is denoted by a * symbol. To switch a view, simply hover on the dropdown arrow, and a list of available views will appear. Note that the viewing options are different for result measure pages and input measure pages.

In Figure 14.14, we've selected the RESULT BENCHMARK VIEW in the dropdown list. In this particular view, users will be given additional breakdowns of the benchmark result, including the year-over-year benchmark trend and more granular slices of results by percentiles.

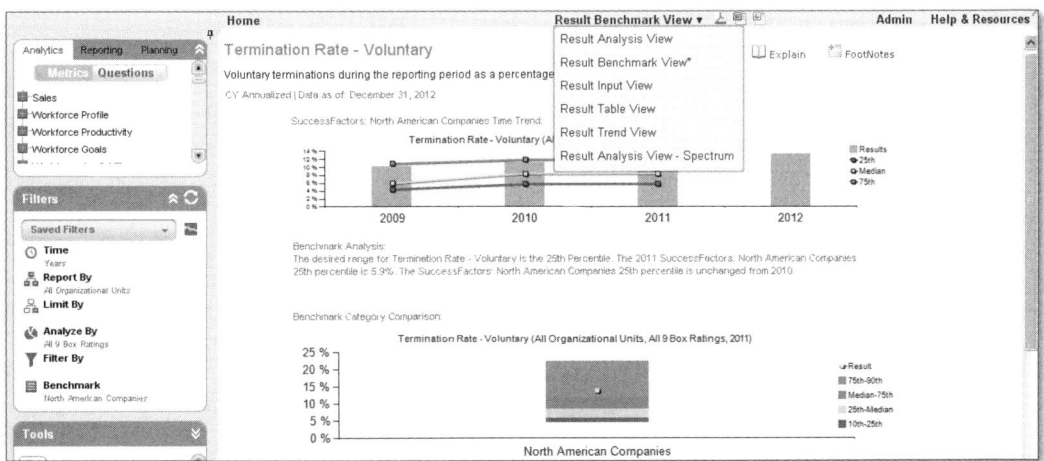

Figure 14.14 Result Benchmark View

Benchmark Chart

The Benchmark Chart is a component of the Benchmark View, as shown in Figure 14.14, and it can also be selected as a charting option in Report Designer. The Benchmark Chart differs from a regular chart in that it shows the benchmark result for the previous four years, provided there are benchmark results for that time period. This trend view allows users to see how the 25th, 50th, and 75th percentiles have changed from year to year, allowing clients to see where their organization's results fell within the percentiles for a specific year. Lastly, the Result Trend View can help organizations understand whether they have been following or deviating from the benchmark trend over the past four years.

Benchmark Scorecard

The final method for viewing benchmarks is the Benchmark Scorecard, which can be found on the REPORTING menu (see Figure 14.15) or in the Report Designer library.

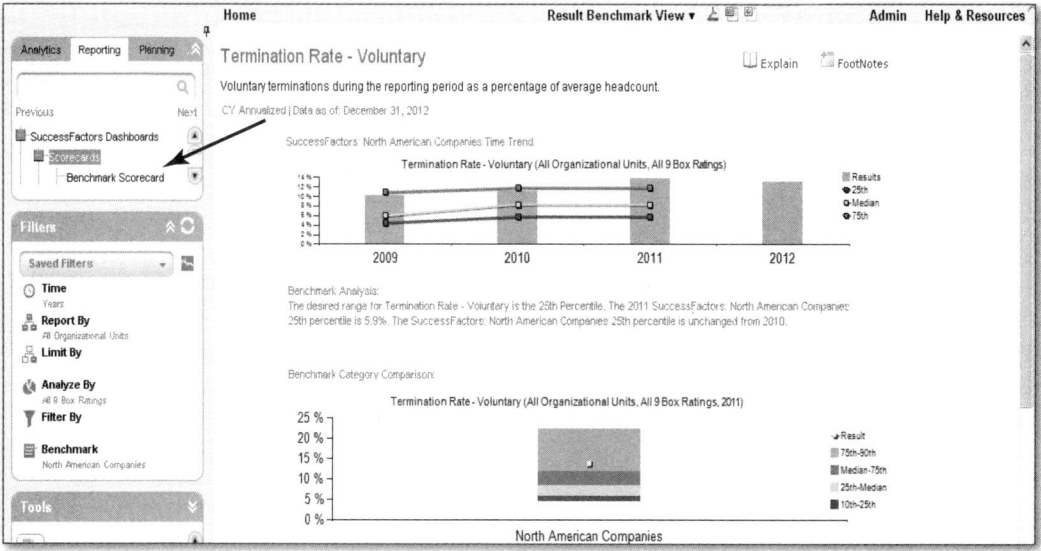

Figure 14.15   Benchmark Scorecard

The Benchmark Scorecard is a standard SuccessFactors dashboard (e.g., out-of-the-box report) that is available to all clients, and it provides a table list of all measures on the site and the corresponding benchmark results. The measures are arranged in the same categories found in the ANALYTICS tab and show the current organizational result, the past four years' benchmark results, and the 25th, 50th, and 75th percentile results for the current year. There is also a column denoting the color-coding associated with your organization's result, and a sample size of the number of organizations making up the benchmark result. Figure 14.16 shows a sample of the Benchmark Scorecard.

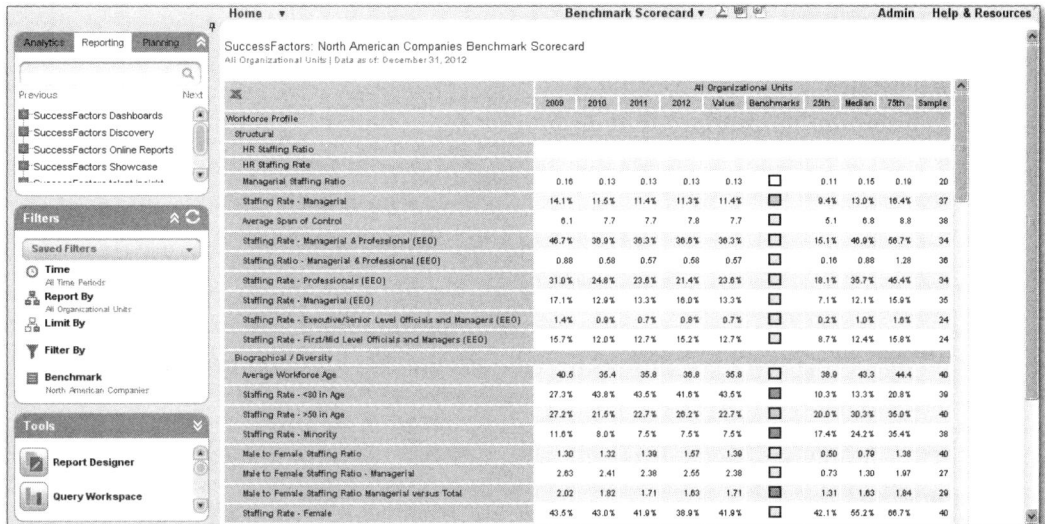

Figure 14.16 Sample Benchmark Scorecard

We've now covered the Benchmarking program in detail, so let's shift our attention to the analytical tools embedded in the WFA application.

14.3 Analytical Tools

The WFA solution includes multiple analytical tools located in the TOOLS section of the Analysis pane, and their purpose is to help to simplify the data analysis and reporting process. Acting as a complement to the standard measure pages and portal pages, the tool includes both basic and advanced analytical tools. Mainly aimed at the power users of the system, all tools are user friendly and intuitive, and play an integral role in creating a repeatable and scalable WFA program.

This section covers the main querying, statistical analysis, and reporting tools that are the crux of the power user's toolkit.

14.3.1 Query Workspace

The querying tool embedded in the WFA application—known as Query Workspace—utilizes a drag-and-drop interface similar to a pivot table in Excel. Users can build custom queries ranging from basic lists to complex combinations of multiple measures and dimensions. This powerful tool is controlled by role-based security, and administrators of the system can determine which user roles should be given access to the querying tool. Typically, access is limited to power users in the HR field, as well as the core WFA team. To access the Query Workspace tool, first locate the tab in the TOOLS section of the Analysis pane (refer to Figure 14.16). After you click on the QUERY WORKSPACE button, a new page loads, and a query displays the data you were last viewing. From here, you can modify the existing query, create a new query, or open an existing query in the folder menu.

Let's look at an example of how to create a new query. Using our example from earlier, we'll create a query for TERMINATION RATE - VOLUNTARY. Figure 14.17 illustrates how to start a new query—by clicking FILE • NEW QUERY.

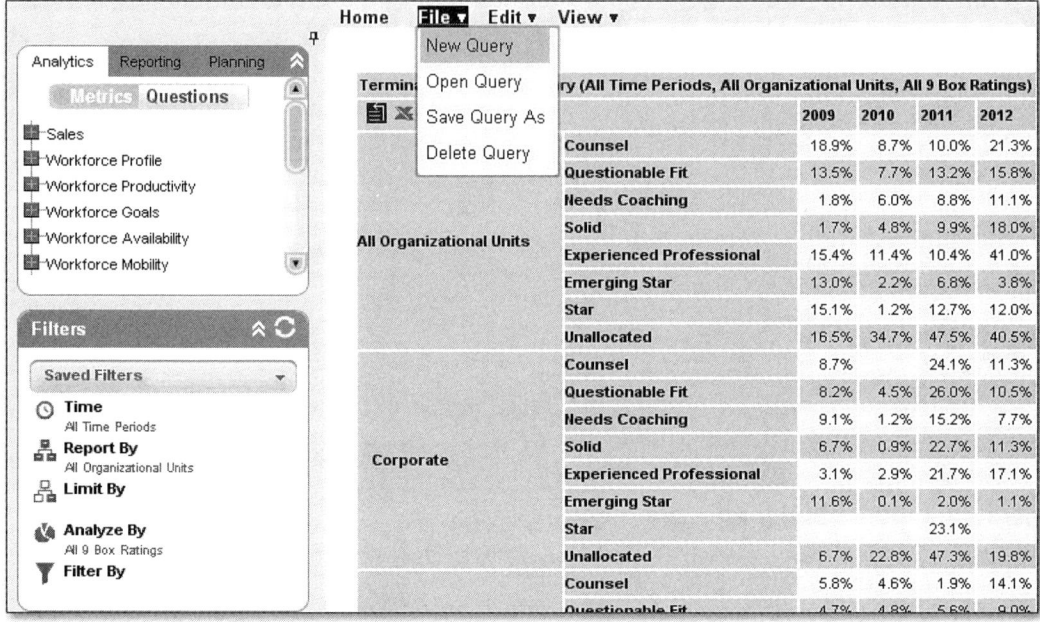

Figure 14.17 Create a New Query

After you click on NEW QUERY, a window appears that allows you to build a custom query. Locate the measure in the metrics catalog on the MEASURES tab, which in this example is located under WORKFORCE MOBILITY • TERMINATIONS • TERMINATION RATE - VOLUNTARY. After selecting the measure, drag it onto the rows and drop it when the rows column turns blue, as depicted in Figure 14.18.

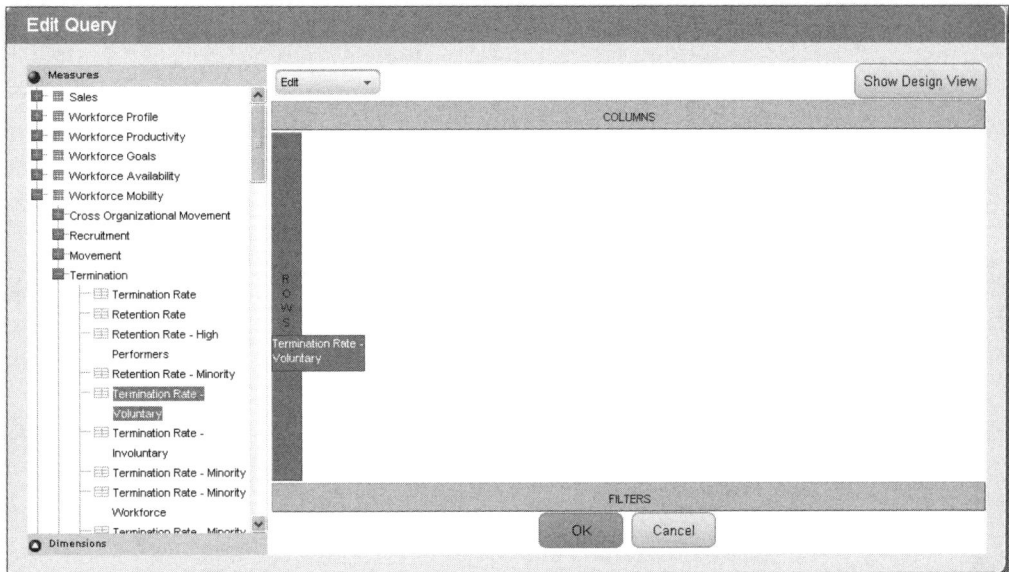

Figure 14.18 Building a Query

After you drop the measure, the data will populate for the most current year of data, which in this case is year-end 2012. As soon as you drop the measure on the rows (see the basic query in Figure 14.19), the MEASURES list will be replaced by the DIMENSIONS list on the left side of the window, and you'll see your result for TERMINATION RATE - VOLUNTARY in 2012.

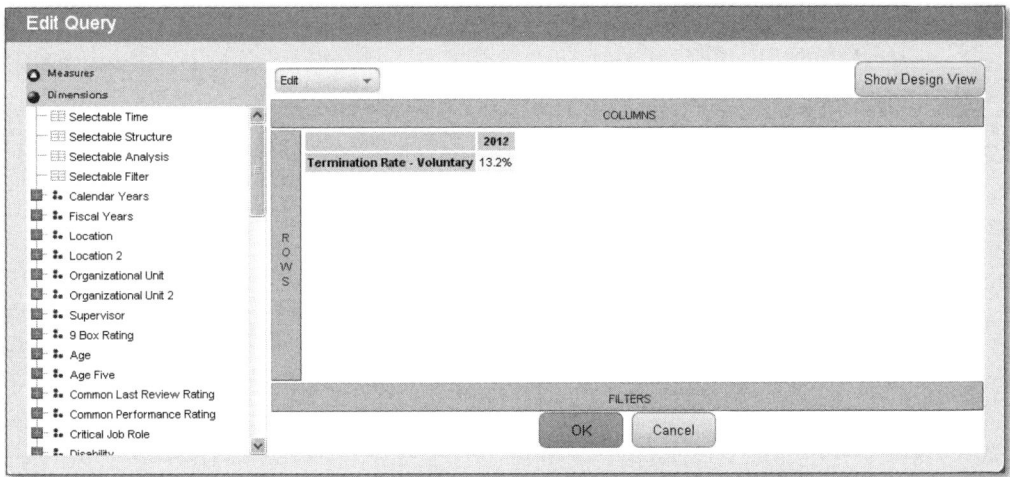

Figure 14.19 Dimension List

Now that the basic query is built, you have limitless options to expand your query. However, the most common additions are to add slices of analysis from the DIMENSIONS list, add additional measures to the rows, or filter by a specific dimension node. Using the example from earlier, let's quickly walk through how to build on this basic query to show 1-<2 year tenure voluntary termination rates by gender in the Healthcare business unit (see Figure 14.20).

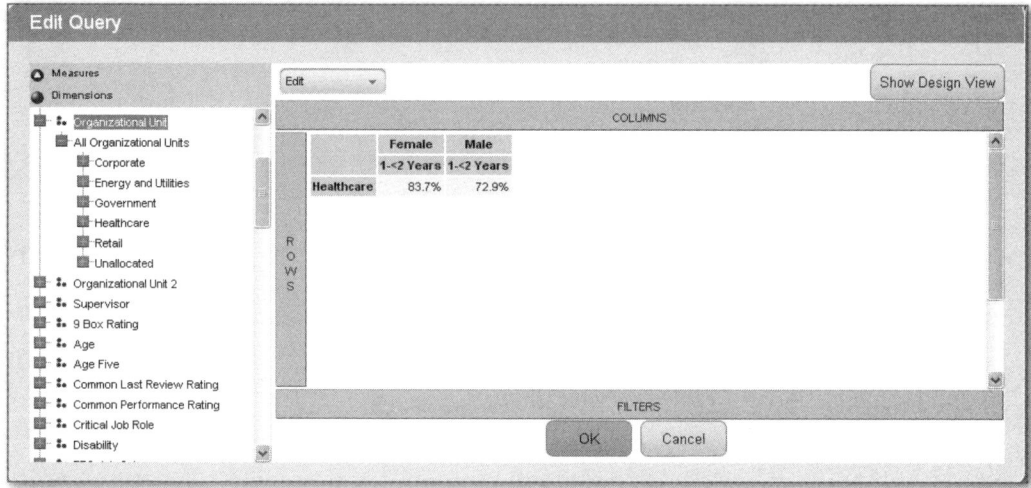

Figure 14.20 1-<2 Year Tenure Voluntary Turnover Rate by Gender (Healthcare)

By clicking on the SHOW DESIGN VIEW button in the top-right corner, you can see the parameters for the query you've defined so far. Note that the drag-and-drop functionality is still applicable in the design view. Use of the design view will allow you to construct a richer, more complex query that enables even closer analysis of the targeted measure. Figure 14.21 shows the design view for your current query; you can toggle back to table view by clicking the SHOW TABLE VIEW button in this right corner.

When you're happy with your query, click on the OK button, and the query will be displayed on the page in a table format. You can export the query by clicking the EXCEL icon on the table (make sure you have clicked OK first!), or you can chart the query by clicking on the VIEW dropdown arrow. Some queries may not be suitable for a chart if there are multiple measures and dimensions on the rows/columns. Lastly, the Drill to Detail functionality does work in queries built in Query Workspace. However, you must make sure to include a measure on both the rows and columns.

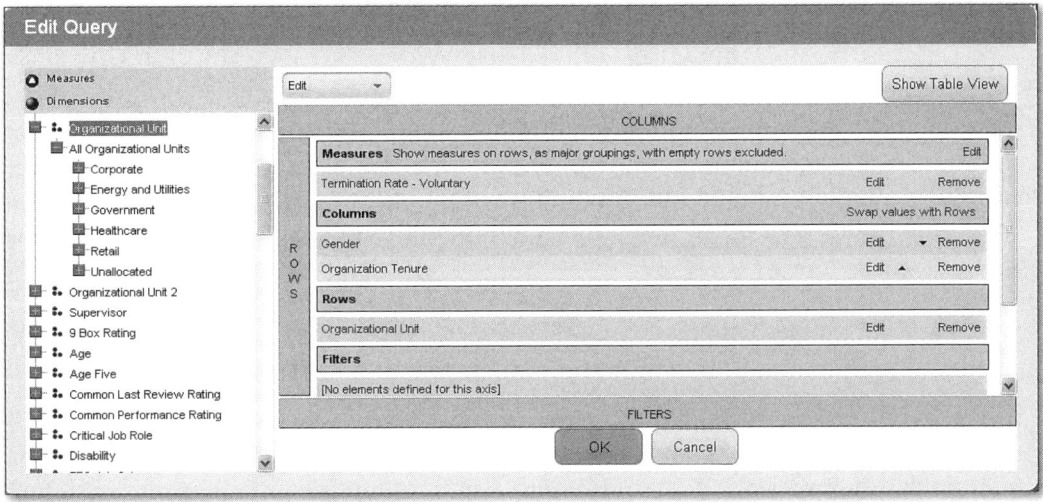

Figure 14.21 Design View

The Query Workspace tool also houses the customer-driven enhancement called Custom Members/Sets (also known as Custom Dimensions). This functionality provides users with the ability to create specific dimension views to be used for analysis and reporting purposes. This is especially useful when there is an ongoing need to view either parts or aggregates of existing dimensions in a custom view. An example of a custom member is if you wanted to report on directors and above as a group, however, your current ANALYSIS OPTION displays results for each individual manager level.

Custom Members/Sets makes it possible to group together the nodes you want to see results for in an aggregate form and can be applied to future queries or reports without having to recreate the view. To access a Custom Member/Set when building a query in Query Workspace, locate the SPECIAL FUNCTIONS folder on the DIMENSIONS list (refer to Figure 14.19). A quick tip is that to see your Custom Member/Set in the SPECIAL FUNCTIONS folder, you must first make it public by clicking on the STATUS button in the MANAGE CUSTOM MEMBERS pane.

In addition to creating custom views for dimensions, you can also create custom measures (also known as custom calculations). Custom measures are created by dragging and dropping inputs and formula operators (e.g., divided by, plus/minus, etc.) into a designer, and the measure builds itself in real time. All custom measures can be saved for future use in queries and reports by enabling the custom measure to be public (also done by clicking SHARE in the MANAGE CUSTOM CALCULATIONS pane). After your custom measure is public, you'll be able to access it in a folder called CUSTOM CALCULATIONS in the QUERY WORKSPACE MEASURE list. One quick tip is to always make sure to validate your formula, which can be done by clicking the VALIDATE button in the MANAGE CUSTOM CALCULATIONS pane. If no errors are detected, then the system will display an "All is valid" message. Validation becomes an increasingly necessary function throughout the lifecycle of the cube and portal as measures and dimensions are added, modified, and occasionally removed as part of the refresh process.

The final component of query workspace we'll cover is folder management, which allows queries to be saved in user-specific folders. It's important to note that all users can edit or access other user's queries, so proper folder management is critical. Queries saved in folders can also be linked to reports in Report Designer, which we'll cover next.

14.3.2 Report Designer

One of the key components of any WFA program is a reporting strategy designed to get key information into decision-makers' hands on a regular basis. The WFA tool enables the reporting process by making the creation of reports, and subsequent distribution, much easier to manage than typical reporting tools. The drag-and-drop interface we saw in Query Workspace is also utilized in Report Designer, making the tool very user friendly. Additionally, clients will find that the reporting process is significantly more efficient because the data is automatically refreshed in every report on a monthly basis. Essentially, clients can build one master report and send it pre-sliced to each different business unit every month with minimal effort. The reduced manual effort through this approach can save significant dollars in your organization, as well as free up your WFA team to do more strategic analyses. Let's now review the key functionality within the Report Designer.

Accessing Report Designer and Existing Reports

To access the Report Designer tool, a user role must have access granted through the Role-Based Permissions (RBP) framework. Similar to other power user tools, the primary users of Report Designer will be the core WFA team. To access the Report Designer, click the REPORT DESIGNER button found on the TOOLS menu in the Analysis pane (refer to Figure 14.16). A new page will refresh displaying the Report Designer Library, which utilizes a similar folder management system to Query Workspace. All users can create as many reports and folders as they wish, however, report "owners" can restrict other users from modifying your existing reports.

In the Report Designer, you are prompted to select a report from the folders or create a new report. The Analysis pane is replaced with a MANAGE REPORTS section, which is where you'll find the NEW REPORT button. Figure 14.22 illustrates the initial access page for Report Designer.

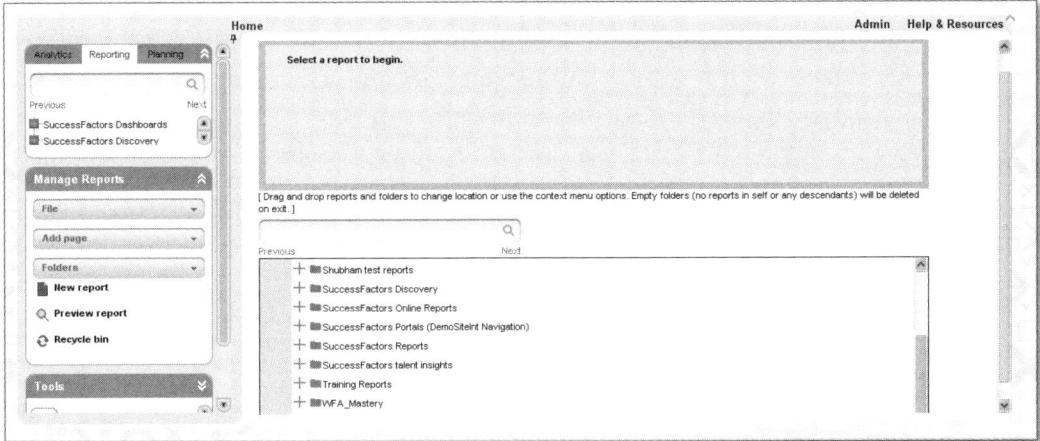

Figure 14.22 Report Designer Access Page

The MANAGE REPORTS section in the Analysis pane houses all of the main reporting functions. Beginning with the FILE dropdown menu, you can choose to link reports to the reporting menu, edit ownership of reports, delete reports (either permanently or put them in the recycle bin if you want to access certain pages again in the future), and edit headers and footers. Next, you can choose to either add a blank page to your report or copy a page from any existing report. The FOLDER dropdown allows you to manage your folders by creating new folders, naming them, or deleting existing folders.

The final button we'll cover in the MANAGE FOLDERS pane is the PREVIEW button, which allows you to view a report on the main site as an end-user would experience. This functionality temporarily moves the report out of design mode and allows the report builder to check that the report features are working as expected.

When you click on an existing report in a folder, the gray box above the folders populates with key information about the selected report such as the report owner's name, the number of pages in the report, the last date/time the report was modified and by whom, and if the report is currently linked to the REPORTING menu. In this view, you can also modify any existing pages in the report you've selected, add new pages to the report, or reorder the pages in the report.

Report Designer Components

Users have complete flexibility in Report Designer to create a multitude of data visualizations, known as components. Components are the building blocks of a report page and can be charts, tables, text, images, or composite queries. All components can be edited to fit a user's preferences, including the font, size, color scheme, and so on. Each of the components has a different purpose that can be used on Report Designer pages, ranging from basic tables to complex queries utilizing formulas and conditional formatting. If you can imagine it, you can build it in Report Designer.

When you add a blank page or copy of an existing page to the report you're building, a new menu appears in the Analysis pane with one tab to add components and a second tab to edit components. Accessing the choices for components is simple because they are all arranged by type in the ADD COMPONENT window, as shown in Figure 14.23.

You'll also notice that there is a new pane below the ADD COMPONENT pane called PAGE PROPERTIES. This is where you can modify the page margins, switch to landscape view, validate that the components on the page are working properly, and enable a grid view to ensure components are properly aligned.

To edit a component, you must first drag and drop one of the component options onto the page. After you do so, a default image will show up in the component box with demo data to illustrate the type of the component you've chosen (e.g., table vs. chart). After dropping the new component onto your page canvas, the ADD COMPONENT menu will be replaced by the EDIT COMPONENT menu.

Now, you have several options for editing your component, all of which can also be accessed by right-clicking on the component as a shortcut. The EDIT COMPONENT menu, shown in Figure 14.24, allows users to do all normal editing activities, such as changing the chart type (e.g., pie vs. bar chart), changing the color scheme, adding data labels or a legend, and adding a chart/table title. You can create a custom color palette utilizing your corporate colors, which you can later incorporate into charts, reports, and so on.

Figure 14.23 Add Component Menu

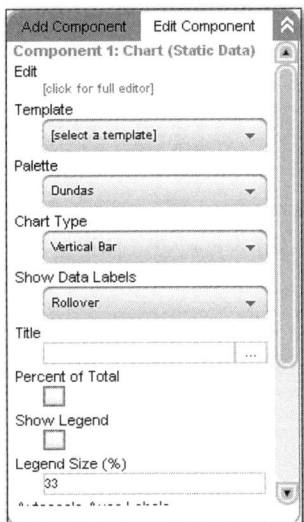

Figure 14.24 Edit Component Menu

In addition, you'll notice a [CLICK FOR FULL EDITOR] link. Clicking this link opens a new edit window that includes an option to link your component to an existing query in Query Workspace. This is a great time-saver because you won't need to rebuild all queries from scratch for reporting purposes. Also, in the full edit window, you have the option to PREVIEW your component to avoid repeatedly clicking in and out of the editor to make changes. Finally, the copy and paste right-click feature works nicely in Report Designer, which can save time editing and formatting components.

Report Distributor

Half the battle of establishing a regular reporting process is automating the report schedule. To eliminate this challenge, the WFA solution has an embedded Report Distributor tool that allows clients to set up "bundles" to be delivered on a regular basis.

The WFA team can determine what information the end user should receive and how often. For example, you may want the CFO to receive a report via email already drilled down to the finance organization on a monthly basis. This feature, which can be found on the TOOLS menu, is a key piece of delivering WFA in a scalable manner across the organization.

In the next section, we'll cover the more advanced analytical tools available in the WFA application.

14.3.3 Analytics Workspace

As your WFA program begins to mature, some analyses might require more powerful statistical analysis tools. The Analytics Workspace feature of the WFA product includes several additional data analysis tools that can be extremely useful for identifying, refining, and visualizing your key findings. Analytics Workspace is controlled through role-based security and is located on the TOOLS menu in the Analysis pane. Note that all queries built in Analytics Workspace can be included in reports built in Report Designer. In this section, we'll give a brief overview of the various tools accessible in Analytics Workspace.

Scatterplots

A scatterplot is a data visualization tool that quantifies a relationship between two measures, or one measure over two time periods, while also analyzing the strength of that relationship through correlation and regression. To access the Scatterplot tool, you must first click on the ANALYTICS WORKSPACE tab in the TOOLS menu, and then click on the SCATTERPLOT graphic. A new page will display a sample scatterplot, and, similarly to other tools within the WFA solution, a user can choose to open an existing query or build a new scatterplot from scratch. When using the Scatterplot tool, you can only view two measures from the same data cube in one query, meaning that measures from different data sources cannot be analyzed together.

Data Highlighting

Data Highlighting is an effective tool for searching through the large amounts of data in WFA. Essentially, this analytical tool allows you to define the parameters of your search, and it will return the results that meet your criteria in a list-based table. The results in the table are drillable, meaning that you can quickly navigate to the measure page for the result you're interested in investigating further.

The data highlighting functionality is particularly useful when there is a specific issue you're trying to hone in on within your data (e.g., business units with voluntary turnover rates greater than 20%). Additionally, you can add expressions using and/or logic that enables more complex searches and thus more refined results.

Significance Testing

While WFA does not require sophisticated statistics to be effective, sometimes there is a need to perform more advanced statistical tests to ensure the data results are significant. For those well-versed in statistics, there is a tool called Significance Testing in the Analytics Workspace that allows users to perform *chi-squared* and *z-tests*. The chi-squared test is used to determine the probability that results are due to chance or whether your results are significant according to the significance level you define (usually 5%). After you have the chi-squared test results, you can choose to perform a z-test to determine whether the results are statistically equivalent for two groups.

Predictive Models

While the Predictive Models tool sits within the Analytics Workspace of the WFA solution, the output is typically leveraged for Strategic Workforce Planning purposes. Essentially, the Predictive Models analytical tool allows organizations to model the relationship of two variables across time, both from a historical perspective and to predict future trends. For example, if you wanted to determine the impact of sales roles on profitability, the tool would show the historical performance of these metrics against each other, as well as leverage an underlying algorithm to predict future performance. This becomes useful during the action planning phase of Strategic Workforce Planning to determine which strategies should be implemented to drive specific organizational outcomes.

In addition, the SuccessFactors Workforce Planning solution allows custom demand models to be built in the Predictive Models tool and then uploaded into demand forecasts for more sophisticated analyses. Demand forecasting will be covered in more depth in Chapter 15.

Career Trajectory

The newest tool to be added to the suite of tools in Analytics Workspace is Career Trajectory, which maps the path, progression, or line of development for individual employees or groups of employees (e.g., organizational unit or location). The upward mobility or succession of employees can then be set against the desired career path to determine if they are within the Career Target Zone (where the organization expects people to be at that tenure level). The goal of this analytical tool is to give greater focus for managing career trajectories as a part of the succession management and employee development process.

All tools within the WFA solution have associated product documentation and can be found in the HELP & RESOURCES section located in the top-right corner of any screen. In the next section, we'll discuss the newest feature of the WFA solution: headlines.

14.4 Headlines

The Headlines feature of the WFA solution is aimed at bringing attention to noteworthy findings in your data by presenting them in common business language (similar to headlines in a newspaper). This innovative feature epitomizes the intuitive aspect of the BizX suite. With the Headlines tile on the SuccessFactors HOME page, workforce insights can be delivered to HR and business managers, providing insight into the performance of their workforce. While traditional workforce analytics applications require managers to comb through hundreds of data points, Headlines continually mines your data according to the parameters that you define, finds hot spots and pain points that are relevant to subscribers, and pushes alerts to them.

The following sections will delve deeper into this game-changing feature of WFA.

14.4.1 Using Headlines

While traditional analytics solutions serve data, charts, and metrics, Headlines serves true "insights" by interpreting metrics and delivering conclusions in common business language. Essentially, Headlines is a mobile device-ready SuccessFactors solution that pulls insights from workforce analytic data automatically and pushes them out to managers who need them.

These insights are communicated in simple human language and offer actionable next steps for any critical issue. Users or administrators can decide which metrics to track by subscribing to alerts that are flagged when a metric goes out of bounds. Metrics can be compared to targets, a prior period, or overall company values.

An example of a Headline alert sent to a manager might be "Your team is losing high-potential employees. 66 exited this month, which is double last month's count," or "Only 60% of your team has completed training." End-users can easily click (or tap, if using a mobile device) to get the details behind the finding to better understand the issue without having to "slice and dice."

In addition to giving end users true insight and guided data interpretation in a compelling way, Headlines also provides options for taking action to mitigate the identified risk. At the bottom of a Headlines page, there is a section populated with targeted strategies for how to address the issue at hand, pulled from an embedded strategy bank that encompasses more than 30 years of HR strategies based on client experiences.

The first time you use Headlines, you'll see a blank page until you add subscriptions. To add a subscription, click on the MANAGE SUBSCRIPTIONS link, and a new MY SUBSCRIBED INSIGHTS page will refresh. If you click on the blue plus button, an ADD CONTENT window will pop up where you can choose from the shared insights that have been defined by your administrator. Users can also deactivate insights in the same window. After you've added one or more subscriptions, you'll see the topmost subscription appear in the HEADLINES tile on your SuccessFactors HOME page. To enable the Headlines tile, go to the ADMIN TOOLS section, and click on the MANAGE HOME PAGE (under SYSTEM PROPERTIES in the old Admin Tools or COMPANY SETTINGS in OneAdmin). From here, move the Headlines tile to the DEFAULT (always shown on HOME page) or AVAILABLE (available via the TILE BROWSER) tab.

Figure 14.25 shows the Headlines tile on the SuccessFactors HOME page, and clearly demonstrates how easily HR and managers can quickly learn the details of concerning workforce issues.

Figure 14.25 Headlines Home Page Tile

14.4.2 Headlines BizX Mobile Integration

The Headlines feature integrates via a mobile tile through the People Insights enhancement in the BizX Mobile application. There are a few important points to note:

- In provisioning for your instance, you'll need to turn on the People Insights feature.
- You'll also need to load the hybrid YOUCALC tiles into your instance (ADMIN • YOUCALC DASHBOARD MANAGER). These tiles must be uploaded as type "Hybrid." After they are uploaded to your instance, you can add them in the People Insight iPad app.

One of the most exciting new features of the Mobile Headlines product is that you can write notes to a colleague on the iPad and send them directly to the other person, as shown in Figure 14.26.

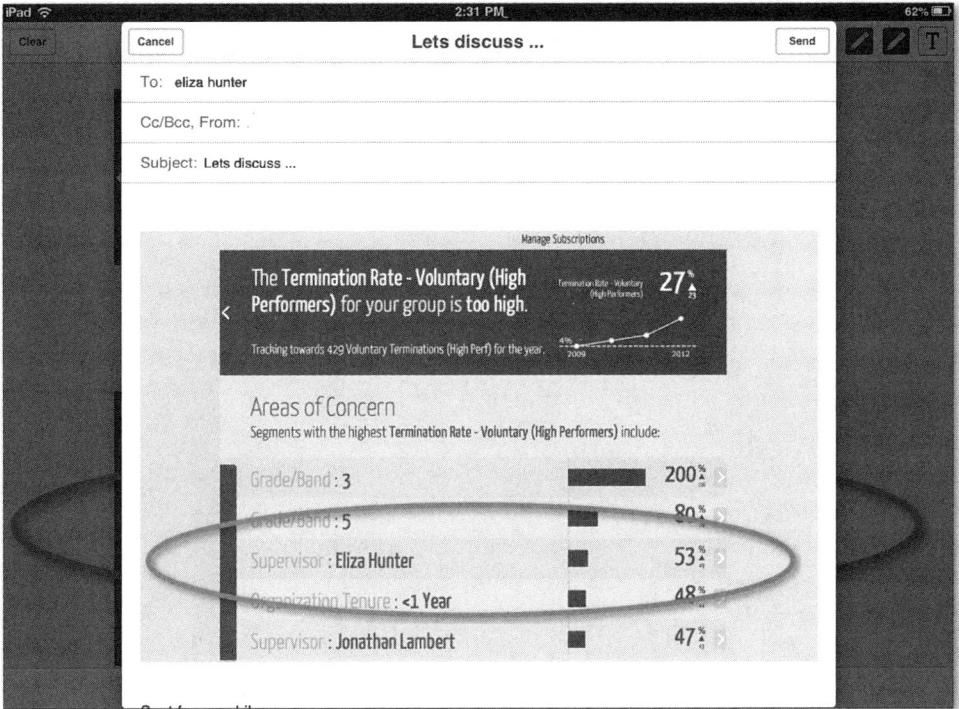

Figure 14.26 Emailing Headlines from an iPad

The Headlines feature of the SuccessFactors WFA solution is revolutionizing the way organizations leverage workforce data to make decisions. People managers need more advice, not more data, and Headlines makes this possible by turning complex data into instant actionable insights.

14.5 Summary

In conclusion, you should now have a thorough understanding of the SuccessFactors WFA solution, and how this innovative technology combined with best practices helps organizations achieve quantifiable business results. By providing clients with a standardized metrics catalog across the various HR domains and business functions, coupled with powerful and intuitive data analysis tools such as Query Workspace or Analytics Workspace, organizations can begin to uncover the insights in their data that translate into cost-savings or increases in revenue. The metric methodology we covered in the beginning of the chapter aids organizations in adhering to the standard definitions and tried-and-true formulas, which in turn allows organizations to communicate metrics in a common language across the business. Further, the Benchmarking program allows clients to make comparisons to external data and is a key differentiator from competitors in the analytics solution marketplace. The Report Designer capability brings all of these data elements together by allowing users to easily create scorecards, dashboards, and standard reports across the business in a scalable and repeatable manner.

Lastly, the Headlines functionality is taking the WFA solution to the next level by acting as an "automated data analyst" that interprets your data, provides guidance on which strategic actions should be considered, and minimizes the time spent discussing data quality while maximizing the time spent on obtaining desirable results. This enhancement has not only made the WFA process more scalable and repeatable but also reduces the amount of time analysts spend combing through the data, allowing them to perform more value-added activities. The SuccessFactors WFA solution continues to make fact-based decision making a part of HR's day-to-day business operations, which is the ultimate goal of WFA.

In the next chapter, we'll cover the five-step SuccessFactors methodology for Strategic Workforce Planning (SWFP). In conjunction with the theory behind WFP, we'll provide an in-depth review of the SuccessFactors WFP technology from both a Strategic Workforce Planning and Operational Planning standpoint.

Organizations often overlook the necessity of strategically planning their human capital to meet the needs of the business in the future, and the result is often expensive interventions to fill talent gaps. SuccessFactors Workforce Planning provides the tools to ensure that organizational strategy can be executed with the right skills, in the right place, at the right time, and at the right cost.

15 Workforce Planning

Strategic Workforce Planning (SWFP) is a process-based business planning activity that often gets overlooked, despite its clear importance in enabling execution of business strategy with the proper staffing of underlying talent management initiatives, now and into the future. Although SWFP has been steadily practiced for more than 30 years in other regions of the world such as Asia-Pacific and Europe, it's still an emerging discipline in North America. Even when utilized as a regular step in the strategic planning process, SWFP often results in plans for the near term rather than looking at whether the organization has the right talent infrastructure in place to meet future demand. Without modeling capabilities, organizations rely primarily on "gut feelings" to make long-term strategic decisions, and more often than not, the resulting plan isn't an accurate representation of the future landscape, nor does it leverage the wealth of historical workforce data that resides in the organization's HCM system.

SuccessFactors Workforce Planning (WFP) provides a platform and a proven process to aid organizations in proactively planning for the types of business challenges associated with critical talent shortages and surpluses. In effect, the solution facilitates the process of matching workforce supply with workforce demand to determine where talent gaps exist, and provides the ability to forecast and model changes to the workforce across the business. The tool also highlights risks, capability skill gaps, cost modeling, and best practice strategies to successfully execute strategy and plan action for the long term.

While SWFP is primarily focused on the next three, five, and ten years, it's still crucial for organizations to operationalize Year 1 and Year 2 of the workforce plan. Consequently, the SuccessFactors WFP solution includes an embedded Operational Planning tool to supplement the SWFP process.

The Workforce Planning application is an extension of the SuccessFactors Workforce Analytics (WFA) module and is fed underlying data from that WFA engine for planning purposes. In addition, the WFA module plays a key role in the ongoing monitoring and reporting of critical areas of the business, which is the final step in the SWFP process. In this chapter, we'll cover the basic methodology and theory behind SWFP, as well as the key functionality within the SuccessFactors WFP application for both Strategic and Operational Workforce Planning. This includes an in-depth review of the key activities in SWFP, such as demand and supply forecasting and gap analysis (Section 15.3), risk identification and action planning (Section 15.4), and what-if financial modeling (Section 15.5).

15.1 Defining Strategic Workforce Planning

Let's begin by defining SWFP as it is mirrored in the SuccessFactors WFP tool. Essentially, SWFP entails creating a process that works for your organization to make sure that you have the right people in the right place with the right skills at the right time, and all for the right price. In theory, if you're doing all of these things properly, you can execute on your business strategy successfully and proactively mitigate risks along the way.

People tend to have different ideas about SWFP and define it differently in their individual organizations (e.g., some organizations consider staffing, budgeting, and headcount planning to be SWFP). However, at its core, the process helps companies understand what is going to happen to workforce supply and demand across a three- to five-year timeframe (typically) and how that will impact the organization's strategic plan. On a related note, it's important to understand what SWFP is *not*: It's not short-term resource planning to fill open headcount, and it's not succession planning where you're planning for named resources.

In general, organizations tend to be better at considering the right place and right time when planning for future demand, but place less emphasis on the right skills and right price. With SWFP, you start to ask questions such as the following:

- Do we know what skills we'll need in the future?
- Do we have sufficient quantities?
- If so, where are they located in the organization (e.g., which business units or job roles)?
- If not, can we build or borrow them, or do we need to buy them from the external labor market?
- Can we buy them, or is there a shortage of that particular skill in the external labor market?

When thinking about price, there are many paths that lead to having the right people in the right place at the right time with the right skills. However, the challenge is figuring out which mix is most cost-effective. In other words, can you answer what your traditional approach costs versus what the alternatives would cost—in both the short term and the long term?

To answer questions like these, organizations need a proven process to guide strategic decision making. Essentially, SWFP focuses on making decisions that will have the most impact, which means making a decision on what you will and will not do. The end goal of SWFP is to move away from firefighting mode to being more proactive about planning for the workforce.

To summarize, the aim of SWFP is to reduce business strategy execution risks associated with workforce capacity, capability, and flexibility. SWFP is an ongoing process to identify the workforce needs for the future and allows organizations to identify the gap between demand and supply for talent, both in terms of capacity and capabilities. Possibly the most important outcome of the SWFP process is that it provides a view of the degree of business risk the organization is facing, or in other words, the magnitude of the gaps. Lastly, it's a plan to inform business decision making and assign action and accountability. SWFP is the process of answering the "how" with scenario planning, creating demand and supply forecasts to assess the gap(s), forecasting the critical skills and capabilities needed in future roles, and financial modeling to help drive action. In this chapter, we'll cover each of these steps in greater detail.

15 | Workforce Planning

15.2 The Five Steps of SuccessFactors WFP

SuccessFactors WFA provides the foundation for the data used in SuccessFactors WFP and supplies the following core data elements:

- Headcount
- External hires
- Terminations
- Retirements
- Movements (e.g., promotions, transfers)

In addition, the WFP tool also utilizes the same organizational structures and analysis options available on the WFA site to allow users to create meaningful forecasts for critical areas of the organization or critical job roles. Clients can access the WFP application by clicking the PLANNING tab within the Analysis pane on any page within the WFA application, as shown at the top left of Figure 15.1.

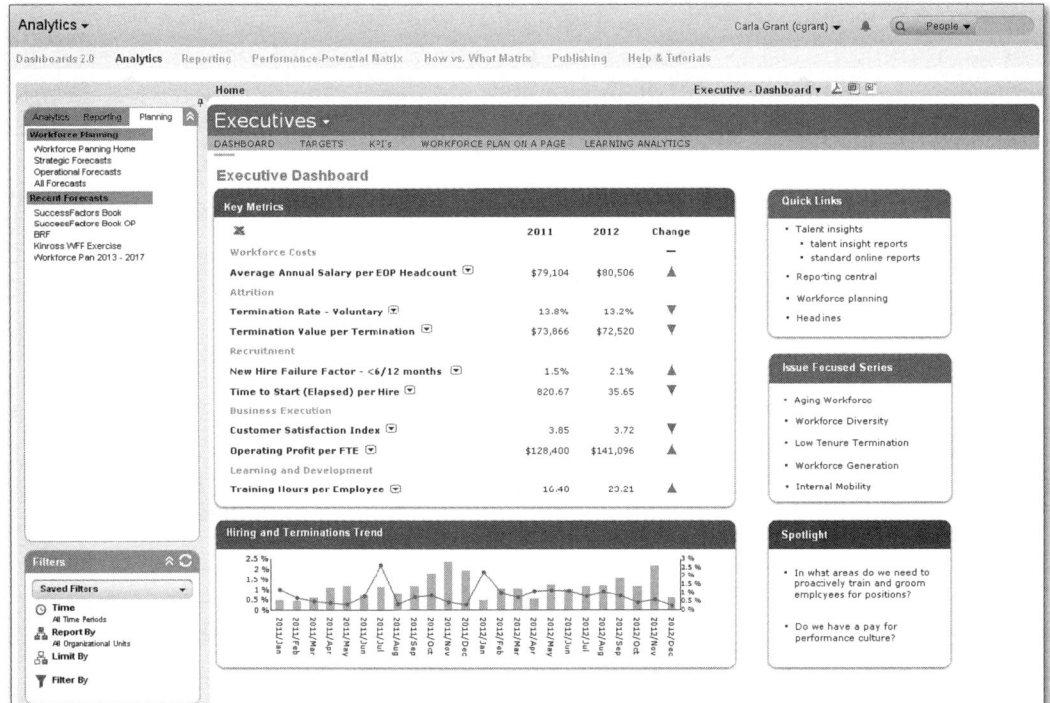

Figure 15.1 Accessing the WFP Application

Because the SuccessFactors WFP application is part of the acquired Infohrm technology (explained in Chapter 14), the product mirrors the Infohrm five-step SWFP methodology:

1. Strategic analysis
2. Forecasting
3. Risk analysis
4. Strategy, impact, and cost modeling
5. Actions and accountability

The five-step process flow can be seen on the HOME screen of the WFP application, as shown in Figure 15.2. Note that in the past few years, SuccessFactors has updated the methodology to include a "pre-step" that is known as the Workforce Planning Foundations and is shown at the base of the staircase. While this isn't an actual step in the process, it was added to act as a blueprint to ensure clients have the critical data elements (e.g., job family framework) and support mechanisms in place before kicking off the SWFP process.

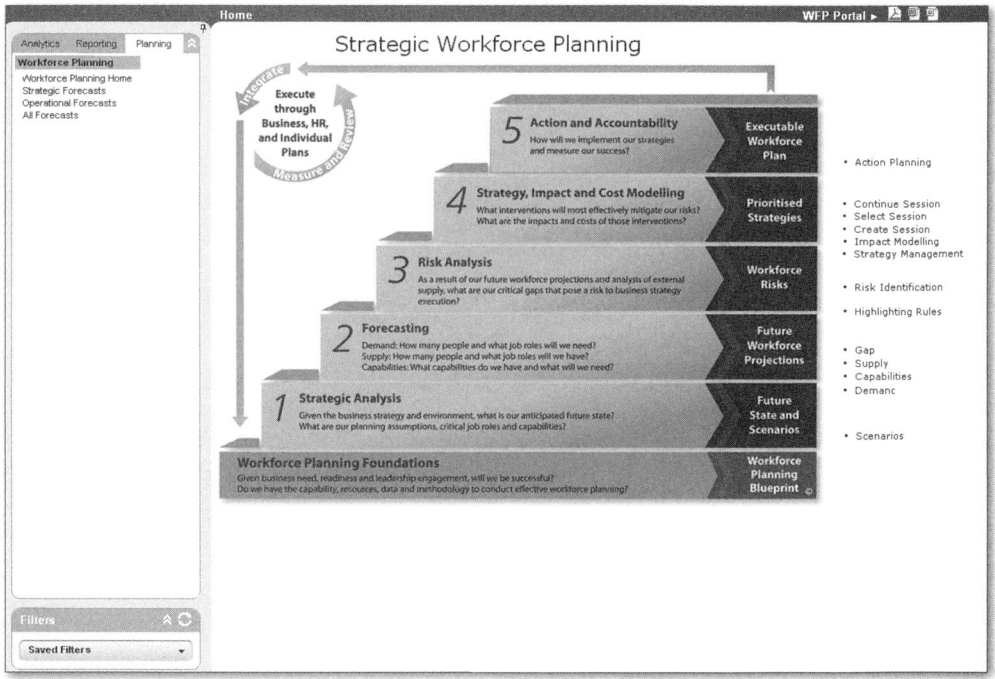

Figure 15.2 The Home Screen of SuccessFactors Workforce Planning

The WFP tool acts as a wizard, taking users through each of the steps to consolidate the qualitative and quantitative data in one forecast for complete, yet simplified analysis. Because SWFP is very much a qualitative process, much of the information is collected in workshop or interview-type settings and then input into the tool. In addition, the HELP button located at the top of every screen is populated with valuable information regarding tips and tricks for navigating the tool and populating the various tabs throughout the WFP process.

Let's walk through each of the phases, beginning with how to create a forecast in WFP.

15.2.1 Forecast List

The first entry point in the WFP tool is the *forecast list*, which can be accessed on the PLANNING tab in the Analysis pane on your WFA HOME page (refer to Figure 15.1). Within the PLANNING tab, there are a few options:

- WORKFORCE PLANNING HOME
- STRATEGIC FORECASTS
- OPERATIONAL FORECASTS
- ALL FORECASTS

For the purposes of this example, we'll look at how to access an existing strategic forecast or build a new one from scratch. When you click on the STRATEGIC FORECASTS link, a new page will refresh that shows all previously built strategic forecasts, as shown in the center of Figure 15.3.

From here, you can edit or copy an existing forecast by clicking the EDIT dropdown, or you can build a new forecast from scratch by clicking the NEW dropdown. The forecast details for the selected forecast are shown on the right-hand side of the screen in the SUMMARY window. Directly below the SUMMARY window is another box called EXPLORE FORECAST, which contains quick links to the various phases of the five-step methodology (see Figure 15.3). Also, each forecast within the list is color-coded, with green denoting a completely built forecast, yellow indicating that the forecast is in the process of being built, and gray showing incomplete forecasts.

15.2 The Five Steps of SuccessFactors WFP

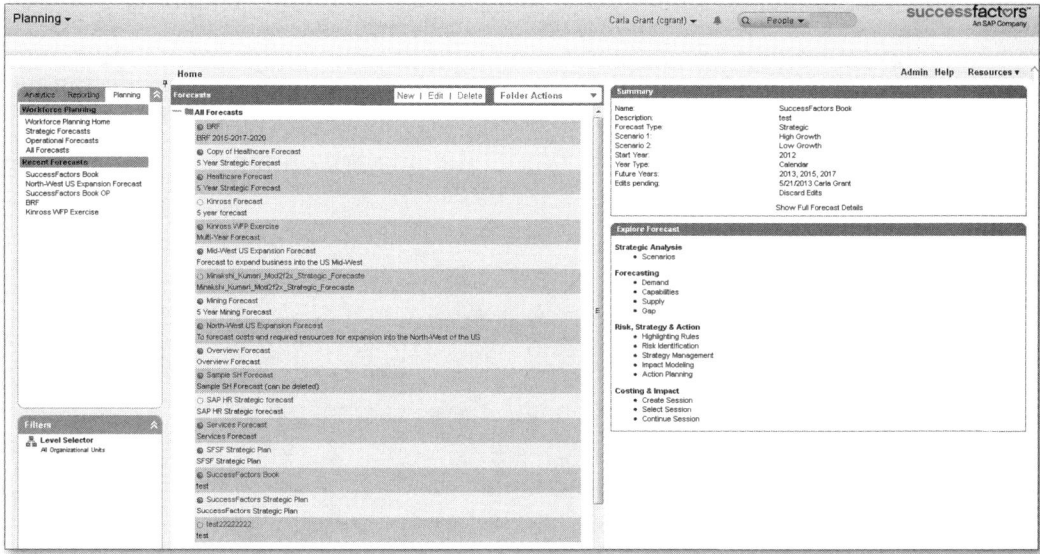

Figure 15.3 Strategic Forecast List

Users can build as many forecasts as they like, but keep in mind that all users can see all forecasts. The WFP tool does give administrators the ability to determine what level of access users of the system will have—either full access that can build forecasts (power users), or a more limited WFP role that allows users to only modify the demand or supply numbers of existing forecasts.

In the next section, we'll walk through the steps of building a new strategic forecast.

15.2.2 Creating a Strategic Forecast

Within the WFP solution, strategic plans are called *forecasts* and fall into three types of forecasts:

▶ Strategic forecast (2+ years into the future)

▶ Operational forecast (6 months to 48 months into the future)

▶ Amalgamate strategic forecast (combine separate strategic forecasts into one)

After a forecast type is selected, a new window will open with six main tabs, which are outlined in the chevron process flow at the top of the screen as shown in Figure 15.4. These six steps to build a strategic forecast include defining all data elements that will be analyzed, as well as the future scenarios that we'll plan against:

429

15 | Workforce Planning

1. FORECAST BASICS.
2. SET SCENARIOS.
3. SET DIMENSIONS.
4. SET RETIREMENTS.
5. SET STRUCTURE.
6. BUILD.

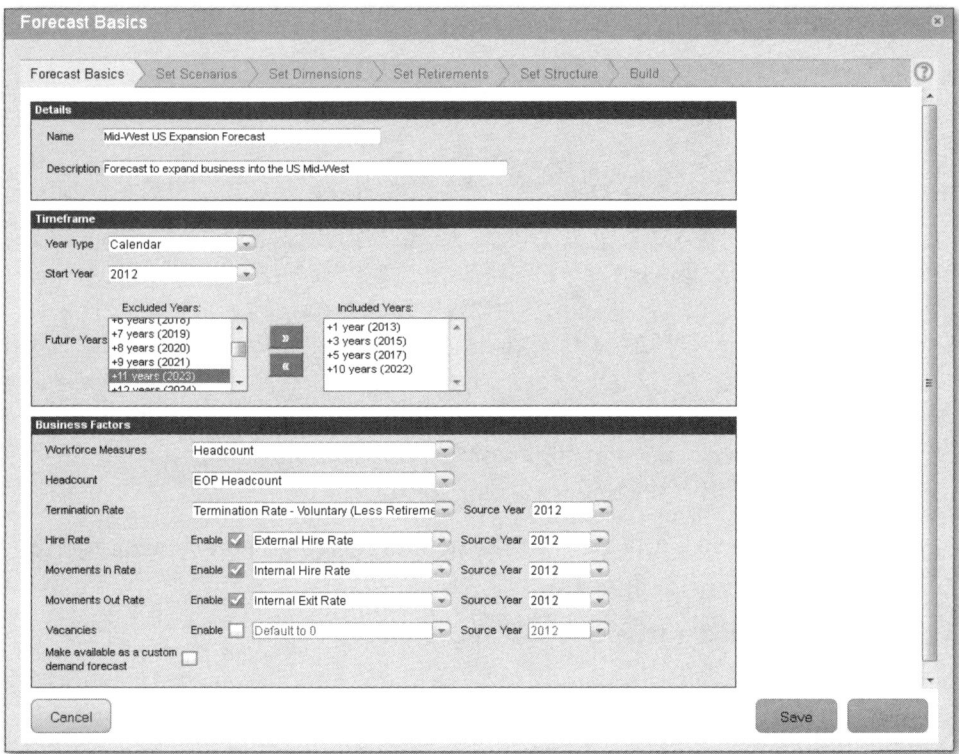

Figure 15.4 Steps in Building a Strategic Forecast

Let's walk through an example of how to build a strategic forecast for a company expanding its retail operations.

Forecast Basics

Again, the first step of creating a strategic forecast is to provide the basic information for the forecast, which can be done by clicking the NEW button and selecting

NEW STRATEGIC FORECAST. Doing so will cause a new window to appear with the title FORECAST BASICS, and you'll be prompted to enter the details and factors of your forecast. Essentially, the information in the following sections and fields will be the backbone of your workforce plan (refer to Figure 15.4).

- DETAILS
  Name and description of your forecast.

- TIMEFRAME
  Year type (calendar or fiscal), start year, and future years you'll be forecasting against.

- BUSINESS FACTORS
  Headcount or full-time equivalent (FTE), termination rate, hire rate, movements in rate, movements out rate, and vacancies.

Starting with the DETAILS section, you'll be prompted to enter the name and description for the forecast. Additionally, you have the option of switching between fiscal or calendar years in the YEAR TYPE dropdown. Please note that you must have fiscal years configured as a dimension in the WFA application for this to appear as an option in the YEAR TYPE dropdown.

The next window is the TIMEFRAME, where you must define the number of years your forecast will include. For the START YEAR field, clients typically select the default option, which shows the current year (in this case, 2012). As an example, for FUTURE YEARS, you would select the values +1 YEAR (2013), +3 YEARS (2015), and +5 YEARS (2017) which means you want to identify any significant risks/gaps in your forecast for next year, within three years, and, finally, five years' time. If you double-click on the year, it will move it to the INCLUDED YEARS window.

The next section that must be populated is the BUSINESS FACTORS, where you choose which underlying measures the tool will leverage from the WFA application. This information will mainly be used to populate the SUPPLY tab with predictions on headcount, terminations, hires, movements, and vacancies based on historical data. For instance, users can choose to forecast against end of period (EOP) headcount or FTE, depending on how headcount is reported in their organization. This section of the WFP tool must be configured to show the measures that you want to make available for users to choose from.

Additionally, different termination measures can be configured to choose from in the TERMINATION RATE dropdown (refer to Figure 15.4), although typically forecasts leverage the voluntary termination rate (less retirements) measure as the standard. The reason this is the most common slice of termination rate for SWFP purposes is that retirements are broken out, which allows users to define the retirement logic in the SET RETIREMENTS tab (covered later in this section).

Another custom termination measure that is commonly used in SWFP is a three-year rolling voluntary termination rate average. This type of measure allows users to take an average over a set number of years, eliminating the possibility of skewing the forecasted terminations due to an unusually high year of turnover.

The additional measures that can be enabled for the forecast are movements in, movements out, external hires, and vacancies. External hire rate is generally included; however best practice states that movement data (e.g., promotions, transfers) should only be incorporated in the forecast if there is a clearly defined career path program for the specific job roles you're planning against. The reasoning here is that in this phase you're defining the available talent supply that you expect to have over the forecast period (here, five years). Therefore, you would only include movement data if you can predict how many employees in a specific job role will be moving through the career path program by the end of the forecast period, meaning that they are available talent to source for filling identified gaps. Lastly, the VACANCIES field can only be enabled if a client has configured the WFA tool to include vacancy rates.

For all data elements after termination rate, users have the option to leverage the underlying WFA data for that specific measure (e.g., external hire rate), or *default to zero*. The premise behind defaulting to zero is called zero-based forecasting and essentially allows you to start with a clean slate for forecasting supply. This is a commonly used method because, in theory, organizations can't count on supply from external hiring (or movements) that has not yet happened, and by defaulting to zero, the tool won't forecast out predicted hires based on historical patterns. Instead, a user can choose to manually override the 0 that is input by the tool, which would make sense for roles that don't have a shortage in the external labor market.

The final piece to consider when filling out the BUSINESS FACTORS section of the forecast is the source year for each data element. Next to each measure, there is a dropdown list called SOURCE YEAR, which shows all of the previous years of historical data that are captured in the WFA application. Using external hire rate as an example, if you were to select 2011 as the source year, the tool will leverage the 2011 external hire rate as a baseline to predict the number of hires for the next five years. However, if 2011 were an unusual year in terms of hires, you might decide to use 2008 as a baseline instead because that was a more "normal" year to represent the organization's hiring patterns.

After you've entered these details, the screen should look like Figure 15.5.

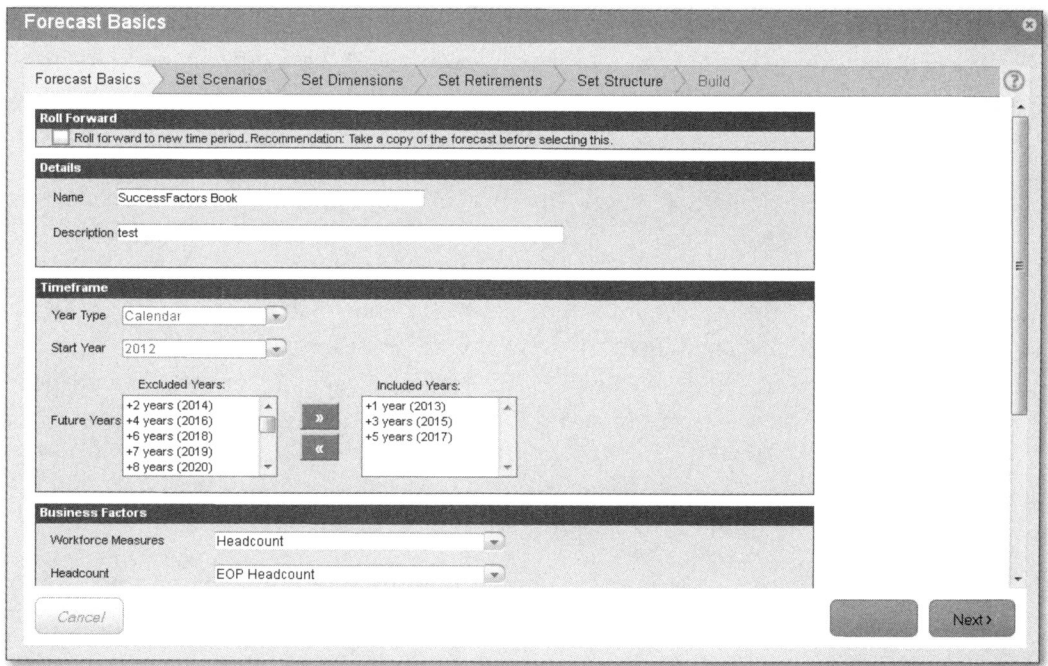

Figure 15.5 Completed Forecast Basics

After you fill out the necessary information, click the SAVE button, and then click the NEXT button to advance to the next tab (SET SCENARIOS).

Set Scenarios

Defining plausible future states, known as scenarios, is a key step in the SWFP process, and it typically takes place in a workshop setting with key business leaders and workforce planners. At this stage of the process, the key stakeholder group comes together to discuss the strategy of their area of the business in relation to the overall company strategy for the forecast period. The objective is to identify a set of unknowns that could potentially affect demand of the critical talent necessary to execute strategy. Simply stated, scenarios are an articulation of what you predict will significantly impact the business during the forecast period.

We develop robust scenarios for the following reasons:

- To understand the drivers of demand to estimate the future demand for labor
- To help identify critical job roles
- To get risks/issues out in the open, including workforce capacity and capability
- To understand the organizational strategy in conjunction with the drivers of change, with a focus on the talent impacts

During scenario planning, the focus is mainly on external business factors that are outside of the organization's control (e.g., regulations, politics, socioeconomic factors, etc.). In addition, because the goal is to limit the number of scenarios to a maximum of three, scenarios should be plausible, rather than possible. Often organizations will start the SWFP process with a "steady-state" scenario, meaning the demand won't change throughout the forecast period. Essentially, the purpose of the steady-state scenario is to show the organization where they will be at the end of the forecast period if they do nothing, which can be a very powerful message. The final step of scenario planning is to obtain sign-off on the scenarios that will be included for forecast purposes.

Because setting scenarios is entirely text-based, the WFP tool allows users to enter in qualitative descriptions of the scenarios. This plays a key role in helping your demand forecasters understand the business goals for the next few years, so the level of granularity is important here. The more detail you can give in each scenario, the easier the job of the demand forecaster will be when they are determining how many people and what skills they are going to need to be successful in the future.

As an example, let's create a common set of two scenarios, one for high growth and a second for low growth. As shown in Figure 15.6, the SET SCENARIOS tab has SCENARIO 1 entered as the default.

By clicking on SCENARIO 1, a new window opens where you can enter in the details and comments that are critical to capture from the scenario planning session. In this window, you can rename the scenario and give a short optional description, so let's change the name to "High Growth." You can add any information that will be helpful to consider during the demand forecasting process into the accompanying text box. Lastly, you can add assumptions common to all scenarios, which are defined as factors that are likely to happen regardless of either scenario playing out.

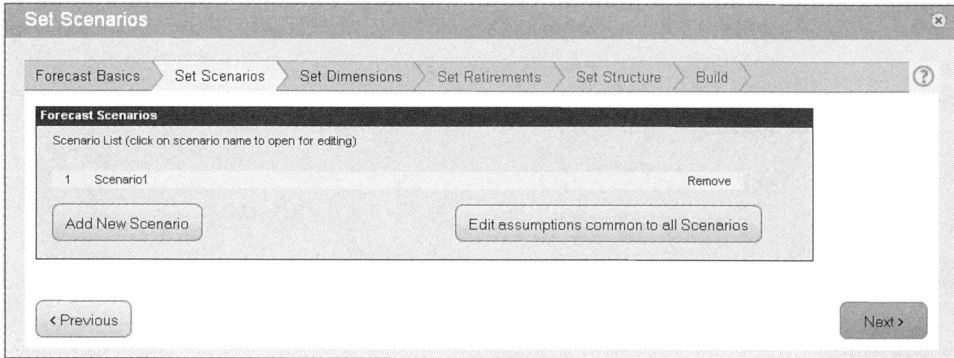

Figure 15.6 The Set Scenarios Step of Creating a Strategic Forecast

After the High Growth scenario is defined, click the SAVE button, and repeat the process for Scenario 2 by clicking the ADD SCENARIO button. When all scenarios are entered, click NEXT to advance to the SET DIMENSIONS tab. After your forecast is built, all scenarios can be accessed on the STRATEGIC ANALYSIS tab in the tool.

Set Dimensions

The third step of building a forecast is to set dimensions. In this step, you can add multiple *dimensions*, which is how you define the critical population that you'll be forecasting against. This is where you determine what those critical jobs roles are and how you're going to analyze them. The most commonly used dimensions for SWFP are job family, grade, or critical job role. Essentially, you're segmenting out the critical population that you've previously identified is at risk over the forecast period. Typically, this is referred to as the Critical Role Identification process and is completed during the initial planning workshops.

For this example, let's say that you're planning for job roles in specific job families, and you want to analyze those that have been marked as critical. By clicking the ADD DIMENSION button, a list of available dimensions that have been configured for the WFP tool will populate in a dropdown list, and you'll add JOB FAMILY. The dimension will populate with the various nodes that have been defined, and users can select/deselect specific nodes to be included in the forecast by highlighting them, or choose to include all nodes by checking the CLICK ON A NODE'S NAME TO SELECT

IT AND ALL OF ITS DESCENDANTS ONE LEVEL BELOW checkbox in the NODE selection window. In this specific example, select all nodes within the JOB FAMILY dimension.

You still need to add a second dimension for CRITICAL ROLES, which you can do by clicking on the ADD DIMENSION button. In this example, you only want to include employees marked YES (critical) and don't want to include employees that are marked NO (not critical) or UNALLOCATED employees, so highlight only the YES node, as shown in Figure 15.7.

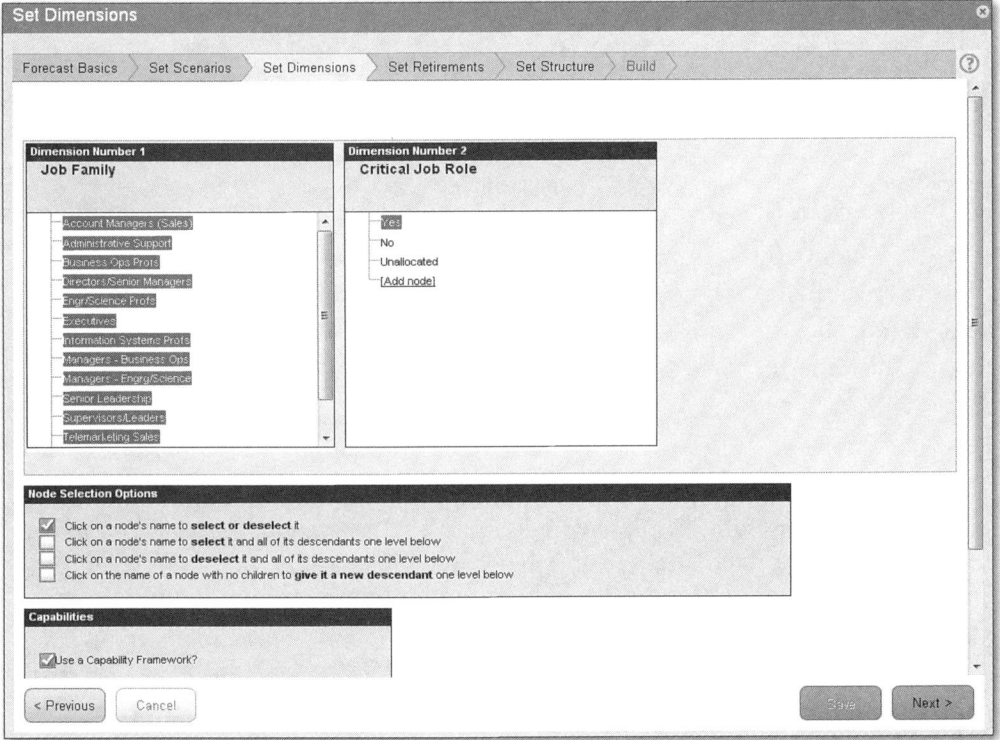

Figure 15.7 The Set Dimensions Step of Creating a Strategic Forecast

All dimensions have an [ADD NODE] link at the bottom of the node list. This is for users to create a placeholder for anticipated future nodes that don't exist yet. For example, under JOB FAMILY, you may not have an existing job family today for a job that you know will be critical in the future, but you can create a place to capture that in your forecast here in the SET DIMENSIONS tab. Because there are no employees in the JOB FAMILY today, there will be no underlying data associated with the new node.

Finally, the order of the dimensions is important because this is how they will appear on your demand spreadsheet. Simply click the left or right red arrows to move certain dimensions up or down in the order list. To delete a dimension, click the red REMOVE X.

One final tip in the SET DIMENSIONS tab is that if you scroll to the bottom of the window, you'll see the option to choose whether to leverage a *capability framework*. By checking the USE A CAPABILITY FRAMEWORK? checkbox, you'll have the ability to forecast by capabilities (also known as skills, competencies, etc.), as well as build a rating scale to rate the current and future skill levels of employees in critical job roles. If you build your forecast without enabling this checkbox, you'll be unable to enter capability demands in the forecasting section of the tool.

The WFP tool does come with an embedded capability framework, which can be selected as the default in the SELECT A FRAMEWORK dropdown. However, most clients opt to enter an organization-specific capability framework into the tool instead. To create a new capability framework, select the CREATE A NEW FRAMEWORK option in the SELECT A FRAMEWORK dropdown.

Next, you'll be prompted to choose an importance scale, which can be either a five- or ten-point scale. Typically, the five-point scale will suffice, although both options are available. The rating scale also includes both a five- and ten-point option. For both, select the five-point scales. We'll cover how to enter in a custom capability framework and assign values to the rating scales in Section 15.3.1 later in this chapter. Click SAVE and then NEXT to move to the next step, which is to set the retirement profile.

Set Retirements

The set retirements step allows you to define the *retirement profile(s)* that can be applied to your critical job roles in the SET RETIREMENTS tab. The default retirement profile will be set to NOT SET and can be defined by selecting the EDIT DEFAULT RETIREMENT PROFILE button in the DEFAULT RETIREMENT PROFILE section. There are two options for defining the retirement profile: FIXED RETIREMENT AGE or MATHEMATICAL APPROXIMATION.

The FIXED RETIREMENT AGE option allows a fixed value to be defined for the retirement age. For example, if you know based on historical data that employees in Job Role X typically retire by age 68, you can set this age as the cutoff.

15 | Workforce Planning

The second option, MATHEMATICAL APPROXIMATION, shows the curved line progression of retirements by defining the start and end age of the retirement wave. Users can either show this in a STRAIGHT LINE or EXPONENTIAL CURVE, with EXPONENTIAL CURVE being the typical selection. From here, you can select the START AGE from the dropdown menu, and define the END AGE as well. The last option is to enable the USE CUTOFF AGE checkbox, which says that all employees will retire by age X. As you change your retirement model criteria, the chart at the bottom of the window will update with a graphical representation of your selection showing the rate at which you can expect employees to retire.

For this example, we chose to enable the MATHEMATICAL APPROXIMATION model with the EXPONENTIAL CURVE, and START AGE of 65 with an END AGE of 75, as shown in Figure 15.8.

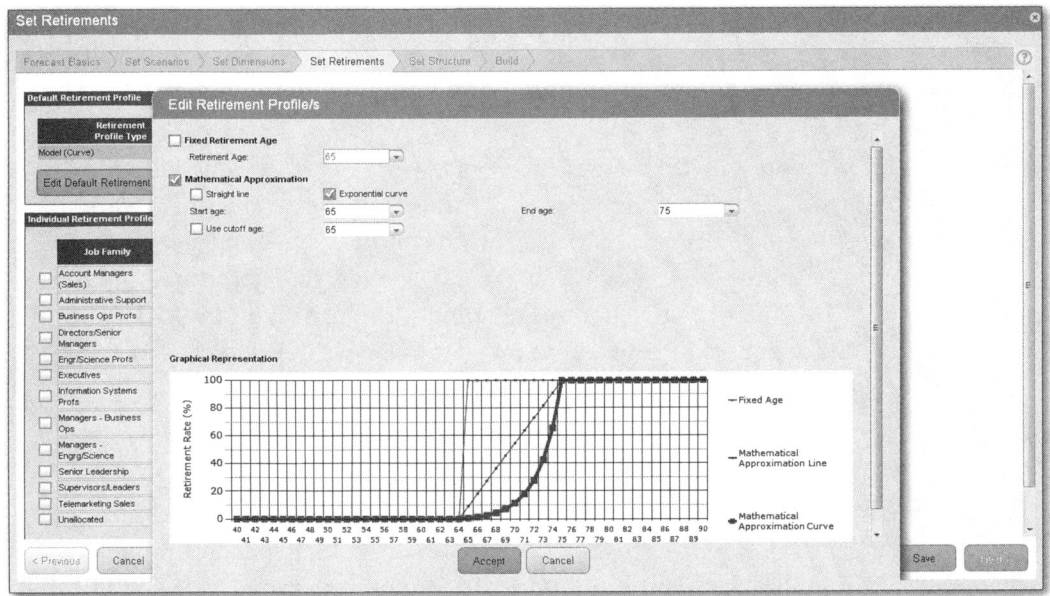

Figure 15.8 Edit Retirement Profile/s Screen in the Set Retirements Step

In addition to defining the general retirement model, you can also set individual retirement profiles for specific job roles in your forecast, which overrides the default retirement model for only the job roles that you assign, as shown in Figure 15.9. This becomes very useful when you're forecasting for a job such as an airplane pilot, where there are regulations specifying the specific age when pilots must retire. Individual retirement profiles can be set at the job family level by checking the box next to the job family, and clicking EDIT SELECTED RETIREMENT PROFILE/S at the bottom of the window.

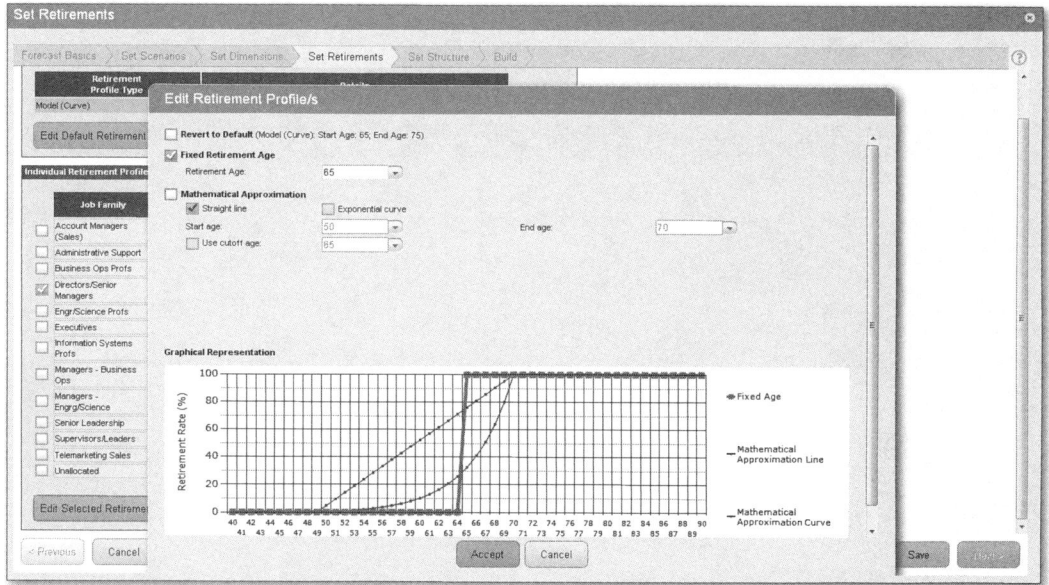

Figure 15.9 Edit Individual Retirement Profile/s

As an example, let's create an individual retirement profile for the directors/senior manager job family. One reason this might be necessary is that perhaps your company has a contractual retirement age of 65, and therefore you don't want to include any employees who meet this criteria in your supply forecast.

In the INDIVIDUAL RETIREMENT PROFILES section, select the checkbox for the DIRECTORS/SENIOR MANAGERS JOB FAMILY, and select the EDIT SELECTED RETIREMENT PROFILE/S button. Enter the EDIT RETIREMENT PROFILE/S screen, and change the FIXED RETIREMENT AGE value to "65". Note that this is the same screen that you used to set the default retirement profile. After clicking ACCEPT to confirm the change, you can see the new retirement model for the DIRECTORS/SENIOR MANAGER JOB FAMILY shown in Figure 15.10.

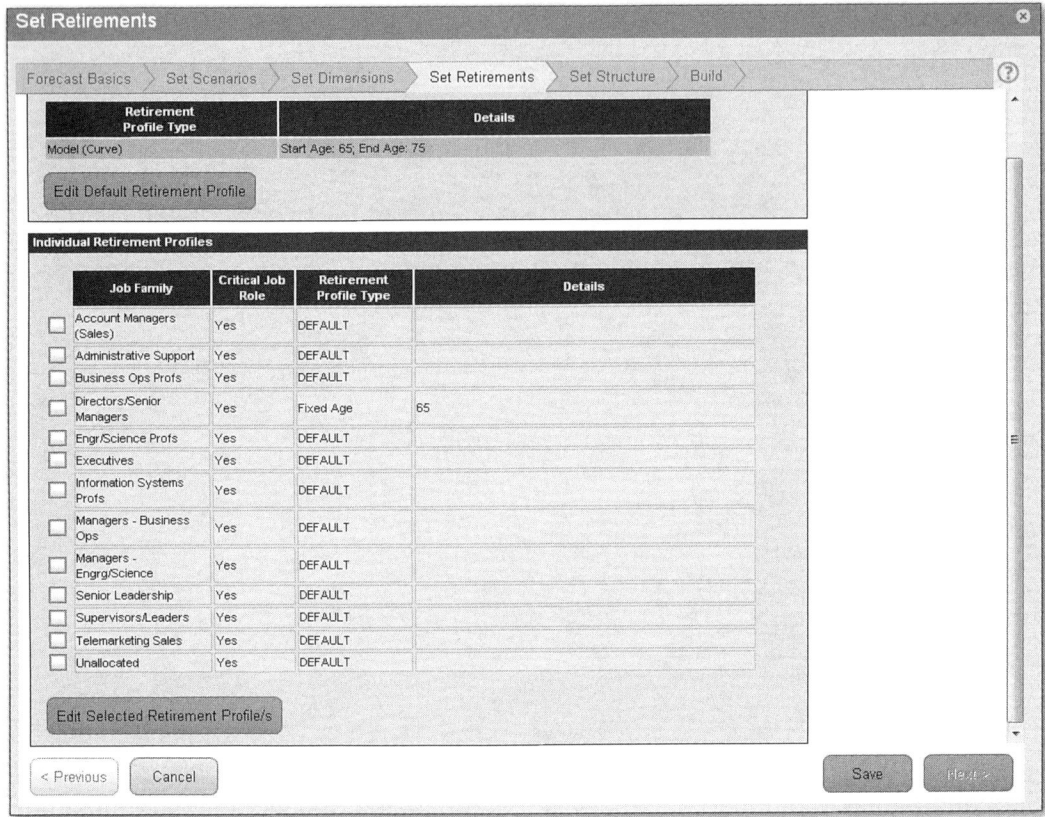

Figure 15.10 Setting Individual Retirement Profile

Click SAVE and then click NEXT, and the tool will move to the next tab: SET STRUCTURE.

Set Structure

In the SET STRUCTURE tab, you can define the organizational structure for your forecast. As defined in Chapter 14, clients can have multiple organizational hierarchies such as cost center structures, supervisor rollups, or location structures. Depending on how the organization reports workforce data, users can choose to apply the structure that most closely represents how the business views the organization.

By clicking on the STRUCTURE dropdown arrow, all available structures will be displayed, but only one can be selected. The most common hierarchy is the organizational unit structure; select it by clicking on the name.

As an example, let's say you are expanding your retail operation into the Midwest region of the United States. First, click on the plus (+) button to expand the top node of the organizational structure called ALL ORGANIZATIONAL UNITS. From here, expand the RETAIL level, and select RETAIL and all departments located one level below, which are denoted by red icons to the left of each node, as shown in Figure 15.11. Also, all existing hierarchies will show a link node called ADD LEVEL, which is used to create a node for a business unit, cost center, location, and so on that doesn't exist today, but you predict will exist in the future.

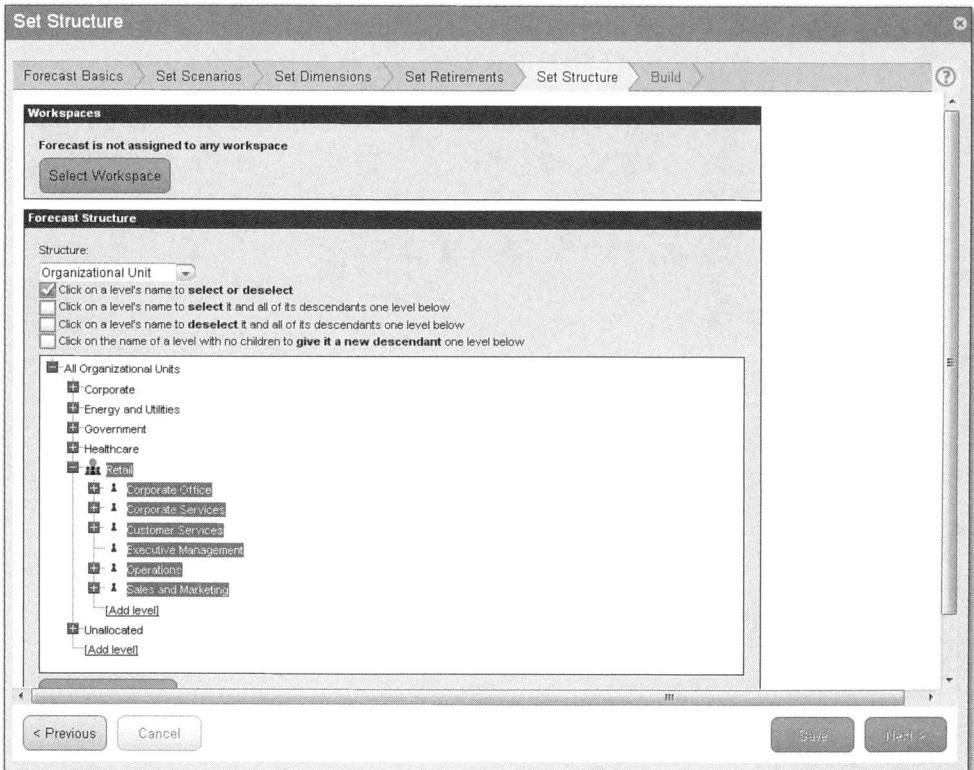

Figure 15.11 The Set Structure Step of Creating a Strategic Forecast

At the bottom of the SET STRUCTURE tab, you'll see the SUMMATION LEVEL EDITING ENABLED checkbox. By clicking this checkbox, users can edit the total level (top level) of the forecast. While all forecast data entered at the business unit or department level will automatically roll up to the top-level node selected, sometimes it's necessary to edit at the total level as well. It's important to take this step at this stage of the process because it can't be enabled after the forecast is built. Check the box, click SAVE, and then click NEXT to advance to the final tab.

Build Forecast

The final step of building the forecast is to verify your forecast selections, and create the forecast using the BUILD FORECAST button. Figure 15.12 shows the final overview prior to the forecast being created. Until the build is complete, your forecast will have a yellow dot next to it in the STRATEGIC FORECASTS list. After the forecast build is complete, you'll receive an email notification, and the dot will turn green in the STRATEGIC FORECASTS list.

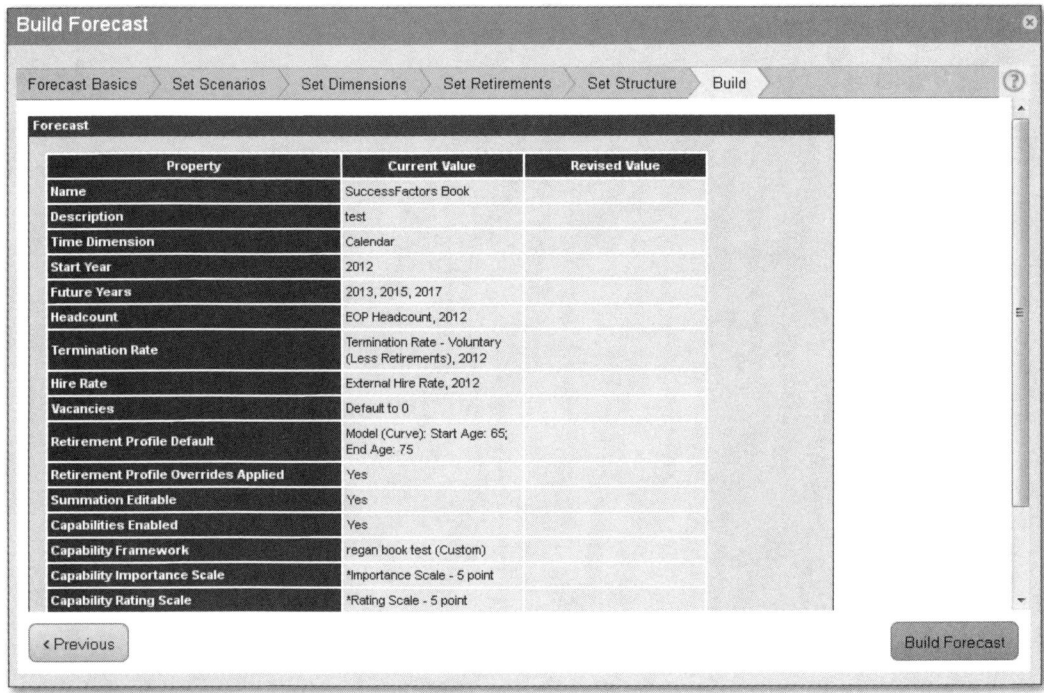

Figure 15.12 The Build Step of Creating a Strategic Forecast

After the forecast is created, you're taken back to the STRATEGIC FORECASTS screen. If you try to edit the forecast after you've clicked BUILD, you'll see a red note at the top of each tab that reads, "This forecast already has data attached to it. Changes will not take effect until after a rebuild."

On the right-hand side of the FORECAST LIST screen, you can see an overall summary of what you've selected, as shown in Figure 15.13. To summarize, you're looking at two different scenarios (high growth vs. low growth), and you're starting in the 2012 calendar year and forecasting out for 2013, 2015, and 2017. Finally, you're analyzing job family by critical roles for the retail business unit, and incorporating the 2012 voluntary termination rate (less retirements).

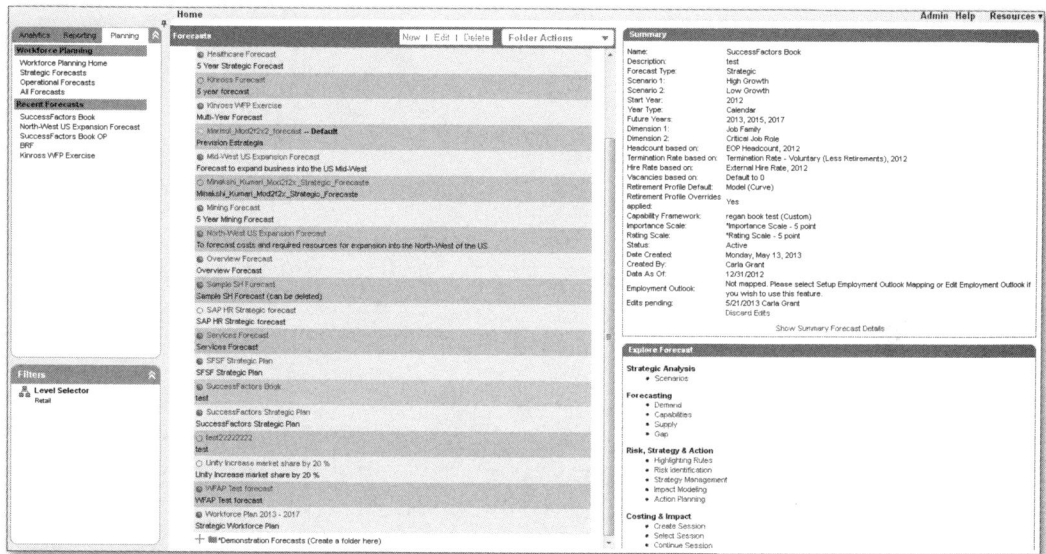

Figure 15.13 Summary View

Now that the forecast has been built, we'll cover the forecasting step in the SWFP process.

15.3 Forecasting

Forecasting is the process of evaluating scenarios to identify any gaps between your existing talent pool and the optimal organizational mix of people and skills that will be needed in the future. In SWFP, forecasting is generally broken down into two separate steps: *demand forecasting* (includes both capability and capacity forecasting) and *supply forecasting*.

15.3.1 Demand Forecasting

Forecasting demand is the process of determining the number of people you'll need in each of the critical job roles that have been identified under each scenario. Critical job roles are defined as those that do the following:

- Conduct the core business of the organization
- May become part of the core business under either scenario
- Have had a high number of vacancies in the past 12 months
- Have been historically difficult to fill
- Require a long training time to develop the skills for the role
- Have the largest number of staff

From a demand standpoint, directors/managers who have expert knowledge of the business are asked to forecast how many people they will need in each critical job role over the next one, three, and five years to meet the demand of each scenario (high growth vs. low growth).

In addition, many organizations not only forecast demand in terms of the number of people needed, but also in terms of the specific capabilities that will be necessary to execute the organizational strategy. In *capability forecasting*, you're looking to differentiate between skills needed today and those in the future.

Typically, the process of determining demand is done in a demand workshop setting or through a series of demand interviews. Lastly, the demand forecasting should be zero-based to estimate demand as if you're starting from scratch. However, it's helpful to understand the current headcount of each critical job role to give forecasters a frame of reference in terms of the amount of growth/downsizing that needs to occur.

After you've collected your demand numbers by critical job role, you can enter the forecast into the WFP tool. To navigate to the FORECASTING screen, select the DEMAND link under the FORECASTING heading in the EXPLORE FORECAST section (refer to Figure 15.13).

When you enter the DEMAND screen, you'll first see a graphical representation of your demand forecast. Because we haven't yet input any demand numbers, the tool automatically assumes a steady-state forecast. This simply means that the demand for each job family over the five-year forecast period remains the same as the starting headcount in 2012 (the beginning year of our forecast). Figure 15.14 shows the steady-state demand forecast for the RETAIL business unit.

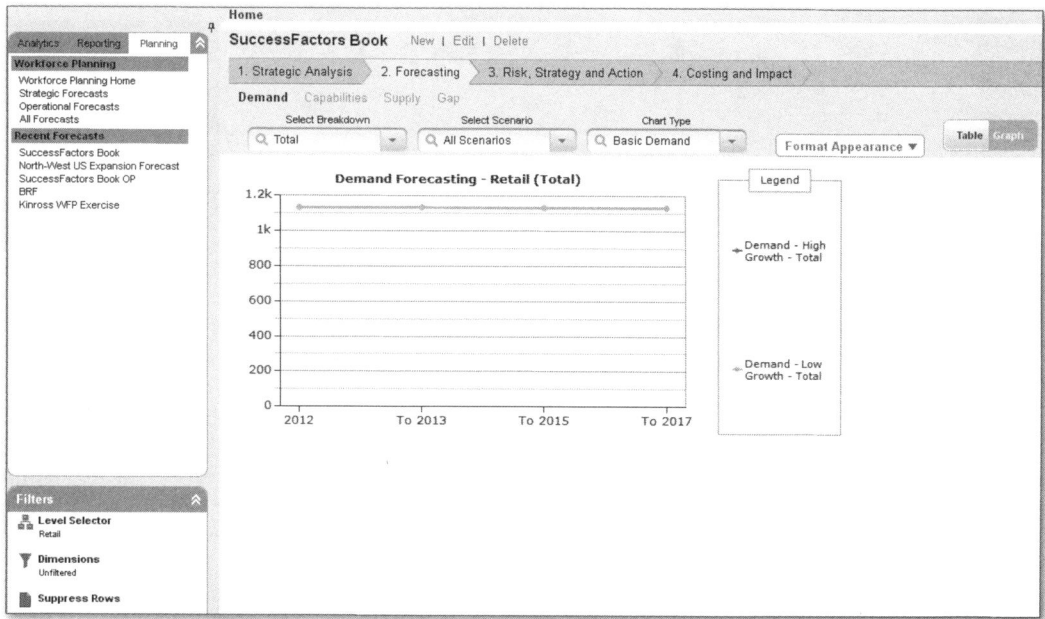

Figure 15.14 Steady-State Demand

By clicking on the TABLE/GRAPH toggle button, the demand forecast can also be viewed as a table. In the table view, you can modify the demand numbers for each critical job family, for each scenario, and for each year of the forecast. The demand page view can be customized to show the data elements or cuts that are of specific interest (e.g., only one scenario, only the first two years, etc.). Similarly, if you want to focus on only one department at a time, you can do so by clicking on the LEVEL SELECTOR in the FILTER pane and selecting a specific node.

Let's say that you want to forecast demand for CUSTOMER SERVICES, and select this node only. Figure 15.15 shows the new demand forecast for each critical job family within the CUSTOMER SERVICES department only. Users can export this demand forecast to Excel by clicking the EXCEL icon in the top-left corner of the spreadsheet (also shown in Figure 15.15). By providing this customized view to Customer Services managers, they can more easily forecast demand for their critical job families (as opposed to seeing the entire Retail business unit). After the headcount demand is finalized by managers for the Customer Services department, you can upload the revised demand forecast into the WFP tool by clicking on the UPLOAD (IMPORT FROM EXCEL) link, eliminating much of the manual data entry.

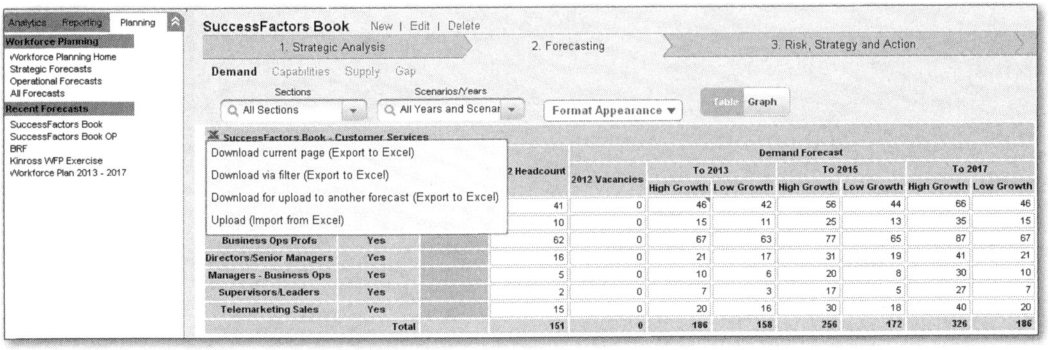

Figure 15.15 Export Demand for Customer Services Department

If a demand forecaster's preference is to modify the demand numbers directly in the WFP tool, you can simply click on a cell and manually override the existing entry in a new window called EDIT VALUES, as shown in Figure 15.16.

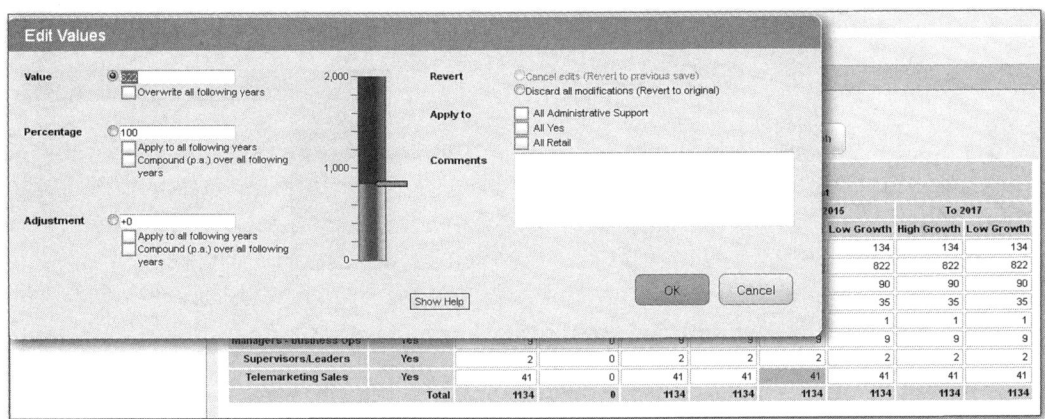

Figure 15.16 Edit Values

Forecasters repeat the process for each critical job family, under each scenario, for each year until the forecast is complete. Often, it's helpful to enter comments in the EDIT VALUES window so that others can quickly understand a forecaster's logic for the demand estimates. This becomes especially useful when you revisit demand forecasts a year or so after the SWFP process is completed and modify/update the demand numbers.

For the Customer Services department example, let's say you want to add +5 headcount and compound this number year over year for each critical job family in the high-growth scenario. For the low-growth scenario, you'll add +1 headcount compounded over the forecast years. Note that this is for example's sake only, and in an actual demand forecast, the numbers would not necessarily follow a straight linear increase. To make these changes, click on the 2013 HIGH GROWTH cell, check the ADJUSTMENT option, change the value to +5, then check the COMPOUND OVER ALL FOLLOWING YEARS option. Repeat the same process for the low-growth scenario, only adding +1 to the value.

After you've accepted all changes, the edited cells will display a red font, and you must click SAVE to move to the next step. If a forecaster enters a comment while editing a value, that cell will have a red icon in the top-right corner, which denotes there is a comment attached. After the demand forecast is saved, the comment icon will turn green, and all cell fonts will revert back to black, as shown in Figure 15.17.

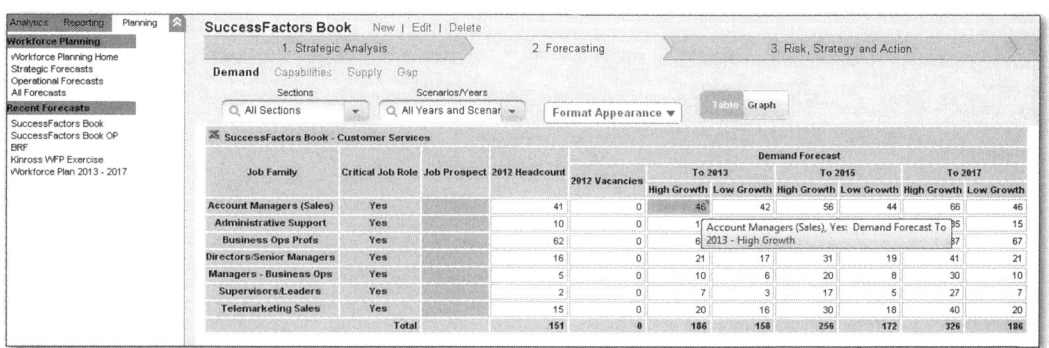

Figure 15.17 Edited Customer Services Forecast

If you toggle back to the GRAPH view of the demand forecast, you can visualize how the different demand forecasts vary for each scenario. Figure 15.18 shows the graphical representation of the demand forecasts for CUSTOMER SERVICES.

15 | Workforce Planning

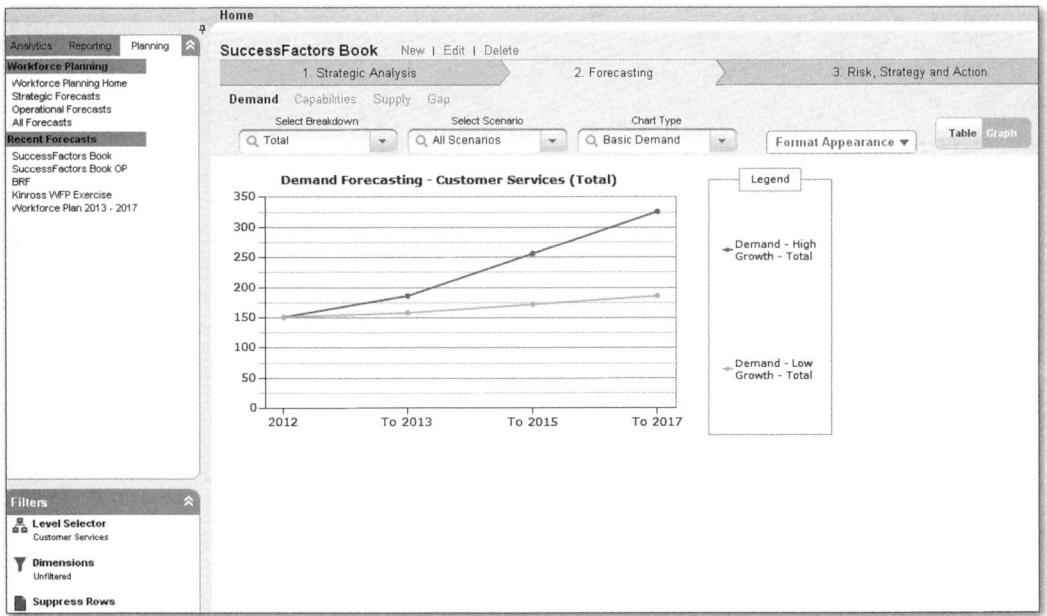

Figure 15.18 Customer Services Demand Graphs

Now that the demand forecast is entered for Customer Services, we can move to the next link in the FORECASTING tab called CAPABILITIES. This tab will only be available if you've enabled the capability framework when building your forecast.

15.3.2 Capabilities

When you click on the CAPABILITY link, a new screen refreshes that shows each critical job family with no capabilities attached, as shown in Figure 15.19.

The first step is to click on the empty cell called [NO CAPABILITIES SPECIFIED], and assign the capabilities for each critical job role that will be important over the forecast period. A new window will open called EDIT CAPABILITIES; if you've entered in a capability framework, it will be displayed here for you to select. To enter a capability framework, click on the EDIT dropdown at the top of the page, and select EDIT CAPABILITIES. A new window will open that allows you to add a two-level framework, as well as customize the importance and rating scales. If your organization does not have an organization-specific capability framework, capabilities can be added on the fly in the CAPABILITY tab. Let's walk through an example of how to add a communication capability to the directors/senior managers job family.

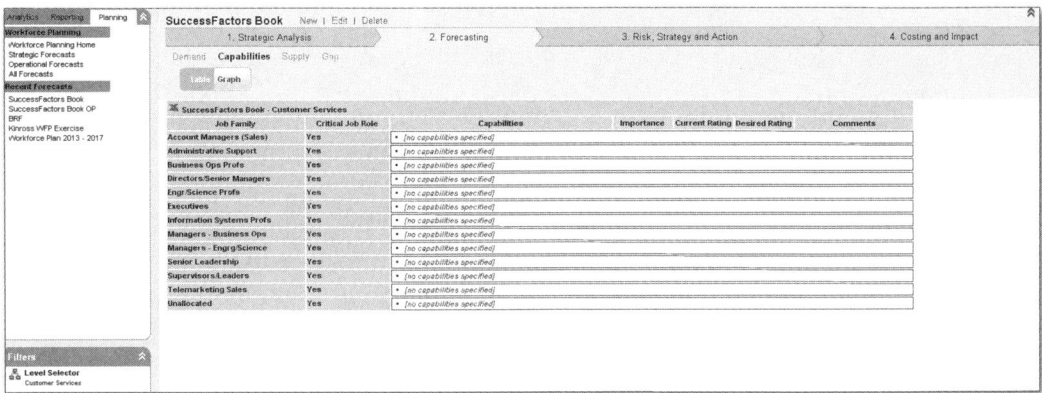

Figure 15.19 Customer Services Capabilities

First, click on the empty [NO CAPABILITIES SPECIFIED] row corresponding to the DIRECTORS/SENIOR MANAGERS JOB FAMILY, which will cause a new window to appear that doesn't have any capabilities listed to assign. Click on OPEN CAPABILITY EDITOR, and click ADD to enter the COMMUNICATION capability (see Figure 15.20). Click OK, and then click SAVE, and the editing window will close and take you back to the main CAPABILITY tab.

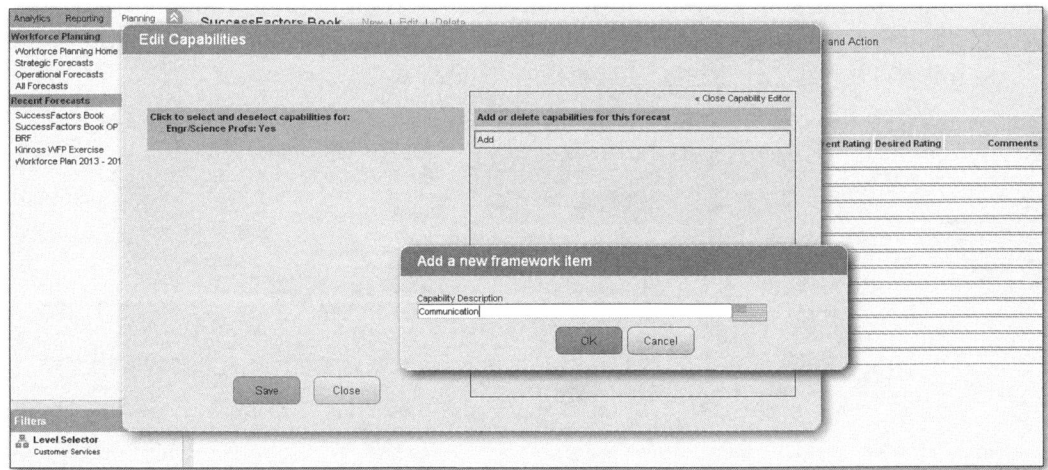

Figure 15.20 Add Communication Capability

15 | Workforce Planning

Now when you click on [NO CAPABILITIES SPECIFIED] for the DIRECTORS/SENIOR MANAGERS JOB FAMILY, COMMUNICATION will be an available capability to choose, and it will turn green with a checkmark signifying it has been successfully applied.

The next step is to assign an importance rating to the COMMUNICATION capability for DIRECTORS/SENIOR MANAGERS by clicking on the empty cell in the IMPORTANCE column. Because you've built the forecast with a five-point rating scale, you can assign a value ranging from 1-NOT AT ALL IMPORTANT to 5-EXTREMELY IMPORTANT to the COMMUNICATION capability, which denotes how critical the capability will be at the end of the forecast period. For directors/senior managers, communication is a very important capability, so assign the highest value (5-EXTREMELY IMPORTANT).

You're also prompted to enter ratings of the capability in this window, which is intended to show the gap between the directors/senior managers' current communication capability level and the desired communication level by the end of the forecast period (e.g., 2017). For directors/senior managers, enter the CURRENT RATING at 4-ABOVE AVERAGE. However, you want them to be at the highest possible level by 2017, so select 5-EXCELLENT as the DESIRED RATING. You can also enter comments about the importance and ratings you've assigned.

Figure 15.21 shows the completed capabilities table for the DIRECTORS/SENIOR MANAGERS JOB FAMILY. Multiple capabilities can be added to each job family and, similar to other tabs in the WFP tool, the capability spreadsheet can be exported to Excel. Users can also toggle between a table and graph view.

Figure 15.21 Completed Capability Row

Now that we've walked through how to forecast capabilities, let's discuss supply forecasting, which can be accessed by clicking the SUPPLY link.

15.3.3 Supply Forecasting

Supply forecasting is where you leverage the measures taken from the underlying analytics engine, meaning that the tool is applying historical rates to forecast estimates for terminations, hires, movements, and vacancies (depending on what you enabled while building the forecast). Similar to the DEMAND tab, when you click SUPPLY, the first screen shows a graphical representation of supply for each critical job family over the forecast period. By clicking the TABLE/GRAPH toggle button, you can view the supply figures in a table, which is the preferred format for forecasting supply.

In the table view, we're starting with the 2012 headcount for each critical job family, and the tool is using the 2012 voluntary termination rate (less retirements) as a baseline for supply into 2013, 2015, and 2017. This measure truly is a baseline, meaning that you can edit the historical supply estimates to more accurately model out expected future patterns. Exactly as you did in DEMAND, you can click on any one of the cells in the supply table to modify the value.

To the right of the current headcount, terminations, retirements, and external hires are incorporated to give a more granular understanding of what the forecast will look like from a supply perspective across the next five years, as shown in Figure 15.22.

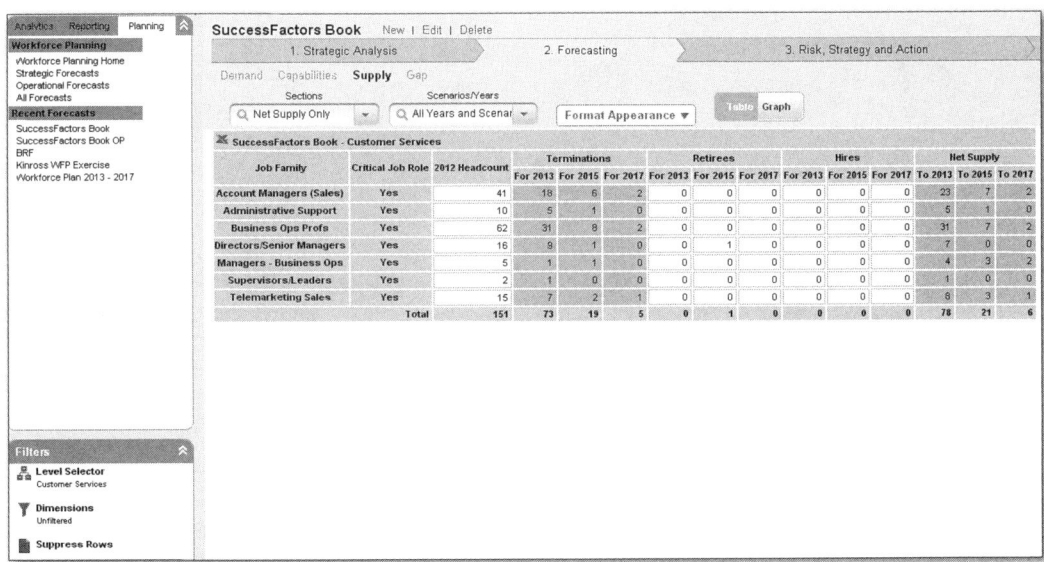

Figure 15.22 Supply Table

Similar to demand, you can view the supply forecast in a graph, and there are a few different charting options. One particularly useful view is the NET SUPPLY EXCLUDING INFLOWS view, which essentially shows you where you'll be at the end of the forecast period if you do nothing differently. In other words, the supply curve is only showing outflows (terminations and retirements), without factoring in any new hires (internal or external) to backfill positions. Figure 15.23 depicts the net supply excluding inflows for Customer Services; by 2017, there will be nearly no one left in the internal talent pool.

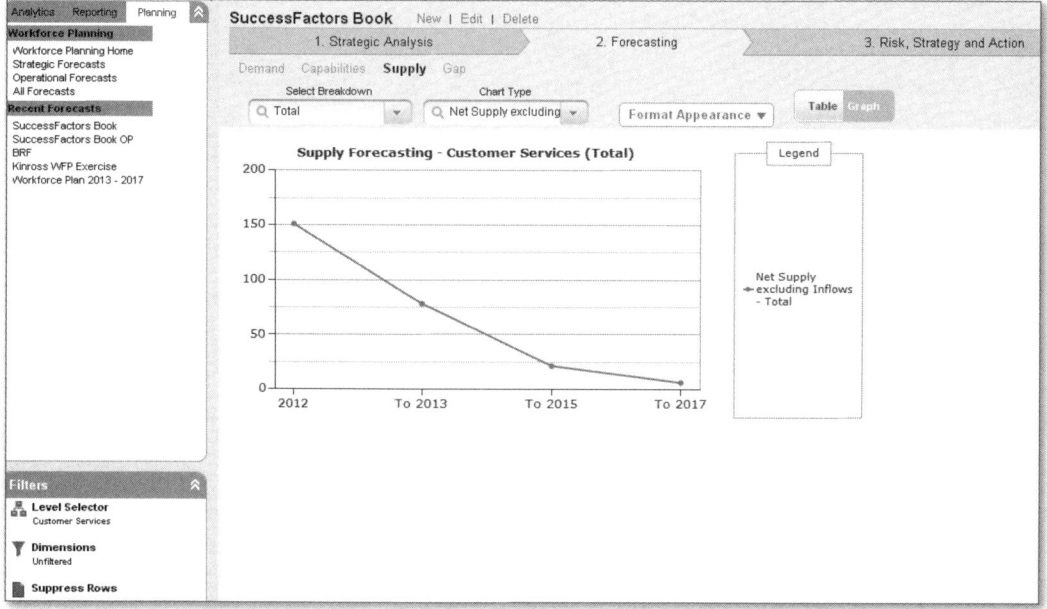

Figure 15.23 Supply Graph

Now that the necessary changes have been made to the supply forecast, let's can move to the final forecasting step: analyzing the gap.

15.3.4 Gap

Gap analysis is a simple calculation of demand minus supply, and it helps you identify the key workforce risks for both capacity (numbers) and capabilities. In the GAP tab, you're pairing together supply and demand and breaking it down by scenario.

Once calculated, you can see the overall net supply, as well as the magnitude of the gap per scenario, either as a shortage or a surplus.

Similar to all tabs within the FORECASTING section of the tool, the GAP tab is accessed by clicking on the GAP link and will show a graphical view on the initial screen. By toggling to the TABLE view, you can see a more granular view of both demand and supply in one table, and the columns shown in the table can be customized by clicking on the SECTIONS dropdown. The last column in the table shows the GAP (SHORTAGE/SURPLUS), and all negative deltas (shortage) are shown in red font, while all positive deltas (surplus) are shown in green. Figure 15.24 shows the GAP table for the CUSTOMER SERVICES department, which identifies shortages across all critical job families regardless of scenario.

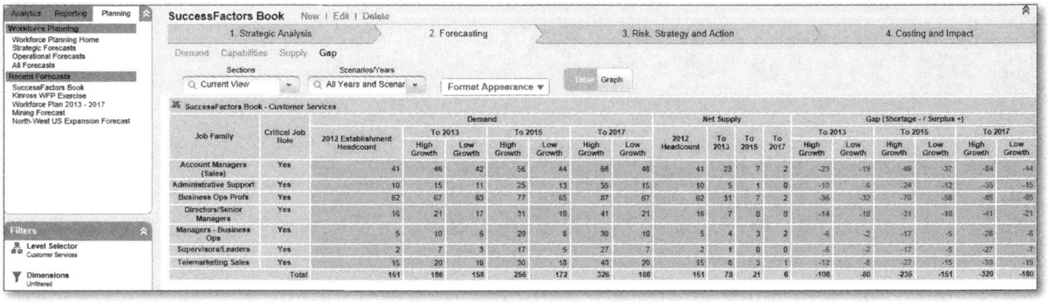

Figure 15.24 Gap Table

Similar to demand and supply, the gap can also be shown in a variety of graphs. After receiving sign-off on both the demand and supply forecasts for each department within the Retail business unit, it's time for the *Risk, Strategy, and Action* phase (also known as the Act Module) which can be accessed by selecting the RISK, STRATEGY, AND ACTION tab.

15.4 The Act Module

At its core, SWFP is a risk mitigation exercise, with the end goal of identifying the highest priority risks an organization is facing in the future, and creating action plans to put in motion today to minimize the impact of risks in the future. After you've identified the gaps, you need to analyze where the largest shortages/surpluses are occurring, and what might be causing them. Typically, there are three main drivers of gaps:

- Growth
- Resignations
- Retirements

By looking at the various data elements on the gap spreadsheet, such as terminations or retirements, you can identify which of these three drivers are causing the gaps. Next, you must prioritize the gaps in terms of significance and impact. Are there large shortages in critical job roles that you know are historically difficult to attract and retain? Or, are the largest gaps in roles you know are easily sourced in the external labor market? You'll also want to consider how the gaps differ by scenario, and what impact changes in capabilities will have on gaps. Ultimately, you're trying to determine the risks that are most likely to occur and that will have the largest impact on your ability to execute your strategy.

In the Risk, Strategy and Action phase, workforce planners can model out the impact of different strategies to mitigate the identified risks. When you first access the Act Module, a screen prompt will appear asking if you want to use the Act default template or start with an empty slate. To leverage the SuccessFactors strategy bank and other best practice defaults, you must click YES.

15.4.1 Highlighting Rules

The first screen is HIGHLIGHTING RULES, which leverages the data highlighting tool embedded within Analytics Workspace in the WFA application (see Chapter 14). The first step is to define the rules that you want the tool to search for in the data. A few common rules are listed here as defaults (e.g., high turnover, significant gaps, and large numbers of forecasted retirements).

Next to the list of rules is a summary window that shows the criteria of the selected rule. To view the criteria of each rule, simply click on the rule description until that row turns green, and the summary window will refresh with the selected rule's details. You can add multiple rules by clicking NEW RULE or edit the parameters of the default rules by clicking EDIT. You must click SAVE after editing a rule to go back to the HIGHLIGHTING RULES screen. For the RETAIL business unit example, let's leverage the three existing default rules, which are shown in Figure 15.25.

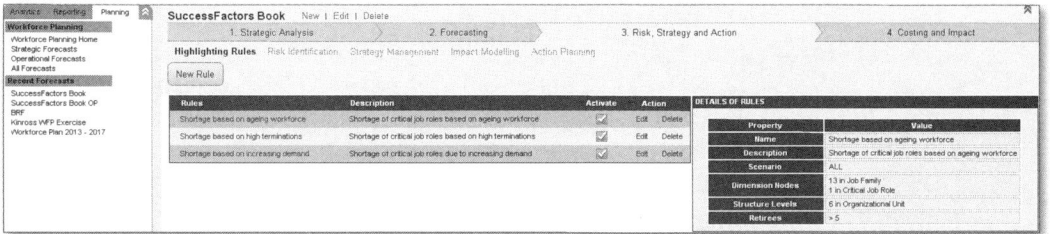

Figure 15.25 Highlighting Rules

15.4.2 Risk Identification

The next link within the Act Module is Risk Identification, which also comes prepopulated with common risks associated with the rules that you defined in the Highlighting Rules section. The risks are listed at the top of the screen, with the selected risk highlighted in green, and a table below showing where in the forecast (by business unit, department, or job family) each specific risk is an issue (denoted by a green cell). New risks can also be added by clicking the New Risk button. Essentially, in this step, the tool has listed out specific risks that map to the rules you've previously defined.

For example, you might have a shortage of critical job roles due to high projected termination rates, as shown in Figure 15.26. If you scroll down, you can easily see where in the forecast this particular risk is an issue because it's highlighted in green.

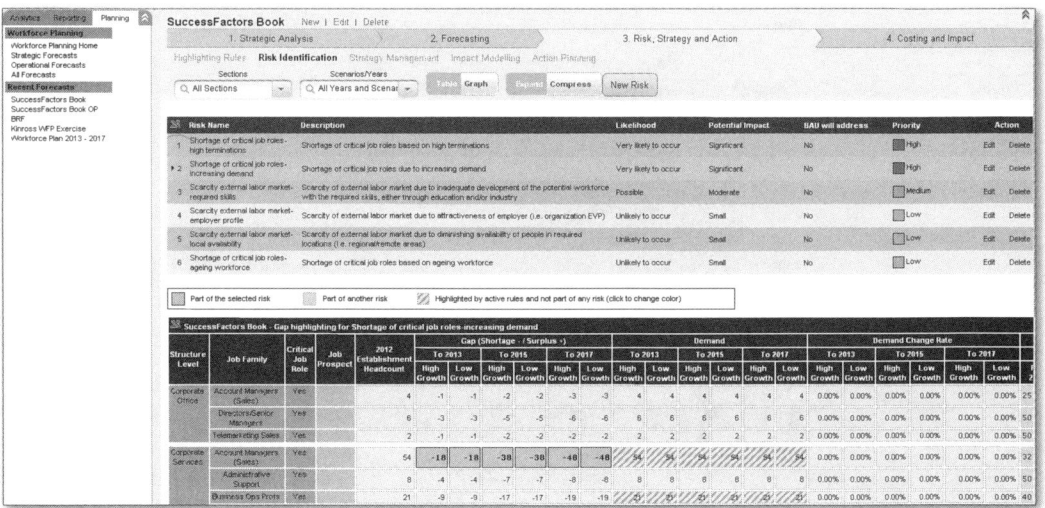

Figure 15.26 Risk Identification

Data highlighting is an easy method of sifting through all of the data in your forecast to quickly highlight the areas with the largest risks. In this case, you can see that account managers in the CORPORATE SERVICES department are at risk for a shortage due to increasing demand, as well as high termination rates.

In Figure 15.26, you can also see that each risk is color-coded in the PRIORITY column. However, the priority level will always default to low (gray color). To change the priority level based on your organization's circumstances, select the risk you want to modify (the row will turn green), and then click EDIT. A new window will appear that shows the description of the risk and requires a rating on the likelihood that the risk will happen, the potential impact, and whether or not business as usual will address the risk. Depending on the risk level assigned, either a red, yellow, or gray color is assigned to the risk. A few quick tips are that risks are listed in order of priority (red to gray), and any cell in the table can be manually overridden and coded according to the specifications a user defines.

The last feature of the RISK IDENTIFICATION section that we'll cover is the graphical view of the risk matrix. By toggling from TABLE to GRAPH view, the risks are shown in a three-by-three matrix utilizing the same color-coding assigned in the TABLE view to visually highlight the highest priority risks. High-priority risks again are defined as the most likely to occur that will have the biggest impact, as shown in Figure 15.27.

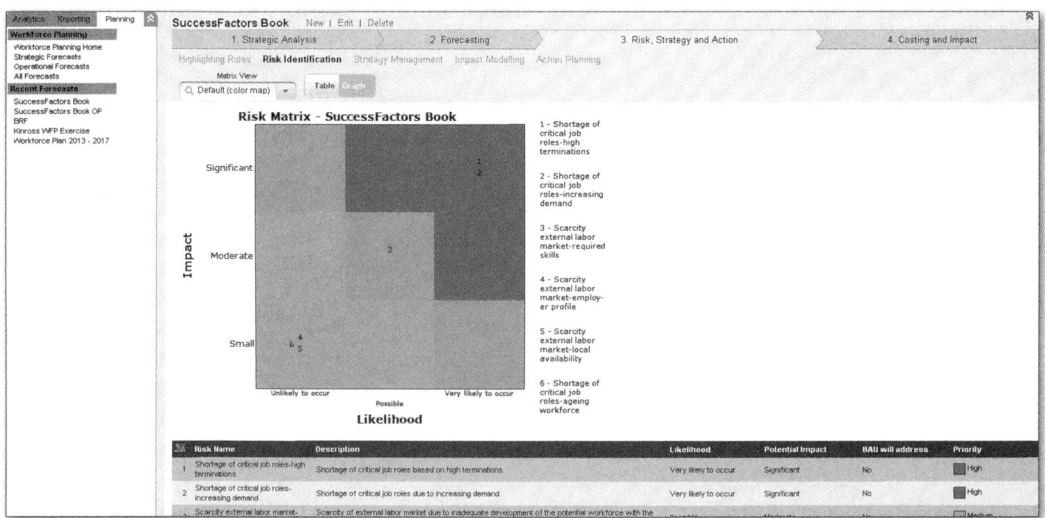

Figure 15.27 Risk Matrix

15.4.3 Strategy Management

Now that you've defined the highest priority risks and where they are occurring in the forecast, you can begin to determine which strategies will be most impactful in terms of mitigating the identified risks. SWFP focuses on making decisions that will have the most impact, which means you'll make decisions on what you will and will not do to address workforce risks related to the following:

- Critical job roles
- Significant capability gaps
- Significant staff surplus/deficit
- Significant turnover in key roles
- Workforce trends such as an aging workforce

By clicking on the STRATEGY MANAGEMENT link, a new screen refreshes with your risk list, as well as suggested tactics for the selected risk (highlighted in green). Tactics are pulled directly from the SuccessFactors strategy bank, which is embedded in the tool and contains more than 30 years of best practice strategies. The full strategy bank can be viewed by clicking on the ADD OR REMOVE TACTICS button, and a new window will open where specific tactics can be checked or unchecked depending on whether you want to include them.

To the right of each tactic is the TACTIC CHARACTERISTICS FOR RISK window, which allows users to rate each tactic on both impact and feasibility. Similar to Risk Identification, the color associated with each tactic will change based on how the tactic is rated. You can toggle between either the RISK or STRATEGY view, depending on the format you prefer. Figure 15.28 shows the STRATEGY MANAGEMENT screen.

After you've assigned and rated tactics for each identified risk, you can toggle to the GRAPH view to see a three-by-three matrix of the strategies that will be most feasible to implement and have the greatest impact. The GRAPH view also includes a legend defining the tactics, as shown in Figure 15.29.

15 | Workforce Planning

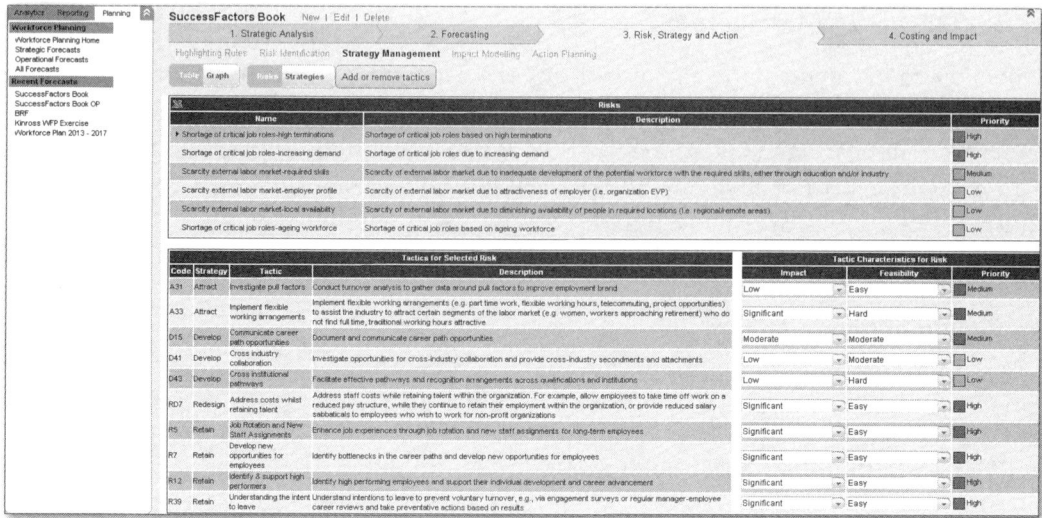

Figure 15.28 Strategy Management Table View

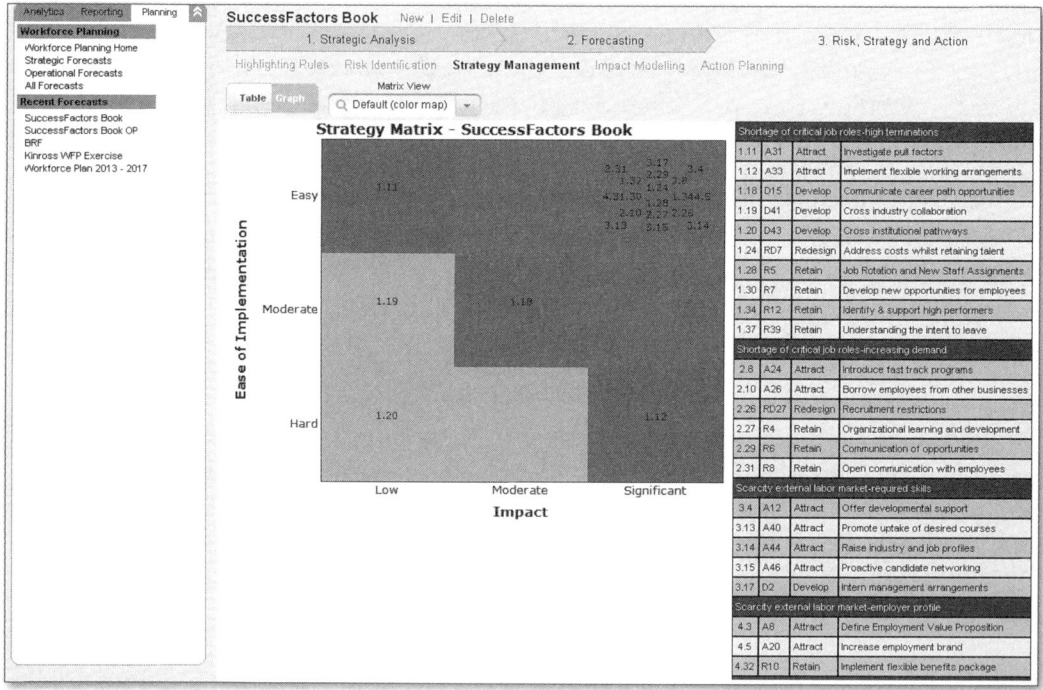

Figure 15.29 Strategy Management Graph View

In the next section, we'll cover how to model the impact of strategies to mitigate the risks already identified in the forecast.

15.4.4 Impact Modeling

Impact modeling can be a powerful tool for identifying which strategies are going to be the most impactful and most cost-effective to implement. Typically, clients create different models by strategy type and can then compare the models side by side to determine which strategy should move forward to the action planning phase.

For example, let's say you've identified a high-priority risk due to high turnover in critical roles. The two strategic options you have to mitigate this risk can be grouped into buy versus build scenarios, meaning you either need to buy talent from the external market or invest in programs to internally develop additional talent. While the specific tactics may vary under each sourcing strategy, impact modeling can help you understand if the benefits of one strategy significantly outweigh the other.

To access the IMPACT MODELING section of the Act Module, click on the IMPACT MODELING link. A blank screen will refresh alerting you that you haven't yet assigned any risks to the model, and therefore it's blank. To assign risks, click on the VIEW/EDIT MODEL DETAILS link in the FILTERS pane, which will generate a list of risks. By clicking on the checkbox next to each risk, the tool will list out the tactics that can be applied, and you can check the ones you want to include in the model.

For the first model, let's select tactics that would apply to a buy sourcing strategy (e.g., RAISE INDUSTRY AND JOB PROFILES, PROACTIVE CANDIDATE NETWORKING, etc.) and then click SAVE. Figure 15.30 shows the complete list of selections.

Now the page will display a table view of where the selected risks and gaps are occurring within the forecast. By clicking on the MODEL dropdown, you can click ADD to save this model, and title it "Buy Sourcing Strategy".

Next, you'll repeat this process by clicking on ADD in the MODEL dropdown menu and naming it "Build Sourcing Strategy". The tool will ask if you want to copy the selected risks and tactics from the current model or start with a clean slate. Because you're changing your strategies, choose to start with a clean slate, and repeat the process of assigning risks/tactics by clicking on VIEW/EDIT MODEL DETAILS and changing your selections to strategies designed at internal capability building. Now, when you click on the MODEL dropdown, you can see both models displayed in the list and can compare them side by side after making edits to each model.

15 | Workforce Planning

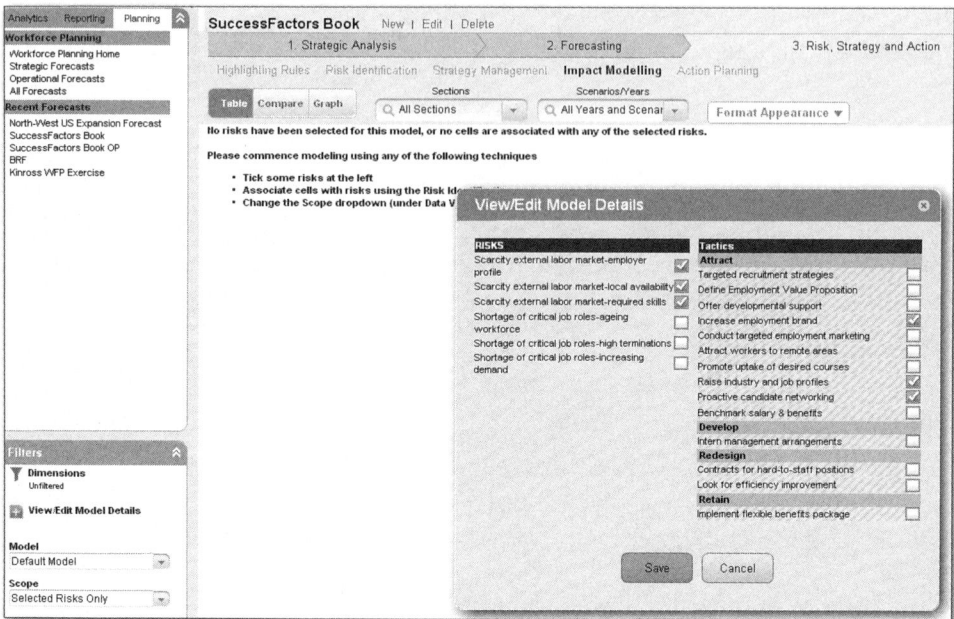

Figure 15.30 Impact Model: Buy Strategy

Similar to demand and supply forecasting, the IMPACT MODELING section allows users to change the numbers in the forecast depending on a specific strategy's expected outcomes. For example, in the buy sourcing strategy, we've chosen to focus recruitment on critical roles, and therefore would expect to see hiring rates for critical roles to change significantly, ultimately affecting the gap.

Let's model this scenario as an example. The first step is to switch back to the buy model, which can be done by selecting BUY SOURCING STRATEGY in the MODEL dropdown in the FILTERS pane. Again, the table view refreshes with the CUSTOMER SERVICES account managers because this is the department you identified with the largest risks/gaps. The default hiring rate is 0%, but let's change this to 3% year over year by clicking on the 2013 cell. Doing so will prompt a new window to open similar to the edit cells window you saw in the FORECASTING section. In this window, you can change the hiring rate to 3% in the value window (change 0 to 3), and check the OVERWRITE ALL FOLLOWING YEARS box.

Before you can exit this window, you must assign this change to a specific tactic in the ASSOCIATE EDITS WITH dropdown menu. For example's sake, associate the hiring increase with the PROACTIVE CANDIDATE NETWORKING tactic, and click OK.

Now your hiring rates are displayed in a red font as 3% for the next 5 years of the forecast, as shown in Figure 15.31.

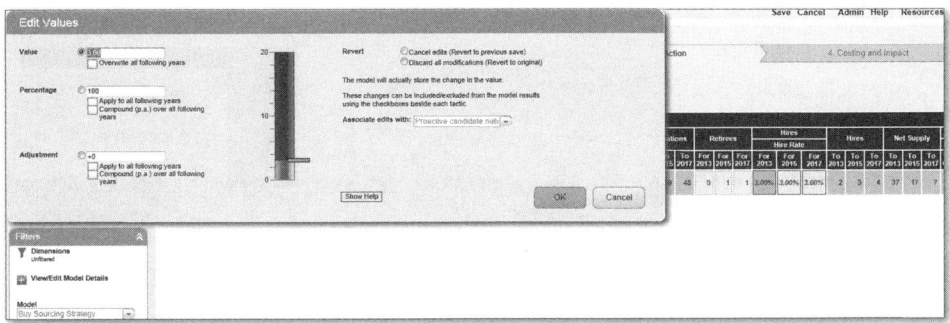

Figure 15.31 Impact Model Change Hiring Rate

The gap is automatically modified as a result of the hiring rate increase; in this example, it has decreased across all years for both scenarios. Before you can move on, you must click SAVE at the top of the screen to confirm the edits and the cell font will revert back to black. Each edited cell will also have a blue border around the cell signifying that the cell has been edited.

After the page refreshes, toggle to the GRAPH view to see a graphical representation of your before/after results for the buy sourcing strategy as shown in Figure 15.32.

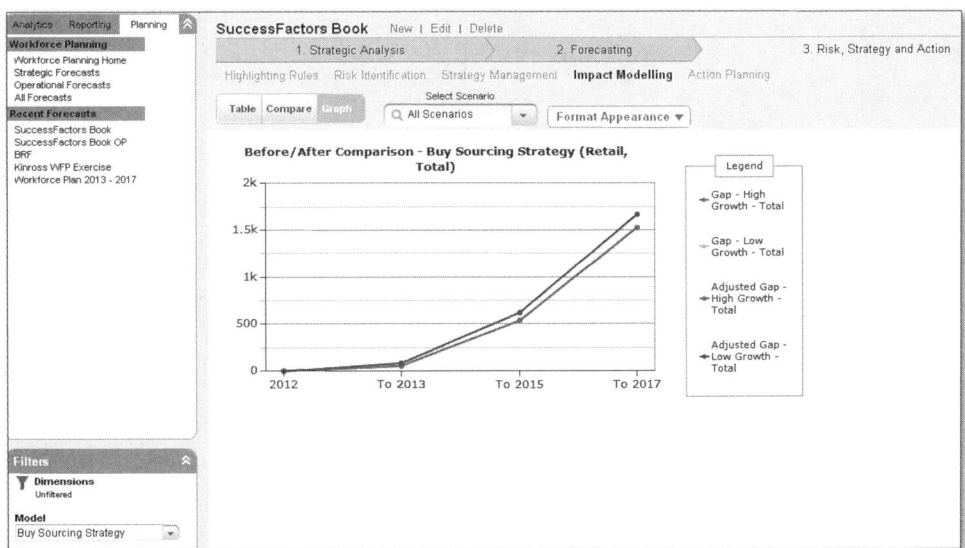

Figure 15.32 Before/After Comparison

After repeating a similar process for the build sourcing strategy, the final step of impact modeling is to do a side-by-side comparison of both strategies. By clicking on the COMPARE toggle, a table view will refresh displaying both models in one view, as shown in Figure 15.33.

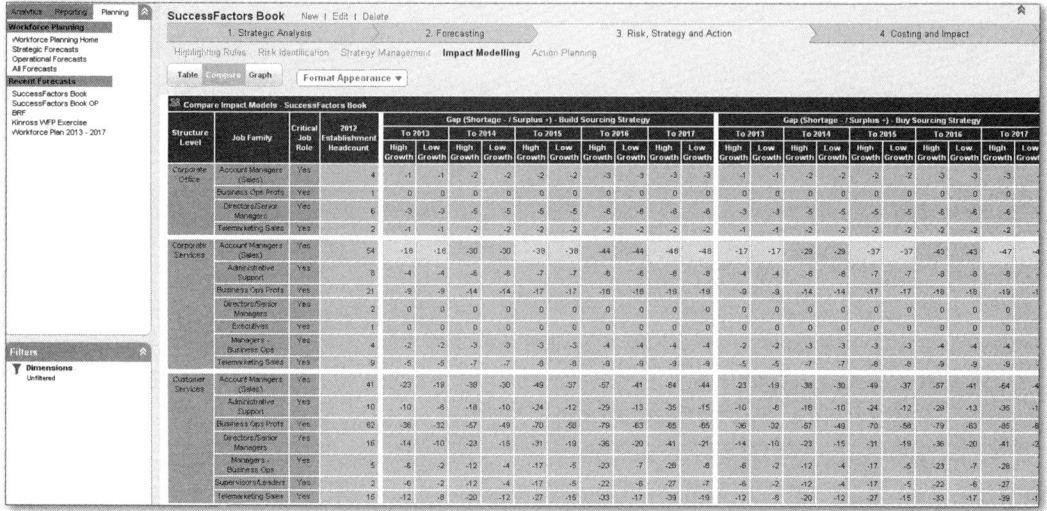

Figure 15.33 Compare Models

Now that you've modeled a few different strategies to reach a decision on which tactics should be implemented, you can build an action plan and assign activities to individuals in the final section of the Act Module.

15.4.5 Action Planning

The final portion of the Act Module is where users can assign responsibility to either individuals or teams to ensure that the selected initiatives are completed in a timely fashion. In effect, this is a great tool to drive accountability and ultimately brings workforce planning from an "exercise" to an "executable strategy." In addition, based on the strategy, you can start to frame the workforce planning discussion in terms of the business. In many ways, this is the beginning of the SWFP process, not the end.

The *action plan* should include an outline of how the strategy will be executed, targets for achievement, the required resources, and timelines and key milestones. Figure 15.34 shows the ACTION PLANNING screen in the WFP tool.

There are several different buttons at the top of the ACTION PLANNING screen. By clicking on TACTIC PRIORITY SETUP, a new window will open that allows users to modify the strategies included from the strategy bank, the tactic priority rating scale, the tactic feasibility rating scale, the associated color-coding, and where the tactic falls on a three-by-three tactic matrix. For example, you might identify a tactic that has a high feasibility of being implemented and will have a significant impact if prioritized. Alternatively, you might identify a tactic that has a low feasibility of being implemented and will have a low impact, so therefore it would not be a priority.

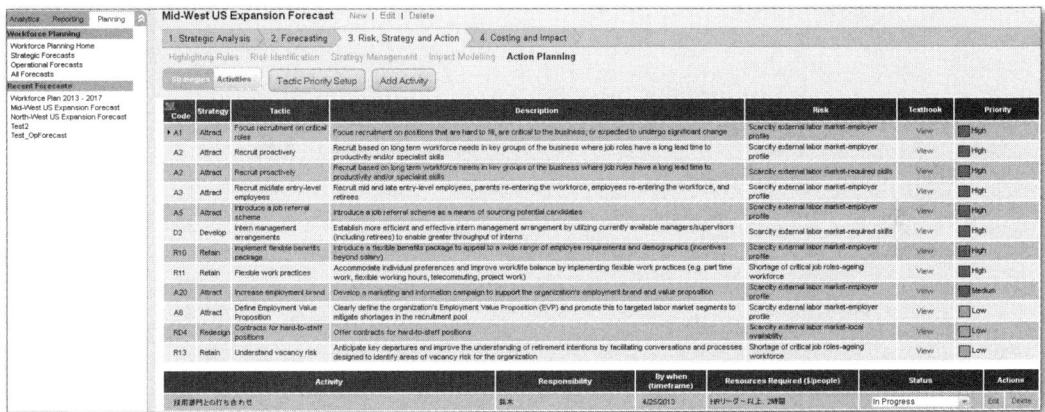

Figure 15.34 Action Planning Screen

For each tactic, activities must be added using the ADD ACTIVITY button. A new window will open called ACTIVITY EDITOR, where you'll enter the name of the person who will be held accountable, the timeline for implementation, and any additional resources needed. Figure 15.35 shows an example of an activity assignment.

After activities have been assigned, you can toggle between the STRATEGIES/ACTIVITIES tab to see different views. Until an activity has been added, the activity view will be unavailable. While the action planning step is the final phase of the SWFP process, some organizations opt to integrate financial data for modeling purposes before determining which strategies to implement. In the next section, we'll cover the Costing and Impact tool, which is also known as the What-If Financial Modeling tool.

15 | Workforce Planning

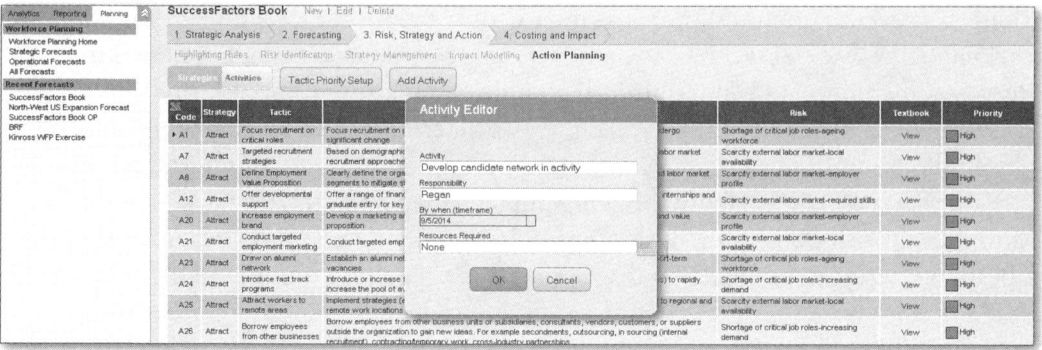

Figure 15.35 Activity Editor

15.5 What-If Financial Modeling

The final tab of the WFP tool is Costing and Impact (also known as What-If Financial Modeling). This section provides context around the financial ramifications of the decisions that you're making today, helps to optimize the composition of the workforce from a financial perspective, and allows organizations to prove that WFP is a necessary business process and not just an HR exercise.

Financial modeling quantifies the financial impact of implementing interventions that address risks to move the business to the desired future state. Organizations that have the Financial Metrics Pack implemented in the WFA application can also configure the financial metrics to flow through to the What-If tool. Essentially, you're connecting the workforce plan and identified future gaps with historic financial and compensation data to model financial variables related to workforce costs, both now and in the future. However, even without the Financial Metrics Pack, users can manually enter the critical financial data elements for modeling purposes.

When you first click into the What-If tool, you're provided with an overall financial dashboard that outlines your company's financial profile (assuming the Financial Metrics Pack is configured) and includes things such as overall total cost of workforce, total operating revenue, and profit per FTE. There is also a chart displaying the cost to fill the gap broken down by the two scenarios across the forecast period. From a financial perspective, all figures take into account measures such as salary growth, composition of the workforce, different costs of training, recruitment, and cost of turnover. The ability to model the numbers to generate different outcomes is what makes the tool truly "What-If?"

464

The FINANCIAL DASHBOARD in Figure 15.36 provides a number of visualizations from a financial perspective. There are also other dashboards that can be viewed, including the following:

- COMPARISON VIEW
- GAP ANALYSIS DASHBOARD
- MARKET COMPARISONS AND PRODUCTIVITY
- EFFICIENCY ANALYSIS

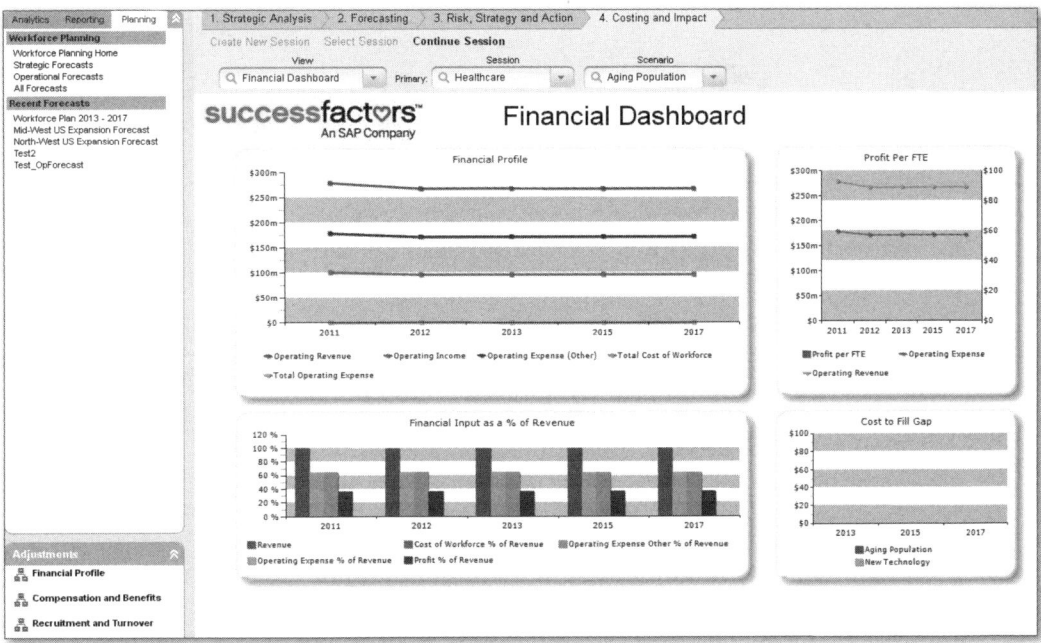

Figure 15.36 Costing and Impact Screen

Let's walk through an example of how to set up a What-If Financial Modeling session for the Retail business unit. The first step is to select the CREATE NEW SESSION link at the top of the screen. A new window will open that prompts you to enter the session details and select the forecast from the existing forecast list. After selecting the RETAIL business unit forecast, you must choose a dimension and a model. For this example, choose to analyze by JOB FAMILY in the BUY SOURCING STRATEGY model, as shown in Figure 15.37. To exit this window, click SAVE.

15 | Workforce Planning

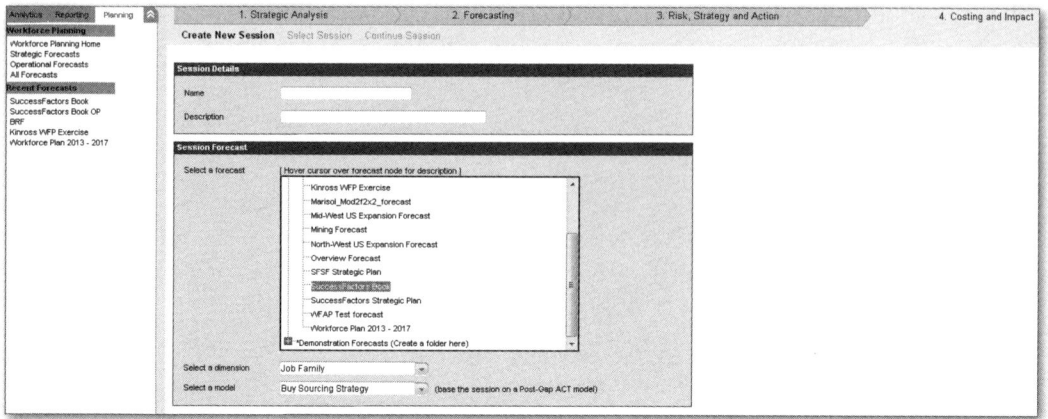

Figure 15.37 New What-If Session

A new FINANCIAL DASHBOARD will refresh based on the data from the Retail Business Unit Forecast. From here, you can begin to model various changes to your workforce to understand the financial implications of these actions by clicking on the three tabs in the ADJUSTMENTS pane (FINANCIAL PROFILE, COMPENSATION AND BENEFITS, and RECRUITMENT AND TURNOVER).

Click on COMPENSATION AND BENEFITS first, which will cause a new window to open showing the job families by AVERAGE ANNUAL SALARY, SALARY GROWTH (%), and BENEFITS (%), as shown in Figure 15.38.

Let's say that your account managers across the next five years are expecting 10% annual salary growth, so you can click on the 5% and change it to 10% in each year. After the change is accepted, the Revised Chart on the right-hand side of the screen (see Figure 15.38) will update to show the financial impact of this salary increase on factors such as operating revenue or total cost of workforce. The Original Chart stays the same, allowing you to compare the before and after effect of this compensation strategy. This ability to make changes dynamically within the tool and then see how the changes will affect the overall organization from a financial perspective is a very powerful tool.

In addition to modeling compensation strategies, you can also start to model different workforce mixes (e.g., temporary vs. permanent vs. contractors) or bonus structures to see the impact on your financial profile. You can do the same type of modeling for recruitment and turnover, and start to factor in things such as cost to fill, turnover costs, and training expenses. Lastly, the FINANCIAL PROFILE tab allows you to model different growth scenarios to determine how increases to operating revenue or expenses will affect your overall financial profile.

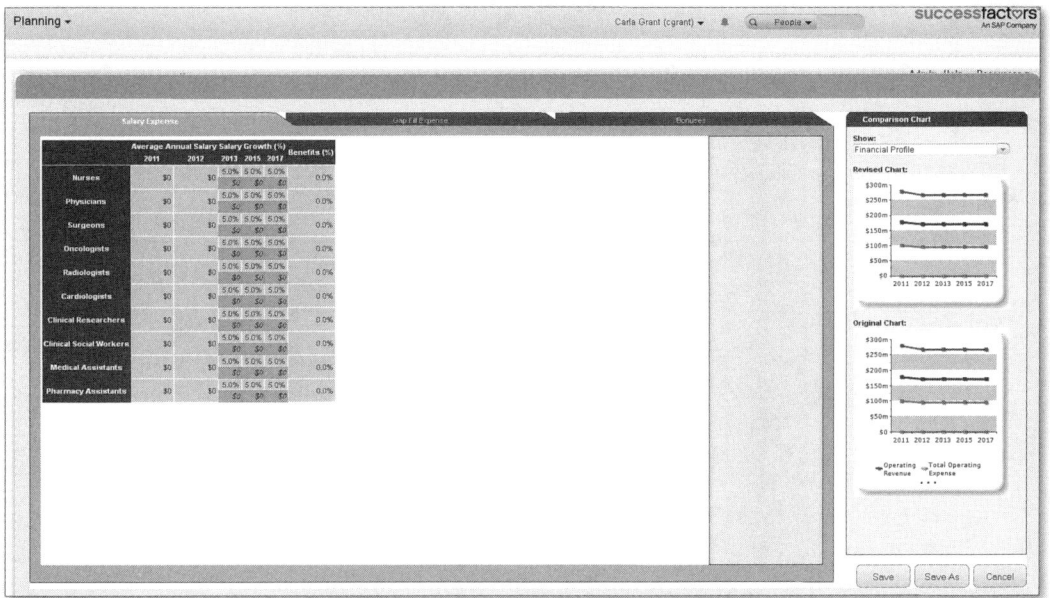

Figure 15.38 Compensation and Benefits

Now that we've covered how the What-If Financial Modeling tool bridges the gap between HR and financial planning, we'll touch on the Operational Planning tool embedded within the SuccessFactors WFP application.

15.6 Operational Workforce Planning Forecasts

Operational Workforce Planning (referred to as Operational Planning) is often known as Headcount Planning, Strategic Staffing, or Budget Planning and can either be a standalone process or a method for operationalizing Year 1 and Year 2 of a strategic workforce plan.

The aim of Operational Planning is to enable each business unit to continue its daily functions by having the right people available to do the work. The process is such that managers forecast how many people they will need to proceed with their day-to-day operations over the next 1-1½ years. Without performing this forecasting as accurately as possible, managers will be less likely to secure the appropriate budget allocation to have the required resources and/or may not have the right people to effectively execute on their near-term goals. Figure 15.39 shows a few key differences between Operational Planning and SWFP.

Figure 15.39 Operational versus Strategic Planning

To meet clients' short-term planning needs, the WFP application includes an Operational Planning tool, which can be accessed on the WFP HOME screen by selecting NEW FORECAST and then NEW OPERATIONAL FORECAST.

For an operational forecast, three sets of parameters must be defined:

- DETAILS section
  NAME and DESCRIPTION fields.
- TIMEFRAME section
  START YEAR and NUMBER OF MONTHS (up to 48) fields.
- BUSINESS FACTORS section
  WORKFORCE MEASURES, HEADCOUNT, TERMINATION RATE, MOVEMENTS IN RATE, MOVEMENTS OUT RATE, MISCELLANEOUS INFLOWS, MISCELLANEOUS OUTFLOWS, and RECRUITMENT SCHEDULE.

Figure 15.40 shows the FORECAST BASICS screen for an operational forecast.

Operational Workforce Planning Forecasts | **15.6**

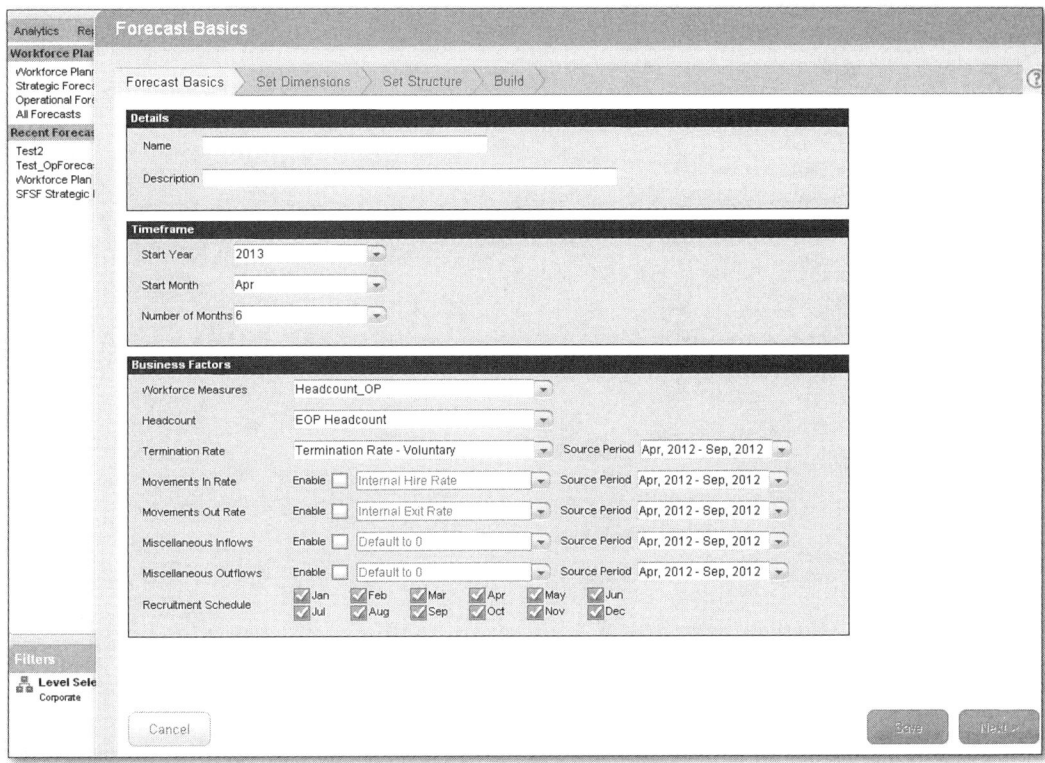

Figure 15.40 The Forecast Basics Screen for an Operational Forecast

Building an operational planning forecast is very similar to the process for building a strategic forecast in that users must define the source data year for enabled data elements when building a forecast. The key difference in Operational Planning is that the source data is by month instead of year (e.g., May 2013 voluntary terminations will be sourced from the May 2012 historical voluntary terminations data). The rest of the forecast building screen follows the same process as building a strategic forecast (e.g., set dimensions, set structure, build).

Using the same selections as the strategic forecast (e.g., job family and critical roles for the Retail business unit), you click BUILD and are taken back to the WFP forecast list. A tip here is to click on the OPERATIONAL FORECASTS link in the PLANNING window on the left-hand side of the screen to only display Operational Planning forecasts. After selecting the forecast, you see in the EXPLORE FORECAST window that there is only one option to click on: OPERATIONAL PLANNING. Click this link,

469

and a screen refreshes with the month-by-month forecast for the next six months, as shown in Figure 15.41.

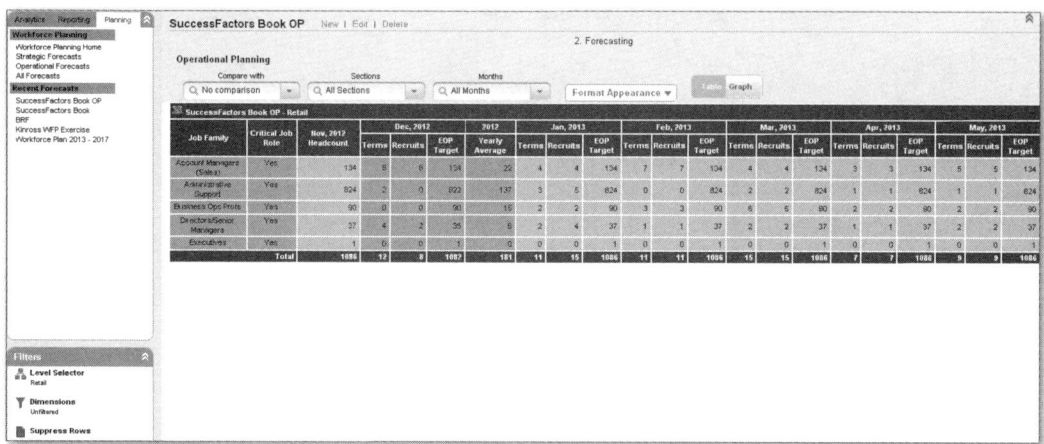

Figure 15.41 Retail Business Unit Operational Plan

In this screen, you can begin to edit the forecasted headcount by job family for the next six months. Note that cells can't be edited at the total retail business unit level, meaning you must click on the LEVEL SELECTOR and drill into a department to make edits. Select CUSTOMER SERVICES for this example.

In this example, December 2012 has already occurred, so the cells can no longer be edited and are highlighted in green. However, all remaining months in the forecast can be edited by clicking on the cell and adjusting the number. The numbers populating the future months again are based on the source month and year that you defined while building the forecast.

If you toggle to the GRAPH view, you're given a quick visualization of where hiring activity increased in previous years, as shown in Figure 15.42.

In this view, you can easily see that January and March are predicted to be your busiest hiring months based on historical data. In theory, if you expect termination patterns to remain consistent, then you can be more proactive in your hiring by starting the recruiting process before you find your organization in firefighting mode.

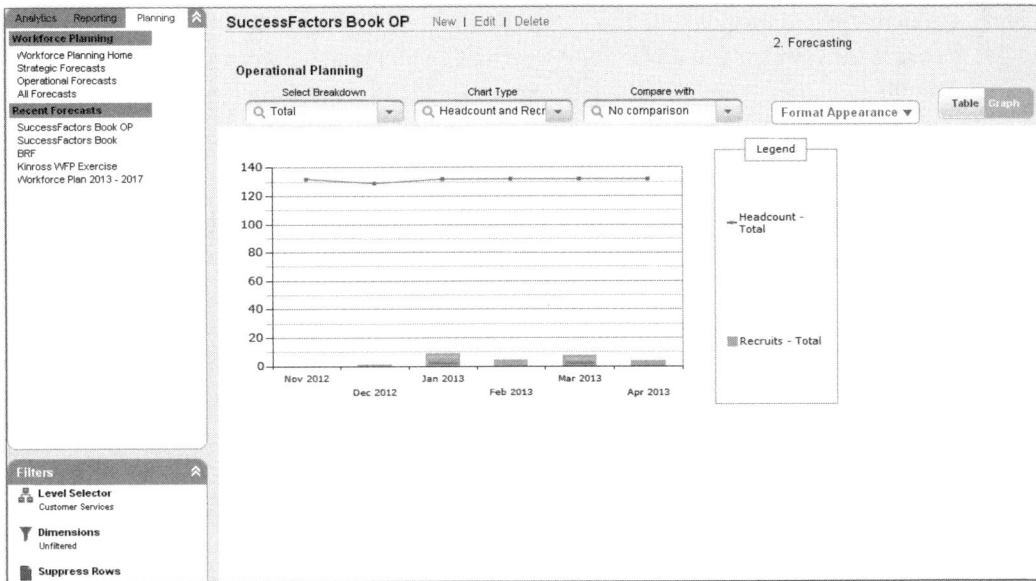

Figure 15.42 Retail Business Unit Graph View

15.7 Summary

Now that we've covered the main features and functionality of the SuccessFactors Workforce Planning solution, you have a thorough understanding of how organizations use this innovative solution to create strategic plans to ensure that you have the right people in the right place at the right time for the right cost. The SuccessFactors WFP methodology has very much evolved while working with hundreds of clients and learning what has helped most organizations do SWFP well. Clearly, SWFP is a qualitative process; even with sophisticated tools and technology, the quality of the workforce plan is going to depend on the key conversations with the business and on the vision and strategy of the organization.

In addition, SWFP is a continuous process that does not stop with the action plan. For the process to be sustainable, it must feed other strategic planning processes undertaken by the business, such as Financial Planning, Operational Planning, and Strategic Planning. Furthermore, prior plans must serve as the basis for future ones, testing old assumptions, and monitoring progress. In effect, this year's plan will serve as the starting point for next year's plan. Throughout the year, an ongoing process for monitoring and reviewing the key elements of your plan is critical and includes regular reviews of the scenarios, changes to company strategy, unexpected internal events, and operational workforce metrics through WFP dashboards and KPI reports.

In the next chapter, we'll cover Onboarding, which assists with bringing new employees into the organization.

Onboarding new employees into any organization can be a complex process with a significant impact on time to productivity and first-year employee retention. Being able to quickly educate, integrate, and prepare new starters for their new roles can significantly reduce costs, and improve engagement, retention, and time to contribution.

16 Onboarding

SuccessFactors Onboarding, which is the most recent addition to the SuccessFactors BizX suite, supports the onboarding of new employees into your organization, as well as offboarding and cross-boarding (transfers).

Onboarding is an automated solution that supports the workflows associated with the onboarding process and provides a one-stop shop of resources, activities, and required documentation for new joiners. It addresses the compliance-driven activities associated with onboarding but also addresses a more strategic set of activities: connecting, informing, and empowering new hires even before their first day on the job with the right tools, content, and connections to start driving business results faster.

It leverages the SuccessFactors BizX platform, as well as existing functionality found in solutions such as Employee Central and SAP Jam and is therefore easy to use and intuitive for individuals to quickly begin onboarding activities. It significantly reduces the time and effort required by managers and HR professionals to manually manage the onboarding process and ensure that forms are correctly completed. SuccessFactors Onboarding also provides a complete set of new hire activities specifically designed to help them assimilate as quickly as possible.

In addition, it acts as a starting point for other HR and talent processes, such as Goal Management, Performance Management, and Learning. And with the possibility to provide access even before the new employee has started with your company, it means that new hires can hit the ground running and begin making a meaningful contribution as soon as they arrive on their first day.

This chapter covers the key features and functionality of the solution. Because this is a new solution, some of the features may have changed between the time of writing and the time of reading. As a result, use this chapter as a guide to the solution as a whole and how it can be applied within your organization.

The Onboarding solution is based on a structured yet configurable onboarding process and contains functionality to suit this type of process. It features the following functionalities:

- Introduction wizard
- Pre-hire verification steps
- Introductory information
- Activities
- Paperwork
- Configurable workflows
- Email notifications
- Integration with Goal Management, Learning, Development, Recruiting Execution, and Employee Central
- Tracking of manager's onboarding process to identify best processes

Now let's run through the key features.

16.1 Pre-hire Verification Steps

Onboarding starts with an email to the new hire, who is invited to begin the onboarding process before they begin with the company. This pre-hire verification step allows the company the option to collect additional information from new hires that may not have been collected during the hiring process, without waiting until employees arrive on their first day. When accessing the system through the email link, new employees are presented with information they have previously provided so that they can verify or update this information, which will feed back into the talent/core HR systems. They are guided through a short wizard with a few simple steps to provide this information in which they see a welcome message and the key features of Onboarding. They then can follow the wizard steps to set a preferred name, upload a photo, and create an introduction message that is shared with the team, manager, and the employee's profile.

Figure 16.1 shows the step of the wizard where employees can define their preferred name, make a recording of it, and upload a profile picture.

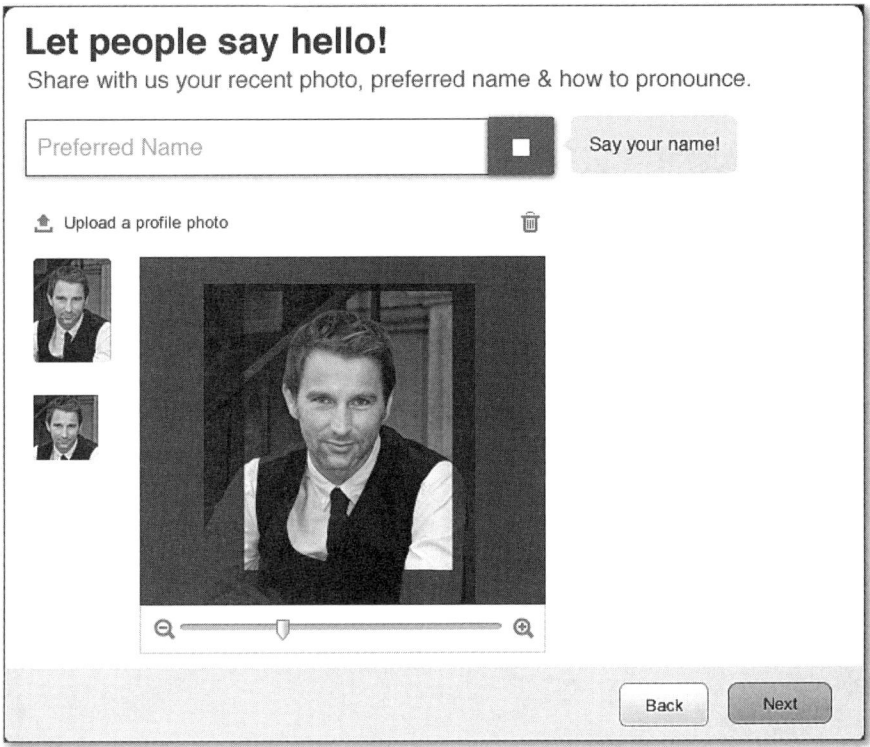

Figure 16.1 Wizard Step to Define Name and Upload Photo

16.2 Introductory Information

The WELCOME page for new hires (see Figure 16.2) provides employees with general introductory information to help them get started with the process. The content on this page is fully configurable and can feature the following types of information:

- WELCOME
- CEO's WELCOME LETTER
- ORIENTATION ROADMAP
- GETTING TO KNOW US

- Benefits information
- Policies

Employees can select the GET STARTED button on the WELCOME page to begin completing the prerequisite paperwork. Any paperwork they do not complete can be completed later. This is accessed via their ACTIVITIES page, which we'll cover next.

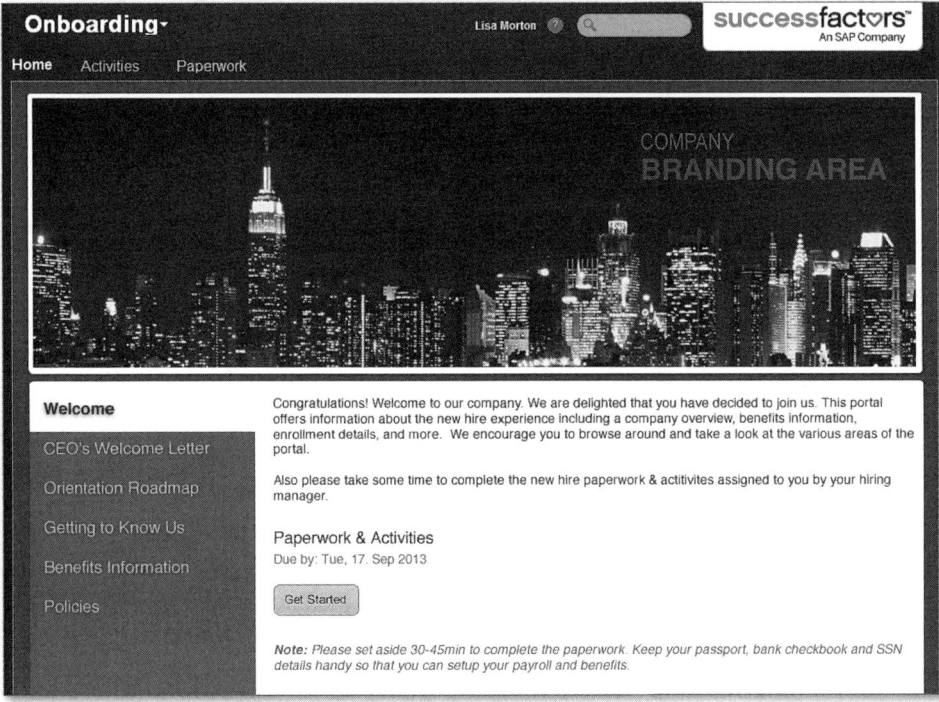

Figure 16.2 Home Page

16.3 Activities

By clicking the ACTIVITIES link at the top of the page, employees can access the ACTIVITIES page, which contains a host of activities that the new starter can perform, all of which are configured specifically for that employee (see Figure 16.3). Here the employee has a number of tiles that provide information or allow the employee to perform an activity. The following tiles are set up by the employee's manager as part of the step-by-step setup wizard:

- INTRODUCTION POSTCARD
  Displays a message from the manager.
- PAPERWORK
  Allows the employee to start the process of completing the prerequisite paperwork for employment.
- UPCOMING MEETINGS
  Displays upcoming events and meetings arranged for the employee (such as an orientation day), which displays the agenda of a meeting when the mouse is hovered over it.
- LINKS
  Contains links provided by the manager.
- LEARNING
  Contains links to the Learning Plan in SuccessFactors Learning.
- JAM GROUPS
  Displays the SAP Jam groups that the employee has been assigned to, either manually by the manager or automatically (with Auto Groups).
- MEETING YOUR BUDDY
  Shows the "buddy" that has been assigned by the manager and displays details when the mouse if hovered over the buddy.
- MEET YOUR TEAM
  Shows the peers of the employee's team and displays details when the mouse if hovered over a team member.
- RECOMMENDED PEOPLE
  Shows recommended people to follow, again with further details when the mouse is hovered over one of the people.

The hover-over details for the last three tiles display the person's name, their position and location, their telephone number and email address, their manager, the size of their team, a button to launch the Org Chart, and a menu to take further actions. From here, employees can email their "buddy" or other team members to introduce themselves.

16 | Onboarding

Figure 16.3 Activities Page

16.4 Paperwork

The PAPERWORK page contains the necessary forms for completing prerequisite employment paperwork, such as e-Verify, I-9, or W-4 in the United States. This part of the process is configurable to include whatever forms the company and local government requires. It is a menu-guided wizard that takes the employee through each form.

Like the ACTIVITIES page, the PAPERWORK page can be accessed from the PAPERWORK link at the top of the page (see Figure 16.4), or from the HOME page if configured.

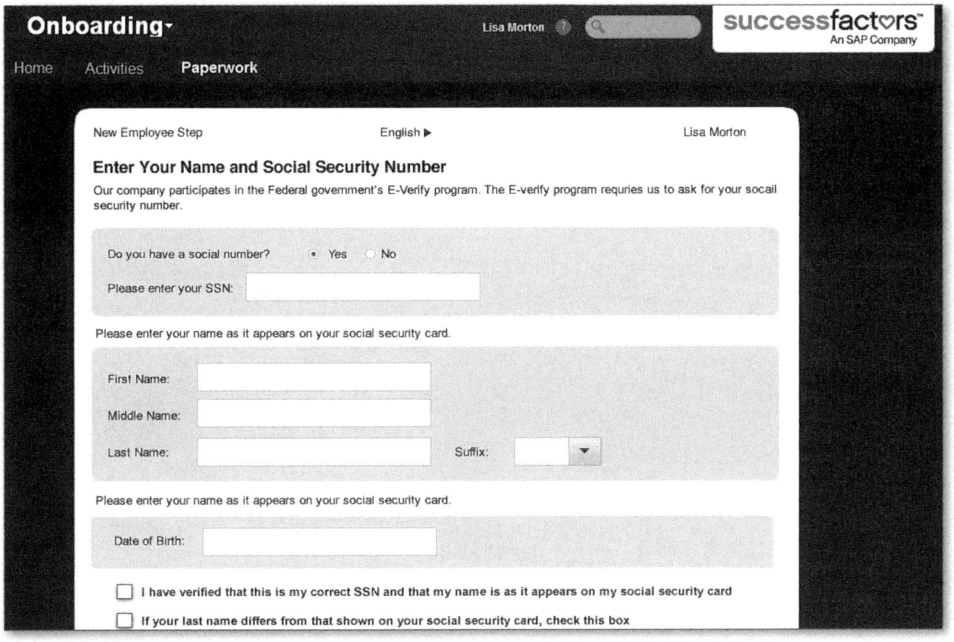

Figure 16.4 Paperwork Page

16.5 Integration

Onboarding features integration with a number of solutions in the SuccessFactors BizX suite. It features employee data used across the suite, as well as integrates with SAP Jam for groups and SuccessFactors Learning for the Learning Plan. Future integration is planned for Employee Central to create users and for Recruiting Execution to begin the onboarding process in Onboarding and use information from the job requisition. Additional integrations with BizX Mobile and other BizX suite solutions are also planned.

16.6 Summary

Onboarding is a value-adding and time-saving solution to enable quick and efficient onboarding of new employees, designed to also improve time to productivity, employee engagement, and employee retention. It removes the manual effort required by managers and HR professionals during the onboarding process and allows employees to become orientated with their new colleagues and working environment before they even set foot in the office.

We've looked at the features and functionality that support this and discussed the integration that exists. You should now have an overview of what the solution offers and what the process is for onboarding an employee with the solution.

In the next chapter, we will take a look at BizX Mobile, the mobile application bundled in with the SuccessFactors BizX suite. We will run through the different processes covered by the mobile app and how it adds value to day-to-day activities performed by HR professionals, managers, and employees.

SuccessFactors' BizX Mobile app is focused on putting the most critical talent management functions in the hands of users when they need them. It takes the virtual teaming concept to the next level by enabling users any time and from anywhere.

17　BizX Mobile

SuccessFactors has taken the ease of its BizX applications and delivered the most critical processes to the mobile device through the BizX Mobile app. This enables employees and managers to stay connected and keep the development process moving forward both at the desk and away from it. The BizX Mobile app is an area of expanding functionality that will continue to be developed as more features are made available. Currently, the BizX Mobile app supports users finding each other through the Org Chart and directory, collaborating via SAP Jam, approving critical recruiting forms and providing candidate feedback, keeping track of pending items from Employee Central, keeping up with Performance Manager To-Do items, and enabling managers to touch base with their employees from anywhere.

BizX Mobile empowers employees and managers to make performance and development an everyday event, not a once a year occurrence. This chapter reviews the features currently available to users via the BizX Mobile app.

Several mobile features that are currently available encompass finding and staying connected to your team and other employees and enabling collaboration among teams on the go:

- Org Chart and Directory
- SAP Jam
- Learning
- Mobile Touchbase

Other features allow managers to stay current with critical processes such as creating performance reviews and approving recruiting actions such as requisitions and offers:

- Recruiting
- Employee Central
- Performance To-Dos

We'll now take a brief look at some of these features and tools.

17.1 Org Chart and Directory

SuccessFactors' Mobile Org Chart and Mobile Directory features, which are shown in Figure 17.1, allow employees to see how their company is connected and organized and find the people they need quickly. The Mobile Org Chart gives a visual representation of how people within the organization are connected.

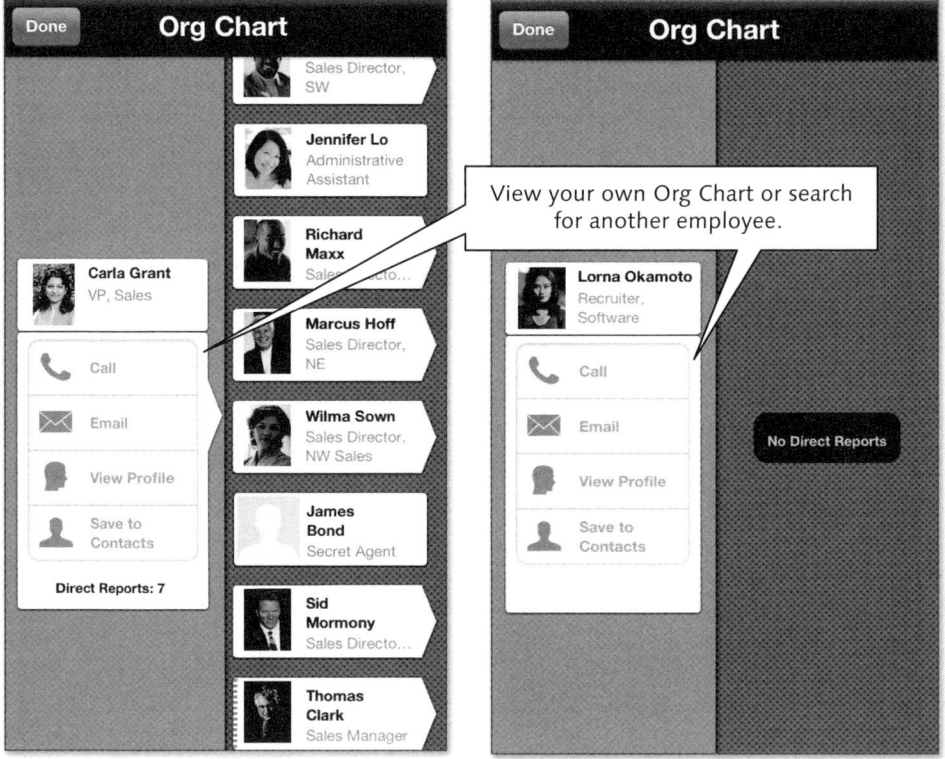

Figure 17.1 Mobile Org Chart and Mobile Directory

The Mobile Directory offers contact details such as phone numbers, email addresses, and instant message details. From the Mobile Directory, employees can reach out directly to contact their colleagues and create new contacts directly on the mobile device.

17.2   SAP Jam on BizX Mobile

Continuous collaboration—the theme of SAP Jam mobile—enables employees to stay connected to and involved with projects and groups right from their mobile device. Employees can set up their notification preferences to receive emails immediately as posts are made to the SAP Jam wall or as a direct message. Posts can be made directly to the SAP Jam wall from the mobile device, or users can reply from their email to reply and post other comments to wall posts.

Active conversations in the feeds encourage engagement and keep employees up to date with dialogue as it occurs and highlights items that have not been viewed yet. The SAP Jam mobile app gives employees access to any group they are a member of and provides tools to move projects forward, right from their smartphone or iPad. SAP Jam content search is a newer feature that puts even more information in the hands of employees when they need it. Allowing users the ability to search for content such as videos, wikis, documents, people, and conversations via the BizX Mobile app reduces the aggravation of having to search through a news feed to find what employees are looking for. Staying connected to the conversation is made easier with feed updates coming right to the mobile device, or even to users' email, so response is almost immediate. In Figure 17.2, users can view their feed and keep up to date on the latest posts, reply to comments and questions, posts blogs, and view documents.

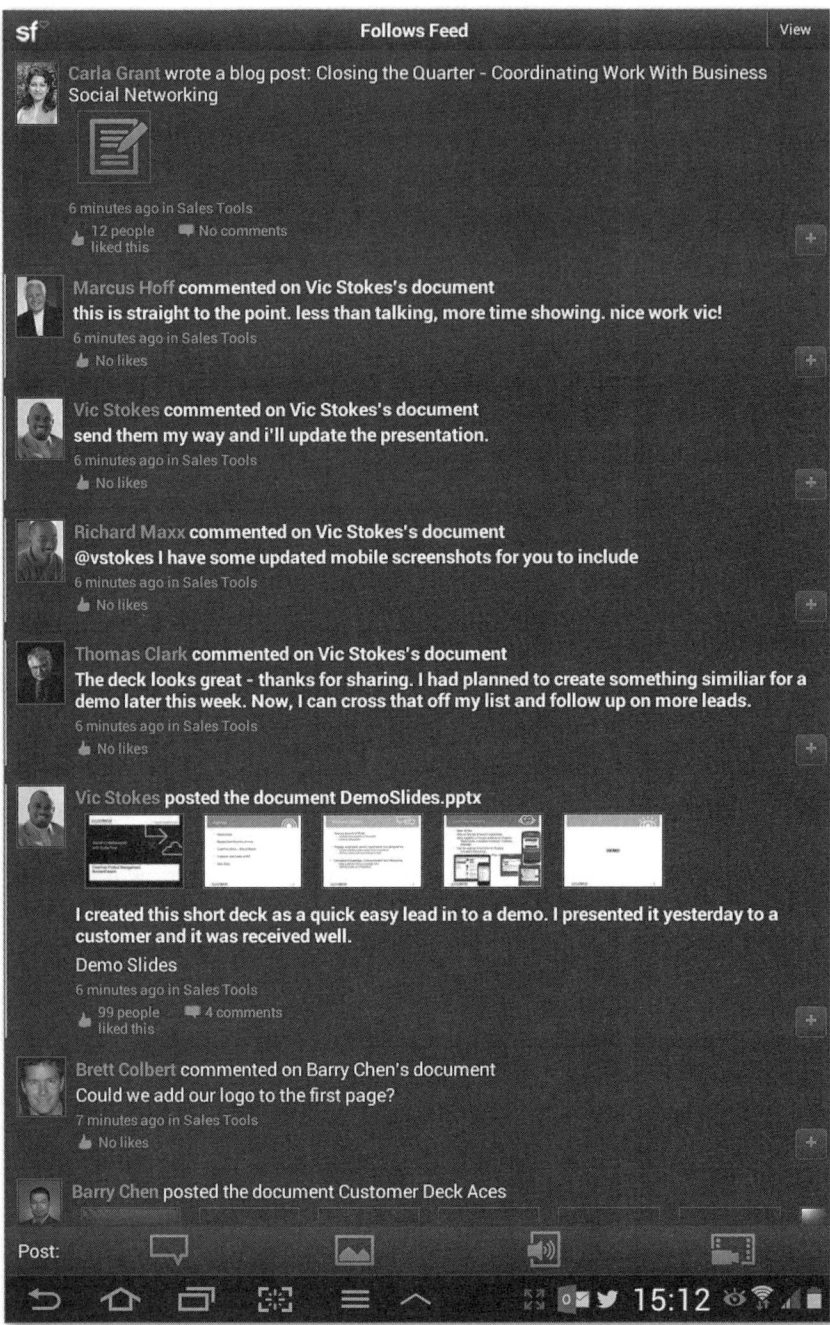

Figure 17.2 SAP Jam Feed on BizX Mobile

17.3 Mobile Learning

Mobile Learning frees users to pursue learning on the go. From the Mobile Learning app, managers can approve courses for their team members, and employees and managers can receive notifications of assignments and upcoming due dates. All employees can access content to learn anywhere, anytime, which can help them get the training they need, when they need it. This can be especially helpful with a dispersed workforce or those in the field that don't have time or opportunity to participate in formal learning in the office or classroom.

Real-time social learning keeps content current because it's constantly being updated. Employees can upload videos and images of white boards and samples, or demonstrate complex procedures right from their mobile device and keep the learning process going, despite being on the road or in an airport. With employees making comments from their mobile device, adding tips and tricks to formal training, they can participate in learning without being tied to a classroom.

17.4 Recruiting

In today's environment, recruiting is a 24/7 process. Candidates view open positions, apply for jobs, and monitor their progression through the process at any time of day and night. Likewise, recruiters often deal with hiring managers and approvers who are traveling or based in different time zones all over the globe. The Recruiting Mobile app keeps the most crucial elements of the recruiting process accessible across the globe and at any time.

For example, requisitions often have an involved approval process to ensure the right positions are advertised and sourced. With requisition approval on the BizX Mobile app, anyone in the requisition approval chain can approve requisitions from their mobile device. Enhanced functionality now supports approval steps that are iterative and collaborative, allowing two or more parties to route the requisition back and forth, or work on it simultaneously, until it's ready to move forward in the process. Configuration on the requisition determines what fields of data are displayed on the BizX Mobile app, providing approvers with only the necessary data.

In today's fast-paced business environment, interviewers need to have a way to provide recruiters and hiring managers with their interview feedback as soon as possible. With Interview Central access on the mobile device, SuccessFactors enables the fastest interview feedback possible. Interviewers can provide candidate ratings by competency, an overall rating, and comments along the way. The side-by-side feature of Interview Central lets interviewers rate candidates against each other in an easy interface. In Figure 17.3, requisition approval and interview feedback are easily performed on the mobile device, keeping the recruiting process moving forward.

Figure 17.3 BizX Mobile Recruiting

After a candidate is selected for hire, approving the official offer becomes a time-sensitive task. BizX Mobile offer approvals again put the right information in the hands of the right people to provide recruiters, hiring managers, and the candidates with the fastest, smoothest hiring process possible.

17.5 Employee Central To-Dos

Just as recruiting is a time-sensitive business process that requires input from multiple people to keep the process moving forward, many HR processes require up-to-the-minute attention. Each Employee Central workflow configuration might require multiple parties' involvement before an employment or compensation action gets approved. The Employee Central To-Do list puts change requests at the fingertips of each approver to keep the personnel action process moving, as shown in Figure 17.4. Approvers can stay informed of pending actions through feeds on items requiring their attention and make the best personnel decisions possible while still on the go.

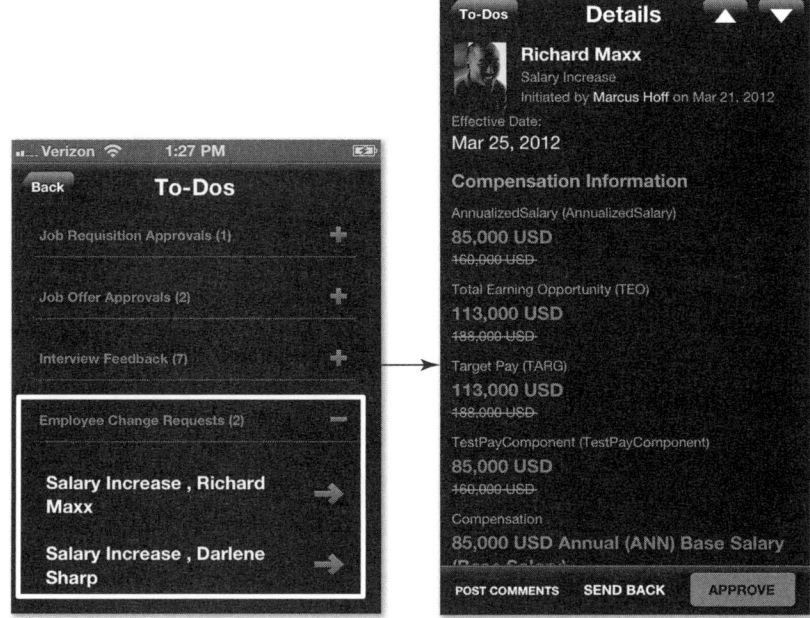

Figure 17.4 BizX Mobile Employee Central To-Dos

17.6 Performance Manager To-Dos

A newer feature of the BizX Mobile app is the Performance Manager To-Do list. Now managers have the capability to complete employee performance reviews by electronically signing them from the BizX Mobile app. They can view overall ratings, add comments to the review, and approve or reject it from their device. Likewise, employees with BizX Mobile app access can sign and confirm their performance reviews from their devices. With push notifications, proactive users can receive email notifications and respond to email without needing to access the BizX Mobile app to-do list.

17.7 BizX Mobile Touchbase

One of the newest and most exciting features of the BizX Mobile app is Touchbase, as shown in Figure 17.5. This innovative tool allows managers to stay in touch with their team at the touch of a button, regardless of distance or time zone. Touchbase enables team collaboration from the device by facilitating the following:

- Setting up meetings with team members and sending recorded messages to them
- Keeping informed of employee goal progress
- Scheduling one-on-one meetings with direct reports
- Sending email agendas for meetings

The multimedia feature of Touchbase enables note-taking and adding photos and videos. Any items created via Touchbase are available to view as comments within Performance Manager and the performance review.

Figure 17.5 BizX Mobile Touchbase

17.8 Data and Security

BizX Mobile enables team management and collaboration on the go within a secure environment. Administrators control who has access to the BizX Mobile app, and, with the user authentication, it can only be accessed from an active user account. Further, access to each component of the BizX Mobile app is permissioned in One-Admin by system administrators, as demonstrated in Figure 17.6. For example, a company can permission all employees to the BizX Mobile Org Chart and Directory and only managers to the Performance Manager To-Dos.

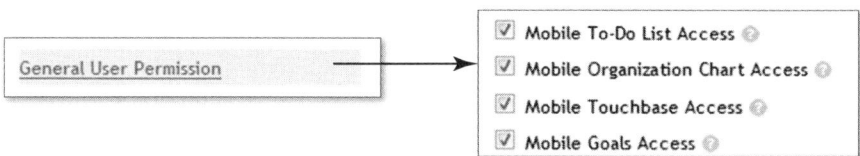

Figure 17.6 BizX Mobile Permissions

An extra layer of security is provided by BizX Mobile PIN activation. Data accessed via the BizX Mobile app remains secure because all data can be erased from the device if it's lost or stolen via a computer. Each user must activate his mobile device from the OPTIONS menu, using the activation code provided by the app and setting his own PIN, as represented by Figure 17.7.

Figure 17.7 BizX Mobile PIN Activation

17.9 Summary

With the collaborative features of BizX Mobile, users are empowered to stay connected to their teams and actively participate in critical business processes regardless of where they may be working on any given day. It delivers the tools they need to find and communicate with each other, stay current with learning needs and activities, and participate in collaborative teams or projects managed via SAP Jam. Managers can keep critical performance-related processes and tasks moving right from their mobile device by signing performance reviews, monitoring goal progress, scheduling Touchbases with their team, and approving critical recruiting forms to ensure the best talent is evaluated for their open positions.

In the next chapter, we'll look at additional resources that are available to customers to access information on the SuccessFactors BizX suite.

In light of the continuous innovation in SuccessFactors software, constant development of strategy, and changes within the market, it's important to ensure that you stay abreast of all the latest information available. A number of resources and channels are available to do this.

18   Further Resources

Due to the nature of cloud software and the evolution of enterprise software, many changes are occurring to the SuccessFactors BizX suite, SAP's strategy, and the overall market. We recommend that you stay as up to date and well informed as possible because the pace of change is quick.

The acquisition of SuccessFactors has garnered great interest from professional services organizations looking to win new projects by portraying themselves as experts. Due to the differing nature of SuccessFactors as a product suite and the lack of access to information, there can sometimes be a difference in understanding of the BizX suite compared to SAP ERP HCM, so it's more important than ever for customers to do their homework and look at a number of sources to get the most accurate and relevant information.

This chapter recommends reliable channels of information for your ongoing research.

18.1   SuccessFactors

SuccessFactors itself does a great job of providing news and new release information on its website (*www.successfactors.com*) and via its Twitter account (*@successfactors*). Customers can also find new release information, detailed product information, training materials, videos, support information, event details, thought leadership topics, and discussion forums at the SuccessFactors Community website (*http://community.successfactors.com*).

SuccessFactors partners can access a wealth of resources via the SuccessFactors Partner Portal (*https://connect.successfactors.com/partnerportal/*), as shown in Figure 18.1. Partners can access a variety of information on products, training, implementation, sales, and marketing.

In addition, SuccessFactors' sales and pre-sales executives can provide up-to-date information on the company's products, as well as information on subscription prices, implementations, and partner recommendations. Customers can get in contact with their regional SuccessFactors representative via their SAP account executive.

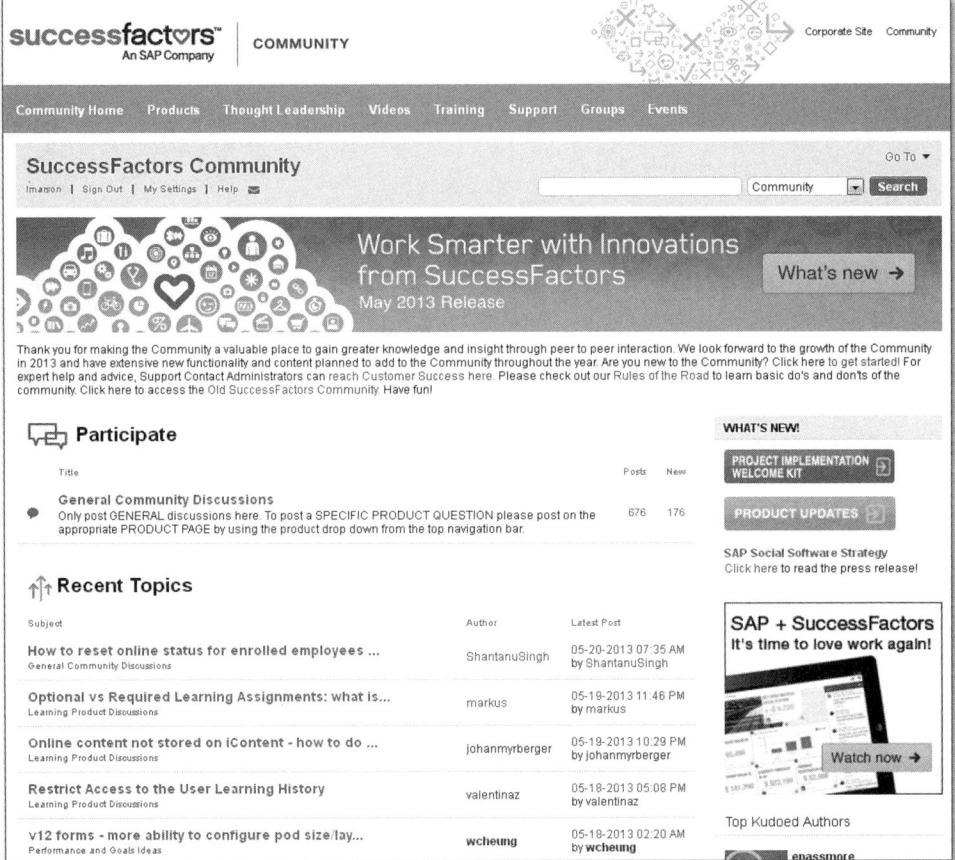

Figure 18.1 The SuccessFactors Community Website

18.2 SAP

SAP continues to improve the release and distribution of information to customers and partners. We recommend several outlets of information that are maintained by SAP.

SAP's sales and pre-sales executives, as well as Solution Management, are a source of the latest information on products, integration, and roadmaps. Although information from this channel can have a strong marketing feel, it's nevertheless a good starting point to understand the capabilities of the SuccessFactors BizX suite and the integration content and technology that SAP is releasing.

The SAP website hosts high-level information on both SAP products and SAP's range of Rapid Deployment Solutions (RDS) packages for integration. The information is extremely high level but can be useful to distinguish SAP's various offerings.

18.2.1 SAP Help Portal

The SAP Help Portal (*http://help.sap.com*) is a useful resource for getting detailed and technical information on SAP's products. Although light on SuccessFactors BizX suite information, the website does host information on the iFlows released for the hybrid scenario and also includes documentation on SSO. The most recent content (*http://help.sap.com/erp_sfi_addon20*) covers both Add-On 1.0 and Add-On 2.0, as shown in Figure 18.2.

18.2.2 SAP Service Marketplace

The SAP Service Marketplace (*http://service.sap.com*) contains solution documentation and SAP notes for the iFlows that have been released for the hybrid model. There are four areas of interest to customers regarding SuccessFactors.

iFlow Administration Guides

The iFlow Administration Guides can be found on SAP Service Marketplace, as shown in Figure 18.3. Access requires an S-username and password. To access the Administration Guides, visit *http://service.sap.com/support,* and log in using your S-username and password. On the top menu bar, select RELEASE & UPGRADE INFO; in the bar below, select INSTALLATION & UPGRADE GUIDES.

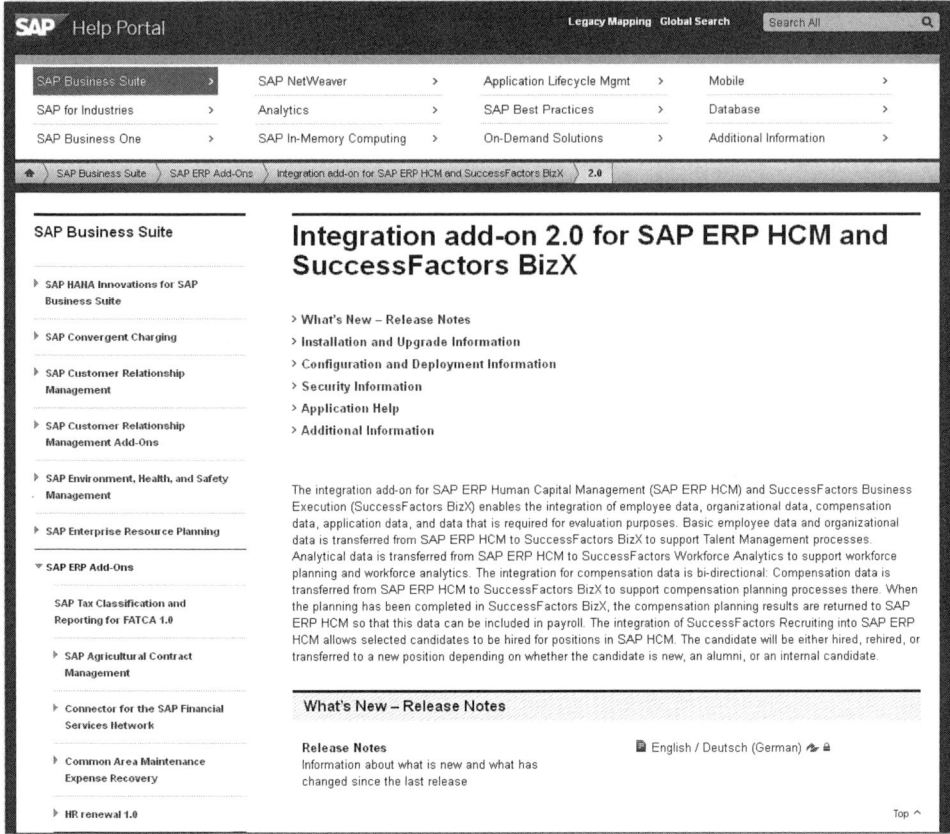

Figure 18.2 Add-On 2.0 Page on the SAP Help Portal

In the navigation pane to the left side of the screen, follow the path INSTALLATION & UPGRADE GUIDES • SAP BUSINESS SUITE APPLICATIONS • SAP ERP ADD-ONS • INTEGRATION ADD-ON FOR SAP ERP HCM AND SUCCESSFACTORS BIZX.

iFlow Release Notes

The iFlow Release Notes can be found on SAP Service Marketplace by visiting *http://service.sap.com/support* and logging in using your S-username and password. On the top menu bar, select RELEASE & UPGRADE INFO; in the bar below, select RELEASE NOTES. In the navigation pane to the left side of the screen follow the path RELEASE NOTES – WHAT'S NEW • SAP SOLUTIONS • SAP ERP ADD-ONS • INTEGRATION ADD-ON FOR SAP ERP HCM AND SUCCESSFACTORS BIZX.

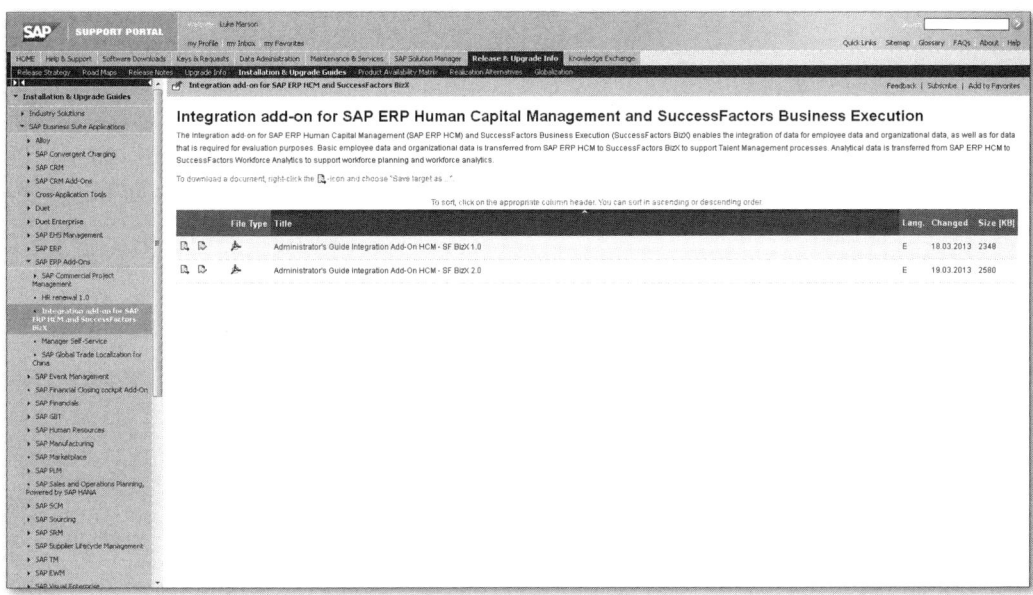

Figure 18.3 iFlow Administration Guides on SAP Service Marketplace

Media Library

The *Media Library* contains a variety of documents relating to SuccessFactors and the iFlows. To access the Media Library, visit *http://service.sap.com/erp-hcm*, log in using your S-username and password, and, in the navigation pane to the left side of the screen, follow the path, SAP ERP • SAP ERP HUMAN CAPITAL MANAGEMENT • MEDIA LIBRARY – SUCCESSFACTORS INTEGRATION.

SAP Notes

SAP regularly releases SAP Notes for corrections to the iFlows. These can be found on the SAP Service Marketplace in the same location as all other SAP Notes. To access these notes, visit *http://service.sap.com/support*, select SAP SUPPORT PORTAL, and log in using your S-username and password.

On the top menu bar select HELP & SUPPORT, and, in the bar below, select SEARCH FOR SAP NOTES & KBAS. In the main panel, enter "PA-SFI-TM" in the APPLICATION AREA text box, and click SEARCH to display all of the SAP notes for the iFlows.

18 | Further Resources

18.2.3 SAP PartnerEdge

The SAP PartnerEdge website (*http://partneredge.sap.com*) is the primary resource for SAP Partners and provides resources for sales, training, solution brochures, and general information. To access the SAP PartnerEdge page for SuccessFactors, as shown in Figure 18.4, visit *http://partneredge.sap.com/cloud*, log in with your S-username and password, and select LEARN MORE under the SUCCESSFACTORS BIZX heading.

Figure 18.4 SuccessFactors BizX Suite Page on SAP PartnerEdge

18.2.4 SAP Community Network

The SAP Community Network (SCN) is the official user community of SAP and has more than 2 million members. The SCN contains a wide range of spaces covering different SAP areas and disciplines with content largely focused around blogs and forum discussions. Within both the SAP ERP HCM space (*http://scn.sap.com/community/erp/hcm/*), as shown in Figure 18.5, and the SAP Social Software space (*http://scn.sap.com/community/socialsoftware*), there is a growing collection of blogs and documents covering SuccessFactors and SAP Jam.

Figure 18.5 The SAP ERP HCM Space on SCN

18.2.5 SAP Jam

SAP and SuccessFactors leverage SAP Jam for social collaboration and knowledge sharing and host a number of groups for partners. As a partner, you automatically get access to SAP Jam, and a number of SuccessFactors product-specific groups will automatically be available along with the SUCCESSFACTORS PARTNER NEWSFLASH group (see Figure 18.6). In addition, selected partners will have access to the SAP group SAP HCM INTEGRATION PARTNER EXCHANGE. This can also be accessed via *http://www.saphcmpartnerexchange.com*.

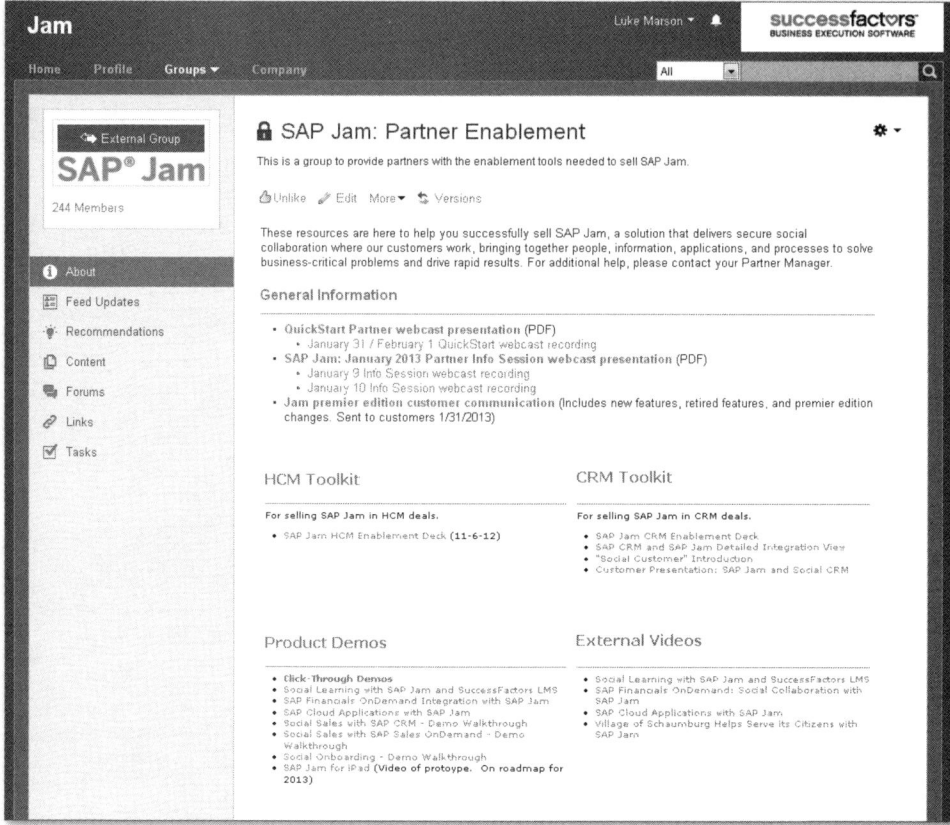

Figure 18.6 The SAP Jam: Partner Enablement Group

18.3 Social Media

Social media plays a large role in disseminating information, and a number of high-profile contributors are involved in this activity. You can use several different social media platforms to source the latest information.

18.3.1 LinkedIn

We recommend you consider joining two groups in LinkedIn: the prominent *SAP and SuccessFactors* group (*http://www.linkedin.com/groups?gid=4278743*), which has more than 6,000 members and is updated with content multiple times daily, and the more customer-centric *SuccessFactors Customer Group* (*http://www.linkedin.com/groups?gid=54022*).

18.3.2 Google Plus

Google Plus is still a heavily underutilized platform with a lot of great features, and this is reflected by the level of engagement on Google Plus pages versus LinkedIn groups. The *SAP and SuccessFactors* LinkedIn group has a presence here (*https://plus.google.com/communities/113841560495002390957*) while SuccessFactors EMEA (*https://plus.google.com/106910022434033585064*) also has a page.

18.3.3 Twitter

Twitter is a special networking site geared around providing tweets (messages up to 140 characters) to followers. Individuals can be followed, or with the help of a Twitter client or app, hashtags (keywords beginning with a # that categorize tweets) can also be followed. We recommend that you follow a few accounts (beginning with @) or hashtags (beginning with #):

- *@SuccessFactors*
- *#SuccessFactors*
- *@SAPHCM*

Additionally, other individuals can be found by searching or by following these hashtags.

During conferences, you can follow hashtags to hear the latest information as it is announced. For example, attendees at the SAPPHIRE show used the hashtag #SAPPHIRENOW. Similarly, the #ASUG hashtag can be used for the ASUG annual conference.

18.3.4 YouTube

SuccessFactors maintains a channel on the video-hosting platform YouTube at *www.youtube.com/user/SuccessFactorsInc*. Additionally, SuccessFactors also has a playlist for videos about its SuccessFactors Community website that can be accessed by selecting the PLAYLISTS tab in its channel.

18.4 Publications

There are a number of professional publications for SAP, including SAP ERP HCM, that regularly publish articles and reports on SuccessFactors, including the following:

- SAPexperts (*http://sapexperts.wispubs.com/HR*)
- SAP Insider Learning Network (*www.insiderlearningnetwork.com*)
- SAP Insider (*http://sapinsider.wispubs.com*)

18.5 Conferences

The regular SAP conferences serve as another great source of information. Informal networking provides an opportunity for customers to talk to other customers or to have off-the-record conversations with experts, consultants, and SAP executives. The following are some of the popular conferences:

- SAP Insider (known as HR2013, HR2014, etc.)
- SAPPHIRE NOW and the ASUG annual conference
- Mastering SAP

18.6 SAP User Groups

SAP User Groups are country-based organizations that are comprised of companies using SAP and SAP partners, such as consulting partners or software developers. They provide a valuable channel of information to members and also provide SAP an opportunity to work with SAP users to improve its software and services.

There are a number of these groups globally, including the following:

- Americas' SAP User Group (ASUG)
- German SAP User Group (DSAG)
- UK & Ireland SAP User Group (UKISUG)

These groups often hold events or provide information to members about SAP ERP HCM topics that include SuccessFactors. ASUG also hosts its annual conference in conjunction with SAPPHIRE and has a strong influence within SAP.

The Authors

Amy Grubb is a founder and principal at Cloud Consulting Partners, Inc., a SuccessFactors consulting partner and full-service HCM consultancy focused on implementing cloud solutions. She has consulted in the HCM space for over 15 years, spending eight years in Deloitte's Human Capital Management practice.

Amy has the unique background of implementing SuccessFactors for more than seven years while also implementing SAP ERP HCM during that same period. She holds three SuccessFactors consultant certifications in Align & Perform, Talent Sourcing, and Talent Management. She currently teaches the Recruiting Mastery course for SuccessFactors University, where she trains consultants to implement Recruiting Execution.

Amy has implemented numerous modules within SuccessFactors, including Performance and Goal Management, Succession Planning, CDP, Recruiting, Compensation, and Learning for clients globally. Her experience with LMS dates to 2000, and she has implemented every market-leading LMS many times over, including Plateau prior its acquisition by SuccessFactors. She is an expert in Learning business process and best practices, and led the development of LearningPrint for Saba™ while at Deloitte.

Luke Marson is an SAP Mentor and principal consultant for SAP ERP HCM and SuccessFactors. His experience covers SAP ERP HCM Talent Management, SuccessFactors, and Visualization Solutions by Nakisa (VSN); he has delivered more than 35 projects in territories across Europe, the Middle East, and Asia to organizations of various sizes and types in different industries and sectors, including oil and gas, defense, retail, manufacturing, the public sector, telecommunications, and media.

He is an active Twitter user (@*lukemarson*), a regular blogger on SuccessFactors, SAP ERP HCM Talent Management, and general SAP ERP HCM topics, and an active contributor to the SAP Community Network (SCN). He has also contributed to numerous articles, reports, and podcasts for SAPinsider Magazine, SAPexperts, and other publications, including the most comprehensive piece written on SuccessFactors to date. He has spoken at numerous international events and in various webinars and podcasts.

Jyoti Sharma is an SAP ERP HCM and principal SuccessFactors consultant and a trained business analyst. She has over nine years of information technology and SAP experience implementing core SAP ERP HCM modules and partnering with customers to formulate and execute business and technology strategies. She has implementation expertise in SuccessFactors, with a primary focus on Employee Central and Employee Central Payroll, though she has also completed the Performance & Goals mastery. Jyoti is widely regarded as an expert in Employee Central, is an active contributor to the SAP Community Network (SCN), has presented at ASUG events, and is an SAPexperts author.

Contributors

Regan Klein is a principal consultant at EPI-USE, where she leads the practice for Workforce Analytics & Planning in North America. Prior to joining EPI-USE, she held a similar role in the Workforce Analytics & Planning Professional Services organization at SuccessFactors, where she managed a portfolio of clients and specialized in helping them leverage their investment in the SuccessFactors Workforce Analytics & Planning product.

She has significant experience delivering workshops, leading Strategic Workforce Planning consulting engagements, and managing strategic deployments and change management for global Workforce Analytics programs.

She is an active thought leader in the space as a presenter at annual Workforce Analytics & Planning conferences and HR.com webinars, and is the founder of the EPI-USE Visionary Series, which provides thought-provoking research on various HCM topics. In addition, she has co-authored several whitepapers and blog articles.

The Authors

Joe Lee is a Talent Management consultant with more than seven years of technical and functional SAP experience in a variety of modules, including Talent Management, SD, MM, WM, FI/CO, and SAP NetWeaver Portal. Originally an ABAP developer, he has experience in functional, technical, testing, and team lead roles. Joe is a contributing speaker at ASUG conferences, as well as a featured Talent Management expert on SAPinsider. He also has deployed both on-premise and cloud-based Talent Management software to private, public sector, and global clients, specializing in third-party integration architecture, Web Dynpro for ABAP, and UI branding.

Atif Siddiqui is an experienced ERP professional specializing in cloud solutions. His areas of expertise are Compensation Management, e-Recruiting, and Performance Management for both on-premise and cloud systems; as someone who also specializes in IT governance, compliance, and regulation, he has also led successful global ERP initiatives in the human resources and finance areas.

Recently he became an active member of the SuccessFactors community in Canada, particularly in the Compensation area. Atif also holds several professional qualifications and certifications in SAP ERP HCM, SAP HANA, cloud security, project management, information systems auditing, and risk and information systems control.

Index

360 Multi-Rater, 49, 223, 238

A

Absence Management feature, 190
Accelerator, 280
Access the WFP application, 426
Action planning, 462
Act Module, 453
Add Activity button, 463
Add Budget Calculation option, 259
Add Budget Rule option, 261
Add Column option, 257
Add Grouping option, 259
Additive formula, 279
Add Members option, 268
Add New Employee option, 148
Add or Remove tactics button, 457
Ad Hoc Report Builder 2.0, 193
Admin Alerts tile, 146
Admin Tools, 135
Advanced Guidelines subsection, 286
Advanced Settings subsection, 256
Agency Portal, 299
AICC, 333
 AICC wrapper, 333
Aligned (cascaded) goals, 225
Analysis by dimensions, 394
Analysis options, 396, 426
Analytical tools, 407
Analytics and reporting, 161
Analytics Workspace, 416
Analyzing your data, 394
Apply Data Updates option, 268
Applying benchmarks, 402
Approval workflow, 273
Ask for Feedback, 234, 235
Assignment record, 280
Association, 167, 196

B

Badge, 206
Balanced Scorecard, 225
Base input measure, 393
Base pay, 241
Base setup table, 249
Benchmark Chart, 405
Benchmark field, 262
Benchmarking categories, 401
Benchmarking methodology, 400
Benchmarking program, 400
Benchmark Scorecard, 406
Benchmark View, 405
Best Practice Goal Library, 225
BizX Mobile, 481
BizXpert, 53
BizXpert methodology, 55
BizX platform, 48
BizX suite, 29, 145
Blog, 382
Bonus, 241
Bonus Calculation Equation option, 281
Bonus cap, 281
Bonus End Date field, 279
Bonus payout calculation, 287
Bonus Plan Multiplier, 280
Bonus Start Date field, 279
Bring Your Own Device (BYOD), 22
Budget, 285
Budget Assignment option, 269
Budget status, 247
Build Forecast step, 442
Business execution, 27
Business goal, 280
 weight, 285
Business Goal Name option, 281

C

Calendar, 322
Calibration, 223, 239, 242
Candidate Data Model, 301
Candidate Profile, 301
Candidate Workbench, 299
Capability forecasting, 448
Capability framework, 437
Career Development Planning (CDP), 49, 359
    Career Path Diagram, 368
    Career Worksheet, 365
    creating development goals, 361
    development goal, 360
    Development Plan, 360
    learning activities, 368
Career Trajectory, 418
Cascade a goal, 229
Cash, 241
Category, 228
CDM
    application, 295
Choose Your Own Device (CYOD), 22
Cloud and SaaS trends, 25
Cloud computing, 22
Column Designer subsection, 283
Column properties, 257
Comments, 271
Company Info option, 158
Company Info page, 208
Compa-Ratio, 251
Compare models, 462
Compensation, 49, 241
    Aggregate Export, 274
    guidelines, 245, 262
    hierarchy, 244
    program, 241
    Rollup, 274
    worksheet, 245
Compensation cycle, 244
Compensation form
    layout, 257
Compensation plan, 246
    template, 244
Compensation Profile, 243
Competency, 232, 361
    model, 50

Conferences featuring SuccessFactors content, 500
Configuration
    Admin Tools, 135
    Metadata Framework, 122
    OneAdmin, 135
    PickList, 127
    rules, 126
Configure Employee Files option, 219
Configure Label Names and Visibility subsection, 283
Content menu, 333
Content object, 333
Core Workforce & Mobility Metrics Pack, 389
    metric categories, 389
Corporate data model, 171
Costing and Impact modeling, 464
Country-specific (CSF) corporate data model, 171
Create Worksheet option, 265
Creating a strategic forecast, 429
Critical job role, 444
Critical Role Identification process, 435
Currency Conversion Table subsection, 249
Currency view, 280
Custom hierarchy, 264
Custom measure, 411
Custom Members/Sets, 411
Cutover, 60
Cycle dates, 266

D

Data-effective history, 286
Data Highlighting, 417
Data migration, 58
Data replication, 198
Define Planners subsection, 264
Defining Strategic Workforce Planning, 424
Delete Members option, 269
Dell Boomi AtomSphere, 72, 112, 199
Demand forecasting, 444
Derived input measure, 393
Design view, 410
Design Worksheet worksheet, 257

Development goal, 360
    Audit History section, 363
    delete, 364
    Detail View, 363
    edit, 363
    publish to Scorecard, 364
    remove from Scorecard, 364
Development Objectives Portlet, 364
Development Plan, 360
    assigning learning activity, 363
    creating development goals, 361
    maintaining goals, 363
    tracking goals, 363
Dimension hierarchy, 393
Display Options option, 270
Domain, 318, 335
Drill to Detail functionality, 398
Drivers of gaps, 454

E

Easy Links, 322
Edit Values window, 446
Eligibility, 285
Eligibility rules, 261
Employee Central, 31, 165
    integration, 111
    reporting, 192
Employee Central Payroll, 165, 197
    integration, 111
Employee Central To-Do list, 487
Employee Data Export subsection, 249
Employee Directory, 208
Employee eligibility, 247
Employee Profile, 203
    Scorecard in Succession, 348
    Talent Profile in Succession, 347
Employee Profile module, 49
Employee Profiles page, 161
Employee Self-Service (ESS), 167
Employment Information view, 183
Employment object, 183
Execution Map, 230
Executive Review, 243, 276, 289
Expressive Public Profile, 204
External career portal, 295

F

Facebook, 218
Filtering, 397
Filter Options section, 277
Financial Dashboard, 465
Financial profile, 464
Five steps of SuccessFactors WFP, 426
Fixed Retirement Age option, 437
Forecast, 278
Forecast basics, 430
Forecast list, 428
Form behavior, 256
Formula box, 250
Foundation object, 170
Full cloud HCM model, 45

G

Gamification, 383
Gap analysis, 452
Generic object, 184
Global Assignment feature, 191
Goal
    Add Goal screen, 226
    alignment, 225
    attainment, 246
    Audit History section, 363
    delete, 364
    edit, 363
    publish to Scorecard, 364
    remove from Scorecard, 364
Goal Execution, 230
Goal Library, 228
Goal Management (GM) module, 223, 49
Goal plan, 224
Go-forward solution, 43
Groups, 379
    auto-membership, 381
    private external, 380
    private internal, 380
    public internal, 380
Guideline, 247

Index

H

Headlines BizX Mobile integration, 420
Headlines feature, 418
Hex Color Code field, 259
Hierarchy-based approval, 273
Highlighting Rules screen, 454
Home page, 146
How vs. What matrix, 214
HRIS element, 167
Hybrid model, 44

I

Impact modeling, 459
Implementing Core Workforce & Mobility, 388
Importance rating, 450
Import key, 257
Individual Development Plan section, 234
Individual Guideline subsection, 285
Individual retirement profile, 439
Input recommendation, 271
Integration, 63, 66, 74, 296
    Add-Ons, 74
    Add-On 1.0, 75
    Add-On 2.0, 95
    Administration Guides, 493
    cookbook, 111
    data integration, 65
    Employee Central, 112
    Employee Central Payroll, 112
    FAST, 64
    flat-file integration, 68
    iFlow, 74
    Integration of multiple SAP ERP HCM systems, 111
    Media Library, 495
    process integration, 65
    Rapid Deployment Solution (RDS), 95, 110
    Release Notes, 494
    SAP BusinessObjects Data Services, 73
    SAP BusinessObjects Data Services adapter, 114
    SAP HANA, 114

Integration (Cont.)
    SAP HANA Cloud Integration, 71
    SAP HCM Integration Partner Exchange, 498
    SAP NetWeaver Business Warehouse, 114
    SAP NetWeaver Process Integration, 69
    SAP Notes, 495
    scenarios, 66
    SFIHCM01, 75
    SFIHCM02, 75
    Social Media ABAP Integration Library (SAIL), 114
    strategy, 63
    support packages for Add-On 1.0, 81
    support packages for Add-On 2.0, 101
    technology, 66
    user experience integration, 65
Interview Central, 485

J

JavaScript Object Notation (JSON), 120
Job board posting, 299
Job Code & Pay Grade Mapping, 246
Job Requisition Data Model, 294
Job structure, 170

K

Kickoff meeting, 56

L

Launch forms, 265
Launch phase, 60
Launch Plan option, 266
Learning, 50
    Career Development Planning (CDP), 368
Learning History, 320
Learning Plan, 319
Legal Scan tool, 233
Licensing, 46
LinkedIn, 218
Live Analytics, 280

Live Metrics, 242
Long-term incentive pay, 241
Lookup Tables, 246
Lump sum, 241

M

Manage compensation form, 265
Management by Objective, 246
Manage Reports, 413
Manager instruction, 281
Manager Promotion Map, 251
Manager Self-Service (MSS), 167
Manager Users subsection, 286
Manage Subscriptions link, 419
Manage Users subsection, 264
Manage Worksheets option, 267
Manage Worksheets section, 265
Mass changes, 186
Mathematical Approximation option, 438
Media Library, 495
Merit, 241
Metadata Framework (MDF), 122, 196
  Hooks, *124, 131*
  Metadata Objects, 122, 124
  PickList, 127
  rules, 126
  Workflows, 131
Metadata Objects, 122, 124
Metric methodology, 393
Metrics Pack, 390
  definition, 392
Mobile Directory, 483
Mobile Learning, 485
Mobile offer approval, 486
Mobile Org Chart, 482
Move Members option, 269
Multiplicative formula, 279
Multiplier Value field, 280
Multitenancy, 119
My Admin Favorites, 147
My Admin Favorites tile, 148
My Info tile, 152
My Subscribed Insights page, 419
My Team tile, 154

N

Navigation, 146
Net supply excluding inflows view, 452
News Page, 323

O

OneAdmin, 135, 148
OneAdmin UI, 171
Onboarding
  Activities page, 476
  e-Verify, 478
  integration, 479
  introductory information, 475
  Paperwork page, 478
  pre-hire verification, 474
  W-4, 478
  Welcome page, 475
  with Jam, 374
Online Report Designer, 194
Operational Planning tool, 424
Operational Workforce Planning forecast, 467
Options, 158
Organization, 318, 337
Organizational structure, 170, 396, 426
Overall Performance Summary section, 234

P

Pay-for-performance, 241
Payout amounts, 289
Pay structure, 170
People Insights feature, 420
People search feature, 160
Performance & Goals, 32
Performance Management (PM) module, 49, 223
Performance Manager To-Do list, 487
Performance-Potential matrix, 214
Performance review, 232
Performance units, 241
Personal Compensation Statement template, 277
Personal Information, 180

PickList, 196
Plan and approve recommendations, 269
Plan Details icon, 289
Plan Details subsection, 259
Plan Instruction option, 259
Plan Setup section, 254
Portlet, 182
Position Management, 356
Position Management feature, 190
Predictive Modeling tool, 417
Prepare phase, 55
Program ID, 279
Program Name field, 279
Promotion, 241
Propagation data model, 197
Proration, 245, 278
Proxy, 158
Proxy Management page, 186
Publications featuring SuccessFactors, 500
Public profile, 204

Q

Quantitative business performance, 278
Query Workspace, 407
Quick Links, 330

R

Range Penetration calculation, 251
Rapid Deployment Solutions (RDS), 493
Rating Sources option, 263
Realize phase, 57
Recruiting Execution (RX), 50, 291
Recruiting Management (RCM), 50
Recruiting Marketing (RMK), 50
Reloadable, 257
Report Designer, 412
Report Designer components, 414
Report Distributor, 416
Requisition approval, 485
Restricted stock, 241
Rewards statement, 242, 290
Risk Identification link, 455
Risk, Strategy, and Action phase, 453

Role-Based Permissions (RBP), 135
Rollup Hierarchy option, 264
Rounding, 281
Route Map option, 255
Route Map Progress section, 247

S

Salary, 241
Salary Pay Matrix, 246
Salary Plans subsection, 251
Salary Ranges option, 251
SAP Community Network (SCN), 496
SAP HANA Cloud Integration, 71
SAP Help Portal, 493
SAP Jam, 41, 162, 371, 497
   auto group, 381
   auto-membership group, 381
   BizX Mobile, 374, 483
   blog, 382
   content creation and sharing, 382
   creating groups, 380
   document, 382
   gamification, 383
   groups, 379
   informal learning, 373
   Jam Admin, 381
   onboarding, 374
   photo, 382
   profile, 376
   sales, 374
   using SAP Jam, 372
   video, 382
   wall, 483
SAP NetWeaver Process Integration, 69
SAP Notes, 495
SAP PartnerEdge, 496
SAP's cloud strategy, 45
SAP Service Marketplace (SMP), 493
SAP StreamWork, 371
Scatterplot, 416
Scorecard, 203, 213
Scorecard module, 49
SCORM, 333
Search Engine Optimization, 292
Section calculation, 280

Secure Sockets Layer (SSL), 74, 133
Security, 133, 256
   authentication, 133
   layer security, 134
   Role-Based Permissions (RBP), 135
Security Assertion Markup Language 2.0 (SAML2), 73, 111, 114
Set Bonus Calculation subsection, 281
Set Dimensions step, 435
Set Number Format Rules subsection, 282
Set Number Formats subsection, 283
Set Retirements step, 437
Set Scenarios tab, 433
Set Structure step, 440
Settings, 254
Setup data, 249
Short-term incentive pay, 241
Significance Testing, 417
Single Sign-On (SSO), 53, 73, 110
Six steps to build a strategic forecast, 429
SMART goal, 228
SMART Goal Wizard, 225
Social collaboration, 371
Social learning, 485
Social Media ABAP Integration Library (SAIL), 114
Software-as-a-Service (SaaS), 23
Solutions consultants, 48
Source Year dropdown, 432
Sourcing analytics, 298
Stack Ranker, 223
Standard and custom fields, 246
Standard Suite Hierarchy option, 264
Status Report screen, 230
Stock Factor, 246
Stock options, 241
Stock Value, 246
Strategic Workforce Planning (SWFP), 423
Strategy Management, 457
SuccessFactors
   about, 27
   acquisition, 29
   architecture, 117
   BizX Mobile, 42
   Compensation, 33
   history, 28

SuccessFactors (Cont.)
   Learning, 35
   Onboarding, 40, 473
   Partner Portal, 492
   Performance & Goals, 32
   Product strategy, 43
   Recruiting Execution, 34
   Roadmap, 43
   security, 133
   Succession & Development, 37, 339
   Workforce Analytics, 39, 387
   Workforce Planning, 38
SuccessFactors on Google Plus, 499
SuccessFactors on LinkedIn, 499
SuccessFactors on Twitter, 499
SuccessFactors on YouTube, 500
Succession data model, 182
Succession & Development, 37, 339
   Ad Hoc Report, 358
   Career Development Planning (CDP) solution, 359
   Development solution, 359
   How vs. What Matrix, 346
   Lineage Chart, 343
   nominating successors, 347, 354
   Performance-Potential Matrix, 345
   Position Management, 356
   reporting and analytics, 358
   Scorecard, 348
   Succession Org Chart, 341
   succession solution, 340
   talent pools, 352
   Talent Profile, 347
   Talent Search, 348
Succession Org Chart, 215
Succession Planning, 49, 339
Summary tab, 271
Supply forecasting, 451
SWFP core data elements, 426

T

Tactic matrix, 463
Tag, 207
Talent Profile, 209, 347
Talent sourcing, 297

Target amounts, 289
Team Guideline subsection, 286
Team Overview subtab, 234
Team Rater, 235
Technical workshop, 57
Template Name field, 254
Testing, 59
Three-by-three matrix, 456
Threshold, 271
Touchbase, 488
Translation, 196

U

UI, 169
Update the Worksheets subsection, 268

V

Validation report, 288
Variable Pay, 241, 278
Variable Pay module, 49
Variable pay plan, 279
Verify phase, 59

W

Warning message, 261
Web 2.0, 206
Weighted business goal, 278
Welcome tile, 151
What-If Financial Modeling, 464
What-if scenario, 278
Workflow, 131, 187, 256
Workforce Planning (WFP), 390, 423, 427
Writing Assistant and Coaching Advisor, 232

X

XML, 167

Y

YouCalc dashboards, 195

Z

Zero-based forecasting, 432

- Understand the Talent Management functions

- Learn how to integrate Talent Management with other modules

- Optimize your Talent Management business processes

Joe Lee, Tim Simmons

Talent Management with SAP ERP HCM

Confused by the term "talent management"? This book will shed some light on the topic – it's your complete guide to understanding and using the Talent Management suite of applications in SAP ERP HCM. You'll find the information you need in order to plan for and understand Talent Management. Each chapter includes screenshots and visual aids to help you understand how all of these pieces are part of the whole, and you'll find real-world examples, case studies, and tricks and tips throughout to help bring the text to life.

388 pp., 2012, 69,95 Euro / US$ 69.95
ISBN 978-1-59229-413-8
www.sap-press.com

- Master the SAP ERP HCM data model, authorizations, infotype framework, interface architecture, and more

- Develop custom reports, apply enhancement techniques, and explore performance programming in SAP ERP HCM

- Get an introduction to integration with SuccessFactors

Dirk Liepold, Steve Ritter

SAP ERP HCM: Technical Principles and Programming

Make this book your day-to-day resource when addressing technical challenges and functional gaps in the SAP ERP HCM system. Dive into custom development using SAP-provided tools and ABAP code, and trending topics for HCM developers or consultants. Improve performance with authorizations, HR Forms Workplace, and ESS/MSS, using case studies to advance your programming work. Take your mastery of technical topics to the next level.

732 pp., 2013, 69,95 Euro / US$ 69.95
ISBN 978-1-59229-431-2
www.sap-press.com

- Learn how to set up an effective forms workflow with HCM Processes and Forms

- Master cutting-edge form functionality and configuration with details on FPM non-Adobe forms

Justin Morgalis, Brandon Toombs

SAP ERP HCM Processes and Forms

Cut through the HR red tape with this comprehensive guide to customizing and implementing ERP HCM P&F. Streamline your most common organizational data processes into one discrete process for optimal HR workflows. Configure and optimize HCM P&F with ease through real-world examples, step-by-step instructions and tips and tricks. This title will teach you to maximize the powerful combination of web based forms, online document storage, and support structural based decision making. Perfect for busy consultants, managers and super users, this is an end-to-end solution that includes configuration steps, overall business scenarios, and the dos and donts of mapping business processes.

344 pp., 2013, 69,95 Euro / US$ 84.95
ISBN 978-1-59229-425-1
www.sap-press.com

- Locate infotypes by SAP ERP HCM module and in numerical order

- Get concise explanations of important infotypes' functionalities and uses

- Learn how and when to create a custom infotype

Christos Kotsakis, Venki Krishnamoorthy, Jeremy Masters

SAP ERP HCM Infotypes

Your Quick Reference to HR Infotypes

How can you effectively manage the hundreds of HCM infotypes at your disposal—or even keep them straight? Find and implement the infotypes your business requirements demand with this guide. Learn when, why, and how to use a particular infotype, when to create a custom infotype, and which infotypes have been updated or replaced. Explore HCM infotypes by application, by task, and in alphabetical order.

529 pp., 2013, 69,95 Euro / US$ 69.95
ISBN 978-1-59229-442-8
www.sap-press.com

- A complete guide to the tax structures, schemas, and rules that drive US Payroll processing logic

- Integrate your organization's payroll with benefits, taxes, and accounting

- 2nd edition, updated and expanded

Satish Badgi

Practical SAP US Payroll

If you're responsible for setting up, configuring, or using SAP US Payroll, you know that even its minor idiosyncrasies can cause headaches and holdups in your HR processes. This book gives you the tools you need to get up to speed on payroll implementation and cutover, time management, and payroll troubleshooting. This new edition includes updated information for SAP ERP 6.0 and EHPs 5 and 6. Balanced coverage of payroll processes, configuration, and real-life scenarios helps you develop applicable skills.

464 pp., 2. edition 2012, 69,95 Euro / US$ 69.95
ISBN 978-1-59229-421-3
www.sap-press.com

Galileo Press

■ Little-known tips and tricks from the SAP experts

Ajay Jain Bhutoria, Cameron Lewis

HR Management with SAP
100 Things You Should Know About...

Have you ever spent days trying to figure out how to generate a personnel report in SAP ERP HCM only to find out you just needed to click a few buttons. If so, you'll be delighted with this book — it unlocks the secrets of SAP ERP HCM. It provides users and super-users with 100 tips and workarounds you can use to increase productivity, save time, and improve the overall ease-of-use of SAP ERP HCM. The tips have been carefully selected to provide a collection of the best, most useful, and rarest information.

298 pp., 2011, 49,95 Euro / US$ 49.95
ISBN 978-1-59229-361-2
www.sap-press.com

Interested in reading more?

Please visit our website for all new
book and e-book releases from SAP PRESS.

www.sap-press.com